The Only
RESUME
and
COVER LETTER
Book You'll Ever Need

---

400 Resumes for all Industries and Positions
400 Cover Letters for Every Situation

Includes Bonus CD with 200 Additional
Resumes and Cover Letters

Adams Media
Avon, Massachusetts

Published by Adams Media, a division of F+W Media, Inc.
57 Littlefield Street
Avon, MA 02322
www.adamsmedia.com

ISBN 10: 1-59869-051-5
ISBN 13: 978-1-59869-051-4

Printed in the United States of America.

J I H G F E D

Contains material adapted from *Adams Cover Letter Almanac, 2nd Edition,*
copyright © 2006, F+W Media, Inc., and *Adams Resume Almanac, 2nd
Edition,* copyright © 2005, F+W Media, Inc.

This publication is designed to provide accurate and authoritative information with regard to the subject matter covered. It is sold with the understanding that the publisher is not engaged in rendering legal, accounting, or other
professional advice. If legal advice or other expert assistance is required, the
services of a competent professional person should be sought.

—From a *Declaration of Principles* jointly adopted by a Committee of the
American Bar Association and a Committee of Publishers and Associations

Many of the designations used by manufacturers and sellers to distinguish
their product are claimed as trademarks. Where those designations appear in
this book and Adams Media was aware of a trademark claim, the designations have been printed with initial capital letters.

This book is available at quantity discounts for bulk purchases.
For information, please call 1-800-289-0963.

How to Use This Book

The Only Resume and Cover Letter Book You'll Ever Need is the most comprehensive collection of job-winning resumes and cover letters available. This single volume contains hundreds of examples of resumes and cover letters that address every level of the job market, all occupations, and all employment situations.

In this collection, you'll discover many examples of both resumes and cover letters from which you can draw the best elements to custom design your own powerful and effective documents. And, by using the CD-ROM that accompanies this book, you can use your computer's word processor to quickly and effortlessly create personalized resumes and cover letters.

The Only Resume and Cover Letter Book You'll Ever Need contains two main sections:

Part I: Resumes is organized by major occupation categories such as: Accounting and Finance, Administration, Computers and Information Technology, Engineering, Health and Medical, and Marketing and Sales. Each category contains dozens of examples of specific resumes arranged by job title. You'll also find the chapter "Resumes for Special Situations," with sample resumes that address unique conditions. There's even a chapter for students with examples of resumes for their particular needs.

Part II: Cover Letters is arranged by situation: Response to a Classified Advertisement, Response to a "Blind" Advertisement, and Letter to an Employment Agency are just three of the cover letter categories. There are also examples of broadcast letters, follow-up letters, and thank-you letters.

To get the most from this book, we recommend that you begin by reviewing the major categories listed in the Contents. Find the chapter(s) that are applicable, and then find a resume or cover letter that best suits your experience, job objective, and employment situation. Those resumes and cover letters that are highlighted with an icon [◉] are found on the CD-ROM included with this book. Insert the CD in the CD-ROM drive of your computer, and use your word processing application to open the resume or cover letter of your choice. You may then modify the document with your own personal information.

It should be emphasized that you need not strictly adhere to one resume or cover letter. The advantage of having so many different styles and formats is that you can pick and choose elements from numerous examples and custom design your resume or cover letter to fit your needs.

Contents

Contents

CHAPTER 21
Response to a Classified Advertisement (Web Posting) 456

CHAPTER 22
Response to a "Blind" Advertisement 459

CHAPTER 23
"Cold" Letter to a Potential Employer 477

CHAPTER 27
Broadcast Letter 628

CHAPTER 28
Resume Letter 641

CHAPTER 29
Cover Letters for Special Situations 650

CHAPTER 30
Electronic Cover Letters (E-mail Format) 687

CHAPTER 31
Follow-Up Letter (After Telephone Conversation) 691

CHAPTER 32
Follow-Up Letter (After Job Interview) 708

Contents

PART I

RESUMES

Chris Smith
178 Green Street
Wise, VA 24293
(703) 555-5555
csmith@e-mail.com

OBJECTIVE   An entry-level position in Human Resources.

SUMMARY OF QUALIFICAITONS
- Trained in basic computer skills.
- Developed interpersonal skills; excellent mediation abilities.
- Proven supervisory abilities; deal equitably with all levels.
- Function well independently and in a team environment.
- Adapt easily to new concepts; adept at handling multiple responsibilities.
- Extensive experience in training; able to explain procedure and garner significant results within a brief time span.
- Charismatic, assertive personality; skilled at commanding the attention of others.

WORK HISTORY

1998-Present   ARMY NATIONAL GUARD, Richmond, VA
Assistant Section Coordinator; Sergeant/ E-5
Coordinate training of soldiers, creating schedules, overseeing adherence to rules, assisting in directing operations.

2005-Present   BENNIE WARD'S STYLE SHINDIG, Winchester, VA
Sales Associate
Provided customer assistance. Acknowledged as one of top salespeople; consistently met/ exceeded sales goals.

2002-2005   MARTELL BLUE SECURITY SERVICES, Salem, MA
Security Shift Supervisor
Handled employee ID checks; secured building; ensured other site call ins. Worked independently on on-site assignments.

1999-2002   VIRGINIA SMARITAN ASSOCIATION, Charlottesville, VA
Fundraiser
Utilized telephone techniques to raise funds for organizations.

1996-1998   FIRST NATIONAL BANK OF LEXINGTON, Lexington, VA
Teller
Processed withdrawals and deposits; tallied vault moneys.

EDUCATION   RICHMOND JUNIOR COLLEGE, Richmond, VA
Associates Degree in Management Science
Major: Business Administration

REFERENCES   Furnished upon request.

Chris Smith
178 Green Street
Troy, MI 48098
(313) 555-5555
csmith@e-mail.com

OBJECTIVE:
To fully utilize over ten years of experience in investment accounting with

SUMMARY:
Experience in monitoring money flow in money market funds and mutual funds, as calculating the yield for various money market accounts, and pricing mutual funds.

EXPERIENCE:

GERGEW SERVICE COMPANY   Iroy, MI
Senior Money Market Accountant   2002-Present
Determined daily available cash, calculated daily yields and dividends. Posted general ledger. RECONCILED trial balance accounts. Acted as liaison between fund traders and custodian banks. Prepared audit schedules. Assisted in training new personnel.

Mutual Fund Accountant   1999-2002
Functions included daily pricing of common stock and bond funds, accruing and reconciling interest and dividend accounts, reconciling trial balance accounts and daily contact with bankers to obtain stock and bond quotes.

TIMBERCREST COMPANY,   Boston, MA
Assistant Supervisor   1996-1999
Prepared schedules for fund audits. Prepared reports for fund managers. Assisted fund accountants with month-end trial balance reconciliation. Trained new personnel.

Fund Accountant   1994-1996
Manually priced funds and posted journals and ledgers through trial balance. Heavy daily contact with brokers.

OTHER QUALIFICATIONS:
LICENSED MICHIGAN REAL ESTATE BROKER, 1993

EDUCATION:
Waterford High School, Waterford, MI
Graduated 1992

CHRIS SMITH, Ph.D.
Curriculum Vitae

178 Green Street
New York, NY
(212) 555-5555
csmith@e-mail.com

Date of Birth: 8/16/78
Place of Birth: Manhattan, NY
Marital Status: Single

EDUCATION:
2005-2006   YORK UNIVERSITY HOSPITAL, New York, NY
Residency in Gynecology
2004-2005   BROOKLYN HEALTH CLINIC, Brooklyn, NY
Internship in Internal Medicine
2000-2004   JOHNS HOPKINS UNIVERSITY, Baltimore, MD
M.D.
1996-2000   LOYOLA UNIVERSITY, New Orleans, LA
B.A., History

CERTIFICATION:
National Board of Medical Examiners – Part I, May 2004; Score 425
National Board of Medical Examiners – Part II, October 2005; Score 400
National Board of Medical Examiners – Part III, July 2006; Score 430

RESEARCH EXPERIENCE:
Investigated the study of a particular protein, which is known to reduce cell fat from 7/9/02 to 10/4/02 in the laboratory of Dr. G. Bartlett, Chairman, Department of Physiology at Johns Hopkins Health Science Center at Baltimore. Experiments were concerned with structural analysis of fats and fat-binding protein isolated from animal blood cells. The project provided experience in techniques for isolation of actin and for characterization of proteins by sodium acetyl iodine-phenalamine powder electrostasis.

EXTRACURRICULAR ACTIVITIES:
1996-1999   Senior Baseball Team, New Orleans, LA
1999-2000   Loyola Baseball Team
1996-2000   Pi Kappa Alpha Fraternity
1996-1998   John Hopkins University Hockey Team
John Hopkins University Rugby Team

PROFESSIONAL AFFILIATIONS:
2002-2006   Member, American Medical Association
2004-2005   Member, Medical Society of the State of New York
2004-2006   Member, Massachusetts Society of Gynecologists/Obstetricians
2004-2006   Member, American Society of Gynecologists/Obstetricians

Chris Smith
178 Green Street
Huntington, WV 25702
(304) 555-5555
csmith@e-mail.com

OBJECTIVE:
A position in small plant management. Willing to relocate and/or travel.

SUMMARY OF QUALIFICATIONS:
More than thirty years of experience encompassing plant management to include sales, production, plant maintenance, systems, personnel, and related functions. Hired, trained, and supervised personnel. Additional experience as Sales Counselor in the educational field. Good background in customer relations and human resources.

CAREER HIGHLIGHTS:

The Westview Schools, Huntington, WV
Career Counselor   2000–Present
Contact and interview teenagers, young adults, and adults with reference to pursuing course in higher education leading towards careers in a variety of business professions (secretarial, accounting, court reporting, business management, public relations, fashions and merchandising, computer and machine operating and programming, machine accounting, etc.). Administer aptitude tests to applicants and advise prospective students as to their aptitudes and best courses to pursue.

Greenbriar Corporation, Huntington, WV
General Manager   1991–2000
Assume responsibility for management of this firm, which originally employed twelve. Selected, set up, equipped, and staffed new facilities; hired, trained, and supervised skilled production personnel; set up incentive plans; quality production and cost controls, systems, plant maintenance; handled payroll, billing, credit and collection, purchasing, and finance.

Rosemont Inc., Charleston, WV
Assistant Plant Manager, Laundry Company   1981–1991
Supervised all personnel in this plant, which employed 250 people. Handled customer relations, complaints, quality control, and related functions.

EDUCATION:

Northeastern University, Boston, MA
B.S.B.A. degree
Industrial Relations and Accounting

Chris Smith
178 Green Street
St. Louis, MO 63130
(314) 555-5555
csmith@e-mail.com

PROFESSIONAL EXPERIENCE:

MARCA INFRARED DEVICES, St. Louis, MO
Manufacturers of infrared sensing and detecting devices.

2004–Present **Administrator**
Control, track, and maintain engineering personnel status, capital expenditures, and perform budget support for engineering departments.
- Automate weekly labor reports to calculate effectiveness and utilization and report against plan.
- Automate calculation of vacation dollars used in engineering budget planning.
- Automate capital equipment planning cycle.
- Act as capital expenditure liaison for all of engineering.
- Maintain engineering personnel status and monitor performance to plan.
- Perform year-end close out on all engineering purchase orders.
- Control, track, and maintain all contractor and consultant requisitions.
- Cross-train in library functions involving documentation ordering and CD ROM usage.

2003–2004 **Documentation Control Clerk**
Controlled, tracked, and maintained all changes to engineering documentation.
- Trained personnel in status accounting function and audit performance.
- Downloaded engineering and manufacturing tracking files from mainframe to Macintosh.

2000–2003 **Documentation Specialist**
Controlled, tracked, and maintained all changes to engineering documentation.
- Generated parts lists and was initial user of computerized Bills of Material.
- Directed changes in material requirements to material and production control departments.

1998–2000 **Configuration Management Analyst**
Controlled, tracked, and maintained all changes to engineering documentation.
- Chaired Configuration Review Board.
- Presented configuration status reports at customer reviews.

1997–1998 **Inside Sales Coordinator**
- Served as first customer contact.
- Directed customer calls and customer service.
- Maintained Literature files and processed incoming orders.

EDUCATION:

B.S. – Biology, Washington University 1997

All Employment at One Company
Vice President

Chris Smith
178 Green Street
Pocatello, ID 83204
(208) 555-5555
csmith@e-mail.com

SUMMARY OF QUALIFICATIONS:
- Over 12 years experience in inventory control management.
- Strong background in customer service.
- Excellent interpersonal skills.

EXPERIENCE:

J.C. RIVINGTON & CO., Pocatello, ID
(An Employee-Owned company since 1985)
Manufacturer/Distributor of premier quality Photo Frames.

2005–Present VICE PRESIDENT Inventory Management/Administrative Services
Monitored the Production/Distribution/Inventory Control Systems, and the Import Purchasing, Product Costing Department. Managed the Distribution, Electronic Data Processing, and Communications Departments.

2001–2005 DIRECTOR Inventory Control/Materials
Managed/Controlled the Production/Inventory Control System including finished goods, Work-In-Process, and Raw Materials, translating Sales Forecasts into production/inventory budgets and plan. Directed and monitored the Purchasing Department, both domestic and foreign purchases including goods purchased for resale. Chaired weekly Production Meetings to set/communicate priorities to Plant, Warehouse, Purchasing, and Customer Service managers. Designed/computerized a Product Costing System initially utilized as a marketing tool.

1996–2001 MANAGER Inventory Control/Materials
Performed Production/Inventory Control managerial functions of Finished Goods, Work-In-Process, and Raw Materials to meet company inventory investment objectives, to provide even production budgets on factory floor, and to meet agreed upon targeted levels of customer service.

1992–1996 OFFICE MANAGER
Supervised, directed, and coordinated Customer Service/Order Department, Communications including Word Processing, Switchboard, and Mail Room, Data Processing, Credit and Collection, Accounts Payable and Accounts Receivable Departments. Established company newsletter.

EDUCATION:

Northwestern College, Orange City, IA
Master of Business Administration, 1992

Iowa State University, Ames, IA
Bachelor of Science in Management, 1990

At-Home Mom Re-entering the Work Force
Interior Design

CHRIS SMITH
178 Green Street
Mesa, AZ 85203
(602) 555-5555
csmith@e-mail.com

Summary of Qualifications
- Strong management background; owned and operated a successful interior design store for nine years.
- Experience in delegating authority; managed retail staff of six, and later performed volunteer work with countless children and adolescents.
- Superior training/teaching skills; patient and supportive, having years instructional background in crafts, swimming, sports, CPR, cooking, etc.
- Communicate well with children.
- Strong team player; enthusiastic attitude motivates increased productivity in others.

Experience

Girl Scouts of America, Mesa AZ   2003–Present (Part-time)
Brownie Troop Leader, ages 10-11
Lead weekly troop meetings; work with girls towards achievements of merit badges in camping, cooking, sewing, and crafts. Organize monthly overnight trips to local campgrounds. Teach practical first aid techniques and CPR. Facilitate discussions on personal safety when unaccompanied by an adult; teach girls methods of dealing with unsolicited attention from strangers, peer pressure, drug and alcohol abuse, and eating disorders. Organize annual cookie drive; profits garnered support Girl Scouts across America in both their performance of community service and their journey towards personal growth.

Weight Watchers, Mesa, AZ   2002–Present (Part-time)
Meeting Leader
Educate and motivate members toward healthy lifestyle changes. The topics change weekly and range from healthful eating habits and exercise to behavior modification techniques. Manage cash and bookkeeping for each meeting.

Baroque Backdrops and Design, Mesa, AZ   1993–2002
Business Owner/Manager (Interior design company)
Performed all aspects of retail and office management, sales, purchasing, closet and space design, estimates, planning, installations, inventory control, brochure designs, and text publishing. Maintained office and inventory control on a Macintosh.

Community Involvement

Parks and recreational department, Mesa, AZ   Spring 1999–Present
Coach girls' softball team, ages 12-14
Saint Martha's Church Choir, Mesa, AZ   2005–Present
Play organ for three services every Sunday morning
CCD Instructor, Mesa, AZ   2002–2003
Taught Catholic doctrine to elementary school children in preparation for Sacrament of First Communion.

Education

Stonehill College, Easton, MA
B.A. Early Childhood Education, 1988

At-Home Mom Re-entering the Work Force
Nursing

Chris Smith
178 Green Street
Upper Montclair, NJ 07043
(201) 555-5555
csmith@e-mail.com

CAREER OBJECTIVE
To utilize my extensive experience in nursing in a challenging position within the health care industry.

PROFESSIONAL EXPERIENCE
2001–2005   MONTCLAIR HOSPITAL, Montclair, NJ
R.N. Staff Nurse
Addictions Treatment Program
Patient care on 40-bed Mental Health Unit, assessing patients in crisis, interviewing and counseling, administering medication, Emergency Room consulting, collaborating with health care providers.
- Assess and evaluate patients with substance abuse problems.
- Responsible for the verification and pre-certification of insurance providers.
- Assess medical complications.
- Lead and co-lead educational groups for patients and their families.
- Collaborate with Treatment Team to implement in-patient and after care plans.

1998–2001   **Staff Nurse/Psychiatric Addiction Emergency Service**
- Assessed addicted and psychiatric patients to determine severity of illness and level of care needed.
- Collaborated with health care providers and medical team.

1995–1997   MONMOUTH COLLEGE/NURSING PROGRAM, West Long Branch, NJ
Instructor/Medical Assisting Techniques
- Instructed students in the arts and skills of office medical procedures.
- Organized and planned curriculum, tested and graded students in written and practical methods.

1992–1996   CITY OF NEWARK SCHOOL DEPARTMENT, Newark, NJ
Substitute School Nurse
- Administered first aid for students in K–12.
- Eye and ear testing, counseling and health teaching.

EDUCATION
JERSEY CITY HOSPITAL SCHOOL OF NURSING, Jersey City, NJ
Registered Nurse: Registration Number 10468, 1987

ACTIVITIES
Volunteer, Cedar Grove Nursing Home, 2000-present.
Forward, Women's Soccer League, 2000-present.

Chris Smith
178 Green Street
Austin, TX 78746
(512) 555-5555
csmith@e-mail.com

OBJECTIVE:
To contribute over eight years experience in administration, promotion, and communication to an entry-level position in **Advertising.**

SUMMARY OF QUALIFICATIONS:
- Performed advertising duties for small business.
- General knowledge of office management.
- Ability to work well with others, in both supervisory and support staff roles.
- Experience in business writing and communication skills.
- Type 55 words per minute.

SELECTED ACHIEVEMENTS AND RESULTS:
Administration:
Record keeping and file maintenance. Data processing and computer operations, accounts receivable, accounts payable, accounting research and reports. Order fulfillment, inventory control, and customer relations. Scheduling, office management, and telephone reception.

Promotion:
Composing, editing, and proofreading correspondence and PR materials for own housecleaning service. Large scale mailings.

Communication:
Instruction, curriculum and lesson planning; student evaluation; parent-teacher conferences; development of educational materials. Training and supervising clerks.

Computer Skills:
Proficient in MS Word, Access, and FileMaker Pro.

WORK HISTORY:
Teacher, Self-Employed (owner of housecleaning service); Floor Manager; Administrative Assistant; Accounting Clerk.

EDUCATION:
Southwestern, Georgetown, Texas, B.S. Education, Summa Cum Laude, 1992
Georgetown Center for Adult Education, Bookkeeping and Accounting, Intermediate Microsoft Word, Introduction to Excel, FileMaker Pro

AFFILIATIONS:
National Association of Advertising Executives.

Chris Smith
178 Green Street
Sioux Falls, SD 57105
(605) 555-5555
csmith@e-mail.com

OBJECTIVE
A position as a day care worker utilizing experience caring for people of all ages.

SUMMARY OF QUALIFICATIONS
- Strong nurturing capabilities, as well as ability to comfort those in time of crisis.
- Excellent communications skills.
- Extremely patient and calm at all times, including high-pressure situations.
- Able to diagnose needs of others.

EXPERIENCE

CHARGE NURSE/STAFF NURSE – ONCOLOGY, DIALYSIS UNIT
Sioux Falls Hospital, Sioux Falls, SD   **January 2004–Present**
- Provide clinical services to 40 patients on the Oncology/Dialysis Unit.
- Delegate work assignments and supervise performance of licensed staff, evaluate nursing activities to ensure patient care, staff relations, and efficiency of service.
- Visit patients to verify that nursing care is carried out as directed and treatment is administered in accordance with physicians.
- Participate in orientation and instruction of personnel and interact with all hospital departments in order to provide patient care.
- Responsible for direct ordering of drugs, solutions, and equipment; maintain records on narcotics.
- Administer prescribed medications and treatments, prepare equipment and assist physicians during treatments and examinations.
- Provide patient education, assess and provide patients' needs, and serve as a resource person for patients and families.
- Hands-on experience with the administration of chemotherapy, narcotic pain control, and other protocols.

REGISTERED NURSE – MEDICAL SURGICAL FLOOR
Brookings Medical Center, Brookings, SD   **January 1998–December 2003**
- Assumed responsibility as Staff Nurse as well as Charge Nurse; supervised a professional nursing staff on a 35-bed floor.
- Covered all areas of surgical/medical clinical treatment and care with other responsibilities similar to above.
- Trained new nurses.

EDUCATION
South Dakota State University   **May 1997**
Brookings, South Dakota
Nursing Certificate/Registered Nurse

CHRIS SMITH
178 Green Street
Aberdeen, SD 57401
(605) 555-5555
csmith@e-mail.com

OBJECTIVE:

To contribute acquired teaching skills at the Secondary Level.

EDUCATION:

SIOUX FALLS COLLEGE, Sioux Falls, SD
Master of Science in Education (January 2006)
Bachelor of Science in Biology (May 2001)

CERTIFICATION:

South Dakota, 9–12 Secondary

RELATED EXPERIENCE:

8/05 – Present   DOWNEY HIGH SCHOOL, Aberdeen, SD
Student Teacher
Assist in the teaching of ninth grade Earth Science. Plan curricula for laboratory experiments and lead post-lab discussions. Administer weekly quizzes. Confer with parents and teaching staff.

9/02–2/05   HAVEN HILLS HIGH SCHOOL, Sioux Falls, SD
Student Teacher
Assist in the preparation of instructional materials for tenth grade Social Studies class. Help teach and evaluate students. Advise students regarding academic and vocational interests.

OTHER EXPERIENCE:

7/02–Present   NORTHERN LIGHTS PUBLISHING CO., Sioux Falls, SD
Freelance Editor

5/00–7/02   Administrative Assistant

MEMBERSHIPS:

Big Sister Program
Volunteer Tutors of Sioux Falls

Career Changer
Fashion Design

Chris Smith
178 Green Street
Decatur, GA 30032
(404) 555-5555
csmith@e-mail.com

OBJECTIVE
To apply my seven years of experience with women's apparel, as well as my educational background, to a career in fashion design.

SUMMARY
- Area of expertise is creativity – from conception and design to marketing and sales.
- Self-starter with involved style of productivity and workmanship.
- Excellent communicator; adept at sizing up situations and developing new ideas or alternative courses of action in order to design, sell, or increase production.

QUALIFICATIONS

Design:
Conceptualized, coordinated, and designed in-store and window displays, including massive front window of major fashion center. Operated within streamlined material budget appropriated by the manager, yet consistently generated award-winning window themes for $2.1 million department store.

Buying:
Attended fashion shows in New York, Milan, and Paris; assisted in the buying process. Perused fashion magazines on off-time; provided head buyer with information about upcoming styles.

EMPLOYMENT

DISPLAY COORDINATOR/ASSOCIATE BUYER, The Tudor Castle, Athens, GA 2002–2007

WINDOW DRESSER, Tanglewood's, Decatur, GA, 2000–2003

EDUCATION

Deverling School of Fashion Design, Decatur, GA
A.A. Fashion Design, 2000

REFERENCES Available upon request.

CHRIS SMITH
178 Green Street
New Brunswick, NJ
(201) 555-5555
csmith@e-mail.com

OBJECTIVE:
Position in INTERNATIONAL CORPORATE RELATIONS, which utilizes and challenges my business experience and knowledge of French Customs, Business Practices, and Language.

SUMMARY OF QUALIFICATIONS:

Communication:
Fluent in French, written and verbal. Knowledge of French culture and customs. Extensive travel in France, Italy, and Germany.

Marketing:
Oversaw marketing, publications, and advertising for Travel Abroad Programs. Wrote and designed camera-ready ads, brochures, and fliers using desktop publishing system. Wrote, edited, and supervised production of departmental newsletter. Developed travel itineraries and budgets. Compiled and edited faculty brochures.

Administration:
Prepared departmental revenue and budget. Monitored registration progress. Processed faculty appointments and tenure reviews. Wrote minutes for administration meetings. Office support for faculty members. Responsible for letters of appointment. Prepared exams and counsel instructor evaluations. Assisted with registration and student inquiries.

Fundraising:
Worked on development proposals and college fundraising campaign. Organized special events.

EXPERIENCE:
RUTGERS UNIVERSITY, New Brunswick, NJ
B.A. in French Language and Culture Studies, 2005
Study Abroad Program, Paris, September 2003–August 2004

REFERENCES:
Furnished upon request.

Career Changer
Public Relations

CHRIS SMITH
178 Green Street
Juneau, AK 99801
(907) 555-5555
csmith@e-mail.com

PROFESSIONAL EXPERIENCE

A position in public relations in which to apply interpersonal, organizational, and conceptual skills.

SUMMARY

- Over twenty years experience in public relations.
- Proven ability to plan and supervise major special events.
- Knowledge of all aspects of media relations.
- Skilled educator and public speaker.

RELATED EXPERIENCE

2005 to Present ALASKANS FOR A CLEANER WORLD, Juneau, AK
Public Relations Coordinator

- Contribute time and creative services to non-profit organization
- Plan and supervise special events
- Organized first annual "A Breath of Life" Walk-a-thon, raising over $15,000
- Handle all aspects of media relations
- Educate public about environmental issues
- Speak at local schools to encourage environmental awareness

2004 to Present MT. JUNEAU MEDICAL CENTER, Juneau, AK
Coordinator, Department of Neurosurgery

- Promote department, oversee public relations
- Coordinate all communications for medical and non-medical activities with department
- Serve as liaison between administrations of two hospitals, physicians, and nurses
- Educate in-house staff, patients, and families on techniques, equipment, and related subjects

UNRELATED EXPERIENCE

UNIVERSITY HOSPITAL, Anchorage, AK
Staff Nurse, Surgical Intensive Care Unit, 2003 to 2005

PRESENTATIONS AND LECTURES

Have given over 25 presentations and lectures to various schools, hospitals, in-house staff, and professional associations

COMPUTER SKILLS

Word, Excel, Photoshop, Quark

EDUCATION

UNIVERSITY OF ALASKA, Anchorage, AK
Bachelor of Science degree in Nursing, 2002

Chris Smith
178 Green Street
Savannah, GA 31401
(912) 555-5555
csmith@e-mail.com

OBJECTIVE:
To obtain an entry-level position in the publishing industry.

QUALIFICATIONS:

Editorial:
- Working knowledge of all aspects of the English language.
- Demonstrated copyediting and proofreading skills.
- Author of self-published book titled *Birding in the South*.
- First-hand knowledge of the book publishing industry.

Prepress:
- Supervise all aspects of book production.
- Assist with layout and formatting process.
- Prepare and organize artwork for reproduction.
- Review and approve proofs.

Operations:
- Manage inventory control.
- Fill orders.
- Coordinate shipping and billing.

Promotion:
- Coordinate preparation and distribution of flier to bookstores.
- Design and place advertisement in *Publishers Weekly*.
- Promote book at local book signing.

Computers:
- Thorough knowledge of Microsoft Word, Access, Excel, Internet Explorer, and Windows.

WORK EXPERIENCE:
1998–Present SAVANNAH SCHOOL DISTRICT, Savannah, GA
Reading Specialist (2005–Present), Implemented the Publishing Center for Students.
Coordinator/Teacher of the Gifted (2002–2005), Advisor for school newspaper.
Teacher, Fourth Grade (1998–2001), Coordinated procedures for Writing Center.

EDUCATION:
College of Charleston, Charleston, SC
Bachelor of Arts in Elementary Education, May 1998

Career Changer

Travel

Chris Smith
178 Green Street
Puyallup, WA 98374
(206) 555-5555
csmith@e-mail.com

OBJECTIVE
A career in the travel industry that draws upon my administrative and communication skills.

SUMMARY OF QUALIFICATIONS
- Over ten years administrative experience.
- Experience booking flight and hotel accommodations for corporate officers and their families.
- Excellent language/communications skills; speak fluent Italian, French, and Spanish.
- Extensive experience in phone inquiries; able to remain calm and diplomatic under stressful conditions.
- Organized and efficient; able to plan ahead with an eye for potential problems; skilled at implementing solutions to ensure maximum effectiveness of plans.

RELATED EXPERIENCE

NOONAN GRAPHICS, Vancouver, WA   2003–2006
Public Relations Assistant
Coordinated the creative and production phases of monthly informative catalog. Answered customer mail; filed out-of-state orders; created a computer filing system on various customer inquiries. Acted as a liaison between international clients and top management; utilized extensive language skills.

BUCHELL AND GORMAN, INC., Puyallup, WA   1999–2003
Administrative Assistant
Provided administrative support and general office assistance. Composed monthly marketing forecast reports; communicated via fax with foreign clients about shareholder status and marketing procedure. Maintained liaisons between client and production staff. Prepared contract bids.

OTHER EXPERIENCE

Insurance Agent, Day Care Worker, Retail Sales Associate, and Front Desk Clerk.

EDUCATION

University of Washington, Seattle, WA
A.S. Business Administration, 1996

East Seattle High School, Seattle, WA
High School Diploma, 1993

REFERENCES

Available upon request.

CHRIS SMITH, Ph.D.

C u r r i c u l u m   V i t a e

**178 Green Street
New York, NY
(212) 555-5555
csmith@e-mail.com**

**Date of Birth: 8/16/78
Place of Birth: Manhattan, NY
Marital Status: Single**

EDUCATION:

2005–2006   YORK UNIVERSITY HOSPITAL, New York, NY
Residency in Gynecology

2004–2005   BROOKLYN HEALTH CLINIC, Brooklyn, NY
Internship in Internal Medicine

2000–2004   JOHNS HOPKINS UNIVERSITY, Baltimore, MD
M.D.

1996–2000   LOYOLA UNIVERSITY, New Orleans, LA
B.A., History

CERTIFICATION:

National Board of Medical Examiners – Part I, May 2004; Score 425
National Board of Medical Examiners – Part II, October 2005; Score 400
National Board of Medical Examiners – Part III, July 2006; Score 430

RESEARCH EXPERIENCE:

Investigated the study of a particular protein, which is known to reduce cell fat from 7/9/02 to 10/4/02 in the laboratory of Dr. G. Bartlett, Chairman, Department of Physiology at Johns Hopkins Health Science Center at Baltimore. Experiments were concerned with structural analysis of fats and fat-binding protein isolated from animal blood cells. The project provided experience in techniques for isolation of actin and for characterization of proteins by sodium acetyl iodine-phenalamine powder electrostasis.

EXTRACURRICULAR ACTIVITIES:

1996–1999   Senior Baseball Team, New Orleans, LA
1999–2000   Loyola Baseball Team
1996–2000   Pi Kappa Alpha Fraternity
1996–2000   Johns Hopkins University Hockey Team
2002–2004   Johns Hopkins University Rugby Team

PROFESSIONAL AFFILIATIONS:

2002–2006   Member, American Medical Association
2004–2005   Member, Medical Society of the State of New York
2004–2006   Member, Massachusetts Society of Gynecologists/Obstetricians
2004–2006   Member, American Society of Gynecologists/Obstetricians

Displaced Homemaker
Administration

CHRIS SMITH
178 Green Street
Grenvil, NE
(402) 555-5555
csmith@e-mail.com

Objective:
An entry-level administrative position.

Summary of Qualifications:

ADMINISTRATION:
Accurate typing at 60 words per minute. Thoroughly experienced in all aspects of office administration, including record keeping, filing, and scheduling/planning.

ACCOUNTING:
Coordinate finances for a middle-income family of five on a personal computer. Process accounts payable in a timely manner without compromising facets of the expenditure budget. Monitor checking account closely.

COMPUTERS:
Outlook, Microsoft Word, Excel, Windows

ORGANIZATION:
Organize a rotating carpool with five other mothers. Make several copies and distribute at least one month in advance.

Organized a monthly women's writing group concerned with reclaiming the feminine voice. Develop writing exercises that address the hidden spiritual elements in modern women's lives. Motivate members to channel stress, uncertainty, and fear into gift of creativity. Act as mentor and friend.

LEADERSHIP:
President of Grenvil Historical Society, an organization of fifteen members concerned with educating the public about Grenvil town history and preserving historic landmarks. Develop calendar of events; invite guest speakers; organize fundraising events. Provide meeting place, as well as materials and refreshments.

Coach a girl's soccer team, ages 7–11, in the Grenvil Youth Outreach Program (GYOR) from September to November. Provide players with the instruction, motivation, support, and outlook that will enable them to come away from each game with satisfaction and pride, no matter what the score.

Notable Accomplishments:
Organized fundraiser to renovate Henry Wallace House; raised over $65,000.
Several short stories published in regional literary magazines, including *The Loft*.

Education:
Grenvil Community College, Grenvil, NE
Courses in Creative Writing, Word Processing, Accounting

CHRIS SMITH
178 Green Street
Baton Rouge, LA 70807
(504) 555-5555
csmith@e-mail.com

Objective:
To provide care in an adult home or child day care environment.

Skills:
Care Providing
- Provide care for paraplegic in a private home setting for five years.
- Maintained a daily log of all medication administered.
- Coordinated a biweekly story hour at two local nursing homes.
- Delivered groceries to homebound seniors twice a week for two years.
- Administered medication.
- Acted as an assistant to seniors in wheelchairs through private and public transportation.

Communication
- Organized the care of an elderly relative within a nursing home for three years.
- Bargained with contractors about the adaptation of private homes for special needs adults.
- Provided counseling to the elderly, clarifying their wants and needs.
- Improved communication with support services for an elderly couple in order to improve their quality of life.
- Organized a pet-visiting hour by acting as a liaison between two nursing homes and the local animal shelter.

Planning
- Organized day trips to local museums, parks, and shopping centers.
- Developed calendar of monthly in-house events for two nursing homes.
- Planned biweekly shopping lists for several elderly individuals according to their physicians' specifications.
- Organized successful "Friends in Deed" program in which mobile seniors visited the homes of their housebound peers.

Education:
Lexington High School, Lexington, KY

Displaced Homemaker
Food Service

CHRIS SMITH
178 Green Street
Cheyenne, WY 82009
(307) 555-5555
csmith@e-mail.com

Objective:
A position in Food Service in the public school system.

Related Experience:

Jameson Homeless Shelter   Cheyenne, WY
Weekday server. Act as liaison between homeless and national food distributor, securing special requests and unanimously favored items.

St. Bernadette's Parish   Cheyenne, WY
Coordinate annual bake sale; provide approximately ten percent of the bakery items sold.

Brady Family   Cheyenne, WY
Act as live-in nanny for eight-year old twin boys; duties include the preparation of their meals and snacks on a regular basis.

Lion's Club Carnival   Cheyenne, WY
Work the concession booths at annual carnival each June; prepare and serve such items as fried dough, sweet sausage, pizza, and caramel apples; maintain a receipt record of profits for event administrators.

Conduct informal cooking classes out of the Payne Community Center kitchen on a weekly basis.

Awards:
Award-winning country style cook.
Placed first in national fruit-based pie competition.
Won cash prize for best pot roast recipe, *Reader's Digest*.

Education:
Cheyenne Community College, Cheyenne, WY
Associate's degree, Home Economics

Interests:
Gourmet cook, Little League softball coach, avid gardener

References:
Available upon request.

Former Small Business Owner
Desktop Publishing

Chris Smith
178 Green Street
Clarksville, TN 37044
(615) 555-5555
csmith@e-mail.com

OBJECTIVE
A challenging position in the field of sales and electronic publishing.

SUMMARY OF QUALIFICATIONS
- More than fifteen years of Art Director/Buyer and graphics design production experience in the publishing field; extensive knowledge of type and mechanical preparation, budgeting, and scheduling.
- Excellent interpersonal, communication, and managerial skills; adept at coordinating and motivating creative artists to peak efficiency.
- Aware of cost management and quality control importance on all levels.
- Self-motivated; able to set effective priorities and meet tight deadlines.
- Productive in fast-paced, high-pressure atmosphere

PROFESSIONAL EXPERIENCE
2002–2006   NO CONTEST GRAPHICS, Nashville, TN
Owner/President, Art Director/Buyer
Coordinate operations, 12-member production staff, freelance desktop publishers and illustrators. Maintain overview of works-in-progress to produce optimum efficiency. Provide advice to personnel in designing materials to appropriately meet client needs; conceptualize product; delegate staff to make decisions. Commission freelance agents by utilizing nationwide illustrator four-color manuscripts using watercolor illustrations, photography, or graphics. Act as liaison between executive personnel and staff. Budget each project; motivate artistic staff and typesetters to meet projected deadlines and remain within cost-efficient parameters. Projects include: greeting cards, care package kits, magazine fragrance inserts, cereal boxes, toy packages, coloring books (cover and contents), holographic bumper stickers, and retail store signs and logos.

2000–2002   NEW JERSEY LITHOGRAPH, Newark, NJ
Head of Typesetting and Design Department
Supervised staff in design and execution of print materials for commercial printer.

EDUCATION
CENTENARY COLLEGE, Hackettstown, NJ
A.S. in Technical Illustration, 2001

ART INSTITUTE OF NEWARK, Newark, NJ
Certified in Graphic Design, 1989

Former Small Business Owner
Environmental Sciences

CHRIS SMITH
178 Green Street
La Jolla, CA 92093
(619) 555-5555
csmith@e-mail.com

OBJECTIVE
A position utilizing my experience in recycling and developing environmentally conscious programs.

SUMMARY OF QUALIFICATIONS
- Acquired the first recycling permit in the City of San Diego for ferrous and non-ferrous metal, aluminum, high-grade paper, and plastic.
- Developed profitable pilot program for community and industrial recycling.
- Recovered non-ferrous and precious metals from waste solutions, photo and electrical scrap.
- Conducted research and formulated chemical process to liquefy Styrofoam in reusable plastic.

EXPERIENCE
2002 to   CALIFORNIA RECYCLE RENEGADES, INC., San Diego, CA
2006   **Owner/President**
Established First Aluminum Recycling in San Diego. Developed programs for expansion from ferrous and non-ferrous metals to high-grade paper, aluminum, and plastic. Conducted pilot program; formulated a network in Sable Park and Briody Hills for voluntary recycling. Provided containers biweekly for aluminum, glass, and newspaper. Picked up and processed material, sending check for proceeds to community associations.

EDUCATION
University of California, Riverside – Bookkeeping
M.A. Business Administration 2000

University of California, Berkeley
B.A. Environmental Science 1998

AFFILIATIONS
Member of Pacific Community Association

REFERENCES
Available upon request.

CHRIS SMITH
178 Green Street
Lawrence, KS
(913) 555-5555
csmith@e-mail.com

FREELANCE PRODUCTION
Writer/Producer/Director/Editor: Training videotape for Child Services of Squaw Valley. Incorporated; tape is designed to instruct current and prospective members of the Council on Children in the most effective and efficient conductance of board functions (2006).

Writer: Series of short videotapes on recreational drinking use for Social Science Research and Evaluation, Incorporated. Program depicts strategies teens may use to avoid problems associated with drinking; to be shown in high schools throughout Kansas. Worked as Camera Operator during production (2006).

Producer/Writer/Editor: Two PSA's for the Kansas Commission for the Deaf, to be aired throughout the state of Kansas (2005).

Camera Operator/Editor: *Missing Buttonholes,* 4th program to be used by Kansas State University's Broadcast Journalism Department (2005).

Producer/Writer/Assistant Editor: Volunteer Recruitment PSA for Specialized Ambulatory Care Clinic, Wichita, KS (2004).

EDUCATIONAL BACKGROUND
KANSAS STATE UNIVERSITY, Manhattan, KS
Master of Science Degree in Broadcasting
- Concentration, Television Production and Writing
- Assistant Director: *Dinnertime Mind Dance* for Cablevision of Lawrence (2005)
- Grade point average: 3.4/4.0
- Awarded $2,000 scholarship from School of Public Communication (2004)

REFERENCES
Excellent references available upon request.

Frequent Job Changer
Copywriter

Chris Smith
178 Green Street
Fort Worth, TX 76114
(817) 555-5555
csmith@e-mail.com

SPECIAL SKILLS

Experienced and competent with Mac and PC systems. Solid communications skills in person and by phone. Possess strong work ethic and enthusiasm. Strong organizational skills.

EMPLOYMENT

Copywriter/Service Director
WDDE Radio Station, Fort Worth, TX   2005–present
- Compose copy for advertisements and promotions.
- Edit client copy, client newsletter and executive correspondence.
- Communicate with clients and listeners by phone.
- Produce commercials.
- Organize and oversee copy and taped spots.
- Delegate on-air personalities for recording.
- Coordinate technical aspects of on-air programming.

Claims Coder
Texas Mutual Inc., Dallas, TX   2003–2005
- Process claims reports and encode data to computer system.
- Review and revise reinsurance files.
- Conduct inventory.
- Balance daily accounts for each computer system.

Mathematics Tutor
University of Dallas, Irvine, TX   2001–2003

OTHER EMPLOYMENT

Graduated Dave Erickson "Public Speaking" course, 2005
University of Dallas, Irvine, TX, 2003, Graduated Summa Cum Laude
Bachelor of Science degree in Education, Minor in English
- Member of Kappa Kappa Gamma Honor Society
- Dean's list four years

SPECIAL INTERESTS

Volunteer at MiCasa, a Dallas Battered Women's Shelter
Surfing, Window Shopping, and Canoeing

REFERENCES AVAILABLE UPON REQUEST

Gaps in Employment History
Editor

CHRIS SMITH
178 Green Street
Sumter, SC 29150
(803) 555-5555
csmith@e-mail.com

Objective:
An editing position within a major publishing house.

Summary of Qualifications:
- More than seven years of writing/editing experience.
- Adept at managing multiple responsibilities simultaneously.
- Experienced at delegating authority and motivating others to ensure efficiency and productivity.
- Computer knowledge includes Excel, Microsoft Word, PageMaker, and Photoshop.

Work Experience:

Editor-in-Chief, Renegade Magazine
Sumter, SC
Selected submissions, edited and wrote headlines for submissions and columns, laid out page, recruited columnist, trained associates from 2004-2006. Frequent copyediting and research.

Associate Editor, Modern Daze Magazine
New York, NY
Wrote articles for both the magazine and its associated newsletter, *Disembodied Voices*. Edited features and department articles from 1998-2002. Read and critiqued assigned articles from contributing editors.

Copy Editor, Heathcliff's Garden Magazine
Boston, MA
Edited news stories, wrote headlines, assisted with layout of page, occasionally solicited advertising and helped with distribution from 1994-1996.

Other Experience:

Writer, professional musician, world traveler.
(Details available upon request.)

Military

Army Corporal (honorable discharge).

Education:

University of Richmond, Richmond, VA
Bachelor of Arts, English, 1985
Le Student Roma, Rome, Italy
Intensive study of Italian language and culture, 2005

Immigrant
Senior Accountant

CHRIS SMITH
178 Green Street
Kankakee, IL 60901
(815) 555-5555
csmith@e-mail.com

EXPERIENCE

K.T. BIRCHWOOD AND SONS, Chicago, IL
Senior Accountant, December 2005–Present
Responsible for G.I. processing reporting, initially for six companies, also bank reconciliation, etc. Involved in preparation for Chapter 11 filing (2006), subsequent reporting requirements, also handling account receivables and internal audits.

ESSEX COMPUTER, LTD., Glasgow, Scotland
Assistant Financial Accountant, 2002–2005
Maintained the general ledger system; oversaw the preparation of the month-end and year-end financial reports, audit reports, budgets, and variance analysis of the monthly financial package for submission to U.S. headquarters. Maintained capital assets, depreciations schedules, and reconciliation of bank accounts. Maintained the operation of the accounts payable system with vendors, also involved in the set-up and modification of a new computer system. Experience using micros, primarily Multi-plan and Lotus. Member of steering committee; selected a new general ledger package, which is currently used at this facility.

S.G.R., LTD., Glasgow, Scotland
Temporary Accountant, 2001–2002
Maintained and reconciled all bank and investment accounts. Performed inventory control. Involved in inter-company accounting with foreign subsidiaries.

UPSCALE ENTERPRISES, Glasgow, Scotland
Accounts Assistant, 1998–2001
Performed all bookkeeping functions of company; creditors (including foreign currency), contract payments, debtors, payroll, management accounts, profit and loss by flight reports, budget, and costing.

EDUCATION

COLLEGE OF COMMERCE, Glasgow, Scotland
Certificate in Business Studies, 1998–2000
Major: Accounting

NOTHERN ENTERPRISE OF CERTIFIED ACCOUNTANTS, Glasgow, Scotland
Exempt-Level I, have passed subjects in Level II.

PERSONAL

Work permit.

Military Background
Intelligence Specialist

Chris Smith
178 Green Street
Appleton, WI 54912
(414) 555-5555
csmith@e-mail.com

Professional Experience

UNITED STATES NAVY   2003–2006
Intelligence Specialist
- Served as intelligence analyst in photographic interpretation for FIRST at NAS Boston and Fleet Intelligence Center Pacific.
- Participated in intelligence operations on month-long active duty assignments.
- Edited and compiled contingency briefs for fleet surface ships at Commander Naval Surface Force, Miami.

UNITED STATES NAVY   1999–2003
Intelligence Specialist
- Served as intelligence assistant at Commander Naval Surface Force, U.S. Pacific Fleet, Miami, 2001-2003.
- Edited and compiled point papers on foreign navies.
- Briefed shipboard intelligence officers on intelligence collection effort.
- Performed various other functions including standing watch, serving as classified control custodian, and clerical and editorial duties.
- Performed administrative duties in Special Security Office at Fleet Intelligence Center Pacific, Los Angeles, CA.

Education

Marquette University, College of Liberal Arts, Milwaukee, WI
Bachelor of Arts in International Politics
GPA in major: 3.5/4.0
Study Abroad: Hamburg, St. Petersburg, Moscow, Paris, 2005
Five-week study of Russian language

Military Training:
Basic Training, Maui, Hawaii, 1999
Intelligence Specialists "A" School, Bangor, Maine, 1999
Shipboard Intelligence School, Miami, Florida, 2000
National Imagery Interpretation Rating Scale School, Miami, Florida, 2000

Additional Information

- Fluent in German, French, Russian
- Received two Naval Certificates of Achievement, 2001, 2005
- Clearance Top-Secret

Chris Smith
178 Green Street
Vancouver, WA 98665
(206) 555-5555
csmith@e-mail.com

CAREER OBJECTIVE
To secure an **Administrative/Supervisory** position in the Human Services field.

SYNOPSIS
Self-starter with involved style of leadership. Excellent communicator with the ability to elicit interest, enthusiasm, drive, and energy using a common-sense approach. Adept at sizing up situations, analyzing facts developing alternative courses of action in order to achieve, even exceed desired results.

QUALIFICATIONS
- Extensive supervisory experience.
- 6 years counseling up to 120 soldiers with subsequent referrals when necessary.
- Exceptional training and instructional skills.
- Strong administrative and organizational abilities.
- Relevant course work in college and U.S. Army professional training.
- Bilingual: English and Spanish.

EXPERIENCE
1998–2006   U.S. ARMY   **Squad Leader/Training NCO**
From initial tour of duty to honorable discharge, details have included military driver, senior gunner, squad leader, acting platoon sergeant, and training NCO.
- Command inspections and training 120-Main Air Defense Battery with an 18-hour worldwide mission in the 7th ID (L.).
- Trained and targeted career progression for soldiers on staff.
- Directly responsible for the discipline, training, morale, and quality of life of one particular soldier.
- Accountable for training records, personnel performance, strength reporting, and weight control.
- Liable for personnel processing, NCO Evaluation Reports, evaluations, awards, in/out processing, legal actions, and orders.

AWARDS

- Army Service Medal
- U.S. Defense Medal
- Four Army Good Conduct Medals
- Four Officer Development Ribbons

EDUCATION
Farmville High School, Farmville, VA
Graduate Diploma, 1998

Chris Smith
178 Green Street
Wise, VA 24293
(703) 555-5555
csmith@e-mail.com

OBJECTIVE   An entry-level position in Human Resources.

SUMMARY OF QUALIFICATIONS
- Trained in basic computer skills.
- Developed interpersonal skills; excellent mediation abilities.
- Proven supervisory abilities; deal equitably with all levels.
- Function well independently and in a team environment.
- Adapt easily to new concepts; adept at handling multiple responsibilities.
- Extensive experience in training; able to explain procedure and garner significant results within a brief time span.
- Charismatic, assertive personality; skilled at commanding the attention of others.

WORK HISTORY

1998–Present   ARMY NATIONAL GUARD, Richmond, VA
Assistant Section Coordinator, Sergeant/ E-5
Coordinate training of soldiers, creating schedules, overseeing adherence to rules, assisting in directing operations.

2005–Present   BENNIE WARD'S STYLE SHINDIG, Winchester, VA
Sales Associate
Provided customer assistance. Acknowledged as one of top salespeople; consistently met/exceeded sales goals.

2002–2005   MARTELL BLUE SECURITY SERVICES, Salem, MA
Security Shift Supervisor
Handled employee ID checks; secured building; ensured other site call-ins. Worked independently on on-site assignments.

1999–2002   VIRGINIA SAMARITAN ASSOCIATION, Charlottesville, VA
Fundraiser
Utilized telephone techniques to raise funds for organizations.

1996–1998   FIRST NATIONAL BANK OF LEXINGTON, Lexington, VA
Teller
Processed withdrawals and deposits; tallied vault moneys.

EDUCATION   RICHMOND JUNIOR COLLEGE, Richmond, VA
Associate's degree in Management Science
Major: Business Administration

REFERENCES   Furnished upon request.

Overseas Employment History
Field Administrator

Chris Smith
178 Green Street
Seal Cove, ME 04674
(207) 555-5555
csmith@e-mail.com

OBJECTIVE A challenging international career where I can contribute extensive experience in administration and management.

CAREER EXPERIENCE

WELBRUN STATE UNIVERSITY, European Region, Berlin, Germany 2005–Present
Field Administrator/Manager
Administer all office activities. Serve as liaison on military based college, resolving military-civilian, faculty-student clashes. Requires ability to maneuver politically, observing military priorities. Coordinate with Education Service Officer, Education Center staff, and faculty in planning educational programs for community. Assist students in course registration and planning individual academic/vocational needs. Process registration forms and financial reports. Maintain/update classroom files and rosters. Initiate/distribute publicity.

UNIVERSITY OF MASSACHUSETTS, European Division, Paris, France 2003–2005
Field Registrar
Managed office in planning/implementing educational program for military community. Initiated innovative marketing policy and personal outreach program; increased student enrollments from 250 to 700 per year. Assisted students as needed; prepared/processed registration forms and financial packets. Reviewed lecturer applications; assisted in transition into area. Planned/organized student tours and field trips.

ILESFORD, Paris, France 2001–2003
Retail Manager
Supervised retail store complex operations including: Retail Store, Barbershop, Pick-up Point, Theater, and temporary concessions. Tripled sales. Monitored Retail Store renovation, inventory, fixed assets, custodial funds, and cash/receipts. Implemented compilation to support inventory budget requirements, projected sales, and annual forecast. Interviewed, hired/terminated, trained, and cross-trained personnel. Acted as liaison between military commander and the community.

THE GUMBLEY SCHOOL, Lancaster, England 2000–2001
Administrative Assistant
Supervised/implemented clearance updating for 2,000 personnel files to improve faculty academic qualifications. Assisted Associate Dean: transcribed edited reports and correspondence, clarified new Academic Affairs procedures/policies, processed/revised/completed reports, catalogs.

EDUCATION **WELBRUN STATE UNIVERSITY**, European Region, Berlin, Germany
M.P.A., Public Administration, Cognate: Counseling 2005

UNIVERSITY OF MASSACHUSETTS, European Division, Paris, France
B.A., Business Management, Cum Laude, 2003

CHRIS SMITH
178 Green Street
Johnson, VT 05656
(802) 555-5555
csmith@e-mail.com

OBJECTIVE

To join a dynamic sales staff with a firm that has a need for a highly motivated representative skilled in retail markets.

SUMMARY OF PROFESSIONAL EXPERIENCE

- Four years of substantial experience in positions as Sales Representative, Retail Sales Manager, and Warehouse Manager with a major retail and wholesale organization.
- Assumed responsibility for divisional sales from $1.4 million to $2.1 million within one year.
- Hands-on experience in sales, inventory control and promotion of chemicals, furniture, clothing, and seasonal products.
- Skilled in developing special merchandising effects to increase product visibility and sales.

WORK HISTORY

Raintree, Inc.
Seasonal Specialty Stores, Raintree Industries, Johnson, VT
Retail Manager (Part-time)   (2005-Present)

- Hire, train, schedule, and supervise a highly productive staff of 11, selling and promoting a diverse product mix.
- Develop, implement, and expand seasonal merchandise and presentations for year-round sales. Greatly expanded product knowledge and sales through use of in store-video and other image equipment.
- Select and purchase all billiard equipment and accessories.
- Prepare inventory projections, work on sales promotions (in-store and chain-wide). Excellent consumer base resulting in strong repeat business.
- Maintain financial control of all debts/credits.

Wholesale Warehouse Manager (Part-Time)   (2004-2005)

- Supervised a staff of 6 and controlled all aspects of shipping and receiving. Directed fleet scheduling maintenance as well as building maintenance control and security for this facility.

Sales Representative (Part-Time)   (1997-2004)

- Increased all aspects of wholesale pool and supply and accessory business. Control of expanding sales and sales force. Established new sales and accounts within New England area.

EDUCATION

Cornell University, Ithaca, NY
B.A. Business Administration, 2003

CHRIS SMITH

178 Green Street
New York, NY 10023
(212) 555-5555
csmith@e-mail.com

Objective:
A challenging mid-level position in broadcasting.

Summary of Qualifications:
Over ten years experience in recording engineering, background vocals, producing, mixing/editing.

Experience:

2005–Present   Vogue Recording Studio, New York, NY
Recording Engineer
- Clarify session requirements.
- Mix and edit demo tapes and albums.
- Maintain and repair audio equipment.
- Support video production department.

2000–2005   WMLC AM, Radio 15, New York, NY
Radio Personality
- Associate Producer and Programmer for live talk shows.
- Audio and sound engineer for commercials.
- Run syndicated talk board operations.
- Produce comedy bits for weekly comedy show.
- Interview call-ins on the air.

Education:
New York University, New York, NY
Studies include broadcasting, public speaking, and audio engineering. School Radio Station General Manager. Braille Tutor.

License: Third Class Broadcasting

Interests: Standup comedy, playing guitar, traveling

References: Available upon request

Personal: Willing to travel

CHRIS SMITH
178 Green Street
Casper, WY 82604
(307) 555-5555
csmith@e-mail.com

OBJECTIVE
An Engineering position in the field of Electro-Optics.

WORK EXPERIENCE
2005–Present JT Technology   Casper, WY
ASSISTANT ENGINEER
- Provide engineering support to various senior and electro-mechanical areas.
- Solve engineering-related problems for production department; assist through direct observation, positive communication, and dynamic interaction between production floor and test engineering management.
- Perform equipment and component testing; troubleshoot malfunctions; assist engineers with special projects and with department support tasks as required.
- Monitor current developments in the engineering fields for possible practical applications.

2002–2005 Charles Technology Corporation   Casper, WY
ASSISTANT ENGINEER
- Supervised various test-engineering projects that required operating specialized equipment, documenting test results and making reports of findings to engineering management.
- Implemented software/hardware modifications and engineering changes requested by company clients.
- Assisted senior engineers with projects and performed support duties as needed.

2000–2002 Dishwashers, Etc.   Green Bay, WI
APPLIANCE TECHNICIAN
- Made household and commercial service calls to troubleshoot malfunctions and engineering changes requested by company clients.
- Assisted senior engineers with projects and performed support duties as needed.

EDUCATION

Associate's of Science Degree in Electronic Technology, 2002
Green Bay Community College, Green Bay, WI
GPA 3.5/4.0

ACTIVITIES

New York Marathon
Placed 5th, Wheelchair Division – 2005

Physically Challenged
Medical Research

CHRIS SMITH
178 Green Street
Arlington, VA 22307
(703) 555-5555
csmith@e-mail.com

PROFESSIONAL EXPERIENCE

2004 to Present   **Research Assistant**
CITY HOSPITAL   Washington, D.C.
Pathology Unit
- Establish protocols and procedures on cell culture and freezing methods.
- Maintain and establish Transgenic, Oscular Meloma Cell Lines, and In Vitro Studies.
- Perform chemotherapy toxicity studies, Cytospins, Dot Blots, DNA Extractions.
- Maintain and breed transgenic SV40, CDI Nude, NIH III, Bg-NU-Xid, and blood sampling.
- Maintain mouse colonies; supervise dissections, autopsy reports, In Vitro injections and record keeping.
- Perform various other laboratory and maintenance processes.

November 2002 to June 2004   **Skin Bank Technician**
ARLINGTON HOSPITAL BURN INSTITUTE   Arlington, VA
- Harvested and processed post-mortem (cadaver) allo-graphs, under sterile technique.
- Processed human/artificial tissue for freezing (auto-grafts, pig skin biobrane).
- Word processing.
- Maintained all laboratory equipment.

1998 to November 2001   **Research Clinical Technician**
FARREL & OKELUND RESEARCH ASSOCIATES   Alexandria, VA
- Performed F.D.A. and I.R.B. pharmacokinetic studies, including statistical analyses of safety and human tolerance studies in bioavailability, bioequivalence, cardiology, alpha and beta blockers, hypertension, neurology, and endoscopy ulcer studies.
- Administered protocols and case report forms.
- Performed various clinical nursing and laboratory duties.

1996 to 1998   **Laboratory Technical Assistant**
ENGLEMAN LABORATORIES   Bethesda, MD
- Performed various clinical laboratory functions.

EDUCATION

Bachelor of Science degree in Biology
Gallaudet College for the Deaf
Washington, D.C., 1996

Retiree Re-entering the Work Force
Principal

CHRIS SMITH
178 Green Street
Arkadelphia, AK 71923
(501) 555-5555
csmith@e-mail.com

OBJECTIVE
To contribute extensive experience and administrative skills to a part-time teaching position.

EXPERIENCE
ARKANSAS PUBLIC SCHOOL SYSTEM

1996 to 2002   **Principle-Retired**
RODHAM ELEMENTARY SCHOOL   Arkadelphia, AR
- Oversaw all operations for entire school.
- Supervised and evaluated teachers and teaching assistants.
- Developed curriculum for mainstream and special needs children.
- Directed staff meetings, oriented new administrative and teaching staff.

1989 to 1996   **Principal**
HOPE CLINTON JUNIOR HIGH SCHOOL   Arkadelphia, AR
- Directed and facilitated all operational procedures.
- Developed curriculum and supervised staff.
- Created and implemented educational program enhancements.
- Directed staff meetings, informed staff of district-ordered changes.

1987 to 1990   **Teaching Assistant Principal**
NOAH JUNIOR HIGH SCHOOL   Arkadelphia, AR
- Served as acting principal and directed operational processes.
- Assisted and supervised teaching staff.
- Interfaced with parents/teachers for educational program development.

1979 to 1987   **Teaching Assistant Principal**
DAMON ELEMENTARY SCHOOL   Conway, AR
- Assisted principal in the coordination of educational programs.
- Purchased books and various educational aids.

1968 to 1979   **Teacher**
CONWAY JUNIOR HIGH SCHOOL   Conway, AR
- Instructed students in math and science.

EDUCATION
JOHN BROWN UNIVERSITY, Siloam Springs, AK
Master's degree: Education, 1992
Bachelor of Arts degree: History, 1959

CERTIFICATION
State Teacher Certification

Short Employment History
Legal Assistant

CHRIS SMITH

178 Green Street
Fairfax, VA 22030
(703) 555-5555
csmith@e-mail.com

SKILLS

Research	Excel
General office skills	Microsoft Word
Writing	Access

WORK EXPERIENCE

Legal Assistant
Parnell & Swaggert
Fairfax, VA   2006–Present
Responsible for corresponding via courier, telephone, letter, and facsimile with clients, attorneys, Secretaries of State, U.S. Dept. of State, and foreign associates in matters of intellectual property law, primarily trademarks. Meet with clients regarding applications/registrations of trademarks and direct either U.S. Commissioner or foreign agent how to proceed. Other duties include: compiling information from other Parnell & Swaggert branches, paying our debt notes and billing clients.

Legislative Intern
Office of Senator Fisher
Fairfax, VA   Summer 2006
Responsible for correspondence, involving casework. Assisted Labor and Human Resources Committee Judiciary Sub-Committee, and Fund for a Democratic Majority. Projects included research, writing; covered hearings and wrote memos.

Legislative Aide
Office of Senator Florio
Washington, D.C.   Summer 2005
Responsible for overseeing communications between Senator Florio and the general public.

EDUCATION

George Mason University, Fairfax, VA
B.A., Law and Society, 2006

HONORS AND AWARDS

Oxford Honor Scholar
Who's Who Among Students, 2004
Student Government Award

CHRIS SMITH
178 Green Street
Raleigh, NC 27611
(919) 555-5555
csmith@e-mail.com

OBJECTIVE:
A long-term position in administration.

SKILLS AND QUALIFICATIONS:
- Five years Accounting, Financial and Administrative experience.
- Computer knowledge includes PC and Mac.
- Outstanding communications and organizational skills.

EXPERIENCE:
11/06–Present   CARMICHAEL ENTERPRISES, Raleigh, NC
Accounting Clerk/Data Entry
Temporary Position
Prepare and maintain all general ledger accounts, records, and files. Input data on various computer systems, including PC and Mac.

6/06–10/06   CHAVEZ INVESTMENTS, Winston-Salem, NC
Customer Service Representative
Temporary Position
Responded to questions and assisted shareholders in regards to their stocks, bond, equity and money markets accounts, as well as tax questions. Approved check disbursement and utilized PC.

11/00–6/06   JOHN HANCOCK LIFE INSURANCE CO., Boston, MA
Purchasing Clerk
Temporary Position
Maintained general supply inventory levels and purchased general supplies and specialty requested items and materials. Negotiated price and coordinated delivery with various vendors. Prepared purchase orders. Assisted in other administrative activities.

4/02–12/04   SCANLON CORPORATION, Chapel Hill, NC
Residential Counselor
Assisted and counseled mentally retarded and emotionally disabled adults in reading, math, personal hygiene, and motor skills.

OTHER EXPERIENCE:
Other temporary assignments have included: Receptionist, Order Entry Clerk, Switchboard Operator, Proofreader.

EDUCATION:
Clydeston Business School Certification, 2006
Kennedy High School Graduate, 2002

Weak Educational Background
Assistant Manager

CHRIS SMITH
178 Green Street
Myrtle Beach, SC 29577
(803) 555-5555
csmith@e-mail.com

OBJECTIVE
To apply skills obtained through experience in supervision of Parking Facilities to the position of Assistant Manager of Parking Facilities.

SUMMARY
- Proven abilities have resulted in the rapid advancement to a supervisory position.
- Self-motivated, people-oriented, consistently responsible.
- Familiar with all prerequisite functions of maintaining a smooth-running Parking Facility.
- Sworn Deputy Sheriff, Birchwood County.

EXPERIENCE

1998–Present **SPORTS AUTHORITY ROLLINS AIRPORT,** Lexington, SC

2003–Present **SUPERVISOR OF PARKING FACILITY**
Oversee collection of all moneys. Maintain public relations and customer service. Resolve all problems. Administer work schedules, payroll, assignments of duties, and various other functions. Attend to snow removal. Represent Port Authority at scheduled court appearances.

2002–Present **PRESIDENT OF LOCAL CHAPTER OF NAGE**
Represent all cashiers and attendants. Settle all problems pertaining to Parking Facilities. Negotiate contracts.

2000–2003 **ASSISTANT SUPERVISOR/CASHIER**
Assisted supervisor. Collected all parking fees. Achieved high standard of customer relations.

1998–2001 **ATTENDANT**
Patrolled and maintained cleanliness standards of Parking Facility. Assisted customers.

OTHER EXPERIENCE
Skilled carpenter's helper; advanced to highest skilled fish cutter within one year and then elected shop steward. (Total experience, 4 years.)
Truck driver, class 2 license to Lead Bartender/Beverage Manager/Assistant Manager. (Total experience, 6 years.)

REFERENCES
Furnished upon request.

Weak Educational Background
Money Market Accountant

Chris Smith
178 Green Street
Troy, MI 48098
(313) 555-5555
csmith@e-mail.com

OBJECTIVE:
To fully utilize over ten years of experience in investment accounting within an allied field.

SUMMARY:
Experience in monitoring money flow in money market funds and mutual funds, as well as calculating the yield for various money market accounts, and pricing mutual funds.

EXPERIENCE:

GERGEW SERVICE COMPANY   Troy, MI
Senior Money Market Accountant   2002–Present
Determined daily available cash, calculated daily yields and dividends. Posted general ledger. Reconciled trial balance accounts. Acted as liaison between fund traders and custodian banks. Prepared audit schedules. Assisted in training new personnel.

Mutual Fund Accountant   1999–2002
Functions included daily pricing of common stock and bond funds, accruing and reconciling interest and dividend accounts, reconciling trial balance accounts and daily contact with bankers to obtain stock and bond quotes.

TIMBERCREST COMPANY   Boston, MA
Assistant Supervisor   1996–1999
Prepared schedules for fund audits. Prepared reports for fund managers. Assisted fund accountants with month-end trial balance reconciliation. Trained new personnel.

Fund Accountant   1994–1996
Manually priced funds and posted journals and ledgers through trial balance. Heavy daily contact with brokers.

OTHER QUALIFICATIONS:
Licensed Michigan Real Estate Broker, 1993

EDUCATION:

Waterford High School, Waterford, MI
Graduated 1992

Accountant
General

CHRIS SMITH
178 Green Street
Loretto, PA 15940
(814) 555-5555

OBJECTIVE

An accounting position offering the opportunity to utilize my professional financial expertise, extensive business expertise, and ability to interact with senior management and with the business community on a worldwide basis.

SUMMARY OF QUALIFICATIONS

- **Accountant** and **Administrative Manager** of medium-sized motor components manufacturing and distribution company serving national and international markets.
- Hands-on expertise with firm of certified Public Accountants and Auditors.
- **Certified Public Accountant** and **Auditor.**

PROFESSIONAL EXPERIENCE

2003– **LISMORE SHIPPING CO., LTD.**, Loretta, PA
Present Accountant

- Managed, developed, and maintained all aspects of finance, accounting, foreign exchange dealings, marketing, and data processing of company and its overseas offices in London and New York.
- Controlled budget, cash flow, and capital expenditure.
- Reviewed, analyzed, and evaluated finances and securities pertaining to advance and shipping for client base of about 200.
- Established and maintained close relationships with bank executives, auditors, and attorneys, ensuring compliance with all regulatory bodies.

1998–2003 **RABINO PRODUCTS,** Meadville, PA
Accountant

- Developed and implemented corporate and project-oriented financial strategies.
- Provided financial overview and leadership for all major operating considerations and activities, including development of business and profit plans.
- Controlled line management for all accounting, production costing, EDP, and financial functions.

1996–1998 **MANNINGS, DAVE, AND BOND,** Pittsburgh, PA
Auditor

- Audited private companies, listed companies, partnerships, and individual businesses.
- Prepared financial statements and schedules.

EDUCATION

UNIVERSITY OF PENNSYLVANIA, Philadelphia, PA
Bachelor's degree, with major in Accountancy, Marketing, and Business Finance, 1996

Accounting Assistant

CHRIS SMITH
178 Green Street
Chicago, IL 60604
(312) 555-5555

OBJECTIVE
A career in the financial field where budgeting experience will be advanced.

SUMMARY OF QUALIFICATIONS
- More than sixteen years of progressive experience in budget control, public relations, and sales.
- Excellent interpersonal and negotiating skills; adept at defusing potential problems.
- Proven oral and written communication abilities.
- Adaptable to new concepts and responsibilities.
- Proficient in handling diverse tasks simultaneously.

PROFESSIONAL EXPERIENCE
STATE TREASURY, Chicago, IL   2000–Present
Accounting Assistant
Administer budget, payroll, and personnel for a 322-person staff and $7 million budget. Attend state house meetings. Act as liaison with Budget Bureau. Pay Treasury bills; ensure payroll coverage. Determine emergency allotment needs. Assist with public relations, opening/closing monthly and yearly budgets, and payroll. Negotiate contract work. Interface with clients from presentations and determining needs through completion of services. Act as liaison with accountants.

CRAVEN TRANSPORT, Midway Airport, Chicago, IL   1995–2000
Budget Director
Set up/implemented $7 million budget and payroll for main branch and subsidiaries. Negotiated contracts with air freight agencies working directly with owner.

NANETTE CONSTRUCTION, Elsah, IL   1989–1995
Budget Director
Actuated original budget for new company; ensured appropriation of moneys for payroll. Administered all office functions utilizing PC-based applications.

EDUCATION
Western Illinois University, Macomb, IL   1987–1989
Major: Business Management

REFERENCES
Furnished upon request.

Accounting Clerk

CHRIS SMITH
178 Green Street
Brimfield, MA 01010
(413) 555-5555

OBJECTIVE

An assistant accounting position in a progressive organization that offers opportunities for advancement.

SUMMARY OF QUALIFICATIONS

- More than three years accounting experience.
- Extensive computer experience.
- Developed interpersonal skills, having dealt with a diversity of professionals, clients, and staff members.
- Self-motivated; able to implement decisions and set effective priorities to achieve both immediate and long-term goals.

EXPERIENCE

4/06–pres.   APPLEDYNE CORP., Brimfield, MA
Accounting Assistant
Prepare, monitor, and maintain computerized accounts payables and receivables. Verify accuracy of purchase orders and invoices. Resolve problem areas. Monitor PC-based accounting system for internal software companies. Implement a billing system to maintain cordial relations with clients, resulting in a 10% increase in new client acquisition. Delegate as troubleshooter. Design an employee check-cashing center within company. Received written commendation from Appledyne president, John Pacs.

4/05–4/06   TERRIO LYCRA CORP., Amherst, MA
Accounts Receivable/Payable Clerk
Maintaining Accounts Receivable/Payable; handled outgoing communications on PC word processing system. Generated/mailed A/P checks.

7/03–4/05   MAYFLOWER DATING SERVICE, Manomet, MA
Accounting Clerk/Assistant to Vice President of Finance
Generated income statements, balance sheets, general ledger, checks, and reports; entered payable vouchers; received/deposited monthly rent checks.

EDUCATION

JASPER COLLEGE, Nashua, NH
B.S., Mathematics, 2003
GPA. 3.0/4.0

COMPUTERS

Proficient in Excel and Microsoft Word.

CHRIS SMITH
178 Green Street
Bakerton, KY 42711
(606) 555-5555

EMPLOYMENT HISTORY

2005 to Present   **CHET HORN INC., Bakerton, KY**
Accounting Manager
- Directed a staff of five. Responsible for the Custody Operations work necessary to maintain client's asset base (International Bond Funds, Equity Funds, Single Country Funds, and Pension Funds).
- Anticipated client needs and responded to their requests. Maintained an excellent service record during a growth period that increased our team's asset responsibility from $6 billion to $7.1 billion in one year.
- Expanded market awareness by attending focus sessions and seminars on the constantly changing foreign markets.
- Improved GCAS productivity by designing the Brown Brothers Monthly Custody Operations Package. Collaborated with the client to test and convert to an automated transmission process. Trained account staff and management peers to utilize bank's online security system.

Account Manager
- Monitored and executed currency and security statements in global markets (including Emerging Markets).
- Supported internal and external audit requests by successfully reconciling all currency and security discrepancies with clients and sub-custodians.
- Accomplished team goals by cross-training with other Account Managers and taking on additional responsibilities, including a weekly review of overdrafts for all funds in the team.

2004 to 2005   **SUNNYVALE AND SON, Lexington, KY**
Fund Accountant
- Settled bond and equity transactions in the United States markets. Prepared weekly and monthly financial statements for mutual funds.
- Assumed sole responsibility for researching past due interest, dividend receivables, and claiming brokers. Reduced the volume by 60% in one year.

EDUCATION

Moorehead State University, Moorehead, KY
Master of Science, 2007 (Expected date of completion)
Concentration: Finance
Cumberland College, Williamsburg, KY
Bachelor of Science, 2004
Concentration: Finance and Economics

COMPUTERS

Software knowledge: Microsoft Word, Excel, Access, FileMaker

Accounts Payable Clerk
General

CHRIS SMITH
178 Green Street
Newark, NJ 07102
(201) 555-5555

OBJECTIVE
Seeking a position in administrative support where acquired accounting skills will be advanced.

WORK EXPERIENCE
5/04 to **BETTY LOU'S LINGERIE**, Newark, NJ
Present **Accounts Payable/Payroll Department**
Light typing, filing, and other general office duties. Key in bills on a PC and print all checks for six different offices. Assist in payroll preparation by calculating all time sheets and related duties.

2001 to **DYNAMO DANCE SUPPLIES**, Newark, NJ
2004 **Accounts Payable**
Set up all invoices to match purchase orders for input into computers. Added up all invoices to match check amounts. Responsible for filing, sorting mail, and general office duties.

1999 to **LEDA AND THE SWAN PET SITTERS**, New Brunswick, NJ
2001 **Administrative Coordinator**
Acted as cashier, light typist, bank depositor, and key punch operator. Handled filing and accounts payable/receivable. Heavy customer contact.

COMPUTERS
Most PC and Mac applications, including Microsoft Word, Excel, FileMaker, Internet Explorer

SPECIAL INTERESTS
Camping, fishing, and jogging.

REFERENCES
Furnished upon request.

CHRIS SMITH
178 Green Street
Burbank, CA 91501
(818) 555-5555

EMPLOYMENT HISTORY

2003 to Present **SIENNA SIGH HERBALISTS,** Burbank, CA
Senior Accounts Payable Administrator
- Manage entire accounts payable function at Corporate Headquarters.
- Coordinate efforts for accounts payable personnel at three branch locations.
- Complete weekly check disbursements for all Sienna locations. Payments averaging in excess of $500,000.
- Inform Corporate Treasury of weekly cash requirements, give input of required vendor payments and credit terms for extremely sensitive cash management function.
- Issue weekly and monthly accounts payable distribution reports, work with Corporate Accountants as to accounts payable interface with the general ledger.
- Maintain total outstanding payable balance, including collection of outstanding credits.
- Manage Japanese accounts payable.
- Cross-train as replacement for Senior Payroll Administrator on APD system.
- Cross-train for filing of federal, state, and unemployment taxes.

Factory Accountant/Accounts Payable (2001 to 2003)
- Recorded and analyzed direct labor and standard costs.
- Posted all invoices to general ledger.
- Maintained and collected all receivables from Sienna's foreign affiliates and outside vendors.
- Assisted in general ledger monthly closings.

1999 to 2001 **THE HOLISTIC HEALING CENTER,** San Francisco, CA
Bookkeeper
- Managed weekly payroll for thirty-seven employees.
- Filed state and federal taxes.
- Maintained human resources duties.
- Oversaw full accounts payable duties.
- Posted cash receipts.
- Composed and posted JE to GL through trial balance.

TECHNICAL SUMMARY

Excel, Word, and various accounting software packages

EDUCATION

University of Nevada at Las Vegas: Bachelor of Science, Accounting, 1998.

Accounts Receivable Clerk

CHRIS SMITH

| 178 Green Street | Newark, NJ 07107 | (201) 555-5555 |

CAREER HISTORY

THE FULLER COMPANY, Newark, NJ   2005–Present
Assistant Manager—Accounts Receivable
- Maintaining $10,000 petty cash fund and $15,000 American Express Travelers' Checks account.
- Documented "proofed" checks and moneys for deposit and coordinated with other departments to resolve problems with checks that failed to clear.
- Posted receivables to electronic spreadsheet and month-end journal entries on a highly technical software application.
- Researched interdepartmental queries and provided results to requester.
- Performed traditional accounting functions.

Financial Associate—Accounts Payable
- Audited documents to include expense reports, invoices, and check requests for payment.
- Generated disbursement instructions for accounts.
- Assigned and maintained vendor identification files through an online computer system.
- Developed and maintained 1099 tax information on vendor.
- Assisted in establishing and validating travel reimbursement programs.

B. PARR AND ASSOCIATES, West Orange, NJ   2003–2005
Bookkeeper
- Performed all accounting functions to include journal entries, accounts payables, receivables, petty cash, deposits, bank reconciliations, and trial balance.
- Calculated payroll deductions and processed payroll.
- Responsible for monthly, quarterly, and year-end payroll and sales tax forms.
- Effective in phone collection of overdue accounts, and generating invoices and statements.

HACKENSACK HOME FURNISHINGS, Hackensack, NJ   2000–2003
Manager/Bookkeeper
- Brought company to full operational status.
- Responsible for inventory, orders, sales, rent-to-own contracts, and supervisor of part-time employees.
- Performed all bookkeeping, banking, sales, payroll taxes, and bank reconciliations.

EDUCATION

Kean College of New Jersey, Union, NJ
A.S. in Accounting, December 1999.

Assistant Portfolio Manager

CHRIS SMITH
178 Green Street
Arlington, VA 22201
(703) 555-5555

PROFESSIONAL OBJECTIVE

Seeking new challenges in **Finance,** where relevant education, experience, and analytical, customer service, follow-up, and problem-solving skills will be utilized and advanced.

CAREER HISTORY

2005–Present   CANNON, SLOAT, ERICKSON, AND BANKS, INC., Arlington, VA
Assistant Portfolio Manager

- Set up all systems and files for Reconciliation Department; assume responsibility for procedures and documentation relevant to this new unit (300 accounts).
- Ensure that all account monies are fully invested and that transaction requests are fulfilled in a timely and accurate manner.
- Personally responsible for portfolio of eighteen accounts.
- Prepare cash flow analyses and verify/submit client quarterly reports.
- Maintain research files of stocks and bonds; assess and select municipal bonds presented by Brokers.
- Interact with bank and in-house Trading Department.

2004–2005   O'CONNOR PRINTING, Alexandria, VA
Promotional Sales Representative

- Generated new business and established new accounts through cold-calling, follow-up, and the provision of detailed service and pricing information.

2003–2005   VIRGINIA STATE REPRESENTATIVE ELECTION COMMITTEE, Charlottesville, VA
Assistant Campaign Manager

- Assisted in the development and implementation of promotional programs; set up and coordinated fundraisers.

EDUCATION

SWEET BRIAR COLLEGE, Sweet Briar, VA
Bachelor of Science degree in **Management/Finance,** January 2003.

Course work included:

Management Information Systems	Managerial Accounting
Financial Accounting	Stock Market Investments
Data Processing Statistics	International Economics
Money and Banking	Monetary Management

Internship: Served VTA Advisory Board as Assistant Budget Analyst.

- Reviewed budget proposals from various departments; broke down and analyzed previous budgets, verified figures, and made recommendations to Budget Director based on results.

Audit Manager

CHRIS SMITH
178 Green Street
Pawtucket, RI 02860
(401) 555-5555

OBJECTIVE

An Audit Management position with the possibility of cross-functional responsibilities in Project Development.

SUMMARY OF QUALIFICATIONS

Versatile, respected management professional with high standards of integrity. Adept at sizing up situations, analyzing facts, and developing alternative courses of action in order to increase productivity. Forms quality liaisons and relationships easily, and instills a high level of confidence at all levels.

PROFESSIONAL EXPERIENCE

Auditing Manager   2004–Present
MINISTRY OF NATIONAL EDUCATION   Hamburg, Germany
- Controlled contract management of an education improvement project.
- Assisted Execution Bureau in establishing Accounting System.
- Controlled all project financial operations; verified financial statements, justification of expenses, requests, and disbursements.
- Established internal control systems for various investment categories.

Financial Advisor   2001–2004
NATIONAL PORT AUTHORITY   Port au Prince, Haiti
- Established control mechanism for financial plans and budgets; monitored the management of all financial resources and established a treasury service.
- Restructured Control and Budget Service; updated accounting procedures.
- Implemented an evaluation system for budget execution; took corrective actions as necessary; updated and restructured the Procurement Service.
- Monitored accuracy and timely transmittal of monthly financial statements; assisted in the establishment of a computerized accounting system.
- Member, Supervisory Board of Management Information Systems; controlled all financial resources.

Chief Financial Analysis/Evaluation and Control Department   1997–2001
MINISTRY OF PLANNING   Port au Prince, Haiti
- Analyzed development projects' annual operations plans, internal and external, physical, and financial project executions.
- Participated in social housing project financed by the United Nations.
- Represented the Ministry at the Management Board of Canadian Government Retrocession Funds.

EDUCATION

BOSTON UNIVERSITY, Boston, MA, B.A. Economics, 1995.

CHRIS SMITH
178 Green Street
Birmingham, AL 35294
(205) 555-5555

OBJECTIVE

A challenging position within the fields of Tax Accounting or Investment.

SUMMARY OF QUALIFICATIONS

- Thorough knowledge of individual income, employment, and excise tax laws and regulations; IRS Service policies; and selected tax forms. Experienced in preparation of individual and employment tax returns. Proficient accounting, bookkeeping, and problem-solving skills.

EMPLOYMENT HISTORY

10/04 to Present   **Taxpayer Service Representative**
INTERNAL REVENUE SERVICE   Birmingham, AL
- Individual income and businesses.
- Explain various IRS bills and notices to taxpayers and set up installment agreements.
- Maintain knowledge of current IRS tax documents, enforcement policies, forms, laws, notices, regulations, Service organization, and policies.
- Develop understanding of "tiered" interview techniques to determine taxpayer's ability to pay outstanding tax obligations.

1/04 to 5/04   **Intern**
PRICE, PATTON, AND TATE   Atlanta, GA
- Posted trades and performed general office and receptionist duties.

Summer 2003   **Sales Intern—China Department**
JAKES DEPARTMENT STORE   Selma, AL
- Provided customer service and resolved consumer and departmental complaints.
- Created displays and initiated sale of merchandise.
- Controlled inventory and trained employees.

Summer 2002   **Ticket Salesperson**
BUDGE BUS TOURS   Montgomery, AL
- Maintained bookkeeping records, deposited currency, and resolved customer complaints.
- Commended for achievement of second highest ticket seller in twelve years.

EDUCATION

ARMSTRONG STATE COLLEGE   Savannah, GA
Bachelor of Arts degree: Management, May 2004

COMPUTERS

Proficient with most PC and Mac applications.

Bank Administrator

CHRIS SMITH
178 Green Street
Boulder, CO 80309
(303) 555-5555

OBJECTIVE

A challenging career where administrative experience, motivation, and a commitment to excellence will be utilized and advanced.

SUMMARY OF QUALIFICATIONS

- Five years of progressive, professional experience; extensive mutual funds background.
- Computer experience includes most PC and Mac applications.
- Developed interpersonal and communication skills, having dealt with a diversity of professionals, clients, and staff members.
- Self-motivated; able to set effective priorities to achieve immediate and long-term goals and meet operational deadlines.
- Adapt easily to new concepts and responsibilities.
- Functions well independently and as a team member; responds best in fast-paced, high-pressure environment.

PROFESSIONAL EXPERIENCE

BOULDER BANK & TRUST CO., Boulder, CO   8/99–7/06

Senior Specialist, 7/04–7/06

Controlled correspondence flow. Maintained input/output data. Completed backlog and time sheets. Supervised support staff. Generated reports. Well-versed in Securities and Exchange Commission rules and regulations.

Priority Response Administrator, 12/03–7/04

Administered/resolved shareholder inquiries; enhanced timeframe. Researched complex and lengthy data maintaining rigid deadlines. Handled general clerical responsibilities; generated reports.

Priority Response Specialist, 8/02–12/03

Dealt with shareowners; provided information on work itemization, research, and adjustments. Handled special projects and clerical functions.

Shareholders Communications Specialist, 2/01–8/02

Communicated directly with shareholders by telephone and letter; provided information on mutual funds, net asset values, policies, and procedures. Analyzed, calculated, and adjusted daily shareholder account activities.

Customer Service Representative, 8/99–1/01

Researched/corrected billing errors; utilized C.R.T. system. Provided account information.

RELEVANT EDUCATION

Certified in ABCD Bank Training Program, 2004

Bank Treasurer

CHRIS SMITH
178 Green Street
Rome, GA 30161
(706) 555-5555

PROFESSIONAL OBJECTIVE
A treasurer position in banking.

SUMMARY OF QUALIFICATIONS
- Extensive experience in Business Development, Commercial Loan Operations, Credit Analysis, Loan Review, Asset/Liability Review, Financial Analysis, and Planning.
- Refinement and implementation of management systems, administrative policies, and operational procedures.
- Experience hiring/terminating, training, scheduling, motivating, and supervising staffs.
- Forecasting, preparing, and monitoring expenditures of operational budgets.
- Exceptional interpersonal, client-service, liaison, and follow-through skills.

PROFESSIONAL BACKGROUND
WYNDCREST BANK, Rome, GA
Treasurer (2004 to Present)
- Manage day-to-day operations and develop new business at branch with staff of sixteen to twenty, and deposit base of $16 million.
- Work with ATM and acquired maintenance skills.
- Hire/terminate, schedule, evaluate, and supervise administrative and support staff.
- Conduct long-range and day-to-day planning for branch.
- Provide customer service through resolution of problems, explanation of bank services and policies, and knowledge of financial planning.

Branch Manager (1999 to 2004)
- Supervised total operation of branch with $7 million deposit base in Rome Center.
- Within three-month period, added 220 deposit accounts and increased deposits to raise branch's deposit base by 244%.
- Trained personnel in Creative Merchandising, Marketing, and Sales Development.
- Implemented turn-around for Winter Square Branch with thirty-six employees and $22 million in assets.
- Streamlined and reorganized Customer Service Operations.

EDUCATIONAL BACKGROUND
PAINE COLLEGE, School of Banking, Augusta, GA
Certification of Completion, 1999
ATLANTA INSTITUTE OF BANKING, Atlanta, GA
Maintained A Average through completion of eight courses, 1999
OGLETHORPE UNIVERSITY, Atlanta, GA
Bachelor of Science in Business Administration, 1998

PROFESSIONAL AFFILIATIONS
Rome Business Association Member

Billing Supervisor

CHRIS SMITH
178 Green Street
Miami, FL 33054
(305) 555-5555

EXPERIENCE

<u>**The Pearl Co.**</u>   **Miami, FL**
Limited Partnerships Accounting and Administration
BILLING SUPERVISOR   9/03 to Present
Created/implemented billing system for reimbursing departmental
salaries, rent, and out-of-pocket expenses. Initiated Accounts
Receivable system. Researched and projected yearly management
fees and cash distributions. Supervised daily preparation of
invoices and reconciling monthly bank statements.

CONTROL ACCOUNTANT   6/01 to 9/03
Monitored daily reconciliation of transfer agent and shareholder
records for Mutual Fund Division. Supervised daily posting
and reconciliation of demand deposit accounts and settlement
with client's share and dollar positions. Reconciled and
reported net changes in Fund daily share positions.

<u>**Bank of Miami**</u>   **Miami, FL**
CASH CONTROLLER   11/00 to 6/01
Monitored incoming shipments of coin and currency, handling
large cash orders from banks and companies. Filled out currency
transaction reports. Distributed and collected moneys from
tellers.

FOREIGN TELLER   3/00 to 10/00
Bought and sold foreign currency and travelers' checks.
Performed wire transfers. Typed bank drafts. Maintained
exchange rates.

COMMERCIAL TELLER   7/99 to 4/00
Cashed and deposited customer checks. Verified signature of
business and individual customers. Typed cashier certified
checks. Trained new tellers. Assisted with automatic teller
machines.

EDUCATION

Rollins College   **Winter Park, FL**
B.S., BUSINESS ADMINISTRATION candidate   2000 to Present

Boca Raton Junior College   **Boca Raton, FL**
A.S., ACCOUNTING   2000
Major: Accounting

CHRIS SMITH
178 Green Street
Albuquerque, NM 87140
(505) 555-5555

OBJECTIVE
A challenging career opportunity in Accounting/Bookkeeping.

SUMMARY OF QUALIFICATIONS
- More than eighteen years experience in Accounting/Bookkeeping.
- Able negotiator/liaison, dealing with professionals, clients, and staff.
- Accurate, organized, and aware of importance of meeting deadlines and maintaining smooth workflow.
- Computer literate.

EXPERIENCE

CHUTES AND LADDERS DAYCARE CENTER, Albuquerque, NM
Agency Bookkeeper   5/06–Present
Handle cash disbursement, verify vendor invoices, and generate weekly checks. Administer General Ledger, fund coding and checkbook maintenance for agency accounts. Record transactions; maintain up-to-date bank balances. Prepare/post disbursements and monthly invoices to state and municipal contractors.

Voucher Bookkeeper   6/05–5/06
Processed current/outstanding for reimbursement for over 300 providers (3,000 payments). Dealt with underpayment/overpayment and rate changes; verified adjustments requests against payment history; issued/recorded advance payment checks. Ensured immediate update of computerized fiscal files and accounts payable to meet rigid deadlines schedule. Assisted providers; verified payments for auditors. Oversaw part-time staff.

Assistant Bookkeeper   4/01–6/05
Supervised current/outstanding invoice payment approval, computerized data input, invoice verification, posting to Ledger, and dispatching checks.

SAWYER REALTY TRUST, Las Cruces, NM
Part-time Bookkeeper
Recorded rent payments, paid banks/vendors, reconciled bank statements.

EDUCATION

NEWBURY JUNIOR COLLEGE, Boston, MA
Associate's degree in Accounting, 1999

MONTREAL UNIVERSITY, DIVISION OF CONTINUING EDUCATION,
Montreal, Canada
Bachelor of Arts degree, Teaching/Education (equivalent)

Bookkeeping Clerk

CHRIS SMITH
178 Green Street
Eden Prairie, MN 55347
(902) 555-5555

OBJECTIVE

A challenging position in bookkeeping.

PROFESSIONAL EXPERIENCE

ASSOCIATES, INC., Eden Prairie, MN
Bookkeeping Clerk, 2006–Present
- Monitor general ledger and investors' monthly reports.
- Oversee A/R and A/P staff to ensure accuracy of accounts.
- Monitor payroll taxes for accuracy and on-time payments.
- Manage multiple accounts for real estate developer with commercial and residential properties in several states.

MORNINGSIDE CO., Hopkins, MN
Bookkeeping Clerk, 2004–2006
- Supervised general ledger through trial balance, as well as A/P, payroll, and payroll tax returns.
- Converted bookkeeping procedures from one write system to in-house computer system.
- Coordinated department's workflow.

Accounts Receivable Clerk, 2003–2004

HAWTHORNE MEDICAL CENTER, Howard Lake, MN
Secretary, Cardiac Care Unit, 2002–2003
- Scheduled patients for appointments and tests.
- Answered phones, troubleshoot problems.
- Transcribed doctors' orders, ordered supplies.
- Maintained patient records, set up charts.

EXCELSIOR CORP., Mankato, MN
Secretary to Vice President, 2000–2002
- Performed office duties such as monitoring personnel files, scheduling, and paying operating expenses.

Receptionist, 1999–2000
- Answered phones, scheduled travel, acted as liaison between management and staff.

EDUCATION

SOUTHWEST STATE UNIVERSITY, Marshall, MN
Accounting Courses, 2003–2004

Budget Analyst

CHRIS SMITH
178 Green Street
Los Angeles, CA 90031
(310) 555-5555

EXPERIENCE

2/06-   **Golden Life Insurance Company**   Los Angeles, CA
Present BUDGET ANALYST
- Balance $1.3 billion budget.
- Reconcile accounts.
- Assist management in budget preparation.
- Conduct training classes on the financial system for upper-level management.
- Prepare comparison of expense to budget reports for executives.
- Submit accounts and IRS filing for the Political Action Committee.
- Generate financial analysts projects.

6/02-   **The Pacific**   Los Angeles, CA
2/06   FUNDING ANALYST
- Prepared contract proposals and illustrative cost calculation.
- Constructed Actuarial Valuation Report for individual clients.
- Determined the minimum and maximum contribution allowable by law for the IRS.
- Assured accuracy of the database.
- Developed plan costs and analyzed actuarial gains/losses.

ACCOUNTING TECHNICIAN
- Managed money market mutual fund for sixty corporate clients.
- Balanced Trial Balance and generated journal entries.
- Maintained, compared, and reconciled the fund on three computer systems.
- Communicated with other departments, field personnel, and clients.
- Prepared financial statements.
- Assisted system analysts in preparation and implementation of new computer system.

EDUCATION

UNIVERSITY OF WASHINGTON   Seattle, WA
Bachelor of Science degree in Finance

ACTIVITIES

Swimming, reading, crafts, travel.

Chief Financial Officer
CFO

CHRIS SMITH
178 Green Street
Marylhurst, OR 97036
(503) 555-5555

EMPLOYMENT HISTORY

2001 to Present   **KALEIDOSCOPE HOTELS, INC.,** Marylhurst, OR
Vice President of Finance and Administration (2005 to Present)
Directed and oversaw the accounting function for thirteen hotels located throughout the Northwest with annual sales in excess of $120 million. Supervised Home Office staff of twenty with extended authority over 100 field employees.
- Directed the annual budget process from original business plan to final approval.
- Administered self-insurance programs for Workers' Compensation by directing attorney selection, investigations, and claim settlements.
- Designed system to track capital spending.

Company (Corporate) Controller (2003 to 2005)
Reported all consolidated financial performance for the divisions of Kaleidoscope, which consisted of hotels, residential apartments, telecommunications stations, and a construction division. Supervised a staff of fifteen.
- Directed selection and implementation of new accounting software for real estate divisions of the company, and new payroll system for entire company which processed payroll for 6,000 employees in seven states.
- Integral member of team that implemented change from a premium-based Workers' Compensation insurance policy to a self-insured one.

Assistant Controller (2001 to 2003)
- Supervised an office staff of ten in the daily accounting function.
- Set up accounting offices in all thirteen hotels in the division.
- Chaired committee that selected automated time and attendance payroll system for entire company which ultimately achieved annual savings of over $500,000.

1998 to 2001   **HUBERT FINE FRANCHISE SYSTEMS, INC.,** Holyoke, MA
Accounting Manager (2000 to 2001)
Responsible for accounting functions and preparation of annual budget for this "spin off" corporation of Marriott Corporation's purchase of the Howard Johnson Company. Supervised a staff of six.
- Worked with Marriott Corporation on pre- and post-acquisition adjustments.

Staff Accountant (1998 to 2000)
Prepared corporate financial statements for senior management and annual audit.

EDUCATION

Oregon State University, Corvallis, OR
Bachelor of Science, Accounting, 1998

COMPUTER PROGRAMS

Microsoft Word, Excel, Access, FileMaker

```
                        CHRIS SMITH
                      178 Green Street
                     Scituate, MA 02066
                       (781) 555-5555
```

EXPERIENCE:

11/05-6/06   NANTASCOT BANK, Scituate, MA
             International Loan Collection Specialist
             Provided and/or coordinated full loan service functions
             to International Corporate, Commercial, and Correspondent
             Financial concerns. Researched and resolved customer problems
             and inquiries. Processed ingoing and outgoing documentary
             collections. Maintained and updated all loan and loan-related
             documentation, including foreign tax credit system.

10/04-6/06   JEREMY PEARL FURNITURE, Weymouth, MA
             Credit Collector (part-time)
             Telephone collections of past due accounts. Informed customers
             in regard to their account status and payment options. Credit
             bureau and fraud account functions. Related typing and data
             entry. Successfully collected 75% of assigned accounts.

12/03-7/04   HOUSE-R-US REALTORS, Weymouth, MA
             Receptionist
             Answered phones and provided customer support. Responsible
             for typing and researching.

7/00-11/03   MASSBANK, Boston, MA
             Trade Service Representative
             Assisted and informed customers regarding debits and credits
             to their accounts. Accurately compiled and updated customer
             files.

EDUCATION:

2001-2003   UNIVERSITY OF MASSACHUSETTS, Boston, MA
             Courses in Personnel Management, English, Communications

1999-2001   QUINCY COLLEGE, Quincy, MA
             Courses in Communications, Typing, English

References Available Upon Request

Credit Analyst

CHRIS SMITH
178 Green Street
Grace City, OH 58445
(216) 555-5555

SUMMARY:
- Five years experience in retail banking and commercial lending.
- Adept at credit/financial analysis.
- Proficient in analysis of financial statements.
- Fluent in Dutch; knowledgeable in conversational and written German.
- Naturalized U.S. citizen.

EDUCATION:
OHIO STATE UNIVERSITY—Graduate School of Management, Columbus, OH
M.B.A., Concentration: Finance, May 2004
Courses included: International Finance, Money and Capital Markets, Investments, Corporate Finance, Corporate Financial Reporting, and Global Macroeconomics.
- GPA in Major: 3.8/4.0

Bachelor of Science, Business Administration, 2000
Concentration: Accounting and Finance

EXPERIENCE:
WISTERIA BANK, Grace City, OH
Commercial Loan Credit Analysis, 2005–Present
Provide analytical services as part of lending team. Analyze/evaluate financial statements. Develop pro-forma statements and cash flow projections. Document findings; prepare independent recommendations on advisability of granting credits for corporate lenders.

Senior Personal Banker, 2003–2005
Assisted in branch administration. Oversaw branch overdraft reports. Reviewed/executed consumer loans. Supervised the vault area; audited tellers; provided customer service.

Personal Banker, 2000–2004
Established/serviced professional clientele accounts. Expedited investments in treasury bills, repurchase agreements, CDs, retirement accounts, and discount brokerage for bank clients. Assisted branch corporate lender weekly on a revolving commercial loan.
- Sold sixteen retirement accounts in one day; resulted in an IRA sales award for branch.
- Achieved several awards for bank product sales.

COMPUTERS: Excel, Word, FileMaker, Access

CHRIS SMITH
178 Green Street
Princeton, NJ 08540
(609) 555-5555

EXPERIENCE: XYZ FINANCIAL CONSULTANTS, Princeton, NJ
July 2005–Present
Financial Consultant, Consumer Markets
- Developed $11 million client base through aggressive prospecting campaign.
- Successfully built portfolios that include stocks, bonds, options, and insurance products for more than 450 clients.
- Implemented financial plans and operations through account development and growth.

October 2003–July 2005
Sales Associate
- Worked directly with the firm's top producer, profiling high net worth individuals for future business.
- Generated $20,000 in commissions for top producer through new account openings.
- Analyzed existing portfolios, assisting in development of accounts.

September 2001–October 2003
Customer Account Representative
- Supervised more than $35,000 accounts in the areas of trade settlement, regulations, and customer inquiries.
- Reported recommendations to upper management.
- Acted as liaison between sales force and New York operations.

RELATED TRAINING: Successfully completed XYZ Financial Consultant Sales Training and Advanced Training programs at Princeton, NJ, headquarters.
Licensed in Series 6, 7, 63, and health and life insurance.

EDUCATION: IONA COLLEGE, Iona, NY
Bachelor of Arts degree in Economics, 2003
Concentration: Business Management

COMPUTER SKILLS: Excel and Microsoft Word

Financial Consultant
General

CHRIS SMITH
178 Green Street
Cookeville, TN 38502
(615) 555-5555

Objective   A challenging position in the field of FINANCIAL COUNSELING, dealing directly with clients developing comprehensive financial plans.

Education   Central Michigan University, Mount Pleasant, MI, 2006
Certificate in Investment Planning.

Northwestern University, Evanston, IL, 2003
Bachelor of Science degree in Business Administration. GPA 3.7, Honors Graduate, Concentration in Marketing.

Experience   Hillside Estates, Kalamazoo, MI 2004–Present
Managing and monitoring all phases of the organization. Applied knowledge of market conditions and sales methods. Interfacing with clients and buyers in the sale and resale of manufactured homes. Interviewed and hired potential employees.

Springhouse Restaurant Springfield, ND 2000–2003
Assistant Manager. Coordinated restaurant operations. Trained and motivated employees in customer relations and the methods of maintaining good employer-employee relationships.

Foreign Friends, Inc., Chicago, IL 2002
Participant in an intensive summer program culminating in four weeks of travel in South Africa. Organized and executed programs to provide immunization shots. Became extremely aware of the need of flexibility in adjusting to changing work situations.

Affiliation   Member of International Association of Financial Planners.

Strengths   Self-motivating; excellent communication skills; able to deal effectively and productively with management, coworkers, and the public; goal oriented; and capable of the sustained effort necessary to take a project from conception to completion.

Interests   Sailing, skiing, scuba diving, hiking, and piano.

References   Available upon request.

CHRIS SMITH
178 Green Street
Seattle, WA 98122
(206) 555-5555

EMPLOYMENT HISTORY

January 2004 to Present

THE ATHENA GROUP, Seattle, WA
Manager of Finance

Manage a group of three associates responsible for producing financial reports, all aspects of budgeting a $51 million office, A/R, A/P, petty cash, expense reports, revenue collection, and monthly closing for an office of 284 associates. Responsible for producing systems that generate the necessary financial information to determine our profitability. Systems track accrual profit, cash profit, expenses by sub-groups, and a new cost accounting systems.

- Upon hiring into this position in July of 2007, had written off $3 million of unbillable or uncollectable business. The office posted a 0% profit. Currently looking to make a 5% accrual profit for this fiscal year.
- Designed a billing tracking system to allow team managers to determine where they stood on a monthly basis for revenue collection. The system projects where the team is in accordance with where they need to be in order to meet the goal of 5%.

Systems Analyst, Finance and Administration

Systems analyst for a network of ten users. Administered COBRA software application—health care/dependent care reimbursement system.

- Assisted in implementing new health care system. Installed remote connection for offsite claims processing.
- User liaison for billing system in place in forty offices throughout U.S. and Canada. Designed training materials, performed on-site training, troubleshooting via telecommunications.

Sept. 2002 to Jan. 2004

FANFARE INTERNATIONAL, Tacoma, WA
Programmer/Analyst/Consultant

- Provided large utility client with database software to track political campaign contributions. System provided feedback on how campaign contributions were distributed versus the way "supported" legislators voted on key issues.

EDUCATION

Longfellow University, Wordsworth, MA
Master's degree in MIS, anticipated December 2009

Barley College, Sioux City, IA
Bachelor of Arts in Economics, 2002
Minor in Computer Science

COMPUTERS

Languages: HTML, Perl, SQL, C++
Applications: Microsoft Word, Excel, FrameMaker, Photoshop
Operating Systems: Mac OS, Windows NT, UNIX
Hardware Platforms: PC and Mac

Financial Planner
Health

CHRIS SMITH
178 Green Street
Tallahassee, FL 32307
(904) 555-5555

EMPLOYMENT HISTORY

2005 to Present **HEALTH PROVIDERS, Tallahassee, FL**
Director, Financial Planning and Reporting
Oversee all aspects of internal and external reporting including preparation of the annual report as well as quarterly and monthly reports of the Board of Directors and Senior Management. Coordinate development of the financial plan and track financial performance against plan. Supervise a department of twelve professionals.
- Successfully guide the financial planning and reporting function through significant transition as management restructured the Corporation to meet customer expectations. Results include Board and Management level reporting structured along business unit and product lines, significantly enhancing effectiveness.
- Selected and implemented Windows-based LAN using advanced database, spreadsheet, and desktop publishing software to create an integrated financial modeling, planning, and reporting process. Reduced analysis and production time by 30%.
- Leader of successful integration project which merged financial operations/staff with corporation. Served as project leader reporting to CFO on all aspects of this six-month integration project. Completed project on time and within budget.
- Directly involved with senior management on an ongoing basis.

2002 to 2005 **THIBERGE TECHNOLOGIES, Miami, FL**
Manager, Accounting/Consolidations
Managed the Corporate Accounting function including foreign and domestic Consolidations for fifteen Subsidiaries. Supervised three professionals and one clerical.
- Successfully managed the transition of the accounting function through decentralization of the entire company within timetable set by senior management.
- Selected, installed, and implemented Micro Control (IMRS) consolidations software at corporate headquarters. Streamlined consolidation process, enhancing accuracy, and reducing closing time by 25%.

2000 to 2002 **INTERNATIONAL CONSULTANTS, Boca Raton, FL**
Assistant Controller
Compiled financial bank and tax reports. Served as principal liaison with bankers and outside auditors. Managed G/L, F/A, Consolidations, and foreign exchange.
- Directed accounting function in a high growth environment. Managed function during expansion, growing from eight to thirty professional and clerical staff.

EDUCATION

Florida University
Bachelor of Science, 1999
Major in Accounting and minor in Computer Science

COMPUTERS

Mac, PC, Excel, Word, Photoshop, Perl, HTML

Insurance Underwriter
General

CHRIS SMITH
178 Green Street
Tempe, AZ 85287
(602) 555-5555

CAREER HISTORY

1994 to
Present

SCRIMSHAW INSURANCE CO., Tempe, AZ

Underwriter, Personal Lines Insurance, 2003 to Present

- Analyzed all personal lines of business to determine acceptability and to control, restrict, or decline according to company's guidelines.
- Handled manually issued policies.
- Assisted in training Administrative and technical personnel either by direct training or set-up of training schedules.
- Facilitated implementation of new programs by training new personnel.
- Kept abreast of changing policies, rates, and procedures—explaining coverage, rules, forms, and decisions to Agents, staff, and insured.
- Briefed Agents on new services to stimulate sales.
- Responsible for all personal lines of business for the states of Arizona and New Mexico.
- Assisted in ensuring achievement of company productivity and profitability objectives.
- Resolved client grievances and misunderstandings.

Assistant Supervisor, Rating and Policy Writing, 1999 to 2001

- Implemented Supervisory Controls—delegated responsibilities, set objectives, and monitored work.
- Evaluated staff performances based on results expected and achieved.
- Conducted audits.
- Implemented new programs through staff briefing, ongoing training, and updating materials.

Senior Rater, 1999

- Rated and coded all lines of business for personal lines.
- Trained other Raters and introduced the Merit Rating Surcharge Program for Arizona Automobile

Unmatched Mail Clerk, Record Department, 1994 to 1999

- Responsible for incoming mail for personal and commercial lines of business.

EDUCATION

- Underwriter Trainee, 2001 to 2002.
- Completed program at Jones Underwriting School in Phoenix, Arizona, and trained for one year to become an Underwriter.
- Ongoing education has included the following classes: Effective Letter Writing, How to Conduct an Interview, Career Workshop, Speed Reading, Xerox Sales Course, Underwriting School (six-week program), Senior Underwriting Seminar, Listening Seminar, and Supervisory Seminar.

Insurance Underwriter
Senior

CHRIS SMITH
178 Green Street
Gallant, AL 35972
(205) 555-5555

PROFESSIONAL BACKGROUND

2000 to Present   **Evergreen INSURANCE COMPANIES, Altoona, AL**
Senior Underwriter Analyst
- Responsible for underwriting complex commercial property referral accounts up to $200 million covering one-half of United States for property and casualty carrier for all lines.
- Advise and provide support for field staff and agents.
- Assist in development of training programs and manuals.
- Interpret state insurance regulations and legislation.
- Review corporate financial data and participate in audits.
- Write underwriting manuals for company personnel explaining underwriting philosophy and complicated insurance concepts.

Senior Property Underwriter
- Evaluated risks and contributed to departmental marketing through personal calls on agents to provide assistance, generate new business, and educate.
- Trained Underwriter Trainees and Underwriters.
- Authorized work from line Underwriters within Branch Letter of Authority.

1996 to 1999   **DALFINO & CONNELLY INSURANCE COMPANIES, Attalla, AL**
Senior Commercial Property Underwriter
- Responsible for underwriting commercial packages for metropolitan and rural agencies in Wyoming and Colorado.
- Promoted from Assistant Commercial Underwriter to Underwriter and to Senior Underwriter.

1994 to 1995   **WALTON INSURANCE COMPANY, Gadsden, AL**
Rate and Code Supervisor
- Managed Rate and Code operations including the insurance of policies and calculation of rates.
- Hired/terminated, trained, scheduled, and supervised staff of fifteen Commercial and Personal Lines Raters.

1991 to 1993   **ALLSURE INSURANCE COMPANY, Birmingham, AL**
Assistant Commercial Packager Underwriter
- Underwrote commercial packages.
- Promoted from Commercial Package Rater to Assistant Commercial Package Underwriter in 1992.

EDUCATIONAL BACKGROUND
BIRMINGHAM-SOUTHERN COLLEGE, Birmingham, AL
Bachelor of Science degree, 1991
Major: Management; Minors: Psychology, Economics.

Junior Accountant

CHRIS SMITH
178 Green Street
Boise, ID 83725
(208) 555-5555

EMPLOYMENT HISTORY
SPUD TRUST, Boise, ID

Junior Accountant (April 2006 to Present)
Supervise the Accounts Payable unit. Prepare monthly journal entries, oversee cash disbursements, expense recording, and petty cash reconciliation. These responsibilities are in addition to the Accounting Technician position.

Accounting Technician (September 2002 to April 2006)
Process Accounts Payable, Agency Commissions and Policyholder Refunds for five companies. Prepare Travel and Entertainment reconciliations for all Vice President expenses as well as reconciliation spreadsheets for all company telephone charges. Responsible for printing all vendor, claims, refund, and agency commission checks; coding invoices, month end closing, filing, 1099 processing, and vendor calls. Handle all telephone inquiries with verbal and written correspondence. Support the secretary for the Vice President of Accounting.

Secretary to Vice President of Finance (December 2000 to September 2002)
Type all correspondence and memos. Type, proofread, and distribute all financial statements. Handle incoming calls to Accounting and Data Processing department and schedule all appointments. Assist in the processing of policyholder refunds, claims, agency commission checks. File accounts payable back-up.

EDUCATION
The Computer Network, Boise, ID
Completed Word Processing Certificate program, November, 1999.
Fluent in Spanish.

TECHNICAL SUMMARY
Excel and Microsoft Word on PCs and Mac

REFERENCES
Available upon request.

Loan Administrator

CHRIS SMITH
178 Green Street
Collister, ID 83706
(208) 555-5555

OBJECTIVE
To obtain a position within a multi-branch bank as a loan administrator.

WORK EXPERIENCE

2006– Bank of Boise, Collister, ID
Present **Loan Administrator,** Commercial Real Estate Division.
Duties include disbursement and tracking of loans, maintenance of the same, and close contacts with customers and legal firms. Administer accounts and maintain contacts within bank and in the Pocatello office.

2003–2005 Garden City National Bank, Garden City, ID
Bank Reconciliation Clerk
Edited journal entries prior to posting. Processed invoices for payment. Determined proper budget account for coding of receipts. Reconciled bank accounts in U.S. currencies. Communicated with banks to clarify and resolve outstanding items as required.

2000–2002 The Tyler Corporation, Narupa, ID
Accounting Assistant, Finance Department
Verified accuracy and proper authorization of bills prior to payment, then processed bills. Reconciled accounts and wrote journal vouchers.

EDUCATION

College of Idaho, Caldwell, ID
Associate's degree, Accounting, 2000

COMPUTERS

Excel, Microsoft Word, Access.

References available upon request.

Loan Servicer

CHRIS SMITH
178 Green Street
Salt Lake City, UT 84117
(801) 555-5555

OBJECTIVE
A challenging position in the Business/Financial area.

SUMMARY
- Developed interpersonal skills.
- Self-motivated and able to function well in high-stress atmosphere.

EXPERIENCE

7/02–Present **THE MORMON BANK,** Salt Lake City, UT
Loan Servicer, Commercial and Real Estate Loans
Prepare customer billing and weekly/monthly reports; resolve customer problems. Set up/maintain customer legal and credit files. Record and adjust income in General Ledger. Process loan payments into computerized system. Maintain tax and insurance Escrow accounts; remit payments to respective institutions. Review loan documents. Responsible for general Portfolio management.

2/01–12/01 **ISLAND OF JAMAICA,** Negril, Jamaica
Cooperative Officer
Responsible for promotion and supervision of cooperative Societies, mainly Commercial Credit Union.

11/98–12/01 **RICHARD'S RESTAURANT,** Montego Bay, Jamaica
Manager
Managed daily retail store functions. Supervised staff and inventory control. Maintained Accounting System; ensured viability and profitability of business.

9/93–9/98 **ISLAND OF JAMAICA,** Education Department, Negril, Jamaica
School Teacher
Instructed children ages 10–13 in Mathematics, English Language, Reading, Social Studies, and History.

VOLUNTEER POSITIONS
Appointed by government to local government administration; Member of Village Council, 5/98–12/01.

EDUCATION
UNIVERSITY OF LIMBURG, The Netherlands
General Certificate in Education
Courses in Cooperative Principles, General Accounting, and Financial Management.

REFERENCES FURNISHED UPON REQUEST.

Management Accountant
Airline

CHRIS SMITH, CMA, CPA
178 Green Street
Houston, TX 77251
(713) 555-5555

EXPERIENCE:

BLUE MOON AIRLINES—1025 Blue Moon Boulevard, Houston, TX

Positions:

Senior Financial Analyst, Flight Operations (3/06–Present)
Manager, Cargo Accounting Automation (11/03–3/06)
Manager, Cargo Payables and Processing (12/01–11/03)
Supervisor, Freight and Mail Audit (9/99–12/01)

Responsibilities and Accomplishments:

- Prepared annual budgets, monthly forecasts, and strategic plans for operating department. Department budget was over $3 billion—25% of total company budget. Increased sophistication and accuracy of budgeting and forecasting.
- Conducted detailed studies to identify cost savings. Contributed to productivity improvements saving $20 million annually. Recommended internal control procedures that saved $250,000 per year.
- Compared actual expenses to budget and investigated variances. Created various computer models and analytical tools to facilitate variance analysis.
- Summarized monthly financial results and reported to upper management.
- Monitored financial performance of sixty cost centers. Provided administrative support for personnel requisitions, capital requests, and budget preparation.
- Calculated monthly revenue. Prepared journal entries and audit schedules.
- Monitored accounts receivable of $35 million and initiated collection efforts.
- Supervised as many as twenty management employees and sixty clerks. Conducted system training for employees. Encouraged participation and empowered employees to take initiative. Developed a positive work environment.
- Integrated Blue Moon Airlines and In Flight Airlines accounting functions following merger.

CERTIFICATION:

CERTIFIED PUBLIC ACCOUNTANT
State of Texas (2007)
CERTIFIED MANAGEMENT ACCOUNTANT
Institute of Management Accountants (2002)

EDUCATION:

RICE UNIVERSITY—Houston, TX
Graduated May 1999—Bachelor of Accounting Science
Student Senate Vice President and Chairman of the Senate Finance Committee

COMPUTER SKILLS:

PERSONAL COMPUTER
Proficiency with Excel, Microsoft Word, and LAN environment.

CHRIS SMITH
178 Green Street
Killington, VT 05751
(601) 555-5555

OBJECTIVE

A position in management accounting.

EDUCATION

University of Vermont, Burlington, VT
Bachelor of Science in Accounting, May 2008
Dean's List Student—GPA: 3.1—Honors Internship Program
Executive Vice President/Fundraising Chairman—Zeta Beta Tau Fraternity: Organized special events that raised over $15,000. Led meetings and coordinated activities. Acted as liaison between faculty and campus community. Served as a Big Brother, Burlington Boy's Club.

TECHNICAL SUMMARY

Excel, Microsoft Word, Access, and numerous accounting packages.

EMPLOYMENT HISTORY

2006 to Present
THE SIZZLER STEAKHOUSE, Killington, VT
Management Accountant
Managed accounting operations and accounts payable department. Ensured use of correct accounts payable factors. Reconciled bank and credit card accounts. Reviewed the general ledger and made adjustments for inter-company transactions. Prepared road tax documents for trucks throughout New England states. Monitored inventory transfers among branch locations.

2003 to 2006
DIAL TONES, Burlington, VT
Manager/Payphone Technician
Performed business and technical activities. Provided supervision, performance evaluations, and training to technical staff of seven—delegating authority to collect revenues, while maintaining equipment. Reconciled bank accounts and handled administrative record keeping.

2002 to 2003
MAPLE TREE ARENA, Burlington, VT
Manager
Directed concession activities for consecutive seasons, including financial record keeping, bank account reconciliation, and food preparation. Directly supervised staff of twenty employees.

VOLUNTEER WORK

THE BURLINGTON SOUP KITCHEN, Burlington, VT
VERMONT VOLUNTEER INCOME TAX ASSISTANCE, Burlington, VT

ACTIVITIES

Achieved Brown Belt Karate status
Uechi Karate Academy—Middlebury, VT
Tennis, Hockey

Payroll Manager

CHRIS SMITH
178 Green Street
St. Paul, MN 55105
(612) 555-5555

CAREER OBJECTIVE
To secure a Senior Level position as Payroll Manager.

EXPERIENCE

2005 to Present

JASMINE HEART, INC., St. Paul, MN
PAYROLL MANAGER
Management of multi-state payroll for 150 shops in North America and ten shops in Canada for well-known apparel and home décor company.
- Act as systems administrator for combined Human Resources and Payroll System (produce 5,500 W-2s and 200 T-4s).
- Act as liaison between Finance, Human Resources, corporation executives, and outside vendors.
- Monitor all payroll tax liabilities, filings, journal entries, accounts payable, and wire transfers for direct deposits.

Accomplishments
- Continued operations of payroll department in Newark, New Jersey, while simultaneously re-establishing department in new St. Paul headquarters.
- Coordinated entire department move to new headquarters and oversaw all human resources payroll-related issues.
- Identified programming errors in Human Resources Payroll System; directed and oversaw corrections.

2001 to 2005

ADAGIO LEASING, INC.   Mankato, MN
PAYROLL MANAGER
Supervised department team of seven. Coordinated a $40 million payroll for 3,000 employees.
- Managed and controlled eighteen separate multi-state payrolls with eight weekly union- and non-union payrolls and nine biweekly payrolls.
- Acted as interface liaison for all payroll coordination and assimilation for executive level financial departments and Internal Human Resources.

Accomplishments
- Allocated six months to correct, organize, and implement eighteen separate payrolls.
- Converted existing manual-worksheet system to full online computerized system.
- Revised procedure for customer audits of Adagio records, thus increasing revenue.

EDUCATION
STATE UNIVERSITY OF NEW YORK AT CORTLAND—B.S., EDUCATION 2003.

COMPUTERS
ADP online payroll system, Excel, LAN, Windows, Mac, and PC

CHRIS SMITH
178 Green Street
Loretto, PA 15940
(814) 555-5555

PROFESSIONAL EXPERIENCE

DEVONSHIRE EQUIPMENT, INC., Loretto, PA   2005-Present
Staff Auditor
- Plan, identify, and test controls; present findings and recommend actions to management.
- Assist in the audits of New England; Northwest; New Jersey; Washington, D.C.; Southeast; and Great Lakes Districts, as well as U.S. Areas General Ledger Group.

BILL CHESTNUT & COMPANY, Greensburg, PA   2003-2005
Staff Auditor
- Participated in audits of $4 billion bank, major manufacturing company, mutual fund, software distribution company, and large, urban transportation company.

GROVE CITY COLLEGE, Grove City, PA   2002-2003
Tutor/Instructor, Introduction to Financial Accounting
- Formulated, administered, and graded exams.
- Tutored individuals in a self-paced course.

LONDON COMMERCIAL BANK, London, UK   2001
Intern
- Conducted over fifty onsite investigations of firms with assets up to $2 million; assessed "fair" valuation of assets.
- Assisted evaluation of $80 million brewery.
- Identified potential bank investments by analyzing financial statements and determining written reports to financial officer.

EDUCATION

Mercyhurst College, Erie, PA
M.B.A., 2005

Grove City College, Grove City, PA
B.A., Economics, 2003

EXPERIENCE

Available on request.

Stockbroker

CHRIS SMITH
178 Green Street
Nashville, TN 37203
(615) 555-5555

OBJECTIVE
A challenging career in trading.

SUMMARY OF QUALIFICATIONS
- Brokerage License, series 7 and 63.
- Two years of progressive, financial experience.
- Developed interpersonal abilities.
- Self-motivated; able to achieve immediate and long-term goals and meet operation deadlines.
- Responds well in high-stress atmosphere.

EXPERIENCE

COPPERDASH ASSOCIATES, Nashville, TN   2/03–Present
Fund Accountant
- Report directly to Portfolio Manager and Traders on investment cash availability.
- Buy commercial paper for private accounts.
- Track stocks and bonds; record dividend/interest payments.
- Monitor/report portfolio security changes.
- Interface with brokers and banks regarding trade settlements.
- Analyze/prepare performance reports for Board of Directors and Shareholders, utilizing market invoices.
- Run industry comparisons.
- Assist Public Accountants, prepare audit papers, price-out daily net worth for NASD, and book accounting transactions (shares, securities, expenses, receipts, disbursements, and dividends).
- Analyze current market condition; forecast dividend/interest payments and fund expenses.

EDUCATION

CAMPBELL COLLEGE, Bules Creek, NC
B.A., Accounting Finance, 2002

OXFORD UNIVERSITY, Oxford, England
One year abroad, 1999

COMPUTERS

Lotus 1-2-3 and Shaw data

REFERENCES

Furnished upon request.

Chris Smith
178 Green Street
Butte, MT 59404
(406) 555-5555

PROFESSIONAL OBJECTIVE

A challenging, growth-oriented position in which professional experience, academic background, technical skills, and a commitment to excellence will have valuable application.

PROFESSIONAL EXPERIENCE

1999–Present **INTERNAL REVENUE COMMISSION,** Sydney, Australia
Tax Inspector/Higher Tax Office

- Review both individual and corporate tax files for completeness and accuracy.
- Consult with tax claims in resolving conflicts and/or resolving inequities resulting from misinformation and/or lack of information at time of initial filing.
- Respond to inquiries on tax matters as to policies and procedures.
- Determine penalties as directed by statute and process claims for collection procedure.
- Strong interpersonal, public relations, and communication skills required.
- Examined corporate payroll records for accuracy.
- Executed collections through direct subscription to the Office of the Collector General.
- Supervised, trained, scheduled, and monitored eleven employees.
- Compiled monthly statistic base for permanent records and data for regional/national reports.
- Monitored job performance and bid selections of traders and vendors.

1992–1999 **THE REVENUE COMMISSION SOCIAL CLUB,** Canberra, Australia
Director

- Managed overall operation of the Club which represented employees of the revenue commissions.
- Maintained facility of two bars, function rooms, gymnasium, saunas, indoor football arena, and ancillary space arenas.
- Hired/terminated, supervised, and motivated staff.
- Oversaw office management, bookkeeping/accounting, and member accounts.
- Arranged for equipment replacement—controlled ordering and bid-purchases.

REFERENCES

Available upon request.

Vice President of Administration and Finance

CHRIS SMITH
178 Green Street
Dodge City, KS 67801
(316) 555-5555

SUMMARY OF QUALIFICATIONS
- Extensive experience in providing administrative, managerial, and operational guidance for the financial services industry.
- Thorough knowledge in managing administrative sales and secured loan programs, preparing budgets, and developing product pricing policies.
- Supervised, trained, and developed staffs of numerous sizes.
- Proficient in monitoring numerous custody accounts in a timely and accurate fashion.
- Participation with affiliates in the capacities of president, executive committee member, speaker/panel member, and general manager.

EXPERIENCE

1/04 to Present   **Vice President Administration-OIC-Custody Services**
THIRD BANK OF KANSAS   Dodge City, Kansas
Manger of the administrative department. Provide handling and record keeping services for corporate, fiduciary, and personal custody accounts with assets totaling $20 billion.
- Prepare budgets and develop product pricing policies.
- Manage administrative sales and secured loan programs.
- Direct administrative processes for a sizable portion of the department's largest and most complex accounts.
- Extensive involvement in the analysis of new accounting systems, to determine customer needs.
- Develop and maintain strong securities operational knowledge.

9/93 to 1/04   **Client Manager—Custody Services**
- Administered over 200 custody accounts, which included direct contact with customers, attorneys, investment advisors, mutual funds, brokers, and accountants.
- Acted as liaison between the operations support areas and the customer contact department. Reported problems and operational errors.
- Participated in the trust systems conversion team, which was responsible for the successful conversion to the online accounting system.

SEMINARS

Harbridge House, Inc.—Senior Management Program
Thomas Blodgett Associates—Consultative Selling Skills Program

PROFESSIONAL AFFILIATIONS
- Member—Executive Committee—Past President—Securities Operations Associations of the Heartland.
- Speaker/Panel Member—Kansas Bankers Association; speaking at various Trust Operations Seminars.
- Past President—Bank of Heartland Supervisors' Association.

Vice President of Finance

CHRIS SMITH
178 Green Street
Buffalo, NY 14212
(716) 555-5555

EXPERIENCE

NIB, Inc.   *Buffalo, NY*
V.P.-Finance   *2004–2006*

Provide administrative leadership to the corporation. Led team in the development of a mission statement, strategic plans, and related business plans to grow company 100% in a three-year time period. Researched, planned, and established a satellite manufacturing plan in less than six weeks. Established full-system integration with the corporate office. Coordinated all legal, tax, and insurance contracts. Developed the company profit sharing, section 125, 401(k), and other benefit plans.

Ryder Group, Inc.   *Poughkeepsie, NY*
Finance Manager   *1997–2003*

Increased levels of management responsibility for financial accounting, analysis, budgeting, credit, and collection for a $4 billion international manufacturing company. Coordinated financial consolidations, analysis, budgeting, acquisition, and divestiture support. Prepared consolidated statements in GAAP and SSAP formats. Supervised four exempt and four nonexempt employees with dotted-line authority over eight Plant Controllers.

Jameil Jones Systems
Cost Accounting Manager   *1995–1997*

Developed cost systems for eight construction branches and two manufacturing divisions. Key member of negotiation team and audit coordinator for the divestiture program involving these divisions. Reviewed and approved standard costs, transfer prices, budgets, physical inventory valuation, and cost estimates. Sales were $62 million. Supervised staff of four nonexempt employees.

Crichton Co., CPA's
Staff Accountant   *1993–1995*

Prepared financial statements, footnotes, and other tax and financial information. Performed compliance testing and the study of internal control. Supervised and reviewed junior accountants.

ACHIEVEMENTS

Management and Treasury

- Founded and operated a successful contract manufacturing corporation.
- Developed investment guidelines, banking relationships, and cash planning programs. These programs reduced corporate borrowing, improved cash flow, and increased other income.
- Led employee meetings in incentive bonus, profit sharing, 401(k), safety, and corporate philosophy.
- Successfully established a new operating division in six weeks.
- Developed a comprehensive risk management program that improved coverage and reduced cost.
- Provided significant shareholder assistance in tax and financial planning.

EDUCATION

New York University, NY
B.A. Accounting, May 1993

Administrative Assistant
Department of Health

CHRIS SMITH
178 Green Street
Milwaukee, WI 53202
(414) 555-5555

OBJECTIVE
To obtain a challenging position as an Administrative Assistant.

SUMMARY
- Highly developed interpersonal skills.
- Self-motivated to ably coordinate daily office functions.
- Knowledgeable regarding technical and medical terminology.
- Familiar with computer operation.
- Responsible for training of new personnel.

EXPERIENCE

5/04–Present **DEPARTMENT OF HEALTH**
Standards and Quality, Milwaukee, WI
Administrative Assistant
Handle incoming calls and mail. Greet visitors. Resolve inquiries. Prepare and type office reports. Maintain supervisor and staff member appointments and travel calendars. Verify, revise, and arrange appointments, conferences, and meetings. Act as liaison to supervisor regarding meetings and conferences. Maintain control records and follow-ups on work in progress. Establish file-coding system. Train incoming staff. Maintain time and attendance records as well as instructional and reference manuals.

7/96–5/04 **VETERAN'S HOSPITAL,** Lacrosse, WI
Claims Development Clerk
Managed clerical functions including: incoming calls; maintenance and update of files, logging, and special determinations reports in all Administrative Law Judge cases; and typing contracts, reports, and general correspondence. Dealt with receipt of checks and attendant recording duties. Computed and interpreted claims processing. Directed inquiries and maintained cordial relations with the public. Trained new clerks.

EDUCATION
1993 JOHN'S CATHOLIC COLLEGE, Madison, WI
Major: Business Management/Human Services, Bachelor's degree

COMPUTERS
PC, Mac, Microsoft Word, Perl

REFERENCES
Available upon request.

CHRIS SMITH
178 Green Street
Albany, NY 12208
(518) 555-5555

OBJECTIVE
To contribute acquired skills to an administrative position.

SUMMARY OF QUALIFICATIONS
- More than four years of professional experience in administration, sales, and coaching/instructing.
- Computer experience includes spreadsheets, word processing, and graphics software programs.
- Proven communication abilities—both oral and written.
- Developed interpersonal skills.
- Ability to achieve immediate and long-term goals and meet operational deadlines.

PROFESSIONAL EXPERIENCE

2005–Present   LOYALTY INVESTMENTS, Albany, NY
Administrative Assistant
Provide administrative support for new business development group; assist CFO with special projects. Ensure smooth work-flow; facilitate effectiveness of fourteen sales consultants. Direct incoming calls, initiate new client application process, and maintain applicant record database. Oversee office equipment maintenance. Assisted in design and implementation of computer automation system. Aided in streamlining application process.

2003–05   THE GYMNASTIC SCHOOL, Albany, NY
Instructor
Planned, designed, and implemented recreational program for seventy gymnasts at various skill levels. Evaluated and monitored new students' progress; maintained records. Coached and choreographed competitive performances; motivated gymnastics team of twenty. Set team goals and incentives to maximize performance levels.

2000–03   GROVER FINANCE, Buffalo, NY
Telemarketing and Sales Representative
Secured new business utilizing customer inquiries and mass mailing responses; provided product line information to prospective clients. Initiated loan application and qualifying process. Maintained daily call records and monthly sales breakdown. Acquired comprehensive product line knowledge and ability to quickly access customer needs and assemble appropriate financial packages.

EDUCATION

Hofstra University, Hempstead, NY
Bachelor of Arts, English, 2000
Concentration: Business; Dean's list, GPA 3.3

REFERENCES

Furnished upon request.

Administrative Assistant
Personnel

CHRIS SMITH
178 Green Street
Pinesville, LA 71359
(318) 555-5555

WORK EXPERIENCE

THE LAPIS CORPORATION, Pinesville, LA   9/03-Present
Personnel Administrative Assistant
• Maintained files.
• Prepared records for offsite storage.
• Designed forms for archives.
• Developed effective space management plan for onsite records.
• Improved tracking system resulting in few lost files.
• Handled employment verifications and designed forms to expedite process.

GLADE GROVE COLLEGE, Baton Rouge, LA   12/99-8/03
Records Coordinator for Development
• Recorded gifts made to the college.
• Maintained files.

Coder   12/96-12/99
• Coded data from surveys.
• Edited computer printouts.
• Performed quality control.

PAISLEY TELECOMMUNICATIONS, New Orleans, LA   6/87-12/96
"Advantage" Coordinator [The "Advantage" is an auto dialer.]
• Tested and programmed each unit.
• Scheduled site visits and installations.
• Kept inventory.
• Assisted customers with questions and problems.

Interviewer   4/86-5/87
• Conducted public opinion surveys.

EDUCATION

Biltmore College, Dallas, TX   1987
Associate's degree in Marketing.

References are available upon request.

Chris Smith
178 Green Street
Stanford, CA 94305
(415) 555-5555

Experience:	**Stanford Law School**
1/06– Present	**Administrative/Research Assistant** Provide support for legal, doctoral candidate. Coordinate manuscript production phases. Research changes in case law pertaining to "Mechanisms of the Supreme Court and Human Rights."
12/05– present	**Administrative Assistant** Edit Stanford Law School journal. Provide administrative support to Editor-in-Chief.
9/05– 1/06	**Administrative/Research Assistant** Utilize database, periodical governmental reports for country-specific research on legal, economic, and political issues. Manage manuscripts from production through publication.
Fall 2005	**Special Events Coordinator** Organized Annual Stanford Law School Alumni Conference.
Education:	
2005	**Michigan State University** BA: International Politics and History. Studied in Madrid, Spain, Fall 2005.
Skills:	Computers—Microsoft Word. Languages—Fluent in Spanish; working knowledge of French.
Interests:	Travel, swimming, inline skating, surfing.
References:	Available upon request.

Administrative Assistant
Wholesale Distributor

CHRIS SMITH
178 Green Street
Dallas, TX 75275
(214) 555-5555

OBJECTIVE
To secure a challenging position as an Administrative Assistant.

SUPPORTIVE QUALIFICATIONS
- Three years as an administrative assistant.
- Four years experience working in the medical/health care arena.
- Two years education and training in Secretarial Sciences.

STRENGTHS

Detail-oriented	Organized
Patient	Prioritize accurately
Positive attitude	Work well under pressure

PROFESSIONAL EXPERIENCE

MUSTANG DISTRIBUTORS, Dallas, TX   **Administrative Assistant**
2006–Present Performed general secretarial tasks, typing reports, and correspondence on Apple equipment; arranged meetings, expense reports, and travel vouchers. Designed computer automation system; assisted in its implementation.

TEXAS MEDICAL CENTER, Austin, TX   **Unit Secretary**
2004–2006 Transcribed doctors' orders for patients' records on computer. Answered telephones in busy office.

GRANITE INVESTMENT RESOURCE CENTER, Dallas, TX   **Data Entry**
2002–2004 Input account transactions and transfers in computer.

SEUSS HEALTH, Houston, TX   **Data Entry**
2001–2002 Input medical information, maintained computer files. Managed nightly upkeep and documentation of triage information, medication, and treatments.

BROWNWOOD HOSPITAL, El Paso, TX **File Clerk, Medical Records Department**
1999–2001 Filed, answered phones, researched patient information for various departments.

EDUCATION

DALLAS COMMUNITY COLLEGE; course work in Secretarial Sciences and Business, 1999–2001.

REFERENCES
Furnished upon request.

CHRIS SMITH
178 Green Street
Washington, D.C. 19180
(202) 555-5555

EMPLOYMENT HISTORY

ADMINISTRATIVE DIRECTOR   2006–Present
Georgetown Medical School, Department of Psychiatry, Washington, D.C.
Coordinate the administrative/logistics aspects of a multi-study research program on the genetic transmission of mental illnesses. Design, implement, and manage a relational database for each of the studies; write and maintain appropriate documentation; produce reports and statistics as required. Identify, assist in the recruiting of, and follow through the protocol study subjects; screen normal controls and family members for medical exclusions; coordinate the chart review process. Develop, organize, and implement administrative procedures and policies; draft the administrative procedures sections of the Study Procedures Manuals. Coordinate medications' and hospitalizations' history review process for psychiatric patients after neuropsychological testing is completed.

COMPUTER EDUCATION COORDINATE   2003–2006
Washington, D.C., Bar Association
Coordinated and administered the Computer College Program to educate attorneys in the uses and advantages of computers in the law office. Developed curriculum, and promoted and implemented educational seminar series; assisted in teaching and presentations; selected sites. Established statewide lawyers' computer-user group; edited and contributed to newsletter; planned meetings and agendas; developed membership; promoted student user groups with law schools.

LEGAL SECRETARY   2002–2003
Randell & Jenks, Boston, MA
Developed and implemented systems to streamline office procedures. Monitored attorneys' daily activities for time records; allocated monthly charges to appropriate cases and matters; drafted bills. Assisted paralegals with assignments. Reorganized attorneys' files.

ADMINISTRATIVE ASSISTANT—EXEMPT STAFF   2000–2002
Catholic University, Washington, D.C.
Coordinated and administered the Professional Summer Program developed for the Navy community. Assisted with catalog preparation and program marketing; prepared and monitored budgets; oversaw lecturer negotiations, site selection, social amenities, and travel management.

EDUCATION

American University, Washington, D.C.
B.A. Economics, 1999

Data Entry Supervisor

CHRIS SMITH
178 Green Street
River Forest, IL 60305
(312) 555-5555

CAREER OBJECTIVE
To secure a Supervisory position in data analysis/data entry.

SUMMARY OF QUALIFICATIONS
- Over thirteen years of data entry and administrative experience.
- Well-developed managerial abilities.
- Proven communication and written capabilities; report writing based on findings in database.
- Strong interpersonal skills, having dealt with a diversity of professionals, clients, and staff.
- Cooperative and flexible team player; equally effective working independently.

PROFESSIONAL EXPERIENCE

MORTEK ANALYSTS, River Forest, IL   2003–Present

2005–Present **Data Analyst III**
Collect data and analyze documents with online database. Retrieve records from the Registry of Deeds, vital statistics. Compile and generate reports of finds. CAST entry and maintenance, CAPS statistical reports production (M204 system). Log and analyze specific calls (TOLLS). Act as liaison to U.S. Attorneys' Office. Gather and analyze case materials; conduct physical case reviews. Act as Interim Supervisor; train, assist, and supervise staff of six.

2003–2005 **Data Entry Supervisor**
Supervised staff of four. Processed data entry inputs and Seizure/Motor Vehicles reports; updated Personnel files and DEAS-Accounting system. Prepared biweekly Progress Reports; maintained relevant records.

BLUE ANGEL ASSOCIATES, Chicago, IL
2001–2003 **Data Entry Operator**
Cooperated with Chief Operator transcribing prescription drug data for reimbursement. Required speed, accuracy, and attention to critical money fields.

AWARDS
- 2003 Merit Award for excellence as a supervisor.
- Presidential Award 2004 for outstanding performance.

EDUCATION AND TRAINING
High School Diploma, 1999

COMPUTER SKILLS
Excel, Microsoft Word

CHRIS SMITH
178 Green Street
Hickory, NC 28601
(704) 555-5555

Professional Objective
A dispatching/management position within the medical field.

Summary of Qualifications
- Four years experience in supervising service technicians, handling public's questions and complaints, and servicing patients' medical equipment.
- Effective in developing rapport with depressed patients.
- Willing to travel or relocate.

Professional Experience
2005 to   GALLIMORE HOME HEALTH CARE; Hickory, NC
Present   **Medical Technician/Dispatch Supervisor**
- Schedule and supervise twelve drivers.
- Handle patients' inquiries and complaints.
- Monitor equipment and supply inventories.
- Service patients' equipment/develop rapport with them.
- Accomplishments: improved efficiency of method of routing drivers and of method of briefing them on their assignments.

2003 to 2005 CARE PROVISIONS; High Point, NC
- Set up medical equipment for patients.

Education
2003   JOHNSON STATE COLLEGE, Johnson, VT
Bachelor of Science, Business Management

Computers
Excel, Microsoft Word, SQL Server, Access

Dispatcher
Terminal/Freight

CHRIS SMITH
178 Green Street
Erie, PA 16563
(814) 555-5555

OBJECTIVE:
A Dispatching position with a growth-oriented organization. Willing to relocate and/or travel.

SUMMARY OF QUALIFICATIONS:
- *Terminal, customer service, human resource, and financial management skills.*
- *Daily reporting, record keeping, and dispatching.*
- *Excellent organizational and communication skills.*
- *Relate well with personnel, management, and clientele at all levels.*
- *Present a positive and productive image of the company.*
- *Ability to promote teamwork for efficient operation of company.*
- *Formulate cost saving procedures to assure effective use of manpower.*

PROFESSIONAL EXPERIENCE:

DISPATCHER—Duffield Freight Inc., Erie, PA (2006–Present)
- Act as dispatcher, set up pick-up and deliveries, update computer, route drivers, customer service, and troubleshoot.
- Check logs for accuracy and DOT regulations.
- Explain procedures to and review work of new drivers to assure accuracy of paperwork.
- Interact with other terminals regarding problem solving.

ACCOUNT EXECUTIVE—Bedelia Transportation Company, Gwynedd Valley, PA (2004–2006)
- Solicited outbound and inbound freight.
- Handled special tariffs and claims, dispatching and setting up freight programs.
- Provided customer profile and customer relations.

LINE DISPATCHER—Sycamore Freight, Haverford, PA (2002–2004)
- Set up manpower and yard schedules of inbound and outbound schedules; determined dispersal of dispatch drivers. Kept customer updated; handled maintenance problems and customer relations.

EDUCATION:

Eastern College, St. David's, PA
Bachelor of Science degree, 2002
Major: Business Administration

CHRIS SMITH
178 Green Street
Erie, PA 16541
(814) 555-5555

Objective:
To provide efficient and effective administrative support.

Experience:

2004–Present	*Redmond Computer, Inc., Erie, PA*

Administrative Assistant to the Chief Executive Officer
Coordinated and prioritized the daily activities of the Chairman of the Board. Performed the administrative functions in support of the CEO. Required an in-depth knowledge of the company, the industry, the financial community, the investors, the customers, the educational community, etc. Interfaced and assisted in the preparation for the Board of Directors meetings. Recorded and distributed the minutes of management meetings.

2001–2004   *Steppenwolf Associated, Pittsburgh, PA*
Administrative Assistant to the President and Chief Executive Officer
Prioritized the daily activities of the CEO. Set up and maintained a "tickler system." Composed and edited correspondence on behalf of the President.

1997–2001   *Jasmine Rain Inc., Beaver Falls, PA*
Administrative Assistant to the Chief Operating Officer
Interacted on behalf of the COO in sensitive customer and employee relationships. Recorded and distributed minutes of the Management Committee. Maintained and distributed monthly department reports.

Education:
2000–Present   University of Pennsylvania Continuing Education Program: Management, Business, Computer Skills, and Marketing. French and Italian. Cutler College: Computer Literacy, Shorthand Refresher, and Medical Language.

Computers:

PC. Word Processing. Proficient in most PC software.

CHRIS SMITH
178 Green Street
Manchester, NH 03104
(603) 555-5555

Experience

2006–Present   Shrike Oil Co., Manchester, NH
Executive Secretary—Sales
- Support the Director of Sales.
- Support Field Sales Representative and Regional Managers.
- Generate sales reports.
- Sales promotions/contests.
- Statistic and data gathering.
- Assist Marketing departments when needed.
- Plan meetings.
- Attend trade shows.

2002–2006   Romeo Associates, Bedford, NH
Administrative Assistant—International Sales
- Supported the Director of Sales and Contracts Administrator.
- Managed all correspondence.
- Supervised export control.
- Managed customer service and repair parts administration.

1995–2002   Jenks Systems, Nashua, NH
Secretary—Marketing
- Maintained personal records.
- Managed travel arrangements.
- Supervised typing correspondence.
- Directed contact with customer base.

Education

1995   • Quinnipiac College, Derry, NH
          Bachelor of Arts; Business Administration
2003   • Seminars: Assertiveness training; Public speaking

Computers

Microsoft Word, Excel, Access

Skills

Typing 80 wpm, Dictaphone, e-mail

Affiliations

Professional Secretaries International

CHRIS SMITH
178 Green Street
Cohasset, MA 02025
(781) 555-5555

OBJECTIVE

A position as a File Clerk in a progressive organization.

SKILLS

Typing 70 wpm accurate   Word Processing
Spreadsheets

EMPLOYMENT

January 2006–Present
Brigham and Women's Hospital, Boston, MA
File Clerk. Type; maintain patient filing system.

September 2005–January 2006
ProTemps Employment, Quincy, MA
Clerk/Typist. Responsible for typing, filing, and general office duties.

May 2004–September 2005
Cohasset Cleaners, Cohasset, MA
File Clerk. Performed clerical duties; processed mail, daily reports, and correspondence; retrieved, updated, and corrected files.

EDUCATION

2004–2005
The Burdett School, Boston, MA
Courses in Typing, Filing, Word Processing, Computers (PC: Microsoft Word, Excel, and Access).

References available upon request.

Inventory Control Analyst

CHRIS SMITH
178 Green Street
Providence, RI 02903
(401) 555-5555

CAREER OBJECTIVE
A technical/administrative support position in inventory analysis.

BACKGROUND SUMMARY

A dedicated, conscientious individual with a solid background in inventory control. Demonstrated ability to identify, analyze, and solve problems. Knowledgeable in all facets of inventory control. Experienced in data entry. Proven ability to work independently or with others. Work well in a fast-paced environment. Organized. Excellent attendance record.

CAREER HISTORY

SULLIVAN DATA SYSTEMS, Providence, RI
Inventory Control Analyst   (2001–Present)
Inventory Control Clerk II   (1997–2001)

- Analyzed, investigated, and resolved inventory discrepancies identified through section inputs and daily cycle count procedures.
- Served as a principal consultant on plant inventory systems.
- Assisted in reviewing and revising physical inventory procedures.
- Coordinated and assisted in conducting physical inventories.
- Created and maintained computerized filing systems. Generated reports from files.
- Assisted in liquidation of excess and used computer equipment.
- Trained new departmental personnel on data entry procedures using a CRT.
- Demonstrated knowledge of Microsoft Word, Excel, and other software applications.
- Created and maintained daily, monthly, and yearly reports for upper management.
- Conferred with management on a daily basis.
- Coordinated projects with coworkers at multiple plant sites.

EDUCATION

Roger Williams College, Bristol, RI, 1983–1987

CONTINUING EDUCATION

Sullivan Data System
ISO 9000 Awareness Training (International Standardization Organization)
QWG (Quality Work Group)

Mailroom Supervisor

CHRIS SMITH
178 Green Street
Biddeford, ME 04005
(207) 555-5555

OBJECTIVE
To secure a full-time mailroom management position.

EXPERIENCE

11/02–
Present

LANCELOT, INC., Biddeford, ME
Supervisor, Mailroom Services
Coordinate incoming mail, disperse inter-building correspondence. Manage courier services and shipping/receiving. Administer employee evaluation/appraisals, schedule hours. Research and account for certified, registered, and express mail. Responsible for office supply procurement. Obtain and maintain lease agreements for electronic machinery and equipment.

2001–2002

BIRCH, INC., Saco, ME
Supervisor, Mailroom Services
Shipped weekly overseas pouches and biweekly payroll to thirty-five domestic offices. Sorted and distributed in-house payroll for 600 employees. Coordinated in-house and U.S. office stock distributions. Acted as building management contact and Chief Fire Warden for 100,000 square feet of office space. Assisted in office relocations throughout U.S.

1999–2001

DATEL EXPRESS, Saco, ME
Courier
Delivered time sensitive packages throughout Boston area. Sorted incoming and outgoing express packages.

1996–1999

PORTLAND FINANCE, Portland, ME
Supervisor, Incoming Mail/Messengers and Stock Distribution
Managed computer facility forms and negotiable forms stored in in-house vault.

EDUCATION

1997–2000

NORTHWESTERN UNIVERSITY, Chicago, IL
Major: Business Administration

1995–1996

UNIVERSITY OF MASSACHUSETTS, Amherst, MA
Major: Business Administration

Office Manager
Construction

CHRIS SMITH
178 Green Street
Rhododendron, OR 97049
(503) 555-5555

OBJECTIVE A management or administrative position that will utilize and challenge proven skills and varied experience.

EDUCATION Willamette University, Salem, OR
B.S., Management, 2001
Spanish minor

EXPERIENCE

2004– **Office Manager**
Present RITTER CONSTRUCTION, Rhododendron, OR
Provide payroll, bookkeeping, personnel, inventory, and job scheduling management for medium-size construction company. Assist in estimating process. Prepare accounts receivable and payable. Maintain good customer and vendor relations.

2001–2004 **Senior Service Representative**
LEHMAN BANK, Monmouth, OR
Opened new accounts and cross-selling of bank services. Conducted branch audits. Performed daily balancing and troubleshooting of ATM system. Extensive customer service and public relations.

1998–2001 **Nurse's Aide**
CUTTER MEMORIAL HOSPITAL, Salem, OR
Directed patient care and nursing support.

1997–1998 **Sales Associate**
BERKOWITZ DRUGS, Salem, OR
Retail sales, responsibilities included customer service, cash register operation, merchandising, and inventory control.

PERSONAL Real Estate Salesperson's License (Oregon)
Notary Public
Experience with IBM PC-based computer systems
Fluent in French, conversational Spanish

Office Manager
General

CHRIS SMITH
178 Green Street
Wayne, NE 68787
(402) 555-5555

OBJECTIVE

To contribute developed skills to a challenging Office Manager/Secretarial position with a progressive organization offering opportunities for growth and advancement.

SUMMARY OF QUALIFICATIONS

- Nearly twenty years office experience including knowledge of typing and word processing.
- Self-motivated; able to implement decisions and set effective priorities to achieve both immediate and long-term goals.
- Bilingual—Spanish and English.
- Excellent communication skills, both oral and written.
- Proven interpersonal skills, having dealt with a variety of professionals and clients.

PROFESSIONAL EXPERIENCE

2006–Present   EMERSON ASSOCIATES, Wayne, NE
Office Manager
Arrange logistics for office expansion and relocation. Establish office procedures and systems. Actuate/implement filing systems, client billing system, and bookkeeping. Order supplies; maintain inventory. Handle word processing and receptionist responsibilities.

1997–2006   RUNNING FAWN HOUSING COMMISSION, Primrose, NE
Administrative Assistant
Functioned as principal support staff person to Executive Director, providing comprehensive administrative and clerical support services. Organized and managed work schedule. Coordinated communication flow with commissions, staff, Mayor's Office, public and private officials, and the general public. Prepared Director's scheduled events; organized and presented information in a useful format. Administered workflow.

1992–1997   COMMISSION ON JEWISH AFFAIRS, Table Rock, NE
Administrative Assistant
Management of office included: typing, recording minutes at commission meetings, handling incoming calls, assisting general public, and maintaining office supplies. Coordinated information release to press, legislators, and interested individuals.

1989–1992   PAULA SHELL HOSPITAL, Broken Bow, NE
Personnel Assistant
Provided administrative support to Personnel Recruiter and Personnel Representative. Screened applicants, checked references, and scheduled interviews. Prepared candidates for typing tests. Answered incoming calls. Typed all office materials and correspondence.

Receptionist
Utilized Word Processor. Greeted and screened applicants.

Office Manager
International Business

Chris Smith
178 Green Street
Sheboygan, WI 53081
(414) 555-5555

SUMMARY OF QUALIFICATIONS
- Supervisory and management experience.
- Fluent in Japanese and French languages; lived, worked, and studied in both Japan and France.
- Broad computer experience includes: Lotus, WordPerfect, IBM, and Apple.
- Self-motivated and detail-oriented.
- Able to motivate staff to facilitate workflow and meet operational deadlines.

EDUCATION
Ithaca College, Ithaca, NY
B.A., International Relations, December 2002

Université de Paris, Paris, France
Courses in French Business and Japanese Language

PROFESSIONAL EXPERIENCE
Leary Company, Sheboygan, WI   2004–Present
Office Manager, Project Development Department
- Supervise staff in diversity of projects. Office communications in Japanese.
- Write and control monthly $200,000 budget.
- Oversee public relations, advertising, association memberships, and donations.
- Coordinate opening of Sheboygan office, interacting with designers, architects, lawyers, and landlord; arranged Opening Party for 300 guests.
- Develop nationwide relocation policy/orientation program for new employees.
- Maintain employee benefits.
- Determine program content, budget, advertising, and student selection for Leary's summer internships in Tokyo for American students.
- Supervise creation of new magazine in Japanese; conducted market research, article research, and writing, layout, and design.
- Conceptualize and develop Japanese Business Library containing 2,000 books for public use.
- Actuate and implement accounting system/program on Excel.

The Rivers Edge Products, Oshkosh, WI   2003–2004
Software Development, Advertising Department
- Assisted in development and marketing of online computer magazine.
- Miscellaneous duties.

Chris Smith
178 Green Street
Montpelier, VT 05602
(802) 555-5555

PROFILE   Office management professional totally involved and dedicated to the services and quality of an organization, while maintaining strong work ethics and standards.

SUPPORTIVE QUALIFICATIONS/ACHIEVEMENTS
- Over four years experience in office management and operations.
- Over twelve years in all areas of legal secretarial work; four years involvement in bookkeeping and payroll.
- Computer Skills: Mac, PC, Windows applications
- Demonstrated training skills; instructed each secretary in policies and procedures of organization—kept them updated on changes in the law, including maintenance of the law library.
- Proven communications and interpersonal skills; writing, speaking, and listening; responsible for event planning, all advertising, and designing letterhead for firms' business stationery.

PROFESSIONAL EXPERIENCE

Duvell and Aldrich, P.C.   Montpelier, VT
Legal Office Manager/Bookkeeper   2002–Present
- Purchase and coordinate installation of all office equipment and its maintenance.
- Hire, supervise, and coordinate schedules of support staff; responsible for the needs of newly hired staff.
- Open, close, and create case files and lists; manage personal injury protection files.
- Maintain account records on computer and hard copy, accounts payable and receivable, financial reports, client funds, and distribute settlement funds.
- Assist operators with word processing, software/hardware programs, and maintain computer reference library and system logbook.
- Provide auxiliary and continued support to attorneys specifically in personal injury law.

Cattail Associates   Johnson, VT
Legal Secretary—Admiralty/Federal/State Workers' Compensation   2000-2002

Artesia, Klebnick, and Rove   Plainfield, VT
Legal Secretary—Small Claims and Collections   1998–2000

Cascade and Jergen   Poultney, VT
Legal Secretary—Business Law   1996–1998

Bird, Spoon, and Mann   Castleton, VT
Legal Secretary—Corporate Litigation   1994–1996

EDUCATION

Johnson State College, Johnson, VT
Candidate for B.S. in Business Administration, 2007

Order Entry Clerk

CHRIS SMITH
178 Green Street
Lincoln, NE 68522
(402) 555-5555

CAREER OBJECTIVE
A position in general clerical or customer services.

CAREER HISTORY

THE BULLFROG COMPANY, Lincoln, NE   2005–Present
Order Entry—Parts Department
- Processed and shipped orders within twelve hours of receipt from Bull Group Field Engineers in the U.S. and abroad.
- Met or exceeded daily deadlines.
- Used computer application to track orders and determine status and availability of parts.
- Generated daily reports on status of orders.
- Prepared and used reports to identify and resolve order processing problems.
- Worked independently.
- Kept supervisors informed on daily basis.
- Established and maintained functional files.
- Invested and resolved complaints from Field Engineers.
- Coordinated with multiple departments and shippers to ensure timely deliveries.

K.T., INC., Norfolk, NE   2002–2004
General Office Administrator
Customer Services
Secretary/Receptionist
- Typed letters and reports.
- Maintained files.
- Answered inquiries about customers' accounts.
- Received payments and balanced statements.
- Posted accounts receivable and payable.

EDUCATION

Marcelle Junior College, Omaha, NE
B.A., Computer Science, Expected 2010.

CHRIS SMITH
178 Green Street
Laramie, WY 82071
(307) 555-5555

QUALIFICATIONS:

- Over twenty-five years Secretarial/Administrative experience.
- Skills: Typing (65 wpm), Dictaphone, multilane phones/switchboard, ten key (110 kspm) digital DECmate computer, bookkeeping, credit checks, and statistical typing.
- Extensive business experience including accounting firms, legal firms, financial firms, insurance companies, transportation companies, medical environments, government agencies, and nonprofit groups.
- Offer common sense, ability to take initiative, quality orientation, and the ability to see a job through.
- Outstanding communications skills . . . Extremely hardworking and dedicated.

EMPLOYMENT: MARSTON CONVENT, Laramie, WY, 2003–Present
Receptionist
Answer phone, greet visitors, and provide information, tours, and literature. Record and monitor thank-you notes for all received donations. Perform light typing, filing, and word processing.

WYOMING PUBLIC TELEVISION, Laramie, WY, 2002–2003
Telemarketer
Solicited donations. Monitored the ordering of informative pamphlets, placards, buttons, T-shirts, etc.

RINALDO RANCH, Laramie, WY, 1998–2003
Secretary
Provided word processing, customer relations, and some accounts payable processing. Implemented new system for check processing; increased prompt payment of client bills.

WOMANPOWER INC., Laramie, WY, 1990–1998
Secretary
Acted as liaison between public and CEO.

STATE HEALTH COALITION, Laramie, WY, 1980–1990
Statistical Typist
Prepared health record documentation of infectious disease patients at State hospital. Managed training of new hires.

EDUCATION: TRAINING, INC., Boston, MA, 1980
An office careers training program in bookkeeping, typing, reception, word processing, and office procedures.

ST. JOSEPH'S ACADEMY, Portland, ME
High School Diploma

Receptionist
Salon

CHRIS SMITH
178 Green Street
St. Louis, MO 63130
(314) 555-5555

OBJECTIVE
A challenging position offering opportunities for growth and advancement.

SUMMARY OF QUALIFICATIONS
- Typing (40 wpm), word processing, and accounting; adept with figures.
- Experience dealing with a diversity of professionals, clients, and staff members.
- Proven communication abilities—both oral and written.
- Adapt easily to new concepts and responsibilities.
- Self-motivated; able to set effective priorities to achieve immediate and long-term goals and meet operational deadlines.

PROFESSIONAL EXPERIENCE
DIETER'S SALON, St. Louis, MO   2005–present
Receptionist/General Clerk
Handled incoming calls; scheduled appointments.
Responsible for cash-flow and weekly payroll.
General clerical duties included some accounting, inventory maintenance, and filing.

CHANTILLY LACE APPAREL, Winslow, MO   2003–2005
Receptionist
Provided customer service.
Assisted in editing sales circulars.
Greeted business associates.

BALZAC'S, St. Charles, MO   2001–2003
Sales Associate/Cashier
Provided customer assistance, registered sales, and responded to telephone inquiries. Security related functions included pre-opening employee and fitting room checks.

REFERENCES
Furnished upon request.

CHRIS SMITH
178 Green Street
Dover, DE 19901
(302) 555-5555

SUMMARY OF QUALIFICATIONS
Administrative professional with high quality skills and experience in the strategic areas of Computer Operations, Customer Service, and Administrative Operations.
- Seasoned administrator and trainer.
- Developed and taught various training sessions on computer hardware/software.
- Reorganized numerous departments to increase efficiency, and reduce expenses and inventory needs.

EMPLOYMENT ABSTRACT

PRATT AUTOMATED SYSTEMS, Dover, DE   2001–Present
Secretary/Receptionist
- Process Accounts Payable invoices.
- Direct incoming correspondence and phone requests to proper personnel.
- Verify accuracy of and submit all employee time sheets and expense accounts.
- Place and follow-up on all equipment orders.
- Demonstrate and train customers on new software programs.
- Create a database with information on customers.
- Maintain computers, scanners, printers, and plotters.
- Operate Source data Systems Computer for input on service records pertaining to awards, advancements, special pay, and emergency data.
- Maintain over 1,000 personnel records.

SOCIAL SECURITY ADMINISTRATION, Newark, DE   1997–2001
Secretary
- Assisted claimants to ensure all SSI claims were processed in a timely manner.
- Maintained files on claimants.
- Performed receptionist duties.

EDUCATION

CURRY COLLEGE, Milton, MA   2002
Course work: English 101, Computer Basics, Mac OS, HTML.

COMPUTERS

Microsoft Word, Excel, Access, Quark.

CHRIS SMITH
178 Green Street
Mitchell, SD 57301
(605) 555-5555

SUMMARY OF QUALIFICATIONS

- Skilled in book production and composition including design composition, production scheduling, desktop periodical production, and photo-typesetting proofreading.
- Developed interpersonal, communication, and supervisory skills, having dealt with a diversity of professionals.
- Self-motivated. Adapt easily to new concepts and responsibilities.
- Function well independently and as a team member; adept at creative problem-solving.

EDUCATION

BLACK HILLS STATE COLLEGE, Spearfish, SD
Bachelor of Arts, December 2004
Major: English; Minor: Psychology

EXPERIENCE

9/03–
Present
HARTNICK GRAPHICS, Mitchell, SD
Assistant to Production Manager
Maintained liaisons between clients and production staff. Coordinated production schedules for in-house and freelance personnel. Prepared contract bids. Administered production status records; expedited completed works. Provided secretarial support and general office assistance. Composed monthly marketing forecast reports; corresponded with international clients regarding foreign government bids and export procedure.

4/99–9/03
ELDERBERRY, INC., Muron, SD
Secretary to Director, Sales and Marketing
Performed all typing, tracked field engineers, and ensured smooth workflow. Handled special projects; completed inventory of engineering supplies.

11/98–4/99
TANGIBLES CORP., Sioux Falls, SD
Public Relations Secretary/Editorial Staff Assistant
Responsible for creative and production phase of quarterly publication. Handled public relations and press releases.

COMPUTERS

Familiar with many PC software programs: Microsoft Word and Excel, Quark, FileMaker.

CHRIS SMITH
178 Green Street
Providence, RI 02908
(401) 555-5555

OBJECTIVE
To contribute acquired administrative skills to a Senior Secretary/Word Processor position.

SUMMARY OF QUALIFICATIONS
- More than thirteen years administrative/clerical experience; type 90 wpm.
- Self-motivated; able to set effective priorities and implement decisions to achieve immediate and long-term goals and meet operational deadlines.
- Proven communication abilities—both oral and written.

PROFESSIONAL EXPERIENCE
CALDYNE ASSOCIATES, Providence, RI   2003–Present
Secretary
Process technical reports, engineering specs, and traffic studies. Type all requisite documents for staff of thirty professionals. Arrange meetings and handle incoming calls. Expedite UPS mailings, FedEx, faxing, and courier services. Type statistical charts, manuscripts, correspondence, and minutes. Order supplies, coordinate daily meetings, arrange luncheons, and administer labor cards.

BRISTOL BANK, Bristol, CT   1999–2003
Secretary/Receptionist
Utilized call director, typed reports, letters, and expense sheets. Reserved conference rooms and ordered supplies. Responsible for calligraphy assignments.

SARGENT AGENCY, Hamden, CT   1996–1999
Secretary
Assigned to School of Public Health. Managed typing of medical charts used in textbooks for Government Funded Medical Program in Iran.

EDUCATION
POLLACK SECRETARIAL SCHOOL, Jackson, TN   1994

COMPUTER SKILLS
Windows, Microsoft Word, Excel

REFERENCES FURNISHED UPON REQUEST.

Shipping/Receiving Expediter

CHRIS SMITH
178 Green Street
Henderson, NV 89014
(702) 555-5555

CAREER HISTORY

THE ALPHA CORPORATION, Henderson, NV
Shipping/Receiving Expediter (2003–Present)
- Entered packing slips, invoices, and other material control information into computer through a CRT.
- Compared and identified contents to packing slips.
- Coordinated with buyers and vendors on problem identification and resolution.
- Scheduled daily deliveries of incoming traffic.
- Transcribed bills of lading.
- Created and implemented and inventory system.
- Conducted physical inventory and updated locations of parts.
- Generated inventory and location reports using Lotus files (self-taught).

Assembler/Material Handler (2000–2003)
- Opened and delivered parts to line.
- Inspected and rejected defective parts.
- Achieved or exceeded production goals.
- Coordinated with coworkers to improve quality of parts.

ROBERT SMITH, INC., Sparks, NV
Clerk (1999–2000)
- Entered purchase orders using a CRT.
- Backed-up computer systems.
- Assisted in maintaining accounts receivable.

Mail Room Clerk (1993–1999)
- Updated and maintained customer files.
- Coordinated and conducted bulk mailings.

EDUCATION

Benton Junior College, Benton Harbor, MI
Associate's degree, Management (1993)

Stenographer

CHRIS SMITH
178 GREEN STREET
REDFORD, MI 48239
(313) 555-5555

OBJECTIVE:

A challenging position as a stenographer in a progressive company.

ACHIEVEMENTS AND QUALIFICATIONS:

- Strong shorthand and speed writing skills at 130 wpm.
- Excel at Gregg Simplified and Diamond Jubilee.
- Proficient with the Pittman method.
- Area of expertise is the transcription, editing, and interpreting of stenographic characters into clear, concise, and precise English.
- Typing skills include word processing at 80 wpm and typewriter production at 65 wpm.
- Recipient of the *Shorthand Award* and *Stenographer of the Year Award* from the Pittman method archives.
- Consistent recognition from the Gregg simplified method archives for excellence in Gregg-style character performance.

EDUCATION:

Salem State College, Salem, MA
A.A. Secretarial Sciences, 2002

Katherine Gibbs Secretarial School, Boston, MA
Executive Secretarial program, 2002

PUBLICATIONS:

Stenographer's Notes, coauthor D. D. Sweeny;
Whole Word Publishing, Boston, MA 2006

Gregg Shorthand Made Simple, coauthor D. D. Sweeny;
Whole Word Publishing, Boston, MA 2006

EMPLOYMENT:

2006–Present   *Harvard University Admissions,* Cambridge, MA, Head Stenographer.

2003–2006   *John Ervine Mutual Life Insurance,* Boston, MA, Stenographer.

Telephone Operator

CHRIS SMITH
178 Green Street
Pompano Beach, FL 33063
(305) 555-5555

PROFESSIONAL OBJECTIVE
A challenging position within the Bell South Corporation in Directory Assistance where progressive experience and excellence will be utilized and advanced.

EXPERIENCE
Southern Bell Telephone/SBT
Pompano Beach, FL

1997–Present
Operator
Responsible for customer calls that can't be directly dialed. Knowledge and skill on the OSDI equipment. Ensure repair orders are called into main office. Assist all callers in a timely, courteous fashion.

1992–1997
411 Directory Assistance Operator
Provide telephone numbers for callers. Ensure numerical accuracy and speed.

EDUCATION AND TRAINING
Winter Park High School, Winter Park, FL
Graduated 1994.

Bell South Telephone Company Directory Assistance Operator Seminar 1992.

Performed training and work routines under the direction of an SBT company mentor 1992.

SKILLS
- OSDI Telecommunications Equipment.
- Data Entry.
- Type 45 wpm.
- Accurate.
- Willing to travel or relocate.

REFERENCES AVAILABLE UPON REQUEST

CHRIS SMITH
178 Green Street
Melrose, CT 06049
(203) 555-5555

OBJECTIVE
To apply skills attained through experience and education to an entry-level position in the field of travel.

STRENGTHS
- Self-motivated and goal-oriented.
- Proven abilities in organization and communication.
- Perform well in high-stress atmospheres.
- Highly developed interpersonal skills, having worked cooperatively with a variety of professionals.
- Experienced traveler.

EDUCATION

Assertiveness Training Courses, The Burke Program, 2006

Computer Programming Workshop
Certified, 2007

University of Bridgeport, Bridgeport, CT
B.A., Public Relations, 2005

WORK EXPERIENCE

TICKET AGENT, Davis Harwin Tours, Ivoryton, CT   2006–Present
Resolved all customer needs. Arranged travel schedules. Handled incoming cash.

MACHINE OPERATOR, Carlisle Sand Inc., Melrose, CT   2004–2006
Duties include sorting and metering mail.

CASUAL DISTRIBUTION CLERK, U.S. Post Office, Hartford, CT   2002–2004
Set up mailroom and appropriate forwarding of packages and mail.

MENTAL HEALTH COUNSELOR, Mystic, CT   1999–2002
Counseled, supervised, and evaluated clients. Arranges special events for youths.

RECEPTIONIST, Warbell Realty, Hartford, CT   1998–1999
Serviced clients. Arranged appointments. Handled incoming calls. Dealt with general office functions.

REFERENCES

Available on request.

Typist

CHRIS SMITH
178 Green Street
Tampa, FL 32714
(813) 555-5555

CAREER OBJECTIVE
A clerical/typist position requiring strong skills in computer literacy.

BACKGROUND SUMMARY
Dedicated trustworthy enthusiastic employee. Loves a challenge and enjoys working with people. Strong background in computer applications. Good humored, friendly, and has a positive outlook. Proven ability to take initiative and adapt to changing priorities.

CAREER HISTORY
Contemporary Data Systems, Tampa, FL, 2002–Present
Secretary and Clerk Typist I–III
- Compiled daily reports and prepared documents using Microsoft Word for Windows.
- Logged, filed, and retrieved Component Engineering Reports.
- Transcribed reports.
- Served as department receptionist: Answered and directed incoming phone calls and messages.
- Ordered office supplies for the entire department.
- Typed purchase orders and expense reports, and recorded and distributed petty cash.
- Sent and distributed fax messages.
- Made travel arrangements and reservations.
- Performed duties of company operator as required.
- Compiled, printed, and distributed various reports.
- Coordinated and distributed part numbers for all engineering departments.

Tampa Sporting Goods, Tampa, FL, 2002–2003
Sales Clerk (part-time)
- Met and serviced customers.
- Responded to customer demands for products and information.
- Maintained inventory levels.
- Participated in showroom reorganization and presentations.
- Conducted physical inventories.

EDUCATION AND WORK-RELATED TRAINING
Attending University of Tampa
B.A. Expected 2008

Contemporary Data System, Excel, ISO 9000.
Type 70 wpm.

Assistant Editor

CHRIS SMITH
178 Green Street
Philadelphia, PA 19103
(215) 555-5555

EXPERIENCE
2004–Present   PUBLICATIONS DEPARTMENT, MUNSON MUSEUM, Philadelphia, PA
Assistant Editor
- Proofread and copyedit scholarly archaeological monographs and museum catalogues.
- Assist editor with all aspects of book production; prepare and organize art work for reproduction and review/approve proofs.
- Identify titles to be reprinted, making necessary editorial changes, obtaining estimates, contracting typesetting, printing, and binding services.
- Recommend and supervise freelance artists. Manage a staff assistant.
- Work directly with authors in regard to editing and artwork.
- Promote materials at various conferences. Select appropriate titles and contract with a combined exhibit group.
- Served as Rights and Permissions Editor.
- Managed inventory control of entire publications stock.
- Supervised order filling; coordinated shipping, billing, and maintenance of circulation records.

1999–2004   VILLANOVA UNIVERSITY, OFFICE OF INTERNATIONAL PROGRAMS FOR AGRICULTURE, Villanova, PA
Assistant to the Director
- Edited and typed grant proposals, research papers, and reports.
- Coordinated preparation and distribution of an international newsletter.
- Served as contact between federal agencies and university departments for sponsored foreign students.
- Coordinated arrangements for visitors, seminars, conferences, and overseas and domestic travel.

1997–1999   **Project Administrator**
- Controlled export trade of endangered floral species within Pennsylvania for U.S. Fish and Wildlife Scientific Authority.

1994–1997   U.S. DEPARTMENT OF LABOR, Scranton, PA
Clerk-Stenographer
- Performed secretarial duties for large technical and professional staffs of the Architecture and Engineering Section and the Community Development Division.
- Served on the Education Committee.

EDUCATION

SWARTHMORE COLLEGE, Swarthmore, PA
Bachelor of Arts degree in English, 1993; GPA 3.8
Academic Honors: Phi Beta Kappa, Phi Eta Sigma, Dean's List

SKILLS

Excel, Microsoft Word, HTML, Perl, Quark, PageMaker. Proficient in Spanish and French.

Author

EXPERIENCE

Writer specializing in women's issues, theater, and the arts.

Books: Best Plays of 2008: A Collection of Theater Reviews (Farber Publishing, forthcoming)
Best Plays of 2007: A Collection of Theater Reviews (Farber Publishing, 2008)
The Evolution of Feminism in the Theater (Farber Publishing, 2006)
The French Woman: Breaking the Stereotype, by Mimi St. Pierre (Bimblass Press, 2003)
A Tale of Caracas, by Esteban Bolivera (Caroline Publishers, 2000)
Plays with corresponding reviews (multiple authors) published by Carolina Publishers in
International Theater, 1997.

Articles: Currently theater columnist for the *New York Review* and editorial writer for *Woman*
magazine. Credits include:

Equality	*Guide to Broadway*	*Our World*
Eve	*Men's World*	*Parent and Child*
Family	*Mother Earth*	*The Renaissance Reader*
The Feminist	*New York Theater Guide*	*Teenage America*
The Great Debate	*NOW*	*Today's Woman*

Corporate
Clients: United Feminists, New York Theater Association.

Editor: 1992–1996: Contributing Editor, *The Feminist*
1988–1991: Copyeditor/Proofreader for various clients.
1985–1987: Manuscript Submissions Coordinator, Nonfiction Division, Carolina Publishers.
1979–1984: Senior Editor, *The Renaissance Reader*
1977–1978: Editor, *Mother Earth*
1975–1976: Assistant Editor, *Our World*

EDUCATION

Adelphi University
Garden City, NY
Bachelor of Arts in English Literature
Minor: Journalism

L'Ecole d'Avignon
Avignon, France
Semester Abroad

Universidad de Cordoba
Cordoba, Spain
Semester Abroad

Broadcast Producer

CHRIS SMITH
178 Green Street
Waukesha, WI 53186
(414) 555-5555

EDUCATION

University of Massachusetts, Amherst, MA
Bachelor of Arts in English, 2005

College of Humanities and Fine Arts, Boston, MA, 2000–2001

TELEVISION PRODUCTION

2004 to 2008   WTOR EDUCATIONAL FOUNDATION, Worcester, MA

Producer
Produced:
Three contract series (twenty half-hour programs for each) for U.S. Marines and Stanford University Commission on Extension Services: "Ideologies in World Affairs," "Computer Science I," and "Computer Science II."

"Fighting Mad"—series of two-hour-long group therapy sessions conducted by Dr. Paula Hershey, Hamline University.

"The 21-Inch Classroom"—History, Geology Pilot

"Bob Bersen Reviews"

Writer/produced:
Half-hour promotional videotape selling ETV for the University of Massachusetts, Amherst.
Half-hour promotional videotape selling ITV for the 21-inch Classroom.

REFERENCES

Available upon request.

Columnist

CHRIS SMITH
178 Green Street
Elmhurst, IL 60126
(312) 555-5555

EDUCATION

Knox College, Galesburg, IL
B.A. in Communications
2001–2005

PROFESSIONAL EXPERIENCE

The Windy City
Current columnist, photographer, and freelance writer for monthly tourist magazine in Chicago. Write 1000-word column each month entitled "Around the Town." 2005–Present.

The Great Outdoors
Wrote copy for seventy-five-page mail-order camping equipment catalog. Wrote and revised hundreds of twenty-five-word sales descriptions. Met tight deadlines in eight-week freelance project. 2005.

The Index
Full-time staff writer for Knox College alumni magazine. Wrote short news briefs and in-depth features, including several cover stories. As the only staff writer, researched and investigated all major articles and initiated several new story ideas. Current freelance writer. 2004.

Along the Shore
Freelance writer for monthly newsletter for cities surrounding Lake Michigan, 2003.

Trailways
Created, edited, and published a newsletter while participating in a hike along the Appalachian Trail. Solicited submissions, edited all copy, and desktop published the newsletter on an Apple computer. 2003.

The Knox Collegian
Full-time editor of campus newspaper. Assigned and edited all articles for weekly publication. Involved in all aspects of publication process, including writing, copyediting, proofreading, desktop publishing, and layout. Managed staff of fifteen. 2002.

Tempo
Intern at newsweekly in Chicago. Responsibilities included proofreading, fast-checking, and writing 250-word news briefs for "Around the World" section. Wrote an in-depth feature on battered women's shelters in the Chicago area. 2002.

References and all works available upon request.

Correspondent

CHRIS SMITH
178 Green Street
Swannanoa, NC 28778
(704) 555-5555

EDUCATION

WAKE FOREST UNIVERSITY, Winston, NC
Master of Arts, Print Journalism, May 1999

SHEFFIELD UNIVERSITY, Sheffield, UK
History Degree, June 1998
Literature Degree, June 1997

PRINCETON UNIVERSITY, Princeton, NJ
Summer Program in Anthropology, 1996

EXPERIENCE

2006–
Present
LE RECORD DU JOUR
French Daily Newspaper

Responsible for writing stories and features on local affairs for the Cultural and the National Sections. Assignments completed on deadline. Travel extensively throughout France and topical point of interest stories. Have been awarded six GLOBE journalism awards for international reporting. Broke several high-profile stories.

1999–2005 *TOKYO RECORD*
Japanese Daily Newspaper—English Edition (second largest in country).

Responsible for writing stories and features on social and political issues throughout the country.

SKILLS

Lotus, WordPerfect, IBM
35mm Photography
½-inch Videotape
Super 8 Movies
Fluent in French, English, and Spanish

PERSONAL DATA

Writing fiction and poetry (novel is pending publication). Traveled extensively throughout the world.

Letters of reference and writing samples will be furnished upon request.

Editor

Events Planner

CHRIS SMITH
178 Green Street
Miami, FL 33054
(305) 555-5555

OBJECTIVE:

A challenging and responsible Events Planning position offering opportunities for direct client contact, where my experience, education, and capabilities can be fully utilized.

EXPERIENCE:

9/03–Present **SEA THE WORLD (INTERNATIONAL CRUISE LINE),** Miami, FL
Passengers: 500 to 2,000
Crew Members: 300–800 from over forty nations.
First Purser (8/06–Present)
Responsible for directing activities of four offices and supervising front office personnel. Act as onboard personnel and accounting departments. Supervise staff of up to ten on embarkation days. On call twenty-four hours per day.
- Prepare manifest, port papers for all ports of call, clearance, crew visas, and act as liaison between ship and country for all customers and immigration procedures for both passengers and crew.
- Resolve passenger problems and collect accounts. Responsible for $250,000 safe for foreign exchange. Prepare payroll.
- Make all travel arrangements for onboard entertainers, changing twice on each cruise, i.e., booking flights, hotel reservations, etc.
- Plan, schedule, organize, and supervise operations for crew benefit events for various organizations at ports of call.
- Oversee all printing/typesetting, i.e., daily programs, literature, menus, maps for shore travel, health programs, invitations, and newsletters.
- Order equipment and supplies for hotel department.
Second Purser—Foreign Exchange (2/06–7/06)
Second Purser—Crew (3/05–1/06)
Senior Assistant Purser (5/04–3/05)
Assistant Purser (9/03–4/04)

6/02–8/03 **THE AMBER HOTEL,** Providence, RI
Front Office Sales Agent
Responsible for taking reservations, solving problems, and checking guests in and out. Handled conventions of up to 250 as well as transient guests.

EDUCATION:

JOHNSON & WALES UNIVERSITY, Providence, RI
SCHOOL OF HOTEL RESTAURANT MANAGEMENT
Bachelor of Science (May 2002)

Information Support Specialist

CHRIS SMITH
178 Green Street
Evansville, WY 82636
(307) 555-5555

OBJECTIVE
A position where I can contribute excellent word processing and administrative skills.

EXPERIENCE
Kimball Equipment Corp., Casper, WY
2005–Present
Information Support Specialist
Offer formal and informal training and assistance in the use of end-user computing hardware, software, and applications, most specifically Excel and Microsoft Word and various graphics packages. Work with user department personnel to ensure adherence to office automation/end-user computing guidelines, standards, and procedures. Coordinated with other Information Services staff to provide appropriate education, hardware, software, and data required to effectively assist users. Perform problem analysis and resolution activities via company help line.

2000–2004
Supervisor, Word Processing, Word Processing Center
Planned, organized, directed, and controlled provision of stenographic, clerical, word/information processing services, and company telephone operators. Supervised thirteen full-time employees. Duties included determining material, personnel, and budgeting needs. Designed workflow systems, defined operating standards, and evaluated overall effectiveness. Established cost and quality controls, and monitored performance to ensure that proper levels were maintained.

1998–1999
Word Processing Specialist, Word Processing Center
Developed thorough knowledge of center procedure and maintenance of records with ability to meet high priority turnaround time. Functions performed included formatting and producing complex documents, records processing, retrieval of data from electronic files, analyzing requirements for and handling special projects, and training center and system personnel in use of information processing equipment. Acted as administrative support specialist and supervisor in their absence.

EDUCATION
Associate's Degree, Business Management, 1998
University of Wyoming, Laramie, WY

REFERENCES
Available upon request.

CHRIS SMITH
178 Green Street
College Park, MD 20742
(301) 555-5555

PROFESSIONAL EMPLOYMENT

May 2000– Present
FREELANCE JOURNALIST AND PHOTOGRAPHER. Cover a variety of current events and general interest topics, including student uprisings in Washington, D.C. and town meetings around Virginia and Maryland.

September 2006– Present
LECTURER, UNIVERSITY OF MARYLAND, COLLEGE PARK. Currently teaching English Composition and Ethics and the Media, eighteen hours a week to first-, second-, and third-year students of journalism.

2004–2006
LIBRARIAN, SMITH COLLEGE, NORTHAMPTON, MA. Coordinated undergraduate library assistance. Organized fundraising and library activities.

August 2001– September 2003
CONTRIBUTING EDITOR AND COLUMNIST, *READER'S PARADISE* MAGAZINE, BOSTON, MA. Published articles on international politics. Authored a fortnightly column "Washington Update" which tracked legislation proposed in Congress.

August 1999– August 2001
CONTRIBUTING EDITOR, PALE MOON PUBLISHING CO., BOSTON, MA. Wrote postscripts and flaps for books, corresponded with authors. Researched and coauthored almanac of resumes for publication in trade market.

EDUCATION

2004–2006
Wardell College, Boston, MA—**MASTER'S OF FINE ARTS, JOURNALISM.**

1994–1998
Georgetown University, Washington, D.C.—**BACHELOR OF ARTS, PHOTOGRAPHY.**

AWARDS

2005
SPRINGFIELD SOCIETY: Received scholarship for being "most likely to contribute to the field of publishing."

Production Editor

CHRIS SMITH
178 Green Street
Bothell, WA 98012
(206) 555-5555

PROFESSIONAL OBJECTIVE

A position in **Production Editing.**

PROFESSIONAL EXPERIENCE

GRAVES EQUIPMENT CORPORATION, Bothell, WA 2006 to Present
Production Editor

- Write and edit weekly newsletter focusing on news and trends at Graves Equipment Corporation and in the GEC-compatible market; major sections devoted to reporting new GEC-compatible hardware and software products and services as well as general news of companies who sell to GEC-based markets.

ZURICH MARKETING GROUP, INC., Seattle, WA 2005–2006
Research Associate

- Assisted development, implementation, and analysis of various surveys pertaining to higher education.
- Developed script, conducted interviews, analyzed results, and wrote reports summarizing research findings.

UNIVERSITY OF WASHINGTON PRESS, Seattle, WA 2003–2005
Manuscript Editor, *Reviews of Genetic Diseases*

- Produced six issues of medical journal; completed work ahead of all scheduling deadlines.
- Organized efforts of editorial committee, scheduled, and edited; coordinated layout with printers.

THE OAKDALE EXPERIENCE, Seattle, WA 1999–2003
Assistant to the Editor

- Wrote weekly column covering science news; researched and interpreted topics of current interest for Editor and contributing editors.
- Edited articles for content and usage, assisted advertisement design, and handled layout and typesetting.
- Acted as liaison for Marketing Director, Editor, and advertisers.

PACIFIC LUTHERAN UNIVERSITY SCHOOL OF MEDICINE, Tacoma, WA 1995–1999
Research Assistant

- Edited three medical textbooks under publisher deadline, coordinated author contributions, and assisted writing.

EDUCATION

Seattle Pacific University, Seattle, WA
Bachelor of Arts in Neuropsychology, 1995

Proofreader

CHRIS SMITH
178 Green Street
Hope, AR 71801
(501) 555-5555

OBJECTIVE

To serve as proofreader for a book publisher.

EXPERIENCE

2004–Present Vigilant Widow Publishers, Hope, AR
Proofreader
Monitor all outgoing business forms, pamphlets, and booklets for mistakes. Train new hires. Manage darkroom. Coordinate efficient darkroom procedures.

2000–2004 Sapphire Runway Photo, Walnut Ridge, AR
Photo Lab Assistant
Proofed outgoing photographs for surface flaws, skin blemishes, etc. Operated printer and EP-2 processor.

1998–2000 John's Photo, Birmingham, AL
Photo Lab Assistant

EDUCATION

Eureka College, Eureka, IL
Associate's Degree, 2000.

COMPUTERS

Microsoft Word, PageMaker, Quark

INTERESTS

Reading, Archery, Photography.

REFERENCES

Available upon request.

CHRIS SMITH
178 Green Street
Tallmadge, OH 44278
(216) 555-5555

SUMMARY:

- Recognized for ability to plan, organize, coordinate, and direct successful fundraising programs, volunteer committees, public relations programs, and educational programs.
- Broad knowledge of legislative procedure.
- Extensive volunteer recruiting and training.

EXPERIENCE:

Ohio Association for Multiple Sclerosis, Akron, OH
Public Relations Manager
Fundraising Director (2006–Present)

- Served as Consultant to seven chapters in Ohio on campaign problems and activities.
- Organized statewide and regional campaign meetings and developed fundraising programs.
- Chairperson for Committee for a Healthier Ohio.
- Special assignments included reviewing all state legislation concerning Association of MS and its programs; staffing Legislative Advisory Committee and following through on specific bills; acting as Training Coordinator for five three-day orientation courses held for new employees.

Campaign Director (2004–2006)

- Administered $1 million campaign, including every aspect of fundraising.
- Recruited 40,000 volunteers.
- Wrote campaign letters; ordered all campaign materials; staffed Campaign Advisory Committee; coordinated and directed chapter-wide meetings; conducted staff meetings.
- Maintained campaign records; tested new materials and ideas; assisted chapter department heads and the executive director.

National Lung Association, Sandusky, OH
Campaign Director (2001–2004)

- Directed complete direct-mail fundraising campaign ($250,000); formulated policy in the areas of scheduling, list building, coding, and testing; cooperated with public relations director in developing campaign materials; trained and supervised up to fifty office volunteers.

EDUCATION:

M.S. degree in Public Relations, 2000—University of Dayton, Dayton, OH
B.A. degree in Government, 1996—Macalester College, St. Paul, MN

Public Relations Assistant

CHRIS SMITH
178 Green Street
Omaha, NE 68114
(420) 555-5555

SUMMARY OF QUALIFICATIONS

Successful administrative experience with major voluntary health agency . . . recognized for ability to plan, organize, coordinate, and direct successful fundraising programs, volunteer committees, public relations programs, educational programs . . . legislative experience and knowledge . . . extensive volunteer recruitment experience . . . supervisory experience with both professional and nonprofessional staffs . . . qualified to work with agencies and institutions as well as civic and industrial leaders in the best interest of the organization . . . active in community affairs.

EMPLOYMENT EXPERIENCE

Nebraska Heart Society, Inc., Omaha, NE
PR Managerial Assistant, 2005–Present
Serve as consultant to the seven chapters in the state regarding campaign problems and activities; organize statewide and regional campaign meetings; develop fundraising programs (bequests); conduct the 2006 and 2007 campaigns for the newly merged Central Chapter (Antelope County); 2007 Chairman for the Nebraska Independent Health Agency Committee (solicitation of State employees); 2007 Secretary for the Combined Federal Campaign (Federal employee campaign); Special Assignments; Responsible for reviewing all State legislation regarding and relationship to the Heart Society and its programs, and bringing specific bills to the attention of the proper committee or individual, Staff the Legislative Advisory Committee and follow through regarding specific bills. Act as Assistant Training Coordinator for four two-and-one-half day orientation courses held for new employees. Assist in developing the course. Speaker at several campaign conferences.

Directorial Assistant (Greater Omaha Chapter), 2003–2005
Supervised all chapter campaign duties as well as assisted the Executive Director with administrative responsibilities such as personnel and budget.

EDUCATION

Dillard University, New Orleans, LA
M.S. degree, Public Relations, 2003

University of Michigan at Flint
B.A. degree, Government, 2001

PERSONAL

Willing to relocate and travel.

Publicist

CHRIS SMITH
178 Green Street
Pullman, WA 99164
(509) 555-5555

OBJECTIVE:

Publicist position at ABC Corporation.

EXPERIENCE:

CNBS TELEVISION, *Confrontations*, Pullman, WA   2006–Present
Production Assistant
Book main guests and panelists. Generate and research story ideas. Conduct video research. Edit teases for show. Organize all production details for studio tapings. Troubleshoot equipment malfunctions. Monitor lighting and TelePrompTer. Coordinate publicity ads in local newspapers.

BARSTOW COMPANY, Seattle, WA   2004–2006
Publicity Assistant
Publicized new books and authors. Assisted in booking media tours (TV, radio, and print). Wrote and designed press releases. Fulfilled review copy requests. Conducted galley mailings and general office work.

WNBN-TV, Tacoma, WA   2003–2004
Production Intern
Assisted producers of a live, daily talk show. Researched and generated story ideas. Pre-interviewed possible guests. Logged tapes. Went out on shoots and wrote promotional announcements. Produced five of my own segments for the show.

THE BENEDICT COUNCIL, UNIVERSITY OF WASHINGTON, Seattle, WA   2002–2003
Promotional Assistant
Implemented promotional campaign for concerts on campus. Wrote and designed promotional advertisements. Initiated student involvement with program.

THE CHERRY HAIKU, INC., Seattle, WA   2001–2002
Art Assistant
Responsible for paste-ups/mechanicals. Operated Photostat camera; coordinated logistics for photo shoots. Participated in "brainstorming" sessions with creative team.

EDUCATION:

UNIVERSITY OF WASHINGTON, Seattle, WA
B.A. Cum Laude, May 2003
Major: Communication
Minor: English

Radio Announcer

CHRIS SMITH
178 Green Street
Baltimore, MD 21217
(301) 555-5555

PROFESSIONAL OBJECTIVE

A rewarding and challenging position as an ANNOUNCER.

EDUCATION BACKGROUND

NORDSTROM BROADCASTING SCHOOL, Baltimore, MD
Received Certificate for eleven-month Broadcasting Program, 1997
Courses included: Announcing, Speech, Technical Lab, News, Sales, and Copywriting.

PROFESSIONAL EXPERIENCE

2004 to Present THE DIVINING ROD, Baltimore, MD
Announcer
- Responsible for providing adult contemporary music and announcing for private club.
- Set up equipment, select music, and engineer show.
- Operated own equipment which includes lighting and broadcasting system.
- Conduct various promotions and accept requests from the audience.

2000 to 2004 WXTS FM, Baltimore, MD
Producer
- Responsible for coordinating adult contemporary music programming, commercials, giveaways, long-distance requests, production, and engineering for Jolene Sunny's Night Show from 6 to 9 P.M.
- Conducted listener music surveys.

1997 to 2000 TRAVELIN' TUNES, Baltimore, MD
Disc Jockey
- Responsible for playing music at weddings, christenings, banquets, etc., all across Maryland.
- Played all varieties of music including: Big Band, Irish, Top 40, and adult contemporary.

PERSONAL

Willing to travel and relocate.

AUDITION TAPE ENCLOSED.

CHRIS SMITH
178 Green Street
Greenville, SC 29613
(803) 555-5555

OBJECTIVE:

To contribute researching and writing skills to a position as **Reporter** or **Editorial Assistant.**

WRITING DISTINCTIONS:

- Superior Scholar Award for "Jack-O-Lantern Dreams," a creative-writing Senior Project, comprised of seven poems and four prose pieces about growing up in a Jehovah's Witness family. Spring 2007.
- Amazon Expedition Article, accepted by *Charleston Record* "Travel" section. Fall, 2006.
- Researched and wrote historical articles for "The Insider's Guide to Greenville."
- Published short stories in *Gnashings*, the Furman student literary magazine. Spring, 2005.

EDUCATION:

FURMAN UNIVERSITY, Greenville, SC
Bachelor of Arts, May 2005
Major: English

SYRACUSE UNIVERSITY, Sydney, Australia   Fall 2003
Concentration: Language and History

WORK EXPERIENCE:

EYE ON GREENVILLE, Greenville, SC
Reporter/Editor
- Researched and wrote articles; assisted in determining editorial content.

English Peer Tutor   Fall 2006, Spring 2008
- Provided one-on-one interaction in basic writing with a freshman student; emphasized grammar and writing skills.

POINT MAGAZINE, Charleston, SC   Summer 2007
Intern
- Assisted writers in research; prepared media kits for potential advertisers.

REACH, Furman journal of student scholarship   Spring 2006
Member, Editorial Committee
- Evaluated and selected articles.

COMPUTERS:

Excel, Microsoft Word, Quark

Symposium Coordinator

CHRIS SMITH
178 Green Street
Sacramento, CA 95823
(916) 555-5555

EXPERIENCE

Fairgate Corporation, Burbank, CA   2006–Present

Symposium Coordinator. Serving as the planner and coordinator of the company's annual supplier symposium. Responsible for setting up and maintaining a supplier database of over 500 records. Responsible to company purchasing teams for the coordination and update of information. Acting as liaison for Fairgate to the Symposium guests. Deadline-oriented position with a strict schedule. Learned the value of attention to details and fine-tuned my ability to handle multiple tasks simultaneously.

Earlcort Enterprises, San Rafael, CA   2004–2006

Creative Consultant. Served in a variety of positions including marketing, advertising and public relations, and the drafting of business plans for a growing list of clients. Extensive communication skills and people skills added to the responsibility of the position.

Jen Brooks and Associates, San Jose, CA   2003–2004

Part-time freelance work for Public Relations Firm. Assignments have included several articles and photographs. Maintain an ongoing relationship.

Sterling Sparrow Salon, Hollywood, CA   2002–2003

Receptionist. Answered phones, greeted customers, handled inquiries, took messages, booked and confirmed appointments. Kept books, compiled daily and weekly sales reports. Handle banking functions, closed out registers. Controlled inventory. Trouble-shot office-related problems.

Sandalwood Fragrances, Ventura, CA   2001–2002

Receptionist. Processed Accounts Payable and Accounts Receivable. Performed computer input and light typing. Answered phones, filed, and performed miscellaneous office tasks.

EDUCATION

Boston College, Chestnut Hill, MA
B.A. English, 2001

OTHER SKILLS

Extensive experience with Mac and PC systems. Proficiency in Excel, Microsoft Word, and Quark.

Television Director

CHRIS SMITH
178 Green Street
New York, NY 10036
(212) 555-5555

PROFESSIONAL EXPERIENCE

2006 to Present
CBS NEWS, New York, NY
Director
- Direct live taping of thirty-minute newscasts.
- Direct all studio personnel, equipment, and scheduling.
- Rotated through several positions in 2007, including Assistant Director, Technical Director, Audio Engineer, and Floor Manager.

2004 to 2006
OWL EYES PRODUCTIONS, Albany, NY
Associate Producer/Production Coordinator
- Coordinated freelance production of television commercials for local and national affiliates.
- Booked talents and handled casting contracts.
- Coordinated travel and wardrobe arrangements.
- Administered budgets for wardrobe, props, and food and beverages.
- Supervised all operations on shooting days.

2004
FREELANCE
Production Coordinator
- Coordinated production of award-winning music video by the Starstruck Souls.
- Coordinated productions of commercial for Paragon Park at Lost Haven Beach, Massachusetts.

2002 to 2004
Production Assistant, Foster Productions, Kingston, NY
- Assisted in the production of industrial and medical films, business presentations, videotaping of plays, fashion shows, etc.

EDUCATION

Syracuse University
Syracuse, NY
B.F.A. in Broadcasting and Film, 2002
Minor: Psychology

INTERESTS

Travel, playing guitar, photography.

Television Production Engineer

CHRIS SMITH
178 Green Street
Sweet Briar, VA 24595
(804) 555-5555

CAREER OBJECTIVE
A position as TELEVISION ENGINEER.

PROFESSIONAL EXPERIENCE

ENGINEERING DEPARTMENT/PRODUCTION ENGINEER   2002–Present
WNPQ—Bristol, VA
Responsible for all technical/engineering aspects of production including lighting, camera operation, and TelePrompTer functioning for studio and location shoots. Supervise tape recording in 1", ¾" VHS, and ½" Beta can modes. Troubleshoot equipment malfunctions. Analyze problems and implement effective solutions including technical and minor repair work. Perform grip work and miscellaneous support tasks as required. Meet all management established production deadlines.

VIDEO POST PRODUCTION/AUTOMATION TECHNICIAN   1999–2002
Rochelle Technical Systems—Lexington, VA
Specialized in programming computer applications to perform multiple tasks carried throughout a network for televisions, VCRs, and control equipment. Edited commercial spots onto two-hour working tapes. Gained a strong background in computer automation and graphics.

PRODUCTION ASSISTANT/INTERN   Summer 1999
Blacksburg Medical Center—Blacksburg, VA
Served as Production Assistant on six Medical Digest shoots, produced exclusively for broadcast on WWLP 22. Handled lighting, TelePrompTer, camera operation, and ¾" broadcast quality tape recording. Maintained highest possible production standards. Resolved malfunctions and technical problems in a timely and cost-effective manner.

INTERN   Spring 1999
Emerald Valley Unit Productions—Sweet Briar, VA
Worked on three camera sets in positions from Grip up to Camera Director. Handled both technical and creative aspects while working in a highly active environment.

EDUCATION AND TRAINING
ASSOCIATE'S DEGREE TELECOMMUNICATIONS TECHNOLOGY, 1999.
Sweet Briar College—Sweet Briar, VA.

COMPUTERS
Microsoft Word and Excel

Translator

CHRIS SMITH
178 Green Street
New Haven, CT 06511
(203) 555-5555

STRENGTHS AND QUALIFICATIONS

- High levels of enthusiasm and commitment to a successful sales, marketing, or communications career.
- Strong leadership qualities; able to schedule priorities and perform/delegate accordingly to effectively accomplish tasks at hand.
- Working knowledge of both written and verbal Japanese and French.
- Broad perspective of Japanese people, culture, and customs, as well as Japanese-American diplomatic relations.
- Computer literate in most popular software, including Microsoft Word, Excel, Quark, and Computer Aided Design (CAD).

JAPANESE-AMERICAN RELATIONS

Served as liaison between Japanese diplomats and the Japanese-American Relations Group and with the Japanese press during Prime Minister's stay.

Translated correspondence and filed inquiries from the Japanese population in the Boston business community.

Organized travel itineraries for Japanese officials visiting the New England area.

SALES/MARKETING/ENTREPRENEURIAL SKILLS

Founded International Resumes, a company designed for the creation of English and Japanese resumes, and ran it from 2003–2005.

Designed and circulated posters, banners, and invitations in order to introduce the Japanese community to New England.

EDUCATION

Yale University, New Haven, CT
M.A., East Asian Studies, expected to be received June 2007.

Harvard University, New Haven, CT
B.A., Psychology and Japanese Studies, May 2003.

EMPLOYMENT HISTORY

2006–Present	**Technical Writer/Junior Programmer**	Universal Programs, Inc., New Haven, CT
2004–2005	**Assistant to the Japanese Ambassador**	Japanese Embassy, Washington, D.C.
Summers 2002–2003	**Sales Representative**	Carlisle's Inc., West Hartford, CT
1999–2000	**Marketing Representative**	A.M. Keegan & Company, Easton, MA

Typesetter

CHRIS SMITH
178 Green Street
Knoxville, TN 37801
(615) 555-5555

EXPERIENCE

Oakridge Industries, Knoxville, TN   2006–Present
Typesetter
Typeset manuscripts for various magazines, advertisements, financial reports, catalogs, graphs, newsletters, etc., and coded all manuscripts.

Butterfield Corporation, Grand Prairie, TX   2002–2006
Typesetter
Typeset manuscript of legal cases for courts and law books.

Alder, Inc., Granbury, TX   1999–2002
Marketing Editor
Oversaw status of work output and interviewed potential employees. Other duties consisted of typesetting manuscripts for various magazine, textbooks, sports directories, and advertisements. Also marked up manuscript in accordance with customer specifications, using computer coding. Experienced in usage of video editing applications.

Camacho and Briar, Inc., Dallas, TX   Summer 1998
Typesetter and Proofreader
Served as a Typesetter and Proofreader for marketing materials, including fliers, advertisements, and posters.

OTHER

Asher and Lynn, Dallas, TX   Summer 1997
Served as a Secretary to the College Editorial Department.

Sunchise and Wright, Dallas, TX   Summer 1996
Served as an Assistant Bookkeeper in the Accounting Department.

EDUCATION

St. Edward's University, Austin, TX
B.A. in English, 1999.

Writer

CHRIS SMITH
178 Green Street
Indianapolis, IN 46205
(317) 555-5555

SUMMARY OF QUALIFICATIONS

- Experienced in the general planning and detailed execution of projects.
- Have written numerous in-house company documents including program proposals, five-year plans, research reports, and executive correspondence.
- Participated in marketing teams which conceived, wrote, and produced direct mail campaigns and support materials for a sales force.
- Flexible in assuming a leadership role, collaborating with colleagues, or supporting a department head or executive.
- Have written and edited over 200 audio-visual scripts and 100 related booklets for science, mathematics, and social studies education.

PROFESSIONAL EXPERIENCE

Writing/ Editing

Writer/Editor

FREELANCE EMPLOYMENT, 2005–Present, Indiana State.

For Business: Wrote numerous planning, policy, and procedural documents; produced in-depth reports which required extensive research and analysis; wrote letters and memos for executive signature.

For Science Education: Wrote clear, accurate audio-visual programs for students; developed useful, informative support materials for educators.

Management/ Publishing

The Ruby Shoes Press, Terra Haute, IN

Editorial and Development Manager   1994–2005

- Began as freelance writer and progressed to the management of company's audio-visual editorial and production.
- Refined and administered annual budget of $300,000 for development of new programs.
- Recruited and supervised ten in-house editors and an average of thirty freelance writers, artists, and producers.
- Conceived, scheduled, and produced over 120 audio-visual programs and an equal number of teaching guides.
- Collaborated on marketing plans for all audio-visual products. Delivered presentations of new products to sales force.
- Developed award-winning programs that ranked among the company's bestsellers.

EDUCATION

NEW YORK UNIVERSITY, New York, NY
Master's degree in English, 1993
- Teaching Fellowship, 1992–1993

COLUMBIA UNIVERSITY, New York, NY
Bachelor of Arts degree in English, 1989
- Minors in Biology and Chemistry.

COMPUTERS

Windows, Microsoft Word, Quark, and PageMaker.

Applications Programmer
Senior

CHRIS SMITH
178 Green Street
Huntington, WV 25701
(304) 555-5555

OBJECTIVE

To contribute relevant experience and educational background to the position of **Computer Programmer/Software Engineer.**

SUMMARY OF QUALIFICATIONS

- Proficient in the design and implementation of program enhancements, including an online message system, database repair/troubleshooting utilities, and a release system to update clients on the current version of software.
- Demonstrated ability in the provision of client support services.

EXPERIENCE

6/2004 to Present   **Senior Programmer—Patient Scheduling System**
TESSERACT CORPORATION   Huntington, WV
A privately owned software company specializing in the needs of the health care industry.
- Design and implementation of new system enhancements.
- Sole development of new generator product. Designed file structure and conducted actual coding based on functional specification requirements.

3/2003 to 6/2004   **Programmer/Analyst**
- Installed software for new clients and provided onsite support.
- Developed online message system for members of the programming group.
- Instituted utilities that aided in the detection and evaluation of client bugs and made repairs to the client database.
- Supported existing clients and resolved critical issues/problems in a timely fashion.

EDUCATION

MARSHALL UNIVERSITY, 2005 to Present   Huntington, WV
Enrolled in Graduate Mathematics program (Part time)

WEST VIRGINIA UNIVERSITY, 2000 to 2004   Morgantown, WV
Bachelor of Science degree: Computer Science Engineering

COMPUTERS

Programming Languages: Java, PHP, ASP.NET, C++, Visual Basic.NET, CGI/Perl, HTML, XML.
Databases: SQL Server, Oracle, Access
Hardware: PC, Mac, UNIX

REFERENCES FURNISHED UPON REQUEST

Applications Programmer
Senior

CHRIS SMITH
178 Green Street
New York, NY 10003
(718) 555-5555

**EMPLOYMENT
HISTORY**

BENTLEY LIFE INSURANCE, New York, NY   2003–Present
Programmer Analyst/Senior Programmer
- Supervised and guided junior programmers in the team on various PC illustration System Projects.
- Developed, maintained, and supported Sales Illustration Systems.
- Developed a Front End System for the Bentley Sales Illustration Systems.
- Wrote the "Illustration Software Illustrations" routine.
- Designed a file transfer process from a PC to a UNIX server.
- Hands-on experience with PC hardware, Windows, and have understanding of Ethernet Networks. Developed an Executive Information System. Became very familiar with production environment.
- Maintained and supported the existing online and batch systems.

SHAW ASSOCIATES, Hartford, CT   2001–2003
Computer Programmer
- Designed product and sales tracking programs for company computer system.
- Monitored product availability and inventory for branch sites, displayed new product releases, and accessed daily proceed information.
- Maintained/expanded client base.

EDUCATION

New York University, New York, NY
Master of Science in Electrical Engineering, 2001
Program emphasis: Software Engineering and Computer Networks

Oxford University, Oxford, England
Bachelor of Science in Engineering (Electronics Option), 1999
Program emphasis: Digital Communications and Engineering Management

**TECHNICAL
SUMMARY**

Hardware: Mac, PC, UNIX
Software: Many PC, Linux, and Mac applications
Op Systems: Windows, Mac OS, Linux
Language: Java, PHP, ASP.NET, C++, Visual Basic.NET, CGI/Perl, HTML, XML

Director of Information Services

CHRIS SMITH
178 Green Street
Ithaca, NY 14850
(607) 555-5555

SUMMARY OF QUALIFICATIONS

- Extensive experience in Visual Basic and Oracle Programming.
- Proven managerial abilities.
- Self-motivated; able to set effective priorities to achieve immediate and long-term goals, and meet operational deadlines.
- Developed interpersonal skills, having dealt with a diversity of professionals, clients, and staff members.
- Function well in fast-paced, high-pressure atmosphere.

EXPERIENCE

NEW YORK INSTITUTE OF CERTIFIED PUBLIC ACCOUNTANTS,
New York, NY   2001–Present
Director of Information Services
Controlled Programming and Systems, Computer Operations, Data Entry, Membership Records, and Membership Promotion and Retention Departments. Implemented complete financial reporting systems, magazine subscription fulfillment, order entry, inventory, invoicing, accounts receivable, CPE course scheduling and evaluations, membership records and dues accounting, computerized production of publications, committee appointments, and sundry applications.

BROMIDE, INC., Albany, NY   1995–2000
Systems Representative
Assisted salespeople in technical presentations for prospective clients; advised and implemented client conversion and installation of new computer systems.

BROWN UNIVERSITY, Providence, RI   1993–1994
Analytical Chemist, Division of Sponsored Research

LIVERPOOL GRAMMAR SCHOOL, Liverpool, England   1992–1993
General Science and Math Teacher

EDUCATION

UNIVERSITY OF DUBLIN, Dublin, Ireland
Bachelor of Science, 1991

LAN Administrator

CHRIS SMITH
178 Green Street
Albuquerque, NM 87104
(505) 555-5555

CAREER SUMMARY

An experienced professional with expertise in the design and development of multi-user database management systems running on a Local Area Network. Skilled in LAN management and user training.

BUSINESS EXPERIENCE

JEFFERSON MANUFACTURING, CORP., Albuquerque, NM   2003 to Present
Documentation Development Coordinator
Analyze, develop, and maintain application software for engineering LAN. Provide training and user support for all applications to LAN users. Maintain departmental PC workstations including software installation and upgrades.

- Reduced data entry errors and process time by developing a program which allowed program managers to submit model number information online.
- Replaced time-consuming daily review board meetings by developing a program which allowed engineers to review and approve model and component changes online.
- Developed an online program which reduced process time, standardized part usage, and which allowed engineers to build part lists for new products and components.

Computer Systems Analyst   1999 to 2003
Responsibilities included database management systems analysis and design, workstation maintenance and repair, and LAN management.

- Reduced process time and purchasing errors by developing an online program, which allowed the purchasing department to track the status of all purchasing invoices.
- Developed a purchase order entry program for the purchasing department, which improved data entry speed and reduced the number of data entry errors.

LAFAYETTE, INC., Albuquerque, NM   1994 to 1999
Engineering Technician III
Prototyped and tested new PC products, drawing schematics, and expediting parts for these new PC products. Designed and coded multi-user database management software for engineering use.

- Expedited the parts for twenty-five or more telecommunications terminal prototypes. Built, troubleshot, and transferred those prototypes to various departments for testing.

EDUCATION

Associate's Electronics Engineering Technology, University of Notre Dame, 1994
Continuing education training courses include, Advanced Digital Electronics, C Language Hands-On Workshop, Visual BASIC Programming, and Structured Analysis and Design Methods.

COMPUTER EXPERIENCE

PC Systems and Architecture, Tape Backup Systems, Local Area Networks, MS Windows, Excel, Access, Visual BASIC, Oracle, and SQL Language.

Manager of UNIX Network Administration

CHRIS SMITH
178 Green Street
Cranston, RI 02920
(401) 555-5555

Experience

Travis Computer, Inc.   **Cranston, RI**
Manager of Network Administration—6/06 to Present
- Manage staff of three Network Administrators and network of 100+ UNIX machines and 250+ users. Network consists of ten server machines, 30+ UNIX workstations, T1 connection to a West Coast company, many X terminals, and exabyte backup.
- Work consists mainly of future planning for growth of a diverse and distributed network and hands-on work with network tools and problem solving.
- Enhance and maintain extensive network tools that allow a network that spans 3 backbones to appear as one entity. Highly automated and user-friendly network.
- Member of team to transition. Travis into several spin-off companies. Entails network design, execution, and subsequent move to new locations.

Network Administrator—4/05 to 6/06
Daily administration of UNIX network including tool enhancement and modification, problem solving, YP maintenance, account creation, mail, news, and installing and upgrading systems.
- Planned and executed a company move at the home office and assisted in planning of company move of the Gulf Coast office. Included space planning and network design and implementation.
- Wrote proposals for graining Datel access, security, and a general plan to move the network into the future.

Lafayette Donlin Laboratory   **Easton, PA**
Member Assistant Staff—7/03 to 2/05
- Software Engineer for real-time integrated, airborne radar system. Code design and generation in C.
- Wrote code that operated hardware over a DVL bus.

Pollack and O'Keefe   **Bethlehem, PA**
Computer Systems Coordinator—1/01 to 6/03
Responsible for computer systems used by CAD, Accounting, Word Processing, and Engineering departments.

Computer Experience

Hardware: PC, Mac, UNIX
Software: Word, Excel, Access, Quark, Outlook, FileMaker
Languages: Perl, Oracle, C++, Visual Basic

Education

Pennsylvania State University   **University Park, PA**
B.S. in Applied Mathematics, 2001.

Manager of Information Technology

CHRIS SMITH
178 Green Street
Raritan, IL 61471
(309) 555-5555

TECHNICAL SUMMARY

Evaluated both hardware and software workstation configurations. Migrated entire organization to Windows Server 2003 network, Exchange 2003, and Microsoft SQL Server. Microsoft Certified Systems Engineer.

EMPLOYMENT HISTORY

L. MULLINS SOFTWARE INC., Raritan, IL

Manager, Product Support (2004–Present)

- Manage the staff and operation of forty technical product support specialists.
- Ensure superior levels of customer satisfaction with Product Support by hiring and retaining talented staff and providing technical and service skills training along with measurable standards of service performance.
- Determine which products and technologies are supported by Product Support Group.
- Responsible for acquiring training for product support specialists on new products and technologies.
- Contribute to various technical publications such as monthly newsletter, biannual software guide, technical notes, and white papers.
- Evaluated and developed in several front-end applications such as Powerbuilder and back-end database solutions such as Microsoft SQL Server.
- Responsible for creating summary, functional specifications, and design specification.
- Developed summary project plans, cost-benefit analyses, and business rationale for completion of each product.
- Monitored project progress. Documented and reported project status to Vice President of Information Services as well as the user community.
- Identified and controlled all project schedule variances with gnatt charts and project management software tools.

FOLSOM AND RUSSO COMPONENTS, SWEETWATER, IL

Manager, End User Computing (1999–2004)

- Managed and implemented local area and all associated applications.
- Developed, implemented, and maintained standards and guidelines for personal computer hardware (PC and Mac) and software.
- Managed hardware and software acquisition.

EDUCATION

Butler University, Indianapolis, IN
Master of Business Administration, 1999
Concentration in Information Systems

University of Illinois at Chicago
Bachelor of Science in Business Management, 1997

Operations Analyst

CHRIS SMITH
178 Green Street
Sunset, SC 29685
(803) 555-5555

OBJECTIVE

A position as a computer operations analyst.

SUMMARY OF QUALIFICATIONS

- More than eighteen years computer experience.
- Dedicated professional; set effective priorities to achieve immediate and long-term goals.
- Self-motivated; able to implement decisions to ensure smooth workflow.

EXPERIENCE

LARCHMONT MUTUAL, Sunset, SC
Operations Analyst, 2006 to Present
Translate information requirements into logical, economical, and practical system designs for large systems; cooperate with users and Senior Operations Analyst. Evaluate corporate requirements; investigate alternatives to identify/recommend best design. Prepare flowcharts; synthesize gathered information and present in logical/manageable components. Write detailed specifications; coordinate system testing; develop practical solutions to problems. Prepare associated documentation, user manuals, and instructions for complete operation of system. Assist junior personnel.

Support Technician, 2000 to 2006
Maintained/monitored Financial Information Services Equipment: PC system and printers.

Senior Quality Reviewer, 1993 to 2000
Scrutinized percentage of claims processed to ensure correct coding of claims; reported statistical errors.

Data Entry Clerk, 1991 to 1993
Processed Data Entry; required knowledge of Medicare operational guidelines and Medical Terminology.

Sales Engineer

CHRIS SMITH
178 Green Street
Olympia, WA 98505
(208) 555-5555

Employment Experience:

Pisces Data Systems, Inc.—July 2000 to Present.
Olympia, WA

Pre-Sales Technical Support:

Support the Eastern Area sales staff, which averages about five reps. Work closely with the sales reps to formulate and implement sales strategies. Working with prospects to understand business problems and propose appropriate technical solutions. Write and deliver technical product presentations. Develop and deliver customer product demos. Design proposed system configuration and write proposals.

Key Achievements:

Managed large data migration effort. Designed and implemented an open-systems migration plan. This effort included: system installation and configuration, development of file migration utilities, conversion of in-house code, conversion of over 50,000 files, and developing and delivering system-administrator and end-user training.

Education:

Washington State University, Pullman, WA
B.S. in Management Information Systems, 2000

Programming Languages:

Perl, C++, Visual Basic

Operating Systems:

UNIX, Linux, Windows NT, Windows Server 2000, Windows Server 2003

Hardware Experience:

PC servers and workstations
Sun workstations
Macintosh

Professional Awards:

MissionCritical Professionals Excellence Award, 2003
MissionCritical Sales Analyst of the Month, 2005

CHRIS SMITH
178 Green Street
New York, NY 11215
(212) 555-5555

WORK EXPERIENCE:

New York Department of Public Welfare—2004–Present
Subcontractor
Designed and developed programs for new, Web-based reporting system plus maintenance programming on legacy systems.
Software used: SQL, ASP.NET, VisualBasic.NET.

Rowe Street Bank and Trust—New York, NY, 2003–2004
Subcontractor
Maintenance Programming on the Trust Accounting System to add tax withholding on interest and dividend income.
Software used: C++, C#.

New York Hospital—Hempstead, NY, 2001–2003
Subcontractor
Program design and development for the existing Medicare billing system.
Software used: Java, Oracle, PL/SQL.

New England Life Insurance, Co.—Elmira, NY, 1999–2001
Subcontractor
Maintenance Programming to handle year-end changes to the agent commission system.
Software used: C++.

Atwood Corporation—Amherst, NY, 1997–1999
Programmer/Analyst
Programming and design on a portfolio management system.
Software used: C++.

E. Walker and Associates, Inc.—Houghton, NY, 1996–1997
Programmer/Analyst Intern
Application programming and program design involving four projects at three separate client locations. Experience in project leadership and user interface.
Software used: C, APL.

EDUCATION:

Houghton College, Houghton, NY
B.S. in Computer Science
Graduated—January 1997

Systems Analyst
Industrial

CHRIS SMITH
178 Green Street
Appleton, WI 54912
(414) 555-5555

SUMMARY OF ACCOMPLISHMENTS

- Set up the interfacing of mini computer to PC in order to archive daily receipts onto optical disks.
- Created a device for a new disk system, and developed a new operating system to handle the new driver.
- Qualified all of Devlin software onto a new computer system.
- Built a new method of handling orders into the system.
- Rewrote accounts receivable program system to handle long-term notes.
- Suggested an improvement in board revectoring at Price Computer, which was later implemented.

EMPLOYMENT HIGHLIGHTS

2004–Present **Systems Analyst** DEVLIN INDUSTRIES, Appleton, WI
Create or change programs; generate new reports and new ways of retrieving information in and out of the computer; responsible for making system more efficient.

2003 **Typesetting Operator** OSHKOSH NEWS, Oshkosh, WI
Interim position with tasks that covered production of all type for several area newspapers.

2000–2003 **Production Assistant** PRICE COMPUTER, Madison, WI
Worked in Production Department on board repair, board revectoring, equipment assembly, and basic production on electronic manufacturing.

PROFESSIONAL AFFILIATIONS

MADISON COMPUTER SOCIETY, ASSOCIATION OF COMPUTING MACHINERY

EDUCATION

MILWAUKEE SCHOOL OF ENGINEERING, Milwaukee, WI. Two Bachelor of Science degrees: Computer Science/Systems and Applied Physical/Astronomy. Graduated, January 2000.

COMPUTER LITERACY

Hardware: PC, Mac, Unix, E-mail Servers, Data Servers and Storage.
Language: C++, Perl, Visual Basic, Java.
Systems: MS Windows, Mac OS, Linux, UNIX.

CHRIS SMITH
178 Green Street
Charlotte, NC 28214
(704) 555-5555

BACKGROUND

Extensive and diversified computer hardware and software knowledge in personal computers. Expertise in prototype computer testing. Excellent investigative and research skills. Self-taught in many programming languages and software applications.

TECHNICAL QUALIFICATIONS

Programming Languages—Borland C++, Java, C#, Visual Basic.
Operating Systems—Windows, Mac OS.
Office Products—Word, Excel, Access.

SUMMARY OF ACCOMPLISHMENTS

- Organized preproduction testing of computer prototype.
- Researched, wrote, and edited test procedures that were used for testing of computer prototypes.
- Correlated and verified technical information and communicative style in test procedures written by engineers and technical writers.
- Wrote database application to track problems found during developmental stages of product, and to generate reports on outstanding issues found during product development.
- Designed storage and retrieval tracking system and cost analysis for manufactured products.
- Developed computer engineering test tools.
- Analyzed, developed, and implemented new work-related quality processes to improve product testing.
- Created software applications that automated work-related processes such as generating status and engineering change request reports.

CAREER HISTORY

Maxmillian Data Systems, **System Engineer,** Charlotte, NC
Gilford College, **Instructor,** Greensboro, NC

EDUCATION

BGS, Duke University, Durham, NC
Majors: Industrial and Systems Engineering; Computer Computational Mathematics; Mathematics.

Technical Engineer

CHRIS SMITH
178 Green Street
Albany, NY 12207
(518) 555-5555

PROFESSIONAL EXPERIENCE

TECHNICAL ENGINEER   2003–PRESENT
MERCER, INC., Albany, NY
Plan, coordinate, and execute hardware, software, and network installation, configuration, maintenance, troubleshooting, and repair operations for service contact clients. Specialize in maintaining Mac, PCs, and peripherals, with emphasis on networking environments.

- *Develop and implement service schedules, systems, and procedures to assure delivery of quality, cost-efficient technical services.*
- *Quickly diagnose causes of system failures and malfunctions to ensure highest operating efficiencies, reliability, and quality performance standards.*
- *Respond immediately to emergency situations with sensitivity to deadlines and customer needs.*
- *Assist network engineers with installation and troubleshooting of Windows 2003 Server systems.*
- *Analyze client equipment and operations to determine servicing and supply needs.*
- *Monitor and maintain cost-effective inventories of supplies, tools, and materials.*
- *Consistently manage time and multiple tasks to meet deadlines, established objectives, and quality performance standards.*
- *Foster clear communication and maintain excellent staff and client working relations.*

MANAGER OF INFORMATION SYSTEMS   1997–2003
KRITEL ASSOCIATES, INC., Schenectady, NY
Directed and supervised all MIS, related activities for a financial services firm supplying critical, timely information to corporate client base. Administered Windows 2000 networks, maintaining peak operating efficiencies and providing user training for all hardware and software applications. Controlled budget costs for purchasing and operations.

LICENSES AND CERTIFICATIONS
Microsoft Certified Systems Engineer—CompTIA A+ Certified, CompTIA Network+ Certified

TECHNICAL EXPERTISE
- **Hardware proficiencies:** HP, Dell, and IBM servers and workstations.
- **Networks:** Ethernet, 802.11a/b/g, 802.1x.
- **Software applications:** Windows 9x/2000/XP, Windows Server 200x, Mac OS, MS Office

Chris Smith
178 Green Street
Chapel Hill, NC 27514
(919) 555-5555
csmith@e-mail.com

EXPERIENCE:
6/06–Present UNIVERSITY OF NORTH CAROLINA, Chapel Hill, NC
Archivist
- Handle daily operations of College Archives, including: cataloging, photo indexing, and reference services.
- Manage school records.
- Work with alumni and local community to expand collection.
- Organize annual alumni weekend events and displays.

9/04–5/06 **Technical Services Librarian**
- Maintained and updated catalog.
- Oversaw retrospective conversion of bibliographic data in preparation for implementation of online catalog.

9/02–8/04 MUSEUM OF SOUTHERN HISTORY, Chapel Hill, NC
Library Assistant
- Transferred newspaper clippings to microfilm.
- Cataloged Civil War era monograph collection.

EDUCATION:
University of North Carolina, Chapel Hill, NC
Master of Science in Library Science, 2004

Wingate College, Wingate, NC
Bachelor of Arts in English, 2000

MEMBERSHIPS:
Southern Personal Computer Users Group
- Program Committee, 2003–2005
- Board of Directors, 2005–Present

ACCOMPLISHMENTS:
Received "Alumni Appreciation Award" for organizing 2008 reunion.

Assistant Dean of Students

CHRIS SMITH
178 Green Street
Pittsburgh, PA 19213
(412) 555-5555
csmith@e-mail.com

OBJECTIVE
A position requiring proven organizational, administrative, and interpersonal skills in an academic environment.

EXPERIENCE
ASSISTANT DEAN OF STUDENTS—Carnegie Mellon University, Pittsburgh, PA   2006–Present
- Supervise housing in four Residence Halls, as well as the Residence Life staff of four professional Resident Directors and fourteen student Resident Assistants.
- Recruit, select, train, and supervise Resident Assistants.
- Plan and arrange social, cultural, and recreational activities of various student groups; meet with student and faculty groups to plan activities.
- Conduct orientation programs for new students with other members of faculty and staff; counsel students on methods for improving their organizations and promote student participation in social, cultural, and recreational activities. Coordinate the preparation and publishing of the student affairs calendar and advertising/press releases.
- Initiate and advise Student Advisory Committee on the campus food service to assure that food service management includes student preferences in daily menus.
- Supervise major campus events; New Student Orientation; Parents' Weekend.
- Interact with Campus Police on various campus-based problems and issues, as well as with Health Services Clinic and Counseling Center, the college food service, housekeeping, and the physical plant.
- Serve on and actively contribute to committees: Student Life and Wellness Committee, the Alcohol Alert Team, and the Drug Task Force.

COORDINATOR OF STUDENT ACTIVITIES—Carnegie Mellon University, Pittsburgh, PA   2001–2006
- Developed a comprehensive student activities program focusing on development of students' leadership skills. Prepared and conducted workshops on Public Speaking, Assertiveness Training, Time Management, and Conflict Confrontation.
- Instrumental in involving International students in campus activities: International Week, International Buffet Dinner (roundtable discussion between American and international students), instituted an international theme on the campus center concourse.

EDUCATION
Master of Education, Program Evaluation and Research, May 2000
University of Pennsylvania, Philadelphia, PA

Bachelor of Arts degree in Psychology, May 1998
Allegheny College, Allegheny, PA

Coach

CHRIS SMITH
178 Green Street
Orono, ME 04473
(207) 555-5555
csmith@e-mail.com

PROFESSIONAL OBJECTIVE
      A challenging position as Hockey Coach at the college level.

PROFESSIONAL EXPERIENCE
    2004– UNIVERSITY OF MAINE, Orono, ME
  Present Assistant Varsity Hockey Coach
- Goaltender Coach
- Scouted opposing teams in preparation for games
- Responsible for recruitment of potential student athletes

2003–2004 SAINT JOSEPH'S COLLEGE, North Windham, ME
      Assistant Varsity Hockey Coach
- Participated in all phases of coaching, training, and preparation of hockey team
- Assisted in recruiting efforts for the 1994–1995 season

ADDITIONAL EXPERIENCE
1999–2002 STATE HOCKEY SCHOOL OF MAINE, Augusta, ME
      Hockey Instructor, Summer program
- Program Director, 1996–1999
- Head Goaltending Director, 1992–1996

    1998 MAXFIELD ALL-AMERICAN HOCKEY SCHOOL, Orono, ME
      Hockey Instructor

    1997 NATIONAL SPORTS CAMP OF AMERICA at UNIVERSITY OF MAINE, Orono, ME
      Hockey Counselor and Instructor

EDUCATION
      UNIVERSITY OF MAINE, Orono, ME
      Master of Science degree in Human Movement, Health, and Leisure, 2002
- Starting Varsity Hockey Goal Tender, 1993–1996
- All-Star Goal Tender, Bangor Tournament, 1993
- Outstanding Goal Tender, Portland Tournament, 1993
- All-East, 1993
- Captain, NCAA Division I Champions, 1996

      Bachelor of Science degree in Human Movement, Health, and Leisure, 1996.

College Professor

CHRIS SMITH
178 Green Street
Malvern, PA 19355
(215) 555-5555
csmith@e-mail.com

SUMMARY OF QUALIFICATIONS

- Ten years teaching experience at college level.
- Academic counselor to students attending Drexel University.
- Six years as a Professor, Drexel University, teaching Criminal Law, Legal Aspects of Criminal Procedures, Crime in America, The Courts and Criminal Procedures, Juvenile Procedures, and Business and Administrative Management.
- Strong communications skills as author, lecturer, teacher, debater, and negotiator dealing with individuals and groups in the disciplines of law and business administration.
- Excellent relationship builder with students, faculty, and administration.

EXPERIENCE

Professor, Drexel University, Philadelphia, PA (2004–Present)
Conduct college-level courses in Business and Legal Studies to university students and serve as academic advisor for students. Prepare and present lectures to students on law and business practices; research and compile bibliographies of specialized materials for outside reading assignments; stimulate class discussions. Plan, coordinate, and participate in special events involving university and community officials. Member of Student Affairs faculty committee.

Assistant Professor, Dickinson College, Carlisle, PA (1999–2003)
Taught seven core courses in Business Administration and Law Enforcement. The latter included Criminal Law, Legal Aspects of Criminal Procedures; Crime in America; The Courts and Criminal Law, Legal Aspects of Criminal Procedures; Crime in America; The Courts and Criminal Procedures; and Juvenile Procedures. Planned lectures, administered examinations, and assisted students outside of classroom.

EDUCATION

John Carroll University, University Heights, OH
Juris Doctor degree, 2008

North Carolina State University, Raleigh, NC
Bachelor of Science in Criminal Justice, 1995

Day Care Worker

CHRIS SMITH
178 Green Street
Delaware City, DE 19706
(302) 555-5555
csmith@e-mail.com

EDUCATION:

University of Delaware, Newark, DE
Bachelor of Arts, 2008
Major: Early Childhood Education; GPA in Major: 3.5/4.0

CERTIFICATION:

Delaware State K-5

TEACHING EXPERIENCE:

Head Teacher: City Child Care Corporation, Delaware City, DE
September 2006–Present
Taught educational and recreational activities for twenty children, ages five to ten years, in a preschool/play care setting. Planned and executed age-appropriate activities to promote social, cognitive, and physical skills. Developed daily lesson plans. Observed and assessed each child's development. Conducted parent/teacher orientations and meetings. Organized and administered various school projects.

Teacher: Little People Preschool and Day Care, New Castle, DE
June 2005–August 2006
Taught educational and recreational activities for children, ages three to seven years, in a preschool/day care setting. Planned, prepared, and executed two week units based on themes to develop social, cognitive, and physical skills. Lessons and activities were prepared in Mathematics, Language Arts, Science, and Social Studies. Observed and assessed each child's development and followed up with parent/teacher discussions.

Student Teacher: Rolling Elementary School, Newark, DE
January–May 2005
Taught and assisted a kindergarten teacher in a self-contained classroom of twenty-eight students. Planned and instructed lessons and activities in Mathematics, Science, and Social Studies.

Teacher's Aide: YMCA Day Care Center, Wilmington, DE
June–August 2004

Teaching Intern: Freud Laboratory School, Newark, DE
January–May 2003

Teaching Intern: Green Meadow Elementary School, Newark, DE
January–May 2002

Teaching Intern: Delaware State College Day Care Centers, Dover, DE
October–December 2001

Developmental Educator

CHRIS SMITH
178 Green Street
Jamaica, NY 11413
(212) 555-5555
csmith@e-mail.com

OBJECTIVE

A senior-level position in development and/or alumni relations with a nonprofit organization or institution.

SUMMARY OF QUALIFICATIONS

- Ten years of experience in development with nonprofit service organizations, universities, and educational institutions catering to the arts.
- Experience ranges from Secretary to Director of Development.
- Expertise in mass media communications, special events organization, budget planning, and multi-office coordination for national development program.
- Well qualified to assume full responsibility for directing and supporting a well organized development or alumni relations program.

EXPERIENCE

DIRECTOR OF DEVELOPMENT—Paisley Star School for the Arts Development Office, Jamaica, NY
Director of Development   **2003–Present**

- Coordinate all fundraising, public relations, alumni relations, and publications for this private Boarding and Day secondary school for students in the arts, while actively developing Trustee, Alumni, and Parents' Association Boards.
- Supervise a support staff of eight as well as volunteers in the planning, organization, and running of reunions, special events, and innovative functions with great success.
- Wrote, designed, and coordinated the production of publications, composed mass media communications, and instituted a new newsletter; increased annual fund by 100%.
- Key participant in $8 million capital campaign structuring, set-up of special committees, etc.; laid groundwork for entire campaign for the enhancement of educational programs.

Assistant to the Director of Development   **1999–2003**

- Assumed full responsibility for the set of systems, procedures, and direction of the Alumni Annual Fund. Administered direct mail, processed responses and returns, acknowledged donor gifts, and maintained current records of approximately 10,000 alumni.
- Served as Ad Book Coordinator for the Annual Paisley Star Gala Dance Performance. Sold and wrote ads and program copy, designed layout, and coordinated printing production. Ad book garnered several thousands of dollars in additional revenue.
- Extensively involved in public, community, and alumni relations as well as media releases and relations.

EDUCATION

- Bates College, Lewiston, ME
  B.A., Communications 1997

Foreign Language Teacher

CHRIS SMITH
178 Green Street
Echo, Oregon 97826
(503) 555-5555
csmith@e-mail.com

OBJECTIVE

A teaching position with an established university seeking the services of a highly commended educator, with total capacity in the teaching and translation of French.

TEACHING EXPERIENCE

Teacher of French Literature and Language: 2006–Present
Smith College, Northampton, MA

Professor of French Language: 2005–2006
Faculty of Literature and Human Science, University of Vermont, Burlington, VT
- Continually active in all aspects of the education process and administration.

Head of French Language Department: 2000–2005
College of Translation, Pratt University, Brooklyn, NY
- Teaching, Translation, French and Persian Literature, Art, History.
- Full curriculum—all aspects of administration—public service.

Professor of French and Persian Language and Literature: 1995–2000
College of Translation, New York University, New York, NY
- Teaching, Translation, French and Persian Literature, Art, History.
- Full academic schedule—research, writing, public service.

Educational Advisor: 1993–1995
Stoughton High School, Stoughton, MA
- Full academic schedule—active in school affairs.

EDUCATION

Ph.D., Harvard University, Cambridge, MA: 1990
- French Literature

M.A. *(Highest Honors),* Hood College, Frederick, MD: 1988
- French Literature

B.A. *(Highest Honors),* University of Illinois at Chicago: 1986
- French Literature

Guidance Counselor

CHRIS SMITH
178 Green Street
Irvine, CA 92717
(714) 555-5555
csmith@e-mail.com

OBJECTIVE

To secure a position as a guidance counselor in grades K–8.

EDUCATION

UNIVERSITY OF CALIFORNIA   Irvine, CA
M.Ed., Counselor Training/Psychology
Concentration on *School Guidance in Primary Grades*
• Certification upon graduation: May 2007

PEPPERDINE UNIVERSITY   Malibu, CA
B.A., Psychology; Minor, Sociology   May 2004

QUALIFICATIONS

• Experience with children with behavioral problems and handicaps including deafness, mental retardation, cerebral palsy, and eating disorders.
• Proven adaptability and expertise working with multicultural populations, particularly Hispanic students.
• Fluent in American Sign Language; conversant in Spanish.
• Excellent communication and interpersonal skills, verbal and written.
• Organized; meet deadlines.

EXPERIENCE

ADAIR SCHOOL   Irvine, CA
Intern/Guidance Counselor, K–8   2004–Present

UCAL/IRVINE   Irvine, CA
Research Assistant   2003–Present
• Conducted extensive research at the Institute for People with Disabilities.

PEPPERDINE UNIVERSITY HOSPITAL SCHOOL   Malibu, CA
Volunteer/Recreational Therapist, Ages 2–21   2002

PROFESSIONAL AFFILIATIONS

• Counseling Association of California.
• PTA, California Chapter.

EXCELLENT REFERENCES AVAILABLE ON REQUEST

CHRIS SMITH
178 Green Street
Deltona, FL 32738
(207) 555-5555
csmith@e-mail.com

EDUCATION

ECKERD COLLEGE, St. Petersburg, FL
Bachelor of Science degree
Major: Elementary Education
Specialization: Moderate Special Needs

FLAGLER COLLEGE, St. Augustine, FL
Major: Speech Pathology and Audiology

PROFESSIONAL EXPERIENCE

MEADOW BROOK ELEMENTARY SCHOOL, Deltona, FL   2005–Present
Head Teacher, Resource Room, grades 4–6.
Major emphasis on successfully mainstreaming learning-disabled students into regular education, Social Studies, Science, and Mathematics classes. Established close working relationships with regular education staff to modify curriculum to meet the needs of special education students. Coordinated, designed, and implemented individual IEP goals in Reading and Language Arts. Supervised instructional aides.

JAMIE FENTON SCHOOL, Pine Coast, FL   2003–2005
Head Teacher, self-contained language/learning-disabilities program, grades K–5.
Designed and implemented individual IEPs, responsibly arranged and chaired COREs for each student. Coordinated efforts of each specialist involved on TEAM. Developed curricula in all content areas. Effectively established excellent rapport with regular education staff which earned recognition of the special education class. Screened potential candidates for program, reporting directly to the SPED administrator. Supervised student teachers and instructional aides.

BORDEN HOME AND SCHOOL FOR BOYS, Winter Park, FL   2002–2003
Head Teacher, self-contained emotionally disturbed and learning disabilities class, ages 8–12.
Developed positive behavior modification techniques to coincide with success-oriented group and individual lesson plans. Integral member of TEAM, coordinated IEPs, case-conferences, parent contact, and psychological support. Supervised student teachers.

THE SOUTHERN HOME FOR RUNAWAYS, Orlando, FL   2000–2002
Head Teacher, self-contained emotionally disturbed and learning disabilities class, ages 10–15
Developed and successfully implemented IEPs. Planned and presented curriculum. Supervised and trained student interns.

Library Technician

Chris Smith
178 Green Street
Norwood, MA 02062
(781) 555-5555
csmith@e-mail.com

EDUCATION:

Simmons College, Boston, MA
M.S., Library Science, Graduated Cum Laude 2004.

Northeastern University, Boston, MA
B.S., Computer Science, Graduated 1998.

AREAS OF EFFECTIVENESS

- Analysis
- Research
- Numerical Ability
- Troubleshooting Skills

EXPERIENCE

BOSTON PUBLIC LIBRARY, Boston, MA   2003–Present
Systems Coordinator

- Ensure all PCs are up and running on a 24-hour basis.
- Troubleshoot, run codes, keep systems operating smoothly.
- Train librarians and library staff on use of systems.
- Provide instant access to newsprint publications on microfiche; maintain terminals.
- Assist librarians to develop materials to aid the public.

THOMAS CRANE LIBRARY, Quincy, MA   2000–2003
Computer Assistant

- Assisted Systems Coordinator in maintaining all PCs and Mac computers.
- Ensured smooth running of all UNIX systems.
- Assisted librarians and public in the use of PCs and Mac computers.

PROFESSIONAL AFFILIATIONS

- Library Technicians of Boston.

Music Teacher

CHRIS SMITH
178 Green Street
Boston, MA 02114
(617) 555-5555
csmith@e-mail.com

PROFESSIONAL OBJECTIVE
Seeking a position as a college-level music teacher.

PROFESSIONAL EXPERIENCE

Teaching
- Juilliard School, New York, NY   2006–Present
  Taught private guitar lessons. Co-led workshops in jazz improvisation and ensemble techniques in New York City High Schools.
- University of Pennsylvania and Temple University, Philadelphia, PA   2005
  Co-led two day workshops in jazz performance.
- Des Moines House of Music; Studio East Music; West Music, New York and Rock Hard Music, NY   2004

Performance
- Guitarist concert with the Bugles, Don Wrensly, Mel Fanfare, the Joe Bob Brown Band, and Prudence Jackson and the Waifs.
- Guitarist, Dirt and Wine and Enrique Smith's Dream, University of Pennsylvania and the inaugural ball for the governor of Pennsylvania.
- Recordings include: guitar work on themes for the Boston Bruins; a documentary film *Whimsy of the Codependent Heart,* and more than a dozen demos and jingles for independent producers.

Musical Direction/Writing
- Music Director, *On the Trellis,* Boston, MA, 2006, Pelican Productions.
- Cowriter and Music Director, *Cry, Sapphire Girl, Cry,* University of Michigan, 2003, as part of the artist-in-residence program.
- Cowriter and Music Director, *Warm Rain: One Woman's Battle with Body Acceptance,* Devlin Theater, San Francisco, CA; Mechely Theater, New York.
- Music Director and Composer, *Buttercup Hates Acorn, A Love Story,* San Francisco Theater.
- Cowriter and Arranger of fifty songs in the pop and jazz fields.

EDUCATION
- Juilliard School, New York, NY. Professional Music Diploma, May 2004.
- Berklee College, Boston, MA. Jazz arranging, harmony, and improvisation, 2002.
- University of Pennsylvania, Philadelphia, PA. Bachelor in Musical Theory and Composition, 2001.

CERTIFICATION/RECOGNITION
- Certified Teacher in New York Private Secondary Schools, 2005.
- Julliard Scholarship Recipient, 2004.
- Outstanding Soloist Award, Montreal Jazz Festival, 2003.

Physical Education Teacher

Chris Smith
178 Green Street
Toledo, OH 43606
(419) 555-5555
csmith@e-mail.com

SUMMARY OF QUALIFICATIONS

Enthusiastic and positive attitude, experienced in making group presentations and teaching a wide range of students of all ages. Strong analytical and problem-solving abilities, welcoming new challenges. Goal- and results-oriented, able to motivate others to perform at their highest levels. Combine mathematical background with writing, planning, and organizational abilities. Eager to learn new skills and procedures.

COACHING EXPERIENCE

BRENNEN HILL SCHOOL DISTRICT, Toledo, OH   1997–Present
Emphasize building self-esteem and character through developing realistic expectations and high standards. Serve as mentor and role model in assisting students to reach their goals.

Head Winter Track Coach—Junior High   1999–Present
- Team finished four seasons undefeated.
- Five teams recorded first place finishes in Brennen Hill District Competitions.

Head Boys' Basketball Coach—Junior High   2001–Present
- Teams recorded two undefeated seasons.
- Achieved three additional first place finishes in B.H.S. League.

Head Football Coach—Junior High   2001–Present
- Team achieved three undefeated seasons with one additional first place finish in their league.

EDUCATION

Baldwin College, Berea, OH
Master's degree in Education, 1996

CERTIFICATION

Ohio, Secondary Mathematics Education

CHRIS SMITH
178 Green Street
Williamsburg, VA 23185
(804) 555-5555
csmith@e-mail.com

OBJECTIVE
A challenging HIGH SCHOOL ADMINISTRATIVE position.

PROFILE
- Offer Master's Degrees in School Administration and Biology/Immunology enhanced by fifteen years of teaching and student guidance experience combined with a ten-year corporate Marketing and Management background.
- Facilitator of the Discipline Committee. Initiated, organized, and orchestrated numerous class trips and education expeditions with durations of up to two weeks.
- Self-started with strong planning, controlling, organizing, and leadership skills. Consistently meets deadlines and objectives; works well under pressure.
- Articulate and effective communicator with proven ability to work with diverse populations of students at a variety of academic levels. Consistently maintain excellent relations with students, parents, faculty, and administration. Works well as part of a team or independently.
- Task record for identifying complex administrative problems; resourceful in developing and implementing creative solutions resulting in increased productivity with enhanced sensitivity to costs and efficiency.

EDUCATION
MASTER OF SCIENCE IN SCHOOL ADMINISTRATION, 2006
College of William and Mary—Williamsburg, VA

MASTER OF SCIENCE IN BIOLOGY/IMMUNOLOGY, 2000
James Madison University—Harrisonburg, VA

MASTER OF SCIENCE IN SCIENCE EDUCATION/ENVIRONMENTAL SCIENCES,
1996

BACHELOR OF SCIENCE IN BIOLOGY, 1980
Drew University—Madison, New Jersey

(continued)

PROFESSIONAL EXPERIENCE (continued)

HEAD TEACHER 1998–Present
The Adams School Williamsburg, VA
Responsible for planning, developing, preparing, and implementing an effective science curriculum, management, and student assessment. Devise and prepare daily lesson plans, materials, teaching aids, and demonstrations to effectively convey critical concepts and factual knowledge in Biology, Physical Science, Physics, Earth Science, and Oceanography. Develop engaging daily classroom presentations; assign work projects; review and discuss lesson objectives and class performance. Stimulate and motivate students by generating excitement and enthusiasm; encourage exploration of new concepts, joy in learning, and pride in performance. Provide clear explanations, creative approaches, and extra tutoring as required. Compose and administer exams and grade student performance. Advise and counsel individual students in academic areas and on aspects of student life. Communicate with parents on their child's progress, fostering excellent professional relations. Interact positively with faculty members and administrators. Provide educational leadership through serving on committees and executing special projects to further high educational standards.

HIGH SCHOOL TEACHER 1997–1998
West Harris High School Harrisburg, VA
- Presented Biology and Physical Science classes at the high school level.

MIDDLE SCHOOL TEACHER 1996–1997
Reede Middle School Harrisburg, VA
- Taught an Earth Science curriculum to eighth grade students.

TEACHER 1991–1993
Melbourne Academy Madison, NJ
- Instructed students in Biology, Marine Biology/Ecology.

LICENSES AND CERTIFICATIONS
VIRGINIA * NEW JERSEY PERMANENT CERTIFICATION IN BIOLOGY, CHEMISTRY, EARTH SCIENCE, AND PHYSICAL SCIENCE.

CHRIS SMITH
178 Green Street
Salt Lake City, UT 84112
(801) 555-5555
csmith@e-mail.com

EDUCATION:

University of Wisconsin, Milwaukee, WI
B.S., Education, 1992

Montclair State College, Upper Montclair, NJ
General Curriculum, two years

CREDENTIALS:

Life Language Learning Disabilities, Utah
Learning Disabilities and Emotional Disturbance, K–12, Wisconsin
Teaching Emotionally Handicapped Certificate, New Jersey
Multiple Subject Teaching Credential, K–12, Oregon

EXPERIENCE:

Salt Lake Independent School District, 2003–Present
Valley Middle School, Salt Lake City, UT
Teacher—Self-Contained, Severe Emotional Disabilities Classroom

Streaming Meadows Psychiatric Hospital, Summer 2004
Salt Lake City, UT
Ninth Grade Summer School Teacher—Multiple Subjects

Cedar City Independent School District, 2001–2003
Cedar Middle School, Cedar City, UT
Special Education Teacher
Behavior Adjustment Classes for Severely Emotionally Disabled Children.
• Participated in Curriculum and Staff Development.
• Revised Grade Six Special Education Mathematics Curriculum Guide.

Social Vocational Services, 1999–2000
Group Home, Medford, OR
Home Manager
• Supervision, IPP implementation for six autistic children.

Madison Schools, 1997–2000
Madison Grammar School, Madison, WI
Primary Behavior Disorder Teacher, grades 1–3

Milwaukee Public Schools, 1993–1997
Marquette Elementary School, Milwaukee, WI
Continuing Substitute (Grade 2)

Teacher
Kindergarten

CHRIS SMITH
178 Green Street
Winesburg, OH 44690
(614) 555-5555
csmith@e-mail.com

OBJECTIVE
To contribute developed skills to a challenging teaching position.

SUMMARY OF QUALIFICATIONS
- More than nine years teaching experience—ages 3 months to 6 years. Relate well with children.
- Able to present materials interestingly, making the introduction to learning fun. Utilize music.
- Practical knowledge of Spanish.
- Proven interpersonal skills, having worked with and supervised a diversity of professionals, clients, and staff.
- O.F.C. and Infant Toddler qualified.

EDUCATION
KENT STATE UNIVERSITY, Kent, OH
B.S., Education, 1995
Major: Early Childhood Education
Staff-certified to teach kindergarten through grade 8.

PROFESSIONAL EXPERIENCE
1/96–Present   O'DONNELL CENTER PRESCHOOL, Winesburg, OH
Head Teacher, Kindergarten, 1998–Present
Supervised teachers, Youth Corp. Workers, and Student Volunteers. Planned and conducted daily curriculum. Cooperated in overall planning of preschool program. Observed/recorded behavior and progress of children; planned individual education follow-up to prepare students for first grade.

Perceptual Motor Instructor, Infant/Toddler to Age 5, 1996–1998
Planned/implemented special training periods, recorded progress, evaluated needs, submitted weekly reports. Cooperated with Special Education Coordinator on program goals and scheduling needs of individual children. Motivated staff in this specialized area.

Assistant Teacher, ages 3–5, 1/96–6/96

9/95–12/95   RETTMAN SCHOOL, Cincinnati, OH
Student Teacher, Pre-Kindergarten and Grade 3

RELATED ACTIVITIES
9/96–3/97   DUVAL CENTER, Dayton, OH
Preschool Teacher, Family Religious Education Program
Interpreted Spanish Language. Tutored English as a Second Language.

CHRIS SMITH
178 Green Street
Charleston, SC 29424
(803) 555-5555
csmith@e-mail.com

EMPLOYMENT

1993 to
Present

IMMACULATE CONCEPTION SCHOOL, Charleston, SC

Fifth Grade Teacher, 1998 to present

- Assisted in setting up the new curriculum; selected materials, designed learning area, and advised on physical setup of classroom.
- Develop and implement curricula, lesson plans, special projects, and exercises to increase dexterity, alertness, and coordination.
- Committee Chairperson for School Accreditation Ceremony.
- Member, Handbook Committee; compile, write, and analyze school policies and regulations.
- Director of School Bowling League (1999 to Present); recruit chaperones, set and collect dues, organize outings, and coordinate total program for 125 to 190 Fourth through Eighth graders. (Previously acted as League Treasurer and Chaperone, 1993 to 1999.)
- Organize and coordinate annual Sports Banquet.

Fourth Grade Teacher, 1993 to 1998

- Developed curricula and lesson plans and instructed in Reading, Mathematics, Science, Spelling, Language, Art, and Religion.
- Participated in and conducted parent-teacher conferences, advising parents on child's progress, and how best to reinforce education.

1989 to
Present

RANE'S DRUG STORE, Charleston, SC

Sales Clerk/Cashier, full time summers and part time through the year

- Responsible for cashing out and verification of receipts.
- Prepare sales reports and break downs per department by analyzing and tabulating merchandise-coded receipts.
- Train and supervise part-time employees and new hires.
- Conduct vendor inventories on a regular basis to facilitate timely and efficient ordering and purchasing.
- Set up displays and implement in-store promotions.
- Assist in opening and closing operations.

EDUCATION

CLEMSON UNIVERSITY, Clemson, NC

Bachelor of Science Degree in Education, Early Childhood Education, 1993.

- Minored in Mathematics/Educational Mathematics.
- South Carolina Teaching Certificate.

REFERENCES

Furnished upon request.

Teacher
Elementary School

CHRIS SMITH
178 Green Street
Harrisonburg, VA 22807
(703) 555-5555
csmith@e-mail.com

OBJECTIVE

Seeking a career continuation as an **Elementary Education Teacher** where education, experience, and developed skills will be of value.

EDUCATION

GEORGE MASON UNIVERSITY, Fairfax, VA
Bachelor of Arts, Cum Laude, in Elementary Education, 1999
- Dean's List (two semesters).
- Academic Scholarship.
- Education Society, member 1995–1999.

EXPERIENCE

1999 to
Present

JAMES MADISON ELEMENTARY SCHOOL, Harrisonburg, VA
Faculty Member
- Experience in teaching kindergarten and first grade in the areas of reading, math, social studies, arts, and music.
- Participate in the selection of textbooks and learning aids.
- Plan and supervise class field trips. Arrange for class speakers and demonstrations.

1997 to 1999

FAIRFAX YMCA, YOUTH DIVISION, Fairfax, VA
Program Assistant/Special Event Coordinator
- Oversaw summer program for low-income youth.
- Budgeted and planned special events and field trips, working with Program Director to coordinate and plan variations in the program.
- Served as Youth Advocate in cooperation with Social Worker to address the social needs and problems of participants.

Fall 1998

GEORGE MASON ELEMENTARY SCHOOL, Fairfax, VA
Student Teacher
- Taught third grade in all elementary subjects.
- Designed and implemented a two-week unit on Native Americans.

Spring 1998

FAIRFAX KINDERGARTEN, Fairfax, VA
Student Teacher
- Generated a unit on Ezra Jack Keats's storybooks.

Fall 1997

ALLEN SCHOOL, Fairfax, VA
Student Teacher
- Concentrated on instructing lower level reading and math groups, and conducted whole class math lessons.

CHRIS SMITH
178 Green Street
Tacoma, WA 98416
(206) 555-5555
csmith@e-mail.com

PROFESSIONAL OBJECTIVE
Seeking new challenges in the instruction of Mathematics and related courses at high-school level.

EDUCATION UNIVERSITY OF WASHINGTON, Seattle, WA: Master's degree in Secondary Education, 1997

EVERGREEN STATE COLLEGE, Olympia, WA: Bachelor of Arts Degree in Mathematics, 1994. Graduated Cum Laude.

Teaching Certification, Washington

PROFESSIONAL EXPERIENCE
1994 to   TACOMA HIGH SCHOOL, Tacoma, WA
Present   Chairperson, Mathematics Department, 1999 to Present
- In addition to responsibilities as Math instructor, direct the Math Evaluation Committee for accreditation by the National Association of Schools and Colleges.
- Develop evaluative report for submission to accreditation board; report details and assesses present and future goals, programs, plans, and professional performance/development.
- Select and approve all departmental texts; write course descriptions and upgrade as indicated.
- Approve all purchases, justify expenditures, and develop/monitor budget.
- Provide input to the hiring/renewal process; evaluate staff teachers.

Mathematics Instructor, 1994 to Present
- Instruct grades 9–12 levels in Trigonometry, Algebra I and II, Geometry, Pre-Calculus, and Business Math.
- Teach Honors Algebra I, Geometry, and Pre-Calculus; initiate, develop, and conduct special Remedial Math Program and after-school tutorial sessions for math students with problems.
- Conduct summer school sessions in Remedial Math and SAT preparation (eight weeks each).
- Develop curricula and lesson plans, select texts, and design tests.
- Serve as Junior Varsity Baseball and Basketball Coach and Varsity Assistant Coach for Baseball and Basketball teams; Athletic Trainer for sports teams (Football, Baseball, and Basketball).

Teacher
High School

CHRIS SMITH
178 Green Street
Baltimore, MD 21218
(301) 555-5555
csmith@e-mail.com

PROFESSIONAL EXPERIENCE

1985–Present   ST. JUDE HIGH SCHOOL, Baltimore, MD
Teacher—Dean of Discipline

Teach primarily Social Studies to students in grades 9–12. Responsible for organizing activities for ninth grade cluster; field trips to museums and to Africa for African-American studies. Serve on numerous committees and boards for multicultural activities. Increased Parent Involvement Committee from ten to eighty parents. Act as Career Cooperative Teacher for student teachers from Harvard School of Education, orienting and training in teaching practicum.

Summers,   HIGH SCHOOL STEP PROGRAM AT JOHNS HOPKINS, Baltimore, MD
1987–Present   **Counselor**

Supervised seventy-five high-school students. Responsible for helping bridge gaps, orientation, acclamation, and placement of inner-city students to the possibility of a college education, in-college, and post-college experiences.

1995–2002   MORTIMER PUBLIC HIGH SCHOOL, Baltimore, MD
Teacher—Adult Education

Taught Geography and World History to adults pursing their GEDs.

EDUCATION

LOYOLA COLLEGE, Baltimore, MD
Master of Arts degree in History
Other relevant courses and training included: Secondary School Principal, Legal Aspects of Education Administration, and Testing and Evaluation.

WAYNE STATE COLLEGE, Detroit, MI
B.A. in French, minor in Chemistry.

CERTIFICATION

Maryland Teaching Certificate.

CHRIS SMITH
178 Green Street
Bel Air, MD 21015
(301) 555-5555
csmith@e-mail.com

EDUCATION

Loyola College, Baltimore, MD   12/06
Bachelor of Arts degree in English: Professional Writing
Honors: Cum Laude (3.21), Dean's List six of eight semesters

EXPERIENCE

Goden Academy, Baltimore, MD   1/06 to Present
Tutor
Teach English to a senior Japanese student concentration on special grammar and compositional needs six hours per week.

Ridge Heights Elementary, Baltimore, MD   11/05 to Present
Teaching Assistant
Instruct group of five second and third grade students in writing and creative expression.

WPIT, Boston, MA   9/04–7/05
News Journalist Intern
Spent a week in the news room, field reporting, and attending music and promotion meetings at Boston's number-one radio station. Communicated with traffic center and sourced news stories.

Loyola College, Baltimore, MD   Summer 2004
Writing Skills Tutor
Assisted the students with their writing and managed the writing skills center during daily hours.

Camp Lalcots, Bethesda, MD   Summer 2003
Special Needs Counselor
Planned and supervised daily events. During summer camp, aided in the care and feeding of children from ages 6–15.

Loyola College, Baltimore, MD   9/02–5/03
Peer Counselor
Assisted students in social and personal development regarding their adjustment to college life. Led group and individual counseling sessions.

COMPUTERS

Microsoft Word, Access, Excel

Chemical Engineer

CHRIS SMITH
178 Green Street
Rochester, NY 14623
(716) 555-5555
csmith@e-mail.com

WORK EXPERIENCE:

SANFORD CORPORATION, Rochester, NY   1998-Present
Chemical Process Modeling Engineer

Carbon Dioxide Process Simulator
- Applied knowledge of thermodynamics; reactor design; phase separation; fluid compression and expansion; process control to complete simulation from preliminary coding.
- Wrote operations manual.

Computer Models for Hydraulic Devices
- Researched, designed, coded, and tested detailed models for submersible centrifugal and hydraulic pumps.

Drilling Control Simulators
- Revised and developed computer models for oil well simulation.
- Utilized knowledge of fluid mechanics, mathematics, and computer programming.
- Wrote operations manuals.

SKILLS:

- Extensive research experience; quantitative and qualitative analysis of dynamic systems, inorganic chemistry.

EDUCATION:

Bachelor of Science in Chemical Engineering, May 1997
Rochester Institute of Technology, Rochester, NY
Honors: Magna cum laude graduate, member of the Engineering Honor Society of America.

MEMBERSHIP:

American Society of Chemical Engineers. Student Chapter Vice President, 2007-Present

PERSONAL:

Willing to relocate.

Electrical Engineer
Managerial

CHRIS SMITH
178 Green Street
New London, NH 03257
(603) 555-5555
csmith@e-mail.com

PROFESSIONAL OBJECTIVE

A leadership position supporting product development or engineering utilizing knowledge of electrical, electronic, and mechanical design.

BACKGROUND SUMMARY

Progressive engineering management experience from project manager, group leader, section manager, to engineering manager over four sections and forty people. Responsible for consumer product development from inception to discontinuance covering mechanical, electromechanical, and electrical design.

PROFESSIONAL EXPERIENCE

The C. Marlowe Company, New London, NH
Engineering Manager 2001–Present
- Created International Technical Engineering responsible for technical coordination and support to multiple global manufacturing sites.
- Created Alpha Test Engineering responsible for creating preproduction engineering prototypes for global marketing use. Planned, hired, and trained the staff, provided for procurement, logistics, facilities, and capital equipment.
- Managed $0.6 million in expense budget +$2–9 million in preproduction engineering prototypes per year. Provided definition input to all proposed products as well as resource allocation, scheduling, planning, control, problem reporting, and solving support.
- Developed major portions of the Quality documentation system for Engineering to comply with ISO 9000.
- Participated in Engineering Documentation Control conversion from manufacturing to stock, from assemble to order. The first product under this system had 700,000 planned configurations.

The Kipling Company, Wolfeboro, NH
Product Design Engineer 1996–2001
- Oversaw design engineering for over 200 consumer and PC products, both in assembled form and in kit form.
- Prepared and monitored expense and capital budgets.
- Prepared cost feasibility studies, analysis of design, and product financing.
- Monitored product safety and regulatory compliance and product cost and development schedule.
- Responsible for adding $9 million of new product revenue out of $90 million total business.

EDUCATION

- New Jersey Institute of Technology, Newark, NJ
  Bachelor of Science, Electrical Engineering, 1995

Electronics Engineer
Experienced

CHRIS SMITH
178 Green Street
Los Angeles, CA 90007
(213) 555-5555
csmith@e-mail.com

BACKGROUND SUMMARY

Over eleven years of extensive computer/electronics experience. Versed in both digital and analog electronics with specific emphasis on computer hardware/software. Special expertise in system and component evaluation. Network supervisor responsible for installing/maintaining LAN system. Excellent communication skills including written, verbal, and interpersonal.

PROFESSIONAL WORK EXPERIENCE

Stevenson Data Systems, Los Angeles, CA   1996–2006
Components Evaluation Engineer   2005–2006

Responsible for the characterization and evaluation of, and approved vendors list for: Power supplies, oscillators, crystals, and programmable logic used in desktop and laptop computers. Evaluated and recommended quality components that increased product profitability. Created and developed power supply test plan used for evaluating third party power supplies. Interacted with vendors to resolve problems associated with components qualification. Technical advisor for Purchasing. Promoted to Engineer II.

Design Evaluation Engineer   2004–2005

Evaluated new computer product designs, solving environmental problems on prototype computers. Conducted systems analysis on new computer products to ensure hardware, software, and mechanical design integrity. Designed hardware and software for PCI bus programmable load board used for environmental testing. Performed reliability life testing on computer systems. Installed/maintained 20-user, Windows 2003, LAN system. Examined system and subsystem susceptibility to electrostatic discharge in order to meet industry standards. Analyzed complete power and load of computer system and subsystem to verify power and load estimators.

Assistant Engineer   1996–2004

Performed extensive hardware evaluation on prototype computers, tested prototype units for timing violations using the latest state-of-the-art test equipment, digital oscilloscopes, and logic analyzers. Performed environment, ESD, and acoustic testing. Designed and built a product saver used to protect units under test during environmental testing. Designed and built a power-up test used to test prototype computers during cold boot.

EDUCATION

Bachelor of Science in Electrical Engineering   University of Southern California   2005
Associate in Engineering Electronics   University of Southern California   1996

Engineering Consultant

CHRIS SMITH
178 Green Street
New York, NY 10027
(212) 555-5555
csmith@e-mail.com

PROFESSIONAL EXPERIENCE

CONSULTING ENGINEER 2006–Present
The Maupin Consulting Group New York, NY

Provide professional consulting services to large- and medium-sized corporations with accountability for project management including planning and coordinating client conferences; facilities inspections; developing and implementing recommendations focused on improving efficiencies and cost control in areas encompassing material management, productivity, customer service delivery, maintenance, and general operations. Analyze and diagnose clients' operational structure. Assess financial operating parameters and schedule progress. Develop and implement improved internal controls. Recruit and train talented management to drive the company's strategic plan. Evaluate existing design and fabrication methodologies, manufacturing processes, tooling, mechanical assembly, inspection, and statistical process controls. Troubleshoot; identify actual and potential problem areas, and implement solutions to ensure maximum effectiveness. Draw on resource networks in related industries, agencies, and professional organizations to assist the client in meeting professional needs. Effectively manage time and multiple tasks to consistently meet deadlines. Foster and maintain excellent staff, customer, and community relations.

LOGISTIC ENGINEER/MECHANICAL ENGINEER 2003–2006
The Duessa Corp. Manhattan, NY

Performed broad, multifunctional responsibilities encompassing management of engineering aspects of parts design, development, testing, and developing documentation for maintenance of the company's frigates. Directed, monitored, and controlled production of engineering documentation, including quality control, efficiency, and project cost considerations. Troubleshot logistics or mechanical problems and implemented effective solutions consistent with the overall Maintenance Plan recommendations. Provided ongoing technical assistance and advice, engineering leadership, and business support.

INDUSTRIAL ENGINEER 2001–2003
Crow, Jones, and Grey, Inc. Albany, NY

Performed research utilizing large database containing customer order information. Identified product-flow patterns. Incorporated machine utilization, product handling, in-process inventory, and customer delivery factors.

PRODUCTIVITY/MANAGEMENT SERVICES ANALYST 1998–2001
City of Buffalo Buffalo, NY

Analyzed/developed formal reports. Made and implemented recommendations for improvements in cost management and work efficiencies for municipal service delivery. Evaluated vehicle and equipment usage, inventory controls, and computer systems needs. Performed numerous related operational/economic studies.

EDUCATION

Master of Industrial Engineering, 1998
Rensselaer Polytechnic Institute, Troy, NY

Bachelor of Mechanical Engineering, 1995
Polytechnic Institute of New York, Brooklyn

Facilities Engineer

CHRIS SMITH
178 Green Street
Broomfield, CO 80021
(303) 555-5555
csmith@e-mail.com

OBJECTIVE: A challenging position in facilities engineering, project engineering, or engineering management.

EXPERIENCE: Facilities Engineer—Breckenridge Company, Broomfield, CO
(2001–Present)
Supervise all phases of maintenance and engineering for this specialty steel company, which employs 800, and covers a 60-acre facility.
- Direct multi-craft maintenance, utilities, engineering, and construction departments.
- Supervise staff of 100 people and ten supervisors in all phases of maintenance and engineering.
- Plan and install maintenance program and directing all improvement and/or new construction projects starting from studies for justification to project start-up.
- Represented the company as general contractor on project and saved approximately $4 million of the original estimates submitted by outside contractors.
- Direct technicians and supervisor on the design, construction, and maintenance of equipment and machinery.
- Established standards and policies for testing, inspection, and maintenance of equipment in accordance with engineering principles and safety regulations.
- Prepared bid sheets and contracts for construction facilities and position.
- Full responsibilities for a budget of approximately $10 million annually.
- Extensive involvement in labor relations with various trades.

Project Engineer—Gibraltar Corporation, Loveland, CO
(1997–2001)
- Planned and implemented modernization program including the installation of bloom, billet, bar, rod, and strip mills as well as the required soaking pits and reheating furnaces.
- Directed a multi-craft maintenance force of approximately 250 craftsmen and supervisors.
- Planned and installed a maintenance program which reduced equipment down-time and increased C/P/T savings substantially.

ASSOCIATIONS: Member of American Iron and Steel Engineers Association.

EDUCATION: University of Colorado at Boulder, Boulder, CO
B.S., Mechanical Engineering, 1997.

Field Engineer

CHRIS SMITH
178 Green Street
Oaklawn, IL 60453
(708) 555-5555
csmith@e-mail.com

OBJECTIVE: A position as *Senior Field Engineer*—Electronics Systems. Willing to travel and/or relocate. Preference: Foreign assignment.

ACHIEVEMENTS AND QUALIFICATIONS:

More than ten years experience with an internationally known field engineering corporation in both the U.S. and abroad.

- Engineering, cost, and administrative responsibility for digital systems and support personnel.
- Maintained and operated special purpose computers.
- Supported various spacecraft launches.
- Initiated and/or implemented various cost reduction programs resulting in over $20,000 savings in reduced labor and material costs.
- Supervised and coordinated all field engineering functions.
- Served as technical advisor and instructor of formal training to engineers and technicians.

EXPERIENCE: Colfax Corporation, Oaklawn, IL

Senior Field Engineer (2000–Present)

Design modifications, which will improve operations while reducing costs of systems. Install design changes as required by NASA. Support various spacecraft launches from the eastern and western launch facilities, and perform M&O for Apollo Lunar Seismic Experiment Package (ALSEP) operations. Handle cost reduction program on the station as required by NASA. This required full responsibility for assuring that Bermuda (MSFN) adheres to its quarterly budget. Serve as Assistant Project Control Centers' Supervisor with responsibility for maintenance and operations of fifteen control centers. Supervise the activities of approximately 200 engineers and technicians; review modifications designed by control center engineers. Provide formal classroom training to newly arrived engineers and technicians. Train engineers and technicians in the maintenance and operation of the R&RR system; initiated 24-hour operations.

Broadmoor Corporation, Detroit, MI

Field Engineer (1992–2000)

Supervised maintenance and alignment of test equipment, preventative maintenance, and operations. Installed design modifications in the Digital Data Assembly System, and the Analog-to-Digital Preselector System. Wrote training material; conducted formal training classes on overall system maintenance and operations.

MILITARY SERVICE:

U.S. Army Security Agency
Rank: Sergeant Major (1987–1992)

TRAINING AND EDUCATION:

Lawrence Institute of Technology, Southfield, MI
Bachelor of Science, Electrical Engineering, 1997

Additional course work and training includes:
Application Programming, Antenna Position Programming, Tracking Data Processor, and Apollo Timing System.

Manufacturing Engineer

CHRIS SMITH
178 Green Street
Seattle, WA 98103
(206) 555-5555
csmith@e-mail.com

SUMMARY

Manufacturing engineer with extensive experience in a development and new product introduction environment. Areas of expertise include design for manufacturability (DFM) of high-density surface mount printed circuit/wiring boards (PWB) and managing contract PWB fabrication.

TECHNOLOGY

- Type 1 (SMT both sides), type II (SMT both sides and PTH), and type III (SMT single side and PTH) PWB assemblies.
- High-density, large (22" x 11"), 6 mm lines and spaces, micro via, high-aspect ratio, fine pitch, 0.093" thick, dry film solder mask, impedance controlled PWBs.
- Range of SMT components include PQFPs (fine pitch technology), PLCCs, SOPs, and discrete chips.
- Futurebus+/Metral and HD+/Litton interconnection technologies.

EXPERIENCE

2005–Present   **Kai Pacific Computer, Inc.,** Seattle, WA
Manufacturing Engineer
Review and modify design of assemblies for manufacturability. Specify the fabrication and assembly process and create assembly instructions for PWBs. Manage PWB fabrication and assembly vendors. Design tooling and fixturing required for assembly and repair of new products. Improved PWB design and manufacturability by creating design guidelines. Solved manufacturability problems of PWBs by influencing engineering to make package type, orientation, and spacing modifications. Improved in-circuit/ATE testability of PWBs by reducing tooling hole tolerance and increasing test pad diameter. Managed and coordinated prototype PWB fabrication and assembly vendors to bring in eight different surface mount PWB assemblies built to an aggressive schedule. Wrote the specification for and managed the design and build of a test station for boundary scan and functional testing and de-bug of PWB assemblies. Evaluated and prepared Kai Computer's vendors in Japan for volume manufacture of new products, which entailed travel to Japan. Improved PWB assembly quality and turn-around time by influencing the vendor to add new equipment.

2001–2005   **Saturn Computer, Inc.,** Auburn, WA
Manufacturing Engineer
Purchased tooling and fixturing required for production and repair of existing products. Solved design, production, and material availability problems of existing products through initiating engineering change orders (ECOs) and temporary variance authorizations (TVAs). Managed the testing and shipment of a surface mount video upgrade product. Created a surface mount PWB fabrication specification.

EDUCATION

1997–2001   **University of Iowa,** Iowa City, IA
Bachelor of Science in Mechanical Engineering (BSME)

Marine Engineer

CHRIS SMITH
178 Green Street
Newport, RI 02840
(401) 555-5555
csmith@e-mail.com

SUMMARY

- Marine/Mechanical Engineer: More than 4 years of progressively responsible hands-on and management experience in the maintenance, repair, modification, overhaul, and installation of heavy marine equipment and machinery.
- Expertise with electrical, water, fuel, lubrication, hydraulic, power plant, motor control, and related systems and major components.
- Experience includes AC/DC light and power systems, generations, controllers, starters and transformers, communications systems, general electronics, consoles, and computers.

EXPERIENCE

First, Second, Third, ASSISTANT ENGINEER   Nordica, Inc.
                                                                            Newport, RI

First Assistant Engineer: *(M/V Maine Sunshine)*: 2006–Present
- Responsibilities aboard this 15,000 h.p. diesel ship with two twin V-14 Enterprise engines and 125 p.s.i. Vaporphase waste heat boiler; supervisor of up to eight assistants in the administration of matters affecting physical operation of the ship, from start-up to shut-down of the main propulsion plant.
- Assigned/scheduled/inspected work; set up preventative maintenance programs; handled inventory management/control, stores/parts/consumable ordering; burning of heavy fuel of required continual troubleshooting/problem-solving in the maintenance of propulsion system. Hands-on management included 80% of all engines.

Second Assistant Engineer: 2005–2006
- Supervised four assistants in the maintenance of boilers and auxiliary equipment; responsible for fueling, storing, and purification of fuel, test/maintenance of correct boiler water and/or main jacket water, and maintenance, repair, overhaul, or replacement of related systems and components.

Third Assistant Engineer: 2004–2005
- Supervised three assistants, handled small electrical maintenance, start-up/shut-down of fresh water distillery system, transfer and storage of water, and operation, maintenance, and repair of the lubrication system, including storing, transfer, and purification.

EDUCATION

Bachelor of Science, Rhode Island Maritime Academy, Providence, RI; 2004.
- Marine Engineering.
- Naval Science Award for Highest Naval GPA by Engineering Student.
- Graduated with Honors.

Mechanical Engineer
Costing and Standards

CHRIS SMITH
178 Green Street
Taylorsville, IN 47280
(812) 555-5555
csmith@e-mail.com

OBJECTIVE   A position in quality control/assurance or inspection with a manufacturer of quality engineered products.

EDUCATION   Valparaiso University, Valparaiso, IN
Bachelor of Science degree in Mechanical Engineering, 2000

Senior Design Project: Stress analysis and final drawings for hydroelectric waterwheel and for variable speed transmission. Received Hestinger Award for work in heat transfer and thermodynamics.

Undergraduate Teaching Assistant. One of three students selected to weekly lectures and grade examinations for junior Thermodynamics (M.E. 345).

EXPERIENCE   **MECHANICAL COSTING AND STANDARDS ENGINEER**
Katsel Corp., Ltd., Terre Haute, IN   **(2005–Present)**
As Costing and Standards Engineer, managed the costing and standards application and implementation. Maintained parts list data to first, second, and third, other levels of critical product structure file including subassemblies to complete system. Converted new products, newly released by engineering to sales staff, for order entry, and interacted with accounting department on cost roll-up examination and tracking.

As Mechanical/Industrial Engineer, proposed cost reducing changes to manufacturing. Conducted time study of a complicated manufacturing process; drafted floor plans for manufacturing. Planned large scale changes in fifteen workstations to increase efficiency. Recommended changes, which were incorporated, and project was successfully completed.

MECHANICAL DESIGNER
Enginuity, Staunton, IN   **(2000–2004)**
Design support stands for heat control devices. Perform quality control sample, testing of synthetic fibers. Monitor effects of extreme temperature on manufacturing equipment.

REFERENCES   Available upon request.

Nuclear Engineer

CHRIS SMITH
178 Green Street
Tuscaloosa, AL 35401
(205) 555-5555
csmith@e-mail.com

CAREER OBJECTIVE
A challenging quality assurance position in the nuclear power industry.

SKILLS/ACHIEVEMENTS
- Experienced in all aspects of nuclear power plant operation including, chemistry, radiological controls, health and safety issues, quality assurance, training, and project management.
- Highly proficient in identifying actual and potential problem areas, and in implementing solutions to ensure maximum safety, and operational and cost effectiveness.

PROFESSIONAL EXPERIENCE
RUCKER ISLAND NUCLEAR FACILITY, Tuscaloosa, AL
ENGINEER LABORATORY DIRECTOR   2006–Present
Coordinated all aspects of operations for the Nuclear Power Training Division. Directed and supervised staff of eight additional trainees in daily reactor and systems maintenance activities. Maintained analytical and radiation monitoring equipment; effected adjustments and repairs as necessary; supervised replacement of reactor components. Ensured compliance with strict quality assurance standards.

ENGINEERING LABORATORY TECHNICIAN   2004–2006
Coordinated Laboratory Division operations. Supervised staff in implementation of chemistry procedures and radiological controls including adjustments, and minor repair and major replacement projects. Responded immediately to emergencies; made adjustments, implemented repairs, and submitted detailed reports of findings; acted as Quality Assurance Inspector.

OPERATOR   2002–2004
Responsible for smooth operation of nuclear plant facility; duties included monitoring readings, record keeping, troubleshooting problems or abnormal test results, and making adjustments and repairs as needed. Served scheduled watches as Engineering Laboratory Technician and instructed various training exercises; made effective oral presentation of information; answered technical questions; oversaw hands-on drill activities and assisted with grading student performance.

EDUCATION AND TRAINING
ASSOCIATE OF SCIENCE IN NUCLEAR TECHNOLOGY, 2005
Tuskegee University, Tuskegee Institute, AL

BACHELOR OF SCIENCE DEGREE IN TECHNICAL ENGINEERING, 2001
Auburn University, Montgomery, AL

Petroleum Engineer

CHRIS SMITH
178 Green Street
Orem, UT 84058
(801) 555-5555
csmith@e-mail.com

SUMMARY OF QUALIFICATIONS
- Extensive knowledge of geological formations and conditions.
- Educational background in geology and environmental engineering.
- Ability to perform statistical analyses and present data effectively.

EXPERIENCE

AMEREXPLORE CORP., Provo, UT
PETROLEUM ENGINEER   2004 to 2006
Responsible for exploration in Colorado, Wyoming, Nevada, Oregon, Washington, Arizona, and New Mexico. Studied and evaluated geological formations and conditions related to petroleum generation, migration, and accumulation. Developed drillable petroleum prospects by predicting favorable locations of accumulation. Oversaw drilling operations in Washington and Oregon with twenty to twenty-five person operating staff.

TAMARACK, INC., Salt Lake City, UT
INTERN   2003
Observed and participated in exploration of mines surrounding Great Salt Lake. Tested petroleum samples gathered. Recoded results of exploration and presented paper to upper-level managers of company.

EDUCATION

UTAH STATE UNIVERSITY
Master's degree in Environmental Engineering, 2002

UNIVERSITY OF UTAH
Bachelor's Degree in Geology, 1999

REFERENCES
Available upon request.

Product Engineer

CHRIS SMITH
178 Green Street
Troy, NY 12180
(518) 555-5555
csmith@e-mail.com

Experience   MDK Incorporated, Troy, NY
Product Engineer (12/06–Present)
Engineer for cable products designed for high-speed applications. Responsibilities include product extension, electrical analysis, release of proposals and products, approval of tools and dies, resolving manufacturing problems, quality assurance, and interacting with customers.

Engineering Analyst (2/05–11/06)
Corporate staff member responsible for electrical engineering computer software packages used internationally. Provided consulting, support, and training of electrical analysis software used to design interconnects. Developed software interface. Evaluated new software packages. Administered UNIX environment and specified optimal configurations for engineering packages.

Development Engineer (9/03–2/05)
Designed computer board-to-board connection specializing in the electrical characterization of the interface. Provided computer modeling to determine capacitance, inductance, impedance, effective dielectric, propagation delay, and crosstalk for multiple conductors. Performed laboratory testing of samples using oscilloscope, TDR, and spectrum analyzer. Used CAD software to represent 3D models of connector proposals and construct mechanical layout.

Engineer Trainee (Summer, 2003)
Worked with development engineering group. Designed and performed procedure to test filtered connector's response to load conditions.

Computer   Operating Systems: UNIX, Linux, Windows
Experience   Languages: C++, Java.
Software: Many PC- and Mac-based applications.

Education   Master of Science in Engineering anticipated, August 2007
Rensselaer Polytechnic Institute, Troy, NY
Currently pursuing an advanced degree in computer and electrical engineering.

Bachelor of Science in Electrical Engineering December 2002
Hofstra University, Hempstead, NY

Associate of Arts in Engineering May 1999
Elmira College, Elmira, NY

Assistant Store Manager

CHRIS SMITH
178 Green Street
Mantua, NJ 08051
(609) 555-5555
csmith@e-mail.com

OBJECTIVE: To utilize skill in administration, management, and personnel toward further responsibilities in professional administration.

SUMMARY OF QUALIFICATIONS:
- Experience with financial administration of retail sales and service operations.
- Management of high-volume retail operations. Includes supervision of merchandising, asset management, customer service, and maintenance. Effect creative marketing programs and maintain compliance with corporate procedure.
- Skill in direction and development of individual and team personnel. Responsible for training, schedule, and motivation of staff personnel.

EXPERIENCE:

Assistant Store Manager   **1998 to Present**
LORAX SUPERMARKETS   Woodbury, NJ
- Responsible for control and administration of financial transactions in retail environment. Includes control of cash flow and expenses, internal audit and protection of corporate assets, and establishment of seasonal budgets.
- Manage schedule and procedure of over 175 personnel. Directly supervise all customer services, lottery sales, display merchandising, maintenance, sanitation, and employee training.
- Received awards for best cash variance and payroll percentage. Set goals and adjust departmental budgets by sales projections. Perform internal audits, control expenses, and protect assets.
- Worked part time 1998–2002. Promoted to Assistant Manager in 2005.

COMPUTERS:

Microsoft Word, FileMaker, Excel

EDUCATION:

Bachelor of Science in Business Management   **2002**
STOCKTON STATE COLLEGE   Pomona, NJ

VOLUNTEER:

Reader Program at Children's Hospital, Red Cross Blood Donor, Youth Tutor League.

REFERENCES:

Available upon request.

Assistant Vice President
Commercial Finance

CHRIS SMITH
178 Green Street
Brooklyn, NY 11210
(718) 555-5555
csmith@e-mail.com

PROFILE

- *Offer Master's training in Public Communication and a B.A. in Economics with distinguished academic performance. Top of class in Brooklyn Master's program; valedictorian of baccalaureate class, 2000.*
- *Business accomplishments include P & L responsibility as Assistant Vice President of LeBrock, Inc. Generated $25 million in revenues through negotiating purchases of commercial paper and effective structuring of real estate loans.*
- *Outstanding Sales Producer for LeBrock—secure 20% of all company annual revenues in an organization of fifteen individuals with financial authority.*
- *Characterized as driven and dedicated to an ideal of quality product and performance. Known for combining creativity, resourcefulness, and initiative to build a solid record of professional achievement.*

PROFESSIONAL EXPERIENCE

ASSISTANT VICE PRESIDENT   **2006–Present**
Brent LeBrock, Inc.   Brooklyn, NY
Coordinate and execute all aspects of revenue development, operations, finance, and contract management of a commercial financing enterprise in the food industry generating $50 million in yearly transactions. Develop and maintain a viable network of business and commercial real estate. Provide consultation to clients in matters of law, finance, and related documentation. Structure attractive financial packages; effectively negotiate terms for commercial paper transactions, mortgages, leasing, and insurance. Monitor and ensure compliance with financial and legal aspects of all client contracts. Troubleshoot and resolve complex situations.

Formulate and establish procedures facilitating peak operating efficiencies, cost effectiveness, and high employee morale. Select and develop support staff in all aspects of activities. Maintain MS systems including computer database, accounting, and business software. Participate in corporate planning and development of effective business strategies, facilitating clear communication between Operations, Legal departments, and managing partners.

ASSISTANT MANAGER   1996–2006
The Bastille Stores, Inc.   Washington, D.C.
Drove sales and supervised all aspects of operations for the Bastille's highest volume Washington, D.C., store, generating $1.9 million in annual sales. Significantly increased sales volume and overall customer satisfaction levels.

EDUCATION
MASTER OF ARTS IN PUBLIC COMMUNICATIONS, anticipated 2007
BACHELOR OF ARTS IN ECONOMICS, 1996
*Class Valedictorian * Summa Cum Laude * Alpha Sigma Lambda Honor Society*
BROOKLYN COLLEGE—Brooklyn, NY

Branch Manager
Restaurant

CHRIS SMITH
178 Green Street
Arvin, CA 93203
(805) 555-5555
csmith@e-mail.com

SUMMARY

- Fifteen years of successful experience in management at three franchise restaurants, including financing, contractual agreements, corporate and personal relations, property management, facilities design and layout, advertising, promotion, and community relations.
- Experience also includes purchasing; inventory control and management; personnel hiring, training, scheduling, and evaluation; security; policy; and procedure.
- Proven record as top salesperson. Consistently awarded top sales manager honors.

PROFESSIONAL EXPERIENCE

1994–Present   **PIZZA PALACE**
Branch Manager   **(THREE LOCATIONS)**
During this period managed three Pizza Palace restaurant franchises, generating annual sales of over $3.5 million. Managed work force of more than 250. Actively involved in all aspects of successful business operations, including: marketing, advertising, and public relations; financing; personnel hiring, training, management, scheduling, and relations; property maintenance, repair, modification, and management; operations and inventory control; financial management; and associated aspects of administrative detail.

1990–1993   **BUSINESS PRODUCTS, INC.**
Store Manager   **Bakersfield, CA**
Supervised twenty-five sales associates for growing office supply company. Kept all records of commissions. Acted as liaison between upper-level management and associates.

1987–1989
Sales Associate
Sold office supplies to various small and large businesses in the Southern California area. Highest earned commission, 1988 and 1989.

EDUCATION

California Polytechnic State University, San Luis Obispo, CA
Bachelor of Arts degree: 1986
- Concentration in English.

REFERENCES
Available upon request.

CHRIS SMITH
178 Green Street
Helena, MT 59601
(406) 555-5555
csmith@e-mail.com

OBJECTIVE

A senior administrative position which would take advantage of twenty years of varied, in-depth background.

CAREER SUMMARY

Executive primarily skilled in banking operations and data processing systems. Strong background in retail banking, marketing, planning, budgeting, and P & L management. Demonstrated record of developing and implementing solutions to multidimensional complex operational problems.

EMPLOYMENT

Calliope Savings Bank, Helena, MT   **2006–Present**
PRESIDENT/CEO
Originally hired as Executive Vice President and subsequently elected President/CEO in June of 2007.
Company provides check processing, consulting, and other services to forty banks. Developed and conducted corporate planning strategy meetings. In addition to having overall responsibility for operations, also responsible for financial management and P & L for the company, which presently employs sixty-five people and processes 30 million checks per year. Company turned profit within two years of start up. Developed data processing delivery system analysis; recommendations were adopted by ten banks.

The Prudent Savings Institution, Billings, VT
VICE PRESIDENT—HEAD OF BANKING DIVISION   **2004–2006**
Under the direction of Chairman of the Board, responsible for administrating, planning, and directing retail banking activities. Conferred with senior management and recommended programs to achieve bank's objectives.

VICE PRESIDENT—MARKETING   **2002–2004**
Administered and directed marketing activities of the bank. Organized and planned actions impacting on various publics supporting banks' markets. Worked with the divisions and outside agencies to develop plans which supported division's objectives. Supervised the following; liaison with advertising and public relations firms; the development and sales of bank services to various businesses; and development and control of the advertising and public relations budgets.

(continued)

EMPLOYMENT (continued)

VICE PRESIDENT—SAVINGS DIVISION	**1999–2002**
ASSISTANT VICE PRESIDENT—SAVINGS DIVISION	**1995–1999**
PROGRAMMER	**1992–1995**

EDUCATION

Bowdoin College, Brunswick, ME
B.A., English, 1988

Colby College, Waterville, ME
M.A., Finance, 1992

SPECIAL EDUCATION

Graduate School of Savings Banking
NAMSB—Carroll College 1995

Management Development Program—NAMSB
University of Montana 1997

Marketing School
Rocky Mountain College 1999

Various courses in: Economics, Finance, Law, Public Speaking, Speed Reading, and Banking.

PROFESSIONAL ACTIVITIES

Contributor, *Hiking for Stress Relief*
Contributor, *Horizons in Corporate Clout*
Rocky Mountain College 2001–2007
Assistant Professor of Business, University of Montana

HOBBIES

Hiking, jogging, and mountain climbing.

Chief Operations Officer

CHRIS SMITH
178 Green Street
San Diego, CA 92106
(619) 555-5555
csmith@e-mail.com

OBJECTIVE: The opportunity to be associated with a dynamic, progressive organization in need of an experienced executive qualified in the fields of training, recreation, and/or education.

SUMMARY OF QUALIFICATIONS:
- Planning and supervising air operations for training activities.
- Manpower, equipment, and facility coordination.
- Personnel training, evaluation, and scheduling.
- Administration and supervision of the maintenance and preparation of records, reports, and correspondence.
- Troubleshooting and resolving operational and training problems.
- Extensive experience as instructor, lecturer, and administrator.

EXPERIENCE: U.S. Navy, San Diego, CA   2000-2006
Chief, Operations Plans Division
Responsibilities:
- Coordinate the preparation, production, and revision of combat mission folders.
- Develop alert force procedures.
- Organize a smooth functioning administration and operational division to accomplish the requirements within the severely limited allotted time.
- Maintain detailed knowledge of all aspects of plans to include maintenance, logistics, and communications weapons.
- Direct the staff of enlisted and officer personnel.

EDUCATION: University of Notre Dame, Notre Dame, IN
B.A. Degree
Major: Political Science

MILITARY: United States Navy
Second Lieutenant 2006
Served in Operation Iraqi Freedom, Stationed in Turkey
Honorable Discharge, May 2006

COMPUTERS: Excel
Microsoft Word
Logistics Radar Equipment

PERSONAL: Willing to relocate.

Claims Examiner

CHRIS SMITH
178 Green Street
Caldwell, ID 83605
(208) 555-5555
csmith@e-mail.com

OBJECTIVE: A challenging and responsible position where my experience as a Claims Examiner for Medical Assistance recipients and provider liaison can be utilized in support of company goals.

SUMMARY: Over eight years experience in positions of increasing responsibility with rapidly growing Health Maintenance Organization includes the following:
- Organization and establishing policies for Medical Assistance Organization.
- Extensive customer service and provider communication.
- Staff supervision and coordination.
- Auditing and quality control.
- Utilizing Com Tec and Disc Corp computer system.

EXPERIENCE:

2001–Present **IDAHO HMO,** Boise, ID
Quality Control Coordinator (2006–Present)
Maintain daily, weekly, and monthly statistics on twenty-five claims examiners, reporting claim error through paper tracking and daily audit report. Interact with State Health auditors yearly. Make adjustments to claims and maintain relationships with providers.

Senior Claims Examiner/Unit Leader (2004–2005)
Trained and supervised three claims examiners, processing claims for 15,000 Medical Assistance recipients. Responsibilities included coordination of benefits, determination of eligibility, extensive provider relations, and customer service communication.

Claims Examiner (2002–2003)
Created new position, organizing and establishing policies for a Medical Assistance Organization which grew from 250 members in 2002 to its present 15,000. Processed medical and dental claims, referrals, encounters, and eye and prescription claims. Maintained heavy telephone contact with customers. Negotiated rates with providers and Health Partners administration.

2000–2001 **NEW LOOKS,** Caldwell, ID
Assistant Manager
Trained and supervised staff of twenty employees for women's clothing store. Responsible for sales, customer service, inventory, payroll, merchandising, management reporting, and problem solving.

CHRIS SMITH
178 Green Street
Roanoke, VA 24018
(703) 555-5555
csmith@e-mail.com

EXPERIENCE:

2003–Present **STARON PROMOTIONAL CORP.**   Roanoke, VA
Controller
Financial responsibilities: Accounts Receivable/Payable, verify and authorize invoices, establish and approve credit lines for clients and suppliers, process payroll, compile and audit monthly, quarterly, and yearly cash disbursement and financial reports.
Import and export responsibilities: Comply with customs and importing regulations, coordinate all aspects of import and export shipments.
Other responsibilities: Process daily banking transactions, open and negotiate domestic and international Letters of Credit, calculate salespeople's commissions.

2000–2003 **MILITARY OF TURKEY**   Istanbul, Turkey
Contract Administrator
Prepared quotations and performed administration of high-dollar contracts for American companies. Position included financial follow-up on the execution of contracts, and administration of technical and contractual modifications.

1998–2000 **TURKISH EMBASSY**   Washington, D.C.
Buyer—Procurement Mission
Performed high-dollar procurement of aviation systems and spare aircraft parts. Gained experience in all aspects of purchasing process, utilizing computerized purchasing systems. Served as liaison between Turkish Users and U.S. Vendors, handled negotiation of prices and conditions.

1996–1998 **UNIVERSITY OF TURKEY**   Istanbul, Turkey
Teaching Assistant
Research Assistant and Student Advisor in School of Business Administration, Financial Studies.

EDUCATION: **UNIVERSITY OF TURKEY**   Istanbul, Turkey
Graduate School of Business Administration
M.B.A., 1998—Major: Finance

TURKISH INSTITUTE OF TECHNOLOGY   Istanbul, Turkey
B.S. in Industrial and Management Engineering, 1991
Graduated with Honors

REFERENCES: Available upon request.

Director of Operations

· **CHRIS SMITH**
178 Green Street
Tacoma, WA 98447
(206) 555-5555
csmith@e-mail.com

SUMMARY

- Over fifteen years in shopping center management.
- Twenty years in retail.
- Strong background in shopping center operations: budget development, expense control, negotiating service/systems contracts, communications, and administration.

EXPERIENCE

1990 to Present

HILLSTON MANAGEMENT CO., INC.
Tacoma, WA

Director, Shopping Center Operations (2003–Present)

- Oversee operations for ten high-volume shopping centers.
- Hire, train, and motivate Operations Managers.
- Prepare budgets and control expenses for each center.
- Negotiate and award company-wide security, maintenance, and other service contracts.

General Manager, Whitman Mall (2000–2002)

- 1.5 million sq. ft. center in Tacoma, WA.
- Managed leasing, maintenance, security, promotions, advertising, budget development, expense control, and accounts receivable.
- Fostered effective tenant and public relations.

General Manager, City Mall (1998–1999)

- 800,000 sq. ft. center in Seattle, WA.
- Coordinated tenant construction, pre-opening activities, and grand opening.

General Manager, Pacific Mall (1990–1997)

- 600,000 sq. ft. center in Walla Walla, WA.

1985–1990

HEAD SALES CORP.
Tacoma, WA

Credit Operations Manager—Central Office
Store Credit Manager—Tacoma, WA

EDUCATION

Pacific Lutheran University, 1990
B.S., Business Administration

District Manager

CHRIS SMITH
178 Green Street
Chickasha, OK 73023
(405) 555-5555
csmith@e-mail.com

OBJECTIVE:

A district management position. Willing to travel and/or relocate.

PROFESSIONAL EXPERIENCE:

JESSAMINE BOOKSTORES, INC., Chickasha, OK
District Manager, Oklahoma   2006-Present
- Oversee all operations of ten retail bookstores in Oklahoma.
- Advise store management on personnel functions, merchandising, loss prevention, and customer service; communicate and ensure compliance with company policies, procedures, and programs.
- Open new stores; hire staff; oversee initial set-up.
- Research competition relative to title selection, pricing, merchandising, and sales programs.

WHIPPOORWILL BOOKS, New York, NY
District Manager, West Coast   2003-2006
- Managed operations as above for total of five districts in Los Angeles, San Francisco, San Diego, San Gabriel, and San Fernando.
- Performed extensive hiring, training, and developing of store managers.
- Set individual store and district sales goals.
- Named District Manager of the Year for Western United States, 2005, 2006.

Store Manager, New York   2001-2003
- Oversaw daily store operations; hired, trained, and developed personnel; performed merchandising functions; tracked and reported sales; handled inventory, bookkeeping, cash administration, etc.

Assistant Manager, New York   2000-2001
- Assisted manager in day-to-day operations; managed store in his absence.

EDUCATION:

Southwestern University, Georgetown, TX
Bachelor of Arts in English Literature, May 1999

COMPUTERS:

FileMaker, Microsoft Word, Excel.

Executive Marketing Director

CHRIS SMITH
178 Green Street
Alexandria, LA 71301
(318) 555-5555
csmith@e-mail.com

OBJECTIVE

A senior management position.

QUALIFICATIONS

- Thoroughly familiar with the design, installation, implementation, and/or conversion of data processing systems for major areas of bank operations that require in-depth knowledge of departmental function.
- Well qualified in areas of planning and setting objectives, sales and customer relations, and training programs dealing with both company and banking personnel. Establish and currently maintain excellent contacts with business and industry.
- Proven expertise in personnel management, employee training, and marketing. Innovative ability in application development, problem definition and solutions, and the ability to manage working teams.

EXPERIENCE

Heidelburg Computer Corporation, Alexandria, LA
Executive Marketing Director   1997–Present
General Information:
Began as a trainee assigned to work with units specifically designed for banks. Continues in this area through punched card accounting and computer-oriented data processing hardware and software. Promoted to Executive Marketing Director with responsibilities including:

- Supervise staff of eight (marketing, systems engineers, customer education, field engineers) and direct efforts of productive sales and systems engineering team.
- Work with three major accounts (commercial banking, teleprocessing network of mutual savings, and a major bank holding company); provide services involving annual revenue of over $4 million.
- Coordinate sales support activities, troubleshoot problem areas, and resolve problems by working in close cooperation with company's divisions (field engineering, systems design division, supply division, administrative staff, local branch management).
- Organize top-level presentations for sales involving million-dollar company/customer commitments.
- Maintain top-level contracts with customer organizations, and advise on matters pertaining to long-range overall system planning.
- Direct investigative effort prior to system design, and instruct customer/personnel.
- Serve as consultant and advisor to other marketing personnel in the organization.
- Serve as a guest lecturer at Heidelburg schools.

EDUCATION

Fort Lewis College, Durango, CO
Bachelor of Science, Business Administration, 1987

CHRIS SMITH
178 Green Street
Baltimore, MD 21239
(301) 555-5555
csmith@e-mail.com

OBJECTIVE To maximize professional and organizational skills in a general management position.

RELEVANT EXPERIENCE

1/06–Present

GENERAL MANAGER
Sweet Dreams Furniture Company, Baltimore, MD
Manage staff of five. Analyze market and target direct market areas. Perform spreadsheet analysis utilizing Excel; i.e., budget analysis, projections, payroll, and bookkeeping. Created custom forms and tables through Access database.

7/04–12/05

BUSINESS/OFFICE MANAGER
Rosek & Flo Bake Shops, Baltimore, MD
Coordinated the effectiveness of staff members' functions with the implementation of a computerized purchasing and billing system. Supervised a staff of ten–thirteen, including interns. Performed Human Resources management duties, i.e., recruitment, selection, training, and development; benefits, policies, and procedures. Increased sales by 75% and reduced cost 30%, utilizing marketing techniques. Negotiated purchases of computer equipment and contracted alternative delivery systems. Maintained public relation contacts with local and regional media, and implemented new marketing promotions. Office procedures also included taxation, bookkeeping, coding, and billing.

SKILLS

Proficient in Microsoft Word, Excel, Access, and PageMaker.

EDUCATION

Dickinson College, Carlisle, PA
BACHELOR OF ARTS, Human Resources, May 2004
Dean's List
Editor-in-Chief of the Yearbook, 2003–2004

INTERESTS

Baking, Sailing, Reading Poetry.

References Available Upon Request.

General Manager
Nightclub

CHRIS SMITH
178 Green Street
Hyannis, MA 02601
(508) 555-5555
csmith@e-mail.com

PROFESSIONAL EXPERIENCE

AMBER REIGN, Hyannis, MA   2001–Present
General Manager
- Manage all nightclub/restaurant operations. Volume $10,000 per night.
- Maintain all accounting, cash, bar/food/inventory cost, payroll, and administrative controls.
- Monitor sales at ticket outlet and supervise ticketing system.

Achievements
- Conceived, opened, and managed Amber Reign, increasing overall volume by 60%.
- Developed "Hear Them Roar," a Women's Comedy Competition which became a successful repeat promotion at Amber Reign and later went on to a national tour in 2007.

CAPE COD CUTIES, Hyannis, MA   1997–2001
General Manager
- Managed all aspects of this growing chain of New England hair salons.
- Supervised staff of twelve employees, ensuring efficient customer service in this high-volume, tourist-oriented selling space.
- Hired/fired staff. Responsible for payroll/accounts payable utilizing IBM PC.

EDUCATION

University of Massachusetts—Boston
Course work in General Management Practices, Business and Finance, Accounting, 2001–2002.

Aquinas Junior College
A.S. Marketing, 1996

COMPUTER SKILLS

Microsoft Word
Excel
FileMaker

REFERENCES

Furnished upon request.

Hospital Administrator

CHRIS SMITH
178 Green Street
Detroit, MI 48203
(313) 555-5555
csmith@e-mail.com

PROFESSIONAL OBJECTIVE

A challenging, growth-oriented position in **HEALTH CARE MANAGEMENT/ ADMINISTRATION.**

PROFESSIONAL EXPERIENCE

THE DETROIT MEDICAL CENTER, Detroit, MI

Hospital Director, 9/03–Present
- Supervise and coordinate administrative services for City public health care program.
- Handle health care and hospitalization for indigents, low-income, and welfare patients, consistent with care afforded insurance and fee-for-service patients.
- Troubleshoot staff/general administration conflicts and issues.
- Resolve policy issues; develop reports and documents for budgeting proposals and expenditure control.

Central Administrator, Emergency Services, 4/97–9/03
- Coordinated all administrative details of Emergency Room health care.
- Assisted medial team in providing prompt support services for the health care delivery system.
- Supervised ward secretaries, interpreters, and ancillary personnel.
- Prepared budget and monitored expenditures.

Unit Manager, 6/95–4/97
- Provided administrative support to Intensive Care Units, Operating Rooms, and Medical/ Surgical Floors.
- Handled vendor relations and inventory control.
- Supervised secretarial staff and ancillary personnel.

ADDITIONAL EXPERIENCE

- Additional experience includes Central Administrator, Night Admitting Manager, and Ward Secretary, 1987–1995.

EDUCATIONAL BACKGROUND

UNIVERSITY OF DETROIT MERCY, Detroit, MI
M.S. degree: Health Service Administration, 1995

MICHIGAN HOSPITAL ASSOCIATION, Detroit, MI
Certificate: Management Development, 1991

MICHIGAN STATE UNIVERSITY, East Lansing, MI
B.A. degree: English, 1987

BOARD MEMBERSHIPS

Elected to Board of Directors, Department of Public Health, 9/08–Present.

Import/Export Manager

CHRIS SMITH
178 Green Street
Pueblo, CO 81004
(719) 555-5555
csmith@e-mail.com

<u>CAREER HISTORY</u>

2003 to
Present

THE MORIN COMPANY, Pueblo, CO
<u>Import/Export Manager</u>, 2006–Present
- Handles established and all new calls/sales for European, Japanese, and U.S. exports.
- Prepare price quotations and government tenders; advise on delivery and order specifications.
- Write new product proposals and manufacturing documents, determining needs and coordinating assembly of all necessary materials.
- Process orders, credit memos, letters of credit, substitutions, return authorizations, and product complaints.
- Maintain extensive written, verbal, and fax communications with U.S. and overseas customers and dealers; provide product delivery information.
- Liaison with all facets of corporate and subsidiary operations including warehouse, manufacturing, advertising, marketing, research and development, and the legal department.
- Ensure proper and timely filling and delivery of each order; resolve collections problems and accountant discrepancies.

<u>Administrative Assistant, International Marketing</u>, 2004–2006
- Provided back-up to eight worldwide International Marketing Assistants and three Marketing Managers; cross-trained in all clerical and Marketing functions.
- Handled European business overflow for assistants and managers; processed orders, invoices, and requests.

<u>Bilingual Executive Secretary to the General Manager of European Exports</u>,
2003–2004
- Provided general secretarial support in all marketing/distribution functions.
- Translated all Spanish and Portuguese documents; made all travel arrangements.

<u>EDUCATION</u>

UNIVERSITY OF COLORADO, Boulder, CO
Bachelor of Arts degree in Spanish, graduated *Cum Laude,* 2002

<u>SKILLS</u>

Mac and PC proficient, fluent in Spanish, knowledge of Portuguese

Insurance Claims Controller

CHRIS SMITH
178 Green Street
Birmingham, AL 35229
(205) 555-5555
csmith@e-mail.com

PROFESSIONAL OBJECTIVE

Seeking greater opportunity for achievements in the field of Accounting Management in the Insurance and Financial areas.

PROFESSIONAL EXPERIENCE

1996 to Present

SHELDON INSURANCE AGENCIES, Birmingham, AL

Claim Control Supervisor, 2002 to Present

Responsible for maintenance coordination of existing claim support systems, development of financial and operational reports from new claim processing system, and establishment and performance of all draft controls and related analysis.

- Coordinate required IRS reporting for claim payments and abandoned personal property review.
- Monitor balances and collection of sundry ledger receivables.
- Develop accruals for liabilities.

Operations Accountant, 2000 to 2002

- Performed confirmation of processed premium transactions. Instrumental in hard development of expense budget and calendarized plan.
- Reported directly to management; provided analyses of monthly plan variances.
- Developed premium reporting specifications and enhancements on an as-needed basis.
- Monitored aging of all receivables and letter-of-credit balances.

Senior Operations Analyst, 1997 to 2000

Generated required premium accruals for unprocessed transactions. Coordinated development of management reports with staff. Performed ongoing analyses of financial results.

Financial Analyst, 1996 to 1997

Provided financial systems reports to field underwriting offices. Prepared short- and long-range plans and expense budgets, as well as the monthly serving carrier profit and loss statement.

1994 to 1996

CROWELL COMPANY, INC., Auburn, AL

Management Report Analyst

Created standardized and specially requested financial exhibits for senior management.

EDUCATION

1995

AUBURN UNIVERSITY, Auburn, AL

B.S., Accounting

Inventory Control Manager

CHRIS SMITH
178 Green Street
Fort Bragg, NC 28307
(919) 555-5555
csmith@e-mail.com

PROFESSIONAL BACKGROUND

2003 to   DEPARTMENT OF DEFENSE, Logistics Division, Supply Branch, Ft. Bragg, NC
Present   <u>Commodity Manager,</u> inventory Control
- Supervise staff of ten; train, schedule, evaluate, and delegate responsibilities—monitor work done and give final approval upon completion.
- Coordinate procurement and delivery of military supplies including electronics, modules, boards, guidance systems, tanks, aircraft, weapons, petroleum products, and spare parts.
- Receive bills of lading and resolve discrepancies with original orders.
- Input receipt of materials into database and monitor inventory.
- Interpret government rules and regulations regarding ordering and receipt of supplies; ensure proper application of all other procedures and policies.
- Review damaged item listings, determine whether to repair, and ship to repair shop.
- Complete financial paperwork ensuring orders are within budgetary requirements.
- Complete paperwork for inventory, shipping, purchasing, accounting, and end-of-month reports.
- Received awards for "Outstanding Performance," 2005, 2006.

2000 to   NATIONAL GUARD, Raleigh, NC
2003   <u>Communications Supervisor</u>
- Coordinated all communications and electronic suppliers for the North Carolina National Guard.
- Trained, scheduled, evaluated, and motivated as many as forty workers.
- Developed and implemented innovative system for ordering supplies and tracking inventory control.
- Input data and monitored inventory via computerized system.
- Forecasted, prepared, and monitored expenditures of operational budget.

EDUCATIONAL BACKGROUND

Asheville High School, Asheville, NC, 2000.

TRAINING

Supply Systems; Storage Management; Logistics Organization; Equal Opportunity; Application of Management Improvement Techniques for First Line Supervisors; Procurement; Financial Management in Stock Control Systems; Management of Materials Handling Equipment.

CHRIS SMITH
178 Green Street
Fort Wayne, IN 46803
(219) 555-5555
csmith@e-mail.com

EXPERIENCE

GARY YMCA — Gary, IN
ASSOCIATE EXECUTIVE DIRECTOR — 2006–Present

Supervision
Supervised seven full-time program directors and nonexempt administrative staff. Recruited, hired, trained, and evaluated full- and part-time staff. Organized and conducted staff meetings and training events. Responsible for career development for full-time professional staff.

Management
Financial management of $2 million multi-department annual budget. Developed and projected new annual budget, balanced and allocated funds, and ensured branch departments met financial goals. Operations management of program areas: Adult Fitness, Aquatics, Youth Sports and Fitness, Gymnastics, Day Camp, Fitness Center, Membership, Member Services, office administration, and facility maintenance. Administered safety and risk management procedures for the branch.

Fundraising
Chaired 2006 Annual Support Campaign. Community Gifts Chair of the 2007 Annual Support Drive. Organized campaign activities, recruited and trained volunteers, managed telephone solicitations, developed prospects, and implemented related administrative procedures.

Program/Services
Managed multi-program areas, scheduling, enrollment, and member evaluations. Established program guidelines and criteria. Managed and supervised membership department and front desk area, program registration, and member services/relations.

Community Relations
Responsible for administration and allocation of scholarship/financial aid funds. Assisted in volunteer development program. Direct responsibility to branch Board of Directors and program committees. Responsible for Public Service Announcements and public relations via presentations at various community organizations.

Promotions and Marketing
Planned and managed promotion budget, promotional print scheduling, hired graphic contractors, and media advertisers. Created, planned, and implemented in-house promotions. Collected and analyzed database of demographics and trends related to marketing membership and programs.

SENIOR PROGRAM DIRECTOR AND PHYSICAL DIRECTOR — 2001–2006
Direct supervision and management of the following departments: Adult Fitness Center, Corporate Fitness, Gymnastics, Youth Physical, Day Camp, and Community Services. Supervised approximately fifty part-time employees and one hundred volunteers. Conducted program and membership open-house promotions.

EDUCATION

GARY COMMUNITY COLLEGE — Gary, IN
Continuing education courses in marketing, MIS, and organizational communication — 2001

DEPAUW UNIVERSITY — Greencastle, IN
Bachelor of Science, Physiology and Biology — 2000

Manufacturing Manager
Automotive

CHRIS SMITH
178 Green Street
Woodstock, VT 05091
(802) 555-5555
csmith@e-mail.com

OBJECTIVE:

A position in manufacturing with a firm in need of an individual with a broad technical as well as management background in the machining and manufacturing fields.

EXPERIENCE:

Manufacturing Manager

Gladstone Motor Company, Montpelier, VT   2004–Present

- Oversaw modernization and reorganization of this engine plant contracted for remanufacture of Dane Motor Company engines.
- Set up controls for workers in manufacturing departments and machine shop which included grinding, boring, and honing operations.
- Initiated improved quality control system to meet Dane specifications for full-year warranty. System resulted in reduction of rejects to less than 4% on 500–600 engines completed monthly.
- Established purchasing policies utilizing second and third sources for parts, which resulted in Baur-Dane assuming more competitive pricing position.
- Classified purchasing details on eighty different production engines; implemented inventory control; greatly improved ordering efficiencies; and set up effective marketing service policies.

Accomplishment: Through expanded automation effected a labor cost reduction of $12 million annually. This was on $82 million in annual sales and the difference between a loss and substantial profit for management.

Manufacturing Manager

P.I.L. Engineering Company, Inc., Colchester, VT   2001–2004

- Supervised production machine shop, which subcontracted to manufacture precision machine parts and assemblies for the electronics industry.
- Developed and implemented manufacturing cost control and quality control programs; successfully developed business to $8.2 million in annual sales.

General Manager

Ferou Maintenance, Rutland, VT   1998–2001

- Shouldered full responsibility for this tractor-trailer maintenance company servicing the Shaw Line Haul Fleet consisting of 500 trailers and 200 tractors traveling New England and upper New York State.
- Recruited and hired sixty mechanics operating on three shifts.
- Initiated many vehicle design changes, which were adopted by the Stanza Motor Company.
- Designed unique field service trucks on which specifications were written for national application.

Operations Manager
Distributor

CHRIS SMITH
178 Green Street
Upper Arlington, OH 43221
(614) 555-5555
csmith@e-mail.com

OBJECTIVE   A management position where experience, education, and communication skills will be fully utilized in a growth-oriented environment.

SUMMARY OF QUALIFICATIONS

- Comprehensive knowledge of all functional areas of business operations.
- Strong initiative in decision-making and assumption of responsibilities.
- Self-starter capable of motivating others.
- Excellent communication and organization skills.
- Effective time management.

PROFESSIONAL EXPERIENCE

ORMON EQUIPMENT COMPANY, Columbus, OH
Operations Manager, 1997–Present

- Directed all administrative functions for distributor of machinery.
- Hired, fired, motivated, and evaluated staff of up to fifteen office, sales, and warehouse.
- Ordered all equipment and supplies.
- Managed accounts payable/receivable and financial statements; proved effective in collection of outstanding accounts.
- Generated sales to national and Midwest-area client firms.
- Provided information to engineers on appropriate equipment to meet their needs, within budgetary limits.
- Worked with purchasing agents; expedited customer service needs.
- Coordinated sales reports with available inventory.
- Scheduled all shipments, ensuring on-time delivery.

HATTRICK EQUIPMENT RENTALS, Grove City, OH
Assistant Supervisor, 1993–1996

EDUCATION   CAPITAL UNIVERSITY, Columbus, OH
Bachelor's degree in Accounting, 1992

REFERENCES   Available upon request.

Operations Manager
Human Services

CHRIS SMITH
178 Green Street
Phoenix, AZ 85023
(602) 555-5555
csmith@e-mail.com

PROFESSIONAL EXPERIENCE

2002 to Present

LASSITER HUMAN SERVICES, Phoenix, AZ
Operations Manager, 2004 to Present
Manage and coordinate all touring activities including scheduling, travel and accommodations planning, and international support for 150 students traveling to approximately 200 cities annually.

- Integral member of management team involved in goal planning, forecasting, cast evaluation, and problem solving.
- Lead and provide guidance to cast members.
- Manage, train, and support up to fifteen public relations representatives in the program's marketing effort.
- Train, supervise, and evaluate operations interns.
- Select and train advance cast personnel in specific city travel and performance guidelines, including logistics, scheduling, cultural information, and team communication.
- Direct and facilitate planning meetings; act as liaison between cast members, management, and sponsors.
- Logistics Coordinator for city-to-city travel in twenty countries on five continents; ensure safety compliance.
- Conduct daily status/informational meetings.
- Maintain Operations Department budget.
- Interview cast applicants, and assess and determine eligibility and qualifications.
- Currently assigned to the training and development of Health Services Coordinators; developed new training program to accommodate shift in coordinator's role and created present training manual; oversee health care of 550 crew, staff, and trainees; train participants to deal with emergency situations, illness, nutrition, and the unique problems encountered in foreign countries.

Health Services Coordinator, 2002 to 2004
- Assumed increasing operations responsibilities.
- Oversaw the health and nutritional needs of the cast and staff during tour, including health maintenance, emergencies, direct care, and coordination with physicians.
- Directed meal planning, budgeting, and preparation.
- Presented self-health care seminars.

1999 to 2002

KEEGAN MEDICAL CENTER, Lake Havasu City, AZ
Staff RN/Rehabilitation and Medical Unit
- Assumed Charge responsibilities when necessary.
- Practiced Modular Nursing; directed and supervised aides and LPNs in direct patient care.
- Selected member, Stroke Education Committee, involved in the implementation of patient/family educational programs.
- Interdisciplinary Team volunteer, Hospice of the Southwest, 2000 to 2002.

EDUCATION

University of Arizona, Tucson, AZ
B.S. Nursing, 1998

CHRIS SMITH
178 Green Street
Helena, MT 59601
(406) 555-5555
csmith@e-mail.com

OBJECTIVE: A **Senior Management** position which would take advantage of more than twenty years of varied, in-depth background.

CAREER SUMMARY:

Executive skilled in Banking Operations and Data Processing Systems. Strong background in Retail Banking, Marketing, Planning, Budgeting, and P & L Management. Demonstrated record of developing and implementing solutions to multidimensional complex operational problems.

CALLIOPE SAVINGS BANK, Helena, MT

2006– *President*
Present Originally hired as Executive Vice President and subsequently elected President in June of 2006. Company provides check processing, consulting, and other services to forty banks. Developed and conducted corporate planning and strategy meetings. In addition to having overall responsibility for operations, also responsible for financial management and P & L for the company. Company presently employs sixty-five people and processes 30 million checks per year. Company turned profit within two years of start-up. Developed data processing system analysis . . . recommendations were adopted by ten banks.

1995–2006, THE PRUDENT SAVINGS INSTITUTION, Billings, MT
(Asset size: $1 billion)

2004–2006 *Vice President—Head of Banking Division*
Under the direction of Chairman of the Board, responsible for administering, planning, and directing the retail banking activities of the Bank. Conferred with Senior Management and recommended programs to achieve Bank's objectives. Responsibilities included: Personnel, Salary Administration, Budget Administration, Performance, Planning, Sales Management, and other duties related to operational areas.

2002–2004 *Vice President—Marketing*
Administered and directed marketing activities of the Bank. Organized and planned actions impacting on various publics supporting Bank's markets. Worked with Divisions and outside agencies to develop plans which supported Division's objectives. Supervised the following: liaison with Advertising and Public Relations firms; the development and sales of Bank services to various businesses; and development and control of the Advertising and Public Relations budgets.

1999–2002 *Vice President—Sales Division*

(continued)

CAREER SUMMARY (continued)

1995–1999   **Assistant Vice President**—*Savings Division*

1989–1995   **Programmer**

EDUCATION:

BOWDOIN COLLEGE, Brunswick, ME
Bachelor's degree, English, 1988

COLBY COLLEGE, Waterville, ME
Master's degree, Finance, 1992

SPECIAL EDUCATION:
Graduate School of Savings Banking

NAMSB—Carroll College—1995
Management Development Program—NAMSB

University of Montana—1997
Marketing School

Rocky Mountain College—1999
Various courses in: Economics, Finance, Law, Public Speaking, Speed Reading, and Banking.

PROFESSIONAL ACTIVITIES:

Contributor, *Hiking for Stress Relief*	Present
Serve on *Horizons in Corporate Clout*	Present
Assistant Professor of Business, Rocky Mountain College	2001–2007

HOBBIES:

Hiking, Jogging, Mountain Climbing

REFERENCES:

Furnished upon request.

CHRIS SMITH
178 Green Street
Dunnellon, FL 34433
(813) 555-5555
csmith@e-mail.com

OBJECTIVE

A position requiring comprehensive product management, product/protocol development and clinical research/nursing skills to obtain FDA product approval.

EXPERIENCE

Estrade, Inc., Dunnellon, FL   **October 2006–Present**
Product Manager
- Provide a comprehensive coordination of all product development activities, from research to market; fulfill the ultimate objective of a commercially marketable product.
- Devise, implement, and evaluate training and educational materials for providers of ALT services.
- Follow up on the continuous assessment and evaluation of product application needs and ALT provider needs through collaboration with multidisciplinary team (clinical research, process development, research and development, and regulatory affairs).
- Assist in the strategic planning for the development of further applications for ALT and the adaptation of cell processing techniques for other clinical indications.
- Assemble and manage multidisciplinary project teams for product development of each application of ALT.
- Prepare and present the clinical aspects of protocols to physicians' investigative groups.

Manager—Clinical Services   **October 2004–September 2006**
- Developed, managed, and provided ongoing evaluation of clinical training and staff development plans for use in fifteen company-operated outpatient treatment centers and participating clinical research facilities throughout the country.
- Participated in the hiring, orientation, and technical training of clinical personnel. Provided ongoing assessment of clinical performance including annual performance evaluations.
- Designed and implemented Clinical Quality Assurance/Quality Improvement Plans for use in company-operated outpatient treatment centers.

St. Theresa's Hospital   **July 1998–September 2004**
Staff RN
- Provided primary nursing care of critically ill pediatric patients in a tertiary care facility. Responsible for patient and family education, discharge planning, and home care placement.

EDUCATION
Boston College, Chestnut Hill, MA
Bachelor of Science degree—Nursing, 1998

COMPUTER LITERACY
Windows, Microsoft Word, Outlook, ACT. Work with systems consultants on the design and implementation of data management systems including remote access.

Program Manager

CHRIS SMITH
178 Green Street
Shawnee, OK 74801
(405) 555-5555
csmith@e-mail.com

BACKGROUND SUMMARY
Extensive experience in customer relations with a major manufacturer of electronic kit products. Special program management skills utilizing the team concept for product development. Program manager for successful federal contracts and the development of four commercial microcomputer systems.

CAREER HISTORY
RICOCHET DATA, Shawnee, OK   2005–Present
Program Manager
Develop and coordinate short- and long-range plans for the design and introduction of new microcomputer products.
- Create work breakdown structure. Identify required resources.
- Develop master charts to track major milestones and critical path activities.
- Served on a management task force assigned to develop a set of work instructions for the introduction of outsourced products.
- Reduced product time to market by 25%.

LORENZ COMPANY, Oklahoma City, OK   1991–2005
Computer Sales Coordinator   2000–2005
Provided customer assistance in selecting the computer components best suiting their requirements.
- Evaluated customer needs and recommended the best hardware and software solutions.

Retail Store Manager   1996–2000
Managed the Lorenz factory retail store providing sales and service for over 200 products.
- Generated gross annual sales in excess of $2 million for four consecutive years.
- Managed a sales and service staff of eight people.
- Provided superior customer service and support.

Product Technical Consultant   1991–1996
Provided technical consultation to customers via telephone and letter on any problem they might experience during the assembly and operation of their kit.
- Maintained sixty to eighty customer contacts per day.
- Developed an in-depth technical knowledge of the product line.
- Improved customer relations.

EDUCATION
Oral Roberts University, Tulsa, OK
B.A. Management, 1999

Phillips University, Enid, OK
Certification: Broadcaster Transmitter Service
Certification: Radio and Television Service

CHRIS SMITH
178 Green Street
Bozeman, MT 59715
(406) 555-5555
csmith@e-mail.com

PROFESSIONAL EXPERIENCE

2006–2006   FERRIS CONSTRUCTION CORPORATION   Bozeman, MT
Project Manager/Superintendent
Oversaw daily field and office operation of a construction corporation handling commercial
and residential projects.
- Provided onsite management and quality control to ensure projects met time and budget requirements, and were built in accordance with contract documents.
- Coordinated and scheduled subcontractors and suppliers.
- Worked closely with architects and engineers in reviewing drawings and specifications.
- Scheduled, conducted, and participated in project meetings.
- Oversaw cost control, coding, and payroll.
- Prepared budgets, estimates, bids, proposals, schedules, contracts, subcontracts, and work scopes.
- Negotiated subcontract agreements, purchase orders, and general contracts with clients.

2003–2005   SONORA ASSOCIATES   Anceney, MT
Superintendent
Managed all aspects of commercial construction projects.
- Coordinated subcontractors and suppliers.
- Provided quality control on various projects.
- Worked closely with designers, engineers, and architects to ensure projects were built in accordance with contract documents.
- Supervised carpenters, laborers, and subcontractors.
- Generated daily and weekly progress reports.
- Reviewed subcontracts and implemented operations.

1998–2003   M. CARDILLO & SONS CONSTRUCTION COMPANY   Belgrade, MT
Carpenter Foreman
Oversaw all daily carpentry-related operations.
- Provided quality control.
- Hired, trained, and supervised up to ten carpenters/helpers.
- Logged time for payroll.

1992–1997   Various Contractors throughout Montana
- Gained experience in union/nonunion, rough/finish, and residential/commercial construction. Later developed specialty in finish work.

LICENSURE   Montana Supervisor's License #325925

EDUCATIONAL BACKGROUND
MONTANA STATE UNIVERSITY, Bozeman, MT
Construction Management, 1992

Regional Manager

CHRIS SMITH
178 Green Street
Wheatland, ND 58079
(701) 555-5555
csmith@e-mail.com

SUMMARY OF QUALIFICATIONS

- A high-energy, self-motivated, self-starter with the ability to develop and establish an efficient, highly productive workforce.
- Expertise in staffing, training, motivation, and evaluation of personnel to assure adherence to quality service, product specifications, and customer satisfaction.
- Active participation in development of Manager Training Program and Employee Certification Program.
- Sound knowledge of sales projections, budgets, cost-control systems, and standardized procedures designed for stable operations and bottom-line profits.

EXPERIENCE

REGIONAL MANAGER
The Supreme Eatery, Hunter, ND   **2005–Present**

- Responsible for management of ten stores. Oversee performance of approximately 150 employees including managers and assistance managers. Report to Director of Store Operations.
- Work with store managers on budgets, and management tracking. Open new stores and negotiate and set up contracts for purchasing foods, beverages, and maintenance with local vendors and service companies.
- Worked with Training Manager on a Manager Training Program and Employee Certification for all employees designed to teach product specifications and procedures for customer service and quality product preparation.
- Conduct coaching, counseling, and motivational sessions, and work with store managers on budget responsibility and projections.
- Developed checklist for opening, closing, safety, sanitation, security, and daily operations for use by managers in each unit.

ASSISTANT GENERAL MANAGER
The Roadside Restaurant, Gardner, ND   **2004–2005**

- Started as an Assistant Manager and was promoted to Assistant General Manager.
- Directed all personnel operations including the recruitment, training and evaluation, and pay administration for seventy-five employees.
- Assisted in Employee Certification Process for fifty employees. Achieved total certification within two months. This resulted in increased efficiency and improved employee morale.
- Maintained inventory levels and supervised ordering. Increased sales by instituting daily specials and a Sunday Brunch. Significantly streamlined operations and lowered costs while maintaining high quality standards.

EDUCATION

North Dakota State University, Fargo, ND
Bachelor of Arts in English Literature, 2003

Retail Store Manager

CHRIS SMITH
178 Green Street
Los Angeles, CA 90035
(310) 555-5555
csmith@e-mail.com

OBJECTIVE: A **Retail Management** position.

EXPERIENCE:

6/04–
Present

RETRO RECORDS CORPORATION, Los Angeles, CA
Manager   5/05–Present
- Operated Retro's largest volume store (approximately $50,000 per week).
- Hire, train, and coordinate a staff of twenty-six.
- Direct sales floor activities.
- Handle all merchandise, inventory control, ordering, cash control, and maintenance functions.
- Coordinate special promotions and events.
- Prepare daily sales reports.
- Interact with corporate personnel on all levels.
- Assist in developing local marketing and advertising strategies.

Assistant Manager   6/03–4/05
- Oversaw full range of retail management responsibilities.
- Assisted in merchandising.
- Opened/closed store; handled customer service complaints and cash control.
- Supervised and motivated employees.

4/01–5/03

SANTA ANA SHOPS, Santa Ana, CA
Assistant Manager
- Handled hiring, merchandising, and cash control for this small convenience store.
- Supervised fifteen employees.
- Opened and closed market.
- Prepared bank deposits and daily sales reports.

ACHIEVEMENTS:

Won two merchandising display contests.
Received the "Super Spinner" Sales Award for exceeding sales goals, 2006.

REFERENCES:

Furnished upon request.

Service Manager

CHRIS SMITH
178 Green Street
Mill Valley, CA 94941
(415) 555-5555
csmith@e-mail.com

SUMMARY OF QUALIFICATIONS

- Expertise encompasses all phases of Field Service support and reports including Labor distribution, contract, billable, and warranty service report processing, expense, accounts payable, parts orders, warranties, repairs, maintenance orders, and related documentation.
- Effectively provide administrative support to District Service, Zone Manager, and Service Technicians.
- Extensive customer contact in troubleshooting, and resolving problems pertaining to service disputes or service contract renewals.

EXPERIENCE

SERVICE COORDINATOR
Western Services Group, Oakland, CA   2003–Present

- Provide administrative support to District Service Manager and six Service Technicians servicing approximately 200 hospitals. Train and supervise assisting personnel.
- Monitor open incidents, report calls, and maintain and monitor Field Service Engineers tracking logs.
- Involved in daily contact with customers to troubleshoot and resolve problems pertaining to billing, unpaid tax balances, excessive charges or short payments, warranties, service contact renewals, and other service-related matters while maintaining good customer relations.
- Generate and maintain service-related and quotation correspondence. Process contract proposals, agings, contract agencies, and contract terminations. Prepare warranty certificates to assure insurance of commissions to correct salesmen.
- Maintain Return Authority log encompassing credit, inventory, and repair exchange inventory, and issue or monitor credits to service customers.
- Audit travel and expense reports, process general vouchers, hours for payroll, and purchase orders for vendors.

ACCOUNTS RECEIVABLE/CREDIT AND COLLECTION AGENT
Sampson and Company, San Francisco, CA   1994–2001

- Advanced from Accounts Receivable Clerk to progressively more responsible positions involving finance, credit/collection, and record keeping for domestic and foreign markets.
- Responsibilities included: Cash receipts, disbursements, adjustments, closings, preparation of worksheets, computer input, and projection of cash flow.
- Handled collection for one parent company and three subsidiaries. Decreased outstanding accounts receivable balances substantially and retained excellent customer relations.
- Directed credit investigations. Successfully resolved all disputes.

EDUCATION
Santa Clara University, Santa Clara, CA
Bachelor of Arts degree, Human Services, 1993
Minor: Business

Transportation Manager

CHRIS SMITH
178 Green Street
Flushing, NY 11385
(718) 555-5555
csmith@e-mail.com

PROFESSIONAL OBJECTIVE

A challenging, growth-oriented position in **TRANSPORTATION INDUSTRIES.**

PROFESSIONAL EXPERIENCE

2001–2006 **MARCONI SYSTEMS,** Flushing, NY
Shift Supervisor/Chief Operator
- Supervised shift of ten employees in monitoring, repairing, and installing electronic protective systems for both domestic and corporate clients.
- Maintained control console for incoming calls on a guard-express with on-call duty, 24 hours daily, in emergency situations.
- Reviewed client needs and made recommendations as to what services best met customer requirements.
- Expedited emergency services to a 75,000 individualized program.
- Strong interpersonal and communication skills required.

1996–2001 **NEW YORK STATE LABORATORIES,** Elmira, NY
Maintenance
- Maintained general laboratory with regard to safety and sanitation within a strict health environment.
- Maintained inventory control of supplies and equipment orders and re-order storage units.
- Responded to departmental work orders on special needs and maintenance repair.

MILITARY

UNITED STATES ARMY
Hatteras, North Carolina
Rank: E-4, Honorable Discharge.

EDUCATION

DUNCAN INSTITUTE OF TECHNOLOGY, New York, NY
Studies: Engineering and Drafting, 1994

NEW YORK SCHOOL OF STEAM ENGINEERING, New York, NY
Certificate: Steam Engineering, 1993

NEW YORK TECHNICAL HIGH SCHOOL, New York, NY
Diploma, Engineering/Drafting, 1992

LICENSURE Auxiliary Police Officer

Vice President
Construction

CHRIS SMITH
178 Green Street
Laconia, NH 03102
(603) 555-5555
csmith@e-mail.com

OBJECTIVE
An Executive Management position in
REAL ESTATE OPERATIONS/DEVELOPMENT/MARKETING.

SELECTED CAREER HIGHLIGHTS

- *Multidisciplined Professional:* Real Estate background encompasses Business Development, Strategic Planning, Marketing, and Construction Project Management.
- *Marketing Edge:* Developed a vital network of business and industry contacts instrumental in Raze's acquisition of key contracts with the China Society, Jen Bright, and Weld Corporations.
- *Technical Expertise:* Offer BSME with proven abilities to estimate costs and design and install electrical, telecommunications, fire and life safety, and related technological systems.
- *Project Executive:* Full profit and loss accountability for key client projects involving scheduling, cost accounting, cash flow analysis, purchasing, and professional systems.
- *Human Resources Management:* Recruit, assign, motivate, and evaluate management and support staff. Develop and implement progressive policy for 500 employees.
- *Cost Conscious:* Developed innovative cost-saving programs including cellular telephone service and Raze's T-Bar Systems.
- *Sales Achiever:* Reputation for excellent sales presentations. Closed the largest single sale within Meyer for an infrared control system.
- *Skilled Negotiator:* Dealt successfully with U.S. and Asian corporate representatives. Handled prime contractor negotiations, secured an equity position with RSSO for Raze's 150-room Manhattan Ritz Hotel.

PROFESSIONAL EXPERIENCE
RAZE REALITY & CONSTRUCTION COMPANY, INC.—2001–Present
SENIOR VICE PRESIDENT/
EXECUTIVE VICE PRESIDENT AND PROJECT EXECUTIVE:
RAZE CONSTRUCTION CORPORATION   Laconia, NH
Coordinate and execute a variety of construction management projects for a leading real estate development firm specializing in hotel, office, and commercial facilities construction and renovation. Home office responsibilities include driving marketing and sales efforts, developing and presenting proposals with cost estimates, and negotiating terms of customer contracts with domestic and international corporations. Provide quality preconstruction consulting, design, and project management services. Provide critical strategic planning; execute project staging and logistics.

Field services include all aspects of design, planning, and execution of assigned construction and tenant installation projects for commercial clients. Analyze existing and proposed designs with a specialty in electrical and telecommunications systems; suggest improvements to plans, methods, and materials. Schedule projects, select and procure materials, and assign personnel and engage qualified subcontractors. Oversee all phases of project execution; approve engineering/design changes; troubleshoot and resolve complex technical problems, consistently meeting project deadlines and highest possible quality standards. Maintain clear communications and positive relations with clients, subcontractors, and the community.

(continued)

- Head of Raze Technologies Group, handle all technology-related installations on trading floors, security, life safety, and high-tech wiring systems.
- Serve on Raze's Personnel and Marketing committees.
- Highly skilled in use of computer systems; utilize numerous software programs for effective project scheduling and cost accounting applications.
- Expert troubleshooter; identify complex problems; resourceful and inventive in implementing creative solutions with enhanced sensitivity to cost, efficiency, and deadlines.

Projects include:

- *FOUR CROWS: Managed construction of the 350-room, four-star luxury hotel, tallest in the world.*
- *THE CHINA SOCIETY: Executed this below-sidewalk expansion with extreme sensitivity to ongoing operations.*
- *DURITZ HOUSE HOTEL: Executed room renovations, new ballroom and lobby in original Art Deco style.*
- *THE HORATIO HOTEL: Undertook gut renovation including new room construction, public spaces, and ballroom.*
- *SCHULTZ HOTEL: Developed architectural and systems design alternatives and cost estimates for extensive renovation.*
- *PENELOPE INN: Local Law 16 upgrade.*
- *GUSTAV KLIMT CENTER: Completed an infrastructure upgrade; installed security and building automation.*
- *HOTEL MONROE in Boston.*
- *MYOKO AMERICA: Handled bidding and purchasing of cabling and installation for trading floors of U.S. branch of Asian trading company.*

PROJECT MANAGER   1991–2000
LINDSEY, KEENE, INC.   North Conway, NH
Estimated project costs, sourced and negotiated purchasing, scheduled, and directed and coordinated a variety of quality office building projects, ensuring compliance with regulatory requirements and highest quality standards. Controlled and managed overhead and project budget costs; approved selection of subcontractors, systems, and materials decisions. Performed cost accounting and administrative tasks ensuring peak profit performance.
Projects include:

- *BIDLAW INSURANCE: Managed construction in two company buildings.*
- *SPECIFIC OIL: Oversaw construction for corporate guest facilities.*

ADDITIONAL EXPERIENCE

ADJUNCT ASSISTANT PROFESSOR   2005–Present
Boston University Real Estate Program   Boston, MA

EDUCATION
BACHELOR OF SCIENCE IN MECHANICAL ENGINEERING, 1991
Massachusetts Institute of Technology, Cambridge, MA

Additional courses, workshops, and seminars include:
Several REAL ESTATE topics and MANAGEMENT seminars.

Warehouse Manager

Confidential Resume of
CHRIS SMITH
178 Green Street
Hoboken, NJ 07030
(201) 555-5555
csmith@e-mail.com

SUMMARY OF QUALIFICATIONS
- Large volume warehouse experience.
- Special handling requirement experience.
- Inventory, quality control, and sanitation abilities.
- Experience in truck fleet operations.

EXPERIENCE

9/03 to
Present   AMERICAN CRYSTAL COMPANY, Hoboken, NJ

5/05 to
Present **Warehouse Manager**
- Supervise staff of seventeen.
- Manage a 25,000-square-foot warehouse with seven bays and three forklifts.
- Schedule all employees.
- Handle all special freight requirements.
- Oversee rate negotiations, breakage, and inventory control.
- Service company-owned retail locations as well as a variety of distributors.
- Direct rerouting and management of a twelve-truck delivery fleet.

9/03 to
5/05 **Warehouse Supervisor**
- Supervised four warehouse managers who were required to supply weekly reports regarding productivity numbers, expenses, overtime, and overall operations.
- Operated and directed activities in four warehouse operations representing supervision of thirty-two people and 35,000 square feet of warehouse space.

6/01 to
9/03   CORNUCOPIA SHOPS, Hoboken, NJ
Assistant Warehouse Superintendent
- Supervise 175 warehouse employees in a 50,000-square-foot warehouse.
- Worked with both inbound and outbound dry groceries and nonfoods; shipments totaled over fifty trailers a day moving 275,000 cases per week.
- Prepared employee schedule.
- Oversaw shipping, receiving, and inventory control.

EDUCATION

Hoboken Community College, Hoboken, NJ
A.S. Business Administration, 2001

DR. CHRIS SMITH
CHIROPRACTOR

178 Green Street
Dedham, MA 02026
(781) 555-5555
csmith@e-mail.com

PROFESSIONAL HISTORY
Greater Boston Chiropractic Center, Boston, MA
Chiropractic Therapy, 2000–Present

- Provide spinal manipulation and handle necessary muscular-skeletal needs of sports-injured patients.
- Alleviate pain in elderly and work-related injured patients.
- Assist the industrial-accident injured in regaining strength and stamina.
- Provide information for insurance companies, worker's compensation, and third party billing procedures.

EDUCATION
Palmer College of Chiropractics, Davenport, IA
M.D., degree
Graduated, 2000

University of Massachusetts, Boston, MA
B.S., Pre-Med
Graduated, 1998

CERTIFICATION/PROFESSIONAL AFFILIATIONS
Certified by the Commonwealth of Massachusetts

American Chiropractic Association
Massachusetts Chiropractic Society
Greater Boston Chiropractic Society
Sports Injury Council of the American Chiropractic Association

PUBLICATIONS
Spine, October 12, 2006, Volume 9.
"Correlation of Spinal Biomechanics and Childhood Asthma."

Journal of the ACA, May 3, 2004, Volume 19, Issue 5.
"Further Effects of Calcium on Geriatric Osteoporosis Patients."

Dental Assistant

CHRIS SMITH
178 Green Street
Poughkeepsie, NY 12601
(601) 555-5555
csmith@e-mail.com

OBJECTIVE

A position as a Medical Assistant or related position of responsibility where there is a need
for clinical as well as administrative experience.

SUMMARY OF QUALIFICATIONS

- Over five years of experience as a Dental Assistant and Medical Receptionist in direct patient care and patient relations.
- Honor Graduate as Medical Assistant from National Education Center.
- Sound knowledge of medical terminology and clinical procedures.
- Certified in: First Aid, Cardiopulmonary Resuscitation, Electrocardiography.
- Additional experience as Receptionist/Secretary with an executive search/management consulting firm, financial management company, and realty firms.

HEALTH CARE EXPERIENCE

Dr. Herbert Dickey, M.D., Brooklyn, NY   **2005–Present**
- Perform accounts payable/receivable.
- Schedule patients for appointments.
- Prepare patients for surgical procedure; record temperature and blood pressure, insert intravenous units, and administer sedatives.
- Provide postoperative care; record vital signs every ten minutes until consciousness; establish patient comfort; provide necessary information to patients regarding new medications/possible side effects.

Drs. William and Joseph Janell, New York, NY   **2004–05**
- Began as Dental Trainee, advanced to Dental Assistant.
- Sterilized instruments, processed X-rays, scheduled appointments, and maintained patient relations.

Externship
Internal Medicine Associates, Brooklyn, NY   **2005**
- Multidisciplinary practice, including gastroenterology, rheumatology, endocrinology, and cardiology.
- Took vital signs, performed urinalysis, EKGs, and blood chemistries. Maintained patient charts.

EDUCATION

State University of New York, Birmingham, NY
A.S. Biology

COMPUTERS

Microsoft Word, Excel

Dental Hygienist

A

CHRIS SMITH
178 Green Street
Upper Montclair, NJ
(201) 555-5555
csmith@e-mail.com

OBJECTIVE

A full-time position as a Dental Hygienist in a private practice.

EMPLOYMENT

Dr. Rettman, D.M.D., Upper Montclair, NJ
Dental Hygienist   (2003 to Present)
- Provide prophylaxis treatment to patients in a variety of situations: teeth cleaning, gum massage, oral hygiene education, and periodontal scaling.
- Monitor radiographs. Administer Novocain prior to painful procedures.
- Provide secretarial assistance: telephones, paperwork, scheduling, etc.

Dr. Grohowski, D.M.D., Princeton, NJ
Dental Assistant   (2000 to 2003)
- Assisted dentist in prophylactic procedures: provided necessary tools, sterilized equipment, and comforted patients.

EDUCATION

Kelly School of Dental Hygiene, New York, NY
A.S. in Dental Hygiene, 2000
Course work included: Chemistry, Radiology, Nutrition, Periodontology, Pathology, Anatomy, Dental Equipment, Oral Embryology, Psychology, and Pharmacology.

LICENSURE

New Jersey Dental Hygiene License
National Board Dental Hygiene Exam (written 90)
N.E.R.B. Dental Hygiene Exam (clinical 93, written 90)

REFERENCES

Available upon request.

Dental Hygienist

B

CHRIS SMITH
178 Green Street
Simi Valley, CA 93063
(805) 555-5555
csmith@e-mail.com

OBJECTIVE

Seeking a full-time position as a Dental Hygienist in a private practice with a strong emphasis on prevention.

EDUCATION

Cooper School of Dental Hygiene, University of California
A.S. in Dental Hygiene, 2003
Course work included:

Chemistry/Biochemistry	Anatomy/Physiology
Radiology	Oral Embryology
Nutrition	Dental Materials/lab
Periodontology	Psychology/Sociology
Pathology	Pharmacology

Dental Hygiene Lecture and Clinical Rotations:
Waterville School, Veteran's Administration Hospital

LICENSURE

California Dental Hygiene License
National Board Dental Examination (written 90)
N.E.R.B. Dental Hygiene Examination (clinical 95, written 84)

EMPLOYMENT

2004–Present Dr. Race Banner, D.M.D., Eastham, MA
Dental Hygienist
- Perform prophylaxis, periodontal scaling, hygiene education, sealants, and radiographs. Occasional assisting and reception; related paperwork and scheduling.

1998–2004 Dr. John E. Quest, D.M.D., Bourne, MA
Assistant/Receptionist
- Provided general clinical and office support on a temporary basis.

PERSONAL

- Member, American Dental Hygiene Association.
- National Student Dental Hygiene Association, Past Member, Class Historian.

REFERENCES

Available upon request.

CHRIS SMITH, D.M.D.
178 Green Street
Bellingham, WA 98225
(206) 555-5555
csmith@e-mail.com

EXPERIENCE

2007–Present   **Owner—General Practice**
ZILAH DENTAL ASSOCIATES   **Bellingham, WA**
- Purchased large dental practice through a leveraged buyout.
- Determined and successfully implemented long-term growth strategies.
- Supervised a staff consisting of two other dentists and six support personnel; providing comprehensive care for over 2,000 patients.
- Doubled practice's growth through the implementation of a strategic marketing program.
- Led the office in steadily increasing production and revenues.
- Updated practice and computerized equipment.
- Presently facilitating transition of practice to new owner.

2006–2007   **Director/Dental Assistant**
                                                                   Unit/Clinical Instructor
SEATTLE UNIVERSITY DENTAL SCHOOL   **Seattle, WA**
- Supervised clinic with rotating groups of seven dental students and eight support personnel.
- Evaluated student performance, analyzed financial viability of clinic, and instituted plan to increase profitability.

2004–2006   **Dentist**
UNIFIED DENTAL CENTERS   **Moses Lake, WA**
- Provided comprehensive dental care and trained staff members.
- Allocated marketing budget.

2003   **Instructor of Clinical Periodontics**
UNIVERSITY OF WASHINGTON   **Seattle, WA**
- Supervised small groups of students during their first course with patients.
- Developed lesson plans, demonstrated periodontal procedures, and evaluated student performance.

EDUCATION

2000–2004   **UNIVERSITY OF WASHINGTON, SCHOOL OF DENTAL MEDICINE**   Seattle, WA
Chairman of Ethical Board, Director of Veterinary Dental Rotation, clinically rated top 5% of classes, American Student Dental Association Student Representative.

2002–2004   **SEATTLE TECH**   Seattle, WA
Bachelor of Science degree: Biology, 2002

Dietitian

CHRIS SMITH
178 Green Street
Atlanta, GA 30350
(404) 555-5555
csmith@e-mail.com

WORK EXPERIENCE:

Dietitian
Ellsworth Hospital, Atlanta, GA   **2006–Present**
- Confer with medical and multidisciplinary staffs.
- Prepare nutritional care plans.
- Interview patients.
- Maintain and document patients' medical records.
- Instruct patients and their families.
- Perform miscellaneous duties as a member of the hospital support team.

Dietary Aide
Bentley Nursing Home, Atlanta, GA   **2005–2006**
- Assisted in preparation of patient food trays.

Office Assistant
Morehouse College, Atlanta, GA   **2004–2005**
- Served as Receptionist for main office.

Library Assistant
Morehouse College Library   **Summer 2004**
- Worked in circulation and periodical sections.

EDUCATION:

Morehouse College, Atlanta, GA
B.S. degree, 2005
Major: Consumer and Family Studies
Minor: Sociology

RELEVANT COURSES:

Human Nutrition; Family Financial Decision-Making; Professional Preparation; Principles of Food I and II; The Four Food Groups; Interpersonal Communications; Social Psychology; Human Relations.

INTERNSHIP:

Dowdell County Extension Service, Atlanta, GA (Fall 2004)
- Wrote weekly food advice column, "Eat Up!"
- Developed chart and gave presentation on the major nutrients.

Emergency Medical Technician

CHRIS SMITH
178 Green Street
Visalia, CA 93291
(209) 555-5555
csmith@e-mail.com

QUALIFICATIONS

- Work well under pressure in crisis situations.
- Thorough knowledge of all Emergency Medical procedures.
- Certified, CPR and Heimlich Methods of Resuscitation.
- Proven capabilities in adhering to standard methods of assisting in emergency childbirth and heart attacks.
- Demonstrated skills in application of dressings, including burn dressings, tourniquets, oxygen, and IVs.
- Familiar with procedures for critical burns, shock, gunshot wounds, and physical manifestations of child abuse and domestic battering.
- Provide emergency treatment for rape victims while staying within the guidelines of the law.
- Excellent knowledge of all main streets and secondary routes; strong sense of direction and map-reading abilities.

LICENSES/CERTIFICATIONS/TRAINING

Certified, EMT License	Visalia Hospital, 2005
License #4490223	State of California, 2005
Recertification Credits	California General Hospital, 2006

EMT EXPERIENCE

DOLAN AMBULANCE SERVICES — Visalia, CA
Head Emergency Medical Technician — 2005–Present
Provide emergency response and care to primarily elderly patients with bone fractures, strokes, heart attacks, and injuries sustained in falls. Assist in standard hospital and legal procedures for fatalities and post-mortem crisis management.

RUSSELL AMBULANCE SERVICES — Los Angeles, CA
Emergency Medical Technician — 2005–2005
Assist in providing emergency response to 911 calls; emergency care to patients involved in traffic accidents, heart attacks, strokes, falls, and industrial accidents.

Health Services Coordinator

CHRIS SMITH
178 Green Street
Charleston, SC 29411
(803) 555-5555
csmith@e-mail.com

PROFILE
More than ten years of office experience in hospital settings. Accurate, detail-oriented, and reliable. Excellent communication with strong customer service skills and ability to work effectively in high pressure environment. Skilled in grant writing. Excel in accounting, bookkeeping, and mathematical calculations.

EXPERIENCE

Resource Coordinator, THE BAPTIST HOSPITAL, Charleston, SC   5/06–Present
Create and implement statistical reports for nursing-home placement, utilizing spreadsheet software. Design a database file system to update nursing homes and rehabilitation facilities. Coordinate luncheons to introduce rehabilitation facilities and services to physicians. Work closely with physicians to identify patients who require referrals to long-term care facilities. Attend patient care rounds on all adult Med/Surg, and conduct psycho-social assessments. Meet with social workers and family members to discuss nursing home placement. Organize and implement system to coordinate appropriate community beds and organize two health-care teams. Coordinate discharges and maintain accurate records of referrals and transfers. Visit and identify all facilities.

Unit Coordinator, CHARLESTON CITY HOSPITAL, Charleston, SC   2004–2006
Supervised activities on hospital floor. Compiled and updated all medical records for patients; maintained all lab work and records. Received admissions and arranged discharges. Maintained inventory of supplies, and ordered when necessary.

Financial Coordinator, HALFWAY HOME, INC., Charleston, SC   2002–2004
Prepared payroll for sixty clients. Created and implemented new budget utilizing Excel. Designed file system for budget and performed accounting duties. Trained and supervised mentally disabled employees. Maintained and created job folder files for vendors. Processed purchase orders.

EDUCATION

FURMAN UNIVERSITY, Greenville, SC   2005–Present
B.S. in Human Services Management Candidate, 2007

CLEMSON UNIVERSITY, Clemson, SC   2004–2006
Business Administration Program, two years

COMPUTER SKILLS   Excel, Microsoft Word

CHRIS SMITH
178 Green Street
Decorah, IA 52101
(319) 555-5555
csmith@e-mail.com

OBJECTIVE

To secure a challenging and responsible position that utilizes my supervisory skills and Home Health Care experience.

EXPERIENCE

HOMECARE INCORPORATED Decorah, IA

2006–Present Case Administrator

Manage the daily clinical operation of CPMS (Clozaril Patient Management System), monitor laboratory results, and manage staff. Recruited to program at its infancy. Selected to develop, test, and implement new home care system.

- Coordinate patient services, including blood draws and drug delivery.
- Establish and maintain service schedule for staff consisting of RNs, LPNs, phlebotomists, and pharmacists.
- Assist in recruitment, selection, and evaluation of RNs and LPNs and phlebotomists.
- Administer training and orientation for clinical staff.
- Generate monthly Quality Assurance reports and audit records and computer files.
- Monitor and report lab results to physicians for review and documentation.
- Identify and resolve service-related incidents. Report and maintain record of incidence as described by quality assurance guidelines.
- Support marketing/sales teams of pharmaceutical companies.
- Assisted in selection and development of office/pharmacy.

2005 Nurse Clinician

Provided professional nursing support for home-bound patients in need of infusion therapy services.

- Worked closely with Nursing Supervisor, agency staff, and referring physicians.
- Attended to full range of patients, including those with AIDS.
- Provided patient, family/caregiver education.
- Educated members of nutrition support, oncology, and IV teams in providing professional services.

2001–2005 **SIOUX CITY HOSPITAL** Sioux City, IA

Staff nurse for the medical/surgical units.

- Responsible for assessment, planning, implementation, and evaluation for primary care patients.
- Acted as resource nurse for staff of a fifty-bed unit, with immediate responsibility for 12–15 patients.
- Supervised LPNs and ancillary staff.

EDUCATION

2001 SIOUX CITY HOSPITAL SCHOOL OF NURSING
Sioux City, IA

References Available Upon Request.

Lab Technician

CHRIS SMITH
178 Green Street
Hoxie, KS 67740
(913) 555-5555 (work)
(913) 555-5555 (home)
csmith@e-mail.com

OBJECTIVE:
Seeking a position as a TECHNICIAN/COORDINATOR that utilizes my skills and experience.

EXPERIENCE:

2005–
Present
KANSAS GENERAL HOSPITAL, Topeka, KS
Medical Media Technician Coordinator, 2002–Present
Coordinate, set up, and implement media services for hospital personnel and BU Medical School students and faculty. This includes supervising 3–8 Media Technicians. Complex medical and educational photography, processing, and slide-reel set-up. Set-up and direction of medical videos and video equipment. Set-up, operation, and demonstration of medical equipment to medical students. Diagnostic troubleshooting, coordination, and problem-solving. Departmental troubleshooting and problem-solving. Conduct Hematological and Seratological medical testing. Work closely with undergraduate and graduate medical students, interns, faculty, physicians, and hospital staff.

Laboratory Supervisor
Coordinated laboratory operations, including media technology, analysis of test results, reporting, and record keeping. Troubleshot and resolved departmental problems.

2002–2005 **Laboratory Technician**
DAMON CORPORATION, Shawnee Mission, KS
Conducted hematology and serology testing, as well as test sample photography. Recorded, analyzed, and communicated results to physicians, patients, and their families.

1999–2002 **Media Research Technician**
MAYFARB INSTITUTE, Wichita, KS
Produced synchronized audio and slide programs on medical and medical-educational topics. Conducted career research. Served as a reference and research guide for institute staff and Harvard Medical School affiliates.

EDUCATION:

B.A., Media and Communications, 1999

References Available Upon Request.

Medical Technologist

CHRIS SMITH
178 Green Street
Milwaukee, WI 53201
(414) 555-5555
csmith@e-mail.com

SUMMARY

A Certified Medical Technologist seeking a challenging position in a private industry setting.

PROFESSIONAL BACKGROUND

2005 to Present
MILWAUKEE HOSPITAL, Milwaukee, Wisconsin
Senior Medical Technologist
- Responsible for conducting laboratory tests and operating equipment at nights for all departments in hospital.
- Primary function with Chemistry and Hematology Departments.
- Data entry via CRT to obtain test results.

2003 to 2005
BIOCARE, Ashland, WI
Medical Technologist
- Conducted laboratory tests at Children's Hospital in Ladysmith, WI.
- Operated Nova for electrolytes, Coulters, and Fibrometer.

2000 to 2003
KIPLING HOSPITAL, Ripon, WI
Medical Technologist
- Conducted testing for several departments and operated Astra, Coagamate, and ELT.

1997 to 1999
DIALTEK, De Pere, WI
Medical Technologist
- Operated Coulters and utilized computer information in Hematology Department.
- Fielded calls for entire department.

1995 to 1997
AL KARTOUM, M.D., La Crosse, WI
Private Hematologist Intern
- Operated hematology laboratory using haemacount machine, leitz photometer, and EKG machine.

EDUCATIONAL BACKGROUND

UNIVERSITY OF WISCONSIN AT MADISON, Madison, WI
A.S. in Medical Technology, May 1996

PROFESSIONAL LICENSES

H.E.W. Certified Medical Technologist #3259050
Certified Laboratory Assistant #BID01359

Nurse
Cardiac

CHRIS SMITH
178 Green Street
Kingsport, TN 37660
(615) 555-5555
csmith@e-mail.com

PROFESSIONAL BACKGROUND
Danforth Women's Hospital, Knoxville, KY
Charge Nurse—C.T.I.C.U. and C.T.P.C.U. (Cardio-Thoracic Intensive and Progressive Care Units), 2005–2006
- Conducted development staff meetings.
- Supervised and evaluated all staff.
- Coordinated ICU (ten beds) and PCU (fifteen beds).
- Performed respective audits and monthly documentations.

Staff Nurse—Heart Transplant Unit, 2007–2008
- Participated in Clinical Practice and Staff Education Committees.
- Wrote standards for nursing practice, stages approximately for various levels of experience with emphasis on setting objectives for improvement; held monthly meetings to evaluate performance of department; targeted problem areas and set up resolutions.
- Conducted seminar on Patient Presentation and Utilization of the Nursing Process and on Pacemaker Care.
- Invited to guest-lecture at Centre College. Gave presentation on "Care of the Patient with a Cardiac Valve Replacement."

Centre College, Danville, KY, 2005–2007
Clinical Instructor
- Supervised third year nursing students in medical/surgical/clinical setting.
- Taught clinical approach to cardiovascular physiological nursing one hour per week.

EDUCATION

Registered in Nursing, 2005
University of Colorado, Boulder
Bachelor of Science, Nursing, 2004
- Dean's List, 3.5/4.0 GPA.
- Participated in departmental meetings and briefings to insure effective interaction between UCB nursing students and City of Boulder personnel.
- Compiled and submitted proposals to the city government; stated objectives, targeted population, and projected budget and benefits program.
- Coordinated with American Heart and Lung Association, American Cancer Society, and Boulder City Hospital to facilitate set-up of equipment and placement and staffing of stations for dissemination of Health Awareness materials.
- Post-project evaluation and statistical analysis.

CHRIS SMITH
178 Green Street
Cherry Fork, OH 45618
(513) 555-5555
csmith@e-mail.com

SUMMARY OF QUALIFICATIONS:

Intensive Care Unit
- Working closely with recently graduated interns at major metropolitan trauma certified hospital.
- Accurate reporting and recording of lab values with follow-up medical treatment.
- Recognizing life threatening arrhythmias and means of treatment for patients placed on cardiac monitors.

Post Anesthesia Care Unit
- Caring for arterial lines, monitoring BP and MAP, drawing arterial blood gases and other labs, and interpreting and reporting abnormal values to physician for medical management.
- Providing specialized nursing and medical care in seventeen-bed unit for anesthetized patients following surgical procedures in the operating room.
- Calculating and recording cardiac output SVR and cardiac indexes.

EDUCATION:

UNIVERSITY OF CINCINNATI, Cincinnati, OH
Bachelor of Science in Nursing (1999)

MUSKINGUM COLLEGE HOSPITAL, New Concord, OH
Trauma Certificate (2006), Critical Care Course (2004)

EXPERIENCE:

OHIO STATE UNIVERSITY HOSPITAL, Columbus, OH
Staff Nurse, Post Anesthesia Care Unit and Trauma Unit
(10/05–Present)
Night Charge Nurse, making assignments and utilizing on-call nurses when necessary. Trauma certified for major trauma unit in the City of Columbus. PACU often turned into ICU for patients unable to get an ICU bed in high crime area location. Experience in treating patients recovering from surgery for gunshot and stab wounds.

Staff Nurse, Medical Respiratory Intensive Care Unit

VIRTUE HOSPITAL, Dayton, OH
Nursing Internship, Medical-Surgical Unit (8/03–10/05)
Nurse's Aide (7/02–8/03)

REFERENCES:

Excellent references available upon request.

Nurse
Medical/Surgical

CHRIS SMITH
178 Green Street
Boston, MA 02115
(617) 555-5555
csmith@e-mail.com

PROFESSIONAL OBJECTIVE
A position as a professional Registered Nurse in Medical/Surgical, Intensive Care, Emergency Room, and/or Ambulatory arenas.

SUMMARY OF QUALIFICATIONS
- Specialize in ventilators, tracheotomy care, burn patients with extensive dressings, and IV therapy.
- Expertise in coordinating discharge planning and home care with doctors, nutritionists, physical therapists, occupational therapists, and social workers; strong on documentation and follow-through.
- Outstanding interpersonal and communication skills.
- Proven written and teaching/demonstration skills for extensive education regarding tracheotomies for in-home care.
- Coproduced educational videos for new staff with specialized information.

PROFESSIONAL EXPERIENCE
2006–Present **BOSTON HOSPITAL, Boston, MA**   **Staff Nurse, R.N.**
Thoracic Surgery
- Coordinating staffing issues, budget responsibilities, and QA monitoring.
- Attend workshops, coproduce and act in educational videos; write working brochures for patients and families.
- Perform primary nursing care; communicate directly with doctors and other health care professionals.
- Participate in extensive post-op care with multiple problems.
- Deal directly with the families regarding hospital policies.

2004–2006 **ST. JOAN'S HOSPITAL, Medfield, MA**   **Professional Registered Nurse**
- As Charge Nurse, provided leadership of forty-bed Medical/Surgical unit with telemetry and provided IV therapy.
- As LPN, employed direct patient care with administration of medications.

EDUCATION

UNIVERSITY OF MASSACHUSETTS, Amherst, MA
B.S. in Nursing, Graduated 2007 with Nursing GPA of 3.2/4.0.

DEAN JUNIOR COLLEGE, Franklin, MA
A.S. in Nursing and Applied Science, Graduated 2004.

Major Course Work:
Nursing Research Seminar—Focusing on qualitative, quantitative, and historic research methodology pertaining to nursing.
Community Health Nursing—A study on community and family environment.
Nursing Leadership and Management—An emphasis on nursing administration and budgetary responsibilities.

CHRIS SMITH
178 Green Street
Lodi, CA 95240
(209) 555-5555
csmith@e-mail.com

SUMMARY

- **Psychogeriatric Nurse:** Progressively responsible and sophisticated clinical nursing experience; including responsibilities as Geriatric, Orthopedic, Plastic Surgery, Ophthalmology, Acute Medical, General Surgical, and Medical-Surgical Nurse in Hospital, Clinical, and Professional Health Care settings.
- **Bachelor of Science Degree, Nursing and Psychology,** with continuing education toward a Master's Degree.
- Expertise includes patient care involving both pharmacological and behavioral modification methods of treatment, as well as for drug and alcohol abuse, congestive heart failure, hospice care, pulmonary disease, and other severe medical or psychological conditions.

PROFESSIONAL NURSING EXPERIENCE

2004–Present   Midvale Counseling Services
PSYCHOGERIATRIC NURSE CLINICIAN   Lodi, CA

- Psychiatric and Psychological Counseling Center specializing in a full range of Mental Health Services. Service various area geriatric facilities in the provision of individual therapy for up to forty geriatric residents, groups, and family members/week for depression, llfestyle adjustment, grieving, and other physical and psychosocial needs.
- Perform medication assessments and consult with physicians about medication regimens. Provide nurse teaching and support services for staff regarding the identification and meeting of patient medical and psycho-social needs.

1999–2004   Unified Medical Center
RN/EVENING CHARGE   Fresno, CA

- Supervised up to eight, while responsible for forty-five-bed unit in this health care facility specializing in care for severe med-stress patients. Responsibilities encompassed admission assessment and care planning, including behavior modification and limit setting.
- Worked closely with Osteopathic Physicians and Psychiatric Staff in the care and assessment of patients requiring treatment for drug and alcohol abuse, manic depression, and acute psychosis.

EDUCATION

Berlin College of Nursing, Green Bay, WI
Bachelor of Science degree 1999

Nursing Administrator

CHRIS SMITH
178 Green Street
Providence, RI 02903
(401) 555-5555
csmith@e-mail.com

PROFESSIONAL EXPERIENCE

2006–Present VISITING NURSE ASSOCIATION OF PROVIDENCE, Providence, RI
Supervisor of Specialty Home Health Aides
Supervised forty HHAs who care for pediatric patients with HIV.

2003–2006 **Reimbursement Specialist,** Northeast and Providence District Offices
Managed and evaluated all clinical documentation for Medicare and all third party related Medicare payers. Worked in cooperation with managers, clinicians, patients' accounts, and clerical staff to ensure quality documentation.

2000–2003 **Staff Nurse**
Provided skilled nursing assessment of primary patients and family needs. Utilized appropriate resource personnel and agencies in a collaborative effort to provide continuity of care to patient and family. Worked with liaison nurses to discharge patients to home with appropriate services and realistic expectation of third party reimbursement payers.

1999–2000 RHODE ISLAND PARAMEDICAL REGISTRY, Providence, RI
Visiting Nurse
Responsible for the home care of chronically ill children to give the primary caretakers physical and emotional respite.

1998–1999 THE CHILDREN'S HOSPITAL, Cranston, RI
Staff Nurse in cardiovascular/surgical intensive care unit. Provided surgical and medical management of critically ill children in collaborative effort with medical team. Supported parents and provided discharge teaching for comprehensive home care utilizing primary nursing.

1995–1997 KINGSTON HOSPITAL, Kingston, RI
Staff Nurse in pediatrics with charge responsibilities for a twenty-bed ICU. Provided surgical and medical treatment for children ages 3–17 years. Incorporated levels of development and psychological needs in teaching discharge goals. Counseled parents about disease process and child's needs.

EDUCATION

SALVE REGINA COLLEGE, Newport, RI, B.S. in Nursing; Graduated 1994.
Summer Externship, Rollins Hospital, Orlando, FL, 1993.

Nursing Home Manager

CHRIS SMITH, MSW, LICSW
178 Green Street
Sandy Springs, SC 29677
(803) 555-5555
csmith@e-mail.com

PROFESSIONAL EXPERIENCE

Haversham Home, Sandy Springs, SC

Nursing Home Manager   2006–Present

- Coordinate provisions of home care for elderly as part of state-funded program.
- Train, supervise, develop, support, and review staff of seven to eight managers.
- Review service plans for appropriations, cost, and compliance with DEA regulations.
- Determine client eligibility by need, age, and finances.
- Act as liaison to service providers and community agencies.
- Lead group meetings with case managers.
- Plan and implement training programs; serve as member of Training Committee.

Case Manager   2002–2006

- Developed comprehensive service plans for elderly clients; assessed needs, determined eligibility.
- Coordinated in-home care, oversaw provision of all aspects of care.
- Advocated for client in obtaining benefits and services; identified available services.
- Administered case load of eighty to ninety; prepared individual case records and reports.

The Department of Youth Services, Suffolk, VA

Social Worker   2000–2002

- Performed casework, community service work, outreach, individual and family crisis counseling, and coordination with community agencies.

EDUCATION

Licensed Independent Clinical Social Worker, October 2000

Master of Social Work, 1999
University of California, Davis, CA

Bachelor of Arts in Social Studies, 1997
University of Dubuque, Dubuque, IA

Nursing Supervisor

CHRIS SMITH
178 Green Street
Giants Pass, OR 97526
(503) 555-5555
csmith@e-mail.com

AREAS OF EXPERTISE

- Policy and Procedures Development.
- Budget Preparation and Implementation.
- Development of and instruction in formal education training programs.
- Administration and supervision of patient care department.
- Development of education/training of auxiliary staffs.
- Personnel Recruitment/Administration (licensed/non-licensed).
- Direct Patient Care (medical/surgical).
- Geriatrics (long term/community care).

EXPERIENCE

Brixton Life Care Center
Director of Nursing Services   *2005–Present*

- Coordinate and direct all services related to direct patient care. Coordinate outpatient services rendering the life care residents in conjunction with director of Resident Care Services.
- Actively participate in all admission and discharge planning.
- Coordinate and oversee emergency services through the facility Digitizer (call service between the Life Center apartments and the medical building).
- Formed and actively participate in Restorative Service Committee for coordination of Rehabilitative Services.

Treehill Clinic
Director of Nursing Services   *2002–2005*

- Troubleshot and upgraded facility to a Level I–II (skilled care). Brought facility to successful relicensure.
- Hired a Staff Development Coordinator; reorganized and expanded staff to 130 licensed and non-licensed personnel including new supervisors. Enforced ongoing policies and procedures with regard to maintaining continuity with supplemental staff.

Day Supervisor   *1999–2002*

- Supervised delivery of patient care, including management and supervision of licensed and non-licensed personnel in this 200-bed geriatric, long-term, multilevel skilled facility.

EDUCATION

Colby College School of Nursing, Waterville, ME
Bachelor of Science in Nursing with Honors, 1999

Georgia School of Nursing, Atlanta, GA
Graduated, 1995 – Registered Nurse

CERTIFICATION

ANA—Certification Nursing Administration, 2000

Occupational Therapist

CHRIS SMITH
178 Green Street
Topeka, KS 66621
(913) 555-5555
csmith@e-mail.com

OBJECTIVE To contribute excellent treatment planning skills to the position of **Staff Occupational Therapist.**

EXPERIENCE

2006 to Present
DIXON REHABILITATION CENTER   Hillsboro, KS
- Independently assessed clients with stroke and head trauma, ages ten to sixty.
- Initiated individual client treatment clinical therapy, utilizing standard disability interventions and physical management techniques.
- Monitored, identified, and resolved client behavioral problems.
- Participated in rehab and clinical rounds and family conferences.
- Co-led a shopping and community re-entry group.
- Facilitated community field trips.
- Performed client treatment, notation, billing, statistical recording, and assisted in training of O.T. Aide, on a daily basis.

2004–2006
WILD THORN CHILDREN'S CENTER   Sterling, KS
- Functioned as dyadic group leader for E.D. pre-adolescents with diagnoses of conduct, personality, and affective disorders.
- Structured developmental group with parallel/project format utilizing cooking, games, leather, and woodworking modalities.
- Observed, monitored, and reported individual group interaction.
- Drafted weekly progress notes.

2001–2004
CURTIS SCHOOL FOR THE BLIND   Wichita, KS
- Evaluated, planned, and established individual treatment interventions for clients with congenital disabilities and MR, Rubella, CP, Lepers, and FTT diagnoses.
- Utilized Neurodevelopmental, Biomechanical, SI, and Developmental methods.
- Coordinated program aids to implement treatment and documented quarterly progress notes.

EDUCATION

NEW YORK UNIVERSITY, College of Allied Health   New York, NY
Master of Science degree: Occupational Therapy, 2001 GPA: 3.8/4.0
Merit Scholarship, NYU College of Allied Health, 2001
Selected as Student Speaker for annual NYOT Conference, 2000

PROFESSIONAL AFFILIATIONS

Member—American Occupational Therapy Association
Member—Kansas Association for Occupational Therapists

Optician

Chris Smith
178 Green Street
Los Angeles, CA 90066
(213) 555-5555
csmith@e-mail.com

CAREER OBJECTIVE

A challenging Senior Level/Management position as a **Ophthalmic Dispensing Optician.**

SUPPORTIVE QUALIFICATIONS

- Expertise in every optical environment: Private Practice, Optometric Practice, Large Retail Outlets, Ophthalmological Groups, and large eye-specialty hospital.
- Broad-based knowledge of multidiscipline opticianary, low vision, binocular telescopes, microscopes, pediatric and geriatric opticianary, and specialty lens designs.
- Extensive knowledge of the latest technology in lens designs.
- Fellow, National Academy of Opticians; California State Optician Licensed.

HIGHLIGHTS OF PROFESSIONAL EXPERIENCE

2004–Present   Los Angeles Eye Infirmary, Los Angeles, CA
Director of Optical Services
- Ensured adherence to hospital, state, and federal guidelines.
- Prepared financial reports; designed department budget.
- Responsible for purchasing of all lenses and frames.
- Supervised staff of five.

Accomplishments
- Redesigned entire optical shop, laboratory, and dispensary.
- Updated equipment to state-of-the-art machinery.
- Cut turnaround time by 75%.
- Consistently stayed within or well under designated budget.
- Completely revamped line of inventory to more updated line of frames.
- Responsible for bringing outside clientele to hospital optical facility for the express use of our services.

1999–2004   THE PUPIL PLANET, Santa Ana, CA
Optician
- Quality control, dispensing eyeglasses, and frame sales.
- Contact lens fittings.

1995–1999   DIPIETRO OPTICAL COMPANY, Los Angeles, CA
Optician
- Laboratory work.
- Eyeglass dispensing; stock control.

MILITARY

U.S. AIR FORCE—Three years Optical Lab Technician—Honorably Discharged.

EDUCATION

BURBANK COMMUNITY COLLEGE, Burbank, CA, A.S. Ophthalmic Dispensing, Graduated 1995.

Pediatrician

CHRIS SMITH, M.D.
178 Green Street
Washington, D.C. 20020
(202) 555-5555
csmith@e-mail.com

PROFESSIONAL OBJECTIVE

Admittance into the Internal Medicine Residency Program of a teaching hospital.

SUMMARY OF QUALIFICATIONS

- Fifteen years of professional experience in Pediatrics/Emergency Medicine.
- Six years as Emergency Room Physician including one year as Chief of the Department.
- Four years of experience as President of a freestanding emergency medical and surgical service.
- Completed American Board of Quality Assurance and Utilization Review examinations.
- Developed and directed a medical and support staff serving approximately 5,000 families.
- Currently Senior Resident—Washington D.C. Medical Center.
- Board eligible in General Pediatrics, 2005.

EXPERIENCE

SENIOR RESIDENT   2005–Present
Washington D.C. Medical Center, Washington, D.C.

- Monitored intensive care, emergency, and inpatient services.
- Supervised staff of fifteen including residents, interns, and medical students.
- During day assignments, supervised three interns and six medical students (pediatric ward) with indirect responsibility for surgical patients. Extensive bedside teaching, rounds, conferences, and lectures.
- Conducted research on intensive care on Validation of Admitting Leprosy Patients into Intensive Care. Developed a Quality Assurance Plan for the Department of Pediatrics.
- Board Eligible in General Pediatrics, September 2005.

PEDIATRICIAN   1993–2005
R. MacDonald and Smith, Inc., Washington, D.C.

- Since 1993, established and developed a health care delivery practice for infants, children, and adolescents. Directed a staff of twenty nurses and administrative support personnel providing services for approximately 5,000 families.
- *Note:* Liquidated practice to accept Senior Residency Program.

PRESIDENT   1998–2002
Emergency Medical and Surgical Service of the Capitol, Washington, D.C.

- In conjunction with three other physicians, planned, organized, and directed a freestanding emergency center. Center successfully grew to employ a support staff of eighty, including associate physicians, nurses, technicians, and administrative personnel.
- Selected site, equipped, staffed, and expanded the Center into a total self-contained operation including: laboratory, x-ray, fluoroscopy, occupational medicine, emergency room, and other health care services. Center was an 8 A.M. to 11 P.M., seven-day week operation which serviced from 200–300 patients per day.

(continued)

- In addition to direct medical care, monitored financing, budgets, personnel, and related business management activities.
- In 2002, resigned and liquidated holdings to concentrate on rapidly growing private practice.

CHIEF OF THE DEPARTMENT OF EMERGENCY MEDICINE/
EMERGENCY ROOM PHYSICIAN 1993–1998
Memorial Hospital, Washington, D.C.
- Functions included all aspects of emergency patient care including physician and nurse coordination in both adult and pediatric care. Handled approximately 80,000 emergency visits per year.
- **As Chief of the Department of Emergency Medicine (1997–1998), and Emergency Room Physicians,** was also responsible for quality assurance, utilization reviews, administrative functions, and financial control.

EDUCATION
American University, Washington, D.C.
Master of Public Health 1992
Area of concentration: Maternal and Child Care

Children's Hospital, Washington, D.C.
Pediatric Internship/Residency 1986–1989
Palona Istak Award, Department of Pediatrics

Valparaiso University, Valparaiso, IN
Doctor of Medicine, 1986
B.A., Chemistry, 1984

PROFESSIONAL ASSOCIATIONS AND ACTIVITIES
Member—American College of Utilizations Review Physicians
Member—American Medical Society
Member—Cook County Medical Society
Certified by National Board of Medical Examiners, 1992

Pharmacist

CHRIS SMITH
178 Green Street
Lafayette, LA 70504
(318) 555-5555
csmith@e-mail.com

PROFESSIONAL EXPERIENCE

2004 to Present   **Pharmacist**
ZERTEX ALLIED HEALTH SERVICES   Lafayette, LA
- Review and fill prescriptions and enter orders in computer.
- Coordinate total intravenous therapy program for nursing homes.
- Supervise staff and conduct purchasing procedures.
- Provide consultation for patients and nursing home staff on drug therapy and regulations.
- Simultaneously coordinate hospital and retail pharmacy services.

2002 to 2004   **Pharmacist**
BEAUCHAMPS HOSPITAL   New Orleans, LA
- Dispensed drugs to and counseled inpatients and outpatients.
- Advised professional staff regarding drug information, interactions, etc.
- Trained new technicians in pharmacy computer operations.
- Assisted in decentralization of pharmacy services.
- Distributed unit doses, prepared intravenous and chemotherapy admixtures.
- Assisted in inventory control and performed various related duties.

2000 to 2002   **Clinical Pharmacy Clerkship**
VETERAN'S HOSPITAL   Baton Rouge, LA
- Worked with team of physicians and other health professionals on rotation through various hospital departments.

1999 to 2000   **Pharmacy Extern**
CUPID'S PHARMACY   Natchitoches, LA
- Assisted in the provision of pharmacy services, including: dispensation of medications, advising patients on usage of prescription and nonprescription drugs, monitoring patient profiles for interactions, medication compliances, inappropriate therapy, etc.
- Assisted in the processing and pricing of third-party prescription reimbursement claims.

EDUCATION

Bachelor of Science degree: Pharmacy, 2000
TULANE UNIVERSITY   New Orleans, LA
Louisiana Registered Pharmacist #34217
Georgia Registered Pharmacist #36954

PROFESSIONAL DEVELOPMENT AND AFFILIATIONS

Member—Louisiana Society of Hospital Pharmacy.

Pharmacy Technician

CHRIS SMITH
178 Green Street
Moss Point, MS 39563
(601) 555-5555
csmith@e-mail.com

QUALIFICATIONS:

- Experience includes large metropolitan hospital, smaller community hospital, and retail experience.
- Skilled in all aspects of medication preparation and pharmacy operations.
- Excellent knowledge of medications/pharmaceuticals.
- Strong communication skills; computer experience.

EXPERIENCE:

2006–Present **Pharmacy Technician**
KENSINGTON MEDICAL CENTER, Moss Point, MS
Perform pharmacy functions for satellite pharmacy serving the surgical and medical floors (100 beds). Pick up and enter orders on computer. Fill and deliver orders. Check and replenish medical carts. Maintain narcotics controls, deliver IVs. Maintain computerized inventory controls and conduct monthly medication room audits. Communicate with physicians, nurses, and administrative personnel.

2001–2006 **Pharmacy Technician**
LAUREL GENERAL HOSPITAL, Laurel, MS
Full range of hospital (seventy-five beds) and convalescent (100 beds) pharmacy responsibilities. Utilized computerized pharmacy system and administrative and documentation procedures. Prepared new medication and IV orders for hospital and convalescent families. Prepared upkeep of daily orders for patient charts and MARS including allergies, special procedures, diet, treatments, lab procedures, and diagnosis. Recorded strengths and dosages on "patient profile" forms. Priced and organized incoming stock. Prepared daily physician's orders, MARS, month-end, and Department of Welfare reports and forms. Communicated with pharmaceutical reps.

1998–2001 **Pharmacy Technician**
ST. MARTHA'S HOSPITAL, Jackson, MS
Filled medicine orders and recorded strengths and amounts on "patient profile" forms. Priced and organized incoming stock, prepared invoices for payment, and interacted with pharmaceutical reps. Prepared Department of Welfare forms and maintained accurate, long-term patient files.

1996–1998 **Pharmacy Clerk**
THE MERIDIAN CENTER, Pascagoula, MS
Received in-person and telephone orders for prescriptions. Conferred with physicians regarding accuracy and clarification on prescriptions. Maintained invoice and inventory information. Prepared Department of Welfare Forms. Updated *Physician's Desk Reference*. Shared bookkeeping and general office responsibilities. Position required customer service and communication skills.

EDUCATION:

Mississippi State University at Starkville
B.S. in Pharmaceutical Procedure, 1995

Physical Therapist
Orthopedic

CHRIS SMITH
178 Green Street
Franklin, IN 46131
(317) 555-5555
csmith@e-mail.com

PROFESSIONAL OBJECTIVE
A career opportunity in PHYSICAL THERAPY.

CLINICAL EXPERIENCE
MIDWEST MEMORIAL HOSPITAL, Indianapolis, IN
Orthopedic In- and Out-Patient Clinic   2005–2006
* Develop treatment plan for ten-patient caseload.
* Work extensively with chronic pain and cardiac patients.
* Present in service on hip and knee prostheses.

DEARBORN COUNTY HOSPITAL, Richmond, IN
Cardiac Rehabilitation   2003–2005
* Acted as program coordinator for exercise regimen.
* Provided individualized treatments using modalities such as ultrasound, electric stimulation, massage therapy, and stretching/strengthening exercises.
* Coordinated aquadynamics program for chronic pain patients.

CINNAMON MOUNTAIN, Mishawaka, IN
Pediatric Rehabilitation   2001–2003
* Coordinated the treatment of amputee children and children with congenital birth defects; created the "Alive with Pride" program that is now functional at thirty national hospitals.
* Encouraged regular exercise by developing child-oriented play program.
* Directed teacher workshops at local elementary schools.

EDUCATIONAL BACKGROUND
INDIANA UNIVERSITY, Bloomington, IN
Bachelor of Science in Physical Therapy, 2005
Awarded Indiana University Scholarship
Course work included Pediatric Therapy

GOSHEN COLLEGE, Goshen, IN
Biology Major; Chemistry, French, Calculus, 2002–2003

SPECIAL PRACTICUM
INDIANA UNIVERSITY, Bloomington, IN
* Performed independent research evaluating back and shoulder strength of musicians who were suffering from tendonitis or bursitis.
* Presented findings to Physical Therapy Department; later published in the *Indiana Journal of Medicine* (vol. X, pp. 20–24, August 2005).

Psychiatrist

EDUCATION

Harvard University Medical School, Cambridge, MA
M.D., 2000

University of Massachusetts, Boston, MA
B.S., Pre-Med, 1996

CERTIFICATION/PROFESSIONAL AFFILIATIONS

Certified by the Commonwealth of Massachusetts

American Medical Association
Massachusetts Psychiatric Society
Greater Boston Psychiatric Society
Council of the American Psychiatric Association

PUBLICATIONS

American Journal of Medicine, August 12, 2005. Volume 9.
"Correlations of Neurological Biomechanics and Headaches."
New England Journal of Medicine, May 30, 2006. Volume 19, Issue 5.
"Further Effects of Prozac on Depressed People."

PROFESSIONAL HISTORY

Borewood Hospital, Framingham, MA
On-Call Psychiatrist, 2005–Present

- Assist permanent staff with severely ill psychiatric patients as needed.
- Sit in on individual and group therapy. Attend staff meetings. Dispense medication.
- Responsible for administrative reporting and preliminary diagnoses as needed.

Greater Boston Psychiatrics Center, Boston, MA
Psychiatrist, 2000–Present

- Provide outpatient psychiatric care to patients in low-income households and dispense medication as necessary.
- Provide treatment for grieving patients who have lost a spouse or child.
- Participate in group therapy sessions at Veterans Administration Hospital, Jamaica Plain; assisting Vietnam and Desert Storm veterans with post-traumatic stress syndrome.
- Provide information for insurance companies, HMOs, and third-party billing staff.

Respiratory Therapist

CHRIS SMITH
178 Green Street
Wellesley, MA 02181
(617) 555-5555
csmith@e-mail.com

PROFILE:
Demonstrated extensive professional achievement in not only respiratory therapy but also in the organization and coordination of the administrative end of the Respiratory Therapy Division of Massachusetts General Hospital.

Areas of Strength:

Highly Organized	Pleasant Bedside Manner	Strong Work Ethic
Creative Problem Solver	Crisis Management	Administration

EXPERIENCE:
Massachusetts General Hospital, Boston, MA
Respiratory Therapy Division Administrator   2004–Present
- Responsible for smooth running and operation of Respiratory Division.
- Handle all incoming information from physicians, surgeons, other hospitals, and HMOs.
- Interview, hire, and train RT Division staff; evaluate and write personnel reports.
- Administer RT on the floor as necessary; assist anesthesiologist and physicians during surgery.

Respiratory Therapist   1992–2003
- Responsible for daily suctioning of vented patients, checking arterial blood gases.
- Administer inhalers and nebulizer treatments.
- Recommend therapies and Bi-pap vents.
- Set up and secure trach-masks.
- Work with doctors and specialists listening to breath sounds; auscultate breath sounds.

EDUCATION:

Simmons College	Boston, MA
B.S., Nursing	1989

Massachusetts General Hospital School of Continuing Medical Education	Boston, MA
Respiratory Therapy Training	**Certified R.T.,** 1991

AFFILIATIONS:
New England Society for Respiratory Therapists

Speech Pathologist

CHRIS SMITH
178 Green Street
Providence, RI 02918
(401) 555-5555
csmith@e-mail.com

EDUCATION

Brown University, Providence, RI
Master of Education in Human Development and Reading, 1997
Cape Town University, Cape Town, South Africa
Bachelor of Arts with Honors in Speech Pathology and Audiology, 1994

PROFESSIONAL EXPERIENCE

2001 to Present ST. CHRISTOPHER'S HOSPITAL, Providence, RI
Clinical Supervisor, Bennet Hospital Satellite Speech and Language Program
- Started and directed Speech and Language Program under aegis of Bennet Hospital.
- Market program; designed brochure, performed on radio talk shows, administer all advertising.
- Provide in-service consultation to hospital staff, students, various agencies, and organizations.
- Hire, supervise, orient, instruct, and discipline employees, graduate students, and clinical fellows.
- Conduct quality assurance; appraise performance.
- Evaluate, diagnose, and treat inpatients/outpatients, adults/children with variety of communication disorders.
- Provide supportive and educational counseling.
- Develop policies and procedures, perform various managerial and administrative tasks.
- Perform Speech, Hearing, and Language screening.
- Develop augmentative communication systems for non-verbal population.
- Conduct aural rehabilitation for elderly.

1998–2001 BENNET HOSPITAL, Providence, RI
Staff Speech-Language Pathologist, Speech, Hearing, and Language Center
- Evaluated, diagnosed, and treated inpatients/outpatients, adults/children with variety of communication disorders including: apraxia, aphasia, dysarthria, head injury, fluency, voice, neurological impairments, language, mental retardation, phonology, laryngectomy, dialectical variances, hearing impairments, cleft palate, and cerebral palsy.
- Ran preschool language group.
- Participated on Stroke Team.
- Provided in-service consultation to staff and agencies.

1995–1998 PRIVATE PRACTICE, Cape Town, South Africa
Speech Pathologist
- Assessed, diagnosed, and treated adults and children exhibiting variety of communication disorders.
- Conferred with physicians and schools.
- Provided supportive/educational parent counseling.

CHRIS SMITH, M.D.
178 Green Street
Providence, RI 02903
(401) 555-5555
csmith@e-mail.com

EXPERIENCE

PROVIDENCE GENERAL HOSPITAL, Providence, RI
Staff Heart Surgeon
Appointed May 2003

RESEARCH EXPERIENCE

2004   INSTITUTE OF CHILD CARE, Harvard University, Cambridge, MA
Worked within Department of Developmental Anatomy. Conducted research on cardiac anatomy and pathology. Research led to awarding of Master of Science degree in Medicine.

2003   DEPARTMENT OF ANATOMY, University of Rhode Island, Kingston, RI
Conducted histochemical research on the urinary tract.

2002   MAXWELL HOSPITAL, Davis, CA
Conducted research on cardiac anatomy, within the Cardiac Anatomy Laboratory.

2000   CHILDREN'S HOSPITAL, Davis, CA
Conducted part-time research in cardiac pathology.

1997 to   STANFORD UNIVERSITY, Stanford, CA
1999   Received general surgical training, at Burnt Oak Hospital, General Hospital, and Abbey Road Hospital.

1990 to   CHILDREN'S HOSPITAL, Pepperdine Medical School, Malibu, CA
1994   As a medical student, performed research on congenital heart disease during elective periods.

EDUCATION

2002   UNIVERSITY OF CALIFORNIA, Davis, CA
1999   STANFORD UNIVERSITY, Stanford, CA
1996   PEPPERDINE UNIVERSITY, Malibu, CA
Doctor of Medicine Degree, M.D.

POST-GRADUATE TRAINING

2000–2002   Surgical Residency: City Hospital, Davis, CA
1997–1999   Surgical Internship: Good Fellow Hospital, Stanford, CA

LICENSURE

Rhode Island #MD-075261-E
Board Eligible: General Surgery/8

Veterinary Assistant

CHRIS SMITH
178 Green Street
Marylhurst, OR 97036
(503) 555-5555
csmith@e-mail.com

OBJECTIVE
To obtain a position as an Animal Health Technician.

EXPERIENCE

PIAGETTI ANIMAL CARE CLINIC   Marylhurst, OR
Neonatal Intensive Care Nurse   2003–Present
- Monitor patients and schedule work, personnel, and supplies.
- Perform pre- and post-operative care and emergency care.
- Collect and ship blood samples.
- Organize labs for veterinary students and for clinical instruction.
- Monitor ventilation and vital statistics of premature and critically ill animals.
- Collect blood, perform intravenous and arterial catheterization. Intubation of endotracheal and nasogastric tubes.
- Member of Emergency Ventilation Team.

Surgery Staff Nurse   2004–2006
Administered pre- and post-operative surgical care.
- Prepared animals for surgery.
- Administered antibiotics.

Rotating Staff Nurse   2003–2004
- Assisted clinicians and students in treatment of patients.
- Room nursing: pre- and post-operative management of patients.

CERTIFICATIONS
Licensed Animal Health Technician, 2003
Veterinary Medicine, University of Portland, 2005
Applied Dentistry for Veterinary Technicians, 2005

EDUCATION
University of Oregon, Eugene, OR
B.A. Animal Health Technology, 2002

University of Portland, Portland, OR
A.S. Animal Health Technology, 2000

Assistant Vice President of Human Resources

CHRIS SMITH
178 Green Street
Longview, TX 75601
(903) 555-5555
csmith@e-mail.com

PROFESSIONAL EXPERIENCE

RENFIELD CORPORATION, Longview, TX   2006–Present
Assistant Vice President—Human Resources
Responsible for professional recruitment, human resources planning, benefits and compensation, employee relations, EEO/AA compliance and reporting, and service quality consultation.
- Spearhead a project team for the development of a home for runaways.
- Evaluated the effectiveness of thirty incentive pay plans, recommending changes tied to service quality and saving over $3 million in unproductive payouts.
- Reduced professional staffing costs by 10%, saving $400,000.

PHINEAS COMPANY, Killeen, TX   2001–2006
Director of Human Resources
Professionalized the human resources function by more cost-effective recruiting, designing a formal compensation program, implementing a performance management process, and inaugurating management and employee training.
- Analyzed pay practices and designed a more appropriate compensation system, including an executive bonus plan, which was linked to performance goals, saving an estimated $300,000 in salary costs.

LANCOWSKI CORPORATION, U.S./Japan   1997–2001
Senior Consultant, Organization Effectiveness
Facilitated the implementation of Total Quality using employee involvement and supportive human resources systems; worked with executive and management teams in planning organization changes, and trained forty facilitators and 2,000 employee teams in quality and problem-solving processes.

EDUCATION
M.S. Industrial Relations/HR Management
New York University, New York, NY, 1996

B.A. Economics/Psychology
Eugene Lange College, New York, NY, 1994

PROFESSIONAL AFFILIATIONS
Southwest Human Resource Planners Group
Association for Management Excellence

SPECIAL ACCOMPLISHMENTS
Vice President and Cofounder of the Longview Quality Club.
Invited lecturer and adjunct faculty at two Longview universities.
Authored ten articles in leading professional journals and publications.
Elected member of the Executive Leadership Committee, 1999–2000.

Compensation Manager

CHRIS SMITH
178 Green Street
Portales, NM 88130
(505) 555-5555
csmith@e-mail.com

CAREER SUMMARY

A Human Resources Manager with extensive experience in maximizing corporate, team, and individual performance through progressive human processes. Diversified generalist experience in strategic human resource planning, employee relations, employment, compensation, training, and organizational development.

CAREER HISTORY

BANK OF NEW MEXICO, Portales, NM
Compensation Manager (2006–Present)
Managed the Compensation and Payroll functions, including Job Analysis, Salary Administration, Employee Payroll, and Personnel Records. Utilized the job evaluation system and implemented a total HRIS conversion.

Compensation Representative (2004–2006)
Provided employee relations support and consultation to three departments. Specific activities included development, implementation, and administration of compensation function. Responsible for all compensation activities, including position analysis and evaluation, benchmarking, salary surveys, and merit budget recommendations.

Employment Manager and Employee Relations Counselor (2003–2004)
Developed recruitment sources, college programs, internal staffing, outplacement, and provided employee counseling. Interpreted personnel policies for employee effectiveness.

M-N-M PLACEMENT AGENCY, Santa Fe, NM
Placement Counselor (2003–2004)
Recruited, screened, and placed candidates for permanent positions. Advertised, interviewed, and placed candidates for temporary assignments, as well as generated new business activity through cold sales calls.

EDUCATION

UNIVERSITY OF NEW MEXICO, Albuquerque, NM
B.A. Political Science, 2004

PERSONAL

Willing to relocate.

REFERENCES

Available upon request.

Employer Relations Representative

CHRIS SMITH
178 Green Street
Provo, UT 84604
(801) 555-5555
csmith@e-mail.com

CAREER HISTORY

2006 to Present   **DEPARTMENT OF EMPLOYMENT AND TRAINING**   Provo, UT
Supervisor

- Assign and review applications, placement, initial claims, and claims processing adjustments.
- Evaluate subordinate performance through both qualitative and quantitative analysis. Ensure compliance with established procedures.
- Recommend improvements in operations for enhanced public services.
- Supervise preparation and maintenance of statistical records. Ensure accurate reports.

2004 to 2006   **DEPARTMENT OF UNEMPLOYMENT**   Provo, UT
Claims Adjudicator

- Interviewed employers; gathered information; determined status in claims cases.
- Analyzed/interpreted Utah Employment Security Law to ensure information completeness.
- Verified/supplemented case data via file searches and data base assessment.
- Trained new personnel.
- Maintained weekly case log and purge files, ensuring timely handling.

2002 to 2004   **STEPHEN JOLIE JEWELS**   Sandy, UT
Assistant Manager

- Supervised/assisted with all facets of retail and wholesale operations.
- Hired, trained, scheduled, and supervised personnel.
- Prepared daily balances; managed cash.
- Planned and implemented in-store displays/promotions.
- Coordinated advertising with media outlets.

EDUCATION

SMITH COLLEGE, Northampton, MA
Bachelor's degree, Management 2002

AFFILIATIONS

- National Conference of Women—Secretary, 2004
- American Association of Business Managers, 2003–Present
- Smith College Alumni Association

Employment Consultant
Specialized

CHRIS SMITH
178 Green Street
Fort Worth, TX 76112
(817) 555-5555
csmith@e-mail.com

SUMMARY OF QUALIFICATIONS:

- Supervisory/administrative experience with educational, recreational, vocational, and community programs.
- Actively involved in programs to motivate, counsel, and tutor college freshmen.
- Superior communication skills and the ability to maintain cooperative spirit from individuals and groups of all age levels.

EXPERIENCE:

Consultant, Murdock Corporation, Fort Worth, TX
2006–Present
Serve as a consultant on matters pertaining to effective methods for developing job openings and serving as a source of manpower supply to industry. Involved in planning, programming, and implementing training programs for the hardcore unemployed. Work as liaison between government agencies, industry, and the community.

Supervisor, The Metropolitan League, Dallas, TX
2003–2006
Served as a Member of the Personnel Committee, the function of which was to set up a policy for the operations of the League. Supervised the operation of the Metro League office. Screened and tested prospective employees and matched skills and talents with several areas of employment. Worked with government agencies and industries to solicit jobs for unskilled, unemployed youths.

Recreational Supervisor, Dalton Neighborhood Action Program, Dallas, TX
2001–2003
Coordinated recreational activities in seven parks and supervised twenty employees.

Counselor, Berns House, Edna, TX
1999–2001
Coordinated sports programs for several teenage social clubs; counseled and tutored teenagers.

COMMUNITY ACTIVITIES:

Elected to serve on the Board of Homeless Advocates, a nonprofit organization formed to foster the socioeconomic levels of individuals and small business aspirants in the Dallas and Fort Worth areas. Investigated business ideas and individuals, providing funds for those with entrepreneurial potential in the greater Forth Worth area.

EDUCATION:

Bishop College, Dallas, TX
M.A., Psychology, 1998

Boston University, Boston, MA
B.A., African-American History, 1996

Facility Manager

CHRIS SMITH
178 Green Street
Suquamish, WA 93982
(206) 555-5555
csmith@e-mail.com

OBJECTIVE

Human Resources Management: Facility Manager.

EXPERIENCE

WOODLAND HALFWAY HOUSE, INC., Suquamish, WA
Facility House Manager   2006–Present
- Manage upkeep of the facility, assigning weekly maintenance and repair details.
- Supervise and assign office spaces and monthly collection of rents.
- Maintain inventory control of supplies, equipment, key control, first aid, and hygiene kits.
- Provide final desk coverage, sign-in and sign-out logs by occupants and verified incoming calls.
- Respond to programs involving informal counseling.

Volunteer Night Counselor
- Responsible for nightly desk coverage.
- Maintained occupant sign-in/sign-out logs and worked with counselors in crises intervention programs.

CITY OF SEATTLE, Seattle, WA
Contract Administrator   2004–2006
- Monitored assigned programs by conducting quarterly on-site visitations and reviews.
- Reviewed monthly invoices and executed quarterly and final analysis of performance standards.
- Researched budget requirements and advised on budget revision requests.
- Participated in annual program planning and proposal review process.

Interviewer/Vocational Counselor   2002–2004
- Provided ongoing vocational counseling to CETA eligible clients and acted as liaison with program administrators.
- Clients represented ex-offenders and unemployed.
- Administered tests and referred applicants to various CETA training programs.
- Responsible for documentaries, reports, and records on progress of programs.

EDUCATION

RANDLE HILL COMMUNITY COLLEGE, Randle, WA   2002
Studies: Human Resources/Criminal Justice/Accounting I/II

References available upon request.

Job Placement Officer

CHRIS SMITH
178 Green Street
Kensington, MI 56343
(313) 555-5555
csmith@e-mail.com

OBJECTIVE: A position in Industrial Relations and/or Human Resources.

EXPERIENCE: The New Division, Kensington, MI
Job Placement Officer   2005–Present
Establish and maintain contact with various civic, cultural, and community organizations; actively participate in the development of programs designed to improve industrial and community relations through vocational training programs, QJT, and equal employment opportunities for the residents of Kensington and surrounding communities. Participate in programs, staff activities, community meetings, and conferences; prepare in-depth reports on proceedings. Establish contacts with prospective employers, union, public and private agencies, and associations to develop job opportunities for community residents. Recruit trainees from the community and instruct them in good grooming and proper procedures for applying for a position.

Emmanuel Agency, Minneapolis, MN
Job Placement Officer   2002–2005
Conducted individual and group counseling of underprivileged youth for the purpose of developing positive attitudes and conduct for entry into the job market. Studied information on current labor trends and investigated areas of referrals. Maintained liaisons with available placement agencies throughout the city.

Borden's Boys' Club, Minneapolis, MN
Athletic Director   2000–2002
Developed and implemented recreational programs for approximately 700–800 boys, ages 7–15. Supervised staff of ten. Maintained all equipment and materials; established excellent relationships with participating children, parents, and other community agencies.

AFFILIATIONS: National Association of Human Resource Administrators
National Association of Job Placement Officers

EDUCATION: Clarke College, Dubuque, IA
Bachelor of Arts degree, 2000
Major: Psychology

REFERENCES: Excellent references available upon request.

Labor Relations Specialist

CHRIS SMITH
178 Green Street
New York, NY 10027
(212) 555-5555
csmith@e-mail.com

OBJECTIVE
A challenging career continuation where labor relations experience will be utilized and advanced.

SUMMARY OF QUALIFICATIONS
- Over fifteen years of human resource and labor relations experience.
- Fluent in written and verbal Spanish and English.
- Available to travel.
- Developed interpersonal and communication skills, having dealt with a diversity of professionals, clients, and staff members.
- Self-motivated; able to set effective priorities and implement decisions to achieve immediate and long-term goals and meet operational deadlines.
- Adept at anticipating and innovatively resolving potential problem areas

PROFESSIONAL EXPERIENCE
THE CITY OF NEW YORK DEPARTMENT OF HEALTH   1999–Present
Labor/Management Relations Analyst
Represent over 4,000 employees. Investigate and mediate disciplinary actions taken by supervision against employees; conduct grievance hearings. Collect, compile, and evaluate labor/economic data; write reports; present findings at City Hall hearings. Provide assistance in policy formation, implementation, planning, and dissemination. Aid and advise management staff with interpretation and application of collective bargaining agreements, supplemental agreements, personnel policies and practices, and grievance policy. Act as liaison with union representatives. Research and determine appropriate adherence to labor contract terms. Prepare documentation for evidence and mediate in diverse hearings. Interact with staff members, union representatives, and management; develop recommendations; design agreements.

NEW YORK COMMISSION AGAINST DISCRIMINATION   1997–1998
Field Representative
Investigated alleged discrimination practices. Utilizes paralegal training and analytical writing skills. Wrote recommendations and case dispositions.

NEW YORK HISPANIC LEGISLATIVE CAUCUS   1995–1997
Legislative Assistant
Served as liaison among Hispanic community, sales legislators, and business interests. Liaison responsibilities extended statewide to over 200 agencies. Organized and conducted legislative research projects. Interacted with senior staff researchers. Cooperated with Caucus in implementation of community outreach and general counseling needs.

EDUCATION
FORDHAM UNIVERSITY, Bronx, NY
B.S. degree, 1994
Concentration: Government

Personnel Consultant

CHRIS SMITH
178 Green Street
Denver, CO 80208
(303) 555-5555
csmith@e-mail.com

PROFESSIONAL EXPERIENCE

National Equipment Corporation   **Denver, CO**
Personnel Consultant, Software, Inc.   *2000–Present*
Provide consultation to and leadership for senior staff members and their management teams. Advise on organization and business issues, including needs assessment diagnosis, transition planning, and problem solving. Develop positive and proactive employee relations, effective communications, employee advocate role, and participative management, third party negotiation, interpreting company policies and procedures, employee development, compensation and benefits, and training design. Recommend organizational design and reorganization to maximize utilization of workforce. Design and/or facilitate group development activities, i.e., team-building programs. Communicate Affirmative Action/EEO policies and procedures to include: profile, climate, goal-setting, identification of problem areas, and planning. Consult on effective management practice and behaviors, particularly in the areas of performance appraisal and reward system, and human resource planning.

Training Consultant, Sales Training Development, Bart and Rogers   *1994–1999*
Consulted with product groups and other clients to determine training needs. Performed needs analysis and established program objectives. Recommended training solutions. Identified methods of introducing new information to increase job competence. Devised and documented training. Developed basic training materials and coordinated efforts of outside consultants and vendors. Assembled and organized all conceptual materials into course design. Determined effective instructional technique. Arranged for design and printing of material and preparation of audio-visual aids. Assisted in conducting pilot programs to train instructors. Evaluated and refined course materials in an effort to find optimum solution to training challenges.

State of Colorado   **Denver, CO**
Staff Assistant, Bureau of Employment   *1994*
Devised in-service staff development programs for state employees. Coordinated implementation with union and management. Planned career ladder education programs for upward mobility for state employees.

EDUCATION

M.Ed., 1993, University of Denver Graduate School of Education, Denver, CO
Administration, Planning, and Social Policy Program

B.A., 1989, Colorado College, Colorado Springs, CO
Major: History

Personnel Manager

CHRIS SMITH
178 Green Street
Franklin, IN 46131
(317) 555-5555
csmith@e-mail.com

PROFESSIONAL BACKGROUND

PERSONNEL MANAGER
Cronin Construction, Franklin, IN
July 2006 to Present
- Adjust Human Resources policy to needs of expanding company.
- Develop Human Resources goals and objectives.
- Manage Human Resources budget.
- Handle employee relations.
- Direct employment and recruitment efforts.
- Manage company benefits and compensation.
- Compile statistics for employee benefits handbook.
- Assist in development of training programs.

PERSONNEL ADMINISTRATOR
Moschella Management Corporation, Franklin, IN
July 2004 to July 2006
- Initiated affirmative action program.
- Compiled policies and procedures manual for Human Resources Department.
- Coordinated recruitment program with agencies and attended job fairs.
- Created advertising campaign for recruitment program.
- Developed and packaged new employee orientation.
- Implemented additional benefits, i.e., tuition reimbursement and employee referral program.

MANAGER OF PERSONNEL/PAYROLL
Purdue University School of Management, West Lafayette, IN
May 2003 to June 2004
- Supervised administrative and technical support staff.
- Interviewed, hired, and terminated personnel.
- Negotiated salaries, budgets, and business plans.
- Analyzed and resolved personnel grievances.

ASSISTANT MANAGER
Atwood Industries, Beloit, WI
September 2001 to May 2003
- Hired and terminated personnel; handled salary negotiations.
- Implemented billing and credit procedures (accounts payable and receivable).
- Served as liaison among client companies, East Coast office, and Home Office.

NOTABLE ACHIEVEMENTS
Developed and managed Human Resources role as company grew from 140 to 275 employees. Completed course work in media presentations and computer applications (Excel, Microsoft Word, PowerPoint).

EDUCATION
Bachelor of Arts degree in English, 2001
Beloit College, Beloit, WI

Recruiter
Human Resources Department

CHRIS SMITH
178 Green Street
Boise, ID 83725
(208) 555-5555
csmith@e-mail.com

OBJECTIVE   A position in recruiting with a progressive, expanding firm offering growth potential within the organization's structure. Willing to relocate and/or travel.

ACCOMPLISHMENTS
- Established excellent relationships with employment agencies from California to Massachusetts; increased quantity and quality of resumes received by 200%.
- Developed monthly mailer directed to agencies.
- Implemented new administration procedures, increasing clerical productivity by 95% and reducing personnel department overhead by 30%.

EXPERIENCE   Professional Recruiter—TAB/GTK Corporation, Boise, ID
August 2006–Present
- Recruit sales and marketing support personnel.
- Plan and execute field recruiting trips to major cities, seminars, career centers, conferences, and universities.
- Design and implement college recruiting programs.
- Establish and maintain working relationship with select employment agencies.
- Prepare statistical reports relating to department expenditures and provide recommendations for eliminating excessive cost and overhead.
- Assist in the development of employee communication programs.

Personnel Manager—Bannen Boot Company, Syracuse, NY
May 2004–August 2006
- Established first complete personnel program including developing all procedures, records, programs, sources of hire, and all administrative functions related to the recruiting and hiring of personnel.
- Established a child-care service in-house.
- Worked on human relations problems arising with the introduction of newly established standards and work procedures.
- Developed new employee orientation programs including visual aids and prepared tests.
- Developed and maintained employee recreation program, music and PA system, bulletin boards, etc.

EDUCATION

Syracuse University, School of Communications, Syracuse, NY
B.S. degree, Public Relations, 2004. Minor: Sociology.

CHRIS SMITH
178 Green Street
New London, CT 06320
(203) 555-5555
csmith@e-mail.com

OBJECTIVE

To contribute managerial skills to a challenging position as a Recruiter.

SUMMARY OF QUALIFICATIONS

- Extensive public relations work, dealing with all levels of employment.
- Self-motivated; able to organize, analyze, and meet operational deadlines.
- Respond well in high-pressure atmosphere.
- Capable of handling a diversity of responsibilities simultaneously.

EXPERIENCE

NORMAN DEPARTMENT STORES, New London, CT
Manager of Executive Recruitment, 6/02-1/06
Oversaw college recruiting process, annual budget $75,000. Presented campus recruitment workshops; developed internship program. Hired/recruited support and merchandising staff. Organized Senior Executive involvement. Received award for overall achievement and outstanding performance in Human Resources, 3/07.

Department Manager, 9/00-6/02
Merchandised children's clothing and accessories. Analyzed/marketed $2 million inventory. Coordinated inventory control. Trained/developed staff of fifteen sales associates in customer service skills and selling techniques. Achieved 20% sales increase over one-year period. Chosen Manager of the Year for excellence in responsibilities, 2001.

SEINFELD'S, Reading, CT
Selling Supervisor Trainee, 6/00-8/00
Coordinated merchandising and overall appearance of Men's Department. Evaluated sales data. Controlled inventory and placement of incoming merchandise. Executed price revisions.

EDUCATION

CONNECTICUT COLLEGE, New London, CT
B.A., Spanish Modified with Government Studies, May 2002

Training Coordinator

CHRIS SMITH
178 Green Street
Orangeburg, SC 29115
(803) 555-5555
csmith@e-mail.com

SKILLS

- *Human Resource Development:* Articulate and effective communicator and trainer. Inspire a team commitment to company goals, management objectives, and high quality performance standards.
- *Computer Systems:* Skilled in use and development of data collection and spreadsheet programs for accounting, statistical analysis, and reporting functions. Assisted in computer systems installation and full training of employees.
- *Troubleshooter:* Analytical with an established track record for identifying complex problems; resourceful and inventive in developing and implementing creative solutions with enhanced sensitivity to cost, efficiency, and deadlines.

EXPERIENCE

TRAINING COORDINATOR   2005–Present
Silver Guard Insurance Agency   Orangeburg, SC
Develop training curriculum, aids, and materials to instruct staff in division operations, corporate policy, and procedure, and to maintain ongoing personnel development in knowledge of current practices, increase job performance skills, and maintain quality assurance for all office operations.

- Conduct highly effective classroom sessions and hands-on training encompassing billing, benefits, insurance industry regulations, and relevant legal issues.
- Specialize in investigating and settling medical malpractice cases.

MANAGER   2003–2005
Orange Community Medical Center   Orangeburg, SC
Managed and supervised daily credit and collections operations with responsibility for client billing and managing free care programs. Controlled operating budget and contributed to overall budget planning. Analyzed accounts status and implemented appropriate collections procedures; facilitated clear communications with service vendors; worked effectively with attorneys in cases involving legal proceedings.

ASSISTANT MANAGER   2001–2003
Contemporary Temps   Hartsville, SC
Collected insurance statistical data; implemented cost avoidance programs and conducted training for temporary employees in billing procedures, government benefits programs, health-care benefits issues, and insurance industry regulations.

EDUCATION

BACHELOR OF SCIENCE IN BUSINESS ADMINISTRATION, 2001
Coker College—Hartsville, SC

Vice President of Human Resources

CHRIS SMITH
178 Green Street
Daytona, FL 32114
(904) 555-5555
csmith@e-mail.com

OBJECTIVE

Executive-level position in Human Resources Management.

PROFESSIONAL EXPERIENCE

Vice President, Human Resources

Ann Davis Laboratories, Inc., Daytona, FL   2006–Present

Direct a staff of eight in the design and delivery of HR programs and services for the $175 million biotech/pharmaceutical business.

- Operated at Executive Staff Level in directing the business and resolving organizational issues.
- Changed existing Personnel Department into a streamlined HR department with bottom-line accountability.
- Recruit difficult to fill positions in an extremely competitive recruiting environment. Reduced turnover by 15%; managed cost per hire to below 30% for exempt hires.
- Introduced new performance compensation program—structure development, management guides and training, distribution curve, common reviews, and new survey participation. Formulated management incentive programs. Reconstructed field operations incentive program which greatly improved performance/morale.
- Formulate and administer new HR policies; employee suggestion system and opinion survey; various other employee motivational and communication programs.

Director, Human Resources

Olsen Laboratories, Inc., Sebring, FL   2001–2006

- Directed large staff (forty-five–seventy-five) in providing all HR services and programs to the Corporate Headquarters organization.
- Introduced and directed a corporate centralized employment function operating as an in-house sourcing unit to reduce costs and streamline operations.

Corporate Compensation Manager

McCormick, Inc., Tampa, FL   1996–2001

- Directed worldwide compensation programs including manufacturing facilities in the United Kingdom for the European sales force.

EDUCATION

M.A., Organizational Communications, Flagler College, St. Augustine, FL, 1997
B.A., Liberal Arts, University of Miami, Miami, FL, 1995

Assistant Attorney General

CHRIS SMITH
178 Green Street
Madison, SD 57042
(605) 555-5555
csmith@e-mail.com

EXPERIENCE:

**OFFICE OF ATTORNEY GENERAL
FOR THE STATE OF SOUTH DAKOTA**   Madison, SD

2006–Present   **Assistant Attorney General, Criminal Bureau**
- Prosecute false claims in Insurance Fraud Unit, including larceny, motor vehicle fraud, and perjury.
- Argued before Supreme Judicial Court and Appeals Court on Commissioner of the Department of Employment and Training v. Nicole J. Ross, 145; and D.E.T. v. Michael Meyers, 66.

2004–2006   **Special Assistant District Attorney**
- Prosecuted criminal cases at district court in conjunction with Urban Violence Strike Force; prosecutions included rape and armed assault with intent to murder.

2001–2004   **SEAVER, MADDEN, AND BERMAN**   Aberdeen, SD
Attorney
- Prepared and presented civil and criminal motions before District and Superior Courts.
- Acted as co-counsel at trial; drafted memoranda, civil pleadings, and appellate briefs.

2000–2001   **WADE COUNTY DISTRICT ATTORNEY'S OFFICE**   Rapid City, SD
Student Prosecutor
- Prosecuted criminal cases from arraignment to disposition.

Summer
2000   **Legal Intern**
- Researched and drafted memoranda for presentation in both criminal and civil actions.

EDUCATION:

2001   **HARVARD UNIVERSITY LAW SCHOOL**   Cambridge, MA
Juris Doctor
Honors: Dean's List
           Phi Delta Phi National Honors Fraternity
           Top 10% of Class

1998   **PRINCETON UNIVERSITY**   Princeton, NJ
School of Business and Economics
B.S. in Business Administration
Honors: Dean's List

CHRIS SMITH, Esq.
178 Green Street
San Francisco, CA 94105
(415) 555-5555
csmith@e-mail.com

EDUCATION

GOLDEN GATE UNIVERSITY, San Francisco, CA
Doctor of Law, 2006
- Semifinalist, Golden Gate Moot Court Competition.

NEW COLLEGE OF CALIFORNIA, San Francisco, CA
B.A., Communications, *Magna Cum Laude,* 2006
- Departmental Honors in Communication.
- Dean's List.
- Communications Department Teaching Assistant (faculty appointment).
- Captain of the Debate Team.

LEGAL EXPERIENCE

KELLY, JACKSON, & JAMES   San Francisco, CA
Associate   2006–Present
- Served as Associate in the Commercial Law Department. Represent financial institutions, debtors, and bankruptcy trustees in all phases of complex litigation and restructuring transactions. Possess substantial transactional and litigation experience in various facets of communication law; special emphasis on musical, artistic, and literary property matters. Deal specifically with cases involving copyright registration and licensing litigation as well as negotiation of trademark licensing; litigation of false advertising, unfair competition, and defamation claims, and the negotiation and formulation of management agreements for entertainers.

FRANCIS, PARKER, MARKS, & WILLIAMS   Los Angeles, CA
Summer Intern   2005

BOSLEY, HUDSON, & ANSON   San Francisco, CA
Summer Intern   2004

VOLUNTEER WORK
- Serve on the Board of Directors of San Francisco General Hospital.
- Offer pro bono legal services to nonprofit organizations serving the arts.

References Available Upon Request.

Attorney
Environmental Law

CHRIS SMITH
178 Green Street
Bangor, ME 04401
(207) 555-5555
csmith@e-mail.com

Admitted to Maine Bar, 2002
Admitted to Indiana Bar, 2001

EDUCATION
INDIANA UNIVERSITY, Bloomington, IN
Master of Studies in Environmental Law and Public Policy, Magna Cum Laude, 2002
Juris Doctor, 2001
Environmental Action Group; National Lawyers Guild Indiana Chapter

ROCKFORD COLLEGE, Rockford, IL
Bachelor of Arts, 1998 Major: Sociology, Cum Laude
Editor, Environmental Newsletter

PROFESSIONAL EXPERIENCE
MAINE ENVIRONMENTAL RESEARCH GROUP, Waterville, ME   July 2003–Present
Environmental Program Director/Attorney
Coordinate environmental programs; develop policies; oversee campaign activities and staff. Draft legislation. Provide legal counseling. Develop media relations. Serve on state's acid rain and recycling program advisory committees. Initiated and successfully lobbied for statewide moratorium on mandatory recycling. Strengthened state's acid rain regulations.

SOLO PRACTICE   August 2001–June 2003
Practiced before Water Resources Board. Negotiated small claims settlements; conducted title searches; advised clients on permitting processes.

LEGISLATIVE COUNCIL, 2000 Indiana General Assembly, Indianapolis, IN   Spring 2000
Intern
Conducted legal research. Wrote memoranda. Presented testimony and drafted legislation primarily for House and Senate Health and Welfare and Government Operations committees. Worked with legislators' public and private interests. Addressed issues including toxics regulation, employment discrimination, and health care financing.

LAND USE CLINIC, Indiana University, Bloomington, IN   Fall 2000
Investigated and analyzed Indiana design review ordinances. Searched records; attended administrative proceedings; interviewed planning officials; submitted report with recommendations for improving existing state enabling statute.

INDIANA ENVIRONMENTAL CONSERVATION BUREAU, Indianapolis, IN   Fall 1999
Semester in Practice, Dept. of Hazardous Waste
Served on legislatively mandated advisory committee. Acted as liaison to Attorney General's office on uncontrolled hazardous waste cases. Addressed issues including pollution liability insurance, water protection, and nonhazardous waste disposal.

CHRIS SMITH
178 Green Street
Alva, OK 73717
(405) 555-5555
csmith@e-mail.com

PROFESSIONAL EXPERIENCE

2005–Present	Alva School Department	Alva, OK

Chief Negotiator for $375 million public agency, reporting directly to the Superintendent of Schools on collective bargaining issues with fifteen unions of over 10,000 employees.
- Primary contract administration advisor for managers in 130 schools.
- Conduct or supervise all administrative hearings.
- Develop content and present training workshops for management staff.
- Oversee private sector labor relations with bus drivers union.
- Supervise and evaluate five-member support staff.
- Design and implement modernization of office procedures.

2003–2005	Alan Pettybone, Esq.	Lawton, OK

Principal
- Retained by the City of Lawton to provide management labor relations representation.
- Duties included: developing negotiation strategies, extensive hearing practice, and rendering legal opinions to personnel on labor relations issues.

2000–2003	Hollyhock, Stiller, and York	Langston, OK

Associate
- Primary focus on labor law and litigation.
- Represented plaintiffs and defendants in general civil litigation cases in federal and state courts.

1997–2000	J.D. Simpson and Wrenwright	Alva, OK

State Attorney
- Represented union members before government agencies, commissions, and arbitrators.
- Drafted memorandums of law and wrote advisory opinions to legal staff.

EDUCATION

COLUMBIA UNIVERSITY LAW SCHOOL	New York, NY

J.D., June 1996

COLUMBIA UNIVERSITY	New York, NY

B.A. HISTORY, Magna Cum Laude, 1993

Correctional Officer

CHRIS SMITH
178 Green Street
Sabattus, ME 04280
(207) 555-5555
csmith@e-mail.com

OBJECTIVE:

A challenging and responsible position in Law Enforcement, Criminal Justice, or related field where my education, experience, and capabilities can be fully realized.

EDUCATION:

BANGOR POLICE ACADEMY, Bangor, ME
Act 120 Certificate with 90% average (2002)

CERTIFICATIONS:

- NRA, shotgun and firearms; Monadnock PR 24; VASCAR plus.
- CPR First Aid.

EXPERIENCE:

2005–
Present

MAINE STATE PRISON, Lewiston, ME
Correctional Officer
Responsible for control of fifty prisoners. Conduct population counts, cell checks, and searches. Supervise dinner and yard duty. Monitor prisoner visitation. Issue money orders for prisoners. Assignments have included escorting special prisoners and serving as outside hospital guard. Prepare and file incident reports.

2004

BIDDEFORD POLICE DEPARTMENT, Biddeford, ME
Part-Time Police Officer

2003

SOUTH PORTLAND POLICE DEPARTMENT, South Portland, ME
Part-Time Police Officer
Responsible for routine patrol, issuing criminal arrest citations, and testifying in court.

2000–2002

FIRST FEDERAL SAVINGS BANK, Cape Elizabeth, ME
Security Guard

VOLUNTEER:

Volunteer Firefighter; Cape Elizabeth Fire Co.

CHRIS SMITH
178 Green Street
Trenton, NJ 08625
(609) 555-5555
csmith@e-mail.com

SUMMARY OF QUALIFICATIONS
- Thorough knowledge in the provision of security and administrative support services, within judicial and supreme court arenas, involving preparation of cases for trial proceedings, maintenance of official records, liaison functions between court and government agencies, and custody/traffic direction processes.
- Adept with personnel management functions, requiring orientation, training, supervision, production of work schedules, and delegation of talks and evaluation.
- Superior communication, organizational, public relations, and interpersonal skills; function well in high pressure arenas; regarded as a dedicated, trustworthy, and loyal employee; able to prioritize assignments to meet operational deadlines.

PROFESSIONAL EXPERIENCE
STATE OF NEW JERSEY—Judicial Court, Trenton, NJ
Chief Court Officer, 2005–Present
- Coordinate general security procedures during court proceedings and in justice lobbies, accompany justices to outside engagements, and manage public traffic.
- Serve as liaison for court and government agencies; transmit pertinent data.
- Produce work schedules; delegate responsibilities for staff; supervise in the execution of duties; train, coach, and develop, as necessary.
- Prepare courtroom for trial proceedings, locate and supply precedent information for judges and counselors, and record courtroom activity.

STATE OF NEW JERSEY—Judicial Court, New Brunswick, NJ
Court Officer, 2000–2005
- Attended court sessions and provided security for courtroom and judicial lobbies.
- Maintained court session and attorney appearance records and documents.
- Monitored activities of individuals held in custody and ensured public safety.
- Announced commencement and termination of court proceedings.
- Answered incoming calls, obtained mail, and distributed to justices.
- Received visitors; inspected guest credentials, and directed to designated areas.
- Scheduled appointments for judges and provided courier services, as needed.

EDUCATION
CALDWELL COLLEGE, Caldwell, NJ
A.S., Criminal Law, 2000

Firefighter

CHRIS SMITH
178 Green Street
Palos Heights, IL 60445
(312) 555-5555
csmith@e-mail.com

SUMMARY OF QUALIFICATIONS:
- Emergency Medical Technician and volunteer firefighter.
- Able to remain calm and take control in emergency situations.
- Have held numerous elective offices.

EDUCATION:

DEERFIELD COMMUNITY COLLEGE, Deerfield, IL
Emergency Medical Technician, 2003.

Certified by the Illinois Department of Health.
Illinois Association of Arson Investigators Certificate, Forensic File Photography.
Chicago Electric Company Fire Academy.
Gas and Electric Firefighting, 1989–90.
Deerfield Fire Academy, Firefighting I, II, III, 1988–89.

TRINITY VOCATIONAL-TECHNICAL SCHOOL, Deerfield, IL
Communications Technician, 1989–91.
Photographic Technician, 1988–89.

WORK EXPERIENCE:

1988–
Present **PALOS HEIGHTS FIRE COMPANY**—Life Member
Firefighter, Emergency Medical Technician
- Ambulance Lieutenant, 1993, 2005—conduct training drills.
- Ambulance Captain, 1994.
- Ambulance Auxiliary Secretary, 1994.
- Photographer, 2002–Present.

2004–
Present **INTERNATIONAL FIRE PHOTOGRAPHERS ASSOCIATION**

1988–
Present **DEERFIELD FIREMAN'S ASSOCIATION**

1994–1998 **MIDWEST AMBULANCE,** River Forest, IL
Assistant Manager/Crew
- Scheduled ten full-time and eight part-time Emergency Medical Technicians for emergency and hospital transportation of patients. Serviced Burn Center at River Forest Medical Center.

CHRIS SMITH
178 Green Street
Sundance, WY 82729
(307) 555-5555
csmith@e-mail.com

OBJECTIVE

A position in security.

PROFESSIONAL EXPERIENCE

FIELDSTONE BANK   Sundance, WY
Bank Guard   2006–Present
- Responsible for ensuring safety and security of customers, bank employees, and bank assets.

WILLOW MEAD ART MUSEUM   Wolf, WY
Security Guard   2004–2006
- Responsible for patrol, surveillance, and control of facilities and areas.
- Maintained reports, records, and documents as required by administration.

CITY OF ROCK SPRINGS POLICE DEPARTMENT   Rock Springs, WY
Property Clerk   2002–2004
- Responsible for security, transfer, and storage of personnel effects/properties as evidence in trial and court cases.

CITY OF GILLETTE SCHOOL DEPARTMENT   Gillette, WY
Transitional Aide   1998–2002
- Responsible for ensuring safety of students and security of school property at Madison Park High School.

THUNDERBEAT CONSTRUCTION   Crowheart, WY
Weigher of Goods/Track Foreman   1997–2000
- Weighed materials and supervised track construction at University of Wyoming.

PINEDALE & SONS   Miami, FL
Mason   1995–1997
- Performed variety of duties including masonry, stucco, finishing work, and foundations for general contractor.

EDUCATION

UNITED STATES COAST GUARD, Miami, FL
Certificate, Interactive Query Language, 1995.
Certificate, Advanced PMIS, 1994.
Certificate, Coast Guard WP School, 1993.
Winter Park High School, Winter Park, FL 1993.

Law Clerk
Criminal Law

CHRIS SMITH
178 Green Street
Des Moines, IA 50311
(515) 555-5555
csmith@e-mail.com

EDUCATION

DRAKE UNIVERSITY LAW SCHOOL, Des Moines, IA
Juris Doctor, June 2005
Class Rank: 5 out of 300.
Honors: Dean's List all semesters.

CENTRAL UNIVERSITY OF IOWA, Pella, IA
B.A., American History, 1995
Internship, Washington, D.C., Office of Rep. William McCarthy,
September–December 1995.

EXPERIENCE

WARD WESTON, AND WOLCOTT, Des Moines, IA
2005–2006 **Law Clerk**
Researched and wrote motions and memoranda, prepared discovery, and trial assistance for three attorneys specializing in criminal law.

ADDISON AND HAYES, Des Moines, IA
2004–2005 **Law Clerk**
Responsibilities included preparation of discovery and trial assistance.

FULTON ADJUSTMENT SERVICE, Des Moines, IA
1997–2004 **Road Adjuster** (two years)
Office Manager (one year), Portsmouth, NH
Suit Supervisor (nearly three years)
Responsibilities included investigation, negotiation, trial preparation, or settlement of first and third party insurance claims, particularly automobile and general liability. Some Workers' Compensation and property cases.

CAROLINA AND CO., Pella, IA
1994–1996 **Road Adjuster**
Handled third party liability and Workers' Compensation claims.

INTERESTS

Baseball, soccer, and jazz.

CHRIS SMITH
178 Green Street
Irving, TX 75061
(817) 555-5555
csmith@e-mail.com

BAR   TEXAS JUDICIAL COURT, 2006
STATUS   U.S. District Court for the District of Texas, 2006

EXPERIENCE   TRIAL COURT OF TEXAS, Irving, TX

Law Clerk to the Justices   2006–Present

Provided legal research and writing assistance with respect to substantive and procedural issues at various stages of civil and criminal proceedings to approximately twenty justices.

IRVING DISTRICT COURT, Irving, TX

Student Prosecutor   2005

Prosecuted misdemeanors under supervision of District Attorney's Office.

TEXAS JUVENILE COURT, Irving, TX

Law Clerk   2005

Drafted proposed findings of fact and conclusions of law in care and protection cases, conducted research, and assisted in a case management project.

UNIVERSITY OF DALLAS LAW SCHOOL, Irving, TX

Legal Research, Reference and Government Documents Assistant   2005–2006

Assisted in instruction of Legal Research course, assisted attorneys and students with legal research, helped maintain reserve materials, and updated collection.

KING'S PRESS, Kingsville, TX

Reporter, Feature Writer and Copyeditor   1999–2005

Covered government, law enforcement, education, health issues, the environment, entertainment, and social trends.

EDUCATION   UNIVERSITY OF DALLAS, Irving, TX

Juris Doctor, *Magna Cum Laude,* 2006, GPA 3.5
Honors: Editor, law review
          Dean's List

TEXAS A&M UNIVERSITY, Kingsville, TX

B.S. Business, *Cum Laude,* 2004, GPA 3.3
Honors: Dean's List

TEXAS CHRISTIAN UNIVERSITY, Fort Worth, TX

B.A. English and Journalism, 1999, GPA 3.2
Honors: Dean's List

Law Student

CHRIS SMITH
178 Green Street
Ithaca, NY 14853
(607) 555-5555
csmith@e-mail.com

EDUCATION

Cornell Law School, Ithaca, NY
Juris Doctor to be awarded, May 2007

City University of New York, NY
Bachelor of Arts in English, May 2004
Gold Key National Honor Society
Yearbook Editor

EXPERIENCE

Cornell Law Library, Ithaca, NY
Research Assistant   2005–Present
- Assist law students, lawyers, and faculty with library research.
- Maintain and update newspaper clippings file of recent Supreme Court decisions.
- Train and supervise staff of five work-study students.

New York Attorney General's Office, New York, NY
Legal Intern   Summer 2005
- Acted as aide to Assistant Attorney General during courtroom proceedings, pretrial conferences, interviewing witnesses, and legal research.
- Prepared discovery motions, typed briefs, provided legal counsel in and prepared witnesses for grand jury testimony.

OTHER EXPERIENCE

CITY UNIVERSITY OF NEW YORK, ENGLISH OFFICE, New York, NY
Secretary/Receptionist   2003–2004

THE BAD SEED RESTAURANT, New York, NY
Bartender   Summers 2002–2003

REFERENCES AVAILABLE UPON REQUEST

CHRIS SMITH
178 Green Street
Danville, KY 40422
(606) 555-5555
csmith@e-mail.com

OBJECTIVE

To acquire a **Legal Secretarial** position, preferably, but not limited to, Civil Litigation or Criminal Law, where my experience and commitment to excellence will be fully applied.

SUMMARY OF QUALIFICATIONS

- Fifteen years experience as a legal assistant/secretary in civil litigation.
- Ten years part-time experience in general practice.
- Computer literate: PCs and Macs.
- Notary Public.
- Supervisory skills, delegate and distribute workload evenly among secretarial staff.

HIGHLIGHTS OF LEGAL EXPERIENCE

2004–Present   LAW OFFICES OF LANGSTON & GREY, Lexington, KY   **Legal Secretary**
Responsibilities include organizing pre-deposition conferences with doctors, attorneys, and involved parties; handling, canceling, and rescheduling; setting up motions for court hearings; trial papers and schedules; researching files for necessary documentation and proofreading; notarizing legal documents.

1994–2002   THEODORE F. LOGAN, Danville, KY   **Legal Secretary**
Part-time evening duties involved court and client scheduling, typing legal documents, drafting wills, letters, and complaints in general practice law office.

1990–1993   CUMBERLAND INSURANCE, Lexington, KY   **Secretary**
General secretarial tasks; typing correspondence and reports, filing, and phones.

EDUCATION

CENTRE COLLEGE, Danville, KY Paralegal Studies, 2003–2004
Also participated in Communications Skills Workshop for Paralegals.

DANVILLE COMMUNITY COLLEGE, Danville, KY
Relevant training and coursework in legal issues and computers.

PERSONAL

Baseball, cooking, and travel.

Loss Prevention Manager

CHRIS SMITH
178 Green Street
Stillwater, OK 74078
(405) 555-5555
csmith@e-mail.com

OBJECTIVE
A position in loss prevention management.

PROFESSIONAL EXPERIENCE

Vedder Toxic Waste — Norman, OK
Loss Prevention Manager — 2006–Present
Ensure proper operation of physical building security, alarms, and camera-surveillance system. Prescreen and train loss prevention staff; enforce policies and procedures; devise incentive programs. Implement inventory control audits and investigations. Apply energy maintenance program to reduce equipment costs and repair, and improve efficiency.

Oklahoma State University Store — Stillwater, OK
Loss Prevention Manager — 2004–2006
Developed loss prevention department, manager, and staff training; conducted comprehensive needs assessment, recommended improvements; credited error notice system; implemented $3 million antitheft system; decreased cash register shortages 93% over six-month period. Executed Merchant Alert Program with local merchants and police.

Oklahoma City University Store — Oklahoma City, OK
Loss Prevention Manager — 2002–2004
Redesigned departmental goals and direction. Developmental training and professional standards; created storewide, loss-prevention awareness and in-house training; implemented cash register error notice program. Produced monthly employee newsletter.

Spruce Crest, Inc. — Stillwater, OK
Operations Manger — 2001–2002
Maintained operations for $5 million service; directly managed forty-to-fifty member supervision/support staff. Hire and terminate, train, schedule, and oversee personnel; delegate responsibilities. Respond to client needs and queries; act as liaison with vendors. Provide cost analysis, budgeting, specifications/proposals, and service maintenance contracts for commercial accounts.

EDUCATION

Albright College — Reading, PA
Master's degree, Private Law — 2000
Allegheny College — Meadville, PA
Bachelor's degree, Liberal Arts — 1998

Ombudsperson

CHRIS SMITH
178 Green Street
Waukesha, WI 53188
(414) 555-5555
csmith@e-mail.com

SUMMARY OF QUALIFICATIONS
- Over ten years of progressive, professional human services experience.
- Proven abilities in training, program development, and analysis of policies.
- Extensive knowledge of long-term care issues.
- Developed interpersonal skills, having dealt with a diversity of professionals, clients, and staff members on all levels.
- Tested communication skills, both oral and written.

PROFESSIONAL EXPERIENCE
WISCONSIN ELDER CARE, INC., Waukesha, WI
Long-Term Care Ombudsperson Program Director, 2003 to Present
- Developed local Ombudsperson Program in forty-six nursing and rest homes in fourteen cities and towns; required close cooperation with administrators and facility staff members.
- Investigated and resolved problems of long-term care residents.
- Recruited, trained, and supervised staff of thirty volunteers; developed ongoing training program for Ombudsperson staff.
- Presented workshops and lectures.
- Refined data collecting and recording system.
- Actuated and implemented inquiry recording system.
- Developed comprehensive information and resource packet.
- Cooperated in team effort to develop and implement several special projects.
- Established productive and effective relationships with state and local agencies; executive office of Elder Affairs, Department of Public Health, Department of Mental Health, Home Care Corporation, and Councils on Aging.

Case Manager, 1999 to 2003
- Assessed physical, environmental, and emotional status of applicants; evaluated existing support systems; determined financial eligibility.
- Advocated for clients; handled crisis intervention.
- Developed and implemented client service plans.

EDUCATION
UNION COLLEGE, Schenectady, NY
Master of Science in Human Services and Gerontology, 1999

SALVE REGINA—THE NEWPORT COLLEGE, Newport, RI
Bachelor of Science in Health Services, 1997

Paralegal
Corporate Law

CHRIS SMITH
178 Green Street
St. Paul, MN 55104
(612) 555-5555
csmith@e-mail.com

EXPERIENCE

2004 to Present

BRODERICK & HOLMES, St. Paul, MN
Corporate Paralegal, 1999–Present
- Solely responsible for ensuring corporate compliance with Minnesota General Laws, meeting, and filing requirements for 750 clients.
- Determine interstate corporate business status and handle registration process.
- Extensive contact with State Department of Revenue Compliance Bureau to verify corporate tax standing.
- Draft corporate votes, liquidations, and dissolution plans, various agreements and supporting documents.
- Familiar with UCC financing statements; research liens in connection with corporate acquisitions and financing.
- Supervise, train, and develop administrative staff.
- Determine and collect corporate data for implementation of computerized information system.
- Responsible for organization of new corporations including preparation of articles of organization, drafting of bylaws, and issuance of stock.
- Guide legal interns in department procedure and scheduling.
- Trained on Lexis-Nexis legal research systems.

Legal Recruiting Coordinating, 2000–2004
- Aided in recruiting effort in all areas of practice.
- Scheduled interoffice interviews.
- Reviewed attorney and summer associate candidates.
- Coordinated recruiting effort in law schools; contacted placement agencies and established positive working relationships.
- Prepared all materials for hiring committee meetings.

EDUCATION

MACALESTER COLLEGE, St. Paul, MN
Bachelor's degree in Marketing, 1998
(GPA 3.85)

CARLETON JUNIOR COLLEGE, Duluth, MN
Associate's degree in Secretarial Sciences, 1993
(GPA 3.75)

Ongoing professional development includes: managing complex financial transactions, organizational structure seminar, and national association for legal placement's annual recruitment conference.

REFERENCES

Furnished upon request.

Paralegal
Real Estate Law

CHRIS SMITH
178 Green Street
Jackson, MS 39217
(601) 555-5555
csmith@e-mail.com

PROFESSIONAL EXPERIENCE

2002–Present   OLIVER, FIELDING, & OLIVER, Jackson, MS
Legal Assistant
- Provide paralegal services to attorneys in residential real estate sales within Mississippi and surrounding states.
- Monitor transactions from start to final settlement statement; order and review titles, obtain plot plans and municipal lien certificates, research background, and work successfully against deadlines.
- Prepare loan documents.
- Determine outstanding utility and tax bills.
- Ensure completion of mortgage payments by previous owners.
- Serve as liaison for clients, banks, and attorney; schedule meetings, identify documents necessary for all parties.
- Coordinate all post-closing functions, complete title insurance forms, send final payments to banks and municipalities, and disburse funds.
- Maintain constant communication with all parties involved throughout the entire process.

1996–2002   HALPERN INSURANCE AGENCY, Jackson, MS
Subrogation Clerk, 2001–2002
- Negotiated payments with attorneys on Third Party Liability cases; reviewed medical records.

Operator, Third Party Liability Dept., 2000
- Provided subscriber information to customers, assisted in completion of questionnaire.

Senior Clerk, Hospital Claims Dept., 1996–1999
- Reviewed claims, made payments for patients with nerve and mental disorders.

EDUCATIONAL BACKGROUND

BELHAVEN COLLEGE, Jackson, MS
Certificate in Paralegal Studies
- Introduction to Paralegal, American Legal System, Criminal Law, Litigation, Utilization of Legal Materials, and Real Estate Law.

HALPERN INSURANCE Courses:
- Legal Terminology, Contractual Terminology, Mathematical Skills.

SKILLS   PC literate, word processing, and typing (55 wpm).

Paralegal
State Department

CHRIS SMITH
178 Green Street
Rindge, NH 03461
(603) 555-5555
csmith@e-mail.com

PROFESSIONAL OBJECTIVE

To obtain a position in the **Paralegal** field.

PROFESSIONAL EXPERIENCE

2005 to Present SECRETARY OF STATE, AWARDS DIVISION, Rindge, NH
UCC Corporations Clerk
Locate Uniform Commercial Code and obtain corporate documents for lawyers. Work with Limited Partnerships and trust. File Annual Reports and Articles of Organization.

2003 to 2005 MILAND, GARLAND, AND TEEK, Manchester, NH
Local Searcher
Obtained documents for clients across the country. Documents Uniform Commercial Code, Mortgages, Plaintiff and Civil Probate Court, and Land Court UCCs. Obtained Federal and State Tax Liens, Bankruptcy, Registry of Motor Vehicles, and Marriage Certificates.

2001 to 2002 BLUE NOTES, Madrid, Spain
Salesman
Responsible for inventory control, customer service, billing, and management liaison.

1997 to 2001 UNITED STATES AIR FORCE, Madrid, Spain
Administrative Personnel Management Clerk
Resolved all Personnel Problems or Requests: re-enlistment, extension of tour in Europe, relocation within the United States and Europe, return of dependents to the United States or Europe, and ensured receipt of awards, tracking of personnel, all records of accidents and injuries. Routed incoming Top Secret Messages. Typed correspondence for Commanding Officer. Honorably Discharged.

EDUCATION AND TRAINING

2005 FRANKLIN PIERCE COLLEGE, Rindge, NH
Certificate in Paralegal Studies.

1999 Thirteen weeks training at Fort Bragg, NC, assisting 109th Signal Battalion. Trained in Computer Science, using Microsoft Word, Access, and Excel.

Police Officer
Campus

CHRIS SMITH
178 Green Street
Baltimore, MD 21210
(410) 555-5555
csmith@e-mail.com

PROFESSIONAL EXPERIENCE

2000 to Present JOHNS HOPKINS UNIVERSITY POLICE DEPARTMENT, Baltimore, MD
Patrol Officer
- Protect life and property on and about the campus of Johns Hopkins University.
- Uphold laws and codes of the state of Maryland and Johns Hopkins University.
- Patrol on foot and via automobile; utilize strong observational skills.
- Cooperate with other law enforcement agencies; act as Deputy Sheriff, Essex County.
- Maintain community relations; give seminars on drunk driving.

1998 to 1999 BUCKMAN ASSOCIATES, Bethesda, MD
Head of Security
- Managed all aspects of security for hotels and adjoining properties.
- Hired, terminated, scheduled, supervised, and evaluated personnel.
- Provided all policing functions with emphasis on defusing potentially violent situations.
- Cooperated extensively with Baltimore and Bethesda Police Departments.
- Promoted from starting position as Patrol Officer.
- Received standing offer of return for emergency or full-time employment.

1993 to 1997 TOWN OF ROCKVILLE POLICE DEPARTMENT, Rockville, MD
Patrol Officer
- Performed all aforementioned policing functions.
- Oversaw proper use of Chapter 90 sheets and citations.
- Interacted and communicated with town officials.
- Kept records; maintained data.

EDUCATION AND TRAINING
Graduate, Baltimore Police Academy, 2000
Graduate, Rockville Police Academy, 1993

CERTIFICATIONS AND LICENSURES
- License to carry firearms.
- Emergency Medical Technician, National Certification.
- Certification in radar usage.

REFERENCES
Available upon request.

Police Sergeant

CHRIS SMITH
178 Green Street
Houston, TX 77030
(713) 555-5555
csmith@e-mail.com

PROFESSIONAL OBJECTIVE
A position as a police sergeant in which professional background, management skills, and commitment to excellence will be effectively utilized.

PROFESSIONAL LICENSE
Certified Protection Professional

PROFESSIONAL BACKGROUND
HOUSTON CITY POLICE DEPARTMENT, Houston, TX
Sergeant/Chief Polygraphist   2001–Present
- Develop objective, establish procedures, set policies, and maintain standards for two units.
- Supervise, train, schedule, and evaluate twenty-five employees.
- Forecast, prepare, and monitor budgets for both units.
- Order supplies and equipment.
- Design and execute workshops on fingerprints and polygraph techniques to maintain efficiency.
- Restructured record filing and material handling systems.
- Utilized computer to evaluate fingerprints.

Commander   1997–2001
- Maintained resident and building security in fifty-building, 5,000-resident Southwest Housing Project in Houston.
- Inspected premises to maximize crime prevention.
- Established goals with residents and adjacent commercial establishments.
- Reduced thefts, assaults, and property destruction by 55%.

Sergeant/Patrol Supervisor   1995–1997
- Directed 150 police officers in all aspects of their duties.

EDUCATIONAL BACKGROUND
Austin College, Sherman, TX
Bachelor of Science, Law Enforcement, 1993.

CHRIS SMITH
178 Green Street
Wise, VA 24293
(703) 555-5555
csmith@e-mail.com

PROFESSIONAL EXPERIENCE

2003 to **WCVT-TV (NLC-Channel 3)**, Wise, VA
Present **Account Executive/Sales Department**   2005–Present
- Established and maintained new and existing corporate accounts representing more than $1.5 million in new clients.
- Initiated and developed marketing strategies and target grids for the second ranked TV station in fifth largest market for effective sales programs/promotions.
- Aided with potential clients in developing effective marketing strategies and programs.

Associate Director/Sales Manager   2004–2005
- Production Department Stage Manager for Noon, Five O'Clock, and News at Ten newscasts, all public affairs programs, editorials, and news cut-ins.
- Assembled sets and operated chyron machine.

Production Intern   2003
- Wrote hard news, feature stories, scheduled and interviewed guests.
- Researched materials and packaged tapes for production.
- Operated TelePrompTer.

2001–2003 **UNIVERSITY OF VIRGINIA**, Charlottesville, VA
Producer, Television and Radio Station WNUV-Channel 62   2002–2003
- Responsible for researching materials for mini-documentary.
- Scheduled and interviewed guests for round-table discussions.
- Wrote and edited scripts and edited master tape.

Production Assistant   2001–2002
- Performed as camera technician, stage manager, and chyron operator.
- Assembled lighting and audio equipment.

EDUCATION

RANDOLPH-MACON WOMAN'S COLLEGE, Lynchburg, VA
B.A. degree, Communications/Mass Media   2004
Magna Cum Laude. Concentration: Economics and Afro-American Studies.

HONORS/AFFILIATIONS

Recipient, Virginia Chapter, National Association of TV Arts and Science Award. National Achievement Award. National Association of Women Journalists. National Association of Media Workers.

Account Representative

CHRIS SMITH
178 Green Street
Clarksville, TN 37042
(615) 555-5555
csmith@e-mail.com

CAREER OBJECTIVE

A position as an account representative calling on a background in marketing, management, and computer graphic design.

QUALIFICATIONS

Computer graphic design using QuarkXPress program and Illustrator. Scanning techniques using the Ofoto and Mictotek Scanners, and Adobe Streamline. Complete knowledge of camera and print production.

EMPLOYMENT

MAPLE SKY ADVERTISING—Clarksville, TN   6/06–Present
Account Representative

Account Representative and troubleshooter for several different advertising accounts, including the creation, development, and management of each account. Projects include newspaper inserts, production, billboard, and advertising, along with radio and other forms of media advertising. Assist in the creation and design of special advertising.

BLACKTHORN GARDEN CENTER—Clarksville, TN   2/03–6/06
Assistant Manager

Managing up to twenty employees while meeting the wants and needs of our customers. Advertising of current seasonal merchandise, through many different media, and purchasing inventory representative of many different distributors.

EDUCATION

- Graduated Cum Laude, Centenary College, Hackettstown, NJ
- B.S. in Business Administration, December 2002.
- Major Field: Marketing.
- Minor Fields: Management, Psychology.
- GPA: 3.5/4.0
- Honors: *Who's Who in American College Students*.
- Financed 90% education through part-time employment, scholarships, and loans.

REFERENCES

Available upon request.

Advertising Assistant

CHRIS SMITH
178 Green Street
Buckeye, WV 24924
(304) 555-5555
csmith@e-mail.com

OBJECTIVE

An entry-level position in the Advertising Department of an established corporation offering advancement potential based on performance excellence.

CAPABILITIES BRIEF

- Mass Communications.
- Advertising and Promotion.
- Marketing and Sales Support.
- Customer Relations.
- Sales and Sales Management.
- Film and Video Production.

SUMMARY

- **Bachelor of Arts degree in Advertising:** Basic knowledge of Mass Marketing and Communications; Consumer Oriented; Computer Literate.
- Three years of full- and part-time employment experience in positions of supervisory responsibility.
- Excellent verbal and written communication skills; experienced in personnel relations, brochure and documentary film production; high aptitude for the acquisition of new business technologies.

EDUCATION

Bachelor of Arts Degree, University of Massachusetts, Amherst, MA, 2007
- Advertising major.
- Core GPA 3.48/4.0; Dean's List of Distinguished Students.
- Relevant courses include Organizational Communication—Interpersonal Communication—Advanced Mass Media—Advanced Video—Customer Motivation—Advertising—Writing for Film, Radio, and TV—Graphic Design.
- Assisted in the production of an independent documentary film *Now I Lay Me Down to Sleep* about the homeless. Acted as script advisor, camera person, and sound assistant.
- Extracurricular activities include: Captain, Lacrosse Team (1996–2007); Varsity Tennis (2005); Contributing Editor for Little Green school newspaper.

EMPLOYMENT EXPERIENCE

Fanfare, Inc.   2006–2006
Assistant Manager   Northampton, MA
- Provided support services for the Operations Manager, including Determination of Costs and Analysis of old and current account.
- Oversaw distribution of warehouse inventory to branch offices.
- Scheduled and dispatched truck fleet.
- Documented billing and posting of union labor.
- Devised daily cut sheets.
- Operated Texas Instrument Computer System.

Advertising Manager

CHRIS SMITH
178 Green Street
Nashville, TN 31210
(615) 555-5555
csmith@e-mail.com

OBJECTIVE
A challenging career in Advertising.

PROFESSIONAL EXPERIENCE
2006 to   USA OLYMPIC PUBLICATIONS, Nashville, TN
Present   Advertising Manager
- Sell advertising space for a publication distributed at Olympic Conventions. Sell rental contracts for booths at trade shows, etc.
- Design fliers and brochures as part of promotions for conventions and trade shows. Handle other promotional work as assigned.
- Initiate, organize, and promote trade show for Tennessee merchants and for others interested in area trade and commerce. Contact merchants to rent booths, send promotional materials to buyers, and contract for media advertising.
- Coordinate and secure facilities and services for trade show project of approximately $150,000.

2004 to   GOOD MORNING NASHVILLE NEWS, Nashville, TN
2006   Executive Secretary to the Advertising Manager
- Prepared statistical analysis of advertising lineage for use in assessing competitive ranking.
- Typed, answered the Call Director, and performed general secretarial duties for sales personnel as assigned.
- Provided resource contact and encouragement to States Staff.

2001 to   DEPARTMENT OF SOCIAL SERVICES, Memphis, TN
2004   Legal Secretary
- Handled correspondence, telephones, and general secretarial work, as well as light research.

1999 to   RYE BROOK COMPANY, Madison, TN
2001   Typist
- Typist of documents usually 40 to 50 pages long; compiled and typed statistical information for analyses.

INTERESTS   Rock climbing, gardening, '70s trivia.

REFERENCES   Furnished upon request.

Assistant Account Executive

CHRIS SMITH
178 Green Street
Kutztown, PA 16233
(717) 555-5555
csmith@e-mail.com

SYNOPSIS Area of expertise is in Advertising Production with a proclivity for TV and Magazine Production. Self-starter and excellent communicator with ability to project and elicit interest, enthusiasm, and drive using a common-sense approach. Adept at sizing up situations, analyzing facts, and developing alternative courses of action to increase productivity and exceed desired results.

SUPPORTIVE QUALIFICATIONS
- Seven years advertising experience; handle accounts up to $3 million.
- Strong client service: professional; diplomatic; supportive; excellent interpersonal skills with clients, management, staff, public, and media.
- Always meet deadlines with accuracy and quality; able to deal with extended pressure; strong on follow-through.
- Proven supervisory skills: organize, prioritize, and delegate tasks; effectively train staff in new concepts and procedures.

EXPERIENCE

THE MERCER GROUP, Meadville, PA
Assistant Account Executive   2006 to Present
Direct all phases of client services for national account, primarily based in the Mid-Atlantic Region. Plan media and placement. Direct creative services, copy, and design.

Account Supervisor—Account Coordinator   2005 to 2006
Oversaw Coordinating Department; trained, guided, and directed staff of five while monitoring ad placement system. Assisted in creation of advertising campaigns and acted as liaison among client, agency, and media vendors, including selection, budget, and advertisement placement.

THE ARIEL AGENCY, Newark, NJ and *MERTON, KASS, & HOWE,* Pittsburgh, PA
Advertising Internship   2004
Responsibilities included compiling market research, writing press releases, producing traffic reports, working media events, and assisting in advertising production.

EDUCATION
Rutgers University at Camden; B.A. in Mass Communication, minor in English.

PROFESSIONAL AFFILIATION
The Advertising Club of Pennsylvania, 2005 to Present.

COMPUTER SKILLS
Microsoft Word, Quark.

Director of Subsidiary Rights

Chris Smith
178 Green Street
Kansas City, MO 64110
(816) 555-5555
csmith@e-mail.com

EXPERIENCE

Chesapeake Company, Kansas City, MO

2006–Present *DIRECTOR OF SUBSIDIARY RIGHTS*
Negotiated subsidiary rights licenses for Trade and Reference publications in hardcover and paperback reprint, book club, large print, motion picture, merchandising, mechanical, and audio recording. Oversaw the administration of departmental contracts and accounting noting systems. Prepared monthly forecast and quarterly budget reports. Supervised a secretary and two interns.

2005–2006 *MANAGER OF SUBSIDIARY RIGHTS*
Negotiated subsidiary rights licenses for Trade and Reference publications in hardcover and paperback reprint, book club, and large print. Supervised administration of departmental contracts and accounting noting systems. Prepared monthly forecast and quarterly budget reports.

2003–2005 *SUBSIDIARY RIGHTS COORDINATOR*
Negotiated specialty book club and large print licenses. Administered the internal monitoring and processing of all subsidiary rights contracts and monies. Coordinated and fulfilled all manufacturing requests from licenses, including foreign and domestic coproducers. Generated all contractual reversions. Supervised an assistant.

2000–2003 *SUBSIDIARY RIGHTS ASSISTANT*
Assisted the subsidiary rights coordinator with submissions, preparation of various reports, and fulfillment of manufacturing materials to licensees. Provided general secretarial support.

1997–2000 *ADMINISTRATIVE ASSISTANT*
Provided general secretarial support within the subsidiary rights department. Researched rights histories and availability of rights.

EDUCATION

Bernadette Tibbs Business School
Kansas City, MO 1995–1997

REFERENCES

Available upon request.

Insurance Agent

CHRIS SMITH
178 Green Street
Erie, PA 16505
(814) 555-5555
csmith@e-mail.com

OBJECTIVE

To join the management team of an organization in need of comprehensive expertise in establishing, implementing, and managing insurance programs in a non-carrier environment.

EXPERIENCE

SENIOR SUPERVISOR CLAIMS   2004–Present
Bimscala Risk Management   Pittsburgh, PA

- As Senior Supervisor, Claims, was accountable for all claims service provided by the Workers' Compensation and Liability units. Oversaw the delivery of a quality product which developed client confidence in the claims handling ability of Bimscala.
- Responsibilities encompassed direct claims handling, reporting, and negotiating high exposure claims; conducted periodic claims reviews and loss report reviews.
- Established all opening reserves on cases and advised adjusters as to what specifics were needed. Instituted authority levels. Reported claims to excess carrier.

DIRECTOR OF RISK MANAGEMENT   2003–2004
Apenwood and Co.   Scranton, PA

- Analyzed risk of potential loss to clients' assets and revenues.
- Consulted on property and casualty insurance for clients of various industries.
- Interacted directly with corporate financial and general management offices to establish insurance policies and procedures.

CLAIMS MANAGER   2002–2003
Jared Barkly, Inc.   Reading, PA

- Administered Workers' Compensation claims for Regional District; processed claims, hired independent adjusters, physicians, and attorney.

EDUCATION

Grove City College, Grove City, PA
Master of Arts in Speech and Business Communications, 2002

Mansfield University, Mansfield, PA
Bachelor of Science in Visual and Verbal Communications, 2000

LICENSE

Licensed Insurance Agent, The State of Pennsylvania—#1068

Market Research Analyst

CHRIS SMITH
178 Green Street
Ossipee, NH 03864
(603) 555-5555
csmith@e-mail.com

OBJECTIVE   To apply marketing and problem-solving skills in a marketing research/analysis position for career growth.

EXPERIENCE

2006 to   BRIODY ASSOCIATES, Derry, NH
Present   **Market Research Analyst**
Build consumer behavior models for corporate clients using multivariate techniques including regression and discriminant analysis, and cluster analysis. Analyze data from national probability survey to identify purchase intents and patterns for business to consumer direct marketers. Organize and present marketing information to executive staff for in-house promotions and press releases.

2001 to 2006   THOMSON AND COMPANY, Manchester, NH
Market Researcher
Member of Survey Research Group addressing all marketing research needs, i.e., marketing segmentation, concept testing, and product usage and awareness. Interviewed and gathered data from managers in a wide variety of industries including consumer goods, high technology, banking, retailing, and health care. Pre-tested, edited, and coded in-depth questionnaires.

1999 to 2001   STEVEN ICE, INC., Derry, NH
Market Researcher
Identified target markets, constructed complex questionnaires, conducted telephone interviews, compiled and analyzed the data, organized and conducted a focus group within market segment, analyzed and dovetailed the results from two data-gathering approaches, tested original assumptions, and wrote and presented a report to management including recommendations for future action.

EDUCATION

BABSON COLLEGE, Wellesley, MA
Master of Business Administration, Honors, 1999
PRINCETON UNIVERSITY, Princeton, NJ
Bachelor of Arts, Psychology, Honors 1997

AWARDS

- Awarded U.S. Medal for Management Excellence, 2005
- Business Board Member of Princeton Yearbook Publication, Inc., 1997

SKILLS   IBM and Mac, Lotus 1-2-3, and Microsoft Word.

Marketing Assistant

CHRIS SMITH
178 Green Street
Terre Haute, IN 47804
(812) 555-5555
csmith@e-mail.com

OBJECTIVE

A position that will further develop my superior marketing skills.

EXPERIENCE

Marketing Assistant, The Art Lover's Institute
Indianapolis, IN   2/06–Present
- Temporary position assisting the Manager of Public Information on the exhibit "Proud Triangles: Gay Life in America."
- Executed the distribution of exhibit posters and organized the development of displays merchandising products to promote the exhibit at local retailers.
- Coordinated press clippings and releases about the exhibit.

Assistant Box Office Manager, Terre Haute Performing Arts Center
Terre Haute, IN   6/05–1/06
- Managed daily operations for a staff of twenty operators responsible for customer service and the sale of all tickets in a theater seating 5,000.
- Compiled all financial statements on a daily and monthly basis for each performance in the theater averaging ten performances per month, including daily deposits and revenue from outlet sales on secondary ticketing systems.

Gallery Assistant/Window Exhibit Coordinator, Jim Cannon's Art Implosion
Bourbon, IN   5/04–6/05
- Developed marketing plan for fine art prints and coordinating notecards.
- Developed client base and serviced accounts.
- Coordinated special events relating to current exhibits, opening receptions, and artist signings. Handled press releases.

EDUCATION

Valparaiso University, Valparaiso, IN
Bachelor of Arts, 2006
Arts Administration with a concentration in marketing and communications.

SKILLS

Proficient with many Mac and PC applications, including: PageMaker, Word, Excel, and Access.

Marketing Intern

CHRIS SMITH
178 Green Street
Washington, D.C., 20020
(202) 555-5555
csmith@e-mail.com

SUMMARY OF QUALIFICATIONS

- Successfully completed finance/marketing internship in Maastricht, the Netherlands.
- Performed market research for new Pinchot Fat Free Cakes.
- Computer Skills: MacIntosh; IBM PC and compatible systems.
- Excellent interpersonal and communication skills with verbal, written, presentation, and foreign language translations.
- Multilingual: Fluent in Dutch; conversant in German, French, and Italian.
- Familiar and comfortable with multiethnic populations; well traveled and have resided and studied in Amsterdam, Munich, and Rome.
- Demonstrated marketing/public relations, events planning, and fundraising capabilities.

EXPERIENCE

LION BANK   Maastricht, the Netherlands
Finance/Marketing Intern   Spring 2006
Dealt with portfolios, stocks, and bonds. Provided translations. Assisted with research on the Maastricht Treaty and the potential financial ramifications of a unified Europe. Selected as part of the Johns Hopkins-Maastricht Exchange Program as one of only seven students chosen to participate.

BANKS' HEALTH FOODS   Richmond, VA
Market Research Intern   Summer 2005
Assisted with new product research for Pinchot Fat Free Cakes; worked extensively on IBM system.

SWEET BRIAR PRODUCTS, INC.   Annapolis, MD
Research and Development Intern   Summer 2007
Worked for new product development research team.

JOHNS HOPKINS ALUMNI ASSOCIATION   Rockville, MD
Fundraiser   Summer 2006
Coordinated the procedure and implementation of securing funds for tutoring facility, career, and alumni center.

EDUCATION

JOHNS HOPKINS UNIVERSITY   Baltimore, MD
B.S., Political Science; Minor, International Relations   Anticipated Spring 2007

JOHNS HOPKINS—MAASTRICHT   Maastricht, the Netherlands
Student Exchange/Internship   Spring 2006

Marketing Manager

CHRIS SMITH
178 Green Street
El Paso, TX 79925
(915) 555-5555
csmith@e-mail.com

OBJECTIVE

A position in **Sales/Marketing Management.**

EXPERIENCE

DENNISON PRESS, El Paso, TX
Trade Division
Marketing Coordinator   2006–Present
- Develop and supervise implementation of all Dennison marketing plans with the sales and marketing departments.
- Prepare and manage the annual marketing budget of $2 million.
- Supervise marketing assistant.
- Manage scheduling and production of all sales and marketing materials.
- Provide marketing information at biannual sales conferences and coordinate book presentations.

Professional Division
Children's Books Department
Editorial Administrator   2005–2006
- Managed revisions from manuscript preparation to bound book. Resolved author questions and problems. Ensured manuscript conformity to budgetary and scheduling constraints.
- Directed supplement program of over seventy books from budget management to project completion with specific emphasis on electronic manuscript preparation.
- Supervised and trained editorial assistant.
- Provided information to marketing department for direct mail promotions and reviewed copy for accuracy and content.

Children's Books Department
Editorial Coordinator   2003–2005
- Supervised the supplement program.
- Conducted editorial market research and assessed results with senior editors.

Children's Books Department
Editorial Assistant   2002–2003
- Provided general support for senior editors.
- Fulfilled various author requests.

EDUCATION   Baylor College, Waco, TX
B.A., English major, Economics minor, 2001

SKILLS   Proficient in Microsoft Word, Excel, and Quark.
Working knowledge of the French language.

Product Developer

CHRIS SMITH
178 Green Street
Hattiesburg, MS 39401
(601) 555-5555
csmith@e-mail.com

OBJECTIVE   A progressive career in **Product Development and Sales.**

MAJOR QUALIFICATIONS
- Nine years managerial, seven years sales, and six years buying experience.
- Perform point-of-sale forecasting.
- Proven training record with ability to make complex concepts and items approachable and user friendly to customers and staff.
- Innovative in merchandising and display.
- Success and expertise in parallel exporting.

PROFESSIONAL EXPERIENCE

2006–Present   **THE TWO WHEEL EXCHANGE,** Starkville, MS   **Product Developer**
Supervise up to twenty-five employees.
- Direct all Product Development Operations, including the fabrication and testing of prototype cycles.
- Conceive, develop, and build bicycles for the physically handicapped.
- Fabricate, develop, and supervise construction of a wheelchair bike for Bill Milton in his annual New York Marathon bid.
- Teach evening classes on bicycle repair/maintenance.
- Manage and equip a cycling team sponsored by the Two Wheel Exchange.
- Open and close store, scheduled and trained staff, and ordered bikes.

2003–2006   **GIGI'S, INC.,** Hattiesburg, MS   **Management/Sales**
Ensured the smooth operation of a prestigious, 150-year-old store.
- Ordered and distributed several lines of merchandise.
- Coordinated product training and development.
- Opened and closed store; ensured safety of cash drawer; inventory and displays.
- Maintained strong customer relations.
- Ordered supplies, maintained inventory, developed creative window displays.

2001–2003   **HARVEY DAWSON MOTORCYCLES,** Boston, MA   **General Manager**
Responsible for the special ordering and purchasing of Harvey Dawson motorcycles in the United States.

EDUCATION

NORTHEAST MISSOURI STATE, Kirksville, MO.
Bachelor of Arts, Marketing, 2000.

Purchasing Agent

CHRIS SMITH
178 Green Street
Bountiful, UT 84040
(801) 555-5555
csmith@e-mail.com

EMPLOYMENT

PURCHASING AGENT   2005–Present
Data Basix, Bountiful, UT

- Purchase PCs, laptops, and peripherals.
- Maintain open-door status reports for Montgomery, Sprint, and Miyako products and expedited orders, as necessary, pertaining to inventory control.
- Return defective and obsolete inventory products.

PURCHASING AGENT   2004–2005
Radient, Inc., Lark, UT

- Purchased laptops, PCs, and peripherals. Interacted with sales and marketing departments, with total responsibility for overseeing all order processing, scheduling, and inventory control function. Handled general supplies purchasing for the entire company.

REGIONAL DISTRIBUTION SUPERVISOR   2003–2004
Rybell Corporation, Teasedale, UT

- Purchased laptop computers, as well as software and peripherals to be sold to individuals and companies up through *Fortune* 500. Handled all purchasing for ten retail outlets in Utah and Nevada. Successfully worked with vendors to maintain best and most current pricing. Supervised and trained a staff of eight in buying, order processing, and billing; and five in warehouse administration and maintenance for the Western Region.
- Started as a Buyer: responsible for annual purchases of $17 million in computer equipment and peripherals, monitoring inventory, and preparing forecasts for a perpetual inventory system. Company sold; retained and promoted to Regional Distribution Supervisor by new management.

BUYER   2000–2003
O'Donnell Corporation, Oasis, UT

- Purchased electronic components for a collision avoidance radar system used by both commercial and military shipping, from manufacturers and local distributors. Functioned as Assistant to the Mechanical Buyer. Purchased all office and miscellaneous supplies.
- Started as a Purchasing Secretary responsible for administrative support to Purchasing Agent and liaison to outside vendors. In 2001, based on performance, was promoted to position of Buyer.

EDUCATION

University of Colorado at Boulder
B.A., Business Administration, 2000

Real Estate Appraiser

CHRIS SMITH
178 Green Street
Winona, MN 55987
(507) 555-5555
csmith@e-mail.com

SUMMARY OF QUALIFICATIONS

Professional experience includes the following areas:

- Assessing property and real estate value for insurance claims, adjustments, and repair.
- Successfully marketing services to *Fortune* 500 companies.
- Project and office management, supervising estimators, superintendent, and construction crew.
- Demonstrating estimating software in Northern regions and following up with problem solving assistance.

EXPERIENCE

2006–Present **WINONA CONSTRUCT**   Winona, MN
Vice President/Appraiser

Manage two estimators, a superintendent and twenty-member construction crew; assessing damages, preparing estimates and proposals for insurance companies, and supervising reconstruction activities.

- Call homeowners, real estate companies, insurance company representatives, and adjusters, promoting company's services.
- Achieved average annual sales of $950,000 with new clients.
- Provide demonstrations and training to groups of ten to thirty persons in computer estimating software package, traveling to Maine, Florida, Georgia, and Massachusetts. Followed up with problem solving services.
- Traveled to Los Angeles area to write estimates for apartment complexes damaged by earthquakes as special assignment.

2003–2006 **NORTHERN STAR RESTORATION COMPANY**   Minneapolis, MN
General Manager

Worked closely with management companies and apartment complexes, managing restoration work for new company, hiring and supervising subcontractors, and supervising jobs from start to finish.

1999–2003 **ST. PAUL LIFE & CASUALTY**   St. Paul, MN
Property Claims Representative (2000–2003)

Appraised all types of residential properties and investigated all types of damages to home, including water, fire, vandalism, and "natural disasters." Determined value of claim and prepared report. Exceeded monthly claims quota by 40%.

Inside Auto Adjuster (1999–2000)

Investigated cause and perpetuators of accidents, dealing with attorneys, police officials, auto adjusters, and clients.

EDUCATION

1999 **BROWN UNIVERSITY**   Providence, RI
Bachelor of Arts in Education

Real Estate Manager

CHRIS SMITH
178 Green Street
Lawton, OK 73703
(405) 555-5555
csmith@e-mail.com

EXPERIENCE

DIRECTOR OF REAL ESTATE DEVELOPMENT

Wildoak, Inc., Lawton, OK   2004–Present

Responsibilities and Accomplishments:

- Started a real estate development division which grew to a professional and support staff of thirty, and generated contracts of $12 million.
- Manage development projects from inception to final use. Assign, manage, and direct company and contract professionals including controller, architects, estimators, designers, engineering, and sale staff.
- Implement large scale development of single family detached home neighborhoods which range in price and market segment from first time buyers, upwardly mobile buyers, to luxury communities. Play a key role in directing all areas of projects.
- Plan and manage projects through the most efficient methods, functioning as a General Contractor or working through a General Contractor.
- Interact with individual and corporate clients; local and staff officials; inspectors, attorneys, and contractors; utilities, financial institutions, and real estate brokers for the planning, development, financing, and marketing of large scale investments.

VICE PRESIDENT—PLANNING AND FINANCE

Village Realty, Inc., Muskogee, OK   1996–2004

General Information:

Started with this firm in real estate sales in 1996, and was involved in all phases of marketing and sales of residential and commercial properties. Based on performance was promoted to Manager of Sales and Marketing, and subsequently, Vice President of Planning and Finance, 1999.

As Vice President of Planning and Finance

- Assumed full responsibility for the planning, finance, sales, lease, or rentals of all company development and construction projects. Supervised a staff of eighteen in accounting, sales, construction, and building management.
- Conferred and negotiated with financial institutions and private investors to obtain financing. Created and coordinated financial packages for new developments or expansions.
- Attended planning and zoning board hearings and meetings, and successfully obtained zoning approval to proceed with what resulted in a successful condominium complex.

EDUCATION

Oklahoma State University, Stillwater, OK
Bachelor of Arts degree in Management/Economics, 2000
Honors: Dean's List
Cumulative Average: 3.5/4.0

Regional Sales Manager

CHRIS SMITH
178 Green Street
Toppenish, WA 98948
(509) 555-5555
csmith@e-mail.com

PROFESSIONAL OBJECTIVE

A position in **Regional Retail Management** in which my strong interpersonal and organizational skills will have valuable application.

PROFESSIONAL EXPERIENCE

THE GIVING TREE, Seattle, WA   2004 to Present
Northwest Regional Manager
- Supervise all operations of ten stores.
- Regional warehouse accountability; supervise all inventories.
- Hire, fire, train, supervise, and develop district managers.
- Handle sales planning, administer loss prevention program.
- Coordinate extensive marketing and merchandising functions.

DEVONSHIRES, Lacey, WA
Regional Manager   2001 to 2004
- Oversee operations of ten stores in metropolitan area.
- Train district managers; hire, fire, train, supervise, and develop managers.
- Coordinate sales planning, loss prevention, programs, extensive marketing, and merchandising functions.

District Manager, Portland, OR   1999 to 2001
- Oversee operations of eight stores in metropolitan area.
- Promoted from Manager in under six months.

Manager, Forest Grove, OR   1998 to 1999

Assistant Manager, Salem, OR   1996 to 1998

TINY TOTS, Beloit, WI   1994 to 1996
Assistant Manager

EDUCATION

Beloit College, Beloit, WI
Bachelor of Arts in Philosophy, 1996
Magna Cum Laude

REFERENCES

Available upon request.

CHRIS SMITH
178 Green Street
Shreveport, LA 70460
(318) 555-5555
csmith@e-mail.com

OBJECTIVE

A position in Sales Administration where I can contribute proven administrative and marketing skills.

WORK HISTORY

SOUTHERN TRAVEL, Shreveport, LA   2006–Present
Sales Administrator to Regional Vice President
Assist sales personnel with outside sales and telemarketing to National/Group Association. Create and proof camera-ready ads and color brochures. Act as liaison for sales stuff and passengers. Process travel orders and correspondence. Direct incoming invoices, outgoing commission checks, and passenger payments. Maintain records. Availability Coordinator for travel programs. Provide customer service. Utilize Trans-National Reservation System.

BEAUREGARD'S BRIGADE, Baton Rouge, LA   2004–2006
Sales Manager
Managed/controlled all facets of $1.1 million annual volume men's clothing business. Hired, trained, and motivated eighteen-member staff. Achieved 19% increases in sales over one-year period.

Manager
Managed daily operations for national video store including the selection, training, and evaluation of ten sales associates. Successfully introduced profitable line of creative slogan T-shirts. Coordinated all advertising and displays.

ORSON'S PRIDE, New York, NY   1999–2002
Manager
Managed Accessories Department of this $2.2 million international women's clothing store.

EDUCATION

FORDHAM UNIVERSITY, College at Lincoln Center
New York, NY
B.A. in Marketing, 2002

Sales Assistant
General

CHRIS SMITH
178 Green Street
Fort Worth, TX 76112
(817) 555-5555
csmith@e-mail.com

EXPERIENCE:

2005– REGENCY CORPORATION, Dallas, TX
Present **Sales Assistant:** Act as liaison between customer and sales representative. Provide customer service via telephone. Ascertain order accuracy. Track and expedite orders. Cooperate in team endeavors.

2002–2005 THE MUSIC MAKER, Inc., Houston, TX
Sales Associate: Coordinated sales efforts of a staff of six for a large musical instruments dealership. Developed and maintained working relationships with manufacturers and customers. Supported top account executives. Maintained open files to ensure greatest customer satisfaction.

2000–2002 CITY OF DALLAS, TREASURER'S DEPARTMENT, Dallas, TX
Research Assistant: Assisted in the collection of delinquent real estate, personal property, and motor vehicle excise taxes. Matched instrument of taking against daily tax title receipts. Processed petitions of foreclosure for the legal section and title searches.

1999–2000 TRAFFIC AND PARKING DEPARTMENT, Dallas, TX
Senior Claims Investigator: Investigated and expedited claim settlements relating to ticket disputes and information requests.

1998–1999 SHERMAN BANK FOR SAVINGS, Sherman, TX
Bank Teller: Interacted with customers, processed all money and check transactions, balanced all transactions at the end of each shift. Developed a working knowledge of money market funds and IRA accounts.

EDUCATION:

Austin College, Sherman, TX
A.S. Business Management, 1998

Texas Institute of Banking
Completed courses in Bank Organization and Business English, 1996

CHRIS SMITH
178 Green Street
Nashua, NH 03060
(603) 555-5555
csmith@e-mail.com

EXPERIENCE

2005–Present DIXON WALSTON RESEARCH, Nashua, NH
Sales Assistant: Support brokers and clients. Handle research, word processing, and incoming calls.

2004–2005 CHAUNCY CO., INC., Derry, NH
Personal Department Assistant: Verified employment, assisted employees to solve everyday problems, set up personnel files, typing, phones, data entry, and issuing check cashing cards to employees and registered representatives.

2002–2004 RUMNEY HEALTH, INC., Westmoreland, NH
Counselor/Office Clerk: Verified eligibility of members, entered data on intake forms, set up appointments, heavy telephone work, various office forms, release of medical claims.

2001–2002 STEVE ANGELINO FITNET, Manchester, NH
Receptionist: Monitored switchboard, opened medical charts for patients, entered data in computer, updated information as necessary, and met and greeted members.

1999–2001 CRYSTAL LAKE LAW, Crystal Lake, NH
Receptionist/Office Assistant: Heavy telephone work, typed various legal documents, filed office forms, translated legal documents from German into English.

EDUCATION

1994 **Bertha Tibbs Secretarial School,** Plymouth, NH
Options Program

1997 **The Austrian Institute,** Vienna, Austria
Degree in translation
German/English, English/German

SKILLS

Typing (60 wpm), Shorthand (60–70 wpm), Word Processing, knowledge of other word processing systems, fluency in German, and good verbal and written communication skills.

REFERENCES

Furnished upon request.

Sales Manager
Engineering

CHRIS SMITH
178 Green Street
Providence, RI 02912
(401) 555-5555 (Days)
(401) 555-4444 (Evenings)
csmith@e-mail.com

CAREER SUMMARY

Sales professional who, for seven years, has solved problems and met customer needs to consistently generate top sales. Acknowledged for pursuit of personal and professional growth through study and application of proven ability to create win-win opportunities for all parties involved.

RELEVANT EXPERIENCE

EAGLE TECH, INC.   Providence, RI

2005–Present *Sales Manager*

- Marketed and sold engineering solutions and graphic equipment including workstations, terminals, printers, software, and other related peripherals.
- Generated a $350,000 order for color printers from Dublin Aircraft which was a result of business relationships cultivated with key corporate contacts.
- Convinced a major account on value of new terminal even though the required driver was not yet available. Persuaded the account to pressure their software vendor to write the driver for the terminal. Result: Closed a $400,000 sale of 40 terminals.
- Trained and supervised a new service technician to provide sales support. He was subsequently promoted for outstanding performance.
- Recognized as top sales performer in eastern half of the United States and inducted into "Leaders." Achieved $4.1 million in sales and exceeded quota of $3.6 million.
- Orchestrated sales efforts with the U.S. Navy and a government contractor to implement a war gaming system. Commitment to service with rapid follow-up resulted in sales of $600,000. Anticipate additional sales of at least $1.4 million.

2003–2005 **LEONARD FINN CORPORATION**   Newport, RI
Territory Manager
- Managed a remote territory while supervising sales and equipment installation in a wide range of companies throughout nine counties.
- Sold conversion from Mac system to the National Bank of Rhode Island, producing a sale of $75,000.

2002–2003 **PEARSON PROBLEM SOLVERS, INC.**   Bristol, RI
Direct Marketer/Manager
- Created and implemented sales plan to promote inventory control system for retailers.

EDUCATION

COLBY COLLEGE, Waterville, ME
B.S., Marketing, 2001

CHRIS SMITH
178 Green Street
Salt Lake City, UT 84102
(801) 555-5555
csmith@e-mail.com

OBJECTIVE

To contribute exceptional sales ability, account management, and communications skills to a challenging Sales Representative position.

SUMMARY OF QUALIFICATIONS

- Thorough knowledge in the provision of sales services, account acquisition, and management; consistent enhancement of product and industry knowledge; reactivation of dormant accounts; and the development of successful sales techniques.
- Consistently meet and exceed sales quotas.
- Accumulated over six years experience within a major hardware/software company.

EXPERIENCE

2/06 to Present   **Sales Representative**
GRASSVILLE SYSTEMS   Salt Lake City, UT

- Sell computer hardware and peripherals to corporate accounts and dealer channels.
- Acquisition new accounts; maintain and reactivate existing accounts. Coordinate cold calling; process orders and sell service accounts.
- Devise solutions for customer computer needs and after-sales support.
- Sell PC desktops and laptops.

7/04 to 1/06   **National Sales Representative**
NIMBUS COMPUTERS   Provo, UT

- Acquired new accounts, maintained and reactivated existing accounts.
- Instituted solutions for customer computer needs and after-sale support.
- Sold Macintosh and PC desktop and laptop systems.

12/01 to 6/04   **Sales Associate**
SUEDE BOGGS COMPANY   Salt Lake City, UT

- Facilitated promotional activities, dealt with customers.

EDUCATION

NEW HAMPSHIRE COLLEGE, Manchester, NH
Bachelor of Arts: Communications, May 2002.

COMPUTERS

IBM, Macintosh

Sales Representative
Technical

CHRIS SMITH
178 Green Street
Savannah, GA 31404
(912) 555-5555
csmith@e-mail.com

OBJECTIVE

The opportunity to join a rapid-growth organization that has the need for a technical sales executive with an established track record in handling state of the art electronic equipment.

EXPERIENCE

REGIONAL MANAGER   2006–Present
Dunsinane Corp., Savannah, GA

- Distribution management for Southern region of factory authorized dealers. Distribution maximization, appointment and quota assignment.
- Manage distributor sales hour and program commitment. Interview sales candidates.
- Consultant to professional engineers and architects. Formulated school and health care project specification and systems design, conduct product line presentations for consulting firms.
- Employed distributor computer project specifications and quoting system. Visit problem installations, troubleshoot, and report failures.

SALES ENGINEER   2003–06
Patridge and Killarney, Atlanta, GA

- Monitored the marketing and sale of communications systems.
- Researched, evaluated, and selected subcontractors and negotiated contracts for the installation of systems. Handled customer relations and provided technical support during and post installation.
- Achieved 120% of quota.

LEAD SENIOR ELECTRONIC TECHNICIAN   2000–03
Hepburn Communications, Americus, GA

- Trained junior technicians on custom built test fixtures as well as company procedures and products; set up and repaired test fixtures. Tested, debugged, and repaired hospital communications modules utilizing analog, digital, and microprocessor-based electronics.

ELECTRONIC TECHNICIAN   1998–2000
Patterson Research, Statesboro, GA

- Worked with production control, production, and service departments on the test and repair of equalizers and noise reduction units for consumer high-fidelity applications. Used oscilloscopes, spectrum analyzers, distortion analyzers, signal generators, and custom designed test equipment.

EDUCATION

Savannah State College, Savannah, GA
B.A. Electronics Technology 1998

Kennesaw College, Marietta, GA
A.A. Business Management/Marketing 1995–96
- Worked part-time installing and repairing audio/video equipment.

Salesperson

CHRIS SMITH
178 Green Street
Lancaster, PA 17064
(717) 555-5555
csmith@e-mail.com

OBJECTIVE:

A challenging position in sales.

EDUCATION:

LESLEY COLLEGE, Cambridge, MA
B.A., Politics and History, 2005
Minor: English

SALES EXPERIENCE:

PETITE'S PET LAND, Pittsburgh, PA   2005–2006
Salesperson
Sold merchandise. Developed ongoing customer relationships, enhancing future sales. Developed special seasonal sales. Handled cash transactions and kennel care.

THE TIRE BARON, INC., Beaver Falls, PA   Summer 2005
Upper Bay/Lower Bay Technician
Sold merchandise. Provided customers with technical advice. Trained new employees.

THE SUBVERSIVE PAGES BOOKSTORE, Erie, PA   Summer 2004
Salesperson
Sold merchandise. Provided customer service. Purchased materials and monitored books.

UNRELATED EXPERIENCE:

UNITED PACKAGERS, Boston, MA   Summer 2005
Material Handler

LESLEY COLLEGE, Cambridge, MA   Summer 2007
Maintenance Technician, Buildings and Grounds

ACCOMPLISHMENTS:

Fluent in French
Student Government Representative, 2007–08
Founder, Debate Team, 2005

Tele-Interviewer

CHRIS SMITH
178 Green Street
Jonestown, MS 38639
(601) 555-5555
csmith@e-mail.com

OBJECTIVE

A diversified position where there is a need for an organized, communicative individual skilled in interacting with, selling to and/or training company/customer personnel.

SUMMARY OF QUALIFICATIONS

- Over five years of experience in telemarketing, tele-interviewing, and customer service for projects involving industrial, commercial, and consumer products, communications, and license regulatory issues.
- Well organized, good time manager, and persistent in achieving or exceeding set objectives.
- Excellent communication skills and the ability to interact with people in sales, training, fundraising, and other programs for profit and/or nonprofit corporations.

EXPERIENCE

TELE-INTERVIEWER
The Telemasters, Inc., Yazoo City, MS 2004–Present

- For this data collection/research company, call companies throughout the United States, establish correct contact, update records, and conduct telephone interviews for a variety of surveys dependent upon client needs.
- Train new tele-interviewers on effective interviewing techniques for completion of questionnaires.
- Responsible for calling prospective customers to explain type of service or merchandise offered.
- Utilize telemarketing techniques to persuade customers to purchase or follow up on products or services available.
- Record names, addresses, purchases and/or reactions of prospects solicited; used city and telephone directories to develop lists of prospects.
- All positions require ability to interact with people in a wide variety of work or community environments to obtain accurate data upon which research and/or sales projections are based.

EDUCATION

University of Southern Mississippi, Hattiesburg, MS
Bachelor of Science in Elementary Education (With Honors), 2004
Cumulative average: 3.5/4.0

References available upon request.

Telemarketer

Chris Smith
178 Green Street
Saint Petersburg, FL 33713
(813) 555-5555
csmith@e-mail.com

OBJECTIVE

A position in inside sales, preferably in the telecommunications industry.

QUALIFICATIONS

- Outstanding selling and closing capabilities with proven track record.
- Excellent listener; patient and sensitive to clients' needs.
- Calm under pressure; meet deadlines; meet all sales quotas.
- Proven problem-solving skills.

EXPERIENCE

2006– ESP Telecommunications, Saint Petersburg, FL
Present **Telemarketing Professional**
Cold called residential consumers, discovered their domestic/international calling needs, recommended programs. Consistently achieved at least 125% of sales goals.

2005–2006 Kaybee Education Group, Miami, FL
Marketing Assistant
Cold called high-school and college students selling diagnostic college and graduate school entrance exams.

2004–2005 Bill Wonka Quality Car Wash, Cambridge, MA
Bookkeeper
Performed bank reconciliations, trial balances, and general ledger.

AWARDS AND ACCOMPLISHMENTS

- Inducted into national club of Top Ten Percent, 2005.
- Awarded Golden Ring Award for meeting sales goals throughout 2006.

EDUCATION

Quincy College, Quincy, MA
B.S., Finance, 2004

COMPUTERS

Lotus 1-2-3, Windows, Pascal, Microsoft Word, PageMaker

Travel Agent

A

CHRIS SMITH
178 Green Street
Joliet, IL 60435
(815) 555-5555
csmith@e-mail.com

OBJECTIVE

A challenging career continuation where computer and travel experience will be utilized and advanced.

SUMMARY OF QUALIFICATIONS

- More than seven years of progressive, professional Computer Operator/Travel consultant experience; proven verbal sales skills.
- Detail-oriented, self-motivated; able to set effective priorities and implement decisions to achieve immediate and long-term goals and meet operational deadlines.
- Developed interpersonal skills, having dealt with a diversity of professionals, clients, and staff members.
- Comfortable in fast-paced, high-pressure atmosphere.

PROFESSIONAL EXPERIENCE

SURGE AND SIEGE TRAVEL, INC., Joliet, IL   2004–Present
Air Coordinator
Coordinate air/ticketing requests and tour departures utilizing computer systems. Resolve client problems and special requests. Verify international and domestic fares; input pricing data. Issue tickets and final itineraries. Maintain/file all pertinent materials. Assist with special projects; prepare reports.

GOTTA FLY TOURS, Wheaton, IL   2002–2004
Computer Operator/Supervisor
Responsible for all computer operations. Administered ticket stock and accountable documents. Managed office accounting. Supervised personnel. Group leader for Caribbean familiarization trips. Actuated/implemented system which eliminated computer costs.

QUICK TRIP TRAVEL, Evanston, IL   2001–2002
Travel Consultant
Arranged individual and group travel. Generated invoices.

EDUCATION

MIDWEST TRAVEL SCHOOL, Chicago, IL
Graduated third in class, 2001.

DEPAUL UNIVERSITY, Chicago, IL
Bachelor of Arts, History, 2000.

WINDY CITY COMMUNITY COLLEGE, Chicago, IL
Associate of Arts, Geography, 1998.

CHRIS SMITH
178 Green Street
Plymouth, MA 02360
(508) 555-5555
csmith@e-mail.com

OBJECTIVE A challenging position within the Travel Industry.

SUMMARY OF QUALIFICATIONS
- Ten years of experience acquired during employment and educational training within the travel industry.
- Thorough knowledge of various reservation transactions, including: booking, bursting, ticketing, interfacing with contracted vendors to ensure realization of customer reservation specifications, sales, and customer service.
- Competent familiarity with Mac and PC computer systems.
- Proficient in general office duties.

EXPERIENCE
2005 to Present   **Support Agent**
AS THE CROW FLIES TRAVEL   Plymouth, MA
- Burst tickets and ensure correct formatting of ticket transaction data.
- Book hotel reservations and direct customer package specifications.
- Process ticket transactions.
- Provide sales services and develop sales strategies.
- Respond to customer inquiries for general and package information.

2002 to 2005   **Sales Representative/Accountant**
BUZZWORD TRAVEL   Hyannis, MA
- Extensive accounting tasks in basic bookkeeping.
- Monitored the selling of corporate and leisure accounts.
- Researched and processed credit checks.
- Verified international and domestic fares.

2000 to 2002   **Tour Guide**
SILVER SENTINEL TRAVEL   Provincetown, MA
- Organized tour schedules for international students. Booked local cruises.
- Acted as assistant to company accountant. Performed general bookkeeping duties.

EDUCATION TRAVEL SCHOOL OF NEW ENGLAND, Springfield, MA, 2000

QUINCY COLLEGE, Quincy, MA, 1999
Completed travel and marketing courses, 2000

Vice President of Marketing

CHRIS SMITH
178 Green Street
Conyers, GA 30208
(404) 555-5555
csmith@e-mail.com

EXPERIENCE:

Shockley Associates, Inc., Conyers, GA
Publisher of *Anarchists in Love Comedy Magazine*

Vice President of Marketing   2006–Present

Manage all corporate day-to-day operations, including production, distribution, sales, marketing, and administration.

- Increased annual sales by 10% while achieving net profit margins in excess of 35%.
- Strengthened company management structure by recruiting key personnel for production, distribution, and accounting operations.
- Saved $70,000 annually and improved production schedule by switching printers.
- Reduced accounts receivables to average of thirteen days.
- Improved effectiveness of distribution operation through daily contact with distributors and stores.
- Capped growth in production staff through aggressive work flow management.

Barton, Quivers, and Spunk, Athens, GA
Testing and Consulting Firm

Vice President   2002–2006

Responsible for the strategic, sales, and business management of the company's publications operations.

- Doubled annual division sales to $2 million in 2002; increased sales by 400% in five years.
- Created $400,000+ in annual ad placements for parent company at no cost.
- Increased total advertising pages 30% over two years, versus 30-40% decreases for competitive publications.
- Built technical seminar business from scratch to $275,000 in annual revenues; developed seminars.

Edgewild Laboratories
Pharmaceutical Manufacturer

Marketing Representative   2000–2002

Sold proprietary pharmaceuticals and OTC medications in hospital and pharmacies.

- Doubled annual sales in two years, from $200,000 to $400,000.
- Achieved 110% of budget in first year.

EDUCATION:

New York University, New York, NY
M.S., Marketing, 2000

PERSONAL:

Willing to relocate.

Vice President of Sales
Furniture

CHRIS SMITH
178 Green Street
Hartford, CT 06106
(203) 555-5555
csmith@e-mail.com

PROFESSIONAL EXPERIENCE
WILLIAMS COMPANY

VICE PRESIDENT OF SALES
HARTFORD, CONNECTICUT   2002–Present
Drive sales/marketing and all aspects of operations for a furniture dealership generating $50,000,000 in annual revenues. Formulate corporate policy, engage in long- and short-range business planning; devise and implement effective marketing strategies and sales campaigns. Responsible for branch profits and loss performances while maintaining $7,000,000 in yearly sales activity focused on the corporate market and the design community. Manage human resource issues, budget controls, purchasing, and sales/marketing.

- Increased sales from billings of $2,500,000 in 2002 to $4,000,000. Initiated the practice of visiting all customers in the interest of fostering and maintaining excellent client relations.
- Single most profitable division in the Williams organization in numerous years with a record for steady volume growth.
- Select, train, and motivate a staff of fifteen branch personnel in all assigned duties.
- Develop and conduct in-depth sales trainings encompassing policy and protocols, product knowledge, sales and customer service techniques.
- Cultivate and maintain profitable relationships with 100+ furniture manufacturers.
- Effectively apply detailed knowledge of the relationships of manufacturing and distribution.

ACCOUNT MANAGER
HACKENSACK, NEW JERSEY   1995–2002
Developed new and existing business within corporate and small business accounts. Directed a staff of junior sales representatives and support personnel in marketing furniture products. Provided personal consultation to clients and prospects.

EDUCATION
University of Pennsylvania, Philadelphia, PA
B.A. Management,1995

COMPUTERS
Windows, Microsoft Word, and Excel.

Astronomer

CHRIS SMITH, Ph.D.
178 Green Street
Jupiter, FL 33477
(407) 555-5555
csmith@e-mail.com

OBJECTIVE: A senior level position as **LEAD ASTRONOMER,** preferably in a university setting, utilizing research and computer-assisted as well as telescopic-lens equipment.

PROFILE: Versatile Physicist and Astronomer who through twelve years in education and privately funded organizations has demonstrated proven effectiveness in the calculations and measurements of stars' magnitudes. Strong ability to write and transform technical data into interesting and informative reading.

EDUCATION:

Massachusetts Institute of Technology, Cambridge, MA
Ph.D., Contemporary and Ancient Astronomy   2005
- Doctoral Thesis: "The Effect of Gamma Gamma Rays on Man in the Moon Marigolds," 2003. Published by Bob Adams, Inc., 2004.

Oxford University
M.S., Astral Physics   2000
- Doctoral Thesis: "The Hubble vs. Jodrell Bank: A Question of Perspective."

Rensselaer Polytechnic Institute
B.S., Astronomy   1997

EXPERIENCE:

NASA, Cape Canaveral, FL   2004–Present
Head Researcher
- Monitor progress of telescopes as they relate to supernovae, the moon, and the planets.
- Investigate binary stars and their movements.

Harvard University, Cambridge, MA   2001–2004
Research Assistant
- Conducted experiments and provided findings in 200-plus–page reports on the magnitude of old stars; monitored their demise.
- Ensured smooth running of the lab and orderly maintenance of telescopes; ordered equipment and supplies.

PUBLICATIONS:
- "Pulsars and Black Holes: Relatives or Diametric Opposites?" *New England Science Journal,* March 2006.
- "Moon Rock or Hard Rock: Our Moon in Music." *Rolling Stone Magazine,* February 2003.

CHRIS SMITH, Ph.D.
178 Green Street
Wellborn, TX 77881
(409) 555-5555
csmith@e-mail.com

OBJECTIVE

A position as a Chemist utilizing my education and experience with microcomputer systems in a laboratory setting.

PROFESSIONAL EXPERIENCE

Menden Corporation, Bryan, TX
Chemist I—Instrumentation and Computer Science (2006–Present)
Developed laboratory microcomputer systems for instrument automation and custom and specialized instrumentation/test equipment. Programmed technical applications on various microprocessors, minicomputers, and mainframe systems.

- Engineered a patented design and coordinated construction of ten particle size instruments for Quality Control and Research saving $150,000 over commercial alternatives while providing improved performance and reliability. Received Award for Technical Excellence.
- Designed and built a continuous viscometer detector for gel permeation chromatography to provide absolute molecular weight and branching data. Design was later commercialized by Cook Associates.

EDUCATION

Texas A&M University, College Station, TX
Ph.D., Chemistry, Anticipated, 2012

Baylor University, Waco, TX
M.S., Chemistry 2006

Austin College, Sherman, TX
B.S., Chemistry 2004

Chemistry Research Assistant

CHRIS SMITH
178 Green Street
West Hartford, CT 06117
(203) 555-5555
csmith@e-mail.com

OBJECTIVE:
To use extensive experience in recombinant DNA technology to help solve molecular biological problems.

EXPERIENCE:

2000–2005   RESEARCH ASSISTANT
New England Cancer Institute, Hartford, Connecticut
Performed DNA sequence analysis, S1 Mapping, plasmid and miniprep DNA purifications; made plasmid constructions.

1992–1999   CHEMIST
Drew Chemical Co., Hartford, Connecticut
Developed chemical synthetic procedures and isolation schemes for various nucleotides, nucleosides, and their derivatives.

1988–1991   GRADUATE STUDENT
Department of Physiological Chemistry, University of Connecticut, Storrs, Connecticut
Developed biochemical procedures for study of ribosome structure with respect to the RNA component.

1984–1987   RESEARCH ASSISTANT/TECHNICIAN
Department of Chemistry, Western Connecticut University, Danbury, Connecticut
Researched fungal cell metabolism; isolated plant alkaloids and their bacteria; performed various organic syntheses.

EDUCATION:
Master of Science—Physiological Chemistry, 1991
University of Connecticut, Storrs, CT

Bachelor of Science—Chemistry, 1984
Fairfield University, Fairfield, CT
Emphasis in the field of biochemistry.

Farm Manager

CHRIS SMITH
178 Green Street
Ayer, MA 01432
(508) 555-5555
csmith@e-mail.com

OBJECTIVE

To acquire a career continuation in **farm management** including animal husbandry.

AREAS OF EXPERTISE

✓ Animal Husbandry/Livestock   ✓ Crop/Produce
✓ Lambing/Foaling   ✓ Dairy Production
✓ Accounting

PROFESSIONAL EXPERIENCE

2003–Present   La Grange Farms   Ayer, MA
FARM MANAGER
Responsible for the operation of a livestock and produce farm; its marketing and accounting tasks; selling beef, lamb, and produce to supermarkets, restaurants, and roadside vegetable stands.

1990–2003   Cory-Copia Farms   Lexington, MA
ASSISTANT FARM MANAGER
Handled all livestock, dairy cows, and goats; assisted in lambing season checking for newborn foal diseases and malformations. Raised lambs and hens; baled and sold hay.

1985–1990   Pleasure Acres Farm   Brigham, KY
FARM HAND
Grew up on family owned and operated dairy and livestock farm; baled hay, collected eggs from hens, milked cows; assisted in the birth of cows and horses; assisted father and uncle in marketing meat and dairy produce to restaurants, supermarkets, and local dairies.

EDUCATION

Bunker Hill Community College, Charlestown, MA
Business Management Certificate   2002

Lexington Community College, Lexington, MA
A.S., Animal Husbandry   1994

Forest Scientist

CHRIS SMITH
178 Green Street
Olympia, WA 98502
(206) 555-5555
csmith@e-mail.com

-EXPERIENCE-

WASHINGTON STATE PARK, Olympia, WA   7/06–Present
Director of Buildings and Grounds
- Handle administrative duties for 850-acre state park.
- Oversee an annual operating budget in excess of $500,000.
- Supervise field surveys and database development.
- Prepare bid documents for contractual services.
- Consult and coordinate scientists, engineers, and other professionals for special projects.
- Develop maintenance schedules for pruning, pest and weed control, fertilization, and pH adjustments. Maintain park records, inventories, and maps.
- Propagate desirable trees and/or plants from seed or cuttings to increase or replace plants in the park collection.
- Provide information to horticulturists, arborists, students, teachers, and the public regarding plants and trees in the park.

WINSTON-SALEM PARK COMMISSION, Winston-Salem, NC   7/03–6/06
Forest Scientist
- Designed and supervised the layout and implementation of horticultural plantings for several state-owned parks and land reservations.
- Supervised total maintenance program.
- Researched and sought sources for tree and plant acquisitions.
- Planned pest control program.
- Handled overall curation of the collections.

PRINCESS GARDENS, Winston-Salem, NC
Worked summers and weekends during college, gaining experience in all phases of planning and planting public display gardens.

-EDUCATION-

WAKE FOREST UNIVERSITY, Winston-Salem, NC
Bachelor of Science in Environmental Science   2003

-COMMUNITY ACTIVITIES-

Save America's Plants (SAP), Washington Chapter—Vice President
Forest Conservation Society—Board Member, Chief Spokesperson for the Northwest Region

Forester/Park Ranger

CHRIS SMITH
178 Green Street
Felda, FL 33930
(407) 555-5555
csmith@e-mail.com

OBJECTIVE

A challenging career as a Forest Ranger where environmental and horticultural experience, education, and skill, combined with motivation and a commitment to our forests; will be utilized and advanced.

EXPERIENCE

FOUNTAIN OF YOUTH NATIONAL PARK   Felda, FL
Manager, Agrarian Development   1999–Present
- Monitor and evaluate areas of agriculture, timber/forestry, and agrarian-based industries.
- Provide consultations to U.S. Wildlife Department with regard to national and regional objectives and priorities.
- Examine all aspects of forestry/timber credit, marketing, labor, and productivity, with strict adherence to territorial logging and replacement of new pine and oak shoots.
- Generate field support for project budgetary controls on lumber projects; negotiate pricing and products with mill contractors.
- Extensive involvement in environmental protection of forests, land, fisheries, and wildlife activities.
- Document existing state of forest destruction and increase public awareness through public relations; conducted start-up group of concerned citizens and schoolchildren through field trips, lectures, films, and videos.

MYLES STANDISH STATE FOREST   Plymouth, MA
Manager, Planning and Development   1992–1999
- Performed case studies on marketing forest and public recreation areas, including inefficiencies concerning fisheries, wildlife, fire prevention/firefighting techniques, and cost of educating both public and private sectors.
- Appraised financial and economic projects for expanding public recreation areas with feasibility studies; monitored water supply, drainage and irrigation, flood protection, and ground water.

U.S. PEACE CORPS—SALIM ABBAS RESERVATION   Malaysia
Case Worker—Forester   1989–1991
- Evaluated areas of lumber, fisheries, and wildlife; examined and planned turf management.

EDUCATION

University of Massachusetts   Amherst, MA
M.S., Forest/Plant Science and Management   1998
B.S., International Agriculture   1989

Geophysicist

CHRIS SMITH
178 Green Street
Canyon, TX 79015
(806) 555-5555
csmith@e-mail.com

SUMMARY OF QUALIFICATIONS

- Planning, coordinating, and directing geophysical exploration programs and acreage evaluation, worldwide.
- Serving as a company representative in negotiation and problem resolution to contractors, industry committees, foreign governments, consortiums, and other individual companies.
- Experience in areas involving strategic planning, profitability analysis, organizational design, and preliminary acquisition studies.

EXPERIENCE

SENIOR EXPLORATION GEOPHYSICIST
The International Petroleum Company, Amarillo, TX (2004–Present)
- Full responsibility for geophysical exploration and evaluation of the Plateau of Tibet.
- Instrumental in the selection of lease blocks for application by International Petroleum.
- Responsible for projects ranging in value from $75,000 to 2 million and equipment valued in excess of $1.5 million, while supervising up to fifty people under extreme working conditions at locations both domestic and foreign.
- Originated a well logging cost-saving operation which saved as much as $100,000 per well on wells in the Persian Gulf.
- Served as company representative in exploration committees of oil company consortiums and to various service companies in contract negotiation and supervision.
- Instrumental in development of amphibious surveying operation which saved the company over $100,000 per month on eight month project.
- Helped set up and manage the first company production digital recording geophysical crew.

SENIOR COMPUTER GEOPHYSICIST
Oil Works, Inc., San Antonio, TX (2000–2003)
- Worked in nearly all field and office positions on company geophysical crew.
- Worked on staff of geophysical crew, using digital equipment and processing on a production basis.
- Completed assignments at numerous locations in Texas, New Mexico, and Mexico.

EDUCATION

FLORIDA INTERNATIONAL UNIVERSITY, Miami, FL
Bachelor of Science degree in Geological Sciences, 1996

BRIGHAM YOUNG UNVERSITY, Provo, UT
Master's degree in Geology-Geophysics, 1999

Laboratory Assistant

CHRIS SMITH
178 Green Street
Manchester, NH 03102
(603) 555-5555
csmith@e-mail.com

PROFESSIONAL OBJECTIVE

A challenging and rewarding position as a Laboratory Assistant in the field of Molecular Biology.

EDUCATION

NOTRE DAME COLLEGE, Manchester, New Hampshire
Master of Science degree in Microbiology, 2005

ST. ANSELM COLLEGE, Manchester, New Hampshire
Bachelor of Science degree in Biology, 2006
- Dean's List.
- Natural Sciences Department Award.
- Senior Class President.
- Named to *Who's Who in American Colleges and Universities*.

EXPERIENCE

ST. ANSELM COLLEGE, Manchester, New Hampshire
Laboratory Assistant to Microbiology Department Head, 2005–Present
- Prepare all media and cultures for microbiology classes.
- Order supplies for department, monitor inventory.
- Act as informal tutor, help other students.

DURHAM MEDICAL ASSOCIATES, Durham, NH
Laboratory Technician for four doctors, 2006–2005
- Initiated running of laboratory; organized equipment and materials.
- Ran tests for patients, reported on same-day basis.
- Ordered supplies; maintained inventory.

REFERENCES

Available on request.

Meteorologist

CHRIS SMITH
178 Green Street
Bar Harbor, ME 04609
(207) 555-5555

OBJECTIVE:

To secure a position as a Meteorologist at an International Airport or for Local Television.

EXPERIENCE: MAINE OCEANOGRAPHIC INSTITUTE, Bar Harbor, ME

Meteorologist 2002-Present
- Analyze and interpret data gathered by surface and upper-air stations, satellites, and radar, and those effects on the surface and subsurface of the ocean and coastline; prepare reports and forecasts.
- Prepare special forecasts and briefings for air and sea transportation, fire prevention, and air pollution.
- Observe and record weather conditions, including upper-air data on temperature, humidity, and winds using weather balloon and radiosonic equipment.

WAYN-TV, Bar Harbor, ME

TV Meteorologist/Announcer 2006-Present
- Weekend TV weather forecaster and announcer for local cable TV.
- Broad-based knowledge of TV broadcasting and forecasting weather for seasonal climate conditions affecting Bar Harbor tourism and/or natural disasters that affect the harbor's special ecosystem.

PORTLAND AIRPORT, Portland, ME

Meteorologist 2002-2004
- Part-time and on-call emergency situation staff member at small airport.
- Observe and record weather conditions utilizing weather balloon and radiosonic equipment.
- Prepare specific, timely forecasts for air transportation.
- Assist in forecasting for hurricanes, northeasters, and natural disasters.
- Conduct pilot briefings.

EDUCATION: CORNELL UNIVERSITY, Ithaca, NY

B.S. and M.S. degrees in Meteorology 2000, 2002

Excellent References Available On Request

CHRIS SMITH, Ph.D.
178 Green Street
Los Angeles, CA 90041
(213) 555-5555
csmith@e-mail.com

PROFESSIONAL EXPERIENCE

2004 to Present
SUN LABORATORIES, Los Angeles, CA
Manufacturing Research Associate II
- Developed expertise in research through production via process experimentation and operation of pilot plant equipment.
- Performed large-scale fermentation, protein purification, and other processes under GMP regulations.
- Developed system for preparing media.
- Performed related protein assays.

1989 to 1999
GRAYSON RESEARCH CORPORATION, Los Angeles, CA
Research Technician, Cell Propagation Department
- Optimized growth parameters of fibroblast and epithelial cellines.
- Scaled up culture from 25-cc T-flasks up through to 40-L fermentor microcarrier cultures; worked independently.
- Established media unit for exclusive use of department.
- Set up perfusion system.

Technician-2, Media Department
- Filtered and sterilized various media under GMP regulations.

Assistant Supervisor, Glassware Department
- Supervised department of fifteen employees.
- Prepared, sterilized, and distributed tissue culture glassware to different departments.

EDUCATION

Ph.D. Program in Biology, 2004
California Institute of Technology, Pasadena, CA
Course: Biochemistry, Molecular Biology, Protein Chemistry

Master of Liberal Arts in Biology, 2001
Occidental College, Los Angeles, CA
Concentration: Immunology

Bachelor of Science in Agricultural Engineering, 1989
Huntington College, Montgomery, AL

Zoologist

CHRIS SMITH
178 Green Street
Lexington, KY 21345
(606) 555-5555
csmith@e-mail.com

OBJECTIVE

A challenging position as a zoologist in the natural habitat of studied subjects or in the laboratory.

EDUCATION

Boston University, Boston, MA
M.S., Zoology, September 2003.

Northeastern University, Boston, MA
B.S., Zoology with a concentration in Genetics, June 2000.

Internships: Center for DNA Research, Cambridge, MA; Spring 2000.
Truman Thoroughbred Stables, Hamilton, MA; Spring 1999.
Stoneham Zoo, Stoneham, MA; Spring/Fall 1999.
Center for Genetic Research, New York, NY; Summer 1998.
Chacombe Kennel, Cohasset, MA; Spring/Fall 1997.

EMPLOYMENT

2006– Uphill Thoroughbred Stables & Stud, Lexington, KY
Present **Genetics/Breeding Specialist**
- Work directly with doctors of veterinary medicine and racehorse trainers in the breeding and grooming of top quality thoroughbreds for racing and dressage.
- Investigate genetic factors, forecast crossbreeding and artificial insemination considerations of specific mares and studs.
- Provide vets, trainers, owners, and investigators with pertinent information regarding the designated forecasts, mating seasons/procedures, and expected inherited traits.

2000–2006 Center for DNA Research, Cambridge, MA
Researcher
- Studied the effects of altering proteins in compositions of DNA.
- Closely monitored mutations and aberrations in basic cellular structure.
- Reported findings to doctors and researchers in public and private sectors; interfaced with the media.
- Coordinated teams for various experiments and procedures.

REFERENCES

Furnished upon request.

CHRIS SMITH
178 Green Street
Dillon, MT 59725
(406) 555-5555
csmith@e-mail.com

OBJECTIVE

To contribute acquired skills to a retail position.

SUMMARY OF QUALIFICATIONS

- Developed interpersonal skills, having dealt with a diversity of professionals, clients, and staff members.
- Adept at cashiering and reconciling cash.
- Proven communication abilities—both oral and written.
- Function well independently and as a team member.
- Self-motivated, able to set effective priorities to achieve immediate and long-term goals and meet operational deadlines.

EDUCATION

BURDEN JUNIOR COLLEGE, Missoula, MT
Major: Criminal Justice   B.A. Candidate, 2007

WORK HISTORY

YOUR STORE, Dillon, MT   2006–Present
Cashier
Provided customer and personnel assistance. Handled cash intake, inventory control, and light maintenance. Trained and scheduled new employees. Instituted store recycling program benefiting the Dillon Homeless Shelter.

RONDELL IMAGE, Helena, MT   2005–2006
Data/File Clerk
Assisted sales staff. General office responsibilities included data entry, typing, and filing invoices.

TARPY PERSONNEL SERVICES, Bozeman, MT   2004–2005
General Clerk
Duties included shipping and receiving, and filing invoices.

TELESTAR MARKETING, Great Falls, MT   2003–2004
Telephone Interviewer
Conducted telephone surveys dealing with general public and preselected client groups in selected demographic areas. Required strong communication skills.

REFERENCES

Furnished upon request.

Caterer

CHRIS SMITH
178 Green Street
Las Vegas, NV
(505) 555-5555 (Work)
(505) 555-4444 (Home)
csmith@e-mail.com

ACCOMPLISHMENTS
- Named "Best & Brightest New Business Owner" by the Entrepreneurial Expo, 2005.
- Coordinated and implemented CCC Employee Training Program, voted "Most Effective" by the Restaurant Association of New Mexico.
- Catered the Governor's Dinner, 2005.

PROFESSIONAL EXPERIENCE

6/05–
Present

CHRISTINE'S CATERING COMPANY, Las Vegas, NV
Owner/Manager
- Manage operations and service, handling $30,000 per week in sales.
- Organize weekly work schedules for staff of thirty-five.
- Troubleshoot staff and client problems.
- Create innovative incentive programs to motivate staff and improve customer service.

9/03–5/04

CAMPUS CATERERS, Hobbs, NV
Banquet Supervisor
- Coordinated banquets for up to 450 guests.
- Organized dining area.
- Trained new employees.
- Supervised staff of fifteen.

6/03–8/04

THE OASIS COUNTRY CLUB, Las Vegas, NV
Server
- Handled cash and credit card transactions.
- Resolved customer complaints.
- Trained new bus and wait staff.

EDUCATION

COLLEGE OF THE SOUTHWEST, Hobbs, NV
Bachelor of Science in Management, 2005.

ASSOCIATIONS

Southwest Restaurant Association, member since 2005.
The National Caterer's Guild, member since 2005.

CHRIS SMITH
178 Green Street
Boston, MA 02116
(617) 555-5555
csmith@e-mail.com

PROFESSIONAL OBJECTIVE

To obtain a position as a Pastry Chef in a restaurant environment.

PROFESSIONAL EXPERIENCE

2006 to Present   THE WILLARD HOTEL   Boston, MA
Assistant Pastry Chef
- Work directly with executive pastry chef. Monitor the baking, mixing, and finishing of cakes, pastries, and a full range of bakery products on an as-needed basis.
- Includes work for Special Orders, banquets, special functions, and the Hotel Restaurant. Schedule and management of personnel. Supervise a four-member staff.

2005   CATERING BY C. SMITH   Everett, MA
Pastry Cook
- Worked concurrently with above position, helping out during the busy season, on a half-time basis, with the baking and finishing of breads and pastries.

2004 to 2005   THE BANNEN INN   Bangor, ME
Rounds Cook
- Cooked dishes to order as needed. Streamlined workflow, acted as a management liaison, scheduled shifts and provided inventory control and the troubleshooting of related problems on an as-needed basis.

2003 to 2004   LE HOTEL DE VIVRE   Bangor, ME
Pastry Cook
- Assisted the manager with all phases of shop management; the production of baked goods, the servicing of accounts, etc. Performed the baking, mixing, and decoration of cakes. Provided inventory control.

2001 to 2003   KIKI COUNTRY CLUB   Boston, MA
Sauté and Broiler Cook
- Performed all associated prep work, including handling stations and cooking food items.

EDUCATION

2002   AMERICAN PASTRY ARTS CENTER   Medford, MA
Course in Chocolates and Candy
- Understudy of Sid Cherney

2001   GOURMET INSTITUTE OF AMERICA   Boston, MA
A.O.S. Degree
- Earned Certificates in Food and Management Sanitation.

Chef
Pastry

CHRIS SMITH
178 Green Street
Eugene, OR 97401
(503) 555-5555
csmith@e-mail.com

OBJECTIVE
To contribute extensive experience, educational background, and culinary skills to the position of Pastry Chef within a restaurant environment.

SUMMARY OF QUALIFICATIONS
- Thorough knowledge in the preparation of an extensive assortment of baked goods, including: pastries, cookies, puddings, muffins, breads, and specialties.
- Consistently utilizing creative talents to develop attractive presentations, and proficient in the production of original creations.
- Competent in organizing production to maximize use of available space.
- Able to direct workflow in an accurate, timely, and efficient manner.
- Recipient of numerous Culinary Awards for superior creations.

EXPERIENCE

1/06 to Present   *Pastry Chef*
THE BEVENSHIRE HOTEL   Eugene, OR
- Plan and prepare three desserts on a daily basis for Faculty Club.
- Produce truffles and special pastries for Dean's House.
- Prepare desserts for in-house groups, serving 100–200 people.

10/04 to 1/06   *Pastry Chef*
DELTA PINES BAKERY & CAFE   Corvallis, OR
- Prepared an extensive assortment of desserts, rotating on a weekly basis, including cakes, cookies, cobblers, puddings, tarts, special-order desserts, and wedding cakes.
- Mixed puff pastry, croissant, and Danish doughs.
- Created breakfast pastries and breads for lunch specials.

3/02 to 10/04   *Pastry Chef*
THE PLUMROSE RESTAURANT   Corvallis, OR
- Planned and executed monthly menu which included six desserts, two sorbets, two ice cream dishes, and two fresh breads, daily for lunch and dinner.
- Ordered all bakery and dairy supplies and created brunch breads.
- Prepared desserts for retail store and special orders.

EDUCATION

6/96
ESTERBROOK INN   New York, NY
American Culinary Federation: Certified Cook

10/99 to 7/02
- Butcher Assistant, Rodeo Ranch, six months
- Soup and Sauce preparation, six months
- Garde Manager, ice and tallow sculpture, six months
- Pastry Assistant, one year

Cosmetologist

CHRIS SMITH
178 Green Street
Marion, IN 46952
(317) 555-5555
csmith@e-mail.com

PROFESSIONAL EXPERIENCE

2005–Present **LATITIA GREEN ACADEMY,** Marion, IN
<u>**Instructor**</u>
- Provide instruction to all levels in cosmetology theory and practical applications.
- Develop lesson plans in all subjects; administer tests; give demonstrations.
- Motivate and counsel twenty-student classes; evaluate tests and performances.

2002–Present **LE SALON DESIREE,** Lafayette, IN
<u>**Owner/Operator**</u>
- Hairdresser/Cosmetologist performing all relevant functions.
- Arranged for promotion of business and maintained good customer relations.

1998–2002 **DYE HEALTHY SALON,** Muncie, IN
<u>**Hairdresser**</u>
- Performed hairdressing, manicuring, skin care, hair coloring, and hair styling.

1997–1998 **BORELLI MORALIO SALON,** Lisbon, Portugal
Hairdresser
- Provided hairdressing, skin care, facials, permanents, and hair coloring.

1995–1997 **ZACHARY DRAKE'S SHOP,** Lisbon, Portugal
Hairdresser
- Serviced customers with hairdressing, manicuring, skin care, facials.

EDUCATION

WINNIFRED ACADEMY, Muncie, IN; Completed Cosmetology course work. Received License #1 (#1372), 1999.
BONNY LASS BEAUTY ACADEMY, Lisbon, Portugal; Completed one-year course in Cosmetology, 1995.

PERSONAL

Bilingual in English and Portuguese. Managed a grocery store in Lisbon, Portugal, for three years.

REFERENCES

Furnished upon request.

Customer Service Representative
Credit

CHRIS SMITH
178 Green Street
Volga, SD 57071
(605) 555-5555
csmith@e-mail.com

CAREER DEVELOPMENT

Credit Office Representative, **The Gillis Corporation, Volga, SD** (October 2006–Present)
- Work with customers to resolve problems concerning billing.
- Assist sales staff with questions on transactions and billing.
- Responsible for cash reconciliation from all registers in store.

Customer Service Representative/Medical Underwriter (June 2002–September 2006)
Desmond Insurance Company, Sinai, SD
- Responsible for underwriting/enrollment of insurance applications and requisitions for change.
- Dealt directly with applicants advising them of enrollment options, plan design features, billing processes, and resolution of problems.
- Handled enrollment/underwriting reports; provided marketing/installation support.

Employment Interviewer, **State of South Dakota** (June 2001–May 2002)
Department of Labor, Brookings, SD
- Interviewed job applicants in unemployment office.
- Reviewed applicants for job placements; fielded job openings from local employers, and assisted employers in filling job orders.
- Received job orders over phone and entered them in computer to facilitate selection and referral process.
- Attended classes on Public Speaking and Interviewing Techniques.

OTHER EXPERIENCE

Shoe Sales Representative—Tilden Department Store, Aurora, SD (Summers 1997–2000)
- In conjunction with the above, worked for this Department Store assisting customers in selecting footwear; cashiering, totaled department daily sales amounts, trained new associates.

Arlington Day Camp, Arlington, SD (September 2000–May 2001)
- Supervised and coordinated activities for children. Prepared schedule and payroll for all employees.

President and Founder—Brookings Baby-Sitting Service, (September 1997–May 1999)
Brookings, SD
- Established baby-sitting service for local residents in Brookings area. Acted as referral service for associates. Created business protocol and guidelines.

EDUCATION

South Dakota State University, Brookings, SD
Bachelor of Arts degree in Health Care, 2001

CHRIS SMITH
178 Green Street
Carson City, NV 89703
(702) 555-5555
csmith@e-mail.com

PROFESSIONAL OBJECTIVE

A challenging, growth-oriented position in the fast-food industry in which academic training, work experience, and a commitment to excellence will have valuable application.

EMPLOYMENT

2005–Present   THE PIZZA PLACE, Carson City, NV
Server
- Participate in opening of new store outlets.
- Assist with public relations, food service, and register control.
- Resolve conflicts in high-pressure environment.

2003–2005   NEVADA TELEPHONE, Las Vegas, NV
Data Input/Repetitive Debts Collection/Commercial
- Responsible for commercial account installation and verification of records and old accounts for new service.
- Maintained computer for bill revisions through referrals.
- Executed customer services, fielded inquiries, and consumer services.

Summers   BLACKTHORN DAY CAMP, Plaistow, NH
2000–2002   **Recreation Director**
- Planned, programmed, and supervised camp activities for summer outdoor education and camping services for juvenile coeds.
- Supervised cabin group, counseled, and instructed in aquatics, sports, and special events.

1997–1999   SISYPHUS GROCERY, Manchester, NH
Cashier/Produce Section
- Maintained produce inventory, cash control, public relations, and in-house advertising for special sales and events.
- Strong communications and interpersonal skills required.

EDUCATIONAL BACKGROUND

MANCHESTER HIGH SCHOOL, Manchester, NH
Diploma, College Preparatory, 2004
Varsity Sports (four years), Blue Key Club.

Flight Attendant
Reserve

CHRIS SMITH
178 Green Street
Peoria, IL 61603
(309) 555-5555
csmith@e-mail.com

PROFILE
Certified flight attendant with over four years experience working overseas/domestic flights. Specialized training in CPR and emergency evacuation/crisis procedures. Fluent in Russian and English; knowledgeable in German language.

SKILLS
Communication

- Bachelor of Arts degree in Communications.
- Developed interpersonal skills, having dealt with a diversity of professionals, clients, and associates.
- Fluent in Russian and English; knowledgeable in German language.

Customer Service

- Over five years experience in retail and sales, dealing with a wide variety of clients.
- Adept at handling customer complaints and problem-solving.

Specialized Training

- Certified flight attendant.
- CPR certified.
- Participated in three-day intensive training seminar: "Reacting in an Emergency."

PROFESSIONAL EXPERIENCE
9/06–Present   WANDER IN WONDER WORLD AIRWAYS, O'Hare Airport, Chicago, IL
Flight Attendant, overseas/domestic flights
- Assist in customer boarding.
- Supervise equipment/supply loading.
- Ensure passenger safety and comfort.
- Maintain passenger manifest and seating allocations.
- Handle bilingual safety instructions and travel problems (emergency landings, etc.).

OTHER EXPERIENCE
2006   THE CRAFTY BOUTIQUE, Orlando, FL, **Salesperson/Manager's Assistant**

2005–2006   BEST BET BUSINESS TEMPS, Chicago, IL, **Account Representative**

2004–2006   THE TAX TASKMASTER, Normal, IL, **Sales Assistant**

2002–2004   THE CHASIN BANK, Joliet, IL, **Teller/Customer Service Representative**

EDUCATION
FANTASTIC FLIGHTS TRAINING CENTER, Orlando, FL
Received Flight Attendant Certificate, 2006
ILLINOIS COLLEGE, Jackson, IL
B.A. in Communications, August, 2004

PERSONAL
Extensive travel including Europe, Asia, and the United States. Willing to relocate.

Hairstylist

CHRIS SMITH
178 Green Street
Menoken, ND 58558
(701) 555-5555
csmith@e-mail.com

OBJECTIVE:

A position with a leading hair salon.

SUMMARY OF QUALIFICATIONS:
- Certified hairstylist.
- Ability to work efficiently, thus reducing customer waiting time.
- Coordinated promotional events with local radio stations, including the first annual "Much Ado about Hair-Dos and Don'ts."
- Named "Most Promising Hairstylist" by the *Bismarck Gazette*.

PROFESSIONAL EXPERIENCE:

2003–Present **The Hair Studio, Mandan, ND**
Hairstylist
- Skilled in various hair cutting techniques such as texturing.
- Working knowledge of permanents, body waves, and spiral perms.
- Use prepared dyes; also create colors desired by clients.
- Perform waxing services.
- Style hair for local fashion shows: French braids, twists, floral weaves.
- Doubled base-clientele within first two months.
- Answer phones and schedule appointments.

1999–2002 **Hair America, McKenzie, ND**
Hairstylist
- Performed duties as above.
- Independently sold hair care products.
- Manicured nails.

EDUCATION:

National Hair Academy, Bismarck, ND
Hair Styling Certification, 1999

INTERESTS:

Skiing, Scuba Diving, Mystery Novels.

REFERENCES:

Available Upon Request.

Hotel Clerk

CHRIS SMITH
178 Green Street
Halstead, KS 67056
(316) 555-5555
csmith@e-mail.com

OBJECTIVE

To contribute developed customer relations and administrative skills to a challenging position in a hotel.

SUMMARY OF QUALIFICATIONS

- Developed interpersonal skills, having dealt with a diversity of clients, professionals, and staff members.
- Detail- and goal-oriented.
- Function well in high-stress atmosphere.
- Knowledgeable on both Mac and PC computer systems.

CAREER HISTORY

THE OLIVER HOTEL, Whitewater, KS   2006–Present
Hotel Clerk
Resolved guests' needs. Controlled reservation input utilizing PC computer system. Handled incoming calls. Maintained daily reports involving return guests, corporate accounts, and suite rentals. Inspected rooms.

WALDEN HOTEL, Walton, KS   2003–2006
Hotel Clerk
Trained personnel. Handled telephone bookings. Maintained daily and monthly reports tracking demands and guaranteed no-show billing. Utilized computer for inputting group bookings and lists.

READ ALL ABOUT IT, Newton, KS   2001–2002
Sales Asscociate
Assisted customers. Maintained stock. Opened and closed shop. Tracked best-selling novels, and made recommendations to customers.

BETHEL COLLEGE, North Newton, KS   1998–2000
Secretary
Responsible for general clerical duties. Resolved inquiries. Assisted in locating guest speakers.

EDUCATION

BETHANY COLLEGE, Lindsborg, KS
Bachelor of Science: Sociology, 1998

REFERENCES

Furnished upon request.

Hotel Concierge

CHRIS SMITH
178 Green Street
Milwaukee, WI 53233
(414) 555-5555
csmith@e-mail.com

PROFESSIONAL EXPERIENCE

2005 to
Present

JAMESON HOTEL, Milwaukee, WI
Concierge, 2006–Present
- Promoted to establish Concierge Department in 350-room luxury hotel.
- Responsible for setting tone and image of hotel through providing guest services, including tourist information, tour arrangements, and hotel and airline reservations.
- Procure theater and symphony tickets.
- Arrange car rentals and limousine hires.
- Handle and route guest mail and faxes.
- Make restaurant recommendations and dinner reservations based on comprehensive knowledge and contact with area restaurants and management.
- Supervise/manage forty-person hotel staff including Concierge Department Assistants, Mail and Information Clerks, Bell Staff, Doormen, Valet Parking and Hotel Garage Staff, and Telephone Operators.
- Flexible schedule includes weekends and evenings.
- Extensive knowledge of all areas of hotel operation.
- Interact with other hotel departments to ensure full guest service.
- Diplomatically and effectively resolve guest grievances/problems; compose responses and make follow-up phone contact.
- During hotel's promotion, handled all guests from check-in to check-out; coordinated 2,500 museum tickets, consulting with guests on preferred times.
- Assist in hotel promotions and marketing strategies; coordinate all Bridal Package arrangements.
- Administer emergency lifesaving procedures as necessary; work well under pressure and in difficult situations.
- Ability to function in a variety of capacities within the hotel structure.

Bell Captain, 2005–2006
- Supervised all Bellstaff and Doormen.
- Acted in role of Concierge prior to establishment of Concierge Department.

Doorman/Bellman, 2005
- Greeted guests; fostered positive impression of establishment.

EDUCATION

Sorbonne University, Paris, France: Summer 2000
Marquette University, Milwaukee, WI: 1999–2001

ADDITIONAL

Working knowledge of French.
Certified in CPR and First Aid.

Hotel Manager
Housekeeping

CHRIS SMITH
178 Green Street
Charleston, WV 25314
(304) 555-5555
csmith@e-mail.com

OBJECTIVE
To contribute developed customer relations, managerial, and accounting skills to a challenging position in hotel management.

SUMMARY
- Capable manager and motivator of staff.
- Function well in high-stress atmosphere.
- Detail- and goal-oriented.
- Highly developed interpersonal skills.
- Developed innovative and efficient system of reconciliation.
- Skilled in utilization of various computer systems.

EXPERIENCE

2005–Present   DONNELY HOTEL, Charleston, WV
Assistant Manager, Housekeeping
- Manage 100 employees.
- Ensure standards of guest rooms.
- Prepare biweekly and monthly housekeeping inventory.
- Develop budget worksheets utilizing FileMaker.
- Assist in weekly labor forecasting and scheduling.
- Certified in Interaction Management.

2003–2005   NEWPORT HEIGHTS HOTEL, Montgomery, WV
Chief Night Auditor/Manager On Duty
- Managed technically proficient and hospitality-oriented staff.
- Supervised reconciliation of all Front Desk and Food and Beverage transactions.
- Maintained hotel computer system. Required weekly reorganizations and various other functions.
- Compiled and distributed Daily Business Summary, using Excel.
- Administered overnight operations of Front Desk, Security, and Food and Beverage outlets.
- Nominated Manager of the Year, 2004.

2000–2002   **Night Auditor**
- Coordinated check-in and check-out of all guests.
- Assisted in reconciliation of all transactions.
- Cooperated in implementation of Food and Beverage cashiering system.
- Developed and implemented efficient system to reconcile Food and Beverage transactions.
- Dealt with preparation of Daily Business Summary.

EDUCATION   WEST VIRGINIA STATE COLLEGE, Institute, WV
Course: Principles of Accounting I & II, 2000.

CHRIS SMITH
178 Green Street
Colchester, VT 05446
(802) 555-5555
csmith@e-mail.com

PROFESSIONAL OBJECTIVE
To obtain a challenging position in the field of Restaurant or Food Service Management.

PROFESSIONAL EXPERIENCE

2006 to Present   BURGER CHEF, Colchester, VT
Manager
- Responsible for Shift Scheduling, Personnel Management, Inventory Control, maintenance of Physical Plant and Lockbox.
- Supervise up to twenty employees per shift.
- Responsible for all cash received per shift.
- Completed Management Training Program.

2003 to 2006   BLACK DIAMOND ICE CREAM CORPORATION, Mount Snow, VT
Shift Supervisor
- Controlled Shift Management, Personnel, Cash Deposits, Opening and Closing, Inventory Control, and Management Reports.
- Promoted to manager from cook.

2001 to 2003   GRIMSHAW LOUNGE, South Burlington, VT
Manager
- Supervised staff of thirty employees per shift.
- Monitored food costs and filed reports.
- Planned weekly menu, made changes where necessary.

2000 to 2001   THE YEE-HAH RESTAURANT, Brattleboro, VT
Manager
- Responsible for Night Shift Management, Special Function Catering, and Kitchen Personnel.
- Hired and trained staff, monitored payroll, and supervised banquets.

EDUCATION
1998 to 2000   CHURCHILL CULINARY ARTS SCHOOL
- Successfully completed two-year course of study.

COMMUNITY ORGANIZATIONS
- Volunteer time and cooking skills at Snacks on Tracks and the Boys Club of Colchester.

Sanitation Inspector

CHRIS SMITH
178 Green Street
Rockford, IL 61110
(815) 555-5555
csmith@e-mail.com

OBJECTIVE: Seeking a challenging position in the Sanitation Field where experience and proven sanitation skills will have valuable application.

PROFILE: Registered sanitation inspector with over twenty years of experience. Proven effective in strict adherence to issues of public health and safety.

EXPERIENCE:

Colorado Board of Health, Denver, CO   1995–Present
Chief Sanitation Inspector
- Ensure all department regulations are adhered to in an orderly, strict, and timely fashion; supervise staff of twelve.
- Conduct inspections in restaurants, retail food stores, bath and massage establishments, and funeral parlors.
- Provide documentation to Board of Health; distribute warning and/or terminate existence if establishments fail inspections.

Chicago Health Department, Chicago, IL   1985–1995
Sanitation Inspector
- Participated in exams and regulatory inspections of restaurants, supermarkets, funeral parlors, commercial buildings, and housing facilities in the greater Chicago area.
- Ensured all inspections were within regulations of the Illinois General Laws, State Sanitary Codes, and Local Ordinances.

Chicago Health Department, Chicago, IL   Fall 1984
Internship—Inspector's Offices
- Accompanied and assisted inspectors in their rounds of restaurants and fast food facilities, hospital kitchens, and shelters.

EDUCATION:

University of Chicago, 1985
B.S., Environmental Health and Sciences
Certification: Registered Sanitation Inspector, 1985

Waitperson

CHRIS SMITH
178 Green Street
Kaneohe, HI 96744
(808) 555-5555
csmith@e-mail.com

EXPERIENCE

THE PALMS, Kaneohe, HI   5/06–Present
Head Waiter
- Managed, opened, and closed high-volume restaurant. Hired, terminated, trained, scheduled, and supervised wait staff.
- Reconciled cash intake.

PALUA SAILS RESTAURANT, Kaneohe, HI   5/04–5/06
Head Waiter
- Provided efficient service to full bar and serving area.
- Chosen Employee of the Month.

CANDLE IN THE WIND, Honolulu, HI   10/03–5/04
Barback
- Handled customer service and cash intake.
- Assisted with liquor inventory.

BLUE HAWAII RESTAURANT, Honolulu, HI   7/02–10/03
Busboy
- Organized large dining room.
- Trained new bus people.

ADDITIONAL TRAINING
- Certified in the SIPS Program for responsibly serving alcohol.
- Attended Restaurant Association training session.

EDUCATION

HAWAII LOA COLLEGE, Kaneohe, HI
Major: Liberal Arts
Degree Expected: 2008

INTERESTS

Photography, parasailing, surfing.

Case Worker/Legal Advocate

CHRIS SMITH
178 Green Street
East Troy, WI
(414) 555-5555
csmith@e-mail.com

PROFESSIONAL EXPERIENCE

2005–
Present **Case Worker/Legal Advocate, The Women's Safe Place**   East Troy, WI
Night manager of shelter for abused women and their children. Monitor 24-hour hotline and authorize admitting residents on an emergency basis. Organize, prepare, and present seminars to high school students on domestic violence and lead discussions to raise awareness. Assist Associate Director in planning public relations and fundraising events. Assist women in completing Temporary Restraining Orders. Provide support and access to legal resources to women in crisis situations. Advocate for women before judges in family court proceedings. Act as Coalition observer during domestic violence legal cases and report outcomes to staff.

2003–2005 **Associate Editor/Program Coordinator**
Baby's Breath Press   Madison, WI
Developed, wrote, and edited articles for monthly business management newsletter. Writing involved combining multiple sources of information and organizing pertinent facts for a business-oriented audience. Developed and wrote articles with outside authors involving case studies on management-development within their organizations. Assisted editorial department in planning content of newsletter by selecting topics for publication. All work performed in a strict deadline-oriented environment. Worked with the fifty people who presented at the annual conference by assisting them with their presentations.

2002–2005 **Writer, *The Republic***   Madison, WI
Researched a variety of sources incorporating various philosophies and wrote articles on women's issues for a quarterly literary magazine in Madison.

EDUCATION

2003 Beloit College   Beloit, WI
Bachelor of Arts in Sociology, Concentration in Economic Stratification and Social Hierarchies. Courses include Poverty and Crisis, Gerontology, and Women in Society. Independent study topic: "The Feminization of Poverty in the United States." Member of the Phi Beta Kappa honor society. Member of student-run Volunteers for a Better World program. Codirected campus food drive. Contributing writer for the Vanguard Press.

Counselor
Career Changer

CHRIS SMITH
178 Green Street
Washington, DC 20008
(202) 555-5555
csmith@e-mail.com

OBJECTIVE

A challenging and progressively responsible position in COUNSELING.

EDUCATION

American University, Washington, D.C.
Bachelor of Science in Psychology and Sociology, 1995

Coursework included the following:

Drugs and Society	Death and Mourning
Sociology of Medicine	Psychology of Women
Speech Pathology	Experimental Psychology

STRENGTHS

Fluent in German; mature, sound decision-making skills; ability to establish trusting relationships with individuals; keep accurate records; relate positively with people from diverse backgrounds; strong communication skills; enthusiastic; genuine desire to be of service to people.

EMPLOYMENT HIGHLIGHTS

American University, Washington, D.C.
Record Coordinator Create, maintain, and update academic records. Assess student charges. Instruct and assist students in registration procedures. Act as liaison with academic and administrative offices. Supervise activities of part-time personnel.
(1996–Present)

Natack & Company, Washington, D.C.
Assistant Controller/Full Charge Bookkeeper Directed activities of all bookkeeping personnel, including training and orientation. Prepared quarterly reports and financial statements.
(1986–1994)

REFERENCES

Furnished upon request.

Counselor
School

CHRIS SMITH
178 Green Street
Fort Lauderdale, FL 38314
(305) 555-5555
csmith@e-mail.com

PROFESSIONAL OBJECTIVE

A counseling position in which my education and bicultural experience will have valuable application.

PROFESSIONAL EXPERIENCE

1999 to Present — AMERICAN SCHOOL OF RECIFE, Recife, Brazil
Counselor, International Primary School
- Administer psychological and educational testing for students ranging from pre-kindergarten to fifth grade.
- Counsel students, families, and teachers.
- Design remedial and therapeutic plans.
- Lead group activities for self-image enhancement and behavior modification.
- Work with teachers in preventive strategies for social and disciplinary problems.

1998 to 2000 — INSTITUTE OF AMERICA, Sao Paulo, Brazil
Guidance Counselor
- Counsel individuals and families for students ranging from pre-kindergarten to twelfth grade.
- Designed complete record-keeping system for all students.
- Performed valuable clarification exercises with students.
- Implemented behavior modification programs.
- Administered achievement, vocational, and college-prep tests.
- Made policy on admissions and discipline.
- Worked with teachers on individual educational programs.

1998 to Present — PRIVATE COUNSELING PRACTICES, Miami, Recife, and Sao Paulo
Counselor
- Bilingual English and Spanish counseling.

EDUCATION

Master of Arts in Counseling Psychology, Nova University
Fort Lauderdale, Florida, 1998
Concentration: Community Clinical; GPA: 3.7
Bachelor of Arts in Developmental Psychology, Barry University
Miami Shores, Florida, 1996
Associate of Arts in Human Development, Barry University
Miami Shores, Florida, 1995
Cum Laude Graduate

References available upon request.

Economic Development Coordinator

CHRIS SMITH
178 Green Street
Cambridge, MA 02139
(617) 555-5555
csmith@e-mail.com

PROFESSIONAL OBJECTIVE

To secure a challenging position overseas in **Economic Development** for a non-governmental organization.

SUMMARY OF QUALIFICATIONS

- Several years experience working overseas in developing countries.
- Fluent in Spanish: Foreign Service Level 4.
- Proficient in Japanese: Foreign Service Level 2.
- Empirical Analysis: Hypothesis Testing, Regression Analysis, Accounting, and Budgeting.
- Micro- and Macro-Economic Analysis.

OVERSEAS EXPERIENCE

WORLD FRIENDS, U.S.A./Ethiopia   2006–Present
Economic Development Coordinator
Implemented a rural, small-scale enterprise and credit program. Planned and ran workshops for village councils and entrepreneurs in credit management and accounting. Assisted entrepreneurs with feasibility analysis and loan applications. Did research for senior thesis on rural, small-scale enterprise and credit, which was subsequently sent to S.C.F. in Ethiopia.

INDEPENDENT TEACHER, Bombay, India   2004–2006
English Teacher
Taught English conversation and grammar to students, ages seven through adult, both privately and in classroom.

WORLD FRIENDS, U.S.A./Japan   2000–2004
Proposal Writer
Researched and wrote a position case-study on landlessness in one district of Japan. Contributed to the development of a new small-scale enterprise project.

HELPING HANDS, Ashau Valley, Vietnam   1997–2000
Health Projects Coordinator
Worked on health-related issues including community mobilization for latrine construction and education for strategies to combat waterborne diseases.

EDUCATION

School of Government, Harvard University, Cambridge, MA
Master's degree in Public Policy; concentration in International Development, 1997.

College of Arts and Sciences, Harvard University, Cambridge, MA
Bachelor of Arts in International Development.
Graduated Summa Cum Laude, with distinction, 1994.

Human Services Worker

Juvenile and Family

CHRIS SMITH
178 Green Street
Elmhurst, IL 60126
(312) 555-5555
csmith@e-mail.com

OBJECTIVE

To contribute comprehensive experience and educational background to a challenging position as a Human Services Worker.

SUMMARY OF QUALIFICATIONS

- Thorough knowledge and management of cases for juveniles and families, which required assessment, development of clinical treatment plans, facilitation of crisis intervention procedures, and informal family therapy.
- Developed exceptional counseling skills, motivating several individuals to enter programs for substance abuse treatment.
- Extensive experience and familiarity with child abuse and neglect cases.
- Excellent rapport with children; superior communication abilities.

EXPERIENCE

2003 to Present   **Investigator/Ongoing Case Manager**
SOCIETY FOR THE PREVENTION OF CRUELTY TO CHILDREN   Chicago, IL

- Conduct assessments and develop treatment plans for family caseload.
- Maintain ongoing written documentation of contracts.
- Provide crisis intervention and informal family therapy.
- Serve as advocate for clients in court and with community agencies.

2001 to 2002   **Intern**
FARMINGTON JUVENILE COURT   Farmington, IL

- Established monitor contacts and composed monitor reports.
- Tracked abuse and neglect cases to ensure that status reports and petitions were filed accurately and on time.
- Observed court hearings and trials and established court expectations.

2000 to 2001   **Intern**
PEORIA JUVENILE COURT   Peoria, IL

- Provided individual and group counseling for juvenile offenders in detention.
- Reviewed case files and incident reports.

1999   **Intern**
DEPARTMENT OF MENTAL HEALTH   Gardena, IL

- Assisted mentally challenged adults in the enhancement of motor skills and encouraged the development of self-esteem and self-sufficiency.

EDUCATION

BRADLEY UNIVERSITY   Peoria, IL
Bachelor of Science degree: Human Services, 2002

REFERENCES FURNISHED UPON REQUEST.

Program Coordinator

CHRIS SMITH
178 Green Street
Alexandria, VA 22311
(703) 555-5555
csmith@e-mail.com

OBJECTIVE
The coordination of production for advertising and promotion, mass communication, or related areas.

SUMMARY OF QUALIFICATIONS
- Bachelor of Arts degree in Political Science.
- Coordination of all production activities associated with fundraising through mass mailing programs.
- Grant proposal preparation.
- Fundraising and staff training.
- Contact list maintenance.

PROGRAM COORDINATOR   2005–Present
Watercrest Developers, Alexandria, VA
Responsibilities with this fundraising arm of Watercrest Developers include:
- Provide direct assistance to the Director of Fundraising Programs; emphasis on direct mail aspect of the Annual Giving Program.
- Coordinate planning, copywriting, production, and analysis of program results as well as procedural detail and in-house consultant reports.
- Streamlined procedures for mailings of 80,000 pieces and saved 40% in printing costs through vendor survey and negotiation.
- Conduct market research, copyediting, and consulting-supervision of telemarketing activities and other functions required in the smooth enactment of sixteen annual mailings totaling approximately 300,000 pieces while managing a $600,000 budget. Overall results in 2005: $3.1 million.

FUNDRAISER/SUPERVISOR   2003–2005
Nathan Hawke Associates, Manassas, VA
- Director of fundraising team responsible for initiating and developing contacts with political contributors for conservative parties and organizations.
- Interviewed, trained, and supervised staff of twenty, while managing coordination of workflow.
- Assisted with preparation of promotional letters for campaign fund solicitations.

DEVELOPMENT/ADMINISTRATIVE ASSISTANT   2002–2003
Appleton Art Abode, Appleton, WI
- Assisted in preparation of grant proposals; prepared and reviewed proposals for events at Art Center, while organizing and providing production support for publication of the Appleton News.

EDUCATION
Lawrence University, Appleton, WI
Bachelor of Arts degree, 2001
Major: Political Science

Psychiatric Counselor

CHRIS SMITH
178 Green Street
Otter Creek, FL 32683
(904) 555-5555
csmith@e-mail.com

EXPERIENCE

2005 to Present   **CAUFIELD PSYCHIATRIC HOSPITAL, Usher, FL**
Psychiatric Counselor
Responsible for crisis intervention for both adult and adolescent clients, psychiatric assessments and evaluations, and patient admissions to specific units. Observe suicidal patients on a one-to-one basis and use physical restraint when necessary. Manage and stabilize unit teams in resolving problems. Submit reports.

2002 to 2004   **CROSS CITY HOSPITAL, Psychiatric Unit, Cross City, FL**
Psychiatric Counselor
Handled psychiatric assessments, evaluations, and attendant reports. Conducted adult and geriatric counseling as well as group community meetings. Taught daily life skills. Prepared treatment plans. Monitored vital signs. Dealt with crisis intervention and assessment of suicide risk. Acted as in-service educator.

1999 to 2001   **PRIMECARE, Jasper, FL**
Counselor
Responsible for unit management, primary care, cooking, feeding residents, nursing care, and crisis intervention. Taught daily living skills to facilitate independence.

1997 to 1998   **VERNON HOUSE, Monticello, FL**
Psychiatric Counselor
Taught patient independence at halfway house. Provided crisis intervention, house management, case management, and case prevention in addition to cooking, feeding, and assisting with cleaning.

1995 to 1996   **FLORIDA STATE HOSPITAL, Ponce de Leon, FL**
Counselor
Supervised activities and recreation for twelve boys. Submitted reports. Acted as liaison between center and District Court.

1990 to 1994   **PANAMA CITY HOSPITAL, Panama City, FL**
Psychiatric Counselor
Handled psychiatric admissions and case presentations. Conducted community meetings. Provided in-service education for counselors and nurses.

1988 to 1989   **WEST FLORIDA REHABILITATION CENTER, Pensacola, FL**
Psychiatric Counselor
Provided individual, group, and family counseling, case management, and presentations. Conducted film presentations and discussion groups.

EDUCATION

UNIVERSITY OF WEST FLORIDA, Pensacola, FL
Bachelor of Science in Developmental Psychology, 1988

CHRIS SMITH
178 Green Street
Chalmette, LA 70043
(504) 555-5555
csmith@e-mail.com

EDUCATION

TULANE UNIVERSITY   New Orleans, LA
Master's in Social Work   May, 2002

LOYOLA UNIVERSITY   New Orleans, LA
Bachelor of Arts, Psychology   May, 2000
Research assistant to Dr. Sophie Dillon. Project involved studying intrinsic and extrinsic motivation in children.
Dean's List.

PROFESSIONAL EXPERIENCE

CHALMETTE CHILDREN'S HOSPITAL
Early Intervention Program   Chalmette, LA
Social Worker/Case Manager   August 2002–Present
Member of interdisciplinary team serving children who are at environmental and/or biological risk. Responsibilities include: clinical, concrete, and supportive services, education for families, and developmental stimulation for children. Services provided via home visits and participation in classroom team for children.

NEW ORLEANS TEEN CLINIC   New Orleans, LA
Intern   September 2001–May 2002
Provided individual social work to children and adolescents, including pregnant teens and foster parents. Cooperated with Department of Social Services regarding treatment and placement of children in foster care.

VETERAN'S ADMINISTRATION HOSPITAL OF NEW ORLEANS New Orleans, LA
Intern   September 2000–May 2001
Medical and psychiatric social work involving direct patient care with both individuals and groups at outpatient clinic. Cooperative experience with nationally recognized pain team at New Orleans Outpatient Clinic.

PROFESSIONAL INTERESTS

Adolescent behavior, Gifted Children, Neuropsychology

REFERENCES

Available upon request.

Therapist

CHRIS SMITH
178 Green Street
Houma, LA 70363
(504) 555-5555
csmith@e-mail.com

EXPERIENCE

THERAPIST   2006–Present
Private Practice   Houma, LA
Render quality counseling services to private clientele with varied psychological disorders. Develop rapport and relationships of trust; facilitate clear communication. Assess symptoms and personal information to diagnose problems and devise effective treatment strategies.

- Assess client progress and effectiveness of treatment plans.
- Involve guardians and family members in supporting therapeutic activities.
- Make referrals to specialists or social service organizations as appropriate.
- Maintain knowledge of new developments in the field and applications to personal practice.

COORDINATOR OF PROGRAM SERVICES
COUNSELOR/ADVOCATE   2003–2006
Domestic Violence Services, Inc.   Orono, ME
Provided leadership and management expertise for efficient daily operations of this nonprofit organization specializing in counseling and services for victims of domestic violence. Assessed needs and coordinated delivery of information, referrals, advocacy, and counseling.

- Responded appropriately to hotline calls and emergency situations.
- Provided one-on-one counseling to battered women and children.
- Conducted play groups for children living in the shelter, as volunteer in 2003.
- Served as Intern Advocate for victims before the Orono Superior court.

EDUCATION

MASTER OF ARTS IN PSYCHOLOGY, 2006
Teacher's College, University of Maine, Orono, ME
Master's Thesis: Impact of Classroom Learning on Students' Behavior

BACHELOR OF ARTS IN PSYCHOLOGY, 2003
Colby College, Waterville, ME

Additional courses, workshops, and seminars:
Identification and Treatment of Trauma and Abuse • Rational Emotive Therapy
CareerPro Leadership Seminar • Group Facilitation • Cultural Diversity
AIDS • Drugs and Alcohol Abuse • Supervision and Management Training
Family Therapy • Battered Women Syndrome • Women Portrayed in Media

College Student Applying for an Internship

CHRIS SMITH
csmith@e-mail.com

School Address:
178 Green Street
Skidell, LA 70458
(504) 555-5555

Permanent Address:
23 Blue Street
New Orleans, LA 70128
(504) 555-4444

OBJECTIVE
A summer internship in the book publishing industry.

SYNOPSIS
Self-starter and fast learner with positive attitude regarding goal direction.
Excellent communicator with the ability to project and elicit interest and enthusiasm using a common sense approach. Adept at analyzing and sizing up situations; diligent, hard worker and strong on follow-up. Enjoy developing and implementing new ideas, techniques, and the creative process as a whole.

SUMMARY OF QUALIFICATIONS
- Well-traveled.
- Public speaking.
- Copyediting/proofreading.
- Intermediate-level French.
- American Sign Language.
- Prolific writer; voracious reader.
- Computer skills: Microsoft Word.

EDUCATION

TULANE UNIVERSITY, New Orleans, LA. **Bachelor of Arts in English and American Literature** with a concentration in film. Degree to be awarded May 2007. Dean's List; GPA in major: 3.4.

UNIVERSITY OF MANITOBA, Winnipeg, Manitoba, Canada. Semester Abroad, Fall 2005. Studied photography, literature, Canadian drama/theater.

EMPLOYMENT HIGHLIGHTS

2/05 to Present
THE NEW ORLEANS PEOPLE FIRST PROGRAM, Skidell, LA
Adult Literacy Tutor
Travel to various prisons, nursing homes, boarding houses, and learning centers. Tutor residents in the basic elements of spelling, grammar, and parts of speech. Issue progress reports, bestow awards, etc.

10/04 to Present
TULANE UNIVERSITY, New Orleans, LA
Manager, Film Series

Summer 2005
PETIE'S DEPT. STORE, Skidell, LA. Direct sales, cosmetics.

Spring 2004
TULANE MAILROOM, New Orleans, LA. Mail sorter.

Chris Smith
178 Green Street
Mossyrock, WA 98564
(509) 555-5555
csmith@e-mail.com

PROFESSIONAL OBJECTIVE
A career opportunity in Technical Editing/Writing.

EDUCATIONAL BACKGROUND
WHITWORTH COLLEGE, Spokane, WA
Master of Science Degree in Mass Communications, 2006

WALLA WALLA COLLEGE, College Place, WA
Bachelor of Arts in Communication and Theater, 2005

PROFESSIONAL BACKGROUND
2006 to Present — LOCKWOOD ENGINEERING, Ravensdale, WA
Editor/Writer—Worldwide Business Development Division
- Responsible for editing, writing, format design, and production coordination of bid proposals for government, industrial, and utility engineering and construction contracts.
- Act as liaison between Proposal/Marketing Engineer and graphic arts, word processing, and production departments; monitor and oversee production schedule.
- Organize and maintain up-to-date dummy book throughout several revision cycles.
- Interpret client RFP requirements; determine applicability of proposal response to RFP.

2005 to 2006 — GLACIER PEAK, INC., Nahcotta, WA
Assistant to the Director—Publications Department
- Researched, wrote, and supervised production of employee orientation brochures.
- Edited and proofread most intra-company published materials.
- Special projects included establishment of corporate slide library and preparation of quarterly budget forecasts/analyses.

2003 to 2005 — RUSTLEAF PAGING SERVICES, INC., Deerpark, WA
Assistant to the Manager—Computer Resources Department
- Developed computerized report program to track personnel productivity and department project/task management.
- Monitored customer accounting including answering inquiries and preparing service reports.

TECHNICAL EXPERIENCE
Mac, PC, and UNIX Operating Systems, Relational Data Bases, Spreadsheets, and Word Processing Programs.

Recent Grad School Grad
Criminal Justice

CHRIS SMITH
178 Green Street
Seattle, WA 98102
(206) 555-5555
csmith@e-mail.com

EDUCATION

EVERGREEN STATE COLLEGE   Olympia, WA
M.S., Criminal Justice; G.P.A., 3.5, 2006
WHITMAN COLLGE   Walla Walla, WA
B.A., Psychology; G.P.A., 3.3/4.0, 2005

Honors:
Psi Chi National Honor Society in Psychology
Dean's List six consecutive semesters
Who's Who in American College Students

EXPERIENCE

OFFICE OF THE COMMISSIONER OF PROBATION, Seattle, WA   **2006**
INTERNSHIP
- Assisted with the integration of probation violators into the Seattle Boot Camp; researched and prepared results for the Commissioner on recidivism rate; attended meetings with judges.

BAY HOUSE HOTEL, Seattle, WA   **2005**
INTERNSHIP—SECURITY DEPARTMENT
- Worked closely with Director of Security in developing a fire safety and security manual for evacuations with floor plans and procedures to facilitate emergency situations.

UNIVERSITY OF WASHINGTON, Seattle, WA   **2004**
RESEARCH ASSISTANT—DEPARTMENT OF PSYCHOLOGY
- Assisted Dr. Rocky Clapper, Professor of Research Methods and Psychology in coding and data entry for experiments on drug use in juvenile delinquents.
- Trained in research methods and interpretation of collected data.

EMPLOYMENT

BINNACLE FASHIONS, Seattle, WA   **2003–Present**
COUNTER ASSOCIATE—JUNIOR MANAGEMENT
- Responsible for customer returns/service; nightly financial transactions.
- Oversee employees; vigilant regarding shrinkage problems and loss prevention.

COMPUTERS

PCs and Macs, Microsoft Word, Excel.

Recent Grad School Grad
Finance

CHRIS SMITH
178 Green Street
Whitewater, WI 53190
(414) 555-5555
csmith@e-mail.com

OBJECTIVE
A Mortgage Banking position in Loan Origination or Processing.

EDUCATION
Beloit College, Beloit, WI
Bachelor and Master of Science Degree in Finance and Management. Graduated June 2004 and June 2006, respectively.

SUMMARY OF QUALIFICATIONS
- Current knowledge of all relevant guidelines and regulations.
- Three years experience in loan processing and servicing.
- Excellent capacity to establish informal rapport with correspondent lender, broker, and borrower.
- Above average communication skills, both oral and written.

RELEVANT EXPERIENCE
Loan Processing
- Analyzed incoming loan package documentation to determine necessary requirements for underwriting of loans.
- Ordered and reviewed credit appraisal reports to establish subject property suitability and to determine credit eligibility.
- Verified all assets and employment to show stable savings and career history.
- Examined initial Loan Analysis Worksheets to determine borrower's qualification according to applicable guidelines.
- Reviewed all matters pertaining to the borrowers in order to explain any inconsistencies found.

LOAN ORIGINATION
- Aided potential borrowers by providing product information interest rate figures.
- Determined borrower's maximum loan amount, closing costs, and monthly payments using pre-qualification guidelines.

EMPLOYMENT HISTORY
2005–Present   LOAN PROCESSOR
                 Urban Finance, Whitewater, WI

4/05–7/05   LOAN SERVICING/Temp
                 Milwaukee City Bank

2/04–3/04   LOAN ORIGINATION/Temp
                 Milwaukee City Bank

CHRIS SMITH
178 Green Street
Plymouth, NH 03264
(603) 555-5555
csmith@e-mail.com

EDUCATION

Plymouth State University, Plymouth, NH
M.A. in Marketing, Dec. 2005
Courses include International Marketing, Marketing Research, Business Communications, and Statistics.
Member, National Honor Society
Pratt University, Brooklyn, NY
B.A. in Accounting, 2003

EMPLOYMENT

6/06–Present

THE PLYMOUTH PLAYER, Plymouth, NH
New Hampshire's largest daily newspaper (circ. 30,000)
Marketing Assistant (part-time)

- Design and manage market research to determine the satisfaction of former subscribers with editorial content. Supplement data with focus group research.
- Develop strategic marketing plans. Propose new marketing management strategies and systems; study online news distribution and creation of new print publications.
- Initiate telemarketing campaign to sell ads for a special section. Targeted advertisers outside usual geographic territory. Although 1/10 of salesforce, sold 1/3 of total ads (sold 6.0k of total sales of 20k).
- Selling display advertising space. Meet with advertisers, negotiate prices and design ads.

1/04–6/04

PILGRIM TRAVEL, Plymouth, NH
Discount travel company specializing in trans-Atlantic cruises
Marketing Intern

- Managed nationwide client base. Monitored sales, marketing, research, analysis, reports, and presentations.
- Developed and executed marketing plan. Coordinated marketing communications; published monthly client newsletter; created, marketed, and conducted seminars; and managed direct mail campaigns.
- Analyzed finances of client organizations. Performed analysis of multivariate revenue, insurance revenue, and accounts receivable.

COMPUTERS

IBM: WordPerfect, Lotus 1-2-3, Microsoft Word, Macintosh.

REFERENCES

Available upon request.

Recent Grad School Grad
Sociology

CHRIS SMITH
178 Green Street
Alamogordo, NM 88310
(505) 555-5555
csmith@e-mail.com

PROFESSIONAL OBJECTIVE

To secure a position in Government.

EDUCATION

New Mexico State University, Las Cruces, NM
Master of Science Degree, Sociology, 2006
Courses: Politicians and Society, International Relations, The Global Marketplace.
Thesis: "Personalities and Politics: A Study of the North American Free Trade Agreement."
Bachelor of Science, Sociology, 2001

MILITARY TRAINING

U.S. ARMY, 2003–2006, Athens, GA
Sergeant, U.S. Army
Prepared briefings concerning material management. Supervised and trained staff members to utilize various software packages, and to achieve proficiency in material management specializations. Assigned to Istanbul in the capacity of U.S. Army translator and liaison between military personnel and Turkish officials. Trained and supervised local population and unit members in settlement construction.

OTHER EXPERIENCE

SINGLETON AIR FREIGHT CO., Raleigh, NC 2001–2003
International Cargo Agent
Prepared international documentation, as required, for the transportation of goods by air and sea. Responded to client inquiries regarding available services. Implemented collection procedures, and recorded invoice statements.

NEW MEXICO STATE UNIVERSITY, Las Cruces, NM 1997–2001
Research Assistant, Sociology Department 1999–2001
Conducted research in the area of Gerontology, and interpreted data for the presentation of a report to the Midwest Sociological Society's annual convention.

Teaching Assistant (Office of Minority Affairs) 1997–1999
Tutored minority students in various subjects, including sociology, mathematics, and methods of statistical research for the humanities.

Recent High School Grad
Child Care

CHRIS SMITH
178 Green Street
Jamaica, NY 11451
(718) 555-5555
csmith@e-mail.com

OBJECTIVE

A responsible position as a Nanny.

WORK HISTORY

2006 to   MR. AND MRS. KURT URBAINE
Present   15 Goldstone Road, Jamaica, NY
          Governess
          • Provide full-time care for a six-year old girl.
          • Duties include dressing, tutoring, chauffeuring, running
            errands, housework, cooking, and seeing to the child's
            needs and well-being.
          • Live-in position.

2005   MR. AND MRS. STEVE MCGUYVER
          333 Sunshine Court, Loveland, CO
          Baby-sitter
          • Provided care for an infant girl and toddler twin
            brothers.

EDUCATION

Boulder High, Boulder, CO
Concentration in Psychology, 2006

PERSONAL INFORMATION

          • Interests include: Skiing, Reading, Horseback Riding,
            Traveling, Swimming.
          • Valid Driver's License; Perfect driving record.
          • CPR/First Aid Certified.

REFERENCES

Excellent references available upon request.

Recent High School Grad
Public Relations

CHRIS SMITH
178 Green Street
Gaffney, SC 29341
(803) 555-5555
csmith@e-mail.com

OBJECTIVE

An entry-level position in the public relations and/or media field.

EDUCATION

GAFFNEY PUBLIC HIGH SCHOOL
Graduated with academic degree, 2006

SKILLS

Typing, data entry, PC computer system, Microsoft Word, editing, filing, and clerical skills. Has worked with Video, Video Production, and Editing. Has a pleasant and professional phone manner. Work well with little supervision; energetic, responsible, well-organized, and work well under stress. Capable of light bookkeeping, customer service, and inventory. Enjoy working in a busy environment.

EXPERIENCE

LAUREL PARK CINEMAS, Gaffney, SC

10/05–Present Ticket Agent/Concessions Manager
Greet moviegoers, provide tickets, drop nightly deposit at bank, provide food service. Assume responsibilities of manager in event of his absence; open and close facility, call in nightly sales to national entertainment center, schedule employee shifts, etc.

STATE OF SOUTH CAROLINA: DEPARTMENT OF PUBLIC WELFARE

6/05–9/05 Summer Intern
Wrote and edited articles for the newsletter, edited forms, data entry, greeted people, confirmed appointments, answered phones, and filed manuscripts.

BROADWAY VIDEO, Gaffney, SC

1/04–5/05 Sales Assistant
Took inventory of merchandise, greeted/served customers, placed and took orders, answered phones, and performed general office work.

THE BURGER VASSAL, Gaffney, SC

1/03–1/04 Cashier
Provided customer service, performed monetary transactions, took weekly inventory of food/paper supplies.

CHRIS SMITH
178 Green Street
Goodwell, OK 73939
(405) 555-5555
csmith@e-mail.com

PROFESSIONAL OBJECTIVE

To secure a position in the field of Accounting/Billing.

EDUCATION

UNIVERSITY OF MIAMI, Coral Gables, FL. M.B.A. with concentration in Finance, 2006.
COLLEGE OF THE HOLY CROSS, Worcester, MA. Bachelor of Science Degree in Economics/Finance, 2002.

EMPLOYMENT

2006 to
Present   NAOT, INC., Goodwell, OK   **Accountant**
Responsible for preparation of monthly financial statements and general ledger reconciliations, project management, billing, and maintenance of Timberline software system for all company projects and cost proposals on government and commercial accounts. Payroll, general ledger, daily cash, and accounts payable and receivable.

2003 to 2004   O'CONNOR, RAISTY, & ROSS, Oklahoma City, OK   **Contract Billing Administrator**
Interpreted billing provisions of government and commercial contracts, maintained interactive billing systems, and prepared accounts receivable and sales adjustments. Maintained MIS database, and reconciled mailing list to invoice register.

2002 to 2003   THE MUTUAL CORP., Shawnee, OK   **Coordinator, ABI**
Designed procedures for implementation of new Automated Brokerage Interface. Supervised transformation from manual to computerized operation and trained personnel accordingly. Maintained system software and daily records. Researched and reconciled complex international transactions.

ACTIVITIES

Broadcaster, SportsNet Football for local cable company.
Coached Okie Acorns Soccer Team, B.A.Y.S. League.

COMPUTERS

Excel   DOS
Lotus 1-2-3   Timberline
dBase Plus   WordPerfect

CHRIS SMITH
178 Green Street
Phoenix, AZ 85044
(602) 555-5555
csmith@e-mail.com

PROFESSIONAL OBJECTIVE
A position in the ACCOUNTING department of a growing corporation.

SUMMARY OF QUALIFICATIONS
- Academic training is represented with an M.B.A. degree, an M.S. degree in Taxation, and a B.S./B.A. Degree in Accounting.
- Capable of interpreting complex tax matters with concern for savings plans, investment avenues, and credits.
- Skill in establishing profit and loss projections, cash flow projections, and financial controls.
- Ability to draft, write, and edit technical publications with clarity and conciseness.

EDUCATION

GRAND CANYON COLLEGE, Phoenix, AZ
M.B.A. degree, 2006
Magna Cum Laude
Who's Who in American Graduate Students

HENDRIX COLLEGE, Conway, AR
B.S.B.A. degree with Honors, Accounting, 2001

PROFESSIONAL EXPERIENCE
2006–Present   DEVONSHIRE TECHNICAL SUPPORT, INC., Phoenix, AZ
Assistant Controller
- Establish corporate accounting systems and procedures with the design of a computerized system for current accounting practices.
- Provide audit preparation and write-up; post journal entries to general ledger; compile working papers and monthly financial statements for auditors.
- Responsible for profit and loss projections, cash flow projections, and cash disbursements.
- Prepare all Federal/State tax returns consistent with statutory requirements.

2003–2006   THE SHONDELL CRIMSON CORPORATION, Chandler, AR
Assistant Controller
- Designed and implemented a new accounting system with two-member support staff.
- Maintained accounts payable verification, check writing, and weekly cash flow forecasts.
- Prepared journal entries to general ledger.
- Responsible for Federal/State corporate income tax returns.

2001–2003   IVANHOE EQUIPMENT CORPORATION, Flagstaff, AZ
Accounting Conversion Staff
- Contracted assignment through the Technical Aid Corporation.
- Performed accounting duties and functions during conversion of manual accounts payable procedure to computerized system.

Chris Smith
178 Green Street
Ogden, UT 84404
(801) 555-5555
csmith@e-mail.com

PROFESSIONAL OBJECTIVE

Seeking a position in the Human Resources/Management field.

EDUCATION

BRIGHAM YOUNG UNIVERSITY, Provo, UT
Master of Business Administration, 2006
GPA: 3.74
Honors: Salutatorian of Graduating Class, Academic Scholarship, Social Service
Award for work with disadvantaged teenagers.

UNIVERSITY OF UTAH, Salt Lake City, UT
Bachelor of Public Administration Degree, 2005
Concentration: Financial Management
GPA: 3.50

PROFESSIONAL EXPERIENCE

SUNRIDGE LABORATORIES, Ogden, UT
Supervisor   2005–Present

- Provided personnel with secretarial, transcription, computer equipment operations, and general clerical services.
- Interview, select, and manage support services staff; developed training and facilitating programs for various levels and created a secretarial floater pool.

Technical Employment Representative/Affirmative Action Counselor   2004–2005

- Acted as initial contact for prospective employees; evaluated resumes, conducted preliminary interviews, calculated salaries, etc.
- Participated in job/career fairs.
- Served as Loden Valley Summer Program Administrator.
- Active member of the Loden Valley Affirmative Action Committee.
- Community Relations duties included representing company on various boards ranging from Chambers of Commerce to Social Service agencies.

OFFICE OF MANAGEMENT SERVICES/DEPARTMENT OF PUBLIC WORKS,
Salt Lake City, UT
Intern   2004

- Coordinated complete automation of the Office of Management Services by establishing an "Engagement Plan" outlining the time frame to complete all phases of the system; generated a final report, incorporating the system's effects on user personnel and corresponding recommendations, evaluation of supporting software, and related matters.

Chris Smith
178 Green Street
Lexington, KY 40508
(606) 555-5555
csmith@e-mail.com

CAREER OBJECTIVE
To secure a challenging position within the fields of **Finance, Mutual Funds,** and/or **Investments.**

EDUCATION

TRANSYLVANIA UNIVERSITY, Lexington, KY
Master of Business Administration.
Graduated, Magna Cum Laude, May 2006.

BEREA COLLEGE, Berea, KY
Bachelor of Business Administration.
Graduated, Cum Laude, May 2003.

MARKETING COURSE WORK
STATISTICS * CORPORATION FINANCE * BUYER BEHAVIOR/MARKETING RESEARCH
SALES MANAGEMENT * INTERNATIONAL MARKETING * BUSINESS POLICY/STRATEGY
PROMOTIONAL STRATEGY * ACCOUNTING I AND II * CALCULUS II
PRINCIPLES OF MARKETING * WRITING FOR BUSINESS

SUMMARY OF QUALIFICATIONS
- M.B.A. and Bachelor of Business Administration.
- Internship, course work, and relevant training in marketing.
- Strong interpersonal abilities; professional, organized, cooperative, diplomatic, and trustworthy team player.
- Computer literate: Excel, Access, Word.
- Goal-directed; meet deadlines, good under pressure, and strong on follow-up.

EMPLOYMENT HIGHLIGHTS

Give em the Boot — Lexington, KY
Assistant Manager — 2006–Present
Supervise staff of five, manage customer service, bookkeeping, displays, ordering, and transfers. Tops in sales. Average $5,000 weekly.

SID'S Country Market — Scuddy, KY
Assistant Buyer — 2003–2005
Planned marketing strategies; developed new customer service program; displays; payroll.

ADDITIONAL EXPERIENCE

KENTUCKY OUTLET; LE JOLIE CAFE; TRAN O' MARKETING and BUSINESS CLUBS.

CHRIS SMITH
178 Green Street
Sanford, FL 32771
(415) 555-5555
csmith@e-mail.com

OBJECTIVE

Management, marketing, or sales position in an organization valuing logical and imaginative thinking.

QUALIFICATIONS

Experience in organizing, accepting responsibility, and making decisions. Ability to supervise and deal successfully with others. Valuable experience in gathering, recording, and interpreting marketing research data. Strong academic background in marketing, sales, management, and economics.

EDUCATION

STANFORD UNIVERSITY, Stanford, CA
GRADUATE SCHOOL OF BUSINESS ADMINISTRATION
Master's degree in Business Administration, May 2006.
Major fields of study: marketing, sales, and management.

EMPLOYMENT

CAMAROON SALES, INC. — New York, NY
Research Assistant — 2005–2006
Employed part-time during academic year doing industrial marketing research. Worked on nationwide studies with WATS lines. Learned to be proficient at telephone surveying, editing, and analyzing results. Recommended for position by Chairman of Marketing Department, Stanford University. Delivered report on Industrial Marketing Research for graduate students, New York University.

DEER SPRING BREWING COMPANY — Daytona, FL
Warehouse Assistant — 2004–2005
Assisted in Production, Packaging, and Shipping.

BENNY'S — Boca Raton, FL
Associate — 2004 Summer
Salesman of men's clothing and specialty goods.

COMPUTERS

Excel, Access, Word.

REFERENCES

Available upon request.

CHRIS SMITH
178 Green Street
Greenville, SC 29649
(803) 555-5555
csmith@e-mail.com

OBJECTIVE

A position in medical sales and marketing with a firm that offers the opportunity to utilize technical training and experience.

EDUCATION

Furman University, Greenville, SC
Master of Business Administration, 2006
National Honor Society
Spanish Club
Awarded Partial Scholarship

Clemson University, Clemson, SC
Bachelor of Science degree, Biology, 2004

QUALIFICATIONS

- Nationally registered as MT (ASCP) and CLS (NCA).
- Two years experience as a Blood Bank Medical Technologist and In-Service Educational Coordinator.
- Sound knowledge of biomedical instruments and scientific reagents.
- Hands-on technical experience and effective training and communications skills.
- Additional experience in sales and business procedures.
- A self-motivated achiever who is efficient, well organized, and capable of dealing with people in a sales, service, or support function.

STAFF MEDICAL TECHNOLOGIST
Greenville Union Hospital Blood Bank
Greenville, SC   2004–Present

- Perform all blood bank procedures using a wide variety of biomedical instruments and scientific reagents.
- Serve as Technical Advisor on weekends and week nights to laboratory staff.
- Serve as In-house Educational Coordinator, planning and organizing in-service seminars and workshops on current technology for blood banking.
- Provide didactic and technical instruction to blood bank internists.
- Maintain monthly inventory of blood bank reagents and daily inventories of blood bank donor bloods.
- Monitor quality control of reagents and blood bank instruments.
- Represent the hospital at medical conventions to learn about new equipment and procedures, and subsequently present and instruct hospital personnel in application of the latest equipment and procedures.
- Position requires the ability to carry a heavy workload, work extra shifts, and deal with people in pressured situations in a precise manner.

Chris Smith
178 Green Street
Pittsburgh, PA 15218
(912) 555-5555
csmith@e-mail.com

EDUCATION

Duquesne University, Pittsburgh, PA
Master of Business Administration, December 2006
Concentration in Marketing and Strategic Planning
Worked full-time while taking courses at night.

Swarthmore College, Swarthmore, PA
Bachelor of Science in Engineering, May 1999

EXPERIENCE

2006–Present

Bomarc, Blue, and Spruce, Pittsburgh, PA
Sales and Marketing Manager
Examined new services and changing markets and developed a detailed marketing strategy resulting in the addition of two new business units for the company. Designed and implemented a company sales and marketing campaign targeting emerging markets with new promotional and communication materials. Identified specific action oriented tasks required to sustain growth; resulted in significant improvement in company's overall financial and operating condition. Designed a three-pronged incentive sales program for telecommunications client wanting to protect installed base and increase market share. Developed push-pull marketing program for software company wanting to expand its channels of distribution. Positioned client's products with innovative promotional campaigns. Designed team-building and gain-sharing programs for clients with a focus on quality, cost reduction, and safety.

2001–2006

Dunkeith Woods, Inc., Pittsburgh, PA
Regional Sales Manager
Established and managed Regional Sales Office for this leading compiler and marketer of business and consumer information database used by direct marketing companies. Worked closely with clients to prepare and implement marketing plans for a variety of products and services. Integrated proprietary Database America information with information brokered from other sources to ensure coverage of established markets and test new potential markets. Recommended and provided necessary data processing services, data file maintenance, and customized enhancement programs. Additional responsibilities included prospecting for new business, attendance at trade shows, and conferences and report preparation.

Some College but No Degree
Administration

CHRIS SMITH
178 Green Street
Mitchell, SD 57301
(605) 555-5555
csmith@e-mail.com

OBJECTIVE
To secure an administrative position where supervisory and training expertise will be fully utilized.

QUALIFICATIONS
- Seven years administrative experience.
- Five years experience in the Health Care field.
- Supervised and trained up to ten on staff in Medical Records.
- Organized and revamped medical records filing system as well as Navy personnel filing system.
- Computer Skills: Mac, Windows, and UNIX

STRENGTHS

- Accurate
- Dependable
- Organized

- Enthusiastic
- Calm under pressure
- Strong written communication skills

EXPERIENCE

2006– MILITARY/HEALTH CARE
Present U.S. NAVY / E-4 Specialist   **Switching Systems Operator**
- Performed extensive administrative tasks, including the maintenance of records of Navy personnel. Composed and typed correspondence.
- Set up equipment, antennae, security codes, and ensured communications were established.
- Honorably Discharged.

2002–2004 HUMAN NUTRITION RESEARCH CENTER, Rapid City, SD   **Nurse's Aide**
- Took patients' vital signs, specimens; stock supplies.

1998–2002 S. DAKOTA GENERAL HOSPITAL, Shadehill, SD   **Medical Records Controller**
- Trained and supervised staff.
- Provided record maintenance in File Room.

EDUCATION

NATIONAL COLLEGE, Rapid City, SD 2002–2003
HURON COLLEGE, Huron, SD 2003–2004
Courses in Marketing, Business Administration, Statistics, Computer Science, and Liberal Arts. Volunteer for Student Legal Aid.

Some College but No Degree
Management

Chris Smith
178 Green Street
Walcott, IA 52773
(319) 555-5555
csmith@e-mail.com

OBJECTIVE

To secure a full-time management position.

EXPERIENCE

10/04–
Present

KLINE AND COMPANY, Moline, IA
Supervisor, Mailroom Services
Coordinate incoming mail; disperse inter-building correspondence. Manage courier services and shipping/receiving. Administer employee evaluations/appraisals; schedule hours. Research and account for certified, registered, and express mail. Responsible for office supply procurement. Obtain/maintain lease agreements for electronic machinery and equipment.

3/04–9/04

EXPRESS MAIL, Blue Grass, IA
Courier
Delivered time sensitive packages throughout area. Sorted incoming/outgoing express packages.

1/01–2/03

GASTON, ROSE & BROOKS, Milan, IA
Supervisor, Mailroom Services
Supervise shipment of weekly overseas pouches and biweekly payroll to thirty domestic offices. Sorted/distributed in-house payroll for 500 employees. Coordinated in-house and U.S. office stock distribution. Acted as building management contact and Chief Fire Warden for 75,000 square feet of office space. Assisted in office relocations throughout U.S.

12/97–12/00

P. GEDELLO FINANCIAL GROUP, Bettendorf, IA
Supervisor, Incoming Mail/Messengers and Stock Distribution
Manage computer facility forms and negotiable forms stored in house vault.

EDUCATION

9/95–11/97

SAINT AMBROSE COLLEGE, Davenport, IA
Course work concentrated in Personnel and Human Resources Management. Participant in SAFE Escort Program for Students.

9/94–5/95

LOVAS COLLEGE, Dubuque, IA
Two courses in Communications.

REFERENCES

Furnished upon request.

Transfer Student

Chris Smith
178 Green Street
Rochester, NY 14623
(716) 555-5555
csmith@e-mail.com

EDUCATION:

Cornell University, Ithaca, NY
Bachelor of Science, Earth Science, 2006
Greenpeace Student Representative
Cornell International Club Member

Massachusetts Institute of Technology, Cambridge, MA 2005
Course work in biology, chemistry, and environmental science

WORK EXPERIENCE:

Biobased Materials Center, Forest Products Department, Cornell, Ithaca, NY
Intern 2005–2006
Developed an understanding of the materials science aspects of polysaccharide (cellulose, hemicellulose, chitin) regeneration in the form of hydrogen beads. This research has been focusing on the examination of relationships between the nature of the polysaccharide (chemistry, molecular weight, viscosity, etc.) and important hydrogen parameters, such as gel structure, morphology, bead pore size, flow characteristics, mechanical strength, and reactivity.

Wood Chemistry Laboratory, Forest Products Department, Cornell, Ithaca, NY
Assistant 2007
Assisted professor on chemical modification of lignin with propylene oxide for the synthesis of urethanes and thermoplastic elastomers.
Developed methods for the synthesis of telechelic oligomers from lignin with controlled number and length of arms.
Performed the synthesis and full characterization (chemical, thermal, mechanical, and morphological) of multiphase block copolymers containing lignin and either polycaprolactone, cellulose propionate, or polystyrene, as the hard segments.
Produced blends of thermoplastic formulations of multiphase block copolymers containing lignin as compatibilizers in polymer blends with commercial polymers such as PVC, polystyrene, and cellulose propionate.

American Center of Technology (ACT), Boston, MA
Assistant 2006
Developed projects on alternative energy from biomass residues, mainly sugar cane bagasse. Worked on projects for ethanol production either from acidic or enzymatic hydrolysis of wood, sugar cane bagasse, and manioc.

PERSONAL:

Fluent in English and German, proficient in Spanish, working knowledge of Dutch. Interests include reading, billiards, and running. Willing to relocate.

AFFILIATIONS:

American Chemical Society—member since 2005
International Club, Cornell—member since 2004
Greenpeace—member since 2005

African-American Studies Major

Chris Smith
178 Green Street
Sunapee, NH 03782
(603) 555-5555
csmith@e-mail.com

Education: **Kalamazoo College,** Kalamazoo, MI
B.A. African American Studies, May 2006
Minor: Political Science
Awarded the Lieberman Scholarship.
Member, Volunteers in Action (VIA).

Experience: **Computer Consultant**   *11/05–5/06*
Personal Computer Classroom Operations
• Maintained classroom equipment.
• Assisted users with MS Word and Quark
• Developed knowledge of PC and Mac operating systems.

Resident Assistant   *9/05–5/06*
University Housing Services
• Coordinated activities for fifty international students in residence halls.
• Enforced policies.
• Counseled students.
• Performed administrative duties.

President   *9/04–5/05*
Student House Council
• Volunteer, elected position.
• Facilitated meetings.
• Organized events.
• Worked with other officers.
• Acted as a liaison between resident director and house council.
• Acted as a representative to area government.

Vice President   *2/04–5/04*
Dormitory Council
• Volunteer, elected position.
• Assisted in organizing social events.
• Arranged fundraisers.
• Coordinated activities with other officers.
• Acted as a representative to area government.

Skills: Typing (approx. 60 wpm), MS Word on Macintosh.

Anthropology Major

Chris Smith
178 Green Street
Neopit, WI 54150
(715) 555-5555
csmith@e-mail.com

EDUCATION

Ripon College, Ripon, WI
B.A. Cum Laude with distinction in Anthropological Studies, 2006
Art history courses completed on Greek and Roman Art
Milwaukee Center for Adult Education, Milwaukee, WI
Classes in Calligraphy and Graphic Design, Summer 2005

EXPERIENCE

Ripon Journal of Anthropology
Assistant Editor Ripon, WI
Responsible for production of journal and office management. Feb. 2005–Present
Monitor and maintain production schedule with printers.
Design layout, create templates for journal.
Proofread all articles and book reviews, some reference checking.
Complete occasional artwork as needed.
Office management responsibilities include:
- Order all supplies, approving bills for payment, and answering mail and phones.
- Create and maintain databases for exchange agreements and fundraising activities.
- Type all correspondence with authors and service providers.
- Manage occasional temporary workers.

Wilder View Program
Student Anthropologist Queensland, AUS
Developed a thesis paper at program's conclusion. Summer 2005
Studied gender roles in four Aboriginal tribes within a six-mile area.

Camp Meteetsee
Counselor Fort Kent, ME
Responsible for daily activities of campers aged five to sixteen. Summers 2001, 2002
Coordinated Arts and Crafts Program, organized and ran Music Library.

VOLUNTEER POSITIONS

Capella Alamire
Treasurer Ripon, WI
In charge of bookkeeping for orchestral society. Sept. 2004–Present
Coordinate grant applications.

Ripon Gilbert and Sullivan Society
Coordinator Ripon College, Ripon, WI
Produced *H.M.S. Pinafore* and *Ruddigore*. 2004–2005
Organized Society functions.

SKILLS

Knowledge of Microsoft Word, FileMaker. Basic knowledge of PageMaker, QuarkXPress.
Working knowledge of German and Latin.

Art History Major

Chris Smith
csmith@e-mail.com

School Address: Permanent Address:
178 Green Street   23 Blue Street
Providence, RI 90666   Los Angeles, CA 90666
(401) 555-5555   (813) 555-4444

EDUCATION

PROVIDENCE COLLEGE, Providence, RI
Bachelor of Arts degree in Art History to be awarded May, 2007. Concentration in the History of African and African-American Art. Courses include: New Trends in Modern Art, Introductory Museum Science, and Modern Sculpture.

THE INTERNATIONAL SCHOOL, Nairobi, Kenya
High School Diploma, May, 2003.

EXPERIENCE

9/06 to Present — **_COPLEY SOCIETY OF LOS ANGELES—ART GALLERY,_** Los Angeles, CA
Internship
Assisted customers, sales, setting up displays, and mailings for exhibitions. Some clerical work.

7/06 — **_RAISON CENTER Cultural Center,_** Paris, France
Internship
Learned all facets of the Center, including Publicity, Technical, Planning, House Management, and Art Gallery Departments. Some duties included creation of layouts for concert and play programs, contact promoters, distribution of leaflets on upcoming events, stage lighting, sound, equipment, etc. Hung displays and exhibitions. Solicited subsidiary funding.

7/06 — **_LAPIS GALLERY,_** Lisbon, Portugal
Assistant to the Head of Lapis Tate International Council. Worked on the opening of a Klimt Exhibition entitled "Golden Rebellion." Organized a dinner for 1,000 art-sponsors and artists.

Summer 2002 — **_EUROPEAN TEEN ORCHESTRA,_** Conductor: Leonard Bernstein
General Secretary
Orchestra toured Hamburg, Athens, Hiroshima, Osaka, Hong Kong, and Vienna. Assisted in administrative duties.

LANGUAGES

Fluency in English and French, working knowledge of Spanish.

Biology Major

Chris Smith
csmith@e-mail.com

School Address:
178 Green Street
Oneonta, NY 13820
(607) 555-5555

Home Address:
23 Blue Street
Houston, TX 77024
(713) 555-4444

Career Objective   A permanent position that would allow me to utilize my skills in scientific writing and editing.

Education   Hartwick College, Oneonta, NY
B.S. in Biological Sciences, Anticipated May 2007

Writing Experience

Student Affairs, Hartwick College
Writer
Revise the text and design of Science Section of *The Word*, a 120-page student handbook, and work to incorporate student input into the undergraduate course catalog. May 2005–Present.

The Bunsen Science Newsletter
Copy Manager
Duties included organizing a staff of eight to ten proofreaders, scheduling their hours, and doing some proofreading and copyediting. Act as the authority on style and layout and also participated in editorial decisions. January 2005–January 2006.

Science News Editor
Assigned and wrote science oriented stories, edited, designed the layout, and put together a five-to-seven page section of a monthly science newspaper. October–December 2005.

Production Manager
Supervised an eight-member staff, designed and typeset advertisements, designed the newspaper pages, and oversaw the final production of the weekly color, broadsheet newspaper. February–October 2004.

Activities

Head Orientation Counselor, Hartwick College
Worked with five others to organize and oversee a week-long orientation program for incoming students. Organized and kept a budget of approximately $100,000. September 2004–September 2005.

Jones Lab, Hartwick College
Laboratory Assistant
Prepared and set up equipment for researchers in the laboratory. May 2004–October 2005.

Computer Skills

Microsoft Word, Illustrator, FileMaker Pro, and Excel. Basic knowledge of Photoshop and QuarkXPress.

Business Administration Major

Chris Smith
178 Green Street
Elsah, IL 62028
(708) 555-5555
csmith@e-mail.com

EDUCATION

NORTHWESTERN UNIVERSITY SCHOOL OF PUBLIC HEALTH, Evanston, IL
Part-time studies toward Master of Public Health degree, to be awarded May 2007.

NORTHWESTERN UNIVERSITY, Evanston, IL 2004
B.S., Business Administration/Marketing. Member, Alpha Beta Gamma;
National Business Honor Society. Certificate of Award for Outstanding Business
Administration Graduates. Varsity Soccer.

LARSON COLLEGE, Malibu, CA 2002
A.A., Merchandising/*Certificate in Professional Modeling.* Emphasis on Communication
and Public Presentation.

EXPERIENCE

2005–
Present

RED SAVIOR INSURANCE, Elsah, IL   **Information Consultant**
Trained on all contracts and systems. Assist Department Supervisor as required with
responsibility for work assignments, quality control, and troubleshooting.
- Educate public on applicable BC/BS policies, guidelines, and procedures.
- Resolve complaints and disputes in billing or contract specifications.
- Research and write customer requests for appeal and present findings.
- Identified existing problems and provided research data to ombudsperson which
  contributed to revision of applicable underwriting policy.
- Selected to assist the Consumer Relations Department with inquiries from the media
  and third party inquiries from the Division of Insurance.
- P.A.C.E.: (Public Acknowledgement for Conscientious Effort) Five Awards.

2004–2005   **Senior Information Representative**
- Assisted in training and orientation of new information representatives.
- Interacted directly with Research on legal cases for Law Department.
- Selected to attend training program on new computer system with subsequent
  responsibility to train coworkers.
- Responded to inquiries, identified and researched subscriber problems.
- Drafted series of form letters to accompany payments to participating medical
  providers.

2003–2004   *THE CLOTHES CRITERION,* Chicago, IL   **Sales Associate**
Responsible for customer sales and service. Assisted with new employee training.
- Ranked among top fifteen salespeople in the country.

Classical Civilization Major

Chris Smith
178 Green Street
Louisville, KY 40292
(502) 555-5555
csmith@e-mail.com

OBJECTIVE: To obtain an entry-level position in Administration.

SKILLS: Excellent written and verbal communication skills.
Ability to work well with a variety of people.
Several years of experience as a temporary worker for over fifty employers.

EDUCATION: University of Louisville, Louisville, KY
Bachelor of Arts, May, 2006—Major in Classical Civilization.
GPA: 3.6 in major. Dean's List.

EXPERIENCE:

Cartel, Manpower, Berman, TAC Temps, and Brooks Temporary Services

2005– Involved in a wide variety of temporary employment including warehouse work,
Present carpenter's assistant, plumber's assistant, furniture moving, construction work, plaster and drywall work, security guard, retail clerk, satellite dish installation, office filing, and Goodwill trailer attendant.

Louisville Music Magazine, Louisville, KY

2005– Album Reviewer. Occasionally published as an album reviewer in independently
Present produced music publication.

Jon's, Calvert City, KY

2004–2005 Cashier and Stock Clerk in retail department store.

Appleby Communications, Lexington, KY

2003–2004 Performed various tasks at independent publisher of *Financial Services Times* and *Kentucky Insurance Times*, including paste-up, making copies and media kits, phone reception, small repairs, mail preparation, etc.

ACTIVITIES:

House Program Council, contributor to *Louisville Collegian*, intramural sports.

REFERENCES:

Available upon request.

Chris Smith
178 Green Street
Albany, NY 12203
(518) 555-5555
csmith@e-mail.com

OBJECTIVE

An entry-level position in magazine publishing.

EDUCATION

Millsaps College, Jackson, MS
B.A. Classics, June 2006
Full tuition scholarship on the basis of academic merit.

EXPERIENCE

WRITING CLINIC TUTOR, Millsaps College. Answered questions about individual work. Critiqued rough drafts. Made suggestions for structural and stylistic improvement. September 2005–May 2006.

CLASSICS TEACHING ASSISTANT, Millsaps College. Ran a weekly discussion meeting focused on course readings for Classics 101. Explicated difficult passages. Answered students' questions. Critiqued rough drafts. Semester I, 2005–09.

TEMPORARY OFFICE POSITIONS, including Receptionist, Mail Room Assistant, and Data Entry, for New York Temps, Inc., Albany, NY. Worked with Microsoft Word. Filed and verified auto insurance coverage. Directed calls. Entered client data into computerized archive system. Summers 2004, 2005.

SKILLS

Proficient with Microsoft Word. Type 50 wpm. Trained in BASIC programming. Excellent writing and editing skills. Working knowledge of French.

ACTIVITIES

STAFF WRITER, *Millsaps College News.* Wrote biweekly feature articles on various campus events. Aided in the decision of which issues to cover.

LITERARY EDITOR, *Hetaera,* a literary magazine produced by Millsaps and Belhaven Colleges. Reviewed and rated contributions. Determined what to include in collaboration with other staff members.

EDITOR-IN-CHIEF, *Another COG,* Albany High School, Albany, NY.
Assigned and edited articles. Managed staff of fifteen. Composed editorials, features, and news articles. Created advertisements.

FOUNDER AND EDITOR-IN-CHIEF, *Juggernaut Cover Girl,* an independent satire magazine, Albany, NY. Founded magazine with help of six other high school students. Edited and assigned satirical articles on high school life. Solicited advertising and created advertisements.

Culinary Arts Major

Chris Smith
178 Green Street
Cavendish, VT 05142
(802) 555-5555
csmith@e-mail.com

OBJECTIVE
To contribute acquired culinary skills to a restaurant position.

SUMMARY OF QUALIFICATIONS
- More than four years of progressively responsible food-related experience.
- Bachelor's degree in Culinary Arts.
- Dependable, detail-oriented team worker; capable of following directions precisely.

EDUCATION

CULINARY INSTITUTE OF AMERICA, New Haven, CT
Bachelor's degree in Culinary Arts
Culinary Arts Diploma (2006)

UNIVERSITY OF WASHINGTON, Department of Correspondence Study Nutrition
Course—three semester hours credit (2005)

EXPERIENCE

AUTUMN OAKS INN, Cavendish, VT   2006–Present
Cook
Assist chefs in meal preparation. Responsibilities include cutting meat, making sauces, rotating food, cooking, and serving at special faculty functions of more than 300 patrons.

SHADE HILL INN, Branford, CT   2005–2006
Cook
Prepare breakfast for over 200 patrons daily.

REDWING FOOD SUPPLY, Hartford, CT   2004–2005
Stock Person
Dated and rotated products. Supplied food to homeless shelter cafeterias.

THE WOLFSONG TAVERN, Butte, MT   Summer 2004
Prep Cook
General responsibilities as above.

Assistant Prep Cook   Summer 2003
Busperson   Summer 2002

Earth Science Major

CHRIS SMITH
csmith@e-mail.com

School Address:
178 Green Street
Corvallis, Oregon 97335
Phone: (503) 555-5555

Permanent Address:
23 Blue Street
Portland, OR 98651
Phone: (503) 555-4444

Education

2006–Present

OREGON STATE UNIVERSITY   **CORVALLIS, OR**

Bachelor of Arts Degree to be awarded in June 2010, majoring in Earth Science and minoring in Forestry. Courses of study include: Forest Economics, Range Management, Ecology, Soil Science, Hydrology, Wildlife, and Agronomy. Independent Research topic: The Effect of Hydrolechicin Treatment on Blue Alpine Firs with Pulloma Disease. GPA: 3.7.

Member of the Oregon State Ecological Society. Awarded the Tepper Badge for outstanding achievement in the natural sciences.

Summer 2006

OREGON STATE SOIL CONSERVATION SERVICE   **PORTLAND, OR**

Provided technical assistance to farmers, ranchers, and others concerned with the conservation of soil, water, and related natural resources. Aided in the development of programs designed to maximize land productivity without harm or damage. Developed programs to combat soil erosion.

Experience

Summer 2005

OREGON STATE UNIVERSITY FIELD CAMP   **KLAMATH FALLS, OR**

Planted and maintained trees and rare natural vegetation, recorded and charted growth. Tracked wildlife species and worked to preserve natural habitats for endangered species. Tested soil and water samples.

Part-time 2003–2005

Unrelated work positions include Bus Person, Cashier, and Service Station Attendant.

Interests

Playing acoustic guitar, hiking, camping, and competition swimming.

References

Available upon request.

Education Major

Chris Smith
csmith@e-mail.com

School Address
178 Green Street
Dayton, OH 45469
(513) 555-5555

Permanent Address
23 Blue Street
Oakwood, OH 45873
(419) 555-4444

EDUCATION

University of Dayton   **Dayton, OH**
Bachelor of Arts degree, Summa Cum Laude, May 2006
G.P.A.: 3.6/4.0 Dean's List, First Honors
Majors: Secondary Education, English

HONORS

Selected to speak at Commencement ceremonies
National Education Award, 2006
National Dean's List, 2005–2006, 2006–2007, 2005–2006
Who's Who Among Students, 2006, 2007

ACTIVITIES

Student Admissions Program
Peer Advisement Program
Freshman Assistance Program
School of Education Senate
Student Representative to Educational Policy Committee

EXPERIENCE

Spring   **Substitute Teaching**   **Oakwood High School, Oakwood, OH**
2006   Work as substitute teacher in various disciplines for students in grades 7–12.

Fall 2005 **Student Teaching Full-Time Practicum**   **Kerrigan High, Kerrigan, OH**
Travel to site daily and assume full teaching responsibility for two eleventh-grade accelerated American Literature classes and one ninth-grade fundamental English class. Prepare, lecture, discuss, and evaluate units in literature and writing. Design and present lessons on Puritan writers, focusing on Nathaniel Hawthorne's *Scarlet Letter*. Provide writing instruction for paragraphs and essays.

Fall 2005 **Student Teaching Field Pre-Practicum**   **Central High School, Dayton, OH**

Spring   **Kerrigan High School**   **Kerrigan, OH**
2005   Visit site weekly to observe classes and gain practical teaching experience.

REFERENCES

Available upon request.

English Literature Major

Chris Smith
178 Green Street
Forsyth, GA 31029
(912) 555-5555
csmith@e-mail.com

SKILLS:

- **Writing:** Over three years experience writing articles for various newspapers on topics ranging from politics to theater.
- **Deadlines:** Extremely reliable under pressure, consistently meets deadlines.
- **Computers:** Knowledgeable in many types of computer software, such as Microsoft Word, Excel, and Photoshop.

EDUCATION:

Tift College, Forsyth, GA
Bachelor of Arts in English Literature, May 2006
Minor: Journalism
Magna Cum Laude

EXPERIENCE:

Editor, *The Spectrum*   Sept. 2005–May 2006
Forsyth, GA
Held weekly meetings with up to twenty-five students to select poetry, short fiction, prose, and artwork for school literary magazine published once per semester. Worked closely with printer on page layout and cover design. Made final decisions on submissions. Carefully proofread final product. Distributed magazine to area locations.

Feature Writer, *The Sentinel*   Sept. 2004–May 2005
Forsyth, GA
Wrote weekly articles for Arts and Entertainment Section of campus newspaper reviewing movies, plays, novels, and new music releases. Was also a guest columnist for viewpoint, sports, and news sections.

Intern, *The Forsyth Gazette*   Sept. 2003–Dec. 2004
Forsyth, GA
Contributed weekly articles on current events to local newspaper. Interviewed local businessmen and townspeople for experimental section on area residents.

AFFILIATIONS:

English Society
Society for Academic Excellence
Young Journalists of America

REFERENCES:

Available upon request.

English Major

Chris Smith
178 Green Street
Columbia, MO 65201
(314) 555-5555
csmith@e-mail.com

OBJECTIVE
To contribute developed skills to a challenging position in the publishing field.

SUMMARY OF QUALIFICATIONS
- Four years publishing experience.
- Completely bilingual in English and Spanish; some knowledge of French.
- Extensive computer experience (formerly a Computer Science major): PC, Mac, and UNIX.
- Proven writing skills; authored hundreds of pages of fiction in the past three years.
- Excellent communication abilities; lectured to a wide variety of audiences in a museum setting.

EDUCATION

DOWLING COLLEGE, Oakdale, NY
B.A. English, Magna Cum Laude, May 2006

COLLEGE ACTIVITIES

Plume, Literary Magazine   Fall 2005–Spring 2006
Editor (from Spring 2005), **Production and Business Coordinator**
Responsible for composing magazine budget and arranging specifications with printers.

Freelance Writer   Spring 2004–Spring 2005
Published book and movie reviews, essays, and short stories in different campus publications.

Dowling College Pictures   Spring 2004
Founding Member/Screenwriter
Wrote short movie production.

WORK EXPERIENCE

The Damien House Museum, Oakdale, NY   Spring 2005
Museum Assistant
Interpreted exhibits for visitors. Prepared and delivered short talks on historical subjects. Participated in organization of creative educational programs.

Bindings Bookstore, Oakdale, NY   Fall 2004
Sales Clerk/Floor Person
Maintained stock; helped customers make selections; registered sales.

Collectible Canvas Store, Creve Coeur, MO   Summer 2004
Framer
Handled frame and glass cutting, and mounting of prints and artwork.

Food Science Major

CHRIS SMITH
csmith@e-mail.com

School Address	**Permanent Address**
178 Green Street	23 Blue Street
Newport, RI 02840	Hull, MA 02045
(401) 555-5555	(781) 555-4444

OBJECTIVE
A challenging CHEF/MANAGERIAL position in the FOOD SERVICE INDUSTRY.

EDUCATION
JOHNSON & WALES COLLEGE, Providence, RI
A.S. degree—Food Science/Degree to be awarded: 2007
Dean's List student

PROFESSIONAL EXPERIENCE
PHEASANT LANE RESTAURANT, Newport, RI   2006–Present
Sous Chef
Main duties involve capably assisting the owner and Executive Chef in overall operations of this nouvelle cuisine specialty restaurant.
- *Ensure and arrange for selective and adequate ordering of all meat, fish, and produce for the café.*
- *Interview, hire, train, and supervise all new kitchen employees.*
- *Skilled in the preparation and production of quality cuisine, and in the planning, development, and execution of innovative designs.*
- *Conceptualize and design creative and original menus.*

OCEANVIEW INN, Providence, RI   2005–2006
Banquet Manager/Food and Beverage Director
- *Organized functions, including scheduling employees, ordering food and beverages, and overseeing functions.*
- *Organized dining areas.*

RHODE SIDE INNS, Providence, RI   2004–2005
Server
- *Trained new bus and wait staff.*
- *Resolved customer complaints.*

Busperson
- *Set up and dismantled dining area.*
- *Promoted to server within six months.*

Gerontology Major

Chris Smith
178 Green Street
San Francisco, CA 94133
(715) 555-5555
csmith@e-mail.com

EDUCATION:

SAN FRANCISCO STATE UNIVERSITY, San Francisco, CA
Bachelor of Arts in Gerontology, 2006. GPA: Overall 3.1, Gerontology,
3.6. Worked to finance nearly 50% of college tuition.

EMPLOYMENT:

VETERAN'S CLINIC, SAN FRANCISCO, CA   2006–Present
Ward Medical Clerk
- Serve as an administrative aide to the medical personnel on the
  wards.
- Carry out doctor's orders such as ordering lab work, scheduling
  tests, and maintaining accurate patient records.
- Duties require a high level of interaction with staff, patients,
  and family members.

BARBOSA LABORATORY, SFSU, San Francisco, CA   2005–2006
Interlibrary Loan Assistant
- Assisted librarians in interlibrary loan office of main college
  library.
- Processed incoming mail, notified students of receipt of requests,
  and updated transactions on the computer.

VETERAN'S CLINIC, San Gabriel, CA   Summer 2005
File Clerk, Record Retirement Project
- Worked as part of eight-person team on special record retirement
  project.
- Located, consolidated, and packaged inactive medical records for
  shipment to storage.
- Chosen to accurately roster and enter data into word processing
  system.

COMMUNITY SERVICE:

STUDENT PROGRAM FOR CHILDREN'S WELFARE   2005–2007
Big Friend/Little Friend Program
Participated in program to aid disadvantaged San Francisco youth
from the Staron Village housing project.
VELSOR MIDDLE SCHOOL, San Francisco, CA   Fall 2005
TUTOR
Tutored seventh grade boy in need of academic assistance.

OTHER SKILLS:
- Familiar with Microsoft Word and Excel.
- Working knowledge of written and spoken German.

Chris Smith
csmith@e-mail.com

Current Address
178 Green Street
Baltimore, MD 21218
(301) 555-5555

Permanent Address
23 Blue Street
Aurora, ME 04408
(207) 555-4444

OBJECTIVE

To contribute acquired skills and recent educational background to an entry-level administrative position within an organization offering opportunities for growth and advancement.

SUMMARY OF QUALIFICATIONS

- Adapt easily to new concepts and responsibilities.
- Diverse background in both business and outdoor skills.
- Self-motivated; detail-oriented; function well both independently and as a team member.
- Proven communication skills, both oral and written.

EDUCATION

UNIVERSITY OF MARYLAND, College Park, MD
Bachelor of Arts degree, History, expected May 2010.

WORK HISTORY

THE SPORTS SPOT, Baltimore, MD   2005–Present
Sales Associate
Consistently meet/exceed monthly sales quotas in all market areas.

BLUE BAYOU ENTERPRISES, College Park, MD   2004–2005
Owner/President
Conceived, developed, marketed, and sold various products to 30,000 student and faculty population.

BERMAN FOUNDATION, Aurora, ME   Summer 2005
Work Camp Supervisor
Responsible for twelve European University students through Volunteer for Peace Program.

Wilderness Trip Co-Leader   Summers 2003–2004
Co-led a seven-week canoeing and backpacking expedition for ten teenage participants in Northern Maine, 2003, 2004. Co-led a family canoeing trip on the Alaska Wilderness Waterway, ages 12 to 65, 2005.

UNIVERSITY OF MAINE, Orono, ME   Winter 2003–2004
Registrar's Office
Administrator
Processed transcripts; researched reports on the database, responded to student inquiries/complaints. Required familiarity with PC data entry.

International Relations Major

Chris Smith
csmith@e-mail.com

School Address
178 Green Street
Ripon, WI 54971
(414) 555-5555

Permanent Address
23 Blue Street
Charlotte, NC 28277
(704) 555-4444

EDUCATION

RIPON COLLEGE
B.S. in International Relations: GPA. 3.20, Major 3.33
Minor: Marketing
Courses: Marketing Research, Sales and Distribution, Management, Promotional Management, Consumer Behavior, Global Communications, and Social Change in Developing Nations.

OXFORD UNIVERSITY   Oxford, England
Spring 2005
Related Courses: International Marketing and Advertising, and International Economics and World Trade.

*Financed 50% of college tuition as well as all personal expenses through part-time college and full-time summer employment.

WORK EXPERIENCE

JACKSON ELECTRIC COMPANY   Ladysmith, WI
Customer Service Representative   Summer 2005
Worked in the Marketing Department for the Power Integrated Circuits Division of Jackson answering both domestic and international customer inquiries regarding product and pricing. Processed product sample requests, packaged and shipped samples. Developed reports on sample requests and manufacturing orders received for District Managers worldwide. Assisted other marketing personnel in various tasks as required.

THE INTERNATIONAL CONNECTION   Ripon, WI
Evaluation Intern   Spring 2004
Composed, edited, and dispersed to management summaries of project reports for IESC, a nonprofit organization which sends retired corporate executives into third world countries to advise and assist them in efficient production methods.

THE WOODTIP CORPORATION   Ripon, WI
Student Manager   2003–2004
Organized blueprint files, order entering, and materials inventory; handled accounts payable and accounts receivable; worked with materials purchasing; and replaced receptionist for plant which manufactures aircraft engine parts.

ADDITIONAL EXPERIENCE

Ripon College Marketing Club (2003–2005), College Marketing Association (2004–2005), International Relations Club (2005–2006), Circle K Club (2005–2006).

Studied in London, England (2005), and traveled through Western Europe and the United Kingdom. Working knowledge of French.

Linguistics Major

Chris Smith
csmith@e-mail.com

School Address
178 Green Street
Sterling, VA 20165
(703) 555-5555

Permanent Address
23 Blue Street
Westhampton, MA 01027
(413) 555-4444

PROFESSIONAL OBJECTIVE

An entry-level position in linguistic analysis.

EDUCATION

Bachelor of Science in Linguistics, 2006
Roanoke College, Salem, VA
Graduated third in College of Arts and Sciences
Cumulative Average: 3.8/4.0
Howard Payne University, Brownwood, TX

SPECIAL COURSES AND SKILLS

Linguistics courses included Semantics, Syntax, Phonetics, and Psycholinguistics.
Experience with Perl, HTML, Linux.
Speak French at conversational level.
Have taken various mathematics and science courses.

ACTIVITIES

Member, Phi Kappa Phi National Honor Society
Member, The Academy Honor Society, Roanoke College
Staff Writer, Student Newspaper, Howard Payne University
Calculus Tutor, Howard Payne University
Member, Orientation Staff, Howard Payne University
Member, Education Club, Howard Payne University
Tour Guide, Admissions Office, Howard Payne University

PRACTICA

ROANOKE COLLEGE, Salem, VA Winter/Spring 2005
• Studied and evaluated performance of computers.
• Assisted development of classroom applications for phonetics class; assessed needs in six-month practicum.

NEWMANN SCHOOL, Westhampton, MA Summer 2005
• Evaluated disadvantaged students to determine effects of socioeconomic background on linguistic skills and scholastic performance.

Marketing Major

Chris Smith
178 Green Street
Berrien, MI 49104
(616) 555-5555
csmith@e-mail.com

EDUCATION:

University of Michigan at Ann Arbor
Bachelor of Science in Marketing, May 2006
Concentration: Communication Studies
Minor: Sociology
G.P.A.: 3.4/4.0
University of Michigan at Flint
Studies in Liberal Arts/Theater, 2002–2004

AWARDS AND ACTIVITIES:

Dean's List	Stage Troupe
Golden Key National Honor Society Member	Somerville Community Chorus
Student Government Representative	International Leadership Award Recipient
University Chorus	Student Government Advertising Committee

EXPERIENCE:

Rodriguez, Inc., *Ann Arbor, MI*   January–April 2006
Public Relations Intern
- Interned in a large Portuguese jewelry manufacturer.
- Researched information on Portuguese and American precious metal trade.
- Compiled status reports and press releases for the company.

University of Michigan Ad Center, *Ann Arbor, MI*   September 2004–October 2005
Account Leader
- Attended weekly client and team meetings.
- Created copy and produced brochures for Ann Arbor Youth Guidance Center.
- Produced informational slide show and video for Champions organization.
- Compiled weekly status reports for clients and team.

Sacajawea Marketing, *Detroit, MI*   Summer 2004
Salesperson
- Arranged meetings with prospective buyers of knives from reputable company.
- Managed monetary transactions between the company and the client.
- Attended valuable seminars on self presentation and salesmanship.

University of Michigan International Scholar's Office, *Ann Arbor, MI*   Summer 2003
International Orientation Leader
- Participated in a program to welcome international students to Boston University.
- Implemented many techniques of intercultural communication during the session.
- Planned and directed a talent night for the students.

SKILLS:

Speech writing and public speaking.
Proficient in Mac software including Microsoft Word and Photoshop.

Mechanical Engineering Major

Chris Smith
178 Green Street
Dobbs Ferry, NY 13026
(914) 555-5555
csmith@e-mail.com

OBJECTIVE
To obtain an entry-level position in Mechanical Engineering.

SUMMARY OF QUALIFICATIONS
- Excellent grounding in all areas of Engineering with ability and desire to continue learning.
- Outstanding abilities with figures, technical and manual operations.
- Highly developed interpersonal skills.
- Experienced in PC and UNIX operating systems.
- Knowledge of Linux, C++, Visual Basic.
- Working knowledge of Japanese.

EDUCATION

STATE UNIVERSITY OF NEW YORK, New York, NY
Bachelor's degree in Mechanical Engineering, Honors, 2006
Specialized in Design Engineering.

WORK HISTORY

UNITED PARCEL SERVICE, Dobbs Ferry, NY   6/06-Present
General Office Clerk
Responsibilities include: customer service, billing, and credit control.

STONY BROOK BUILDERS, Stony Brook, NY   1/06-1/06
Engineering Intern
Involved in all departments of this Electronics Company including Workshop, Wiring, Soldering, Testing, and Design Departments.

REFERENCES

Available upon request.

Music Major

Chris Smith
csmith@e-mail.com

School Address
178 Green Street
New York, NY 10012
(212) 555-5555

Home Address
23 Blue Street
New Rochelle, NY 10801
(914) 555-4444

OBJECTIVE

To participate in various musical settings as a drummer/vocalist and to perform and record my own original material.

EDUCATION

THE JUILLIARD SCHOOL, New York, NY
Dual Major: **Performance and Songwriting**, B.A. May 2006. Dean's List.
Played piano for school band. Performed in annual Christmas concert to benefit the homeless.

Resident Assistant for Freshman Dormitory for two consecutive years. Organized student activities and field trips. Managed $500-per-semester budget.

ACCOMPLISHMENTS

- Broad based knowledge and comprehensive academic training in music for thirteen years in jazz, rock, pop, Latin, and classical music.
- Principal instrument: Drums with expertise on piano, guitar, voice, songwriting (words and music).
- Strong grounding in harmony and theory.
- Expertise in performance and recording both in the United States and Puerto Rico.
- Own copyright on twenty-five original pieces of Rock Memorabilia.
- Bilingual: Spanish and English, verbal, written, and reading.
- Sat on jury for Spin Digest's International Songwriting Contest, July 2007.
- Appeared and played drums in rock video for famous Puerto Rican group, Los Hombres Guapos, Christmas 2005.

EMPLOYMENT EXPERIENCE

The *"Record" Record,* New York, NY   2005–Present
Served as **Assistant Editor** at this up-and-coming monthly chronicle of rock music's early years. Selected feature artists for impending issues, conducted interviews, researched backgrounds, and assisted in editing final product.

The Salmon Run, New York, NY   2004–Present
Weekly Performer with Band
Acquired weekly performance slot at this star-studded night club. Played one-hour set, opening for such bands as the Dead Onions, Pain Cave, and Burnt Retina.

REFERENCES

Available upon request.

Nutrition Major

Chris Smith
csmith@e-mail.com

Current Address
178 Green Street
Bloomington, IN 47405
(812) 555-5555

Permanent Address
23 Blue Street
Evansville, IN 47712
(812) 555-4444

OBJECTIVE

To utilize acquired skills in biotechnology research toward project responsibility in nutrition/health industry.

EDUCATION

Bachelor of Science in Nutrition
INDIANA UNIVERSITY
Degree Anticipated: 2007
Courses include Organic Chemistry, Anatomy and Physiology, and Food Service Administration.
Thesis topic: "Advances in Refrigeration Techniques and Their Application to the Fresh Meats Industry."

EXPERIENCE

2006 to Present   **Intern**
Nutrition Evaluation Laboratory, Human Nutrition Research
CENTER ON AGING AT INDIANA UNIVERSITY

- Assist seven researchers in routine and esoteric biochemical analysis. Implement ten different non-clinical assays of vitamins, amino acids, and other biomolecules in support of human and animal tissue culture studies. Develop and implement new types of assays and improve existing analytical techniques.
- Interact with investigators and assist in organization and implementation of analysis. Provide literature search and publication of developed methodologies in scientific journals.
- Provide maintenance for a wide variety of laboratory and analytical equipment.
- Train on microprocessor and personal computer driven analytical instruments and robots: Waters hardware and software, analytical, and chromatography software.
- Initiated independent research project concerning detection of non-enzymatically glycated amino acid residues in proteins.

2005 to 2006   **Teaching Assistant**
Department of Biochemistry and Biophysics
INDIANA UNIVERSITY
Bloomington, IN

- Led group of seven students in weekly laboratory experiments.
- Administered quizzes and evaluated lab results.

PERSONAL

Willing to travel.

Occupational Therapy Major

Chris Smith
178 Green Street
Ypsilanti, MI 48198
(313) 555-5555
csmith@e-mail.com

Education

Eastern Michigan University, Ypsilanti, MI
Bachelor of Science, Occupational Therapy, 2006
Dean's list four consecutive semesters.

Clinical Affiliations

LEARNING PREP SCHOOL, Ypsilanti, MI   2006–Present
Assistant Occupational Therapist
Work with students having Developmental Delays, Mental Retardation, and Related Learning Disabilities.
- Interventions include Gross and Fine Motor Therapy, Visual-Perceptual-Motor Therapy, Vocational Training, and Neurodevelopmental Technique in individual therapy.
- Supervised Community Outings, Supervised Visual-Perceptual-Motor Group, and Pre-vocational and Vocational Work Centers.

SPAULDING REHABILITATION HOSPITAL   Summer 2006
Assistant Occupational Therapist
- Caseload included patients with Cardiac and Pulmonary Disorders, Lower Limb Amputations, Stroke, Brain Injury, and Reflex Sympathetic Dystrophy.
- Interventions included Neurodevelopmental Technique, Joint Mobilization, Deep Friction Massage, Computer Assisted Cognitive Therapy, Community Mobility, Home Program Planning, Home Evaluations, and Evaluations in all related areas.

MORING PSYCHIATRIC HOSPITAL   Summer 2005
Occupational Therapy Internship
Work with adolescent, adult, and geriatric patients with Affective, Chronic Thought Process, Social, and Personality Disorders, as well as Substance Abuse Disorders.
- Supervised General Activities Period.
- Administered initial evaluations, vocational readiness evaluations, and leisure planning evaluations.
- Student Project—Occupational Therapy in Psychiatry.

Professional Associations

Michigan Occupational Therapy Association, American Occupational Therapy Association.

Related Work Experience

SUGAR CREEK CHILDREN'S UNIT, Michigan State Psychiatric Hospital
Mental Health Assistant   Fall 2005
Worked with adolescents ages twelve to sixteen on a thirty-patient unit. Responsibilities included Milieu Therapy, counseling, behavioral management, restraint of aggressive or self-abusive patients, and custodial care.

Philosophy Major

Chris Smith
csmith@e-mail.com

School Address
178 Green Street
Charlotte, NC 28277
(704) 555-5555

Home Address
23 Blue Street
Banner Elk, NC 28604
(704) 555-4444

EDUCATION:

University of North Carolina at Charlotte
Bachelor of Arts, Projected May, 2007
Major: Philosophy
GPA: 3.8/4.0
Dean's List seven consecutive semesters.
One of five candidates chosen to assist in teaching Freshman Seminar orientation class.
Self-financed 50% of education.

EXPERIENCE:

9/05–
Present
Cake Decorator
HARPER LEE SUPERMARKETS, Charlotte, NC
Fill custom cake orders and maintain cake shelf on sales floor. Associate of the Month award in August, 2006. Received corporate-wide recognition for cake production idea which increased company cake sales 10%. Represented Bakery in Associate Task Force. Time commitment of thirty hours per week.

9/06–
Present
Learning Center Tutor
UNIVERSITY OF NORTH CAROLINA AT CHARLOTTE
Tutor students on an individual basis in all aspects of writing and literature and the concepts of molecular, genetic, and evolutionary biology. Average of three hours per week.

Summers
2004–05
Store Manager
JERRY K. PANTS, INC., Charlotte, NC
Full profit and loss responsibility for high volume package store employing twenty-five people. Managed purchasing, inventory control, cash handling, financial reporting, merchandising, advertising, special promotions, and personnel hiring, training, and supervision.
- Implemented purchase control system, thus reducing inventory levels by $75,000.
- Achieved average annual sales growth of 20%.

2003–05
Assistant Store Manager
ANCIENT OAK FOOD MARKET, Wilmington, NC
Scheduled and supervised fifteen to twenty staff members and managed daily operations and inventory. Involved in extensive customer service and cash handling during full- and part-time employment. High volume store with up to $300,000/weekly.

Physics Major

Chris Smith
csmith@e-mail.com

Current Address:
178 Green Street
Pasadena, CA 91125
(818) 555-5555

Permanent Address:
23 Blue Street
Milton, MA 02186
(617) 555-4444

EDUCATION

California Institute of Technology, Pasadena, CA
Bachelor of Arts in Physics, to be awarded: May 2008
Additional areas of study include Chemical Engineering, Mathematics, and Systems Applications.
3.42 grade point average.
Golden Key Honor Society. Cycling Team. Varsity Wrestling.

Milton Academy, Milton, MA
High School Diploma, May 2004

SKILLS

Programming experience in:
C++, Visual Basic, Perl, HTML.

Experience with several different machines and operating systems including Mac, PC, and UNIX.

ACHIEVEMENTS

- Chosen by Caflo Limited to develop new currency options trading strategies using advanced mathematical and statistical modeling.
- Developed and wrote an original bond pricing program.
- Served as president of the Physics Club.
- Wrote for *The Pasadena Sun Times,* College Section.
- Entered college at the age of 15.
- Accepted by and participated in the Physics Project at the University of Chicago; received a grade of 'A'.

WORK EXPERIENCE

5/05–11/06   Caflo, Limited, Pasadena, CA

Intern Software Systems Analyst
Helped develop and write a PC-based application to manage the company's accounts.

Sociology Major

Chris Smith
178 Green Street
Belle Chasse, LA 70037
(504) 555-5555
csmith@e-mail.com

OBJECTIVE

To contribute acquired skills and recent educational background to an organization offering opportunities for growth and advancement.

SUMMARY OF QUALIFICATIONS

- Adept at dealing with ethnic relations, handicapped individuals, and emergency situations.
- Proven supervisory skills; able to work in groups.
- Self-motivated; able to set effective priorities and implement decisions to achieve immediate and long-term goals and meet operational deadlines.
- Fluent in verbal and written Spanish.

EDUCATION

DILLARD UNIVERSITY, New Orleans, LA, 2006
B.A., Sociology: G.P.A. 3.0
Minor: Spanish
Independent Study: "The Feminization of Poverty in the United States."
Member of the Phi Beta Kappa Honor Society.
Contributing writer for the Vanguard Press.

PROFESSIONAL EXPERIENCE

2005–06   GRETNA CITY, Gretna, LA
Weekend/Evening Telecommunications Shift Supervisor
- Supervised staff of five handling incoming calls; ensured smooth workflow and prompt attention to emergency situations.
- Notified key personnel of incoming emergencies; coordinated security efforts to ensure hospital safety; initiated appropriate measures during fire alarms.
- Reported shift inadequacies; recommended resolutions.

2004–05   HARVEY MEDICAL CENTER, Harvey, LA
Assistant Translator
- Translated Spanish medical documents; edited previously translated documents.

REFERENCES

Furnished upon request.

Speech Major

Chris Smith
178 Green Street
Bar Harbor, ME
(207) 555-5555
csmith@e-mail.com

EDUCATION

HUSSON COLLEGE, Bangor, ME
Bachelor of Arts in Speech, May, 2006
Course work in: Radio Announcing, Advanced Public Speaking, TV Production, and Interpersonal Communications.

WKPL-FM HUSSON COLLEGE, 2005–2006
Sports Director, two consecutive semesters
Assigned daily sportscasts to all twenty-two department members. Assisted Program Director and Station Manager in scheduling Husson College athletic events to be broadcast. Set up remote broadcast equipment for athletic events. Assigned department members to broadcast events and biweekly, hour-long, phone-in sports talk show.
Won: MOTORMOUTH PRESS AWARD, best sports coverage for a college radio station.

Board Operator, 2005–06
Formatted and hosted local music show. Featured live interviews with local bands. Coordinated ticket giveaways with Promotion Department.
Involved with various other formats.

Class Orator, Husson College Commencement Exercises, May, 2006

WORK EXPERIENCE

CITY OF BANGOR, Public Facilities Department, Bangor, ME   2/05–5/06
Office Clerk
Witnessed/assisted bid openings for city contracting jobs. Delivered/received documents to and from Bangor offices. Reorganized filing system. Handled blueprint orders and general office functions—filing, typing, and mail delivery.

HUSSON COLLEGE, Bangor, ME   10/04–1/05
Social Science Office Assistant
Delivered and received exams and important documents to Campus Copy Room. Made deliveries on campus. Coordinated student evaluations of faculty members.

SUMMER EXPERIENCE

RORHERCH CLUB, Bar Harbor, ME
Bus Boy
DURLET RECREATION CENTER, Bangor, ME
Laborer

Chris Smith
178 Green Street
Ewing, NJ 08625
(609) 555-5555
csmith@e-mail.com

FORMAL EDUCATION

HAMPSHIRE COLLEGE, Amherst, MA. **B.A. in Studio Art/Sculpture,** 2006.
Also extensive studies in Chinese, Environmental Issues, Politics, and Women's Studies.

THE RAINBOW HERMITAGE, Nova Scotia. A humanistic, alternative high school. 2005.

INFORMAL EDUCATION

Lived and traveled extensively in
GREECE * VIETNAM * THE PEOPLE'S REPUBLIC OF CHINA
CANADA * INDIA * UNITED STATES * HONG KONG

LANGUAGES

English * Spoken Mandarin Chinese * French

WORK EXPERIENCE

HEALWELL, Ewing, NJ   2006–Present
Co-leader, Art Therapy Groups
For children, ages four to ten, of battered women.
Child Care Supervision
For children, ages infant to twelve years, whose mothers are in counseling.

REESE PARK EXPRESS, Durango, CO   Summer 2005
Counselor
Coleader for coed, teenage group which explored cultures and wilderness areas of the southwestern U.S.; planned and led backpacking trips.

BUSINESS TIMES, Boston, MA   Summer 2004
Proofreader and Unofficial Copyeditor
Proofread and edited copy for internationally distributed magazine.

HAMPSHIRE COLLEGE, Amherst, MA   Winter 2003
Workshop Leader
Led Sexual Assault Education Program workshops.
Organized Women's Self Defense workshop.

THE SILENT BLOOM, Hanoi, Vietnam   Fall 2002
English Teacher
Developed and implemented lesson plans for four levels of English, from six-year-old beginners to adult intermediates.

Theater Major

Chris Smith
csmith@e-mail.com

School Address:
178 Green Street
Raleigh, NC 27610
(919) 555-5555

Home Address:
23 Blue Street
Asheville, NC 28804
(704) 555-4444

Hair: Dk. Brown   Eyes: Green   Height: 6'2"
Weight: 180   Age: 21   Age Range: 15–30   Voice: Bass

PERFORMANCE EXPERIENCE

Play	Role	Produced By	Year
Love Letters	Andy	Meredith College	2005
Machinal	The Husband	Meredith College	2005
Carousel	Mr. Bascomb	Ferndale River Playhouse	2005
Black Coffee	Cptn. Hastings	Ferndale River Playhouse	2005
Brigadoon	Mr. Lundie	Ferndale River Playhouse	2005
The Wake of Jamie Foster	Leon Darnell	Ferndale River Playhouse	2005
A Bright Called Day	Baz	Meredith College	2005
Oklahoma!	Slim	Meredith College	2005
The Mikado	Chorus	Ferndale River Playhouse	2004
Chamber Music	The Man in White	Meredith College	2004
The Time of Your Life	Dudley	Meredith College	2004
Twelfth Night	Sir Andrew	Meredith College	2004
Becoming Memories	Stephen/Jerry	Meredith College	2003
Guys and Dolls	Arvide Abemathy	The Meadowlark Playhouse	2003
Mirrors	Chip	Ridgehollow Country Players	2003

OTHER EXPERIENCE

Two seasons of cabaret with the Ferndale River Playhouse—singing, dancing, improvisation, comedy sketches; 2004 and 2005.

Two seasons of Ship-Ahoy! children's theater in Ferndale River, NC—improvisational story theater; 2003 and 2004.

Creative Arts at Park summer camp, Rocky Mount, NC—CIT (two years) and counselor (two years) teaching improvisation, playwriting, and creative dramatics to children ages eight to fifteen; 2002–2003.

TRAINING/SPECIAL SKILLS

Bachelor of Arts degree in the Dramatic Arts, Meredith College. To be awarded May 2006.
Acting, Directing—Jasmine Elwood
Improvisation—Maury Firethorn
Theatrical Design—Lark Hartshorne
Stage Combat (epée, hand-to-hand)—Alexander Kennybunk
Playwriting—written/directed *The Sapphire Runaway, Relieving Atlas* at Meredith College
The Sapphire Runaway, produced at Theater Americana in Altadena, CA
Comedy sketches performed at Cabaret in Ferndale River, NC

Theology Major

Chris Smith
csmith@e-mail.com

School Address
178 Green Street
Immaculata, PA 19345
(215) 555-5555

Home Address
23 Blue Street
Clifton Forge, VA 24422
(703) 555-4444

EDUCATION:

Immaculata College, Immaculata, PA
Candidate for Bachelor of Arts degree in Theological Studies, May 2007.
Courses: Religion in Society, Eastern Religions, Church vs. State.
Honors/Activities: Dean's List all semesters. Sailing Club Co-Captain. Editor-in-Chief of campus magazine, *Immaculata Concepts.* Community Task Force Member.

EXPERIENCE:

Teaching Assistant, Immaculata College, Fall 2006.
Selected by Chair of Theology Department to assist in instruction of Introductory Eastern Religion course. Conducted regular review sessions, helped students with papers, facilitated classroom discussions.

Teaching Intern, Immaculata School System, Spring 2005.
Taught special-needs class in math, science, and writing in cooperation with full-time staff member. Prepared lessons, graded daily assignments, organized afternoon activities and field trips. Participated in parent-teacher conferences.

Tutor, Immaculata Tutoring Program, 2007–2005.
Tutored elementary-school children in history and reading for eight to ten hours a week.

SUMMER WORK:

File Clerk, Clifton Medical Center, Clifton Forge, VA. Summers 2005–2006.
Maintained active patient files and assisted office manager with computerized billing of patients and insurance companies.

TRAINING:

Computers: PC and Mac
Languages: Proficient in French; rudimentary knowledge of Latin.

INTERESTS:

Travel, antiques, sailing.

Western Civilization Major

Chris Smith
178 Green Street
Presque Isle, ME 04769
(207) 555-5555
csmith@e-mail.com

<u>EDUCATION</u>

UNIVERSITY OF MAINE AT PRESQUE ISLE — Presque Isle, ME — 2006
Bachelor of Arts degree: Western Civilization
Concentration: European Studies
Secretary of Alpha Chi Epsilon sorority.
Member of the Ski Team. Regular competitor in downhill ski races, including three annual statewide competitions.

INSTITUTE OF WESTERN STUDIES — Paris, France — Spring 2005
Student Exchange Program
Major: French Cultural and Economic Studies

<u>EXPERIENCE</u>

Intern — Bangor, ME — Spring 2006
STEADMAN TRADE
- Marketed imported French products.
- Prospected territories and acquisitioned clientele.
- Performed cold calling and seed sales.
- Developed sales strategies.
- Conducted research to ascertain target market.

Sales Representative/Administrative Assistant — Boston, MA — Summer 2005
BENSONHURST AND DYNELL
- Provided customer and sales assistance.
- Performed various general office duties, including: filing, light typing, greeting guests, responding to customer inquiries, delivering messages, and controlling inventory.

Customer Service Representative — Paris, France — Spring 2005
LA BANC DE FRANCE
- Sold bank products, opened and closed customer accounts.
- Calculated and deposited currency.
- Provided customer service and supervised staff members.

<u>SPECIAL SKILLS</u>

Fluent in French language.
Exceptional translation and interpretation capability.

<u>VOLUNTEER EXPERIENCE</u>

BOSTON UNIVERSITY MEDICAL CENTER — Boston, MA — 2005–Present
Assist handicapped patients with daily living skills.

<u>INTERESTS</u>

Foreign languages, sports, travel.

Women's Studies Major

Chris Smith
178 Green Street
Newark, NJ 07102
(201) 555-5555
csmith@e-mail.com

Education:

Rutgers University, Newark, NJ
Bachelor of Arts in Women's Studies, 2006. Thesis topic: *The Political Economy of Our Domestic Health Care System.* 3.63 Grade Point Average.
Member of Varsity Crew Team. Designed and painted university-sponsored mural with the theme of cultural diversity.

Work Experience:

12/05–6/06   Summer Orientation Leader
Rutgers University, Newark, NJ
- Aided over 400 students in registration process.
- Led groups through rigid itinerary in strict time schedule.
- Provided initial contact to services and advisors for freshman and transfer students.
- Facilitated dialogue on issues following group diversity exercise.
- Presented campus-wide tours to incoming students and their families for university Open House.

9/05–5/06   Editor-in-Chief, Layout and Design Editor, Activities Editor
The Amber Store, Rutgers University
- Successfully worked within a $30,000 budget to create a 400-page publication from scratch.
- Served as accountable leader of student-run organization.
- Interviewed and selected personnel.
- Acted as teacher, advisor, and supervisor to team of eight.
- Established deadlines for book completion and staff contracts based on academic calendar and publisher expectations.

Summer/Winter Breaks:

2005–2006   Teller
Alpine Savings Bank, New Brunswick, NJ
- Achieved excellent balancing record with daily cash flow.
- Processed large and numerous transactions responsibly.
- Promoted bank services and benefits.
- Mastered the Unisys computer terminal.

2003–2004   Snack Bar Staff
Clover Fields, Camden, NJ
- Organized inventory, storage, and daily tasks for new snack bar.
- Assisted in managing front line customer transactions and behind the scenes operations while training new applicants.

Interests:

Enjoy photography, yoga, and collecting nineteenth-century Russian novels.

Aircraft Mechanic

CHRIS SMITH
178 Green Street
Northfield, MN 55057
(507) 555-5555
csmith@e-mail.com

OBJECTIVE

A challenging position in AIRCRAFT MAINTENANCE which allows for broadening professional experience and room for growth toward management.

EDUCATION

NORTHFIELD COMMUNITY COLLEGE, Northfield, Minnesota
Currently attending Applied Science Degree Program in Aeronautics

UNITED STATES AIR FORCE AIRCRAFT MAINTENANCE SCHOOL
Grissom Air Force Base, Indiana
Graduated 170-hour program—KC/RC/EC-135, Periodic
December 2006
Graduated 110-hour program—KC/RC/EC-135, Able Chief
May 2006

UNITED STATES AIR FORCE AIRCRAFT MAINTENANCE SCHOOL
Sheppard Air Force Base, Texas
Graduated 150-hour program in Tactical/Airlift Bombardment
December 2006

AIRCRAFT MAINTENANCE COURSE
Lackland Air Force Base, Texas
Graduated 120-hour program
September 2005

PRACTICAL EXPERIENCE

Trained in maintenance, servicing, and troubleshooting on all areas of KC/RC/EC-135 aircraft from wing tips to landing gear, nose to tail, interior and exterior, including removals and replacements of component parts, repairs, lubrications, refueling, and flight-line launching and recoveries.

Perform inspections of J57-59 Turbo Jet Engines, plus troubleshooting of component parts. Certified in aircraft towing, aircraft power and battery connections and disconnections, and engine cowl removal and installation.

RELATED INFORMATION

Received honorable discharge.

Available immediately . . . Willing to relocate . . . References on request.

Broadcast Technician

CHRIS SMITH
178 Green Street
Burlington, VT 05405
(802) 555-5555
csmith@e-mail.com

OBJECTIVE:
To pursue a technical career in television or video with opportunities for training and merited enhancement.

EDUCATION:
Trinity College, Burlington, VT
Associate's degree in Radio-Television-Film Technology, Dec. 2006
Cumulative GPA: 3.4; GPA in major: 3.7
Selected Radio, Television, and Film Courses: Newswriting and Production, Film Production, Television Production, Community Video and Industrial Production, Writing for Radio-Television-Film, and Station Organization and Operation (FCC Laws).

Film Direction Workshop. Sponsored by the American Film Institute. Covered the essential narrative, visual, and organizational elements of the director's craft. Examined all phases of film production from the special point of view of the director.

Scriptwriting: An informal discussion. Sponsored by the Burlington Film Festival. Workshop explained how a studio system works, and how scripts are submitted and evaluated.

EXPERIENCE:

December 2006–Present
Master Control Room Technician, **KSTG** Channel 68, TTP Affiliate
Responsible for "on-air" switching of various program sources, commercials, promos, and public service announcements. Recorded satellite feeds. Dubbed commercials and movies. Maintained proper transmitter, program, and operational discrepancy logs. Required the ability to perform with accuracy during periods of high stress.

Fall 2006
Internship, **KARR-TV** Channel 3, NLS Affiliate
Operated studio camera and television prompter. Lighted commercials and public service announcements. Operated dimmer board.

Spring 2005
Film Production Class
Wrote, produced, and directed for short films. Acted as camera person for two short films.

Fall 2004
Community Video and Industrial Production Class
Operated a portable camera. Directed two exercise videos.

Building Inspector

CHRIS SMITH
178 Green Street
Prichard, AL 36610
(205) 555-5555
csmith@e-mail.com

SUMMARY OF QUALIFICATIONS

- More than fifteen years of experience ranging from Carpenter Apprentice to general contractor/project superintendent in military, custom, and general construction.
- Most recent eight years of experience as Permanent Building Inspector, with three years as Acting Building Commissioner during absence of incumbent Commissioner.
- Sound knowledge of state building codes and the inspection of all construction projects.
- Expertise in inspecting new and existing buildings and structures to ensure conformity to building, grading, and zoning laws and approved plans as well as specifications and standards.
- Experience working with engineers and architects on design, coordination, and building of construction projects.
- Capable of enforcing full range of building codes and working with all construction and mechanical trades on codes including electrical and plumbing regulations.

EXPERIENCE

PERMANENT LOCAL BUILDING INPECTOR, City of Prichard, AL   (2003–Present)
As Local Inspector:

- Assigned to inspect Mobile District. Position requires application of sound knowledge of state building codes in inspecting residential, commercial, industrial, and other buildings during and after construction to ensure that components such as footings, floor framing, completed framing, chimneys, and stairways meet provisions of building, grading, zoning, and safety laws.
- Interact with all construction and mechanical trades as well as architects and engineers to assure adherence to improved plans, specifications, and standards.
- Prepare reports concerning violations which have not been corrected, interpret legal requirements, and recommend compliance procedures to contractors, craft workers, and owners.
- Maintain inspection records and prepare reports for use by administrative or judicial authorities.

As Acting Building Commissioner:

- During the absence of the Building Commissioner, assume full responsibility for administering and enforcing state building codes as well as all state rules and regulations involving construction in Mobile.

GENERAL CONTRACTOR
Prichard Construction   (1993–2002)

- Formed a company in 1993 and applied education, training, and expertise in building custom style homes for clients insisting on high degree of skill, quality workmanship, and ability to complete projects to schedule and budget.
- Negotiated all subcontracts. Supervised up to twenty-five carpenters and laborers.

EDUCATION

Mobile Junior College, 1991, Mobile, Alabama.
Associate's degree in Industrial Arts.
Completed Apprenticeship with John Skrensky.
Journeyman Carpenter, 1993, Mobile, AL

Drafter

CHRIS SMITH
178 Green Street
Richmond, VA 23201
(804) 555-5555
csmith@e-mail.com

SUMMARY OF QUALIFICATIONS
- Fifteen years experience in various aspects of electronics.
- Broad knowledge of product development; mechanical/electronic detailing, and drawing; regulatory compliances, codes, and standards; and managerial skills.

PROFESSIONAL EXPERIENCE

2005–Present **Supervisor, Drafting Department**—SHAMROCK INDUSTRIES, Richmond, VA
- Monitor all drafting responsibilities, products, and drawings in Optical Division.
- Manage hybrid microcircuit design and drawing for production.
- Assist with documentation of federal licensing/certification for government projects.
- Coordinate all aspects of detailing with schematic capture, wiring, harnessing, cable drawings, and sand casting.

2003–2005 **Drafting Technician and Designer**—GRAPHIQUE CORPORATION, Dallas, TX
- Performed schematical, electrical, and P.C.B. designs and CADD development.
- Responsible for drawings' development and detailing from conceptualization stage through final release.
- Prepared and coordinated ECNs, along with necessary concurrence markups.

2001–2003 **Mechanical Detailer**—ECO-LAST CORPORATION, Hoya, TX
- Analyzed client specifications and aided in initial design development.
- Calculated extrusions and flat patterns for sheet-metal fabrication.
- Utilized basic dimensioning system and datum structure for machine drawings.

2000–2001 **Detailer**—MUNSON MECHANICAL CO., Hemingway, TX
- Prepared sheet metal drawings, component drawings.
- Created artistic illustrations for advertising and marketing purposes.

EDUCATION

VIRGINIA COLLEGE OF ART, Richmond; Drafting and Design—Transferring to WORTH INSTITUTE, Richmond—B.S. in Drafting and Design. Graduation anticipated 2011.

EL GRECO COMMUNITY COLLEGE, Austin, TX; course work in Drafting Technology and Architectural Development.

COMPUTERS

CV/4X, CADD, Xerox Expert Schematic capture systems. Loading digital software from hard drive onto mag maps.

Electronic Equipment Repairer

CHRIS SMITH
178 Green Street
Warwick, RI
(401) 555-5555
csmith@e-mail.com

SUMMARY OF QUALIFICATIONS
Thirteen years of experience as a customer service hardware specialist and field service engineer. Extensive electronics and mechanical background.

EXPERIENCE

2006 to Present   VI-TAL COMPUTERS   WARWICK, RI
Customer Service Repair/Refurb. Technician
Perform system test and configuration of both hardware and software to meet the customer's needs. Track vendor repaired items. Maintain refurb inventory for all product lines. Assist less experienced technicians with software and operating systems. Reduced testing and configuration time by 60% by developing more streamlined procedures.

2002 to 2006   THE BREWMAN CORPORATION   SLOCUM, RI
Customer Service Repair Technician/Group Leader
Repaired product line using UNIX. Repaired and tested all cpu cards, floating point processors, image and bulk memory cards, and a variety of customer products. Utilized as a consultant in customer support.

2000 to 2002   DAMMON LEE INC.   WATCH HILL, RI
Electronic Test/Repair Technician
Repaired and upgraded field service and system test boards. Provided test, repair, and calibration of a variety of high-speed logic boards.

EDUCATION

1998 to 2000   THE GORTEK INSTITUTE
Graduate of a 700-hour computer technology curriculum. Basic electronics, digital concepts, hardware, software, and micro-processor principles.

TRAINING

VI-TAL COMPUTER INC.
UNIX System Administration.

BREWMAN COMPUTER SYSTEMS, INC.
Introduction to UNIX.

DAMMON LEE, INC.
Managing Multiple Priorities.

Landscape Architect

CHRIS SMITH
178 Green Street
Prescott, AZ 86301
(602) 555-5555
csmith@e-mail.com

OBJECTIVE: A challenging and responsible entry-level **Architectural Landscaping** position where my experience, capabilities, and career interest can be utilized.

EDUCATION:

UNIVERSITY OF NEW MEXICO, Albuquerque, NM
Bachelor of Science in Environmental Science Studies to be awarded May, 2007.

UNIVERSITY OF ALBUQUERQUE, Albuquerque, NM
Architectural Landscape Design Program (1995–1998)

ACME GASOLINE CORPORATION, Prescott, AZ
Management; interviewing, hiring, and EEO training (2001–2002)

SKILLS: Strong mechanical aptitude. Experienced with power mower, small tractor, and other small equipment. Knowledgeable in planting and care of trees, shrubs, bulbs, annual and perennial flowers, and vegetables.

EXPERIENCE:

2002–Present **ACME GASOLINE CORPORATION,** Prescott, AZ
Station Manager, Prescott, AZ (2002–Present)
Responsible for all phases of operations for full-service gas station including maintaining appearance standards and landscaping, customer service, hiring and supervising personnel, fuel product, and merchandise ordering.

Shift Manager, Walker, AZ (2000–2002)
Responsible for full-service convenience store including store appearance, customer service, ordering merchandise, cost control, and personnel functions.

Cashier, Alameda, NM (1998–2000)
Maintained station appearance and provided customer service.

1985–1998 **FORD WORKS INCORPORATED,** Alameda, NM
Assistant Manager
Supervised twelve employees. Act as liaison between upper management and associates.

PERSONAL:

Enjoy working outdoors. Own pickup truck.

REFERENCES AVAILABLE UPON REQUEST

Millwright

OBJECTIVE To secure a position as a Millwright.

SUMMARY OF QUALIFICATIONS

- Eight years experience as a millwright.
- Strong mechanical and analytical attributes.
- Highly effective supervisory skills.
- Constructed turbines; overhaul and repair turbines; turbine assembly and alignment.
- Member, Local Millwright Union.

EXPERIENCE

2004–Present HARRISON INC., Fort Wayne, IN   **Millwright**
Supervise staff of four to thirty millwrights. Assemble and disassemble turbines on Gary, IN, job site.

2001–2004 STEEL THE SKY, INC., Kokomo, IN   **Millwright and Foreman**
Oversee plant construction; set and align turbines and pumps; construct air-cooled condenser.

1995–2001 PERFORMANCE AUTOMOTIVE, Notre Dame, IN   **Owner**
Manage sales, service of foreign cars; import autos from Japan; possess emissions certificates and comply with DOT regulations. Fabricate race cars and engines.

EDUCATION

OAKLAND CITY COLLEGE, Oakland City, IN
Automotive Technology; certified and graduated 1995.
INDIANA UNIVERSITY, Bloomington, IN. A.S. Accounting 1993.

COMPUTER SKILLS

PC and Mac applications; Microsoft Word, Excel.

REFERENCES

Furnished upon request.

Chris Smith
178 Green Street
Las Vegas, NV 89154
(702) 555-5555
csmith@e-mail.com

OBJECTIVE:

A position in computer repair with opportunities for advancement.

EXPERIENCE:

2004–
Present
Lakinakis Corporation, Wendover, NV
Customer Service Receiver
Quality Assurance Test Technician
Handled receiving of computer work station units that failed in the field; tested and repaired all computer work stations; ran diagnostic tests and handled troubleshooting on the sub-assembly level.

2003–2004
Ostow Stores, Search Light, NV
Area Specialist/Department Manager
Performed managerial duties for retail camera and electronics department.

2001–2003
Woodruff Electronics, Las Vegas, NV
Field Service Technician
Repaired PCs on-site. Performed preventative maintenance and customer service.

EDUCATION:

2001–2005
New York University, New York, NY
Bachelor's degree in Computer Science
Maintained G.P.A. of 3.9.

1999–2001
Colgate University, Hamilton, NY
Physics Major
Successfully completed four semesters toward a B.A. Achieved a 3.8 GPA before transferring to New York University for completion of studies.

1998–1999
Spinack Data Institute, Brooklyn, NY
Electronics Technology
Received a Certificate in Electronics Technology. Achieved Honors for maintaining a 95+ average.

REFERENCES:

Available upon request.

Research and Development Technician

CHRIS SMITH
178 Green Street
Ames, IA 50011
(515) 555-5555
csmith@e-mail.com

CAREER SUMMARY

An accomplished Research and Development Technician with solid Quality Control experience. Knowledgeable in testing, product specifications, inspection methods, documenting, and electrical/mechanical components. Well developed problem-solving skills. Contributions which improved quality and effectiveness.

BUSINESS EXPERIENCE

SYSTEMS SCIENCE, INC.   2005 to Present
Des Moines, IA
A manufacturing company specializing in desktop and portable computers for the home, business, and educational markets.

Test Specialist
Provide research and development for compliance, testing, verification, and submittals.
- Identified test equipment and procedure, reducing test time from two days to one day.
- Codeveloped basic programs for compliance testing of new equipment.
- Maintained test equipment and components to eliminate measurement error thereby reducing product failure.

TOWNSEND COMPANY   1998 to 2004
Des Moines, IA
Technician
Provided testing for compliance of computers to meet safety standards and requirements. Conducted component evaluation to assure attainment of print specifications. Coordinated incoming Quality Assurance inspection of electrical and mechanical components.
- Developed various test programs for equipment, assuring attainment of product.
- Reduced overall testing time by creating and documenting program to calculate test results.

PREVIOUS EXPERIENCE

Served as Computer Operator for Security in the United States Navy.

EDUCATION

Electronics, Luther College, Decatur, IA, 1995 to 1997

COMPUTER EXPERIENCE

Windows 98, NT, XP, Millennium and Mac OS and most associated applications.

CHRIS SMITH
178 Green Street
Billings, MT 59102
(406) 555-5555
csmith@e-mail.com

OBJECTIVE: A position in construction, project, or related areas of management. Willing to relocate.

EXPERIENCE: <u>Public Works Department, Billings, MT</u>
Chief Surveyor (2006-Present)
Perform highway, watershed, and topographical surveys. Supervise preparation of plans and specifications for all county highways, bridges, park buildings, and related structures. Maintain a private practice as a surveyor handling site surveys, real estate development layout, and topographical surveys.

Office Engineer (2005-2006)
Developed standard designs for retaining walls and reinforced concrete bridge abutments the designs for which are currently still being used.

<u>Job Works Program, Billings, MT</u>
Seminar Teacher (2005-Present)
Instructed construction foremen in construction methods and leadership.

LICENSES: Professional Engineer, Montana
Surveyor, Montana
Builder, Montana

EDUCATION: Montana State University, Bozeman, MT
B.S. degree in Civil Engineering (with honors), 2006. Additional course work in design, programming, and computer-aided design. Maintain state-of-the-art skills through extensive reading on construction and business topics.

HOBBIES: Golf, running, racquetball, music.

REFERENCES: Furnished upon request.

Technical Instructor

CHRIS SMITH
178 Green Street
Alpha, NJ 08865
csmith@e-mail.com

CAREER OBJECTIVE:
Develop training programs in a corporate or academic environment and present the material in a clear and interesting manner.

BACKGROUND SUMMARY:
Fifteen years of experience in the microcomputer industry with skills ranging from system design to Project Management. Special expertise in creating and presenting training programs covering a wide variety of topics.

EMPLOYMENT:
THE RACE BANNEN COMPANY, Rockaway, ME
Program Management Training Specialist/Network Administrator   2004–Present
Prepare and teach classes in program management techniques and the use of program management software. Manage and maintain the computer network for the department of Program Management. Reconfigure the computer network resulting in 60% increase in the efficiency of the electronic mail system. Developed the course material for seven different classes and presented them to over 300 employees.

Program Manager Computers   2002–2004
Coordinated all efforts going into the successful development of computer products from their inception through their discontinuance. The activities managed included electrical and mechanical engineering, publications, purchasing, and regulatory. Successfully managed seven different computer models to market.

Marketing Support Engineer   1999–2002
Possessed working knowledge of computer products. Represented the company at computer trade shows. Answered technical questions from dealers, distributors, and prospective customers. Field tested computer products and performed other "continuing engineering" functions.

Software Documentation Writer   1996–1998
Authored documentation for computer products including a complete revision of the original operating system manual.

SINEAD KIERNEY CORPORATION   1994–1996
Technical Staff
Codesigned a disk interface for word processor to photo-typesetting equipment. Wrote all of the machine language firmware for the design.

EDUCATION:
Ramapo College of New Jersey, Mahwah, NJ
Master's degree in Physics

COMPUTERS:
Programming: FORTRAN, Basic, Assembly
Applications: MS Word, QuarkXPress, Illustrator

Technical Support Specialist

CHRIS SMITH
178 Green Street
Fairbanks, AK 99775
(907) 555-5555
csmith@e-mail.com

EXPERIENCE

1/06–Present   *SASQUATCH HEALTH CARE,* Fairbanks, AK
TECHNICAL SUPPORT SPECIALIST
Structure the submission of test files for electronic billers, according to the required specification manual, which imposed significant changes in physicians' reimbursements. Developed and designed test data formats for telecommunications claim billers, relative to internal technical operations and equipment.

Monitored effective working relationships with external credentialing groups, linking users to meet shared objectives. Formulated and edited technical user-specification manual. Submitted weekly patient accounting check writing jobs on the Tape Operating System controlled by Job Control Language and operated the Series 1 mainframe for electronic billers.

6/05–1/06   **INTERNAL SUPPORT SPECIALIST**
Communicated with physician and health providers desiring to submit patient billing claims on the professional line of business, Medicaid, including initiating the activities related to their acceptance and approval of all billers.

Acted as corporate liaison, communicating and monitoring the providers fraud list for active, suspended, or deceased physicians, and reviewed contracts for credentials of providers anticipating the acquisition of technical billing authorization and a physician provider identification code. Updated and maintained all Alaskan professional input providers and billers authorization file for medical reimbursement billing system.

3/03–6/05   **DATA CONTROL ANALYST**
Serviced local and regional billing agents. Created and maintained a database on the facility line of business for all input files. Distributed hard copies of vouchers for health care services provided by hospital facilities, to aid as balance control documents.

Allocated missing data that controlled the mechanisms for billing tape submissions; analytically identified and resolved data processing problems, and communicated the solution.

EDUCATION

FAIRBANKS COMMUNITY COLLEGE, Fairbanks, AK
ASSOCIATE OF ARTS, Computer Science, May 2005, GPA 3.7

ALASKA INSTITUTE OF COMPUTERS, Fairbanks, AK
DIPLOMA, Computer Programming, May 2001, GPA 3.6

PERSONAL

Willing to relocate.

Telecommunications Consultant
Cable

CHRIS SMITH
178 Green Street
Robbinsdale, MN 55422
(612) 555-5555
csmith@e-mail.com

OBJECTIVE

A challenging position in telecommunications where my international perspective will be utilized.

EXPERIENCE

May 2005–
January
2006

CANADIAN CABLE COUNCIL   **Vancouver, Quebec, and Minneapolis**
Consultant
- One of five consultants assigned to research/recommend a strategic alliance for Canadian Cable Corporation.
- Conducted onsite research at CCC's Vancouver offices and at its home office near Quebec.
- Presented final recommendations in video conference. Recommended alliance with Truglia Corp. to produce a multimedia product in anticipation of the merging of telecommunications and computer technology.

September
2004–May
2005

**THE INTERNATIONAL JOURNAL
OF TELECOMMUNICATIONS**   **Minneapolis, MN**
Market Researcher
- Researched direct-mail advertising as an international marketing tool.
- Examined political campaigns, image design, and information distribution.

May 2003–
August 2004

AROUND THE WORLD CONSULTANTS   **Saint Paul, MN**
Market Research Project Support
- Built database of international publishing and printing firms. Researched list sources, acquired lists, and created, merged, and purged database.
- Conducted, coded, and edited telephone market research surveys to identify and track trends in the electronic publishing and information networking industry.

EDUCATION

SAINT CLOUD STATE UNIVERSITY, St. Cloud, MN
B.S. in Engineering, Minor: French, 2004
- Spent junior year studying and traveling in France.

TRAINING

Seminar in *Global Relations and American Business*.
Training session on the uses of the Internet.

CHRIS SMITH
178 Green Street
Seattle, WA 98105
(205) 555-5555
csmith@e-mail.com

Hair:	Blonde	D.O.B.:	7/20/80
Eyes:	Hazel	Height:	5'8"
Sex:	Female	Weight:	135 lbs.

EXPERIENCE

2006 WHITEWATER COMMUNITY THEATER, Seattle, WA
Mrs. Babson, *Lights, Camera, Action.*

SUMMER ARTS THEATER, Seattle, WA
Karen Arnold, *Life In The Slow Lane.*

NIGHT OWL THEATER, Seattle, WA
Candice Lloyd, *World's End.*

2005 ST. MARY'S CONGREGATION, Black Diamond, WA
Director, Assorted children's plays.

REGGAE FEST, Jamaica
Actor/Director, Several festival performances during this annual national celebration.

CHARLES STREET THEATER, Black Diamond, WA
Therese Dupuis, *The Deal.*

EDUCATION

2006 to Present ACTING UP DRAMA WORKSHOP, Seattle, WA
Advanced Acting, Acting for Stage and Television, Ritual and Performance
Related performances:
- **Carolyn Christian,** *Many Moons.*
- **Sarah Downs,** *Two For Lunch.*
- **Maryanne Walsh,** *Computer Geeks.*
- **Lisa,** *Cranberry With a Twist.*

2006 EMERSON COLLEGE, Boston, MA
Bachelor of Fine Arts, Acting

ADDITIONAL

Bilingual: Fluent in Italian and English.

Art Director

Chris Smith
178 Green Street
Bristol, RI 02809
(401) 555-5555
csmith@e-mail.com

OBJECTIVE:
Freelance or full-time gallery employment as Art Director in an established advertising agency.

EMPLOYMENT:
CURTIS ASSOCIATES/CHERRY HILL, Boston, MA
Art Director, 2006–Present
Major responsibilities included:
- The design, art direction, illustration, and concept-development of black-and-white and full-color promotional samples for black-and-white, color-copying, and ink-jet printing divisions.
- Art direction on photography sessions for direct mail marketing pieces.
- Quality control management on press runs for promotional pieces printed in and out of house.
- Design in-house company morale promotional pieces such as anti-drug abuse posters, company picnic and Christmas dinner/dance posters and tickets, as well as completing most of the paste-up on all projects.

WOLFSONG, INC., Northampton, MA
Assistant Art Director, 2003–2006
Designed and/or rendered full page cooperative free standing insert ads for regional and national name brand pet food companies.
- Designed and/or rendered FSI's accompanying point-of-sales materials (header cards, tear-off pads, soft sheets, and shelf talkers), trade promotions (ad reprints, dealer sell sheets, and marketing lists), and bounce-back coupons.
- Utilized illustrative talents to complete black-and-white product illustrations for bounce-back coupons and ad slicks.

EDUCATION:
RHODE ISLAND SCHOOL OF DESIGN, Providence, RI
Associate's Degree in Specialized Technology (2003)

MONTSERRAT COLLEGE OF ART, Beverly, MA
Completed three-year program in Commercial Art (2001)

SKILLS:

Mac and PC applications; QuarkXPress and PageMaker; inkjet printers, color photo copiers, and retouching and page layout software.

Comedian

CHRIS SMITH
178 Green Street
Miami, FL 33199
(305) 555-5555
csmith@e-mail.com

PROFILE:

Charismatic, crazy, creative, daring, dastardly, hilarious, hyper, hysterical, and of course zany!

PERSONAL:

D.O.B.: 9/5/83	Height: 6'1"
Hair: Brown	Weight: 165 lbs.
Eyes: Blue	Sex: Male

LAST SEEN:

MIAMI	Comedians At Large	Beachside Comedy Review
	Miami Moon	Laughter Unlimited
	Carlisle's Lounge	Give It Up
	Kevin's Connection	Pleasure Island
CHICAGO	Wind It Down	The Funny Farm
	Comedy Central	
DETROIT	Let It Slide	Can You Stand It?
	Barry's Bar & Grill	The Haverill House
SAN FRANCISCO	Wild Child	The Funny Bone
	Check It Out	Tickle My Fancy
ORLANDO	Church Street Station	The Mad Hatter
	Mickey's	

TELEVISION LOSIN' IT
  - Coproducer of local cable program, showcasing a variety of stand-up performers.
  COMEDIANS FOR HIRE
  - Numerous stand-up appearances.

KNOWN ASSOCIATES:

The American Comedians Association

CAUTION:

Mr. Smith is armed with a sharp tongue and a quick wit. He has been known to strike without warning!

Dancer

CHRIS SMITH
178 Green Street
Las Vegas, NV 89154
(702) 555-5555 (Day)
(702) 555-4444 (Evening)
csmith@e-mail.com

TALENTS:
- Ballet
- Jazz
- Modern Dance
- Tap
- Singing
- Acting
- Choreography
- Directing

EXPERIENCE:
DANCING
September 2006–Present: Soloist with Mormon Youth Ensemble. Presentations include:
- "Summer Winds"—Contemporary ballet
- "Peace at Heart"—Modern piece
- "Travels Afar"—Classical ballet
- "Italian Gondolas"—Contemporary ballet
- "Two Stars"—Jazz piece
- "Clouds Above"—Dream ballet, musical
- "The Gosling"—Classical ballet
- "A Little Bit Country"—Modern ballet, musical

CHOREOGRAPHY
- Special events and shows, 2006–Present
- Rocket Dance Club, Las Vegas, NV, 2006–Present
- Copa Cabana Club, Las Vegas, NV, 2006

EDUCATION:
Sierra Nevada College, Incline Village, NV
B.F.A. in Dance and Choreography, 2006

TRAINING:
- Ballet: Nevada Ballet, Nevada Academy of Ballet
- Jazz: Genevieve le Fleur, James Ivan
- Tap: Jackie Rose Studio

DEMO TAPE AVAILABLE UPON REQUEST

Fashion Designer

CHRIS SMITH
178 Green Street
New York, NY 10019
(212) 555-5555
csmith@e-mail.com

OBJECTIVE   A position in apparel and accessory design where illustration, design, and technical skills will be creatively utilized.

SUMMARY   Diversified background offers expertise in:
- **Illustration:** Design sketching and fashion illustration.
- **Sewing:** Tailoring, mass production, fabrication, pattern marking, construction.
- **Design:** Specializing in custom evening wear and women's special occasion and sportswear.

EXPERIENCE   THE NEW COLLECTION, New York, NY
Tailor, 2006–Present
- Specialize in fashionable women's working apparel.
- Provide tailoring, wardrobe consultation, and custom design of suits and evening wear.
- Sketch original designs, create patterns, and construct garments.

Freelance Fashion Designer, 2005–Present
- Create custom clothing for fashion shows.
- Provide wardrobe, fabric, and color consultation.
- Have developed a solid, recurring client base.

COLOR CONTOURS, Albany, NY
Seamstress, 2003–2005
- Fabrication, woolen and knit ponchos and fur accessories.
- Production sewing, Merrow, single-needle and fur machines.

GALLUZO MANUFACTURERS, Saugerties, NY
Assistant Designer, 2001–2003
- Designed for High Street label and line.
- Selected fabric, color, and pattern.
- Achieved minimum production costs on first pattern estimates.

EDUCATION

FASHION INSTITUTE OF TECHNOLOGY, New York, NY
Associate's degree in Applied Science: Fashion Design Major, 2005.

HONORS/EXHIBITS
- Prize-winning garments for design and construction
Fashion Union Fashion Show, 2005
- Best Bikini Design
New York Swimwear Associates, 2005

Film Production Assistant

CHRIS SMITH
178 Green Street
Los Angeles, CA 90049
(213) 555-5555
csmith@e-mail.com

PROFESSIONAL OBJECTIVE

A film production position where I can contribute a broad range of relevant experience and education.

EXPERIENCE

2005–
Present

HOLLY CAN PRODUCTIONS, Burbank, CA
Production Assistant
- Assisted in production of *Chuck's Gals*.
- Shot and edited commercials.
- Research and recommend prop and wardrobe choice.

2005–
Present

Freelancer
- Videotaped improvisational workshop for the L.A. Entertainment Theatre, and comedy sketches for local talent.
- Wrote material for various Los Angeles comedians.
- Wrote jokes published in *Side-Splitters* magazine.

2004–05 **Intern**
- Observed techniques in video editing and preproduction of feature films and slide shows for corporations and universities.

WRITING

- Radio/TV commercial scripts.
- Thirty-five–page comedy.
- Several short narrative sketches.
- Several short comedy films.

EDUCATION

Bachelor of Arts in Film Production
Emerson College, L.A. Program, May 2005

PORTFOLIO

Portfolio of writing and productions available upon request.

Graphic Artist/Designer

A

Chris Smith
178 Green Street
Honey Grove, TX 75446
(210) 555-5555
csmith@e-mail.com

PROFILE

Business and art professional with broad-based knowledge and expertise in a variety of art forms. Excellent organizer and communicator with the ability to project and elicit interest, enthusiasm and energy, using a common sense approach. Over five years professional art experience. Strong conceptual skills; able to translate ideas into realities.

ART/DESIGN EXPERIENCE

MICHAEL JUDGE GALLERY, Dallas, TX   Spring 2006
Displayed and sold several art pieces. Illustrations used in advertisements and gallery logo.

CAROL OATES INC., Keeci, TX   2005–2006
Freelance work for national stationery and social invitation firm.
• Design invitations, personal stationery, business cards, and logos.
• Implemented italic method as well as numerous hand-designed, stylized lettering.

BYRON KATZ, Kress, TX   2004–2005
Freelance calligrapher for national stationery company.
• Design invitations and logos.

BARBARA B. DOLE, Kress, TX   2002–2004
Self-promoting/advertising, freelance calligrapher for local clients.
• Design wedding and party invitations.
• Provide artwork and calligraphy for accompanying accessories.

ACCOMPLISHMENTS

• Designer of logo for Connection Street Gallery, its storefront sign, T-shirts, jackets, business cards and stationery, advertising, and greeting cards.
• Designer of logo for *Brazen Attachment* magazine; artwork for advertising appeared in *Her View.*
• Designer for calligraphic artwork for Texas History Museum.

EDUCATION

CONCORDIA COLLEGE, Bronxville, NY
Bachelor of Fine Arts, 2003

PUBLICATIONS

Missed Grits: How to Cook Southern Favorites No Matter Where You Live, Reni Watts. 2006. Cover Design.

References and Portfolio Available On Request.

Graphic Artist/Designer

B

Chris Smith
178 Green Street
Elk Rapids, MI 49629
(517) 555-5555
csmith@e-mail.com

CAREER OBJECTIVE

A challenging position in the field of COMMERCIAL ART where I can contribute
highly developed graphic design skills and technical aptitude.

RELATED EXPERIENCE

GRAPHIC ARTIST   1999–Present

Packard Army Reserves, Elk Rapids, MI

Serve as artistic support for Army base; create fliers, charts, brochures, tickets, diagrams, maps, and design logos. Document work order requests; plan and organize work to meet all deadline requirements. Purchase materials and supplies; document materials received and perform graphics department inventory. Maintain accurate and timely department records.

GRAPHIC ARTIST/ELECTRONIC DESIGN   2003–Present

Midland Products, Alden, MI

Produce camera-ready art utilizing Mac computer system with laser printing equipment. Proficient in use of QuarkXPress and Illustrator programs. Process film, operate reproduction camera for stats, positive and negative images. Utilize Diffusion Transfer machine. Efficiently organize time and work to consistently meet critical deadlines. Keep artwork and files up to date.

TECHNICAL LINE ARTIST   1999–2003

Marmoset Electric Company, Rapid City, MI

Performed drafting work; inked illustrations. Produced paste-up and mechanical preparation for Detroit Transit Railcar Inspection Manuals.

ARTIST/PASTE-UP   1997–1999

Sharona's Art Emporium, Ellsworth, MI

Created art for slide presentations; designed ads for newspaper; provided computer art for Sharona's computer facility. Set up mechanicals for print orders including business cards and stationery. Ran blueprints, made negatives, and opaqued negatives.

EDUCATION

ASSOCIATE'S DEGREE in GRAPHIC DESIGN, 1995
Kendall School of Design, Grand Rapids, MI

PORTFOLIO AND REFERENCES AVAILABLE UPON REQUEST

Model

Chris Smith
178 Green Street
Acworth, GA 31707
(912) 555-5555
csmith@e-mail.com

Height: 5'9"   Bust: 36"
Weight: 120 lbs.   Waist: 28"
Hair Color: Auburn   Hips: 35"
Eye Color: Green   Dress Size: 6
Age Range: 18–30   Shoe Size: 7

TRAINING

Rick Bass Casting, Modeling and Acting
Joy DeVivre, Modeling and Acting

EXPERIENCE

Fashion Shows BRYDIE'S BRIDAL SHOP, Atlanta, GA
Fashion Show, May 2006.

RAYANNE'S FASHIONS, Albany, GA
Runway Show, July 2005.

Film EBONY'S FINE ARTS SCHOOL, Alphoretta, GA
Modeled for Photography class, Summer 2006.

GOLD MORNING PRODUCTIONS
Extra for three scenes at Downtown Crossing, Boston, MA, October 2006.

Competition EVAN HAWKE MODELING CONTEST, Atlanta, GA
First Runner-up, December 2005.

SPECIAL SKILLS

Sports: swimming, ice skating, snow and water skiing, bicycling, baseball, basketball, tennis, jogging, and aerobics.
Dancing: jazz, tap, and ballet.
Play classical piano.
Familiar and comfortable working with animals (dogs and cats, large and exotic species included).

EDUCATION

Georgia County Community College, Atlanta, GA
Chemical Engineering Studies.

Musician

Chris Smith
178 Green Street
New York, NY 10019
(212) 555-5555
csmith@e-mail.com

SUMMARY OF QUALIFICATIONS
- More than six years orchestral experience as violinist/violist.
- Ability to comprehend administrative needs from the perspective of a performer.
- Acquired skills as orchestra librarian/personnel manager.
- Organizational abilities; detail-oriented.

RELEVANT EXPERIENCE

Orchestra—2nd Violin
- *La Musique, C'est Magnifique!*
  Play, Paris, France
- *White Willows in Glasgow*
  Opera and Ballet, Scotland
- Sun Symphony Orchestra of L.A.
  Los Angeles, California
- The Lighthouse Orchestra
  Bar Harbor, ME
- *Bang a Ceramic Gong: The Tale of a Chinese Emperor*
  Play, Boston, MA

MIDAS TOUCH CHAMBER ORCHESTRA, New York, NY   2005–2006
Personnel Manager. Recruited players. Arranged for substitutes. Assisted Conductor/Music Director. Scheduled recitals, announcements, and member contact regarding changes, problem resolution, etc. Required ability to deal with personality conflicts and musical problems as well as fielding suggestions from members. Instituted rotating string sections. Handled membership payment. Acted as liaison between musicians and union.

EDUCATION

O'BURN INSTITUTE, New York, NY   2006
Teacher Workshop Courses

THE JUILLIARD SCHOOL, New York, NY   2004
Bachelor of Arts, Music

References and Tape Available on Request

Production Tour Manager

Chris Smith
178 Green Street
Boston, MA 02115
(617) 555-5555
csmith@e-mail.com

SUMMARY OF QUALIFICATIONS
- Five years of progressive, professional tour management/production experience requiring ability to coordinate tours, video, TV, fashion and trade shows, and conventions.
- Self-motivated; able to set effective priorities and implement decisions to achieve immediate and long-term goals and meet operational deadlines.
- Capable of organizing projects from initiation through completion; adept at troubleshooting and resolving problems.
- Proven liaison and negotiating skills coordinating worldwide tours.
- Deal with daily expenses, cost projections, and show settlements.

PROFESSIONAL EXPERIENCE

STRANGE MAGIC MANAGEMENT COMPANY, Boston, MA   2005–Present
Tour/Production Manager
Oversaw road tours. Managed finances/budget. Hired outside contractors/road crews. Coordinated travel arrangements, including four worldwide tours. Dealt with visas, freight, hotel accommodations, etc. Acted as liaison with local labor unions and security. Resolved problems as necessary.

MILQUETOAST, LIE TO YOUR MOTHER TOUR   2005
Production Manager
Oversaw/directed six-month worldwide tour.

WENDELL THE PAPERBOY, WHY BOTHER? TOUR   2005
Production Manager
Coordinated all aspects of six-month tour.

NO ARTICULATION, HEART ON YOUR SLEEVE TOUR   2004
Back-Line Technician
Served as Drum Technician. Assisted in stage management. Arranged equipment rental for worldwide tour including: Bangkok, Saigon, and Taiwan. Developed endorsements with instrument companies and backstage catering.

THINK TANK, KISS IN THE RAIN TOUR   2004
Back-Line Technician/Stage Manager
Worked directly under Production Manager on this arena-level tour. Served as Drum Technician.

BURNT RETINA, BREAD & WATER TOUR   2003
Lighting Technician
Dealt with complicated lighting system, rigging, loading/unloading, and working with union crews.

EDUCATION
CURRY COLLEGE, Milton, MA
B.A. Public Relations, 2002

Talent Agent

Chris Smith
178 Green Street
Winterthur, DE 19735
(302) 555-5555
csmith@e-mail.com

OBJECTIVE
To become an artist and repertoire representative for a major field.

EXPERIENCE

Ricochet Management Inc., Wilmington, DE
Personal Manager (2005 to Present)
- Selected six local bands and brought them to national recognition: Top of the Charts, Sights, New York Talk, and Spunk Awards 2006.
- Advised artists on performance and repertoire, resulting in three major-label signings.
- Oversaw and coordinated the production, promotion, and marketing of four major label projects.
- Initiated and devised extraordinary prerelease promotions for a debut album, resulting in immediate college chart movement on release (Kieley and Briody).
- Tour managed three album tours, one regional and the others national, all 20–25% under budget.

Moonchild Records, New York, NY
Label Manager (2003–2005)
- Achieved three regionally Top Ten selling and charting records, and a top selling single in Europe.
- Devised and oversaw promotion and marketing on limited budgets of $10,000 to $15,000.
- Oversaw production, mastering, manufacturing, artwork, and distribution.
- Coordinated career development with artists and their management.

Aural Erosion Records, Los Angeles, CA
Product Manager (2002–2003)
- Created a showcase club for up-and-coming alternative acts: Crudeness, Drink the Foam, Your Mangy Mother, Corporate Mind Wipe, Clubbed Knee, and Four Evil Extraterrestrials and their Dad.
- Conceived entirely new club concept: music format, design, and marketing strategy. Increased revenues from an average $10,000 to over $2 million, and profit on live shows from 52% to 99%.

EDUCATION

Stanford University, Stanford, CA
Major: Public Relations
Master's degree, May 2000

Theatrical Director

CHRIS SMITH
178 Green Street
Chicago, IL 60622
(312) 555-5555
csmith@e-mail.com

OBJECTIVE

A career continuation as a Director of legitimate theatre on or off Broadway.

SKILLS AND QUALIFICATIONS

- Over thirteen years experience stage directing with clear understanding of playwrights' texts and creative analysis.
- Provide theatrical direction to actors attuned to both the Stanislavsky and Method styles of acting.
- Focused on the physical requirements and restrictions of stages ranging from in-the-round, proscenium arch, mechanical stages, and special effects.
- Communicate well with actors in relation to lighting and sound technicians.
- Involved in all aspects of costuming and makeup to enhance actors' performances and facilitate their taking direction accurately and precisely while maintaining their own "voice" and force on stage.
- Able to deal with producers and financial backers in structural, aesthetic, and artistic feasibility of a play.
- Work closely with producers and board of directors on time, focus, budget, creative, and practical expectations among director, actors, and powers-that-be.

SELECTED DIRECTORIAL EFFORTS

- *THE IMPORTANCE OF BEING EARNEST*
- *SUNSET STRIP*
- *FENCES*
- *THE FANTASTIKS*
- *PEARLIE*
- *GREASE*
- *THE WIZ*
- *THE REAL INSPECTOR HOUND*
- *SHADOWLANDS*
- *AGATHA CHRISTIE'S THE MOUSETRAP*
- *EVITA*
- *OLIVER!*
- *BARNUM*
- *THE LITTLE FOXES*
- *WAITING FOR GODOT*

EDUCATION

EMERSON COLLEGE, Boston, MA	M.A., Directing	1995
EMERSON COLLEGE, Boston, MA	B.A., Theatre	1993

References and Portfolio Available on Request

Financial Planner E-Resume

Jamie Brown
123 Main Street • Hometown, NY 00000 • (555) 555-1234 • jbrown@company.com

Financial Planning Qualifications and Credentials

- Over a decade of progressively significant roles and achievements within planning, portfolio management, and client services.
- Personal responsibility for more than $210 million client assets.
- Regularly recognized for asset-based performance and customer service.
- Asset collection, asset allocation, asset management, risk management, tax deferment and minimization, portfolio management, generational wealth transition, trust and estate planning, and private placement funding competencies.
- History of maximizing client portfolio value, generating relationships with high net-worth clientele, and regularly conducting need versus risk analyses.
- Experience hiring, training, and supervising newly hired FCs and FPs.
- Served as trainer and curriculum developer, using traditional lectures, audiotapes, videotapes, and simulation exercises.
- Licensed Series 6, 7, 63 and health and life insurance.

Financial Planning Accomplishments

ABC FINANCIAL CONSULTANTS, Princeton, NJ

Financial Consultant/Financial Planner, 1990–present

Serve within comprehensive financial planning and roles. Oversee individual and group portfolios. Serve as senior manager, supervisor, and trainer within corporate headquarters of firm responsible for over $800 million in client assets.

- Developed $210 million client asset base via prospecting and targeting.
- Successfully built portfolio that includes stock, bonds, options, and insurance products for more than 450 clients.
- Implemented financial plans through account development and growth.
- Gained estate planning, asset allocation, and wealth succession expertise.

Sales Associate, 1988–1990

- Worked directly with firm's top producer, profiling high net-worth individuals.
- Generated $90,000 for top producer through new account openings.
- Analyzed existing portfolio, assisting in development of accounts.

Account Executive Trainee/Intern, 1987–1988

MAPLEWOOD INVESTMENTS, Maplewood, NJ

Prospecting Intern, Summers 1986 and 1987

EDUCATION

IONA COLLEGE, Iona, NY

Bachelor of Arts degree in Economics, 1988

Concentration in Business Management, with courses in: Financial Accounting, Managerial Finance, Corporate Treasury, Insurance, Statistics, and Financial Services.

Pharmaceutical Sales E-Resume

DANA JOHNSON

123 Main Street • Hometown, NY 08456 • (555) 555-1234 • djohnson@company.com

PHARMACEUTICAL SALES QUALIFICATIONS

Interest in: AIDS, Antidepressants, Antihistamines, Arthritis, Cancer, Cholesterol, Diabetes, FDA Approval Stages, Heart Disease, Osteoporosis, and Aging. Knowledge gained via research of: Antiulcerants, Cholesterol and Triglyceride Reducers, Antidepressants, Calcium Antagonists, Plain Antirheumatic Non-Steroidals, ACE Inhibitors, Plain Cephalosporins and Combinations, Antipsychotics, Non-Narcotic Analgesics, and Oral Antidiabetics. Record of success within direct marketing and information-driven sales roles. Confidence nurturing existing relationships and developing new clientele via direct calls using information dissemination strategies. Capacity to understand and share pharmaceutical product and protocol knowledge. Abilities to blend qualitative and communication talents as well as analytical skills to set goals, document impact of sales efforts, and maximize output. Bilingual English-Mandarin abilities and cross-cultural sensitivities.

SALES AND SALES SUPPORT ACHIEVEMENTS

PEARLS AND GEMSTONES CORPORATION, San Francisco, California, 2001–Present

Sales Associate for Loose Diamond Division: Sell and market polished gemstones for an international gemstone and pearl distributor and jewelry manufacturer. Sales methods include appointments onsite, telemarketing, tradeshow exhibiting, and Internet sales. Customers include manufacturers, retail stores, department stores, and catalogs.

Directly involved in sales to house accounts totaling $2.5 million in 2001.

Indirectly involved in sales to salespersons accounts totaling $3 million in 2001.

COMPUTER ASSOCIATES INTERNATIONAL, San Jose, California   1997

Quality Assurance Analyst: Analyzed business applications and RFPs (Request For Proposal) for marketability. Implemented quality assurance for an inter/intranet-enabled, multiplatform, enterprise management solution used worldwide.

Supported customer service and sales representatives in refining product to match customer needs.

BUSINESS EXPERIENCE

BANK OF HONG KONG, Hong Kong, Spring 2000

International Securities Dealing Room Trader: Communicated with customers' desires to execute orders in the areas of American and foreign equities, bonds, and options. Received training in and gained working knowledge of Bloomberg and Reuters information systems.

BANK OF HONG KONG, San Francisco, California, 1997–2000

International Lending Department Credit Analyst: Prepared proposals on prospective customers for credit committee. Conducted business and industry research using Bloomberg, Moody's, and S&P analysts and publications.

BUSINESS, ECONOMICS, AND LIBERAL ARTS EDUCATION

UNIVERSITY OF CALIFORNIA, BERKELEY, Berkeley, California, 1993–1997

Bachelor of Arts, Political Science, with minor in Economics

Served as Intern for Member British Parliament, London, England, Fall 1995. Served as Intern for Senator Barbara Boxer, U.S. Senate, Washington D.C., Summer 1995.

HAAS SCHOOL OF BUSINESS ADMINISTRATION, Berkeley, California, 1993–1997

Management Certificate for completion of Marketing, Accounting, Economics, Statistics, and Computer Science courses. Developed detailed and fiscally sound marketing plan.

PART II

COVER LETTERS

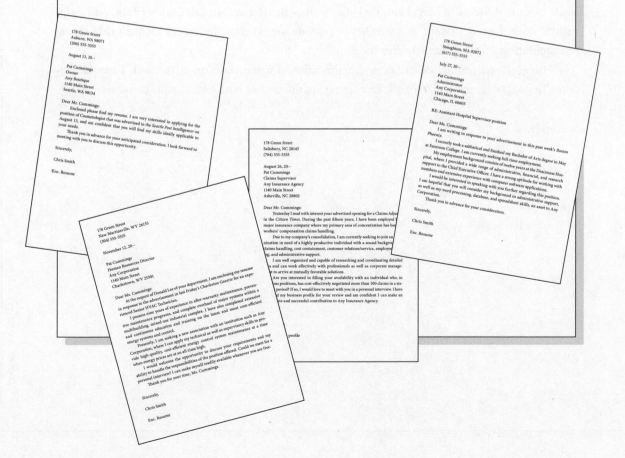

Administrative Judge

178 Green Street
Fox, OR 97831
(503) 555-5555

May 23, 20--

Pat Cummings
Chairperson
Chicago Municipal Court
1140 Main Street
Chicago, IL 60605

Dear Ms. Cummings:

Your advertisement in the May 30 issue of *Lawyers Monthly* is of great interest to me. I feel that I have the qualifications necessary to effectively handle the responsibilities of Administrative Judge.

During the past four years as Assistant Attorney General, I have gained broad experience in the litigation of personal injury actions and workers' compensation claims. In this position, I made extensive use of my legal knowledge as well as my research, analytical, writing, and judgmental skills. I am confident of my ability to provide the expertise necessary for the professional representation of an Administrative Judge.

The enclosed resume describes my qualifications for the position advertised. I would welcome the opportunity to personally discuss my qualifications with you at your convenience.

Sincerely,

Chris Smith

Enc. Resume

Analyst

178 Green Street
Henniker, NH 03242
(603) 555-5555

December 30, 20--

Pat Cummings
Director, Financial Planning
Any Corporation
1140 Main Street
Nashua, NH 03061

Dear Mr. Cummings:

I write in response to your advertisement for an Analyst in the December 28 edition of the *Telegraph*. During the past several years I have been actively involved, in both academic and workplace settings, with financial and business analysis as well as support activities involving corporate business and finance.

Although my present position has provided me with the opportunity for quality professional development as an Analyst and interesting challenges through diverse assignments, I am ready for a change. I am interested in joining a firm in which I can offer my analytical and qualitative skills toward making a substantial contribution to its overall success and reputation.

The enclosed employment profile is a summary of my experience. I would be glad to schedule an interview to discuss your requirements and my ability to handle the responsibilities of the position offered.

Should you require additional information prior to our meeting, please feel free to contact me at the above address and daytime number, or during the evenings at (603) 555-4444.

In the interim, I will look forward to your return response.

Yours sincerely,

Chris Smith

Enc. Employment profile

Assistant Hospital Supervisor

178 Green Street
Stoughton, MA 02072
(617) 555-5555

July 27, 20--

Pat Cummings
Administrator
Any Corporation
1140 Main Street
Chicago, IL 60605

RE: Assistant Hospital Supervisor position

Dear Ms. Cummings:

I am writing in response to your advertisement in this past week's *Boston Phoenix*.

I recently took a sabbatical and finished my Bachelor of Arts degree in May at Emerson College. I am currently seeking full-time employment.

My employment background consists of twelve years at the Deaconess Hospital, where I provided a wide range of administrative, financial, and research support to the Chief Executive Officer. I have a strong aptitude for working with numbers and extensive experience with computer software applications.

I would be interested in speaking with you further regarding this position. I am hopeful that you will consider my background in administrative support, as well as my word processing, database, and spreadsheet skills, an asset to Any Corporation.

Thank you in advance for your consideration.

Sincerely,

Chris Smith

Enc. Resume

Associate Desktop Publisher

178 Green Street
Tacoma, WA 98447
(206) 555-5555

March 10, 20--

Pat Cummings
Managing Editor
Any Corporation
1140 Main Street
Richmond, VA 23225

Dear Mr. Cummings:

In response to your advertisement for an Associate Desktop Publisher, I am sending my resume for your review.

My ten years of computer experience include researching, developing, and documenting the operational procedures of a software seller. I was responsible for all aspects of the manual, from conceptualization to publication. I also coordinated and published the sales and marketing newsletter distributed to key accounts and sales representatives.

Successful completion of such projects requires skills in researching, organizing, writing, and editing. I am proficient in several desktop publishing and word processing applications, including WordPerfect, Microsoft Word, and Corel Ventura.

I will be moving to the Richmond area next week and would be happy to meet with you at your convenience. I will call your office during the week of March 17. Thank you for your consideration.

Sincerely,

Chris Smith

Enc. Resume

Campus Police Officer

178 Green Street
Stanford, CA 94305
(415) 555-5555

February 23, 20--

Pat Cummings
Director of Security
Any College
1140 Main Street
Whittier, CA 92608

RE: Campus Police Officer

Dear Ms. Cummings:

My interest in pursuing and expanding my professional career in law enforcement and security management has prompted me to respond to your advertisement in the March issue of *Careers in Law Enforcement*.

For the past twelve years, my background has been concentrated in security and law enforcement. In my present position, I am responsible for maintaining the highest possible site and operations security for a key United States government defense contractor. From 20-- to 20--, I served in the United States Army where I was responsible for maintaining peak law enforcement/security alertness and the welfare of all personnel. In that capacity, I received numerous letters of commendation for superior job performance. I am a graduate of military police school, I have completed additional law enforcement seminars, and I am currently enrolled in a criminal justice degree program.

Through practical experience, I am well versed in military and international law as well as United States law and procedures. If we could meet in a personal interview, I could discuss further my qualifications and outline the potential contribution I could make to your security office.

I look forward to your response.

Sincerely,

Chris Smith

Enc. Resume

Canine Science Instructor

178 Green Street
Winesburg, OH 44690
(614) 555-5555

February 25, 20--

Pat Cummings
Academic Administrator
Any College
1140 Main Street
Cincinnati, OH 45202

RE: Canine Science Instructor

Dear Mr. Cummings:

My interest in the position of part-time Instructor for courses in animal grooming and behavior training advertised in the February 24 edition of the *Cincinnati Post* has prompted me to forward my resume for your review.

In addition to a Bachelor of Arts degree in Behavioral Sciences, I hold certificates in Kennel Management, Dog Grooming, and Training, and continue to attend seminars in adult dog and puppy training. Beyond my academic pursuits, I have more than six years of hands-on experience teaching group obedience classes for dogs and puppies. I also provide private lessons, behavioral consultations, and training for AKC Titles.

After you have had the opportunity to review my qualifications, I would appreciate meeting with you to further discuss this position. I am well qualified to teach future instructors in courses on animal grooming and behavior training, and feel confident that I can provide the kind of student support expected of instructors at Any College.

Yours sincerely,

Chris Smith

Enc. Resume

Case Manager

178 Green Street
White Plains, NY 10606
(914) 555-5555

December 17, 20--

Pat Cummings
Director of Social Services
Any Agency
1140 Main Street
Hoboken, NJ 07030

Dear Ms. Cummings:

    I am responding to your advertisement in the *Star Ledger* for a Case Manager. My interest is in pursuing and expanding my professional career in the motivation and guidance of juveniles to achieve positive objectives and personal dignity. It is this goal that has prompted me to forward the attached resume for your review and consideration.

    Please note that I have directed and dedicated my efforts, both academically and through the co-op program at Fordham University, to working with juveniles and prison inmates, guiding them through innovative programs in self-preservation. These programs required extensive communication and interaction with boards of trustees, agency personnel, and the Neighborhood Watch campaign. In addition, I have acquired excellent customer/client relations and communications skills, as well as sound knowledge of office procedures, in a variety of full-time and part-time positions.

    I would welcome a meeting to learn more about your work at Any Agency and how I could contribute to your success. I will call next Monday to follow up on my inquiry.

Yours sincerely,

Chris Smith

Enc. Resume

Claims Adjuster

178 Green Street
Salisbury, NC 28145
(704) 555-5555

August 26, 20--

Pat Cummings
Claims Supervisor
Any Insurance Agency
1140 Main Street
Asheville, NC 28802

Dear Mr. Cummings:

Yesterday I read with interest your advertised opening for a Claims Adjuster in the *Citizen Times*. During the past fifteen years, I have been employed by a major insurance company where my primary area of concentration has been in workers' compensation claims handling.

Due to my company's consolidation, I am currently seeking to join an organization in need of a highly productive individual with a sound background in claims handling, cost containment, customer relations/service, employee training, and administrative support.

I am well organized and capable of researching and coordinating detailed data and can work effectively with professionals as well as corporate management to arrive at mutually favorable solutions.

Are you interested in filling your availability with an individual who, in previous positions, has cost-effectively negotiated more than 100 claims in a six-month period? If so, I would love to meet with you in a personal interview. I have enclosed my business profile for your review and am confident I can make an immediate and successful contribution to Any Insurance Agency.

Sincerely,

Chris Smith

Enc. Business profile

Clinical Research Nurse

178 Green Street
Marietta, GA 30060

August 20, 20--

Pat Cummings, R.N.
Head Nurse
Any Hospital
1140 Main Street
Savannah, GA 31404

Dear Ms. Cummings:

I believe I have the combined clinical nursing and research skills that would qualify me as an ideal candidate for the Clinical Research Nurse opening you advertised in *Nursing Today*.

I am a dedicated professional capable of working with physicians and nursing, laboratory, and professional specialty groups, and can offer more than fourteen years of responsible experience ranging from Staff Nurse and Charge Nurse to Clinical Research Nurse with a major teaching hospital.

I hold a Bachelor of Science in Nursing, and my graduate studies have focused on epidemiology and international health. My experience encompasses sound knowledge of nursing quality assurance programs and in-service education programs. Throughout my career, I have worked both independently and as part of a team on studies involving psoriasis, cardiology, AIDS, sickle-cell anemia, amyloidosis, diabetes, and oncology.

Please contact me at the above address, or call (404) 555-5555 to arrange a mutually convenient time for a meeting. I am very interested in joining the nursing staff at Any Hospital and hope to speak with you soon.

Thank you for your consideration.

Sincerely,

Chris Smith, R.N., B.S.N.

Enc. Professional profile

Conference Coordinator

178 Green Street
Racine, WI 53406

December 22, 20--

Pat Cummings
Artistic Director
Any Deaf Theatre
1140 Main Street
De Forest, WI 53532

Dear Mr. Cummings:

The position of Conference Coordinator advertised in the January issue of *Deaf Today* is of great interest of me, and I have enclosed my professional profile for your review.

I am a deaf person who has had the opportunity to complete my undergraduate and graduate studies, and who has worked in responsible positions requiring strong leadership, planning, organizational, administrative, and communication skills. Throughout my career, I have worked with individuals and groups in diverse settings within public, private, artistic, and government sectors.

I am well versed in visual and performing arts as a student, performer, coordinator, instructor, and facilitator with concentration in providing services for, and instructing, the deaf community and the general public. I have the communications, public relations, and people skills necessary to establish an annual conference for Any Deaf Theatre that will meet the criteria of excellence you are looking for in a lasting international artistic exchange. It is a challenging undertaking that I feel I am capable of achieving.

Should you need additional information, please contact me at (414) 555-5555 TTY.

I look forward to your return response.

Sincerely,

Chris Smith

Enc. Professional profile

Cosmetologist

178 Green Street
Auburn, WA 98071
(206) 555-5555

August 13, 20--

Pat Cummings
Owner
Any Boutique
1140 Main Street
Seattle, WA 98134

Dear Mr. Cummings:

    Enclosed please find my resume. I am very interested in applying for the position of Cosmetologist that was advertised in the *Seattle Post Intelligencer* on August 13, and am confident that you will find my skills ideally applicable to your needs.

    Thank you in advance for your anticipated consideration. I look forward to meeting with you to discuss this opportunity.

Sincerely,

Chris Smith

Enc. Resume

Customer Service Representative

178 Green Street
Decorah, IA 51201
(319) 555-5555

September 6, 20--

Pat Cummings
Director of Public Relations
Any Corporation
1140 Main Street
Northampton, MA 01060

RE: Customer Service Representative

Dear Ms. Cummings:

My interest in the above position has incited me to forward my resume as requested in your advertisement published in the *Boston Sunday Globe*.

During the past several years at Fortmiller, Inc., my experience has been concentrated in the areas of billing, credit, collection, and customer service. In my current position as Customer Service Supervisor, I maintain the efficiency and accuracy of complex billing systems. This position also requires generating detailed reports for management. My position has given me the opportunity to set policies and procedures, implement systems, and participate in staffing and training personnel. During my tenure, 55 percent of the entry-level staff I trained advanced to managerial positions within Fortmiller, Inc.

Reading your requirements for the position advertised, I am confident of my ability to provide you with the experience and quality of performance you expect.

Once you have had a chance to review my qualifications, I would appreciate meeting with you for further discussion. I will call within the week to schedule an interview at your convenience.

Yours sincerely,

Chris Smith

Enc. Resume

Dentistry Department Manager

178 Green Street
Gaithersburg, MD 20879

February 10, 20--

Pat Cummings
Chief Administrator
Any Hospital
1140 Main Street
Chapel Hill, NC 27514

RE: Manager—Department of Dentistry

Dear Ms. Cummings:

The position you advertised is of great interest to me, and I hope to convince you of my capability to cost-effectively execute the responsibilities of Dentistry Department Manager.

My experience with Johns Hopkins Medical School's Department of Ophthalmology, Maryland Eye & Ear Infirmary, and Blue Cross/Blue Shield has involved interfacing and dealing with all operations and administrative departments on matters pertaining to fiscal and business reporting. I have extensive experience with MIS and firsthand experience with sophisticated programs designed to accommodate and control the rapid and profitable growth of business.

My business management, staff training and supervision, and administrative experience are essential requirements for maintaining equitable controls for a highly complex business. I can provide cost-effective fiscal management to maintain and increase profitability. Through efficient tracking and control systems, budget planning, and administration, I am able to generate cost savings and greater profit margins.

Should you require additional information, I will be glad to meet with you for further discussion. I can be reached at (301) 555-5555. In the interim, I look forward to meeting with you and joining your management team in the near future.

Sincerely,

Chris Smith

Enc. Resume

Director of Public Works

178 Green Street
Liberty, SC 29657
(803) 555-5555

September 22, 20--

Pat Cummings
District Supervisor
Any Office
1140 Main Street
Charleston, SC 29403

Dear Mr. Cummings:

I am very interested in the position of Director of Public Works for the town of Liberty, as advertised in the September 20 edition of the *Post and Courier*.

During the past thirteen years, I have been actively involved in the management of diverse projects which require the ability to work with engineering, architectural, and construction professionals on public and private rehabilitation, restoration, and construction programs. My experience ranges from concept to signoff as well as the supervision of in-house and field crews on both privately and city/federally funded building and highway contracts.

I am an effective manager and budget administrator, and have the ability to work in harmony with individuals and groups in a busy construction/public works environment where concentration is on community services, safety, and the environment. As a longtime resident of Liberty, I believe I could reflect both personal and local interests in providing quality DPW services. I am confident of my ability to direct an efficient, cost-effective, and productive department.

Enclosed is my business profile for your consideration. I would like to learn more about the position, and will call your office early next week to see if we can schedule a meeting.

Thank you for your time.

Sincerely,

Chris Smith

Enc. Business profile

Editorial Assistant

178 Green Street
Austin, TX 78746
(512) 555-5555

June 4, 20--

Pat Cummings
Vice President
Any Corporation
1140 Main Street
Dallas, TX 75275

Dear Ms. Cummings:

   I am very interested in the Editorial Assistant position listed recently in the *Dallas Morning News*, and have enclosed my resume and a writing sample as an application. I am familiar with Any Corporation's publications, and would love the opportunity to contribute to your efforts.

My accomplishments include:
- Experience editing books and other materials for a wide variety of clients, including Reiling Press, Wilson Smith, and numerous corporate clients.
- Experience writing consumer materials, including chapters for fiction books published by Hollis Press, and a complete nonfiction book entitled *Easy Do It Resumes* (O'Leary Press).

   Should you need additional information or writing samples, please feel free to contact me at the above-listed number. I look forward to joining the editorial team at Any Corporation, and will call your office next week to discuss this opportunity further.
   Thank you.

Sincerely,

Chris Smith

Enc. Resume, Writing Samples

Features Reporter

178 Green Street
Emmitsburg, MD 21727

July 20, 20--

Pat Cummings
Senior Reporter
Any Newspaper
1140 Main Street
Largo, MD 20772

Dear Ms. Cummings:

I am interested in the Features Reporter position advertised in the *Baltimore Sun*. As a recent graduate of Mount St. Mary's College with a Bachelor of Arts degree in Journalism, I am eager to begin a long-term association with a newspaper as a reporter.

As detailed in the enclosed resume, I possess broad experience in various fields of journalism. My internship with the *Emmitsburg News* provided me with the opportunity to sharpen my writing and researching skills. My duties included field reporting, writing copy, and editing a variety of articles, all demanding strict deadlines. My skills in photography made me a greater asset to the *Emmitsburg News*, as I was able to photograph the subjects of stories as well. In addition, while completing my degree at Mount St. Mary's, I worked as Editor of the yearbook and Layout Editor of the student newspaper, where I became proficient in desktop publishing.

I currently have a flexible schedule and am available for an interview at almost any time, given advance notice. I can be reached at (301) 555-5555. I am very interested in reporting for *Any Newspaper* and hope to hear from you soon.

Sincerely,

Chris Smith

Enc. Resume

Field Finance Manager

178 Green Street
Richmond, VA 23220

January 17, 20--

Pat Cummings
Chief Financial Officer
Any Corporation
1140 Main Street
Washington, DC 20002

Dear Mr. Cummings:

I am applying for the Central Area Field Finance Manager position advertised in the *Richmond Times-Dispatch*.

Enclosed you will find my resume, which details the skills necessary to enhance the central area's performance:

- Experience advising *Fortune* 100 and small company senior management on strategy, planning, and budgeting.
- Strong academic preparation and significant work experience in accounting and finance.
- Excellent working knowledge of microcomputer technology.

Finally, one item not on my resume is my desire to enter a high-growth industry with a leader. The Field Finance Manager position offers such an opportunity.

Please feel free to contact me at (804) 555-5555 if you have any questions and would like to meet to further discuss my interest in, and qualifications for, this challenging position.

Sincerely yours,

Chris Smith

Enc. Resume

Film Archivist

178 Green Street
New Castle, DE 19270
(302) 555-5555

July 22, 20--

Pat Cummings
Curator
Any Library
1140 Main Street
Macon, GA 31201

RE: Film Archivist Position; *Moving Picture Pictorial*, July 19, 20--

Dear Ms. Cummings:

I am interested in your advertised position for a Film Archivist. My passion for film and my applicable skills make me confident that I am a qualified candidate.

Currently, I am a reporter for the *Vertov Film Journal*, a monthly entertainment magazine. In addition, I am capable of shooting, printing, and developing 35 mm, black-and-white film. I also have proficiency in digital photography. During my last year at Brandeis University, I researched, wrote, and edited a 100-page senior honors thesis on the filmmaker Sergei Eisenstein. I enjoyed that project immensely, and would enjoy researching film and film-related literature on a daily basis.

I am aware that your library's film archive is the largest in the South. I would welcome the opportunity to employ my talents at Any Library, and am willing to relocate if offered the position.

I have enclosed a resume and a few writing samples for you to look over at your convenience. Thank you for your time, and I hope to meet with you soon to discuss your Film Archivist position even further.

Sincerely,

Chris Smith

Enc. Resume, Writing samples

Gemologist

178 Green Street
Gainesville, FL 36608
(904) 555-5555

June 2, 20--

Pat Cummings
Vice President
Any Institute
1140 Main Street
Tampa, FL 33611

Dear Ms. Cummings:

I was very excited to read about the opening for a Gemologist in the latest edition of your company newsletter. I would like to submit my credentials as an application for this opportunity.

I became interested in the import/export of precious gems several years ago while living in Nepal. Upon my return to the United States, I enrolled in what my research revealed to be the best gemology school, the Gemologist Institute of America, in Santa Monica, California. This year I graduated with honors, and hold the title of Graduate Gemologist.

The enclosed resume summarizes my background, most of which has an emphasis in public relations, sales, promotions, and dealing with people of all socioeconomic levels and cultures. I am presently searching for an opportunity with an institute such as yours, where I might apply my training, skills, and knowledge in the technical and business facets of gemology to our mutual benefit.

After you have reviewed my qualifications, I would appreciate interviewing with you for this position. I am very interested in the opportunity that it provides, and am confident that my training and experience fit your requirements. Please note that I plan to follow up with a call in a few days. In the meantime, should you need additional information, please don't hesitate to call me at the phone number cited above.

Sincerely,

Chris Smith

Enc. Resume

Home Economist/Coordinator

178 Green Street
Reno, NV 89520
(702) 555-5555

July 25, 20--

Pat Cummings
Director, Home Economics Program
Any University
1140 Main Street
Seattle, WA 98109

Dear Mr. Cummings:

My interest in the position of Home Economist/Coordinator described in your advertisement in the *Seattle Times* has prompted me to forward the attached resume for your evaluation.

In addition to earning a Bachelor of Science degree in Home Economics and Nutrition Education, I have completed coursework in psychology and learning development, and have undergone supplemental training at the professional level with each employer since graduation, including a teaching hospital.

I possess excellent verbal, written, and interpersonal skills. In addition, I hold extensive experience with the development and training-related duties of seminars in my areas of expertise, and relate easily to all age groups and socioeconomic levels. As an alumnus of the University of Washington at Seattle and a native of the State of Washington, I am well acquainted with the overall family/business environment in which I would be working.

I will be in Washington on Friday, August 5. I would like to arrange to meet with you at this time to convince you of my ability to successfully fill your position. I will call your office on July 27 to schedule an interview.

Thank you very much for your consideration.

Sincerely,

Chris Smith

Enc. Resume

Hotel Manager

178 Green Street
Traverse City, MI 49684

January 23, 20--

Pat Cummings
District Manager
Any Corporation
1140 Main Street
Marquette, MI 49855

Dear Mr. Cummings:

Enclosed is my resume, which I submit as a candidate for the Hotel Manager position advertised in the *Detroit Free Press* on January 23.

My experience in the hospitality industry is broadly based, and my accomplishments reflect a proven ability to perform in diverse and varied functions. My positions have ranged from Front Desk Clerk and Director of Sales and Marketing, to my current position as Assistant General Manager of a prestigious 3,000-room hotel. In this capacity I am responsible for all operational aspects of the rooms division, including front office, housekeeping, maintenance, reservations, quality control, and communications. In addition, as a member of the executive committee, I am involved in all budgetary and policy decision-making.

I have been involved in hospitality management for ten years, and while my present position is satisfying, the position of Hotel Manager you offer seems to provide the ideal next step, and an opportunity for a long-term association with a new organization.

I would greatly appreciate the opportunity to discuss your requirements, and how I might fulfill them. Please telephone me at your convenience. During the day, I can be reached at (616) 555-5555.

Thank you for your consideration.

Sincerely,

Chris Smith

Enc. Resume

International Buyer

178 Green Street
Knoke, IA 50553
(515) 555-5555

February 3, 20--

Pat Cummings
Senior Marketing Manager
Any Corporation
1140 Main Street
Chicago, IL 60605

Dear Ms. Cummings:

In response to your advertisement for an International Buyer in the February 1 edition of the *Chicago Sun-Times*, I would like to submit my application for your consideration.

As you can see, my qualifications match those you seek:

YOU REQUIRE:
- A college degree
- Fluency in Italian and French
- Office experience
- Typing skills
- Willingness to travel

I OFFER:
- A Bachelor's degree in English from Long Island University
- Fluency in Italian, German, and French
- Experience as a receptionist at a busy accounting firm
- Accurate typing at 60 wpm
- A willingness to travel

I feel that I am well qualified for this position and can make a lasting contribution to Any Corporation. My salary requirement is negotiable.

I would welcome the opportunity for a personal interview with you at your convenience.

Sincerely,

Chris Smith

Enc. Resume

Legal Assistant

178 Green Street
Shoshoni, WY 82649
(307) 555-5555

September 18, 20--

Pat Cummings
Partner
Any Corporation
1140 Main Street
Chicago, IL 60605

Dear Mr. Cummings:

I am writing in response to the Legal Assistant position advertised in the September 17 edition of the *New York Times*. Having recently graduated from New England School of Law, it is my intention to relocate to Chicago. I have enclosed my resume for your consideration.

My work experience and scholastic endeavors have thoroughly prepared me for employment in a firm that specializes in various segments of law. Over the past summer and fall, I have been interning with a small general practice firm where I am entrusted with a great deal of responsibility. I write appellate briefs and memoranda in corporate, contract, and criminal law, and I draft complaints and answers. I also actively participate in attorney-client conferences by questioning clients and by describing how the law affects the clients' suits.

I would appreciate the opportunity to meet with you and discuss how my qualifications could be guided to meet your needs.

Thank you for your time and consideration. I look forward to meeting with you at your convenience.

With best regards,

Chris Smith, Esq.

Enc. Resume

Loan Officer

178 Green Street
Owensboro, KY 42302

March 2, 20--

Pat Cummings
Branch Manager
Any Bank
1140 Main Street
Lexington, KY 40506

RE: Loan Officer Position

Dear Mr. Cummings:

In response to last Friday's advertisement in the *Lexington Herald-Leader*, I have enclosed my resume for your review. As you can see, my qualifications are an ideal match for your requirements.

You require:

- More than five years' experience.
- Skill in personnel and customer service relations.
- Extensive lending knowledge.
- A willingness to travel.

I offer:

- Nine years of rapidly progressive and responsible experience with a service-oriented commercial bank.
- Five years of full responsibility for the management of branch banking operations, training, directing, and coordinating activities of personnel, and establishing and implementing relationship banking programs for quality customer service and satisfaction.
- Skill in the implementation of institution policies, procedures, and practices concerning lending and new business development, and the granting or extending of lines of credit as well as commercial, real estate, and consumer loans.
- A willingness to travel.

I would welcome the opportunity for a personal interview to discuss the details of the position available and my capability to achieve mutual goals. I am well qualified to handle the position, and confident I will make a valuable contribution to your staff. Please contact me at the above address or by phone at (502) 555-5555.

I look forward to hearing from you.

Sincerely,
Chris Smith
Enc. Resume

Masonry Supply Manager

178 Green Street
Waterbury, CT 06708

December 5, 20--

Pat Cummings
General Manager
Any Corporation
1140 Main Street
Hartford, CT 06115

Dear Ms. Cummings:

My interest in the position of Masonry Supply Manager (*Hartford Courant*, November 30) has prompted me to forward my resume for your review and consideration.

During the past ten years, my experience has been concentrated in the masonry and plastering products supply industry with a building materials firm. During my six years as General Manager, I took an old line business, which had undergone several years of poor management, and reversed the trend. I upgraded the firm's image and customer and vendor relations, which subsequently increased the dollar volume and bottom-line profits by 300 percent.

I am presently looking for a position where my experience will make a positive contribution to the start-up or continuing profitable operation of a business in which I am so well experienced.

I will contact you in a few days to arrange a meeting for further discussion. In the interim, should you require additional information, I may be reached at (203) 555-5555 between 9:00 A.M. and 5:00 P.M.

Sincerely,

Chris Smith

Enc. Resume

Meeting Planner

178 Green Street
Rohnert Park, CA 94928
(707) 555-5555

May 11, 20--

Pat Cummings
Vice President, Marketing
Any Corporation
1140 Main Street
San Francisco, CA 94132

RE: Meeting Planner Position

Dear Mr. Cummings:

   After reading your advertisement in the *San Francisco Chronicle*, I believe my qualifications match your requirements for a Meeting Planner.

   During the past seven years, I have held positions requiring communications, sales, marketing, and supervisory skills in people-oriented, retailing, media, and educational environments. I am currently seeking a career opportunity offering a new scope of responsibility and more permanent challenge requiring creative skills as well as follow-through capability as an individual or member of a production team.

   I am a quick study and have good presentation and communications training. I pride myself on the fact that I can readily take direction, and provide organization, creative input, and an enthusiastic approach to the various segments of a position.

   I believe I am the right candidate for the position of Meeting Planner and would like the opportunity to discuss your requirements and my ability to handle the responsibilities of the position offered. I will call your office next Monday to schedule an interview at your convenience.

   I appreciate your time and consideration.

Sincerely,

Chris Smith

Enc. Resume

Newspaper Intern

178 Green Street
Charlotsville, VA 22906

April 7, 20--

Pat Cummings
Managing Editor
Any Newspaper
1140 Main Street
Lexington, VA 24450

Dear Mr. Cummings:

I enclose my resume in response to your listing in the University of Virginia's (UVA) career services office for a internship position with your newspaper. I am currently a junior majoring in English at UVA, and am seeking valuable career experience for the months of June through mid-September. I am hoping to use this summer to explore possible opportunities within the field of newspaper publishing.

The position you outline is one I feel I could enhance with my writing, editing, and expressive skills gained as an English major, as well as my past work experience, which has involved a great deal of organization, discipline, and responsibility. My active leadership and service roles have also helped me develop strong interpersonal and communication skills which I feel would make me a worthy addition to your staff.

I would greatly appreciate the opportunity to discuss with you how I might best meet your needs. I will call your office next week to confirm receipt of my resume and inquire about the publicized opening. In the interim, if you have any questions, please do not hesitate to call me at (804) 555-5555.

Thank you for your consideration in this matter.

Sincerely yours,

Chris Smith

Enc. Resume

178 Green Street
Gastonia, NC 28054
(704) 555-5555

January 16, 20--

Pat Cummings
Personnel Supervisor
Any Corporation
1140 Main Street
Mt. Olive, NC 28465

Dear Mr. Cummings:

I am interested in applying for the Office Receptionist position as advertised in the *Herald Sun*, dated January 16. Attached please find my resume.

My areas of expertise lie in administration, organization, documentation, communications, and cost control. I am a detail-oriented individual and enjoy customer/client interaction. Additionally, I believe that an organization's client relationships are a tangible asset in a world where individualized service and assistance is rapidly declining. My administrative skills include a 70 wpm typing speed and proficiency on multiple word processing programs and spreadsheet applications.

I look forward to hearing from you and learning more about Any Corporation.

Sincerely,

Chris Smith

Enc. Resume

Park Maintenance Supervisor

178 Green Street
Zanesville, OH 43701
(614) 555-5555

August 28, 20--

Pat Cummings
Chairperson
Any Reservation
1140 Main Street
Youngstown, OH 44501

RE: Park Maintenance Supervisor

Dear Ms. Cummings:

Please accept the enclosed resume as my expressed interest in applying for the Park Mainte-nance Supervisor position you advertised in the August 26 edition of the *Vindicator*. For the past twelve years, I have held a senior-level position as Fire Chief of the Zanesville Fire Department.

Although my position is secure, it is strictly administrative and does not allow me to physically participate, as I have in the past, in actual firefighting or other hands-on activities that provide the outdoor work environment I most enjoy. For some time, I have realized that I must make a change, and the position described in your advertisement is what I have been looking for.

I have worked on a family farm, attended a degree program in agriculture, and, by choice, always worked full-time or part-time with tree and excavation services. I am thoroughly familiar with the operation, maintenance, and repair of equipment, and with safety practices for its opera-tion; I also have the necessary background to train and supervise work crews using this equipment. Because my prime interest is job satisfaction, the salary is secondary and negotiable.

I feel confident that I can provide Any Reservation with reliability, dedication, and quality of work performance that will maintain the forested properties in the condition in which parks should be kept and enjoyed.

Since the department is not aware of my interest in making a change, your confidence is appreciated. I look forward to your return response.

Yours sincerely,

Chris Smith
Enc. Resume

Political Staffer

178 Green Street
Bristol, RI 02809
(401) 555-5555

January 25, 20--

Pat Cummings
Director
Any Organization
1140 Main Street
Providence, RI 02908

Dear Ms. Cummings:

I am responding to the Political Staffer position advertised in the January 24 edition of the *Providence Evening Bulletin*.

Currently, I am employed as an Administrative Assistant at the State House in Providence. My primary responsibilities include writing press releases, researching and drafting legislation, and consistent constituent contact. I have also worked with various committees and legislators regarding an array of legislative issues.

I hold a Bachelor of Arts degree from Boston University (BU) in Political Science with a concentration in Public Policy. In addition to my coursework at BU, I worked as an intern at the Lieutenant Governor's office during the spring of 2004 and actively worked for several political and social causes on campus and in the Boston area. I also organized and managed my own successful campaign for Secretary of Student Affairs.

I am eager to continue my political career in the position of Political Staffer for your organization. I have the commitment, energy, and drive necessary to contribute successfully to your cause. I will call your office on January 29 to schedule an interview time that is convenient for you.

Thank you for your consideration.

Sincerely,

Chris Smith

Enc. Resume

Preschool Director

178 Green Street
St. Paul, MN 55105

July 10, 20--

Pat Cummings
Principal
Any High School
1140 Main Street
Minneapolis, MN 55404

RE: Preschool Director Position

Dear Mr. Cummings:

As a Speech/Language Clinician with extensive experience in the management and administration of programs dealing with special needs in education, I feel I have the qualifications necessary to succeed in the position of Preschool Director as advertised in the *Star Tribune*.

During the past eleven years, my experience with a professional, private agency has been concentrated in the area of special needs programs for multiple school districts. Prior to that, my work as a Speech Language Clinician involved the development and implementation of programs directed toward special education for preschoolers through twelfth grade in a public school system.

Although my positions were diverse and my achievements provided professional satisfaction, I am interested in making a new association with a large, highly recognized institution such as Any High School. As Part-Time Preschool Director, I hope to utilize my broad-based experience in special education to make a meaningful contribution to your professional management staff.

The enclosed resume summarizes my background and experience. I would appreciate the opportunity to meet with you to further discuss my qualifications and how I can best contribute to your needs. Please contact me at the above address or by phone at (612) 555-5555.

I look forward to hearing from you.

Yours sincerely,

Chris Smith

Enc. Resume

Product Developer

178 Green Street
Bismarck, ND 58501
(701) 555-5555

February 15, 20--

Pat Cummings
Chief Executive Officer
Any Technology
1140 Main Street
Bismarck, ND 58501

Dear Ms. Cummings:

I read with much excitement in your company newsletter the announcement of openings within your new products development department.

Please note that I have more than ten years of experience in manufacturing R&D, management of new product development, and existing product redevelopment/upgrade. I am especially experienced with complex composite materials, precision metal castings, and PC board industries. In addition, I have extensive experience both as teacher and lecturer at several well-known universities. This expertise is supported by a Ph.D. in Materials Science/Engineering.

I am eager to join the Any Technology team, as its reputation for innovation is unparalleled. I will call to schedule an interview so that we may discuss further my qualifications and your requirements. Thank you for your consideration.

Sincerely,

Chris Smith

Enc. Resume

Production Assistant

178 Green Street
Birmingham, AL 35294
(205) 555-5555

October 2, 20--

Pat Cummings
Vice President, Production
Any Corporation
1146 Main Street
Mobile, AL 36630

RE: Production Assistant Position

Dear Mr. Cummings:

Your recent advertisement in the *Mobile Register* interests me, as my experience matches your requirements.

I would appreciate the opportunity to discuss how I might contribute to your organization. I will call your office the week of October 10 to schedule an interview at your convenience. In the meantime, I may be reached at the above listed daytime phone number or in the evenings at (205) 555-5555.

Thank you for your consideration.

Sincerely,

Chris Smith

Enc. Resume

Program Coordinator

178 Green Street
Holland, MI 49423
(616) 555-5555

September 30, 20--

Pat Cummings
Language Coordinator
Any Institute
1140 Main Street
Detroit, MI 48226

Dear Mr. Cummings:

    I discovered your advertisement for a Program Coordinator, English as a Second Language in the *Detroit Free Press*. I was very much intrigued and am enclosing my resume detailing my relevant experience.

    I feel I am particularly qualified for this job as a result of my double language major in college as well as my current enrollment in two language proficiency certificate programs. I am a person who deeply believes in the importance of language enrichment. I would like the chance to work for an organization that reflects both my interests and my personal commitment.

    Having grown up in a bilingual (Spanish/English-speaking) environment and having studied abroad in both Spain and Mexico, I am well aware of the demands and technical challenges involved in the translation business. Language is forever evolving and new expression and technology breed new linguistic mutations daily. To meet these challenges and maintain my skills, I work on my languages weekly, both by continuing to take language classes and tutoring children in the fundamentals.

    Given the opportunity, I am confident that my skills and language experience could make an immediate and long-term contribution to Any Institute. I would be delighted to discuss my qualifications with you. I will call your office on October 7 to schedule a convenient interview time.

Sincerely,

Chris Smith

Enc. Resume

Project Manager

178 Green Street
Charleston, SC 29411
(803) 555-5555

April 10, 20--

Pat Cummings
Director of Human Resources
Any Corporation
1140 Main Street
Charleston, SC 29411

Dear Ms. Cummings:

In response to your ad for Project Manager in the April 9 edition of the *Post and Courier*, I have enclosed my resume for your review and consideration.

With more than twenty years of construction experience, I am familiar with project management in the role of owner's representative as well as general contractor/manager. I have managed projects regionally and nationally.

I will contact you the week of April 17 so that we may schedule an interview. I look forward to discussing my credentials and the requirements of the position with you.

Sincerely,

Chris Smith

Enc. Resume

178 Green Street
East Point, GA 30344
(404) 555-5555

February 4, 20--

Pat Cummings
Publicity Director
Any Corporation
1140 Main Street
Rome, GA 30162

Dear Ms. Cummings:

I am responding to your advertisement in the *Atlanta Constitution* for a Publicist.

I am confident that I have the skills and experience necessary to successfully meet the requirements of this position. As an Advertising and Promotions Assistant for a major newspaper, I have acquired strong interpersonal and communication skills. In addition, I have extensive experience with a number of computer systems and applications.

As the newest member of your publicity department, I would prove to be a diligent, organized, and enthusiastic employee. Could we meet for further discussion? I would be available at your convenience.

I look forward to your response.

Sincerely,

Chris Smith

Enc. Resume

Publisher's Assistant

178 Green Street
Topeka, KS 66621
(913) 555-5555

January 18, 20--

Pat Cummings
Vice President of Editorial
Any Corporation
1140 Main Street
Topeka, KS 66621

Dear Mr. Cummings:

I am writing in response to your advertisement in the *Topeka Capital-Journal* for the Publisher's Assistant position. Please consider me an applicant for the position.

I believe you will find that my training and varied experience are well suited to this position. My background as an administrative assistant, magazine production assistant, and teacher demonstrate my capacity to handle the challenges of providing superior executive support.

As a current temporary assignment worker with Alltemps in Topeka, I have become highly computer literate in both Macintosh and PC environments and accompanying software programs. I am organized and accurate, master new information rapidly, communicate effectively, and work well with other people.

Thank you for reviewing my credentials. I will call in a week to schedule a convenient time to discuss my qualifications and your expectations.

Sincerely,

Chris Smith

Enc. Resume

Real Estate Sales Associate

178 Green Street
Milwaukee, WI 53201
(414) 555-5555

December 20, 20--

Pat Cummings
Vice President
Any Properties
1140 Main Street
Milwaukee, WI 53201

RE: Real Estate Sales Associate

Dear Mr. Cummings:

I am writing to apply for the above-listed position advertised in *Real Estate Weekly*, December 20, 20--. I am interested in contributing my real estate expertise to Any Properties.

I offer nearly twenty years of intensive experience involving the most sophisticated aspects of commercial and residential real estate sales and leasing, as well as associated areas of real estate development, property management, and rehabilitation. In addition to a current broker's license, I am very well grounded in real estate and business law.

I am considered a highly organized team player, with excellent verbal and written communication skills, an eye for detail, and the necessary persistence to conceive, package, and bring the big deals home.

My resume is a quick summary of my background and professional experience, but I feel that during the course of a personal interview my potential to contribute to Any Properties could be more effectively demonstrated. I will call to establish a mutually convenient time for such a meeting.

Thank you for your consideration.

Sincerely,

Chris Smith

Enc. Resume

Regional Manager

178 Green Street
Dubuque, IA 52001

August 7, 20--

Pat Cummings
Management Supervisor
Any Corporation
1140 Main Street
Peosta, IA 52068

Dear Ms. Cummings:

Please accept this inquiry as my expressed interest in the Regional Manager position advertised in the August issue of *Automotive Monthly*.

During the past twenty-two years, I have developed a successful track record as a professional with internationally recognized expertise in the automotive industries. In the last twelve years, I have specialized in customer satisfaction program development and strategic implementation consulting.

My extensive management experience has encompassed the design and evaluation of corporate marketing strategies and involved the evaluation of policies, projects, and new products. This experience is supported by a B.A. in Economics, an M.A. in Economics, M.B.A. coursework, a D.Sc., and a D.E.S. in Applied Mathematics.

Although my present position provides interesting diversity and challenge, I feel that it is time to move on to other opportunities. The enclosed professional profile provides only a portion of my qualifications and activities which I will be glad to expand on during a personal meeting. I will call your office on Monday, August 14, to schedule a mutually convenient meeting time.

Thank you for your consideration.

Sincerely,

Chris Smith

Enc. Professional profile

Restaurant Manager Trainee

178 Green Street
Grand Junction, CO 81502
(303) 555-5555

November 15, 20--

Pat Cummings
Manager
Any Restaurant
1140 Main Street
Denver, CO 80202

RE: Restaurant Manager Trainee

Dear Ms. Cummings:

Please accept the enclosed resume as an application for your position advertised in the November 14 edition of the *Denver Post*.

During the past seven years, I have held positions of responsibility in banquet/special events catering, function management, and restaurant food service operations.

Currently, I am seeking a new association with a firm that can benefit from my experience in the above areas. I have additional experience in front desk operation; possess good organizational, leadership, training, and supervisory skills; and can provide quality service and performance in a high-volume setting. As my resume indicates, the vast diversity of food service settings with which I have been associated has made me extensively experienced in the management of virtually any type of food, beverage, and kitchen staff.

I have continually heard and read many favorable reviews of Any Restaurant, and I have always enjoyed my own dining experiences there. I would love to join your management team after completing the requisite training program. I will call you next Monday to arrange a mutually convenient time to discuss this opportunity further.

Sincerely,

Chris Smith

Enc. Resume

Sales Representative

178 Green Street
Northridge, CA 91324
(818) 555-5555

April 17, 20--

Ms. Pat Cummings
Vice President
Any Corporation
1140 Main Street
Pittsburgh, PA 15217

Dear Mr. Cummings:

Please accept the enclosed resume as an expressed interest in contributing relevant experience to the position of Sales Representative, as advertised in the *Pittsburgh Post-Gazette*, on Wednesday, April 11.

I have accumulated several years of experience in the development of sales and marketing strategies. I have been involved in a number of diverse employment situations, including a self-owned business, in which I successfully utilized various sales techniques, such as cold calling, telemarketing, and prospecting. In my first two years at FloSoft, I increased our client base by 25 percent. While at the Brian Agency, I was part of a sales team that generated a record-breaking $10 million in one year. In addition, I have held numerous positions where I supervised and developed personnel and assisted in the facilitation of daily operations.

I would welcome the opportunity to meet with you and discuss ways in which my capabilities could be directed to suit your needs. I await your call to arrange a mutually convenient time to meet.

I look forward to talking with you in the near future. Thank you for your time and consideration.

With best regards,

Chris Smith

Enc. Resume

Senior HVAC Technician

178 Green Street
New Martinsville, WV 26155
(304) 555-5555

November 12, 20--

Pat Cummings
Human Resources Director
Any Corporation
1140 Main Street
Charlestown, WV 25301

Dear Ms. Cummings:

At the request of Donald Lee of your department, I am enclosing my resume in response to the advertisement in last Friday's *Charleston Gazette* for an experienced Senior HVAC Technician.

I possess nine years of experience in after-warranty maintenance, preventive maintenance programs, and complete overhaul of major systems within a multibuilding, mixed-use industrial complex. I have also completed extensive and continuous education and training on the latest and most cost-efficient energy systems and control.

Presently, I am seeking a new association with an institution such as Any Corporation, where I can apply my technical as well as supervisory skills to provide high-quality, cost-efficient energy control system maintenance at a time when energy prices are at an all-time high.

I would welcome the opportunity to discuss your requirements and my ability to handle the responsibilities of the position offered. Could we meet for a personal interview? I can make myself readily available whenever you are free.

Thank you for your time, Ms. Cummings.

Sincerely,

Chris Smith

Enc. Resume

Social Worker

178 Green Street
Northridge, CA 91324
(818) 555-5555

July 19, 20--

Pat Cummings
Director
Any Agency
1140 Main Street
Northridge, CA 91324

Dear Ms. Cummings:

In response to your advertisement in the summer edition of the *Social Justice Journal*, I would like to offer my services to fill the vacancy in the Social Worker position. I am confident you will find my experience and abilities qualify me for the position.

I possess extensive diverse and applicable experience. As stated in my resume, I received a Bachelor's degree in Dance Therapy, an interdisciplinary major, which involved extensive research into child psychology as well as artistic ability. While in college, I worked with children in a volunteer program called P.A.L.S., in which we visited and recreated with children in housing projects. I also visited a day-care program to study the psychology behind children's drawings for my senior research project. In addition, in high school, I worked with mentally disturbed adults.

As you can see, my background corresponds to your requirements. I look forward to hearing from you to discuss this job further.

Sincerely,

Chris Smith

Enc. Resume

State Administrator

178 Green Street
Riverside, CA 92521
(909) 555-5555

December 23, 20--

Pat Cummings
President, West Coast Offices
Any Organization
1140 Main Street
Sacramento, CA 95821

Dear Mr. Cummings:

In response to your advertisement in the December 20 edition of the *Sacramento Bee*, please find my resume enclosed for your review. I am very interested in securing the position of State Administrator available at Any Organization.

During the past twelve years, I have held diverse and progressively responsible positions in development for nonprofit service organizations, universities, and educational institutions. These responsibilities have ranged from Secretary to Director of Development.

Throughout this period, I have been heavily involved in development strategies, annual fund campaigns, marketing and mailing programs, and media and public relations. Although these positions have been challenging and broad in scope, I feel that my expertise may be utilized to a better advantage by your organization.

I hope that, after reviewing my qualifications, you will consider me as the right candidate for State Administrator. I am confident of my abilities, and would like to schedule an interview to reiterate my desire for the position. I will call you on December 27 to follow up on my inquiry.

I appreciate your time and look forward to speaking with you.

Sincerely,

Chris Smith

Enc. Resume

Telemarketer

178 Green Street
Omaha, NE 68182
(402) 555-5555

January 22, 20--

Pat Cummings
Director of Marketing and Sales
Any Corporation
1140 Main Street
Lincoln, NE 68522

Dear Mr. Cummings:

   I am responding to your advertisement in search of a telemarketing professional in the *Lincoln Journal* dated January 16.

   The enclosed resume provides details of my solid career experience in marketing and sales. My accomplishments include:

- Managing and directing sales of a national publication to business decision-makers and chief executive officers of major financial, educational, and municipal organizations that resulted in sales of $175,000 over a four-month period.
- Creating and implementing marketing strategy for a family-owned retail establishment that produced a substantial increase in sales.
- Establishing a marketing and public relations plan for a consulting firm that increased client base and significantly enhanced public recognition of the firm.
- Writing, editing, directing, and producing public service television programming that involved timely legal and medical issues.

   I would be pleased to discuss this matter with you in a personal interview and look forward to hearing from you.

Sincerely,

Chris Smith

Enc. Resume

Television Camera Operator

178 Green Street
Pineville, LA 71359
(318) 555-5555

January 18, 20--

Pat Cummings
Production Manager
Any Television Station
1140 Main Street
New Orleans, LA 70018

Dear Ms. Cummings:

I aspire to find a challenging position where I am able to apply my technical and production talents. When I read your job description for a Television Camera Operator in the Sunday *Times-Picayune*, I felt that my background and skills would be a wonderful match for your requirements.

During the past three years, I have worked as a Production Assistant and Technical Operator in a television studio involved in all aspects of video production. I also have written, directed, produced, and edited three short 8 mm films and a music video that was shot using ENG equipment. These projects allowed me to sharpen many skills, such as conceptualization, camera work, and editing. In addition, I have received a Bachelor of Science degree and gained additional experience in video and camera operation from Ellis Technical Training School.

Once given the opportunity to demonstrate my talents, I am sure that I will prove to be a worthwhile addition to your station. Also, I am confident of my ability to quickly move through a training program and soon begin taping. I look forward to the opportunity for an interview and to meet with you in person.

Sincerely,

Chris Smith

Enc. Resume

Travel Agent

178 Green Street
New Britain, CT 06050
(203) 555-5555

January 29, 20--

Pat Cummings
Owner
Any Travel Agency
1140 Main Street
New London, CT 06320

Dear Ms. Cummings:

I am responding to your advertisement in the *Wichita Eagle* for the position of Travel Agent.

As my enclosed resume indicates, I possess eleven years of extensive experience in the travel and tourism fields. As sole owner of a tourism-related business for four years, I oversaw and advised thirty host homes and inns operating in the New England area. I was independently responsible for maintaining accurate business records, purchasing supplies, and writing and editing all public relations materials, contracts, and policy guidelines. I enjoy writing and promoting New England as a premier business and leisure destination, and would welcome the opportunity to broaden my local attention to include the rest of the nation.

In addition, my association with the Greater Hartford Convention and Visitor's Bureau and the Southern Connecticut Bureau, as well as the Connecticut Chamber of Commerce, has considerably heightened my awareness of visitor markets and related disposable income. I believe my knowledge of current visitor trends coupled with my affinity for customer travel make me a qualified candidate for a position as a Travel Agent.

Thank you in advance for your generous consideration. I may be reached at my home phone number indicated above should you desire to contact me. I would be happy to make myself available for a personal interview at your convenience.

Sincerely,

Chris Smith

Enc. Resume

Writing Instructor

178 Green Street
Richmond, VA 23219
(804) 555-5555

June 1, 20--

Pat Cummings
Dean
Any College
1140 Main Street
Winston-Salem, NC 27108

Dear Mr. Cummings:

Please consider this letter and the enclosed resume as an application for the position of Writing Instructor as advertised in the *Richmond Times-Dispatch* last Wednesday.

I have been a college-level teacher of writing for the past eleven years and offer strong writing, editing, and proofreading skills. I am also a writer; my published works include short stories, essays, and poems. Last February, a one-act play of mine was produced in New York City. I also have experience ghostwriting, editing for the *Chapel Hill Review*, and publicity writing for a Raleigh rock group.

I am confident that the above-listed experience distinguishes me as a qualified candidate for your opening. I would be delighted to discuss further how my abilities match your requirements.

I have enclosed a writing sample and can provide letters of recommendation if needed.

Thank you for your attention to this matter.

Sincerely,

Chris Smith

Enc. Resume, Writing sample

Administrative Assistant

To: *patcummings@anyfitnessclub.com*
From: *chrissmith@jobsearch.com*
Subj: Job #ABC004687

Dear Mr. Cummings:

   I am pleased to submit my application for the position of Administrative Assistant with Any Fitness Club. I believe my positive attitude and exceptional people skills, combined with my willingness to work both independently and as part of a team, make me an ideal candidate for this job. As my attached resume indicates, I have more than six years of experience providing administrative and support services to the professional staff of a golf and tennis club in suburban San Diego, where my responsibilities included word processing and data entry, purchasing, inventory control, office equipment maintenance, and assistance with special events and promotions as needed. In addition, I hold an Associate's degree in recreation management and, as a volunteer for the local chapter of the American Cancer Society, have served on the steering committee for the 20-- and 20-- "Run for the Cure" mini-marathon run/walk events, which drew more than 10,000 participants each.

   I would appreciate the opportunity to meet with you to further discuss my qualifications and how I might utilize them to the benefit of your facility and club members. I look forward to hearing from you.

Yours sincerely,

Chris Smith

178 Green Street
La Jolla, CA 92037
(619) 555-5555
chrissmith@jobsearch.com

Business Operations Manager

To: *patcummings@anyfirm.com*
From: *chrissmith@jobsearch.com*
Subj: Job #999888ZYWX

Dear Mr. Cummings:

    I believe I am ideally suited to the position of Business Operations Manager which you posted recently on Careerbuilder.com. I am a seasoned professional with more than eighteen years of business and corporate experience in the areas of cost accounting and financial analysis, procurement and contract administration, negotiations and contract procurement, budget oversight and forecasting, and business impact analysis. Supported by a Master in Business Administration degree in Finance and a Bachelor of Arts degree in Economics, my strengths include the ability to manage multiple projects of a diverse nature and a proven ability to analyze operational units in order to arrive at alternative methods of service delivery. I am equally adept at working with supervisors, colleagues, and subordinates, and have "hands-on" knowledge of computer programs for rigorous analysis, financial reporting, and high-quality presentations.

    My goal is to join a firm that requires immediate use of these skills to either increase a rate of established growth, or to effect a turnaround situation. The attached resume describes my qualifications in greater detail. I will call you within the week to determine when your calendar might permit time for a personal interview. Thank you for your consideration.

Sincerely,

Chris Smith

178 Green Street
St. Louis, MO 63110
(314) 555-4444
chrissmith@jobsearch.com

Concierge

To: *patcummings@anyhotel.com*
From: *chrissmith@jobsearch.com*
Subj: Job #XYZ007800

Dear Ms. Cummings:

    I was delighted to read your advertisement on truecareers.com for the position of Concierge for two reasons: 1) I share your philosophy concerning the role of a concierge in maximizing the overall guest experience, and 2) I believe I am the ideal candidate to fulfill this role at your hotel. My dedication to providing exemplary customer service is evidenced by more than six years of progressively responsible positions in upscale retail establishments and luxury hotel properties. My professional demeanor, organizational abilities, and exceptional attention to detail and follow-through, have garnered accolades from clients and employers alike. I know my way around the Internet and I am especially adept at securing whatever arrangements are necessary to ensure that every guest feels welcomed and well cared for during their stay, and that each one leaves, looking forward to his or her next return.

    I would greatly appreciate the opportunity to learn more about this position and to discuss in greater detail how we might work together for the benefit of your guests. I hope we can get together soon, as I am anxious to share my ideas. In the interim, I attach my resume for your additional information about my qualifications. Thank you for your consideration.

Sincerely,

Chris Smith

178 Green Street
Charlottesville, VA 22906
(804) 555-5555
chrissmith@jobsearch.com

Administrator:
Parks and Recreation Department

178 Green Street
Jaffrey, NH 03452
(603) 555-5555

April 16, 20--

Personnel Manager
P.O. Box 7777
Hanover, NH 03755

Dear Personnel Manager:

The April 13 edition of the *Union Leader* ran an advertisement for a Parks and Recreation Department Administrator. I am very interested in making a significant contribution to convention planning, special event planning, and/or recreation products and services.

As my resume indicates, I offer twelve years of solid experience ranging from Waterfront Director to my most recent position as Program Administrator for all recreational aspects of a municipal parks and recreation department. Currently, I am seeking a new association with an organization that can benefit from my management and administrative expertise. I welcome the opportunity for a meeting.

Thank you for your consideration.

Sincerely,

Chris Smith

Enc. Resume

Assistant Personnel Officer

178 Green Street
Vienna, VA 22211

June 1, 20--

Human Resources Director
P.O. Box 7777
Arlington, VA 22203

Dear Human Resources Director:

I am writing to express my interest in the Assistant Personnel Officer position as advertised in the May 30 edition of the *Washington Post*.

As the enclosed resume indicates, I offer extensive experience, including my most recent position as Assistant Staff Manager at Virginia General Hospital. In this capacity I have recruited and trained administrative and clerical staffs, ancillary and works department staffs, and professional and technical staffs. I have also evaluated personnel, conducted disciplinary and grievance interviews, signed employees to contracts, and advised staff on conditions of employment, entitlements, and maternity leave.

Should my qualifications be of interest to you, please contact me at the above address or by phone at (703) 555-5555. I look forward to hearing from you.

Sincerely,

Chris Smith

Enc. Resume

Catering Manager

178 Green Street
Mobile, AL 36608

October 13, 20--

P.O. Box 7777
Gainesville, GA 30503

RE: Catering Manager

Dear Sir/Madam:

    I write in response to your recent advertisement for a Catering Manager in the *Southern States Service Weekly*. Currently, I am seeking a new position with a firm than can benefit from my ten years of professional experience in the food service industry. Allow me to elaborate.

    I have held positions of responsibility in banquet/special event catering, functions management, and restaurant food service operations. I have additional experience in front desk operations, and I possess good organizational, leadership, training, and supervisory skills. I can also provide quality service and performance in a high-volume setting, and manage food, beverage, and kitchen staff with ease.

    The enclosed resume summarizes my experience. I would like the chance to expand on my qualifications in a personal interview. I am anxious to learn more about your firm and the available position, and to show you how I can meet your requirements.

    Please contact me at the above address or at (205) 555-5555 so that we may schedule a meeting time. I thank you for your time.

Sincerely,

Chris Smith

Enc. Resume

Chief Executive Officer

178 Green Street
Madison, WI 53706
(608) 555-5555

July 24, 20--

P.O. Box 7777
River Falls, WI 54022

RE: Chief Executive Officer position

Dear Sir or Madam:

Selecting the right CEO for a $100 million U.S.–based operation can be a grueling process. I would like to take the stress out of that process by suggesting that you review my qualifications and the experience I can bring to your company.

As Corporate Vice President of Sales, with an established record for the development of approximately $100 million in sales, my responsibilities have covered the gamut of successful strategies and techniques for growth and profitability. My involvement in sales, marketing, staff development, and production interface has been extensive, and my ability to organize and manage is well documented in the goals I have achieved with my present and past employers.

My resume is enclosed. If it is bottom-line results you are looking for, then we have good reason to meet for further discussion and mutual gain. Should you require additional information prior to our meeting, please do not hesitate to contact me.

I look forward to your return response.

Sincerely,

Chris Smith

Enc. Resume

Executive Sous Chef

178 Green Street
Austin, TX 78704
(512) 555-5555

July 7, 20--

P.O. Box 7777
Roanoke, VA 24001

RE: Executive Sous Chef

Dear Sir or Madam:

I am enclosing a copy of my resume for your review and hope it will convince you that I am the right choice for the position of Executive Sous Chef at your facility.

My experience in the restaurant industry goes back to my high school days and has taken me through all phases of the culinary arts in progressively responsible positions. During the past fifteen years, I have had the opportunity to work with Leisuretyme Properties. In my present position as Sous Chef at the Naturne Hotel in Austin, I have responsibility for both the brasserie and Charles Fisheries, which generate combined food revenues of $6 million, and have direct supervision of a staff of thirty.

My experience with Leisuretyme has included extensive work with banquet preparation and special themes for up to 2,500 guests in a facility generating $19 million in banquet business. Because of my ability to organize, train, and work effectively with personnel in quality, high-volume restaurants, I have been able to maintain a low-turnover, conscientious, highly productive work force in an industry notorious for personnel problems.

Based on my qualifications, I feel confident that I can handle the responsibilities of Executive Sous Chef and maintain high-quality food services at your facility. In addition, I am willing to relocate given a suitable opportunity.

Please contact me so that we can discuss how I may contribute my expertise to your organization. I look forward to our initial conversation.

Sincerely,

Chris Smith

Enc. Resume

Field Finance Manager

178 Green Street
Presque Island, ME 04769
(207) 555-5555

February 6, 20--

Professional Staffing
P.O. Box 7777
Bangor, ME 04401

RE: Field Finance Manager

Dear Professional Staffing:

Please accept this letter and enclosed resume as an application for your Field Finance Manager opening advertised in the *Bangor Daily News*.

As a 20-- graduate of the University of Maine's Graduate School of Business, I have more than six years of business and financial analysis experience. This includes two years of domestic and international travel as an Internal Auditor for Manyfoods, Inc., two years of credit analysis at Millbury, and a treasury internship at Envirlab. Since my graduation, I have been working as a Business Analyst in the areas of banking, real estate, and restaurant management.

I have been recognized for my creative spirit and ability to identify practical solutions to current business problems. The following highlights some of my achievements:

- Participated in the due diligence and/or postacquisition reviews related to five acquisitions.
- Planned, coordinated, and/or participated in the compliance and productivity audits of forty-one independent business units.
- Participated in the fraud review of a major business unit.
- Researched, developed, and planned a cash collection reorganization that, when implemented, will save $120,000 per year.

Based on my job experience and educational qualifications, I am confident I can make an immediate contribution to your firm. I would appreciate the opportunity to further discuss my credentials with you in person. Thank you.

Sincerely,

Chris Smith

Enc. Resume

Legal Associate

178 Green Street
Alfred, NY 14802
(607) 555-5555

October 28, 20--

P.O. Box 7777
Conway, SC 29526

RE: Legal Associate

Dear Sir/Madam:

In addition to a Juris Doctor degree, I recently received a Master of Law in Banks and Banking Law Studies with a concentration in International Law. I am looking for the opportunity to join the legal staff of a bank or corporation where I can put my experience in general legal practice and recent graduate degree to practical use as I further develop my legal capabilities.

My expertise is in the supervision of associate and support legal staff in all phases of research, document preparation, and coordination as required for all legal issues. I am well organized, accurate, and conscientious, interface well with individuals and groups, and feel confident that I can be a contributing asset to your firm.

I am most anxious to become a part of your firm and would appreciate meeting with you at your convenience. The enclosed resume is a brief summary of my academic accomplishments and work experience.

I look forward to your response.

Sincerely,

Chris Smith

Enc. Resume

Librarian

178 Green Street
Quincy, MA 02171

July 22, 20--

Personnel Director
P.O. Box 7777
Amherst, MA 01003

RE: Librarian

Dear Personnel Director:

In response to the July 21 advertisement in the *Boston Sunday Globe*, I have enclosed my resume for your review.

In addition to an M.L.S. degree and ALA accreditation, I have twelve years' experience as a Bibliographer and Acquisitions, Special Collections, and Reference Librarian with concentration in history and additional experience in philosophy and religion. In these positions, I provide general and specialized reference services, develop and manage collections, perform faculty liaison work, and conduct bibliographic instruction sessions at undergraduate and graduate levels. I am also experienced in assisting and training others in the use of electronic resources including CD-ROM, the World Wide Web, and other networked information resources for research.

Although my present position provides a challenging and rewarding atmosphere, I am interested in making a change where I can contribute my knowledge and experience in an academic setting. I have the ability to undertake a broad scope of responsibility and work effectively with a diverse population of students, faculty, and staff.

I am anxious to learn more about this position. Should you require additional information, please contact me at the above address or by phone at (617) 555-5555. I look forward to your response.

Sincerely,

Chris Smith

Enc. Resume

Manufacturing Test Technician

178 Green Street
Glendive, MT 59330

June 5, 20--

Human Resources Director
P.O. Box 7777
Billings, MT 59107

RE: Manufacturing Test Technician

Dear Human Resources Director:

I am writing this letter with the expressed intent of applying for your position advertised in the June 3 edition of the *Billings Gazette*. It is my interest to join your engineering staff in an area that allows me to utilize my academic as well as practical experience on new product applications and engineering development.

I offer six years of experience, with three as a Test Technician on top-quality electronic audio systems and as a member of a technical academic team working on a 3,000-line computer program designed to debug software. I also have supervisory and sales responsibility in a retail setting.

Through study and work, I have directed my career toward the full-time profession of engineering and I feel that my education and diversity of environments and responsibility enable me to make a positive and immediate contribution to your organization.

I would like to arrange a personal interview to further expand upon your requirements and my ability to meet them. I can be reached at the above address or between the hours of 9:00 A.M. and 4 P.M. at (406) 555-5555.

I look forward to meeting you.

Sincerely,

Chris Smith

Enc. Resume

Medical Assistant

178 Green Street
Lawton, OK 73505

February 10, 20--

P.O. Box 7777
Platteville, WI 53818

RE: Medical Assistant

Dear Sir or Madam:

My interest in the position of Medical Assistant that you advertised in *Health Support Monthly* has prompted me to forward my resume for your review and consideration.

In addition to ten years of experience as a Home Health Aide, In-patient Claims Representative, and, since 20--, Medical Assistant with Smith Rehabilitation Hospital, I have good knowledge of medical terminology, procedure codes, and medical office systems including related computerized applications. I have an Associate's degree in Sociology, was graduated as a medical assistant, and am currently a candidate for an Associate's degree in Nursing.

My career objective is to develop further my medical and support skills in areas that will give me the opportunity to participate in the administration of quality health care. I would welcome the opportunity to discuss whether my abilities and goals suit your requirements and expectations. Please contact me at the above address or at (405) 555-5555 during the daytime to schedule an interview.

Thank you.

Yours sincerely,

Chris Smith

Enc. Resume

Nurse's Aide

178 Green Street
Cleveland, OH 44143

November 26, 20--

Hiring Coordinator
P.O. Box 7777
Dayton, OH 45463

RE: Nurse's Aide Position

Dear Hiring Coordinator:

In response to the advertisement in the November 12 edition of the *Dayton Daily News* for a Nurse's Aide, please accept the enclosed resume as my initial application.

I am CPR-certified and possess a strong clinical background. The classes I attend as part of Ohio State University's nursing program have given me the formal training necessary for this position. With my experience and education, I am confident that I would be a valuable asset to the nursing staff.

I would appreciate the opportunity to meet with you to further discuss the position offered. I can be reached at the above address or at (216) 555-5555.

I look forward to your reply.

Sincerely,

Chris Smith

Enc. Resume

Optical Manufacturer

178 Green Street
Baltimore, MD 21201

July 23, 20--

Senior Manufacturing Manager
P.O. Box 7777
Bethesda, MD 21211

Dear Senior Manufacturing Manager:

    My interest in the Optical Manufacturer position advertised in the July 20 edition of the *Baltimore Sun* has prompted me to submit the enclosed resume for your review. During the past fifteen years, my experience has ranged from Lamination Technician to Production and Manufacturing Manager in the optical industry. I offer excellent skills in technical sales and marketing support, production and product management, manufacturing management, communications and presentations, and trade show coordination.

    Although my positions have been diverse and challenging, I am currently seeking a new position that will afford me the opportunity to contribute to the growth and profitability of a company with a diverse product line in industrial, commercial, and/or military markets.

    I will be glad to furnish you with additional information pertaining to my qualifications. Please feel free to contact me at the above address or by calling (301) 555-5555.

Sincerely,

Chris Smith

Enc. Resume

Pharmaceutical Administrator

178 Green Street
Rock Springs, WY 82902

September 6, 20--

Human Resources Representative
P.O. Box 7777
Casper, WY 82604

RE: Pharmaceutical Administrator

Dear Human Resources Representative:

I recently spotted your advertisement in the September 4 edition of the *Casper Star Tribune*. I am very interested in becoming associated with an established organization as a Pharmaceutical Administrator and have enclosed my resume for your consideration.

I hold a Master's degree in Hospital Pharmacy Administration and two related Bachelor's degrees. In addition, for the past fifteen years I have had progressively responsible experience ranging from Staff Pharmacist to Pharmacy Supervisor at a 300-bed community hospital. I am well versed in medical terminology; have excellent communications and presentation skills; and work effectively with physicians, clinical staffs, and hospital administration.

Based on my extensive experience in pharmaceuticals, combined with my energy and enthusiasm for a career in the health care field, I believe I am well qualified for this position.

Please contact me at the above address, or call (307) 555-5555 to arrange a mutually convenient time for a meeting, during which we may further discuss your current or anticipated needs and my ability to fill the position.

Thank you for your time.

Yours sincerely,

Chris Smith

Enc. Resume

Production/Materials Control Manager

178 Green Street
Fairfield, CT 06420

July 21, 20--

P.O. Box 7777
Willimantic, CT 06626

RE: Production/Materials Control Manager

Dear Sir or Madam:

Production/materials control management is my forte, and I am looking for a new opportunity where I can put these skills to work for a company interested, as I am, in profitable growth and mutual gain for the long term. Please accept the enclosed resume as my expressed interest in applying for the Production/Materials Control Manager position you advertised in the July 19 edition of the *North Jersey Herald and News*.

I am considered by my associates to be a dynamic, persistent achiever with a composite background of technical, sales, management, and training experience. During the past twenty years my positions have ranged from Production Control Manager to Vice President of Operations and President with world-leading manufacturers of cutting tools, industrial process controls, and electronics. My expertise encompasses selection, training, and development of competent team leaders and support personnel, with hands-on experience in the design and installation of materials.

I would be happy to meet with you to discuss, in detail, your requirements and my ability to handle the responsibilities of the position offered. I am very interested in learning more about your company and I am confident I can provide you with effective and profitable management.

Should you require additional information prior to our meeting, please contact me at the above address or by phone at (203) 555-5555.

Yours sincerely,

Chris Smith

Enc. Resume

Staff Photographer

178 Green Street
Tyler, TX 75799

July 20, 20--

Department of Human Resources
P.O. Box 7777
San Antonio, TX 78297

RE: Staff Photographer

To whom it may concern:

I am responding to your July 18 advertisement in the *San Antonio Express* for a staff photographer.

As you will be able to see from my resume, I hold a Bachelor of Fine Arts degree in photography from the University of Texas. My extensive photography experience includes several years of printing and processing with a variety of black-and-white materials, and custom and production printing of color negatives. In addition, I am familiar with traditional 35 mm, 2-¼, and 4 × 5 equipment, as well as digital formats. I also have experience teaching photography in a bachelor's degree program.

I would very much like to arrange an opportunity to meet with you and review my portfolio. I am confident that I can convince you of my skills as a photographer, as well as my dedication to producing a product of the highest quality.

I can be reached at the above address or by phone during the evening at (903) 555-5555. Thank you for your consideration of my application.

Sincerely,

Chris Smith

Enc. Resume

Teacher

178 Green Street
Newport, RI 02840

May 14, 20--

Search Committee
P.O. Box 7777
Providence, RI 02908

RE: Sixth Grade Teaching Position

Dear Search Committee:

I have enclosed my resume in response to your advertisement in the May edition of *Education in New England*.

During the past several years, I have been preparing myself for a full-time position as a teacher in an established school system, where I can apply my teaching, training, and administrative experience to manage and motivate a classroom of students toward higher education.

As a Student Teacher with the Easton Public School System, I successfully taught literature, public speaking, and creative writing at the secondary level. I received my Bachelor's degree and certification in Elementary Education in 20-- from Stonehill College in Easton, Massachusetts. Also, I have served as a Substitute Teacher in several school districts over a four-year period and have designed, organized, and taught my own summer course for gifted children in the town of Newport for the past two years.

Currently, I am seeking an opportunity with a system that offers continued professional development and the opportunity for advancement in the field of education. I would welcome a personal interview to discuss in detail my ability to handle the teaching position and my compatibility with the rest of your staff.

In the interim, should you require additional information, please contact me at the above address or by phone at (401) 555-5555.

Yours sincerely,

Chris Smith

Enc. Resume

178 Green Street
Toledo, OH 43660

April 11, 20--

P.O. Box 7777
Toledo, OH 43660

Dear Personnel Manager:

I am interested in the part-time position of At-Home Typist for which you advertised in the February 13 edition of the *Toledo Blade*.

My typing speed is 80 wpm. At present, I am a part-time student at Ohio State University and I am confident your company can utilize my available time and impressive qualifications to fulfill your typing needs.

Please consider the enclosed resume as an application.

I have a desktop PC with an Intel Pentium 4 processor, as well as an HP LaserJet printer, and I am proficient in both Microsoft Word and WordPerfect word processing software. I am anxious to put this equipment and my typing skills to work for your organization.

When would it be a convenient time for an interview? Please call me at (419) 555-5555.

Sincerely,

Chris Smith

Enc. Resume

Underwriter

178 Green Street
Klamath Falls, OR 97601

July 9, 20--

P.O. Box 7777
Anchorage, AK 99514

RE: Underwriter position

Dear Sir or Madam:

I am writing with an expressed interest in applying for your advertised position of Underwriter that appeared in Sunday's edition of the *Anchorage Daily News*. I am an experienced professional underwriter with a successful track record in the development of new business, the management of highly productive and diversified underwriting activities, and the support of sales and marketing operations.

I have a record of outstanding success as a Security Underwriter in establishing and maintaining profitable relationships with accounts and agents throughout the Pacific Northwest. In my current position, I have grown marketing and client contacts from a start-up base to $1.7 million in gross premiums.

I am eager to continue my successful track record with a new company that is in need of an aggressive, dedicated professional. I would like to learn more about your corporation and how I can begin to make a substantial and long-term contribution to your success. I would be glad to travel to Anchorage for a personal interview at your convenience.

Please contact me at the above address or at (503) 555-5555 if I can be of further assistance. I hope to hear from you soon.

Yours sincerely,

Chris Smith

Enc. Resume

Accounts Receivable Clerk

178 Green Street
Philadelphia, PA 19134

December 2, 20--

Pat Cummings
Manager, Accounts Receivable
Any Corporation
1140 Main Street
Macungie, PA 18062

Dear Mr. Cummings:

I would like to express my interest in applying my relevant experience and background to a position in the Accounts Receivable department at Any Corporation.

In addition to an Associate's degree in Administration, I possess four years of bookkeeping and general office experience. While at Independence Bank, I performed word processing and data entry involving trust fund information, daily sales records, payroll expenses, and invoices. As an Academic Records Assistant at Drexel University, I was responsible for the maintenance and input of thousands of alumni records. I can type 65 wpm, and am proficient in most major computer word processing programs and spreadsheet applications. Of additional interest, I have a fluent command of the Spanish language, both oral and written, and have a reading knowledge of Italian.

The record-keeping nature of my past experience has given me a facility for detail, patience, and the ability to keep accurate records, all of which I am confident can be successfully applied to an Accounts Receivable position with Any Corporation.

My resume is enclosed for your consideration. Should you have any questions or wish to schedule an interview, please do not hesitate to call me at (215) 555-5555. I look forward to hearing from you soon.

Sincerely,

Chris Smith

Enc. Resume

Administrative Assistant

178 Green Street
Delaware City, DE 19706
(302) 555-5555

January 18, 20--

Pat Cummings
Director, Human Resources
Any Corporation
1140 Main Street
New Castle, DE 19720

Dear Ms. Cummings:

I am interested in applying for an Administrative Assistant position with Any Corporation. I graduated in May 20-- with an Associate's degree in Computer Information Systems from the University of Delaware.

I have worked in the university's main computer room for two years, and I have developed advanced skills in a large number of software packages on both PC and Macintosh systems, including WordPerfect and Word for Windows. More recently, I worked as a receptionist for four months with Cammarata Designs, Inc., where I gained exposure to all facets of administrative work: typing 70 wpm, phone contact, and customer relations. With my educational background, proven academic success, and desire to learn and excel, I am confident I can make a significant contribution to your staff.

My enclosed resume provides additional information about my education and experience. I will be glad to make myself available for an interview at your earliest convenience to discuss how my qualifications would be consistent with your needs. Thank you for your time and consideration.

Sincerely,

Chris Smith

Enc. Resume

178 Green Street
Minster, OH 45865

June 3, 20--

Pat Cummings
Senior Art Director
Any Advertising Agency
1140 Main Street
Dayton, OH 45401

Dear Ms. Cummings:

I am no stranger to hard work, long hours, or tight schedules. To achieve mutual objectives, I am open to training, travel, and new assignments, and will apply dedication and quality performance to whatever tasks I am assigned.

During the past seven years, my experience has been concentrated in directing and coordinating the design, illustration, and concept development of promotional and direct mail marketing pieces for an established advertising agency. I have completed advanced coursework in commercial art and specialized technology.

Although my position is diversified and provides me with challenge and decision-making responsibilities in a creative and highly competitive industry, I feel it is time for a change. I am interested in joining a company, such as Any Advertising Agency, where I can apply my education and experience to develop new skills that will lead to my advancement within your art department.

I have enclosed a resume and project sample. I would welcome the opportunity to present a portfolio of my work and discuss my qualifications in greater detail.

To arrange an interview, please contact me at the above address or by phone at (419) 555-5555 days or (419) 555-4444 evenings.

I look forward to your response.

Sincerely,

Chris Smith

Enc. Resume, Sample

Advertising Sales Associate

178 Green Street
Decatur, GA 30032
(404) 555-5555

August 26, 20--

Pat Cummings
Personnel Director
Any Corporation
1140 Main Street
Augusta, GA 30901

Dear Mr. Cummings:

Given both my sales experience and my objective of pursuing a career in the fast-paced advertising industry, I would like to explore options within the Sales Department at Any Corporation.

I have been involved in sales/customer service with a major U.S. air carrier for four years, in which time I gained the exposure and valuable work experience necessary for success. I have learned the art, as well as the importance of, creating a strong rapport with clients while demonstrating outstanding customer service for successful sales. I have also learned unique approaches to problem-solving and how to handle rejection with renewed optimism and good humor. In addition, I possess exceptional communication and organizational skills. I am proficient in Microsoft Word for Windows and can type effectively at 65 wpm.

I look forward to expanding my career in sales and advertising with Any Corporation. I would certainly appreciate the opportunity to discuss how I might apply my skills and knowledge to benefit your company. I would like to schedule an interview at your convenience, and will call you next week to do so. Thank you.

Sincerely,

Chris Smith

Enc. Resume

178 Green Street
Schaumburg, IL 60191
(708) 555-5555

March 3, 20--

Pat Cummings
Executive Director
Any Performing Arts Foundation
1140 Main Street
Chicago, IL 60632

Dear Ms. Cummings:

   As a studio owner, manager, choreographer, performer, and producer, I feel I have much to offer in support of performing arts.

   In addition to my successful experience, I have been actively involved in public relations and promotional activities. Such work requires the ability to communicate and interface effectively with talented professionals as well as patrons of the arts. I am most effective in the capacity of planner, coordinator, manager, and representative in a creative environment and feel confident that I can contribute to the efforts of a performing arts foundation.

   I have enclosed a professional profile for your consideration regarding any suitable openings. Perhaps we could meet for a personal interview? I would love to share with you my experiences and dedication to the performing arts.

Sincerely,

Chris Smith

Enc. Professional profile

Arts Administrator

178 Green Street
Arlington, VA 22203
(703) 555-5555

June 26, 20--

Pat Cummings
Director
Any Gallery
1140 Main Street
Vienna, VA 22108

Dear Mr. Cummings:

Last weekend I attended the opening of your newest exhibition, "Forming Meaning," and I especially appreciated your commitment to the local art scene. I am currently searching for an opportunity with a reputable gallery, and would be very interested in contributing my skills to your staff.

Please note that in addition to my broad formal education in areas related specifically to art and art education, I hold a Master of Education degree in Administration. I also possess valuable experience in diverse aspects of museum operations, including exhibition and display, media presentation, proposal writing, and associated details of estimation and cost accounting.

I would like to arrange a mutually convenient time for an interview during which we could further discuss your current or anticipated needs.

Thank you for your consideration.

Sincerely,

Chris Smith

Enc. Resume

178 Green Street
Needham, MA 02192
(617) 555-5555

June 18, 20--

Pat Cummings
Human Resources Director
Any Publishing Company
1140 Main Street
New York, NY 10128

Dear Ms. Cummings:

I have four years of publishing experience, including two years of scholarly journal experience in social science, physical science, and engineering which I would like to put to work at Any Publishing Company.

Specifically, I am seeking a position as an Associate Editor, Project Editor, or the equivalent in new book or journal development and administration. Originally from Long Island, I am planning to relocate to the New York area later this summer. Please consider the following highlights from my career:

- Developed a new book series in sociology through all phases of publication: from author contract negotiation to the creation of a series marketing plan.
- Acquired *Earth Day Every Day*, which was nominated for the Fortmiller Foundation's Prize and is already an "academic bestseller."
- Participated in a dynamic engineering program which included the launch of three new journals: *Physical Science*, *Micro Journal*, and the *Journal of Alternative Energy*.

In addition to a strong background in English literature and the social sciences at the University of Notre Dame, my training has included courses relevant to a position in medical publishing: Anatomy, Biology, Physiology, Medical Terminology, Nursing Procedures, and Radiographic Physics.

I will be in New York from July 20 to 30, during which time I would appreciate the opportunity to meet with you. Thank you for your consideration, and I look forward to speaking with you soon.

Sincerely,

Chris Smith

Enc. Resume

Audio-Visual Specialist

178 Green Street
Proctorville, VT 05153
(802) 555-5555

July 7, 20--

Pat Cummings
Personnel Manager
Any Corporation
1140 Main Street
Chicago, IL 60605

Dear Mr. Cummings:

In the interest of investigating career opportunities with your company, I am enclosing my resume for your consideration and review.

As you will note, I have fifteen years of educational and media experience. I am proficient in the operation of a wide variety of photographic, video, and audio equipment. In my current position, I am regularly responsible for processing and duplicating slides, as well as designing and setting up slide presentations, from simple slide-only programs to full-blown synchronized slide and audio productions.

I believe that my qualifications would make me an outstanding asset to your organization. I would very much appreciate the opportunity to personally meet with you at your convenience to further discuss my abilities and the needs of Any Corporation.

I look forward to hearing from you soon.

Sincerely,

Chris Smith

Enc. Resume

178 Green Street
Hunt Valley, MD 21031
(712) 555-5555

January 20, 20--

Pat Cummings
Senior Operations Manager
Any Airline
1140 Main Street
Baltimore, MD 21226

Dear Mr. Cummings:

I am very interested in securing a challenging position in an aviation-related operation, and have admired the fast-growing quality reputation Any Airline has built in the national arena.

I possess nine years of diverse full-time and part-time experience within the airline industry, ranging from Ground Crew and Operations Agent to my current position as Senior Operations Dispatcher for a highly personalized, worldwide courier service. This experience is supplemented by a Bachelor of Science degree in Aviation Science/Aviation Management, and comprehensive advanced training courses in these areas.

My enclosed resume provides a summary of the experience and training I feel can be put to effective use for your company. After you have had an opportunity to review my credentials, I would like to arrange a personal meeting so that I can more fully expand on my immediate and long-term potential. I am happy to make myself available at your convenience.

I look forward to hearing from you.

Sincerely,

Chris Smith

Enc. Resume

Business Consultant

178 Green Street
Medford, WI 54451
(715) 555-5555 (days)
(715) 555-4444 (evenings)

September 12, 20--

Pat Cummings
Chairperson of the Board
Any Corporation
1140 Main Street
Schofield, WI 54476

Dear Mr. Cummings:

In the past several months, I have been studying operations at Any Corporation. By reading your annual report, company profile, and write-ups in several trade publications, I have been able to keep a close eye on both your costs and profits. If you agree that Any Corporation could benefit from an efficient, time-saving plan to cut production dollars, I would like to present my qualifications to you.

I am a skilled business consultant with more than seventeen years of experience concentrated in the advertising field. I believe I can be of assistance to your organization. For your evaluation, I have prepared the attached business proposal that contains a detailed summary of a series of events and observations concerning trends in Any Corporation's operations that could be easily reversed.

I may be reached at either one of the above-listed numbers for a telephone conference, or to establish a mutually convenient time for a personal meeting. At such time, I would be pleased to demonstrate how I might be able to assist in correcting and/or eliminating many of the challenges touched upon in the attached proposal.

Thank you for your consideration.

Sincerely,

Chris Smith

Enc. Business proposal

178 Green Street
Omaha, NE 68102
(402) 555-5555

December 23, 20--

Pat Cummings
Lieutenant Governor
State of Nebraska
1140 Main Street
Lincoln, NE 68502

Dear Lieutenant Governor Cummings:

Over the past fourteen years, I have had diverse and progressively responsible experience in development for nonprofit service organizations, universities, and educational institutions. These responsibilities have ranged from Secretary to the Director of Development.

During this period, I have been heavily involved in development strategies, annual fund-raising campaigns, marketing and mailing programs, and media and public relations. Although these positions have been both challenging and exciting, I now feel that my expertise would be put to better use in a new environment, namely, the State of Nebraska.

I would appreciate the opportunity to discuss with you the contribution I can make to the state administration. I will call your office the week of January 9 to schedule a mutually convenient time to meet.

Thank you for your consideration.

Sincerely,

Chris Smith

Enc. Resume

Chef

178 Green Street
Clarksville, TN 37044
(615) 555-5555

April 15, 20--

Pat Cummings
Manager
Any Hotel
1140 Main Street
Lexington, KY 40508

Dear Ms. Cummings:

During the past six years, my positions have ranged from Sous Chef to Executive Chef of a restaurant continually rated in the top 100 restaurants and food service institutions nationwide. My experience includes associations with country clubs, hotels, resorts, and four-star restaurants where I held a variety of positions including, Waiter, Line Cook, and Sauté Chef.

Because of my ability to organize, train, and work effectively with personnel in quality, high-volume restaurants, I have been able to always maintain a conscientious, highly productive work force. I have expertise in coordinating activities and directing the indoctrination and training of chefs and other kitchen staff to ensure an efficient and profitable food service.

In addition to being an honors graduate of the Culinary Institute of America, I have received several national and regional awards for my creative culinary skills.

The enclosed resume is a brief summary of my qualifications. I would welcome the chance to discuss the culinary opportunities available at Any Hotel, and will call during the week of May 1 to schedule a meeting.

Thank you for your consideration.

Yours sincerely,

Chris Smith

Enc. Resume

178 Green Street
Pueblo, CO 81001

November 7, 20--

Pat Cummings
Product Development Supervisor
Any Corporation
1140 Main Street
Gunnison, CO 81231

Dear Mr. Cummings:

I am interested in a challenging position requiring product management, product development, and clinical research/nursing skills. Any Corporation's research facility has earned a reputation as the most technologically advanced in the field and, for this reason, I am eager to join your staff.

My expertise includes the management of product development from clinical research for FDA approval to commercial marketability. I offer thirteen years of professional clinical experience with major teaching and trauma hospitals as a Staff R.N. and Therapeutic Apheresis Nurse Specialist. My most recent three years have been spent as Project Manager of Clinical Services and Product Manager with a firm specializing in clinical research and product development, concentrating in applications for autolymphocyte therapy (ALT).

I have excellent communication, computer, and writing skills and am well qualified to assume responsibility for clinical, regulatory, and related functions.

I am anxious to discuss how I might contribute to your organization. Please contact me at the above address, or call (719) 555-5555 to arrange a mutually convenient time for a meeting. Thank you for your consideration.

Sincerely,

Chris Smith, R.N.

Enc. Resume

Clinical Service Administrator

178 Green Street
Orono, ME 04473
(207) 555-5555

February 21, 20--

Pat Cummings
Senior Administrator
Any Corporation
1140 Main Street
Portland, ME 04101

Dear Ms. Cummings:

If you are in need of a take-charge professional skilled in clinical service administration as well as quality assurance, utilization review, and risk management, then we have good reason to meet for further discussion.

In addition to a Master of Science degree in Business Administration, I offer thirteen years of progressively responsible, comprehensive experience, including five years in my current position as Director of Service Administration at the medical teaching facility of the University of Maine. In this capacity, I have developed a competent quality assurance support staff, and have provided overall leadership and management for a department that supports and generates input to clinical chiefs in highly technical areas.

The enclosed resume summarizes my qualifications. I would appreciate the opportunity to meet with you in order to discuss in greater detail the mutual benefits of my joining your management team. I will call you on February 28 to schedule a convenient time.

Yours sincerely,

Chris Smith

Enc. Resume

Communications Consultant

178 Green Street
Wayne, NE 68787

November 11, 20--

Pat Cummings
Program Director
Any Corporation
1140 Main Street
Schenectady, NY 12308

Dear Mr. Cummings:

My interest in a consulting position with a communications company offering potential for advancement has prompted me to forward my resume for your review and evaluation.

In addition to a Bachelor of Arts degree in Political Science/Communications, I have three years of concentrated experience in customer contact and service. My positions have ranged from Data Processing Analyst and Brokerage Service Representative to my most current position as New Business Representative. I have exceptional organizational, communication, and interpersonal skills that I am confident could be effectively utilized in a firm such as yours.

If you have room for a highly motivated achiever in your firm, then we have good reason to meet. I feel strongly that my qualifications can be more fully demonstrated during a personal interview. I am able to travel to Schenectady at your convenience for a discussion. I can be reached at the above address or by phone at (402) 555-5555.

Thank you for your consideration and response.

Sincerely,

Chris Smith

Enc. Resume

Computer Programmer

178 Green Street
Bunkie, LA 71322
(318) 555-5555

December 5, 20--

Pat Cummings
Hiring Director
Any Corporation
1140 Main Street
Chicago, IL 60605

Dear Mr. Cummings:

    I am an experienced Computer Programmer and I am ready, willing, and able to join Any Corporation.

    I offer extensive knowledge of five computer languages and strong management, sales, and sales support experience. As a Computer Specialist, I was responsible for the management of a center handling the complete line of IBM computers and peripherals for home and commercial use. In addition to a Bachelor of Science degree in Business Administration, I will receive a certificate in Programming in May 20--.

    I feel confident that, given the opportunity, I can make an immediate contribution to Any Corporation. I would appreciate the opportunity to meet with you to discuss your requirements. I will call your office on Tuesday, December 12, to schedule an appointment. Thank you for your consideration.

Sincerely,

Chris Smith

Enc. Resume

Consulting/Management Specialist

178 Green Street
Franklin Park, IL 60131

June 28, 20--

Pat Cummings
Operations Manager
Any Company
1140 Main Street
Skokie, IL 60076

Dear Mr. Cummings:

Is Any Company currently in need of a hardworking and intelligent Consultant/Management Specialist with more than ten years of experience? If so, then please consider the following qualifications.

During the past eight years, I have been actively involved in the development and administration of health and welfare funds and defined contribution plans, and have developed, designed, and implemented medical practice systems. This proficiency has been applied to both union and company requirements. My professional background is supported by a Master of Business Administration, Employee Benefits Specialist Certification, and current candidacy for a Master of Science in Computer Information Systems.

If I possess what you are looking for, please call me at (708) 555-5555. I eagerly await your reply.

Sincerely,

Chris Smith

Enc. Resume

Controller

178 Green Street
Sioux Falls, SD 57102

July 22, 20--

Pat Cummings
Hiring Officer
Any Corporation
1140 Main Street
Richmond, VA 23219

Dear Ms. Cummings:

During the past eight years I have held numerous progressively responsible positions in the areas of general accounting, business, office management, and project management.

Currently I am seeking a new association with a company where I can apply my experience and skills toward both company and personal goals.

I consider myself to be well-organized, self-motivated, and productive. I am open to additional training and am looking for a position that offers advancement based on ability to perform.

The enclosed resume summarizes my background and experience. I am available at your earliest convenience to discuss my qualifications with you during a personal interview. I can be reached at the above address or by phone at (605) 555-5555.

Thank you in advance for your response.

Sincerely,

Chris Smith

Enc. Resume

178 Green Street
West Palm Beach, FL 33405
(407) 555-5555

April 13, 20--

Pat Cummings
Owner
Any Country Club
1140 Main Street
Sarasota, FL 34236

Dear Mr. Cummings:

 I am writing to inquire about available management positions at Any Country Club. I have been an active member since 20--, and my familiarity with the club and its members would make me an excellent candidate for your consideration.

 I am presently employed in a position that has presented challenges and personal satisfaction for a job well done. However, I feel that my education, training, and experience have prepared me for a broader scope of responsibility, and for this reason I am seeking a change.

 I would like to associate with a quality facility in the hospitality industry that maintains high standards for services offered to guests or members. Based on my education and employment history, I believe I can play a key role in achieving our mutual goals for success and profit by providing cost-effective management.

 The enclosed resume summarizes my qualifications. I would welcome the opportunity to discuss my ability to meet your expectations for club management positions. Please contact me to schedule a mutually convenient time for an interview.

 Thank you. I look forward to talking with you.

Sincerely,

Chris Smith

Enc. Resume

Electrician

178 Green Street
Lawrence, KS 66409

September 14, 20--

Pat Cummings
Staff Coordinator
Any Corporation
1140 Main Street
Topeka, KS 66607

Dear Mr. Cummings:

I am currently investigating availabilities in electrical operations, and would like to submit my qualifications for your review.

Although I am a newly licensed Journeyman Electrician, I have nine years of experience in the field, five as an Apprentice and four as a Journeyman, handling a variety of electrical installations while working with electrical contractors and as a subcontractor. I am capable of working independently or as a member of a team and feel confident in my ability to handle multiple responsibilities and provide quality performance on any assignment I undertake.

The enclosed resume is a brief summary of my experience. I would appreciate the opportunity to further discuss my qualifications, and with that in mind, I will contact your division next Wednesday to schedule a meeting. Should you require additional information, please contact me at the above address or by phone at (913) 555-5555.

I am very interested in joining Any Corporation and look forward to your return reply.

Yours sincerely,

Chris Smith

Enc. Resume

Electromechanical Drafter

178 Green Street

New Castle, DE 19720

(302) 555-5555

November 20, 20--

Pat Cummings

Chief Engineer

Any Corporation

1140 Main Street

Easton, PA 18044

Dear Ms. Cummings:

As a recent graduate with an Associate's degree in Electromechanical Drafting, with concentration in Electromechanical Technology, my goal is to join a firm where I can apply my skills in a drafting environment.

Since 20--, I have held responsible part-time positions as a Marine Technician and a Mason Tender while earning my degree. Able to handle assignments individually or as a team member, I am computer literate, and people-oriented, have good communication skills, and relate well to all levels of authority. Now I am seeking an opportunity for personal development and advancement based on the quality of my technical performance.

My resume provides a summary of my education, background, and experience, but I strongly feel that during the course of a personal interview my potential for making a significant contribution to your firm can be more fully demonstrated. I am hopeful that we can set up a mutually convenient appointment in the near future.

Should you require additional information, please contact me at the above address or phone number. I look forward to your return response.

Yours sincerely,

Chris Smith

Enc. Resume

Engineering Instructor

178 Green Street
Macon, GA 31201
(912) 555-5555

August 20, 20--

Pat Cummings
Headmaster
Any School
1140 Main Street
Evansville, IN 47713

Dear Ms. Cummings:

If you are in need of an Engineering Instructor to teach accredited classroom courses or conduct in-house seminars and training, then we have good reason to meet for further discussion.

I have extensive experience in teaching courses on proposal writing, pricing, component design, and equipment operation and control. My practical expertise is in electromechanical design and the analysis of mechanical systems. In addition, I offer five years of experience teaching engineering.

My experience as an Engineer, Principal Engineer, and Manager, Author, and Technical Writer is extensive. I am skilled in preparing and presenting complex technical reports to corporate clients and/or company management in support of contracts or proposed new developments. Currently, I am interested in joining an educational system where I can impart my engineering knowledge, experience, and writing skills to students in an academic or vocational environment, preferably on a per diem or course assignment basis. I have an excellent grasp of highly sophisticated systems and instrumentation, and I can provide your students with essential technical knowledge and support.

I would appreciate the opportunity to discuss my qualifications. I will call the school next week to schedule an interview. In the meantime, I have enclosed my professional profile for your review. Thank you for your time.

Sincerely,

Chris Smith

Enc. Professional profile

178 Green Street
Hartford, CT 06115

April 2, 20--

Pat Cummings
Vice President, Personnel
Any Corporation
1140 Main Street
New Haven, CT 06511

Dear Mr. Cummings:

Currently I am seeking a position with the international sales/marketing division of Any Corporation. I offer professional expertise in opening new markets, launching new salons/spas, introducing beauty products and services, and training personnel.

I am a Licensed Esthetician who, during the past ten years, has held positions in France as Director of Education for a manufacturer of beauty products sold to select European spas and in the United States as Skin Care Director for an exclusive beauty spa.

I am a multilingualist fluent in French (native speaker) and German, and I feel confident that I could make a valuable contribution toward increasing your product name visibility and market share in today's increasingly global economy.

I would appreciate the opportunity to discuss your requirements for penetrating international markets. Should you require additional information, please contact me at the above address or by phone at (203) 555-5555.

I look forward to your response.

Sincerely,

Chris Smith

Enc. Resume

Executive Secretary

178 Green Street
Allentown, PA 18105

August 5, 20--

Pat Cummings
Human Resources Manager
Any Corporation
1140 Main Street
Philadelphia, PA 19130

Dear Ms. Cummings:

If you are in need of an Executive Secretary who can double as an Administrative Assistant and handle the day-to-day details necessary to keep an operation running smoothly, then we have good reason to meet.

During the past seven years, I have provided administrative support to senior-level officers and account executives in a domestic and international sales and marketing environment. Although this position has been interesting, I am presently considering a position change with a company offering greater responsibility and growth potential than is possible with my present employer.

So that I can be considered for a position with your firm, I am enclosing a copy of my professional profile for your review. I would appreciate the opportunity to discuss my past achievements, along with ways in which I might excel in a future position with Any Corporation.

Thank you for reviewing my credentials. I can be reached at the above address or by phone between 9 A.M. and 1 P.M. at (215) 555-5555.

Sincerely,

Chris Smith

Enc. Professional profile

Field Coordinator

178 Green Street
Greenville, SC 29601
(803) 555-5555

July 10, 20--

Pat Cummings
Chief Executive Director
Any Campaign
1140 Main Street
Clinton, SC 29325

Dear Ms. Cummings:

Are you searching for a dynamic Field Coordinator or Campaign Manager for your upcoming campaign?

During the past two years, both my graduate education at the University of Southern Carolina and my professional experience have been focused on government issues and political campaigns. I have worked as a Campaign Manager, Field Coordinator, Volunteer Organizer, and Fundraiser.

My motivation has always been toward a behind-the-scenes career in politics that would allow me to play a key role in electing qualified candidates, the kind who can make a significant difference for the constituents they represent. As the enclosed resume reflects, I have had experience with numerous campaigns on the local, state, and federal levels. I feel confident that I have the skills necessary to make voters aware of the importance of electing your candidate into office.

I will call your office on Wednesday, July 19, to assure receipt of my letter and to schedule an interview. Thank you for your consideration. I am eager to join your team!

Sincerely,

Chris Smith

Enc. Resume

Financial Associate

178 Green Street
Eugene, OR 97401
(503) 555-5555

October 17, 20--

Pat Cummings
Human Resources Director
Any Corporation
1140 Main Street
Portland, OR 97201

Dear Mr. Cummings:

I am a new graduate with a Bachelor of Arts degree in Political Science who can offer your firm dedication, skill, and a willingness to learn your industry while aspiring to performance-based advancement.

My interests are in business, investments, and finance. In keeping with these, I have developed a strong work ethic, which is evidenced by the fact that I have maintained a part-time job throughout my four years of college. My work has included operating my own successful small business, as well as employment with outside firms and internships related to my career interests. I function equally well working independently or as a member of a team, and feel confident that given the opportunity, I can make a positive difference as a member of your organization.

The enclosed resume summarizes my experience. I am eager to meet for an interview during which I can fully express my capacity and desire to contribute to Any Corporation. I will call your office the week of October 23 to schedule an appointment.

Thank you for your time and consideration. I look forward to speaking with you in the near future.

Sincerely,

Chris Smith

Enc. Resume

Financial Planner

178 Green Street
Gardenia, ND 58739

April 15, 20--

Pat Cummings
Personnel Manager
Any Corporation
1140 Main Street
Chicago, IL 60605

Dear Mr. Cummings:

Having had the opportunity to meet with Deborah Sturgis and the rest of the staff at the Fargo office, I am very much interested in starting my career in finance at Any Corporation.

I am planning a permanent relocation to the Chicago area in the late summer. Therefore, I am submitting my resume for consideration for admittance into your Financial Planner Training Program.

Please note that I am currently completing my senior year at North Dakota University and will receive my Bachelor of Science degree with a major in Accounting and a concentration in Computer Programming this May. Throughout four years of college, and during full-time and part-time employment, I have continued to strengthen my focus in these areas. In addition, I have excellent problem-solving skills and feel that, given the opportunity, I would be both an immediate and long-term asset to your firm.

While my resume is a good summary of my qualifications, I feel strongly that my potential to be of service to your organization could be more fully demonstrated during a personal interview. I plan to be in the Chicago area the week of May 1 and would welcome the opportunity to meet with you. I will follow up with a phone call on April 25 to arrange such a meeting. In the interim I can be reached at the above address or by telephone at (701) 555-5555.

Thank you for your time and consideration.

Sincerely,

Chris Smith

Enc. Resume

Flight Attendant

178 Green Street
Helena, MT 59601
(406) 555-5555

January 3, 20--

Pat Cummings
Attendant Supervisor
Any Airline
1140 Main Street
Phoenix, AZ 85023

Dear Ms. Cummings:

    I am an ambitious, career-oriented, energetic individual with a keen interest in becoming a Flight Attendant for Any Airline.

    I possess six years of diverse business experience in both the retail and hospitality industries. I understand the importance of excellent customer/public relations and support, along with strong communication skills, for maintaining efficient airline operations and a strong, positive public image.

    I feel confident that, given the opportunity, I can make an immediate contribution to the flight system at Any Airline. I would appreciate the chance to personally sit down with you to discuss your requirements and my ability to meet them.

    I look forward to meeting with you.

Yours sincerely,

Chris Smith

Enc. Resume

Foreperson/Ironworker

178 Green Street
Spartanburg, SC 29304

August 4, 20--

Pat Cummings
Personnel Manager
Any Corporation
1140 Main Street
Sioux City, IA 51102

Dear Mr. Cummings:

Please accept the enclosed resume as indication of my interest in securing a position with Any Corporation. During the past ten years, my career has grown steadily. I began as Journeyman Ironworker/Foreman Ironworker with Local #10, and have progressed to Senior Project Manager, with responsibility for constructing commercial and industrial steel buildings in the United States and Canada.

I am an effective negotiator skilled in dealing with subcontractors, vendors, and suppliers, and in the coordination and scheduling of manpower, equipment, and materials to meet deliveries, time schedules, and budgets. I am well qualified to assume responsibilities for projects from pre-job site inspections to final completion.

I would welcome the chance to personally discuss my capabilities and your anticipated requirements. Please contact me at the above address or by phone at (803) 555-5555 to arrange for a mutually convenient time for such a meeting.

Thank you for your consideration and early response.

Sincerely,

Chris Smith

Enc. Resume

Graphic Artist

178 Green Street
Bridgeville, PA 15017
(412) 555-5555

September 20, 20--

Pat Cummings
Director of Human Resources
Any Corporation
1140 Main Street
New York, NY 10108

Dear Mr. Cummings:

I am extremely interested in putting my graphics expertise to work for Any Corporation. Your great successes in the past year, including your six-figure accounts with Kitters Cola and the Mooburger Company, impressed all of us in the advertising business. Now I want to get in on the fun and excitement! Enclosed is a copy of my resume.

I operate from my own computerized studio where I design using the latest graphic-related hardware and software. I offer extensive experience in:

- Designing marketing literature with QuarkXpress, Macromedia Freehand, and Photoshop.
- Preparing complicated files on the Macintosh as final mechanicals, for direct export to the printing company.
- Communicating and working directly with clients, supervisors, and department heads.
- Estimating jobs firsthand and working directly with vendors.
- Directing graphic art departments and supervising projects.

Do my credentials sound suitable for a position at Any Corporation? I would be more than happy to meet with you and show you a portfolio of my work at your convenience. I will call your office next week to schedule an interview. Thank you for your consideration.

Sincerely,

Chris Smith

Enc. Resume

Head Nurse

178 Green Street
Woodland Hills, CA 91367
(818) 555-5555

May 29, 20--

Pat Cummings, R.N.
Director of Nursing
Any Facility
1140 Main Street
Long Beach, CA 90844

Dear Ms. Cummings:

Last week, I read an article in the *Press Telegram* praising Any Facility's excellent staff and patient services among area health care centers. I am looking for a nursing opportunity in the Long Beach area, and this piece confirmed my desire to join your esteemed organization.

I offer more than twelve years of experience ranging from Nursing Assistant and Charge Nurse to Nursing Supervisor for a 120-bed, multilevel nursing facility catering to patients afflicted with Alzheimer's, renal disease, and other chronic geriatric conditions. My experience encompasses diverse areas of health care supervision, including patient assessment and staff development, as well as the coordination of such resident care services as physical therapy, dietary, housekeeping, pharmacy, and social services.

I am interested in joining the staff at Any Facility. I would welcome the opportunity to arrange a mutually convenient time in which we could further discuss your current or anticipated needs in terms of my qualifications.

Thank you for your consideration.

Sincerely,

Chris Smith, R.N.

Enc. Resume

Human Resources Professional

178 Green Street
Grenvil, NE 68941
(402) 555-5555

October 19, 20--

Pat Cummings
Staff Coordinator
Any Corporation
1140 Main Street
St. Louis, MI 63130

Dear Ms. Cummings:

I am writing regarding opportunities your firm may have for experienced human resources professionals.

I have a solid track record as a Human Resources Generalist working in a fast-paced environment with a reputable professional services firm in the Omaha area. I have successfully provided staff planning, recruiting, and employee relations support for several of the firm's key high-technology practices, which provide systems engineering and management consulting services. In addition, I have more than six years of solid accomplishment as a Management Analyst, Systems Analyst, and Environmental Management Consultant providing technical and management services to both government and commercial clients.

I am now seeking new and challenging responsibilities in an organization that would benefit from my background and specific mix of skills. I am willing to relocate and/or travel for the right opportunity.

Perhaps we could meet soon to discuss available openings at Any Corporation? Thank you for your time and consideration.

Sincerely,

Chris Smith

Enc. Resume

Human Services Coordinator

178 Green Street
Washington, DC 20024

November 6, 20--

Pat Cummings
Director
Any Agency
1140 Main Street
Washington DC 20005

Dear Mr. Cummings:

During the past ten years, my experience has been concentrated as an Area Office Manager and Child Advocate Coordinator in the coordination and management of human services information and resources for multicultural, multilingual populations in the Washington, D.C., area.

Currently, I am seeking a new association with an agency, in the public or private sector, which has a need for a qualified professional. I can offer broad experience working with and coordinating the efforts of, public, private, and charitable resources, educational systems, and providers of human services to community residents or company employees.

I am especially interested in the field of human services as I am dedicated to improving the quality of life and learning for the less fortunate. I possess strong organizational, communication, and teaching skills, as well as the ability to work well under stressful or crisis situations.

I would be glad to make myself available for an interview at your convenience to discuss how I might put my knowledge and experience to work for Any Agency. Should you require additional information prior to our meeting, please contact me at the above address or by phone at (202) 555-5555. I plan to make a follow-up call within a few days.

I look forward to speaking with you.

Yours sincerely,

Chris Smith

Enc. Resume

Insurance Salesperson

178 Green Street
Lubbock, TX 79408
(806) 555-5555

July 16, 20--

Pat Cummings
Sales Director
Any Insurance Company
1140 Main Street
Houston, TX 77027

Dear Ms. Cummings:

Currently, I am seeking a new association within the insurance industry where I can apply my combined knowledge experience to the sale of insurance products and services. I am interested in a home office staff or sales position where there is opportunity for increased responsibility and compensation based on personal performance.

During the past thirteen years, I have built a successful career in the insurance industry, first as a Sales Representative with Unlimited Trust Insurance and then for ten years with Lubbock Mutual Life Insurance. In both positions I established myself as a consistent top producer selling a broad scope of insurance and investment products to businesses and individuals.

I have enclosed a resume for your consideration. I am anxious to discuss in greater detail my credentials for contributing to the profitability and increased customer satisfaction of your firm. Please contact me so that we may explore the possibility of a mutually beneficial association. Thank you.

Sincerely,

Chris Smith

Enc. Resume

International Sales Associate

178 Green Street
Los Angeles, CA 90066
(213) 555-5555

April 1, 20--

Pat Cummings
Controller
Any Corporation
1140 Main Street
Boston, MA 02215

Dear Ms. Cummings:

During the past fifteen years I have played a key role in the development of international markets for the sale of capital and laboratory equipment, systems, and services. Currently, I am seeking a new position with a firm that can benefit from my expertise in the development of profitable overseas markets. Any Corporation's commitment to developing overseas accounts makes me eager to join your international team.

Throughout my career in foreign service and international sales, I have developed and currently maintain excellent personal, business, and government contacts with key product movers in pharmaceuticals, cosmetics, and chemical manufacturing; food processors; scientific laboratories; and health institutions worldwide.

My peers and associates consider me to be a goal setter and achiever, and I am confident I can produce the same beneficial results in the development of international markets for your products that I have for my present employer. If you can use an executive who is thoroughly familiar with international market development and sales, I would like to discuss my qualifications with you during a personal interview. At that time, I will be glad to expand on my experience and answer any questions you might have. I will call your office next week to schedule a mutually convenient meeting time.

Sincerely,

Chris Smith

Enc. Resume

Jewelry Designer

178 Green Street
Fresno, CA 93786
(209) 555-5555

August 15, 20--

Pat Cummings
Creative Director
Any Corporation
1140 Main Street
Los Angeles, CA 90053

Dear Mr. Cummings:

Of all the fine jewelry designs being produced today, in my estimation yours is singularly the best. I would like to put my talent as a Jewelry Designer to work for Any Corporation.

I have devoted the past seven years to developing and refining my design skills while maximizing my technical knowledge. In addition to producing my own designs, I currently work as a model maker for Gemmz, Inc., a Fresno-based jewelry maker. Over the course of my career, I have continued to make several significant contributions to the field of jewelry design:

- Three of my designs were featured as part of Gemmz's flagship line at the 20-- International Jewelry Bazaar.
- Developed a buffing method in our Fresno production facility that is being implemented nationwide.
- Earned a fine arts degree in jewelry design.
- Won several design awards.

I would like to discuss some of the options available at Any Corporation and the possibility of my designing jewelry for you. I will call on September 1 to arrange an interview.

Thank you for your consideration.

Sincerely,

Chris Smith

Enc. Resume

Jewelry Sales/Buyer

178 Green Street
Neptune, NJ 07754
(415) 555-5555

July 18, 20--

Pat Cummings
General Manager
Any Store
1140 Main Street
Cherry Hill, NJ 08002

Dear Ms. Cummings:

I am a recent graduate of the Gemological Institute of America with a year of successful experience in the purchase and sale of precious metals, gems, and antique jewelry.

Currently, I am looking for a new position with a major jewelry store where I can apply my sales and customer relations skills to continue my proven track record of increasing profit and market share. During my year at Monahan Jewelers, I was responsible for increasing company sales by 10 percent while creating a substantially larger customer base.

The enclosed resume summarizes my experience. I am very much interested in Any Store because of your top-notch reputation in the field. I am confident of my ability to represent you in an ethical and professional manner, and look forward to hearing from you soon.

Yours sincerely,

Chris Smith

Enc. Resume

Lawyer

178 Green Street
Glendale Heights, IL 60139
(708) 555-5555

February 26, 20--

Pat Cummings
Hiring Coordinator
Any Law Firm
1140 Main Street
Chicago, IL 60606

Dear Ms. Cummings:

I am a 20-- graduate of Chicago-Kent College of Law interested in a position as an Associate with Any Law Firm. I am particularly interested in the firm's real estate, corporate, finance, and litigation departments.

As my enclosed resume indicates, upon graduation I accepted a job with the Chicago-based law firm Glavin and Joyce. As a first-year associate, I worked in the firm's litigation, real estate, finance, and corporate departments. In May of 20--, I accepted a position with the Brussels-based international consulting firm Brunkhorst and Associates. On their behalf, I act as a consultant and advisor on American law as it relates to the offshore funding of U.S. commercial real estate.

Although I enjoy my present position, I would very much like to become associated with an up-and-coming firm such as yours so that I can continue my development as a lawyer. My association with a well-established, full-service law firm would also enable me to better service Brunkhorst and Associates and its clients.

If my qualifications are of interest to you, I would like to visit your offices for an interview. I will contact you Monday, March 4, to discuss available opportunities. Thank you for your attention and I look forward to speaking with you.

Sincerely,

Chris Smith

Enc. Resume

Legal Associate

178 Green Street
New York, NY 10128

July 10, 20--

Pat Cummings
Hiring Officer
Any Law Firm
1140 Main Street
Syracuse, NY 13221

Dear Ms. Cummings:

I am enclosing a copy of my resume for your review. Please consider me for an associate position with Any Law Firm.

During the past three years, I have been employed in several law-related positions while completing my requirements for a Juris Doctor degree at Yale Law School. These positions have given me the opportunity to gain firsthand experience in legal drafting and research in those areas of the legal profession having to do with real estate, corporate finance, and litigation. As a result of my studies, I was admitted to the Connecticut Bar in December 20--.

I would like the opportunity to meet with you for further discussion. I am very interested in joining your firm and would look forward to an interview at your earliest convenience. I can be reached at the above address or by phone between 6 P.M. and 10 P.M. at (212) 555-5555.

Sincerely,

Chris Smith

Enc. Resume

Librarian

178 Green Street
Boston, MA 02215

December 28, 20--

Pat Cummings
Director, Personnel
Any Library
1140 Main Street
Cambridge, MA 02138

Dear Mr. Cummings:

I am an experienced researcher who has worked extensively with archival records and secondary sources. Currently, I am seeking an opportunity to apply my acquired research skills to a full-time position as a Librarian.

My training has emphasized the importance of precise organization and the thoughtful use of evidence to make clear historical arguments, and my work at the Library of Congress, the Boston Public Library, and the Hauptstaatarchiv Stuttgart has shown me the usefulness of these skills in an actual research environment. As a Librarian and as a Consultant at Boston University, I have gained valuable experience supervising staff members, working directly with students and professors, and choosing and instructing departments on new reference procedures. I have also achieved expertise in the following areas: Microsoft Word and WordPerfect software, automated library reference networks, copying, and filing.

I would welcome the opportunity to work at Any Library. While I have enjoyed my time at Boston University, I am eager to put my skills to work in a nonacademic environment.

Enclosed please find a copy of my resume, which summarizes my qualifications. I will be glad to furnish any additional information that you desire, and you may reach me at (617) 555-5555 to discuss opportunities. I look forward to speaking with you.

Thank you very much for your consideration.

Sincerely,

Chris Smith

Enc. Resume

Manufacturer

178 Green Street
Little Compton, RI 02837
(401) 555-5555

August 27, 20--

Pat Cummings
Personnel Manager
Any Corporation
1140 Main Street
Chicago, IL 60605

Dear Ms. Cummings:

During the past fourteen years, my experience has been in all phases of custom casework and millwork manufacturing. Currently, I am investigating new opportunities in the Chicago area where my family and I are planning permanent relocation.

The enclosed resume summarizes my background and experience in the areas cited above. I am highly motivated, profit-oriented, and recognized for my ability to direct a manufacturing function and produce quality goods within cost-budget and time schedules.

I am very much interested in joining your organization, and am currently available for interviews. I will call you on Wednesday, September 6, to confirm that you received my resume and to answer any questions you might have.

Sincerely,

Chris Smith

Enc. Resume

Marketing/Development Executive

178 Green Street
Troy, MI 48098
(313) 555-5555

June 14, 20--

Pat Cummings
Staff Manager
Any Corporation
1140 Main Street
Grand Rapids, MI 49503

Dear Ms. Cummings:

During twenty years of employment with major corporations such as Peters and Miller, B.K. Murphy Company, and Bennett Trade Company, I played a key role in both marketing and the development/introduction of new product lines at national and regional levels.

Currently, I am seeking a new position in which I can utilize my marketing expertise to provide planning and support to a chief executive officer or general manager with marketing responsibility.

The enclosed business profile summarizes my experience in the development, marketing, and sale of food and nonfood products for domestic, overseas, and military markets. I am very much interested in your company and its products and would welcome the opportunity to meet with you at your convenience. In the interim, should you require additional information, please do not hesitate to contact me.

Sincerely,

Chris Smith

Enc. Business profile

Marketing Intern

178 Green Street
Augusta, GA 30901
(706) 555-5555

July 21, 20--

Pat Cummings
Personnel Director
Any Corporation
1140 Main Street
Detroit, MI 48226

Dear Mr. Cummings:

My interest in a marketing internship with your reputable firm has prompted me to forward my resume for your review.

As a fourth-year student and candidate for a Bachelor of Arts degree in Marketing, I am looking for an opportunity to develop my skills in marketing and product management. In return, I offer academic marketing experience, superb written and verbal communication skills, and a keen desire to learn the ins and outs of the marketing business.

I will call your office the week of July 24 to schedule an interview. Thank you for your consideration, and I look forward to speaking with you.

Yours sincerely,

Chris Smith

Enc. Resume

Mechanical Engineer

178 Green Street
Laconia, NH 03102
(603) 555-5555

January 6, 20--

Pat Cummings
Recruitment Officer
Any Corporation
1140 Main Street
Newark, NJ 07101

Dear Mr. Cummings:

For more than twenty years, I have been actively involved in precision machining work encompassing the development of working prototypes, specialty machine building/design, and precision tool/die production for high-speed equipment.

My work is diverse and challenging, requiring talent and technical skill to evaluate needs and solve complex problems. While I have been challenged by my previous experiences, I would like now to join a professional group where I can concentrate my skills on the design and development of prototypes and models for projects on the leading edge of discovery.

I have hands-on experience with the use, maintenance, and programming of all types of mechanical and hydraulic equipment used in precision machining, and can provide you with the quality work necessary for your purposes. The enclosed resume summarizes the details of my education and experience. Should you have any questions, please contact me at the above address or phone. I plan to make a follow-up call on January 16. Perhaps we can set up an appointment for an interview at that time?

I look forward to your return response.

Yours sincerely,

Chris Smith

Enc. Resume

Multimedia Manager

178 Green Street
Cinnaminson, NJ 08077
(609) 555-5555

November 1, 20--

Pat Cummings
Hiring Director
Any Corporation
1140 Main Street
Chicago, IL 60605

Dear Ms. Cummings:

As a member of the Newark Computer Society, I have followed with interest Any Corporation's growth and innovation in the field of multimedia technology. I am currently conducting a job search in the Chicago area, and would like to apply for a position within your management structure.

During the past fourteen years, my experience has ranged from Senior Auditor with Keane & Co. Peripherals to my current position as Vice President/Controller of a $90 million, multiplant CD-ROM manufacturing operation. I believe that my expertise and entrepreneurial insight can be utilized to the advantage of a growing enterprise with a need for effective and efficient financial management and cost control.

If your company can use a profit-oriented and financially astute executive, I would like to discuss my qualifications with you during a personal interview. Thank you for your time and consideration.

Sincerely,

Chris Smith

Enc. Resume

Mutual Funds Broker

178 Green Street
Honolulu, HI 96813
(808) 555-5555

April 14, 20--

Pat Cummings
Controller
Any Corporation
1140 Main Street
Chicago, IL 60611

Dear Mr. Cummings:

I am writing to inquire about employment opportunities within your organization, which, according to *Money Managers' Report*, is the fastest-growing mutual funds broker in the country.

I have been involved in the brokerage business for the better part of the last twenty years. On "Black Monday" I solidified a $1 million lease in the largest mall in the West, and then consummated the agreement during one of the worst economic scares since the Great Depression of the 1930s. I am the only private broker to raise construction money from Warga Property Investors, the top-grossing real estate trust in the world.

I am a highly motivated and principled professional who knows that her energy level, expertise, and commitment to success will produce results. I would be interested in meeting with you to discuss your current or anticipated needs in terms of my qualifications and career objectives. I will contact your office in the coming weeks to schedule an interview.

Thank you for your consideration.

Sincerely,

Chris Smith

Enc. Resume

178 Green Street
Trenton, NJ 08618
(609) 555-5555

April 3, 20--

Pat Cummings
Human Resources Coordinator
Any Hospital
1140 Main Street
Trenton, NJ 08618

Dear Mr. Cummings:

As a recent graduate of the New Jersey Medical Center School of Nurse Anesthesia, I am anxious to explore the possibility of a position within your anesthesia department. My resume is enclosed for your review.

In addition to technical academic coursework and extensive exposure to the administration of anesthetics during all surgical specialties, I have six years of professional experience in med/surg and SICU nursing. Early on, I established, and continue to maintain, an excellent record for dedication, quality of direct patient care, and clinical interface with multidisciplinary health care systems.

I offer a strong work ethic combining flexibility, reliability, and stamina. I consider myself a professional dedicated to providing patients with the highest quality of health care throughout the treatment and recovery processes.

I will call you within the week to schedule a mutually convenient time to meet. Thank you for your consideration.

Sincerely,

Chris Smith

Enc. Resume

Office Manager

178 Green Street
Kingsport, TN 37660

January 11, 20--

Pat Cummings
Director of Human Resources
Any Corporation
1140 Main Street
Yukon, MO 65589

Dear Mr. Cummings:

My interest in associating with an established firm such as Any Corporation has prompted me to forward my resume, which briefly summarizes my experience in office and departmental management.

As Office/Department Manager at Kimco, I was responsible for directing and coordinating the activities of accounting and support personnel in a $10 million manufacturing operation. I concurrently managed the cutting room and handled the purchasing of approximately $5 million in raw materials, supplies, and capital equipment used in manufacturing, sales, and distribution of branded and private label products through mass merchandisers.

This position required entrepreneurial skills and the capability to "wear many hats" in a small, active manufacturing operation. During my six years at Kimco, the company nearly doubled its profits and was able to expand its staff by 15 percent.

I would appreciate the opportunity to discuss, on a one-on-one basis, openings within your company. I can be reached at the above address or by phone at (615) 555-5555. If I do not receive a response, I will call within a few days to arrange a mutually convenient meeting time.

Sincerely,

Chris Smith

Enc. Resume

178 Green Street
Santa Ana, CA 97201
(714) 555-5555

April 10, 20--

Pat Cummings
Staff Director
Any Corporation
1140 Main Street
St. Petersburg, FL 35701

Dear Mr. Cummings:

I am presently searching for a position at the decision-making level in areas of customer service/sales support. I read about Any Corporation's recent expansion in this month's *Investing Now,* and am interested in exploring employment opportunities at your firm.

Please note that my fifteen years of broad-based management experience encompasses a full range of customer service functions. Most recently my talents were put to use as Customer Service Manager for a well-established and growing computer service company providing computer systems, time-sharing business application programs, software packages, and associated support services on an international level. My intensive experience in sophisticated aspects of customer support management includes on-site training of front-line staff and management in diverse computer business and manufacturing applications, and associated sales support activities. I am willing to relocate for the right opportunity.

I would like to arrange a mutually convenient time for a meeting, during which we may further discuss your current or anticipated needs. I will call your office next week to schedule an interview.

Thank you for your consideration.

Sincerely,

Chris Smith

Enc. Resume

Pharmacy Director

178 Green Street
Santa Clara, CA 95053

June 22, 20--

Pat Cummings
Director, Health Care Services
Any Corporation
1140 Main Street
Colorado Springs, CO 80903

Dear Ms. Cummings:

As Assistant Director of Pharmacy with a high-volume, forty-store chain, I have the management and sales expertise necessary to deal with multidisciplinary health care professionals as a member of your management team.

In addition to holding a Bachelor of Science degree in Pharmacy, I am a Registered Pharmacist with eight years of progressively responsible experience encompassing general management and in-house and field sales experience in a rapid growth environment.

I am well versed in regulations controlling therapeutic drug treatment, have sound knowledge of medical terminology, work well in either an independent setting or team effort, and enjoy both the clinical and nonclinical aspects of working with health care products and/or services. Based on my experience and professional credentials, I consider myself well qualified to handle the responsibilities of a management position at your company.

I hope to hear from you to schedule a personal interview at your convenience. I can be reached at the above address or at (408) 555-5555 from 9 A.M. to 5 P.M. weekdays or at (408) 555-4444 on weekends. I am willing to relocate for the right professional challenge and compensation package.

Sincerely,

Chris Smith

Enc. Resume

178 Green Street
Athens, GA 30601
(404) 555-5555

May 29, 20--

Pat Cummings
Manager, Production Department
Any Corporation
1140 Main Street
Atlanta, GA 30340

Dear Ms. Cummings:

My interest in a position in printing or related areas of graphic arts prompts me to forward my resume for your review.

During the past six years, I have been employed with a major insurance company where I rapidly advanced from an entry-level position to Operator of a Xerox 9900 printing system. This experience, combined with my formal education in graphic arts, college-level courses in business administration, and experience in various areas of retail business operations, has equipped me with a sound and varied background. I am confident of my ability to make a creative and productive contribution as a member of your publications and training department.

I will be spending the week of July 29 to August 4 in your area prior to permanent relocation. I hope to meet with you during my visit, and would like to hear from you to set a convenient time and date for an interview. At that time, we will have the opportunity to discuss your requirements and my ability to handle the responsibilities of a position at Any Corporation.

I look forward to your return response.

Sincerely,

Chris Smith

Enc. Resume

Property Manager

178 Green Street
Mill Valley, CA 94941
(415) 555-5555

May 19, 20--

Pat Cummings
Personnel Director
Any Corporation
1140 Main Street
Fresno, CA 93786

Dear Mr. Cummings:

I am writing to investigate opportunities in which I could apply my skills in property management and real estate investments with your company's holdings.

As you will note from the enclosed resume, I have more than fifteen years of experience in general property management, including both residential and commercial properties. During the past five years, I have headed an absentee-owner property management company that has grown from 400 to 750 units while maintaining a vacancy rate below 5 percent. I offer a thorough knowledge of all aspects of property management, from locating, negotiating, and acquiring property through leasing, maintenance, and financial management.

I strongly believe my qualifications would prove to be an asset to Any Corporation. I would greatly appreciate the opportunity to present my skills in a personal interview.

Thank you for your time and consideration.

Sincerely,

Chris Smith

Enc. Resume

Public Relations Assistant

178 Green Street
Wheatland, ND 58079
(701) 555-5555

September 10, 20--

Pat Cummings
Vice President, Human Resources
Any Public Relations
1140 Main Street
Los Angeles, CA 90053

Dear Ms. Cummings:

Please accept the enclosed copy of my resume as a preliminary application for a position with Any Public Relations.

In addition to my degree in Journalism and Public Relations, I have four years of experience working with a modeling/talent agency and modeling school. In both the teaching and model recruitment/placement environments, I have worked with key accounts in areas where image building and high visibility for client services and/or products were the ultimate objectives. Through activities which included the selection and placement of models for union and nonunion television commercials, I honed my abilities to coordinate creative programs and innovative functions involving clients and the general public. As a result, I feel confident that I could successfully apply my experience to a position in your firm.

I will be in the Los Angeles area at the end of the month and will call your office during the week of September 25. I look forward to talking with you.

Sincerely,

Chris Smith

Enc. Resume

Real Estate Banker

178 Green Street
Sunnyvale, CA 94088
(408) 555-5555

August 3, 20--

Pat Cummings
Associate Director
Any Bank
1140 Main Street
Newtown Square, PA 19093

Dear Ms. Cummings:

I am interested in exploring opportunities within the real estate investment/mortgage lending department of Any Bank. Should you be in need of someone with my qualifications, I would be eager to lend assistance to your organization.

In addition to a Bachelor of Science degree in Management with a major in Finance and a real estate sales license, I have diverse experience in positions that have required strong communication and interpersonal skills in dealing with associates, customers, and personnel. My current position as Portfolio Administrator/Fund Accountant is diverse and detailed; however, I am interested in applying my financial background to areas involving new business development and account administration.

I am confident that my skills and abilities could benefit Any Bank. I would appreciate the opportunity to talk with you regarding suitable opportunities within your organization.

Sincerely,

Chris Smith

Enc. Resume

Repair Technician

178 Green Street
Sioux Falls, SD 57105
(605) 555-5555

January 29, 20--

Pat Cummings
Repair Maintenance Operator
Any Corporation
1140 Main Street
Salt Lake City, UT 84111

Dear Mr. Cummings:

Please accept the enclosed resume as an expressed interest in exploring employment opportunities available in the repair and maintenance division of Any Corporation.

I have acquired training and extensive experience in the installation and repair of various heating, electrical, and power systems for commercial, industrial, and residential properties. My employment has required that I develop proficiency in the fabrication of plumbing systems and in the coordination of repair service for equipment malfunctions. In various management capabilities, I have facilitated all administrative and fiscal operations for service companies, in addition to managing personnel. I possess exceptional communication, leadership, and troubleshooting skills. In response to an increasingly multicultural industry, I have acquired fluency in Portuguese and conversational abilities in Spanish and French. I feel that my accomplishments have prepared me to assume the responsibilities demanded at Any Corporation.

I would welcome the opportunity to meet with you and discuss ways in which my capabilities could be guided to suit your needs. Please consider the enclosed resume and direct your response to the above address or telephone number. I will follow up this correspondence with a phone call early next week.

I look forward to speaking with you in the near future. Thank you for your time.

With best regards,

Chris Smith

Enc. Resume

Research Assistant

178 Green Street
Manchester, NH 03104
(603) 555-5555

July 31, 20--

Pat Cummings
Human Resources Director
Any Bank
1140 Main Street
Chicago, IL 60605

Dear Ms. Cummings:

Having majored in Mathematics at Rice University, where I also worked as a Research Assistant, I am confident that I would make a successful addition to your economics research department.

In addition to my strong background in mathematics, I offer significant business experience, having worked in a data processing firm, a bookstore, and a restaurant. I am sure that my courses in statistics and computer programming will prove particularly useful in an entry-level position.

I am attracted to Any Bank by your recent rapid growth and the superior reputation of your economic research department. After studying different commercial banks, I have concluded that Any Bank will be in a strong competitive position to benefit from upcoming changes in the industry.

I would like to interview with you at your earliest convenience.

Sincerely,

Chris Smith

Enc. Resume

Retail Salesperson

178 Green Street
Cherry Fork, OH 95618
(513) 555-5555

July 21, 20--

Pat Cummings
Hiring Manager
Any Corporation
1140 Main Street
Cincinnati, OH 45202

Dear Ms. Cummings:

During the past three years as a Sales Representative with Fits Like a Glove, Inc., I have successfully sold to and serviced retail accounts throughout the Midwest. In this capacity, I established a record for the development of new business and solid client relationships which have generated additional customers and referrals. In addition, as principal owner of a retail establishment, I managed all areas of independent department store operations specializing in family ready-to-wear accessories, athletic wear, and athletic footwear and equipment.

Currently I am looking for a new opportunity where I can utilize my sales, merchandising, management, and communications skills to contribute to the efficiency and bottom-line results of a firm providing quality products and service to a diverse consumer population or dealer network.

Among retailers, Any Corporation's name emerges as the industry leader with respect to aggressive sales techniques. I feel that I can play a valuable role in such an environment.

My resume is enclosed for your review. In the near future, I will call your office to schedule an interview. Thank you for your consideration and I look forward to speaking with you.

Sincerely,

Chris Smith

Enc. Resume

Sales Executive

178 Green Street
Beetown, WI 53802

June 6, 20--

Pat Cummings
Staff Coordinator
Any Corporation
1140 Main Street
Milwaukee, WI 53201

Dear Mr. Cummings:

Your firm has been brought to my attention as one that can provide the challenge, diversification, and stability I am looking for in a company.

For more than fifteen years, I have held progressively more responsible jobs selling industrial and agricultural chemicals, pharmaceuticals, and related products with a multinational manufacturer and distributor. I am an effective time-and-territory manager, have sound knowledge of sales techniques and strategies, and have been successful in new business and marketing development in every position I have held to date.

The enclosed resume summarizes my background and experience. While I am interested in permanent relocation to your area, I am also willing to travel.

I am highly productive, profit oriented, and cost conscious, and can contribute much to increasing your share of the market. I feel that a meeting, at your convenience, could be mutually beneficial. I can be reached at the above address or by phone at (414) 555-5555.

Yours sincerely,

Chris Smith

Enc. Resume

178 Green Street
Hartford, CT 06120
(203) 555-5555

July 14, 20--

Pat Cummings
Superintendent
Any Public School System
1140 Main Street
Bridgeport, CT 06604

Dear Dr. Cummings:

During the past twelve years as Principal of Murray Central High School, I have had the opportunity to provide leadership in a multiracial, multilingual urban high school during a complex, volatile era. Please accept the enclosed resume as an application for an administrative position with the Any Public School System.

My positions with the Murray School System have been challenging and have provided a setting in which I have been able to develop a variety of new programs as well as implement existing programs to create a winning tradition of academic excellence. My primary purpose has always been to motivate students toward educational excellence, higher education, improved self-image, and job preparedness.

In my years with Murray Central High, I have achieved the goals I projected for the school, students, parents, and business and residential communities. Now, I am ready for a change to a school system where I can once again provide the leadership needed to uphold and strengthen educational standards while achieving desired objectives. With my background, experience, proven leadership skills, and dedication to quality education, I am well qualified and prepared to make the same commitment to the Any Public School System.

The enclosed professional profile is a summary of my experience. I look forward to the opportunity to discuss, in further detail, my educational philosophy, my ability to fill your requirements, and why I am qualified for an administrative position with the Any Public School System. I anxiously await your response.

Yours sincerely,

Chris Smith

Enc. Professional profile

178 Green Street
Fort Worth, TX 76114
(817) 555-5555

March 17, 20--

Pat Cummings
Director, Mental Health Services
Any Center
1140 Main Street
Dallas, TX 75206

Dear Ms. Cummings:

My involvement with a number of local counseling centers has given me the opportunity to become familiar with Any Center's work. My observation of your facility and its staff has confirmed my desire to join your organization in a counseling or group leadership capacity.

For the past fifteen years, my experience has ranged from Mental Health Aide to Peer Counselor and Group Leader working with alcoholics, drug abusers, and mentally/emotionally disabled adults. I am a candidate for a Master's degree in Counseling/Psychology, and am well trained in alcohol/substance abuse counseling and the provision of related health care services to individuals and/or groups at all age levels.

I am very interested in joining your staff. I will call your office next week to schedule an interview at your convenience.

Yours sincerely,

Chris Smith

Enc. Resume

178 Green Street
Great Falls, MT 59403
(406) 555-5555

July 3, 20--

Pat Cummings
Director, Human Services
Any Corporation
1140 Main Street
Billings, MT 59107

Dear Mr. Cummings:

My interest in continuing my professional career as a clinical social worker in the geriatric area of human services has prompted me to forward my resume for your consideration.

In addition to graduate work, licenses, and registration in the field of social work, I have nine years of professional experience ranging from Psychiatric Caseworker to Clinical/Research Social Worker at Worthy Hospital. Recently, I conducted research and coauthored a publication on geriatrics, an undertaking that has focused my interest on the problems of aging and the older adult population.

I would appreciate meeting with you for further discussion after you review my qualifications. In the interim, please feel free to contact me if you have any questions.

I look forward to learning more about Any Corporation.

Sincerely yours,

Chris Smith

Enc. Resume

Social Worker
Medical

178 Green Street
Geneseo, NY 14454
(716) 555-5555

April 2, 20--

Pat Cummings
Outreach Director
Any Hospital
1140 Main Street
Oneonta, NY 13820

Dear Ms. Cummings:

I am a newly Licensed Medical Social Worker investigating new opportunities in which to apply my education and experience. I am capable of working independently or as a member of a team, and I feel confident in my ability to handle the responsibilities of the position and to provide quality performance in any assignment I undertake.

In addition, I offer excellent administrative and clinical experience and am anxious to put my skills to work for Any Hospital. With that in mind, I enclose my resume for your consideration.

I look forward to your immediate reply.

Sincerely,

Chris Smith

Enc. Resume

Telemarketer

178 Green Street
Juneau, AK 99801
(907) 555-5555

February 23, 20--

Pat Cummings
Director, Marketing
Any Corporation
1140 Main Street
Anchorage, AK 99514

Dear Mr. Cummings:

I am a highly motivated individual with a proven sales record who is interested in securing a challenging telemarketing position. I have enclosed my resume for your consideration.

During the past ten years, I have been employed as a Telemarketer selling sophisticated products and services to hospitals, clinics, and medical professionals, as well as filtration systems to end-users. During this time, I have successfully increased company sales by 40 percent and have established an impressive customer base. I possess extensive telephone and interpersonal skills, and am proficient with all aspects of office operations, including dBase Plus and Lotus 1-2-3 computer applications.

I feel confident that my experience can be successfully applied to a telemarketing position at Any Corporation. I will call your office next week to discuss this matter further.

Yours sincerely,

Chris Smith

Enc. Resume

Textile Specialist

178 Green Street
Bloomington, IN 47405
(812) 555-5555

April 18, 20--

Pat Cummings
Vice President, Human Resources
Any Corporation
1140 Main Street
Chicago, IL 60601

Dear Mr. Cummings:

During my successful career in textiles, I have advanced to such positions as Director of Wool Procurement for an international corporation and Senior Vice President of a national profit trading center. These responsible positions have provided me with the administrative and management expertise to contribute to the efficiency, growth, and profitability of Any Corporation.

I possess extensive experience in trading, sourcing, and purchasing, as well as new market and business development, import/export coordination, and profit center management. Although my current position has been challenging and rewarding, my decision to relocate permanently to Chicago makes it necessary for me to seek new opportunities with a company, such as yours, that can utilize the full scope of my experience in order to achieve mutual objectives.

I have enclosed a resume for your consideration. As of May 1, I will be residing in Chicago and will be available for an interview at your convenience. I will make a follow-up phone call next Monday (April 24) to schedule a meeting time.

Sincerely,

Chris Smith

Enc. Resume

Underwriter

178 Green Street
Syracuse, NY 13221

April 10, 20--

Pat Cummings
Senior Claims Adjuster
Any Corporation
1140 Main Street
New York, NY 10010

Dear Ms. Cummings:

Currently, I am seeking new opportunities with an underwriter or corporate liability insurance department in which there is a need for expertise in claims settlement.

During the past ten years, my experience in the liability insurance field has ranged from Transcriber to Senior Field Claims Representative. My skills include fact-finding analysis and negotiating settlements, both of which demand strong training and management skills.

The enclosed resume summarizes my background in the areas I have cited above. I am very much interested in Any Corporation and would be glad to furnish you with additional information during a personal interview. I can be reached at the above address or by phone at (315) 555-5555.

Thank you for your consideration.

Sincerely yours,

Chris Smith

Enc. Resume

Upper-Level Manager
Accounting

178 Green Street
Giants Pass, OR 97526
(503) 555-5555

October 21, 20--

Pat Cummings
Controller
Any Corporation
1140 Main Street
Boston, MA 02101

Dear Mr. Cummings:

In the interest of investigating career opportunities with Any Corporation, I am enclosing my resume for your review.

As you can see, my proven record of achievement has led to rapid promotions. During the past fourteen years, my experience has ranged from Senior Auditor with Hans Anderson and Company, Public Accountant, to Controller and, subsequently, Vice President of a $50 million multiplant manufacturing operation.

These positions have been fast-paced, challenging, and broad in scope, requiring strong financial and strategic planning capabilities. I am a CPA with the ability to recognize, troubleshoot, and resolve financial and administrative problems. I feel that my experience and entrepreneurial insight can be utilized to the advantage of a growing enterprise with a need for effective and efficient financial management and cost control.

If your company can use a profit-oriented and financially astute executive, I would like to discuss my qualifications with you during a personal interview. I can be reached at (503) 555-5555, at which time I will be glad to provide you with additional information.

Thank you for your time and consideration.

Sincerely,

Chris Smith

Enc. Resume

Accounting Manager

178 Green Street
Hazelwood, MO 63042
(606) 555-5555

July 18, 20--

Pat Cummings
Director
Any Employment Agency
1140 Main Street
Bridgeton, MO 63042

Dear Ms. Cummings:

The enclosed resume outlines my diverse experience in accounting and finance management. I am in search of an appropriate opportunity in the greater St. Louis area.

The following are some of the strengths and capabilities that I can bring to a position:

- Solid understanding of financial statement preparation and review.
- Proficiency at budget preparation and various written analyses.
- Proven ability to organize department goals to meet overall corporate goals.
- Competency in terms of resource management, including people and systems.
- Strong leadership qualities including upgrading and motivating staff resources.

I would welcome the opportunity to meet with you to discuss my background and credentials. Thank you for your time and consideration.

Sincerely,

Chris Smith

Enc. Resume

Administrative Assistant

178 Green Street
Madison, WI 53706

July 17, 20--

Pat Cummings
Representative
Any Employment Agency
1140 Main Street
Milwaukee, WI 53201

Dear Mr. Cummings:

I am searching for an administrative position in the real estate, international finance, or import/export industry. Such a position seems a good match for my education and achievements, as well as my career interests.

As a B.A. graduate of the University of Wisconsin's School of Business, I have been thoroughly educated in all aspects of the business environment. In addition, I consider myself a highly motivated and ambitious person. While pursuing my academic studies, I was accepted into and participated in the University Study Abroad Program in Tokyo, Japan.

I am interested in pursuing a full-time, entry-level position that would allow me to utilize my computer, administrative, and finance skills, as well as my interests in real estate and travel. I would be willing to relocate, given a salary range of $22,000 to $28,000.

I would appreciate consideration for any suitable opportunities. You can contact me between 8 A.M. and 6 P.M. weekdays at (608) 555-5555.

Thank you for your consideration.

Sincerely,

Chris Smith

Enc. Resume

Advertising/Graphic Design Assistant

178 Green Street
Topeka, KS 66612

April 18, 20--

Pat Cummings
Director
Any Employment Agency
1140 Main Street
St. Paul, MN 55401

Dear Ms. Cummings:

    I am writing with the hope that one of your clients in the field of Advertising/Graphic Design is in need of an entry-level assistant.

    I possess strong verbal and written communication skills and pay close attention to detail, while maintaining a flair for creativity. I feel that I am a well-disciplined, highly motivated person with a strong desire to succeed in Advertising/Graphic Design. To support my enthusiasm, I possess excellent PC and Macintosh computer skills and a typing speed of 55 wpm.

    Thank you in advance for reviewing the enclosed resume. I would be happy to further discuss my experience and qualifications with you in person. Please feel free to contact me at (913) 555-5555 if I can be of further assistance. Once again, thank you for your consideration.

Sincerely,

Chris Smith

Enc. Resume

Claims Processor

178 Green Street
Tarrytown, NY 10591

December 4, 20--

Pat Cummings
Employment Specialist
Any Employment Agency
1140 Main Street
Bronx, NY 10474

Dear Mr. Cummings:

My interest in securing a position of Claims Processor with one of your client companies has prompted me to forward my resume for your review.

In addition to six years of experience as Home Health Aide, In-patient Claims Representative, and, since 20--, Medical Assistant with Marifield Rehabilitation Hospital, I have sound knowledge of medical terminology, procedure codes, and medical office systems, including related computerized applications. I possess an Associate's degree in Sociology, have trained as a Medical Assistant, and am currently a candidate for an Associate's degree in Nursing.

My career objective is to further develop my medical and support skills in areas that will give me the opportunity to contribute to the quality and efficiency of health care. My salary is negotiable, depending on the opportunity.

Should you require additional information, please contact me at the above address or by phone at (914) 555-5555. I can be available for a meeting at your convenience.

Thank you for your consideration.

Sincerely,

Chris Smith

Enc. Resume

Computer Operations Supervisor

178 Green Street
Sinking Spring, PA 19608
(215) 555-5555

July 14, 20--

Pat Cummings
Associate
Any Employment Agency
1140 Main Street
Lancaster, PA 17605

Dear Ms. Cummings:

During the past several years, I have gained broad-based experience in data communications, telecommunications, and personnel supervision with major information resource corporations. Presently, I am looking for a new position that will allow me to combine my computer science and supervisory skills.

Should you be aware of any suitable opportunities, please contact me. I look forward to hearing from you.

Sincerely,

Chris Smith

Enc. Resume

178 Green Street
Sioux Falls, SD 57117
(605) 555-5555

April 5, 20--

Pat Cummings
Director
Any Employment Agency
1140 Main Street
Dayton, OH 45402

Dear Mr. Cummings:

I will be moving to the Dayton area next month, and would like to submit my qualifications for any suitable opportunities available through your agency.

I am an accomplished cook with experience in a wide variety of food service institutions, including restaurants, catering services, and banquet functions. My areas of expertise include all aspects of food preparation, from ordering ingredients to presentation.

As you can see from my enclosed resume, I most recently worked as a Rounds Cook at the McGuiness Inn. In addition to cooking to order, I performed several supervisory duties, such as scheduling shifts, overseeing inventory control, and troubleshooting problems.

I will be visiting Dayton to secure housing arrangements during the week of April 17–23. I would be available to meet with you or a client within this time frame. In the interim, I will call your office next week to see if I can provide you with any additional information.

Thank you in advance for your consideration.

Sincerely,

Chris Smith

Enc. Resume

Cosmetologist

178 Green Street
Arlington, TX 76015

March 4, 20--

Pat Cummings
Associate
Any Employment Agency
1140 Main Street
Fort Worth, TX 76110

Dear Ms. Cummings:

Please accept the enclosed resume as my expressed interest in obtaining your job search assistance.

For the past twenty years, I have been employed in the field of cosmetology, in positions ranging from Hairdresser and Instructor to Owner/Operator of my own salon. I possess a valid cosmetology license and have completed several courses in related subjects. I am thoroughly trained in:

- Instruction of all levels of cosmetology theory and practical applications.
- Store promotions and customer relations.
- Hairdressing, permanents, and hair coloring.
- Manicuring, skin care, and facials.

I am currently investigating opportunities that will allow me to apply these skills in either a training school or salon setting. I would greatly appreciate any assistance you could provide in identifying area employers who might be looking for a professional with my qualifications.

My resume is enclosed. Please feel free to contact me at (817) 555-5555. Thank you.

Sincerely,

Chris Smith

Enc. Resume

Director of Operations

178 Green Street
Dallas, TX 75240

July 26, 20--

Pat Cummings
Director
Any Employment Agency
1140 Main Street
Houston, TX 77251

Dear Ms. Cummings:

If one of your client companies is in need of a person who can handle the day-to-day details necessary to ensure a smooth operation, then we have good reason to meet.

During the past twelve years my experience has ranged from Credit and Collection Manager with a high-tech company to Service Coordinator with a manufacturer of sophisticated medical systems. In these capacities, I provided detailed administrative support to senior-level managers, field service engineers, and other department personnel.

I am currently contemplating a change and would like to be considered for a position with a progressive management team. I have expertise in complex manual- and computer-generated reports, work well independently or as a member of a team, and have extensive troubleshooting, problem-solving, customer service, interpersonal, and communication skills.

Should my qualifications meet the needs of a client, I would be happy to learn of the opportunity. Please note, I am available for immediate, full-time work. I can be reached at (214) 555-5555.

I hope to hear from you soon.

Sincerely,

Chris Smith

Enc. Resume

Executive Assistant

178 Green Street
Mobile, AL 36625
(203) 555-5555

July 18, 20--

Pat Cummings
Associate
Any Employment Agency
1140 Main Street
Birmingham, AL 25202

Dear Ms. Cummings:

    I am an experienced Executive/Administrative Assistant seeking appropriate career opportunities in the corporate arena.

    In addition to five years of staff experience at Bradstreet and Associates, I have worked for three years as an Executive Assistant to the President and Executive Vice President of a software development company. In that capacity, my responsibilities included a variety of assignments, both individual and team projects, writing and typing executive correspondence, and other administrative activities. My word processing and spreadsheet expertise includes Microsoft Word for Windows, Lotus 1-2-3, and Excel, and my technical background enables me to quickly develop expertise in other similar software programs. I am an organized, detail-oriented individual who enjoys staff projects and produces high-quality work. My resume is enclosed.

    Should your client needs and my experience prove to be a good match, I would welcome an opportunity to meet with you.

Sincerely,

Chris Smith

Enc. Resume

Housekeeper

178 Green Street
Melrose Park, IL 60160

March 27, 20--

Pat Cummings
Associate
Any Employment Agency
1140 Main Street
Twin Falls, ID 83303

Dear Ms. Cummings:

My interest in securing a position in housekeeping or related support activities has prompted me to forward my resume for your review.

During the past seven years, my experience has been concentrated in housekeeping and related nonclinical services with a quality professional nursing home operation. I enjoy working with people in a professional or resort environment and feel confident that I can make a contribution, as a member of the housekeeping staff, to the quality image an institution would like to uphold.

I will be spending a week, from April 29 to May 5, with family in your area prior to permanent relocation. I would welcome the opportunity to meet with you or one of your clients at that time.

If I can provide you with additional information, please contact me at the above address or by phone at (312) 555-5555.

Thank you for your consideration.

Sincerely,

Chris Smith

Enc. Resume

Insurance Account Manager

178 Green Street
Las Cruces, NM 88003

October 7, 20--

Pat Cummings
President
Any Employment Agency
1140 Main Street
Albuquerque, NM 87103

Dear Mr. Cummings:

As per your request during our recent conversation, I am enclosing my business profile for your review and for submission to one of your client firms.

My experience as an Account Manager and Office Manager has provided me with expertise in all facets of insurance agency operation. Once oriented to the policies of a new firm, I have the knowledge and skill to assume responsibility for either of the above positions.

Any assistance you can provide in arranging interviews with prospective employers will be most appreciated. Should you require additional information prior to our meeting, please contact me at the address listed above or call me at (505) 555-5555.

Sincerely,

Chris Smith

Enc. Business profile

Insurance Underwriter

178 Green Street
Flandreau, SD 57028

March 4, 20--

Pat Cummings
Director
Any Corporation
1140 Main Street
Chicago, IL 60605

Dear Ms. Cummings:

    During the past ten years, my experience has been in the liability insurance field in positions ranging from Transcriber to Senior Field Claims Representative. Currently, I am seeking a new association with an underwriter or a corporate liability insurance department in which there is a need for expertise in claims settlement, from fact-finding analysis to negotiation.

    I am hoping that among your many clients there may be one or two who are looking for someone who is knowledgeable in the area of corporate liability insurance; if so, I would like to explore the opportunity. I may be reached at (605) 555-5555 during regular business hours or evenings at (605) 555-4444.

    I look forward to hearing from you.

Sincerely,

Chris Smith

Enc. Resume

178 Green Street
Jacksonville, FL 32203

August 7, 20--

Pat Cummings
Partner
Any Employment Agency
1140 Main Street
Tallahassee, FL 32302

Dear Mr. Cummings:

I would like to be considered for a court- or legal-related administrative position with any appropriate clients you may serve. I have recently relocated to Florida from the Washington, D.C. area, and am seeking employment that would utilize my leadership skills, education, and experience.

In Washington, I was the Office Manager for a respected court-reporting firm. All of my primary job responsibilities required organization, attention to detail, writing, and significant computer skills. I have extensive experience working multitasking and in meeting deadlines in a team-oriented environment. As a result, I have developed strong time management and inter-personal skills.

I have enclosed my resume for your review. Should you need additional information, please do not hesitate to contact me at (904) 555-5555. I look forward to hearing from you. Thank you for your time.

Sincerely,

Chris Smith

Enc. Resume

Office Manager

178 Green Street
La France, SC 29656
(803) 555-5555

March 30, 20--

Pat Cummings
Associate
Any Employment Agency
1140 Main Street
Spartanburg, SC 29304

Dear Mr. Cummings:

Finding the right person for the job is often difficult, costly, and at times disappointing. However, if one of your clients is in need of a reliable, competent, and well-organized individual for his or her office management staff, I have the qualifications and dedication for the position.

During the past ten years, I have held progressively responsible positions in office management with manufacturing, distribution, export, and service companies. Recently, I made a permanent relocation to La France, and am interested in joining a company in the greater Spartanburg area that can benefit from my experience.

I have broad experience with manual and automated accounting/administrative systems, customer service, personnel supervision, event/meeting planning, credit and collection, and executive support. I function best in a diverse, busy environment and have established a reputation for being organized and capable of coordinating and handling multiple assignments cost-effectively and to schedule.

The enclosed business profile summarizes my qualifications. Should you know of any suitable opportunities, I would appreciate your consideration.

I look forward to hearing from you.

Sincerely,

Chris Smith

Enc. Business profile

Property Manager

178 Green Street
Salamanca, NY 14779
(716) 555-5555

May 13, 20--

Pat Cummings
Director
Any Corporation
1140 Main Street
Chicago, IL 60605

Dear Mr. Cummings:

In July of this year I will be permanently relocating to the Chicago area. I am forwarding the attached resume for your evaluation because of my desire to contribute my comprehensive experience in real estate/property management to a locally based company.

I have two years of direct experience involving all aspects of the management of 275 apartments and four commercial units in three buildings. My responsibilities include a range of activities, from advertising and promotion of apartments to competitive analysis of rate structures.

My experience also includes contractor negotiations, liaison with government and service agencies, personnel relations, financial management, and other functions basic to the effective management of complex properties.

If you know of any company with a current need for a bright, outgoing property manager with an orientation to sales, please do not hesitate to contact me.

Thank you for your consideration.

Sincerely,

Chris Smith

Enc. Resume

Quality Control Specialist

178 Green Street
South Bend, IN 46619

July 23, 20--

Pat Cummings
Director
Any Employment Agency
1140 Main Street
Memphis, TN 38109

Dear Mr. Cummings:

My interest in locating a position in quality control/quality assurance with a firm in the Memphis area has prompted me to forward this up-to-date resume for your review. I am planning permanent relocation to Tennessee in September and I would appreciate any assistance in finding a suitable employer.

My background includes a Bachelor of Science degree in Biology and Associate's degrees in Math and Science. I also have seventeen months of solid, hands-on experience as a Quality Control Analyst with a manufacturer of instrumentation for environmental analysis. My knowledge in these areas includes all current inspection systems, procedures, and equipment used to maintain standards to critical tolerance. I am certain of my ability to make an immediate, long-term contribution to my employer.

Please contact me at the above address or by phone at (219) 555-5555 if you know of any quality control vacancies or related positions. I look forward to hearing from you in the near future.

Sincerely,

Chris Smith

Enc. Resume

Sales/Customer Service Representative

178 Green Street
Trenton, NJ 08619
(609) 555-5555

November 4, 20--

Pat Cummings
Employment Representative
Any Employment Agency
1140 Main Street
Linwood, NJ 08221

Dear Mr. Cummings:

I am writing to inquire if your agency might be able to assist me in my search for a position in either sales or customer service.

As you can see from my enclosed resume, I have more than seven years of experience in positions ranging from Sales Assistant to Claims Investigator and Bank Teller. Some of my applicable skills include:

- Acting as liaison between customers, staff, and management.
- Investigating and resolving customer requests and problems.
- Tracking and expediting sales orders; ascertaining order accuracy.
- Processing a wide range of financial transactions; maintaining accuracy and balance.
- PC and Macintosh word processing; Lotus 1-2-3 and Excel.

I would be interested in discussing any employment opportunities you feel would be applicable to my skills. Please note that I am willing to travel, and negotiate a salary in the $28,000 to $35,000 range. Do not hesitate to contact me if you need any additional information.

I will follow up this inquiry with a phone call next week.

Sincerely,

Chris Smith

Enc. Resume

Secretary

178 Green Street
Clinton, MS 39060

January 18, 20--

Pat Cummings
Staff Associate
Any Employment Agency
1140 Main Street
St. Louis, MO 63122

Dear Ms. Cummings:

Enclosed please find my resume for your review regarding potential employment with your client community. I would be interested in a secretarial position where I could utilize my administrative and secretarial skills.

I have earned an Associate's degree in the Secretarial Program at Macomb Community College. In addition, my current tenure at Gaudet and Growney has afforded me the opportunity to further develop competent organizational and analytical skills. In the everyday operations of the department, the general merchandise manager relies on me to organize meetings and coordinate all communications to our ten-store chain. These responsibilities have enabled me to expand my general office skills.

Although my employment at Gaudet and Growney has been a positive experience, I am seeking a position that will offer more advancement opportunity.

I possess excellent secretarial and administrative skills. I have nine years of administrative experience working both in the merchandising department and in the executive offices of my current employer. I am also knowledgeable in a variety of software programs. My compensation requirements are in the $25,000 to $35,000 range, and I would be willing to relocate.

I would welcome the opportunity to speak with you regarding my qualifications. I can be reached at (601) 555-5555, ext. 226 (days), or (601) 555-4444 (evenings).

Thank you for your consideration.

Sincerely,

Chris Smith

Enc. Resume

178 Green Street
Minden, NV 89423

May 4, 20--

Pat Cummings
Director
Any Employment Agency
1140 Main Street
Las Vegas, NV 89125

Dear Mr. Cummings:

I understand that your agency provides job placement services in the greater Las Vegas area. Having recently moved here, I would greatly appreciate your assistance in securing a position.

For the past eight years, I have worked in the security industry as a Guard. My interest in this field developed from a position with the Willow Mead Art Museum in Wyoming. As a Security Guard at the museum, my duties included patrol, surveillance, and control of facilities and areas. I also maintained reports, records, and documents as required by administration.

For the past three years as a bank Security Guard, I was responsible for ensuring the safety and security of customers, bank employees, and bank assets. My compensation for that position was in the high $20,000 range.

I look forward to finding a similar position through your agency. I can begin work immediately. Please contact me to schedule interviews at (702) 555-5555.

Sincerely,

Chris Smith

Enc. Resume

Stenographer

178 Green Street
Troutdale, OR 97060
(503) 555-5555

January 3, 20--

Pat Cummings
Representative
Any Employment Agency
1140 Main Street
Portland, OR 97208

Dear Ms. Cummings:

Recently, a friend of mine, Sean Wilson, recommended your agency to assist me in my job search. I understand you successfully found Sean a clerical position last month. I am searching for a challenging position as a Stenographer, to which I could apply the following qualifications:

- Strong shorthand and speed-writing skills at 120 wpm.
- Expertise in Gregg Simplified and Diamond Jubilee methods; proficiency with the Pitman method.
- Experience in the transcription, editing, and interpreting of stenographic characters into clear, concise, and precise English.
- Typing skills that include word processing at 80 wpm.

My experience is supplemented by an Associate's degree in Secretarial Sciences and a certificate of accomplishment from the Executive Secretarial Program at Katherine Gibbs secretarial school.

I would prefer to stay in the greater Portland area, and would ask for a salary starting between $24,000 and $28,000. If you could provide me with any assistance in this regard, I would be most appreciative.

I look forward to hearing from you.

Sincerely,

Chris Smith

Enc. Resume

Waitperson

178 Green Street
Reston, VA 22091
(703) 555-5555

December 19, 20--

Pat Cummings
Representative
Any Employment Agency
1140 Main Street
Vienna, VA 22180

Dear Mr. Cummings:

I am searching for a challenging position in the fast-food industry in which work experience and a commitment to excellence will have valuable application.

Currently, I am working as a Server/Bartender for a 250-seat restaurant in Reston. In addition to my serving duties, I am responsible for register control, assistant shift supervision, and conflict resolution. I work well in both relaxed or fast-paced, high-pressure environments.

I would like to continue my career in food service upon my relocation to your area next month. If you should be aware of any available opportunities, I would appreciate your assistance. Until January 1, I can be reached at (215) 555-5555. After that date, I will be residing at the address and telephone number cited above.

Thank you for your time. I will be in contact soon to confirm that you have received this inquiry and attached resume.

Sincerely,

Chris Smith

Enc. Resume

Buyer

178 Green Street
Charleston, WV 25322
(304) 555-5555

March 7, 20--

Pat Cummings
Executive Recruiter
Any Company
1140 Main Street
Huntington, WV 25755

Dear Ms. Cummings:

I am a creative, innovative buyer who can add excitement to your clients' inventories while generating bottom-line profits.

During the past eighteen years, I have had the opportunity to work in positions ranging from Merchandise Planner to Head Buyer at the headquarters level of major off-price retail chains. I have enjoyed rapid advancement and experienced the challenge of coordinating new concepts and introducing change associated with upscale fashion and trends. Recently, my efforts generated a 75 percent increase in sales and profits.

Currently, I am looking for a new association with a growing chain that will benefit from my experience and successes in identifying fashion trends, developing resources, and negotiating big buys for off-price retail operations. The professional opportunity I am looking for will utilize my market and product knowledge and ingenuity to achieve the same results for your clients as I have for my current employer.

I am interested in positions with a salary range from $75,000 to $90,000 and will relocate for the right opportunity.

Since my current employer is unaware of my current search, your confidence is appreciated.

Sincerely,

Chris Smith

Enc. Resume

Corporate President

178 Green Street
Redmond, WA 98052
(206) 555-5555

December 24, 20--

Pat Cummings
Executive Recruiter
1140 Main Street
Seattle, WA 98103

Dear Mr. Cummings:

I have enclosed a business profile and request your consideration for any current or anticipated search assignments.

During the past twenty years, I have had the opportunity to apply innovative, leadership, and profit-making skills in positions ranging from President of a successful start-up business developed to $7 million in annual sales, to Vice President, Product Management/Business Development, with a $750 million rapid growth computer resale company.

My skill in undertaking new challenges, ability to implement change, and expertise in developing compatible, professional teams during the transition phases of acquisitions, mergers, and consolidations enables me to provide stability and profitability to growth situations. Presently, I am looking for a position change to a company where I have the responsibility for making meaningful decisions and the authority to implement plans to achieve corporate objectives.

My desire is to find an exciting, growth-oriented position. Thus, I would be willing to relocate to secure a salary in the $100,000 range.

Please contact me should my qualifications be of interest to one of your client firms. Thank you for your consideration.

Sincerely,

Chris Smith

Enc. Business profile

Engineering Administrator

178 Green Street
Lansdale, PA 19446

November 4, 20--

Pat Cummings
Executive Recruiter
Any Firm
1140 Main Street
Philadelphia, PA 19114

Dear Ms. Cummings:

I am currently exploring administrative opportunities in the engineering field. Enclosed is my resume for your consideration.

Please note that my seventeen years of practical experience have involved working on major commercial and industrial projects in the Middle East as a Construction Engineer, Construction Manager, and Planning and Systems Engineer. This experience is supported by a multilingual capability, a Bachelor of Science degree in Civil Engineering, a Master of Science degree in Engineering Administration with concentration in Construction Management, and broad experience with computers.

I look forward to discussing with you my potential to contribute to your clients' needs. If you will please contact me at the above address or by phone at (215) 555-5555, I would like to establish a mutually convenient time for a personal interview. My salary has ranged from $75,000 to its most current $95,000, and I am open to opportunities that offer similar compensation.

Thank you for your attention.

Sincerely,

Chris Smith

Enc. Resume

Executive Administrator

178 Green Street
Columbia, SC 29202

December 15, 20--

Pat Cummings
Director
Any Executive Search Firm
1140 Main Street
Spartanburg, SC 29304

Dear Mr. Cummings:

If one of your client firms is in need of an innovative executive with broad experience in product management, business development, and high-tech product service operations, then we have good reason to meet for further discussion.

I am an aggressive professional who enjoys a challenge and is willing to accept the responsibility for capturing my corporate share of targeted and strategic markets. As a leader or member of a professional national and/or international marketing staff, I am confident that I can make the same outstanding contribution to one of your client firms as I have to my present employer.

During the past seventeen years, I have progressively advanced from positions ranging from Senior Sales Representative, Strategic Account Manager, and Marketing Manager to my most current position as Strategic Alliance Marketing and Business Development Manager with an internationally recognized computer company.

Although these positions have been fast-paced and challenging, I feel that my expertise in selling concepts and working with vendors worldwide on the development and execution of joint marketing ventures can be effectively utilized to provide high visibility and develop new applications for increased sales. Please note, I am willing to relocate for the right opportunity.

The enclosed resume summarizes my background and experience in the areas cited above. Should you require additional information, please feel free to contact me at the above address or by phone at (803) 555-5555. I would welcome your acknowledgment and look forward to a meeting at your earliest convenience.

Sincerely,

Chris Smith

Enc. Resume

Labor Relations Specialist

178 Green Street
Kalamazoo, MI 49006

June 15, 20--

Pat Cummings
Executive Recruiter
1140 Main Street
Chicago, IL 60605

Dear Mr. Cummings:

My experience encompasses more than ten years of decision-making responsibility for human resource development, manpower planning, and labor law and relations, affecting hundreds of employees in the public and private sectors. In addition to the training and supervision of sizable staffs, I have been involved in collective bargaining for management, wage and salary administration, employee benefits, safety and training, and making and enforcing labor law considerations.

I am currently interested in a firm that offers stability, growth, and profits. I am willing to relocate if offered a challenging assignment. My salary requirement is $50,000 to $65,000.

I have enclosed my resume for your review. If I may provide you with additional information, please call me at (616) 555-5555. I look forward to discussing my qualifications with you in more detail.

Sincerely,

Chris Smith

Enc. Resume

178 Green Street
New Hope, MN 55428
(612) 555-5555

March 24, 20--

Pat Cummings
Executive Recruiter
1140 Main Street
Minneapolis, MN 55426

Dear Ms. Cummings:

I feel that as an executive in a search company, you might be effective in matching me with the legal staff of one of your client firms.

In addition to a Juris Doctor degree, I recently received a Master of Laws in Banking Law Studies with a concentration in International Law. My expertise is in the supervision of associate and support legal staff in research, document preparation, and coordination as required for all legal issues. I am well organized, accurate, and conscientious, interface well with individuals and groups, and feel confident that I can be a contributing asset to one of your client firms.

I have enclosed a professional profile of my academic accomplishments and work experience. My last compensation was $90,000, although I feel my value has substantially increased with the attainment of my recent degree. Should you wish to discuss my qualifications further, I can be reached at my office at (612) 555-4444, extension 22.

I look forward to working together.

Sincerely,

Chris Smith

Enc. Professional profile

Operations Manager

178 Green Street
Minnetonka, MN 55343
(612) 555-5555

March 23, 20--

Pat Cummings
President
Any Search Firm
1140 Main Street
Minneapolis, MN 55408

Dear Ms. Cummings:

Based on my diverse background and experience with high-end, mid-range, and low-end hardware, software, and network products designed for many industries, I feel confident that I can make a valuable contribution toward new product planning, market development, and expansion at a firm within your client base.

Over the last seventeen years, I have developed and marketed packaged and customized software for many industries in domestic and international markets, but also provided the support products for end-users at all levels. Because of this diversity, I am easily able to transfer my skills to marketing other products.

In addition to a strong marketing and sales background, I have established a record for setting up, staffing, and managing top-producing, profitable district offices.

The enclosed profile is a brief summary of my qualifications. Should you be aware of an advanced marketing and development position within the $70,000 to $80,000 range, please consider my qualifications.

Thank you in advance for your attention to this matter.

Sincerely,

Chris Smith

Enc. Professional profile

178 Green Street
Warwick, RI 02886
(401) 555-5555

August 3, 20--

Pat Cummings
Personal Consultant
Any Search Firm
1140 Main Street
Pawtucket, RI 02860

Dear Ms. Cummings:

In the course of your search assignments, you might have a need for an experienced President/CEO with expertise in all phases of real estate development and construction. If so, I would like to be considered.

During the past twenty years as a Developer of large real estate complexes and President of a major real estate development group, I managed large projects, from site acquisition and master planning through approvals. I have successfully marketed award-winning residential and commercial mixed-usage developments representing $185 million in sales. Currently, I am involved in negotiating site acquisitions, and planning, coordinating, and managing large real estate development/construction projects for both foreign and domestic investors with interests throughout the Northeast.

My positions require strong administrative, management, financial, and interpersonal skills, as well as the capability to negotiate effectively and successfully with financial institutions, regulatory agencies, development professionals, and contractors. Presently, I am looking for a new association with a firm where my expertise can be used to achieve mutual objectives for growth and profit.

My preference is to remain in my present regional location, with which I am most familiar. My current salary is in the low six figures. After you have reviewed my qualifications, I can arrange to meet with you at your convenience.

Thank you for your attention to this matter.

Sincerely,

Chris Smith

Enc. Professional profile

Senior Accountant

178 Green Street
Concord, NH 03302
(603) 555-5555

July 20, 20--
Pat Cummings
Executive Recruiter
1140 Main Street
New York, NY 10022

Dear Mr. Cummings:

I believe that the varied accounting, finance, and general management experience I have gained over the course of my career will be of significant interest to you in your current or anticipated client searches.

As a seasoned, certified Accountant, I have successfully managed general ledger, cash accounting, accounts payable, employee disbursements, and fixed asset operations. As a Manufacturing Plant Controller, I managed the accounting activities and the general administrative functions of a $35 million manufacturing plant. I have:

- Prepared, analyzed, and presented P&L, balance sheet, departmental expense, manufacturing variance, and other operating reports.
- Prepared $2 million annual departmental operating budgets, analyzed results, initiated required operational improvements, and prepared forecasts.
- Developed annual strategic and operational improvements that resulted in a 15 percent increase in efficiency.
- Oversaw human resources, purchasing, payroll, and other plant administrative functions.
- Maintained quality accounting operations by implementing internal controls testing programs.

I have also managed the interface between my group and the data center running my applications, directed the MIS professionals that supported my applications and systems, and managed the enhancement projects that steadily improved day-to-day operations. I am also comfortable with the operation of several different spreadsheet and word processing applications on PC and Macintosh systems.

My resume is enclosed. While my prime interest is in securing a position on the East Coast, I am willing to relocate for the right opportunity and compensation ($80,000 to $95,000).

Thank you for your consideration.

Sincerely,
Chris Smith
Enc. Resume

Vice President of Banking

178 Green Street
Atlanta, GA 30303
(404) 555-5555

December 21, 20--

Pat Cummings
President
Any Search Firm
1140 Main Street
Atlanta, GA 30340

Dear Mr. Cummings:

I am an accomplished Vice President who can significantly contribute to the successful operations of one of your client banking institutions.

I possess extensive experience in multibranch operations, including the following areas:

- Successfully developing and personally marketing new products for small businesses.
- Rewriting and implementing branch system policies and procedures.
- Troubleshooting operations and establishing improved financial controls.
- Budget planning and controls, audits.

My compensation requirement is within the $75,000 to $85,000 range, and I would consider making a long-distance move to a new job location. I have enclosed a professional profile and would be happy to provide additional information if needed.

I look forward to hearing from you regarding placement possibilities.

Sincerely,

Chris Smith

Enc. Professional profile

Vice President of Sales

178 Green Street
Houston, TX 77248
(713) 555-5555
(713) 555-4444 (Fax)

August 2, 20--

Pat Cummings
Recruiter
Any Search Firm
1140 Main Street
Hartford, CT 06102

Dear Mr. Cummings:

Currently, I am considering a move to the Northeast and am pursuing executive positions with profitable, aggressive retail corporations. Your firm has been recommended to me as one that services a wide client base in this area. In this regard, I would request your consideration of my qualifications.

As a corporate Vice President of Sales with an established record for the development of approximately $215 million in sales, my responsibilities have covered the gamut of successful strategies and techniques for growth and profitability. My involvement in sales, marketing, staff development, and production interface has been extensive, and my ability to organize and manage is well documented in goals I have achieved with my present and prior employers. My salary requirements lie in the $200,000 to $250,000 range, plus bonuses.

The enclosed resume highlights my accomplishments. I would welcome the opportunity to discuss my qualifications further should a client wish to consider me for a position.

Thank you for your time.

Sincerely,

Chris Smith

Enc. Resume

178 Green Street
Durango, CO 81301

November 16, 20--

Pat Cummings
Attorney at Law
Any Firm
1140 Main Street
Pueblo, CO 81001

Dear Mr. Cummings:

Recently, Luke Gokey suggested I contact you concerning any assistance you might be able to provide with my job search. I am interested in joining an organization in a position that would utilize my legal, administrative, and managerial knowledge and experience. The enclosed resume will provide you with information concerning my background and abilities.

As indicated, my law-related background is extensive and varied. For twelve years, I have supervised records and staff activities within the Any County Registry of Deeds. Unfortunately, I have reached the plateau of responsibility level within the structure of this position, and am now seeking to continue in my career progression.

I am especially interested in a legal administrative position, preferably with a private firm or corporation. I am willing to relocate and/or travel and am open to negotiation in terms of starting salary.

Should you know of any related openings or contacts to whom I should pass my resume, please do not hesitate to call me at (303) 555-5555. Thank you for your time. I look forward to hearing from you in the near future.

Sincerely,

Chris Smith

Enc. Resume

Advertising Executive

178 Green Street
Neptune, NJ 07754
(908) 555-5555

August 14, 20--

Pat Cummings
Communications Director
Any Agency
1140 Main Street
Hackensack, NJ 07601

Dear Ms. Cummings:

Please find attached my resume. I spoke with Jim Shaffer last week and he suggested I send my credentials to you prior to meeting in person.

As we discussed, I have five-plus years of advanced media, governmental, and business experience. My background provides a broad base of skills that allows me to handle a variety of situations and responsibilities.

I look forward to meeting with you at your earliest possible convenience.

Sincerely,

Chris Smith

Enc. Resume

178 Green Street
Burbank, CA 91501

January 18, 20--

Pat Cummings
Director
Any Corporation
1140 Main Street
Vernon, CA 90058

Dear Mr. Cummings:

At the suggestion of Walter Durrane, I am enclosing my resume for your consideration pertaining to advising or related assignments with Any Corporation.

I have recently retired from a long and successful general medical practice. However, I am interested now in contributing my expertise as a representative for a public agency such as the Fraud Control Unit at Any Corporation. I have had prior experience as an Evaluator and Advisor for insurance companies and attorneys with regard to industrial and insured claims, and I would like to apply these skills to the continuation of my profession.

I look forward to meeting with you to further discuss my ability to fulfill your requirements. In the interim, I may be reached at the above address or by phone at (818) 555-5555.

Sincerely,

Chris Smith, M.D.

Enc. Resume

Assistant Hospital Administrator

178 Green Street
Rapid City, SD 57007
(605) 555-5555

July 4, 20--

Pat Cummings
Hospital Administrator
Any Hospital
1140 Main Street
Rapid City, SD 57007

Dear Mr. Cummings:

Upon completion of my coursework this month, I will be searching for a full-time position in hospital administration. During the past year as a volunteer at your hospital, I have gained a great deal of personal satisfaction and continued interest in working at a facility caring for older citizens. I would like to call upon your experience in this field to assist me in any way possible as I begin my job search.

Although you may already be aware of my qualifications, I have enclosed my resume for your perusal. In addition to a Bachelor of Science degree in Business Administration, I can offer five years of part-time and full-time experience in office administration, accounting, computer operations, and credit/collections that may be beneficial to Any Hospital. I am willing to work in an entry-level position that would allow me to interface with professionals from whom I can learn and further develop my skills to handle greater responsibilities.

I would like to meet with you briefly when I come in to volunteer for the final time on July 17. Any organization/contact names or industry insight you could provide would greatly enhance my search efforts. I will call your office this Friday to arrange a time on the 17th that would be convenient for you.

Thank you for your time, Mr. Cummings.

Sincerely,

Chris Smith

Enc. Resume

Auto Salesperson

178 Green Street
Brooklyn, NY 11201
(718) 555-5555

December 5, 20--

Pat Cummings
Regional Manager
Any Corporation
1140 Main Street
Rochester, NY 14623

Dear Ms. Cummings:

During a recent visit to Rochester, my longtime friend Bill Atwood suggested your name as a valuable contact in the field of auto sales. I understand that your corporation has contracted with Bill's agency several times to promote your regional dealerships. I would like to take this opportunity to ask for any assistance you might be able to provide with my job search.

Due to recent downsizing, I am seeking a new, long-term association with an aggressive, fast-paced dealership. During the past eight years, my positions have ranged from Salesperson to Sales Manager with a high-volume dealership. My expertise is in developing, training, motivating, and managing a top-producing sales team in a highly competitive market. I am an effective communicator with presentation skills designed to generate results when dealing with management, personnel, and the general public. I established and continued to maintain a record of achievement as Salesperson of the Month and Salesperson of the Year for generated sales and margin of profit.

Should your schedule permit, I will be visiting the Rochester area next week and would love to meet with you. Your insight into the market and the future of the industry, as well as any specific advice or contact names you could provide, would be very helpful. I will call your office next Monday to see if we can find a convenient time to meet.

Thank you for your consideration, Ms. Cummings, and I hope to speak with you soon.

Sincerely,

Chris Smith

Enc. Resume

Beverage Manager

178 Green Street
Lexington, KY 40508
(606) 555-5555

April 10, 20--

Pat Cummings
Vice President, Importing
Any Corporation
1140 Main Street
Philadelphia, PA 19130

Dear Ms. Cummings:

It was a pleasure skiing with you and Alex Park last month. Alex has been telling me for years how well we would get along, and it was a pleasure discovering that his instincts were correct. At that time, you urged me to forward a resume, so that you could inform me of suitable career opportunities at Any Corporation and other refreshment dealers.

During the past six years, I have been involved in customer service and operations management for a company that offers complete office beverage services to businesses and manufacturing plants throughout the United States. One of my responsibilities has been testing, evaluating, introducing, and promoting gourmet coffees and beverages to discriminating coffee drinkers. In addition, I managed key accounts and was involved in training personnel in methods of beverage brewing that would assure quality results.

Although my position has been challenging, I feel it is time for me to make a change to the primary segment of the coffee industry, importing and roasting, which I feel can offer me broader responsibilities and opportunities. I would like to apply my combined knowledge and experience in the office coffee service business to operations or sales to institutional accounts and resellers such as office beverage services.

I am pleased to see that Any Corporation is expanding its beverage services to the Midwest. I am confident, due to my years of experience, that I could be a key player in such a growth environment. May we meet to discuss?

Sincerely,

Chris Smith

Enc. Resume

Broadcast Manager

178 Green Street
Menomonie, WI 53818

May 4, 20--

Pat Cummings
Deejay
Any Radio Station
1140 Main Street
Madison, WI 53715

Dear Mr. Cummings:

As you may recall, I am scheduled to graduate from the University of Wisconsin this month. The internship I completed at your station last spring has definitely confirmed my desire to seek a career in broadcasting, and I am writing to ask for your assistance in reaching this objective.

My desire is to participate in the management training program of a progressive broadcaster, studio, or agency seeking a highly motivated achiever who sees success in a ground-floor opportunity that offers enhanced potential for career growth and advancement based upon outstanding performance. As I prepare to graduate, I am attempting to gather contact names and information concerning major players in the industry. I hope to schedule some informational interviews while still in school to begin my job search.

Mr. Cummings, I recall from my time at the station that you are especially knowledgeable about the industry as a member of the Wisconsin Broadcasters Association. Any assistance you could provide in the way of referrals or general advice would be greatly appreciated. Would it be possible to get together for lunch one afternoon after your broadcast? If so, please contact me at (608) 555-5555 to arrange a mutually convenient time to meet. Thank you for your time.

I hope to hear from you soon.

Sincerely,

Chris Smith

Enc. Resume

Business Manager

178 Green Street
St. Joseph, MO 64507
(816) 555-5555

October 5, 20--

Pat Cummings
Executive Vice President
Any Corporation
1140 Main Street
St. Peters, MO 63376

Dear Mr. Cummings:

Thank you for taking the time out of your schedule to speak with me yesterday. It is always a pleasure to speak with a friend of David's. As I mentioned on the phone, I am seeking a new association with a company that can benefit from my experience in the development, implementation, and management of manufacturing and business information systems and networks.

As you know, I have devoted the past sixteen years to senior-level positions and played a key role in designing and managing systems that provide support to all facets of corporate functioning and strategic decision-making on domestic or international levels. To better acquaint you with my expertise and record of success in modern, automated management, manufacturing, and business information systems and control methods, I am enclosing a summary of my qualifications and accomplishments.

If you are aware of a firm in need of a professional with my qualifications, I would appreciate your forwarding my business profile for their review and further discussion.

Should you or a receptive firm require additional information, please contact me at the address cited above or by phone during the daytime at (816) 555-4444. If there is any assistance I can provide you, Pat, please do not hesitate to let me know.

With best regards,

Chris Smith

Enc. Business profile

Commercial Real Estate Sales Executive

178 Green Street
Honolulu, HI 96841

February 20, 20--

Pat Cummings
Staff Coordinator
Any Real Estate Company
1140 Main Street
San Francisco, CA 94111

Dear Mr. Cummings:

Are you in need of a well-organized, highly motivated, profit-oriented representative to market and sell acquired properties? Lee Yang, from your commercial sales division, felt that my qualifications would make me an excellent contribution to your staff.

During the past fifteen years, I have been actively involved in diverse industries with concentration on both residential and commercial properties. I have successfully managed and taken various businesses from foreclosure to profitable and salable properties. My ability to start up, set up, reorganize, and manage profitable business operations also applies to the management of major accounts or territories to increase market share.

Please find my resume enclosed. I would like to arrange a personal interview at your convenience. I am planning to relocate to your area, I am free to travel, and the compensation package is negotiable. Please contact me at the above address or by phone at (808) 555-5555.

I look forward to your return response.

Yours sincerely,

Chris Smith

Enc. Resume

Community Relations Specialist

178 Green Street
Winchester, VA 22601
(703) 555-5555

August 21, 20--

Pat Cummings
Director, Community Planning
Any Organization
1140 Main Street
Virginia Beach, VA 23456

Dear Ms. Cummings:

I am writing at the suggestion of Barbara Winters, a fellow member of the Community Outreach Organization in Winchester. I am currently in search of a long-term association with an organization in the field of community relations. Barbara mentioned her frequent working relationship with Any Organization, and felt your office may be in need of a skilled professional with my qualifications.

During the past fifteen years, my experience has been concentrated in areas of community relations and government affairs working in public sector, university, and private industry settings. I have extensive experience working with various populations and divergent groups, and have been actively involved and successful in troubleshooting and problem-solving during the planning and decision-making processes pertaining to issues impacting communities.

I possess strong presentation, communication, and interpersonal skills, and I have trained, managed, and molded support staffs into efficient and productive teams. Based on my qualifications, I feel confident of my ability to make a significant contribution to your organization.

Although my resume provides a good summary of my background and experience, I would like to arrange a mutually convenient meeting, during which we can further discuss any availabilities within Any Organization. Please contact me at the above address or phone, or by fax at (703) 555-4444.

Thank you for your time.

Sincerely,

Chris Smith

Enc. Resume

178 Green Street
St. Charles, MO 63302
(314) 555-5555

November 6, 20--

Pat Cummings
President
Any Corporation
1140 Main Street
Chesterfield, MO 63017

Dear Mr. Cummings:

I obtained your company name from my client, Fred Mosley, President of ISS, Incorporated. My expertise is in working with small, nonprofit health care and human services organizations, such as ISS, that have problems meeting their commitments because of budget constraints. As an experienced independent consultant, I implement cost-effective techniques to put in place the systems, programs, and controls necessary to generate the dollars to meet and exceed fundraising goals.

During the past twenty years, I have played a key role in the management, planning, and successful execution of projects that require working with decision-makers, committees, volunteer groups, and community organizations on institutional/organizational development. I am qualified to handle such projects, from needs survey to achievement of projected funding objectives, and I am prepared to provide you, or any suitable corporation you are aware of, with this expertise on a per-assignment rather than full-time basis. Depending on your needs, my consulting fees will be quoted on a per-project or hourly rate.

If you are in the process of, or are planning, a campaign, please contact me so that we can arrange a meeting to discuss your requirements. I can be reached at the above address or phone, or by fax at (314) 555-4444. I will be glad to provide you with a client list and documentation of my achievements at that time.

Sincerely,

Chris Smith

Enc. Professional profile

Corporate Treasurer

178 Green Street
Canyon, TX 79016
(806) 555-5555

June 4, 20--

Pat Cummings
Vice President
Any Corporation
1140 Main Street
Cedar City, UT 84720

Dear Ms. Cummings:

    At the suggestion of Tom Poudrier, I am submitting my resume for the Corporate Treasurer position. I have followed your company's rapid growth during the past two years, and read with much excitement your prediction for further expansion in the trade journal *Real Estates*. I wish to be a part of this exciting atmosphere.

    During the past thirteen years, I have compiled a record of success as Vice President/Treasurer of a multicorporate real estate development and management company, and I have ten years of additional experience as Corporate Treasurer and Controller with a nonprofit educational research firm and an electronic manufacturer.

    I am pursuing a new opportunity utilizing my financial and management expertise. My interest is in working in a business or nonprofit environment where my associates and I share the common goal of profitable growth and mutual gain.

    After reviewing my qualifications, I would appreciate your contacting me for a personal meeting. I can be reached at the above address, by phone, or a message may be left at (806) 555-4444. I appreciate your consideration.

Sincerely,

Chris Smith

Enc. Resume

Credit Officer

178 Green Street
Baton Rouge, LA 70821
(504) 555-5555

May 25, 20--

Pat Cummings
Chief Loan Officer
Any Bank
1140 Main Street
LaPlace, LA 70069

Dear Mr. Cummings:

Pursuant to your recent conversation with my father, I am forwarding the attached resume for your evaluation. It is my desire to participate in a leading commercial credit training program as a first step in my commercial banking career. I understand that your loan officer development program is regarded as one of the finest in the industry.

Please note that in addition to receiving my recent Master of Business Administration degree in Finance and Management Policy with honors, I have a Bachelor of Arts degree in Economics and two years of progressively responsible experience working in diverse areas of operations and marketing support with McEllis Industries, Inc.

I would like to demonstrate my potential to succeed with your bank, working as an individual contributor or as a team member, to the achievement of mutual goals and objectives. For this reason, I welcome the opportunity to meet with you in order to further discuss your current or anticipated needs in terms of my qualifications and career objectives. I will contact your office on Wednesday, May 31, to schedule a convenient interview time.

Sincerely,

Chris Smith

Enc. Resume

Director of College Development

178 Green Street
Pittsburgh, PA 15217
(412) 555-5555

June 8, 20--

Pat Cummings
Alumni Development Director
Any University
1140 Main Street
New Haven, CT 06520

Dear Mr. Cummings:

I am glad we had the opportunity to meet at the Educational Development Symposium. I thoroughly enjoyed exchanging ideas about the interplay between the academic and the financial worlds. Your development ideas have enriched the scope of my knowledge and I hope our discussion benefited you as well. As you suggested, I have enclosed a resume to remind you of my background.

In addition to a Master of Education degree in Administration and Supervision and a Bachelor of Arts degree in Business Administration, I offer ten years of experience in positions ranging from Assistant Director of Alumni and Parent Relations with a four-year college, to my most recent position as Director of the Annual Fund with a college preparatory school.

My experience includes a full range of management responsibilities, including full knowledge of the institutional advancement field, public/client relations, development/fundraising, special event planning, marketing/sales, and promotion/advertising.

I am interested in exploring opportunities at other colleges. If you know of any openings, or have colleagues who may be aware of developmental opportunities at other universities, I would appreciate your passing the information along to me.

I hope to speak with you again soon.

Sincerely,

Chris Smith

Enc. Resume

Director of Information Services

178 Green Street
Bellingham, WA 98226
(206) 555-5555

November 19, 20--

Pat Cummings
Director of Informational Services
Any Municipality
1140 Main Street
Bellingham, WA 98226

Dear Ms. Cummings:

After so many years of working in your department, it is with mixed emotions that I greet your departure. While I will regret your absence, I congratulate you on your retirement and the successful conclusion of your years of service.

At your retirement celebration, you said that you had recommended me to the search committee as your replacement. I would be honored to act in this position, and thank you for your recommendation. As you suggested, I hereby remind you of my career history.

During the past fourteen years, I have held positions as Manager of Systems Planning and Development, Principal Systems Analyst, and Manager of Computer Operations with Any Municipality. In this capacity, my responsibilities have included directing the operations of a data processing center serving numerous departments within the city hall complex. In keeping with numerous changes in municipal systems and procedures, my work in data processing has been increasingly complex and required extensive program development, systems analysis, troubleshooting and problem-solving, employee training, and supervision in computer operations.

Allow me to reiterate my interest in contributing my energy and skills to Any Municipality. I am confident that, given this opportunity, I can uphold your high standard of service which, as a result of your efforts, the city has come to expect.

Thank you for your kind consideration.

Sincerely,

Chris Smith

Enc. Resume

Driver

178 Green Street
Cookeville, TN 38505
(901) 555-5555

June 21, 20--

Pat Cummings
Shipping Services Manager
Any Corporation
1140 Main Street
Florence, MS 39703

Dear Mr. Cummings:

Last week I spoke with Brooke Breyfogle, who encouraged me to contact you. My desire to drive for Any Corporation has prompted me to forward the attached resume for your evaluation.

Please note that in addition to six years as a Package Car Driver for United States Shipping, I received intensive training in Diesel Mechanics while a member of the U.S. Marine Corps. I also managed a Marine auto hobby shop where I learned basic auto mechanics. In my current job, I have gained valuable insight into the task of working effectively while on a tight schedule, maintaining good customer relations, and interfacing regularly with employees and management.

I will contact your office on Monday to establish a mutually convenient time for a meeting, during which we may more fully discuss your current or anticipated driver needs in terms of my qualifications.

Thank you for your time and consideration.

Sincerely,

Chris Smith

Enc. Resume

178 Green Street
Mt. Pleasant, MI 48859

July 18, 20--

Pat Cummings
Director, Products and Services
Any Corporation
1140 Main Street
Kalamazoo, MI 49007

Dear Mr. Cummings:

Thank you for taking the time to speak with me on the phone yesterday. I saw your nephew Brenden last night and sent your regards as you requested. Brenden hopes to see you soon, and confirms that he is, indeed, working hard to graduate.

As I mentioned on the phone, I am a candidate for a Bachelor of Science degree in Electrical Engineering, anticipating graduation in May 20--. I have enclosed my resume as per your request. Ideally, I would like to find a position in which I could contribute to a firm's technical products and services through my combined academic and practical experience.

I certainly do not expect that you will be able to provide me with a position, Mr. Cummings, but I would greatly appreciate any leads or contact names you may know of in the field. Additionally, would it be possible to meet? I would love to get your insight into the industry, as well as hear any advice you could provide for my search. Please contact me at the above address or by phone at (517) 555-5555 to arrange a mutually convenient time to get together.

I appreciate your time.

Sincerely,

Chris Smith

Enc. Resume

Elementary Teacher

178 Green Street
Medford, MA 02155
(617) 555-5555

July 18, 20--

Pat Cummings
President
Any Teachers' Association
1140 Main Street
Everett, MA 02149

Dear Ms. Cummings:

Hello! I hope that you are enjoying your new position at the Union. We certainly miss you at Medford Elementary. Many of the students still ask when you are returning, and the teacher's room has been so quiet without you. When are you coming back to visit us?

Pat, I am also writing on a business-related subject. Since the town lost its override appeal this month, I have found myself out of a job. I was hoping that, as Association President, you might know of a school system in need of a classroom veteran.

I am seeking a position that involves teaching and motivating children toward academic success and self-improvement, possibly one in which I can utilize my certification and six years of experience in special needs education. I am especially interested in a professional environment that caters to the development and well-being of children either in an educational or child-care setting.

If you could refer me to any leads you might be aware of, I would be grateful. I have enclosed my resume to assist you in the brainstorming process. I'll call you early next week to talk further.

Thank you for taking the time to assist me. I look forward to catching up soon!

With best regards,

Chris Smith

Enc. Resume

Environmental Services Director

178 Green Street
Provo, UT 84602
(801) 555-5555

November 22, 20--

Pat Cummings
Director
Any Corporation
1140 Main Street
Washington, PA 15301

Dear Mr. Cummings:

My desire to secure a position in the management of large-scale environmental services or related operations with an institution offering enhanced potential for career growth and development has prompted me to forward the attached resume for your evaluation. Mindy LeMouge suggested that you may be aware of such a position.

Please note that in addition to an Associate's degree in Public Environmental Health, and intensive additional professional-level training in this area, I possess eighteen years of progressively responsible experience in the management of environmental services operations for commercial and institutional employers.

My experience encompasses all aspects of departmental management, including the development of policies and procedures, personnel hiring, training, supervision and evaluation, scheduling, customer and vendor negotiations and relations, cost estimation, budget development and management purchasing, payroll, management reporting, inventory control, scheduling, and wage and salary negotiation.

I would appreciate a chance to meet, in which we could discuss the environmental industry. Frankly, I would appreciate any advice you, with your vast experience in the field, could offer me regarding my current job search. I will call your office to schedule a mutually convenient time for such a meeting.

Sincerely,

Chris Smith

Enc. Resume

Field Service Manager

178 Green Street
Belleville, MI 48112

August 20, 20--

Pat Cummings
Human Resources Manager
Any Cancer Institute
1140 Main Street
Boston, MA 02118

Dear Mr. Cummings:

During a recent conversation with Dr. Elizabeth Bradley, a specialist in children's leukemia, I mentioned my interest in the human resources division of Any Cancer Institute, specifically for the Field Service Manager position advertised.

Dr. Bradley has firsthand knowledge of my organizational and management skills, as well as my comprehensive training and experience dealing with the day-to-day management of care control for children. She recommended that I contact you directly, to make you aware of my interest in the position and my conviction that I am capable of handling its inherent responsibilities in order to achieve the goals of Any Cancer Institute.

Although I have forwarded an application to your director of human resources, I am enclosing a copy of my resume for your review. I am planning to relocate permanently to the Boston area and hope to do so as an employee of your facility. Any assistance you can provide is appreciated.

Should you require additional information, please contact me at the above address or by phone at (313) 555-5555 or (313) 555-4444.

Yours sincerely,

Chris Smith

Enc. Resume

178 Green Street
Maryville, MO 64468
(816) 555-5555

May 14, 20--

Pat Cummings
Executive Vice President
Any Corporation
1140 Main Street
Fulton, MO 65251

Dear Mr. Cummings:

I received your name as a key figure in the Missouri banking industry from a mutual friend, Rebecca Meader. I understand that Rebecca is a fellow member of the Fulton Country Club and has often accompanied you on the golf course. She generously offered your services as a contact for my job-search campaign.

For the past fifteen years, I have acted as a top producer in new business development, consumer lending, system implementation, personnel management and training, customer service, and financial counseling. Although my positions have been challenging, at this point in my career, I am exploring new opportunities in which to apply my extensive background and experience in banking and finance.

Please note that in addition to formal education and a degree in Business Administration, I have undertaken advanced study in financial counseling and mortgage banking. I have worked in a $140 million credit union in the greater St. Louis area. I also have extensive customer support and technical coordination experience providing support and training to select client personnel on an IBM-automated ordering system.

I would greatly appreciate your consideration of my enclosed resume for any suitable availabilities at Any Corporation, and would welcome the opportunity to speak with you in a personal meeting. Please feel free to contact me at the above address or phone, or by fax at (816) 555-4444. Thank you for your consideration, Mr. Cummings.

I look forward to hearing from you.

Sincerely,

Chris Smith

Enc. Resume

Finance Manager

178 Green Street
Downers Grove, IL 60515
(708) 555-5555

January 25, 20--

Pat Cummings
Human Resource Director
Any Bank
1140 Main Street
New York, NY 10128

Dear Ms. Cummings:

John Monroe, of First Avenue Bank, informed me that you might be expanding your staff. Based on my comprehensive experience in the field of finance, I can offer your firm a broad range of management and administrative skills in banking.

During the past twenty-five years, I have played a key role in the trust banking industry in positions ranging from Tax Officer to my current position as Chief Trust Officer. Because of my ability to adapt strategies to changing conditions, I was able to apply innovative approaches that increased productivity, accuracy, and profits. As a result, customer service, corporate visibility and image, and customer base were substantially improved.

I am confident I could contribute my expertise to the continued success of Any Bank, and would welcome the chance to discuss career opportunities. I will call your office to schedule an interview.

Thank you for your time.

Sincerely,

Chris Smith

Enc. Resume

Genetic Research Technician

178 Green Street
Baton Rouge, LA 70821
(504) 555-5555

March 13, 20--

Pat Cummings
Director
Any Center
1140 Main Street
Lake Charles, LA 70602

Dear Mr. Cummings:

I am a good friend of Anne Connelly, whom I understand is a colleague of yours at Any Center. Anne thought that, as an experienced veteran in the field of biomedical research, you would be able to offer some valuable assistance with my job search.

I am currently seeking a challenging position as a Genetic Research Technician. In addition to a Bachelor's degree in Biology with a concentration in Genetics, which I received in 20--, I have hands-on laboratory experience as a lab assistant conducting studies related to neuropsychology. I have researched and written class papers on germ line therapy, genetic technology, legal aspects of genetics, and genetics testing in the workplace. I am a highly motivated, career-oriented individual who would like to contribute to an established facility by combining both my academic and practical experience, as outlined in the enclosed resume.

Would it be possible to meet? I would like to briefly solicit your advice and, possibly, gather any further names to contact in the field. I will call your office on Friday to confirm a time.

Thank you for your consideration.

Sincerely yours,

Chris Smith

Enc. Resume

Golf Instructor

178 Green Street
Albuquerque, NM 87190
(505) 555-5555

February 14, 20--

Pat Cummings
Director
Any Golf Club
1140 Main Street
Las Cruces, NM 88003

Dear Ms. Cummings:

As a result of a recent referral from Mr. David Stefan regarding an entry-level opening for an instructor at Any Golf Club, I am submitting my resume for your review.

I possess eight years of education, training, coaching, and playing experience. My involvement with the game of golf began in high school and, since then, my skill level and affection for the sport have increased. Currently, I am seeking a career opportunity that will allow me to use my education and experience to make a positive contribution by maintaining high standards and a professional image within a club environment.

I am very interested in this opening. Could I perhaps schedule a personal interview with you at your convenience? I will contact your offices on Monday, February 20, to discuss an appropriate meeting time.

Sincerely,

Chris Smith

Enc. Resume

178 Green Street
Kilgore, TX 75662
(903) 555-5555

January 16, 20--

Pat Cummings
Finance Manager
Any Corporation
1140 Main Street
Austin, TX 78713

Dear Mr. Cummings:

It was a pleasure meeting you last month while visiting Bob and Cheryl Maxmillian at their home in Austin. As you may recall, at that time I was working as an International Controller of Divinex, a multidivision manufacturer of automatic test equipment. Recent ownership changes have prompted me to seek another association in finance management. When I updated Bob on my search recently, he suggested I obtain your assistance.

I possess more than sixteen years of experience working with foreign manufacturing entities and sales/service subsidiaries, which has involved corporate financial planning and analysis, international reporting, treasury and tax management, and interactive MIS systems for both corporate and divisional financial operations. I am searching for a position that would allow me to utilize my diverse background while providing the opportunity for career growth.

Should you know of any corporations in the Austin area in need of someone with my qualifications, would you kindly forward my resume to the appropriate contacts? Also, I will be visiting Bob and Cheryl in two weeks' time, to meet with industry insiders and continue my search. If your schedule permits, I would like to meet, perhaps for lunch or dinner. I would greatly appreciate your input as a fellow professional in the field. I will contact you next week to find a time that works for you.

Thank you for your assistance. I hope to see you again soon.

Sincerely,

Chris Smith

Enc. Resume

International Marketing Specialist

178 Green Street
Stratford, CT 06497
(203) 555-5555

April 10, 20--

Pat Cummings
Senior Marketing Specialist
Any Corporation
1140 Main Street
Middlebury, CT 06762

Dear Mr. Cummings:

My uncle, Joe McGinness, a former Fiji fraternity brother of yours at Worcester Polytechnic Institute, suggested I contact you to explore career opportunities in our mutual field of interest, international marketing.

I graduated from Fairfield University in May 20--, with a Bachelor of Science in Textile Marketing. I feel that through my educational extracurricular programs and work experience, I have gained an outstanding business foundation upon which I can build my professional career. I consider myself to be a determined competitor. Setting high, yet realistic, goals for myself and seeing them through to their completion is something I pride myself on and which is a key ingredient in my success to date. I am ambitious and willing to devote the extra time that is almost always necessary for worthwhile achievements. Additionally, I would consider travel and/or relocation.

My past experiences have helped me sharpen my interpersonal skills. To me, the marketing field offers unlimited growth potential and a career in which one is directly rewarded for hard work and perseverance. Therefore, I believe marketing is the ideal profession for me, since I am willing to work long and hard to attain success.

I would appreciate a chance to meet with you, at your convenience, to discuss possible career opportunities within your firm or in others in your immediate area. I will call your office during the week of April 17 to confirm an interview time. Thank you for your consideration and for any efforts you may extend on my behalf.

Sincerely,

Chris Smith

Enc. Resume

Legal Assistant

178 Green Street
Johnson City, TN 37614

June 28, 20--

Pat Cummings
Assistant District Attorney
Any Office
1140 Main Street
Nashville, TN 37203

Dear Ms. Cummings:

Lee Ellis, Director of Career Services at East Tennessee State University, gave me your name as a valuable contact within the Nashville law enforcement field. I am a recent graduate of East Tennessee State, which I understand is your alma mater as well. During the past several years, I have been preparing myself for a career in law where I can utilize my dual degrees in Criminology and Psychology in the public or private sector.

As my enclosed resume reveals, in addition to my academic studies in these fields, I have experience as a student Investigative Assistant with the Memphis County District Attorney's office, where I was involved in a variety of investigations and other assigned duties dealing with law enforcement and legal issues. Based upon my performance in this position, I received the highest possible evaluation. I consider myself to be dependable, capable of rapid orientation and training, and skilled at assuming responsibility for assignments as an individual or as a team member.

I am considering attending law school in several years, and would love the opportunity to confirm my interest in law and law enforcement through a Legal Assistant position at an organization such as Any Office. I would greatly appreciate the opportunity to meet with you to discuss availabilities at your office or to receive any referrals you might find helpful. Would your schedule permit a few free moments next week? I will call on Monday to schedule a mutually convenient time.

Should you require additional information prior to our meeting, please contact me at the above address or by phone at (615) 555-5555.

Sincerely,

Chris Smith

Enc. Resume

Leisure Trainer

178 Green Street
Lincroft, NJ 07738
(908) 555-5555

March 1, 20--

Pat Cummings
President
Any Travel Agency
1140 Main Street
Nyack, NJ 10960

Dear Mr. Cummings:

Anna Murphy, co-owner of Kannenberg Travel, suggested you as a top contact in the travel industry. I am confident that as an Educator and Staff Trainer with comprehensive experience in domestic and foreign travel, I have the qualifications necessary for the position of Leisure Trainer. Do you have a need for a person with my expertise?

During my seven years in travel, I have been involved in the development, sales, and marketing of travel products, agency management, and staff development. My experience encompasses diverse travel packages and customized leisure and educational travel.

Currently, I am seeking a new association within the travel industry where I can utilize my combined teaching and travel experience to train new agents in the nuances of providing clients with a quality travel experience and maintaining the agency's high standards. I am interested in Any Travel Agency because your company has committed itself to expanding into Asian travel markets, an area I was just beginning to explore in my last position.

I would like to speak with you. May we meet?

Sincerely,

Chris Smith

Enc. Resume

178 Green Street
New Castle, DE 19720
(302) 555-5555

April 3, 20--

Pat Cummings
Facilities Manager
Any Country Club
1140 Main Street
New Castle, DE 19720

Dear Ms. Cummings:

I enjoyed playing doubles with you and Brian Fee last week. With regard to the open Maintenance Supervisor position you mentioned, I am forwarding my career history. Pat, I am confident that I can provide your facility with top-notch care and maintenance.

My primary technical skills include plumbing, heating, and the general maintenance of residential and commercial properties. I have broad-based knowledge of and experience in construction and mechanical trades such as electrical work, roofing, painting, carpentry, and other areas essential to the cost-effective upkeep of a quality facility. Presently, I am interested in a position in property management where my skills in these areas can be best utilized.

Please contact me so that we may discuss how my experience can benefit your club. If the Maintenance Supervisor position has been filled, I would appreciate if you could forward my resume to other facility managers or other useful contacts.

Thank you for your time.

Sincerely,

Chris Smith

Enc. Resume

Medical Sales Representative

178 Green Street
Odenton, MD 21114
(301) 555-5555

April 20, 20--

Pat Cummings
Sales Director
Any Corporation
1140 Main Street
Emporia, KS 66801

Dear Mr. Cummings:

    I write this letter to remind you of our conversation at the Innovex Medical Sales Trade Conference in California. As you urged me to forward a summary of my credentials, I have enclosed my resume.

    During the past fifteen years, my positions have ranged from Sales Representative to Corporate Vice President responsible for the sales management of diagnostic imaging equipment and consumables to a $70 million health care market. I have established and continue to maintain excellent contacts with physicians, material management directors, directors of purchasing, and other senior decision-makers. My expertise is in developing and managing key accounts in the medical industry, including major hospitals, imaging centers, HMOs, and group purchasing offices. Salary requirements are negotiable. In addition, I am willing to relocate, given a suitable opportunity.

    I am confident that my skills qualify me for a range of senior-level sales positions. Are you aware of any avenues I might pursue to fully utilize my skills? I would appreciate the chance to talk with you. Please contact me in order to let me know when you can take a few moments out of your schedule for a face-to-face discussion.

    It was a pleasure meeting you, and I look forward to speaking with you again.

Sincerely,

Chris Smith

Enc. Resume

Microwave Technician

178 Green Street
Manchester, NH 03105

January 14, 20--

Pat Cummings
Chief Technician
Any Corporation
1140 Main Street
Keene, NH 03431

Dear Ms. Cummings:

In a recent informational interview, Steven Hague of NewMark Industries referred me to your firm. I am interested in joining an organization where I can utilize my strong technical and leadership skills in microwave or related industries.

I have eleven years of experience in the microwave industry working with state-of-the-art microwave communications antennas. My expertise is in test setups for outdoor and indoor test ranges, as well as the design, manufacturing, and repair maintenance of microwave antennas. In addition, I have extensive experience working with customers and inspectors on final tests to FCC regulations. I am well qualified to assume responsibility for managing projects from initial design to final test and operation.

After you have reviewed my background, please contact me so that we may arrange a personal interview to further expand upon your requirements and my ability to meet them. I can be reached at the above address or at (603) 555-5555.

Thank you for your consideration. I await your response.

Sincerely,

Chris Smith

Enc. Resume

Mortgage/Loan Officer

178 Green Street
Conway, AR 72032
(501) 555-5555

April 4, 20--

Pat Cummings
Chief Loan Officer
Any Bank
1140 Main Street
Little Rock, AR 72203

Dear Mr. Cummings:

Recently, I ran into an old college roommate and friend, Ellen Barie. As I am currently considering a new association with a bank or corporation in a Mortgage/Loan Officer capacity, Ellen suggested I contact you. She mentioned that she had worked as a Teller at your Little Rock main branch, and thought you might be interested in someone with my qualifications.

As the enclosed resume indicates, my extensive loan experience has encompassed office supervision and general bookkeeping, with a concentration in credit and collections, within the mortgage, insurance, and banking industries. My current position as a Senior Collections Specialist has provided me with the opportunity to accomplish and exceed a set objective of reducing delinquent loans from $24 million to $10 million within six months. At this point, I feel I have successfully surpassed both company and personal goals, and am searching for new and greater challenges.

I am very interested in the opportunities available at Any Bank. Could we meet for a personal interview? I would be happy to make myself available at your convenience.

Sincerely,

Chris Smith

Enc. Resume

178 Green Street
Kingston, RI 02881
(401) 555-5555

November 19, 20--

Pat Cummings, R.N.
Nursing Director
Any Hospital
1140 Main Street
Bristol, RI 02809

Dear Ms. Cummings:

Are you in need of a nursing professional with extensive clinical, research, and teaching experience? Laura Fogerty, a nurse in your pediatric unit, suggested that I contact you regarding employment opportunities at Any Hospital.

I possess fifteen years of experience in clinical research and direct patient care with an emphasis on neuroscience intensive care, memory disorders, and brain and cognitive sciences. During the past three years, I have functioned as a Staff Nurse assigned to a neuro-intensive care unit.

I am well qualified to teach, counsel, conduct utilization reviews, and/or administer programs related to health care, equipment, or human services—all in appropriate settings. I am capable of making presentations to individuals and groups, skilled at conducting meetings and teaching classes, and have the required communication skills necessary to demonstrate as well as instruct medical professionals and support staffs.

Enclosed please find my business profile. I would be happy to make myself available for an interview to discuss possible openings matching my qualifications. Please feel free to contact me at the above address or daytime phone, or evenings at (401) 555-4444.

I look forward to your return response.

Sincerely,

Chris Smith, R.N.

Enc. Business profile

Payroll Supervisor

178 Green Street
Hayward, CA 94541

June 6, 20--

Pat Cummings
Office Manager
Any Corporation
1140 Main Street
Los Angeles, CA 90017

Dear Ms. Cummings:

I received your name as a contact for my job search from a mutual friend, Steve Herson. I was employed at Steve's bank several years ago, and worked closely with him on many projects. In a recent conversation, Steve mentioned that you might be in need of a professional with my qualifications.

As my enclosed resume indicates, in addition to a Bachelor of Arts degree in Economics, my background encompasses eleven years of progressively responsible and sophisticated hands-on experience ranging from Marketing Research Assistant to Union Benefits Coordinator and Human Resources Administrator. In my present position as Payroll Administrator with a special emphasis on the day-to-day details of financial operations and related areas, I have gained valuable experience and training in important organizational and operational areas of a company's general business operation.

I am very interested in investigating opportunities at Any Corporation and believe I could successfully contribute to your staff. Please contact me at the address cited above or call (415) 555-5555 to arrange a mutually convenient time for an interview.

Thank you for your consideration.

Sincerely,

Chris Smith

Enc. Resume

Power Systems Designer

178 Green Street
Mesa, AZ 85028
(602) 555-5555

August 22, 20--

Pat Cummings
Systems Designer
Any Corporation
1140 Main Street
Tempe, AZ 85284

Dear Mr. Cummings:

Debbie Swanson of Systems Powerphasing recommended I contact you concerning my interest in securing a position in the field of power systems design. I understand that your corporation leads the field in power-related emerging technologies. Debbie spoke highly of your work and thought you could provide me with some useful information.

My background includes seven years of experience in positions as Technical Sales Representative and Medical Equipment Technician with a medical equipment manufacturer, and Power Systems Engineer with a manufacturer of telecommunications earth stations. My most recent experience involves all phases of power systems design projects from proposal preparation and specification to on-site installations, customer training, and full operation.

I am very interested in continuing my career in power design with a new firm. I know that your expertise in the field and knowledge of the current trends would be very helpful in my search. Would it be possible to meet briefly? I can easily make myself available at your convenience, and will call you on Monday to see when we might get together.

Thank you for your generous consideration, Mr. Cummings.

Sincerely,

Chris Smith

Enc. Resume

Production Manager

178 Green Street
Arlington, VA 22229
(703) 555-5555

July 22, 20--

Pat Cummings
Director of Operations Management
Any Corporation
1140 Main Street
Macon, GA 31201

Dear Ms. Cummings:

As Alex Drumlins may have told you, I was caught in Timony's recent downsizing. I am writing to inquire if Any Corporation has any openings in production/operations, or if you can provide industry contacts that I may use in my job search.

My related experience extends throughout the last two decades. In addition to a Bachelor of Science degree in Management, I possess four years of supervisory and production management experience with a large Washington, D.C.–based corporation. While working my way through college, I experienced aspects of many other disciplines and gained valuable insights into corporate structure.

Thank you for your time and consideration. May I hear from you?

Sincerely,

Chris Smith

Enc. Resume

178 Green Street
Northridge, CA 91324

November 27, 20--

Pat Cummings
Director
Any Institute
1140 Main Street
Los Angeles, CA 90053

Dear Ms. Cummings:

Pursuant to my conversation with Alex Franks on November 9, I am enclosing my resume as an expression of my interest in the position of Project Manager.

Through my education and experience in the transportation field, I have dealt with the public in an assistance capacity in both business and community service environments. In each position I have held, my initiative and ability have led to advancement and the assumption of greater responsibilities.

During the preparation of my recently completed thesis, I conducted extensive research on water transportation. (Enclosed please find an abstract from that thesis.) In addition, my current position involves transportation research and computer transportation modeling.

I feel that my skills, eagerness to learn, and motivation to succeed would contribute to a productive association with Any Institute. I would welcome an opportunity to meet with you to discuss ways in which my capabilities may suit your needs. Please consider the enclosed and direct your response to the above address, or phone me at (818) 555-5555.

Your time and consideration are appreciated. I look forward to hearing from you.

Sincerely,

Chris Smith

Enc. Resume, Thesis abstract

Promotions Representative

178 Green Street
Bakerton, KY 42711
(606) 555-5555

March 16, 20--

Pat Cummings
Vice President, Promotions
Any Corporation
1140 Main Street
Knoxville, TN 37902

Dear Mr. Cummings:

Susan Schlegal, Madison Corporation's Promotions Representative, recommended I contact you about the possibility of an opening with Any Corporation. Please accept the enclosed resume as an expression of my interest in joining your organization.

As you can see from my resume, my diverse experience includes administrative duties, telemarketing, coaching, and instructing gymnasts. Ideally, I would like to apply my enthusiasm for athletics, combined with my educational background and acquired business skills, to an organization where my capabilities could be utilized to accomplish mutually agreed upon goals. I feel strongly that Any Corporation is such an organization.

I am confident that my experience and education, coupled with an eagerness to learn and a motivation to succeed, would contribute to a productive association with your company. I would value an opportunity to discuss any current or long-term positions that may be available either at Any Corporation or within the field.

You may contact me at the address cited above, or I will contact you early next week, to arrange a meeting at your earliest convenience.

Your time and consideration are very much appreciated. I look forward to speaking with you in the near future.

Sincerely,

Chris Smith

Enc. Resume

178 Green Street
Cocoa Beach, FL 32932
(407) 555-5555

March 3, 20--

Pat Cummings
District Manager
Any Corporation
1140 Main Street
Stamford, CT 06904

Dear Ms. Cummings:

It was a pleasure to meet you last week at the Realtor's Association. Our conversation has prompted me to write to you. As indicated by the enclosed resume, I have progressively advanced from Property Manager to Senior Area Manager with multistate, multisite responsibility for full residency and profitability of major investment properties. At this point in my career, I am seeking a new and challenging opportunity where my qualifications can be utilized by a progressive investment property and/or property owner/management organization.

I have a record of cost-effective management for individual, client, and company-owned properties including high-rise luxury apartment buildings, multistructure condominiums converted from apartments, and subsidized housing. I am accustomed to working with government agencies and associated regulations.

My expertise in troubleshooting, problem-solving, turning serious rental losses into profitable operations, capital improvement plans, preventive maintenance, and maintenance management has enabled me to provide harmonious tenant, owner, and community relationships and trouble-free operation of properties.

If your organization or any of your colleagues can provide an opportunity for someone with my experience, I would like to explore that possibility in the hope of a mutually beneficial association. May we meet for discussion?

I look forward to talking to you soon.

Sincerely,

Chris Smith

Enc. Resume

Publicist

178 Green Street
Woodland Hills, CA 91367

July 9, 20--

Pat Cummings
Publicity Director
Any Corporation
1140 Main Street
Santa Ana, CA 92701

Dear Mr. Cummings:

Lee Cyndis suggested I write you with regards to support areas of advertising and public relations. I would appreciate any information or advice you can provide about how to search for a publicity-related support position. I have enclosed a resume to acquaint you with my background.

I possess comprehensive experience in the support of direct mail fundraising activity for a major university. My training and expertise also include areas of publicity and public relations, staff training and supervision, program coordination and budget management, market research and copyediting, and management and administration of related detail.

I have excellent writing skills, work well under pressure, and meet deadlines consistently. In addition, I have experience with streamlining operations for enhancing production efficiency at an optimum cost.

I would appreciate the chance to meet with you so that we may discuss how my abilities prepare me for a position in the advertising world. I can be reached at the above address or at (818) 555-5555.

I look forward to speaking with you at your earliest convenience. Thank you for your time.

Sincerely,

Chris Smith

Enc. Resume

Publishing Intern

178 Green Street
Charleston, SC 29403
(803) 555-5555

April 28, 20--

Pat Cummings
Editor
Any Publishing Company
1140 Main Street
Boston, MA 02210

Dear Ms. Cummings:

I will be graduating from the College of William and Mary in May 20--, and am searching for an avenue that will lead me to a career in publishing.

Lee Jones, an Editorial Assistant at Any Publishing, suggested your company as a possible place to gain experience. I will be living in Massachusetts during June, July, and August and I am hoping that you will consider me for a summer internship. I would welcome the opportunity to work full- or part-time throughout the summer months in order to better understand the workings of a publishing house.

As an intern, I could contribute excellent editing, researching, and writing skills. I am familiar with computers and the general library cataloging systems. Additionally, I am an eager and quick learner, and an observer with a creative eye for detail.

My resume is enclosed; writing samples and references are available upon request. I look forward to hearing from you.

Thank you for your consideration.

Sincerely,

Chris Smith

Enc. Resume

Quality Control Engineer

178 Green Street
Daytona Beach, FL 32117
(904) 555-5555

January 24, 20--

Pat Cummings
Production/Operations Manager
Any Corporation
1140 Main Street
Long Grove, IL 60047

Dear Mr. Cummings:

I enjoyed talking with you on the plane from Denver. I only wish that we had met a little earlier, on the slopes of Winter Park. Enclosed is the resume you asked to see. I am very interested in discussing opportunities within Any Corporation.

As a Quality Control Engineer, I played a key role in the growth of Victor, Inc., where I interfaced with all departments including sales, purchasing, manufacturing, and inventory. I am knowledgeable in quality functions and have experience bringing product lines through the transitional stages from research/prototype to full production.

During the past seven years, I have implemented and audited clean room contamination control, electrostatic discharge, and internal auditing programs for semiconductor and engineering facilities.

I am interested in joining the professional staff of a firm where I can apply my experience in quality control engineering and manufacturing. I am innovative, productive, accurate, and work well as an individual or as a team member.

I will be in Chicago for a training conference from April 10 to April 14. I would enjoy meeting with you at that time to talk further. Please let me know if this would be a good time to schedule a meeting.

I look forward to hearing from you soon.

Sincerely,

Chris Smith

Enc. Resume

Research Assistant

178 Green Street
Elgin, IL 60123

July 20, 20--

Pat Cummings, M.D.
Director of Pharmaceutical Research
Any Hospital
1140 Main Street
Cicero, IL 60650

Dear Dr. Cummings:

Susan Burwen of your human resources department recently informed me of an opening for a Research Assistant (Allergic Diseases) in your pharmaceutical division. Susan and I have been longtime friends, and she felt that my qualifications as a Researcher would ideally match your job requirements. Although I have submitted my resume to Susan, I would like to introduce myself to you as well.

As a graduate of the Massachusetts College of Pharmacy and Allied Health Science, where I earned my Pharmacy degree, I have had the opportunity to perform research in laboratory facilities and have received both instruction and hands-on experience in the use of state-of-the-art research techniques and equipment. As a member of a family who, for generations, has been severely affected by allergic diseases, it has always been my professional objective to either research a cure or contribute to discovering a treatment that would alleviate the discomfort of allergy sufferers.

Given the opportunity to become a part of your pharmaceutical laboratory, I will apply my education, laboratory training, and technical skill toward the achievement of your research objectives dealing with gene regulation and allergic diseases. I would very much like the opportunity to meet with you for further discussion. I will call your office early next week to arrange a time that is convenient for you.

Should you require additional information, please feel free to contact Susan Burwen. Also, I can be reached at the address cited above or (705) 555-5555.

Thank you for your time.

Sincerely,

Chris Smith, Ph.D.

Enc. Resume

Restaurant Manager

178 Green Street
Glen Burnie, MD 21060

April 26, 20--

Pat Cummings
Regional Manager
Any Restaurant Chain
1140 Main Street
Silver Spring, MD 20901

Dear Ms. Cummings:

I am writing in response to a referral from a colleague of yours, Jim Murray. Jim was the Assistant Manager of your Baltimore location in 20--, when I worked there as a waitress. When I expressed my desire to return to your organization in a managerial position, Jim enthusiastically responded with several contact names, including yours.

I have enclosed my resume as an expressed interest in exploring available management opportunities at Any Restaurants. In addition to an Associate's degree in Hotel/Restaurant Management, I have five years of experience ranging from Roving Manager with a multiunit restaurant operation to General Manager of a full-service restaurant, lounge, and multiple function/banquet facility. My experience encompasses front- and back-of-the-house management, food and beverage preparation, and personnel training and supervision.

I feel confident of my potential to make a significant contribution to your restaurant chain. My previous experience as a waitress not only provided specific insight into your management operations, but also was very rewarding personally.

After you have reviewed my qualifications, please do not hesitate to contact me at the address cited above or call (301) 555-5555. I would like to arrange a mutually convenient time for a meeting to discuss your current or anticipated needs in terms of my qualifications.

I greatly appreciate your consideration.

Sincerely,

Chris Smith

Enc. Resume

178 Green Street
Sumas, WA 98295
(604) 555-5555

February 7, 20--

Pat Cummings
Eastern District Manager
Any Corporation
1140 Main Street
New York, NY 10028

Dear Ms. Cummings:

It was great to meet you at the DeLux Designer's conference. I hope we have the chance to speak again soon. As you may remember, I am looking for a new opportunity where my excellent sales skills, strong work ethic, and initiative would directly correlate to my growth, advancement, and future within a company.

During the past six years I have had experience in new business development, negotiations, proposal and contract preparation, and interfacing with banks and attorneys.

Throughout my career, I have worked well independently or as a member of a team. I possess sound knowledge of and experience with the sales of tangible and intangible products as indicated in the enclosed resume. I feel confident that I can be an asset to your company as I have for my present and past employers.

My strong interest in Any Corporation makes relocation feasible and salary issues negotiable.

I look forward to our next discussion.

Sincerely,

Chris Smith

Enc. Resume

Sanitarian

178 Green Street
Rockville, MD 20850

May 6, 20—

Pat Cummings
Director
Any Health Department
1140 Main Street
Baltimore, MD 21207

Dear Mr. Cummings:

As per your request when we spoke at last week's district meeting, I am enclosing my updated resume so that I may be considered for the position of Sanitarian with Any Health Department.

During the past seventeen years, I have been professionally associated in various capacities with private and public health care facilities and educational institutions. My activities have not only involved health care provider services, but also required extensive involvement with individuals and groups, both of which required direct interfacing with community, municipal, and public health agencies.

A prime interest for me is to work in an area where my recommendations can make a difference in the quality of care and in the environmental surroundings of people dependent on the decisions made by the staff of a municipal health department. I am equally effective working independently or as part of a team effort, and I hope to be able to apply my skills toward achieving the objectives of the department.

I want to thank you for the opportunity to be considered for the position. Should you require any additional information prior to a personal interview, please contact me at the above address or by phone at (301) 555-5555.

Yours sincerely,

Chris Smith

Enc. Resume

178 Green Street
Birmingham, AL 35294
(205) 555-5555

November 15, 20--

Pat Cummings
Personnel Director
Any Corporation
1140 Main Street
Mobile, AL 36630

Dear Ms. Cummings:

Maureen Deegan suggested I speak with you regarding a secretarial position with Any Corporation. Enclosed is my resume for your consideration. I hope, in reviewing my background, you will find that my qualifications suit your needs.

During the last five years with Stuart Photographers, my responsibilities included assisting on shoots, handling incoming calls, arranging appointments, and light typing. As Service Representative for the Dalton Corporation, I dealt with all customer inquiries and resolved problems in shipping and billing. I am accustomed to working closely with staff and management in a fast-paced environment and enjoy the satisfaction of doing a job well.

Also enclosed is my resume for your review. I am eager to join the staff of Any Corporation and would be glad to make myself available for an interview. I look forward to hearing from you at your earliest convenience.

Sincerely,

Chris Smith

Enc. Resume

Staff Accountant

178 Green Street
Newport, RI 02840

November 15, 20--

Pat Cummings
Director, Career Services
Any College
1140 Main Street
Smithfield, RI 02917

Dear Ms. Cummings:

It was nice meeting you at the alumni luncheon on Monday. If you recall, at that time you offered your assistance in my job search. I would greatly appreciate any help you may be able to provide.

During the past three years, I have been employed as a Staff Accountant with a major corporation with responsibility for maintaining financial statements and monthly closings, and preparing financial reports using Microsoft Excel. During the prior four years, while attending college, I held positions of increasing responsibility in areas ranging from auditing to accounts payable in corporate and nonprofit environments.

These positions have been fast-paced and challenging, and the experience I gained is broad in scope. However, to further my career in accounting and finance, I am investigating new opportunities where I can apply my experience to benefit a company that offers room for advancement based on personal preference.

Should you know of any corporation in need of an experienced accountant, please do not hesitate to forward the attached resume. Also, if you have any questions or can provide any further guidance, I can be reached at (401) 555-5555 or (401) 555-4444.

I appreciate your time, Ms. Cummings.

Sincerely,

Chris Smith

Enc. Resume

178 Green Street
Atlanta, GA 30303
(904) 555-5555

June 4, 20--

Pat Cummings
Headmaster
Any Academy
1140 Main Street
Sarasota, FL 34236

Dear Mr. Cummings:

Diego Arrigo suggested I contact you in reference to teaching positions in the fields of history and social studies. I am not sure if openings currently exist within your school, but I would appreciate any advice or information you could provide about career opportunities in the academic world. As a recent graduate with a Master of Education degree in Secondary Education, and a Bachelor of Arts degree in History, my goal is to become associated with a university or private school where I can apply my education and experience in the field of education.

From 20-- to June 20--, I worked as a permanent Substitute Teacher with responsibility for teaching various secondary-level courses, including history. I possess superior research, computer, leadership, and organizational skills, and I am capable of working independently or as a team member in an educational, administrative, or research environment.

I would appreciate the chance to meet with you. As a young academic, I am interested to hear how your career has progressed to its current point. Please contact me at your convenience so that we may schedule a time to meet.

I look forward to hearing from you.

Sincerely,

Chris Smith

Enc. Resume

Telemarketer

178 Green Street
Wooster, OH 44691
(216) 555-5555

December 4, 20--

Pat Cummings
Director, Telemarketing
Any Corporation
1140 Main Street
Columbus, OH 43216

Dear Mr. Cummings:

Your name was given to me by Leanne Marquis, who I understand has worked with you on several promotional projects. Leanne is a close friend of my mother's, and has been very helpful in assisting me in obtaining an entry-level position in the telemarketing field. Leanne felt that I would benefit from your extensive industry experience.

I possess four years of successful part- and full-time employment in sales administration and support, and have worked most recently in telemarketing, direct mail, marketing, and sales for a variety of product and/or service-oriented companies.

I would like to meet with you briefly to discuss your insights into the industry. Any referrals or advice you could provide as I prepare to launch my job search would be greatly appreciated. I will contact your office on Friday morning to see if we can schedule a few moments together at your convenience.

Thank you for your consideration.

Sincerely,

Chris Smith

Enc. Resume

Transportation Coordinator

178 Green Street
Batesville, MS 38606
(601) 555-5555

January 11, 20--

Pat Cummings
Operations Manager
Any Campaign
1140 Main Street
Tupelo, MS 38802

Dear Ms. Cummings:

I recently completed an extended association with the campaign team to elect Congressman Bob Millis. Now that the election is over, Campaign Director Marsha Herns suggested I contact your office to offer my services as Transportation Coordinator.

I have spent the last eleven years owning and operating my own business—coordinating limousine and luxury car services for business professionals and politicians, entertainment celebrities, foreign dignitaries, and the general public. I have the stamina and enthusiasm to work long hours, possess the experience and ability to handle crisis situations, and am known to be responsible and innovative when it comes to getting the job done as planned and on schedule.

Enclosed please find my business profile. If you are in need of a competent, experienced Transportation Coordinator, I would like to meet for further discussion. I could be available for an interview at your convenience, and would be happy to supply references at that time.

I look forward to hearing from you.

Sincerely,

Chris Smith

Enc. Business profile

Victim Witness Advocate

178 Green Street
Pawtucket, RI 02860

December 1, 20--

Pat Cummings
Bureau Chief
Any Agency
1140 Main Street
Providence, RI 02902

Dear Mr. Cummings:

In a recent telephone conversation, Marcie Waters of the Children's Protectorate Agency suggested I submit my resume for your review regarding the position of Victim Witness Advocate.

Please note that, in addition to a Bachelor of Arts degree in Psychology and fluency in English, Spanish, and French, my most recent experience has been as a Special Police Officer/Security Officer for Puttnick's Department Store. During my term of employment there, I have, on a daily basis, been called upon to employ skillful, sensitive interviewing and counseling techniques during the detention/arrest procedure, from initial apprehension through court appearances. In addition, for more than three years, I have had the opportunity to interact extensively with staff, customers, and families at all levels.

My experience has provided me with the ability to motivate others toward achieving personal objectives while promoting human dignity. I would welcome the chance to discuss available or anticipated professional opportunities within Any Agency. Should you require additional information, I can be reached at the above address or by phone at (401) 555-5555.

Thank you for your attention to this matter.

Sincerely,

Chris Smith

Enc. Resume

178 Green Street
Holdrege, NE 68949

April 9, 20--

Pat Cummings
Managing Editor
Any Newsletter
1140 Main Street
Omaha, NE 68102

Dear Ms. Cummings:

At the suggestion of a member of your staff, I am writing to express my interest in a position with your writing/reporting team.

As a recent college graduate, class of 20--, with a major in Political Science and a minor in English, I have extensive experience in researching, abstracting, and writing accurate, detailed papers on topical issues, using journalistic techniques.

Currently, I am seeking a career opportunity with a publication, such as *Any Newsletter*, where I can combine my writing skills with my keen interest in ecology to research and report on discoveries and events dealing with the environment on a local, regional, or international level. Also, based on my interest in providing effective pollution awareness materials to the general public, I consider myself to be a viable candidate for the position.

Enclosed are my resume and samples of my writing. I am confident of my ability to handle the responsibilities of the position offered. Should you wish to schedule a personal interview, please contact me by phone between 5:30 and 10 P.M. at (308) 555-5555.

I look forward to your return response.

Sincerely,

Chris Smith

Enc. Resume, Writing samples

Account Executive

178 Green Street
Knoxville, TN 37902

July 16, 20--

Pat Cummings
Managing Director
Any Theater
1140 Main Street
Nashville, TN 37203

RE: Account Executive

Dear Mr. Cummings:

Please note that I have ten years of progressively responsible experience, which includes management positions in hospitality services, marketing, promotion, corporate communications, and public and media relations. My focus has been on events planning, press relations, and the implementation of image-building, attention-getting public relations operations and events for several nationally recognized companies. My accomplishments include:

- Increased paid attendance for special events by more than 31 percent as Marketing and Promotions Coordinator.
- Development of city/corporate transportation programs that substantially increased employee participation.
- Prepared and made presentations as Public Relations Representative and Lecturer before Chambers of Commerce and Convention and Visitor Bureaus, as well as during group sales to private, professional corporate organizations.

My current responsibilities encompass hosting a weekly international program on TV Channel 38 and three out-of-state cable stations. My responsibility involves research, script preparation, on-site taping coordination, and on-air interviews.

I have enclosed my resume. My prime interest is in the challenge and personal satisfaction I will derive from achieving your company's objectives. The compensation package is negotiable. To arrange for a meeting, please contact me at the above address or call (615) 555-5555.

Sincerely,

Chris Smith

Enc. Resume

178 Green Street
Chicago, IL 60601
(312) 555-5555

April 9, 20--

Pat Cummings
Chairperson of the Board
Any Clinic
1140 Main Street
Chicago, IL 60601

Dear Mr. Cummings:

I am a certified Chiropractor currently exploring affiliations with established clinics. I have worked in the Chicago area for more than twenty years and, as a result, my reputation for quality care is well known.

Currently, I work as a Chiropractic Therapist with the Chicago Chiropractic Center, a position I have held for the past fifteen years. In this capacity I provide spinal manipulation and handle the musculoskeletal needs of sports injury patients, alleviate pain in elderly patients and those with work-related injuries, and help victims of industrial accidents regain their strength and stamina.

I am also an active member of the following associations:

- American Chiropractic Association
- Illinois Chiropractic Society
- Chicago Chiropractic Society
- Sports Injury Council of the American Chiropractic Association

If my qualifications are of interest to you, I can be reached at the phone number and address above.

Sincerely,

Chris Smith, D.C.

Enc. Resume

Corporate Salesperson

178 Green Street
Newberg, OR 97132
(503) 555-5555

February 9, 20--

Pat Cummings
Vice President, Sales
Any Corporation
1140 Main Street
Portland, OR 97201

Dear Ms. Cummings:

For more than ten years, I have been instrumental in opening, selling to, and servicing accounts as well as establishing corporate accounts in a multistate region. Some of my accomplishments include:

- Opening and servicing accounts that resulted in an increase in volume from $50,000 to $500,000.
- Achieving successful sales exceeding 20 percent of entire account inventory.
- Increasing customer accounts by 10 percent in a six-month period.

Currently, I am seeking a new position with a company that can benefit from the efforts of a self-starter who has not only developed new approaches to sales and has experience with customer-controlled computer inventories, but who has also motivated individuals and groups to achieve desired objectives or quotas as both independent contributors and team producers.

I am a dedicated, highly productive, hard-working individual with the kind of persistence that gets results. I work best in a competitive environment and prefer working with an incentive package.

I would be happy to meet in a personal interview to provide you with more detail as to my qualifications and how they can best serve your company.

Thank you for your consideration and early response.

Sincerely,

Chris Smith

Enc. Resume

178 Green Street
Washington, DC 20013
(202) 555-5555

June 26, 20--

Pat Cummings
Chief Executive Officer
Any Company
1140 Main Street
Arlington, VA 22234

Dear Ms. Cummings:

I am a successful entrepreneur with fifteen years of experience in areas that include planning, organization, setup, start-up, and management of unique and successful retail sales, product development, manufacturing, and marketing ventures.

Most recently, I have been involved in the launching of a gourmet food product within retail accounts and the hospitality industry. This new venture has given me the opportunity to participate, firsthand, in product formulation, development, and package design. And, under my direction, the product increased its distribution by 52 percent and averaged $150 million in sales.

Although my previous positions have been broad in scope, requiring the skills of a well-organized, innovative individual, I am seeking a new association that will afford me the opportunity to participate in high-level decision-making processes and to contribute to the company's growth and success.

I look forward to a new challenge. Please call with questions.

Sincerely,

Chris Smith

Enc. Resume

Fashion Designer

178 Green Street
Colorado Springs, CO 80903

May 13, 20--

Pat Cummings
Manager
Any Corporation
1140 Main Street
Jacksonville, FL 32231

Dear Mr. Cummings:

    I am a veteran of the fashion industry seeking a position with an aggressive, cutting-edge design team. Any Corporation's recent, extensive marketing campaign has confirmed my interest in the company.

    I possess three years of diverse experience as an Art Director and Fashion Designer working with a screen-printing company. In this capacity, my principal responsibility has been creating the art and fashion design of clothing lines for national mass markets.

    I feel that my creative skills and experience in dealing with sales and buyers can be effectively utilized with a firm such as yours. If you have the need for a highly motivated achiever, then we have good reason to meet.

    Please respond at the above address or by phone at (719) 555-5555 to arrange a mutually convenient time for a meeting to discuss my qualifications. A portfolio of my creative work is available for your review.

    Thank you for your consideration.

Sincerely,

Chris Smith

Enc. Resume

Fleet and Transportation Manager

178 Green Street
Altus, OK 73521
(918) 555-5555

April 25, 20--

Pat Cummings
Executive Vice President
Any Corporation
1140 Main Street
Tulsa, OK 74106

Dear Mr. Cummings:

If your firm can benefit from a committed professional with general, financial, fleet, and transportation management experience, then we have good reason to meet.

In addition to a Master's degree in Business Administration, Summa Cum Laude, from Harvard University, and advanced study in dealer management, I offer:

- More than sixteen years of senior-level management experience with P&L responsibility for a composite automotive dealership offering new and used car/truck sales, service, and rental/leasing operations.
- Eight years of additional experience in banking as an investment officer with investment analysis and portfolio management responsibility.
- Expertise in the design, implementation, and installation of computerized accounting systems, as well as extensive experience with financial analysis, budgets, and cost-effective corporate operations.
- Skill in the selection and development of management teams, incentives, and benefit programs to retain the most capable personnel.
- Knowledge of developing cash management and financial programs to provide funding for new or continuing operations to maximize returns on investment.
- Qualifications to function as controller, financial analyst, operations, or administrative manager where corporate management is interested in achieving its objectives of cost-effective operations and increased profitability.

I am in search of a fast-paced, aggressive company that could benefit from my ability to quickly increase growth and profitability. Relocation and travel would be considered. Thank you for your time.

Sincerely,

Chris Smith
Enc. Resume

Freight Supervisor

178 Green Street
Raleigh, NC 27611

September 1, 20--

Pat Cummings
District Supervisor
Any Corporation
1140 Main Street
Fayetteville, NC 28302

Dear Ms. Cummings:

During the past thirteen years, I have been actively involved in positions as Field Manager of Contained Operations and Night Operations Supervisor of freight stations and service centers dealing with domestic and international freight deliveries.

In addition to the supervision of day-to-day operations, my experience encompasses the hiring, training, and supervision of drivers, office and support personnel, and the provision of cost-effective quality service within a multiple service network. I have sound knowledge of computer systems design for freight movement management, and am skilled in both troubleshooting and resolving problems relative to the movement or transfer of materials.

Although my present situation is challenging and diverse, I feel that it is time for me to make a change. I am looking for a new association with a firm that can benefit from my extensive experience with import/export traffic. Depending on the benefits package, salary is negotiable.

I would welcome the opportunity to discuss your requirements and to further outline my qualifications. Should you require additional information, please contact me at the above address or by phone at (919) 555-5555.

Thank you for your consideration.

Sincerely,

Chris Smith

Enc. Resume

178 Green Street

Cedar Rapids, IA 54201

(319) 555-5555

April 10, 20--

Pat Cummings

Chief Account Executive

Any Corporation

1140 Main Street

Wichita, KS 67202

Dear Ms. Cummings:

I am a seasoned Marketing/Sales Executive seeking an association with an aggressive, young firm such as Any Corporation. I offer extensive experience and achievements in marketing, business development, and product management at national and international levels.

During the past ten years, my successes have included:

- Development of sales programs and new businesses to increase penetration, market share, and revenue through advanced, technically sophisticated systems management services.
- Team participation in the development and marketing of new service products for a service business generating $3.7 billion worldwide.
- P & L responsibility for an added-value services business generating $90 million.
- Established record of achievement for producing positive bottom-line results in a high-tech service-oriented business with worldwide markets.

I am well qualified to direct areas that are key to achieving your business objectives. I am prepared to play an integral role in the profitable management of corporate programs designed to broaden your business opportunities on national and/or international levels.

My salary range is in the mid-$70,000 range. However, as my primary interest is in the challenge of the position and your goals, this figure is negotiable.

Sincerely,

Chris Smith

Enc. Resume

Program Manager

178 Green Street
Tulsa, OK 74117
(918) 555-5555

August 12, 20--

Pat Cummings
Director
Any Company
1140 Main Street
Anadarko, OK 73005

Dear Ms. Cummings:

An article in the July issue of *Oklahoma Business Journal* featured Any Company's recent success and growth. As a Program Manager interested in establishing connections with a new, up-and-coming firm, I submit the enclosed resume for your review.

My qualifications include more than twelve years of managing experience with Ricochet Data. In this capacity I developed and coordinated short- and long-range plans for the design and introduction of four new microcomputer products. I also created master charts to track major milestones and critical path activities, directed a management task force to develop a set of work instructions for the introduction of outsourced products, and reduced product time to market by 25 percent.

My work in retail management might also be of interest to you. While employed at Lorenz Company, I generated gross annual sales in excess of $2 million for four consecutive years, managed a sales and service team of twenty people, and provided superior customer service and support.

Should my qualifications match your current or anticipated needs, I can be reached at the telephone number and address above.

Sincerely,

Chris Smith

Enc. Resume

178 Green Street
Appleton, WI 54912

December 14, 20--

Pat Cummings
President
Any Corporation
1140 Main Street
Madison, WI 53713

Dear Mr. Cummings:

During the past thirteen years, working with a full-service real estate and consulting firm, I have acted as:

- Director of Development for consulting services generating $1.8 million in fees.
- Project Manager overseeing major additions and renovations for corporate and institutional clients involving 1.2 million square feet.
- Property/Asset Manager of half a million square feet of company-developed, -owned, and -managed real estate.

My position has been one of diverse responsibilities and challenges. However, I feel it is time for me to make a change to a larger, more aggressive firm where my comprehensive experience in development, property/asset management, and related consulting skills can be better utilized.

In prior positions, as Regional Manager and Loan Officer, I gained broad experience and insight into residential and commercial financing with emphasis on the mortgage and mortgage insurance industries involving institutions and private investors. I am confident that this combination of varied and successful experience can be effectively applied to a firm competing against other major full-service real estate operations.

Should you require additional information, please contact me at the above address or by phone at (414) 555-5555. Since my present employer is not aware of my intent to make a change, I would appreciate your holding this correspondence in the strictest confidence. Thank you.

Sincerely,

Chris Smith

Enc. Resume

Senior Vice President

178 Green Street
Bridgeton, MO 63044
(314) 555-5555

January 3, 20--

Pat Cummings
President
Any Bank
1140 Main Street
St. Louis, MO 63146

Dear Ms. Cummings:

I am currently the Senior Vice President at Central St. Louis Bank where I have been for the past twenty-five years. Please note my credentials:

- Fifteen years of diverse experience ranging from Acting Branch Manager and District Manager to my present position as Vice President.
- Supervised all internal departments including sales/account development, human resources, customer relations and customer service supervision, and product and sales support.
- Increased new business by 25 percent in one year through extensive interface with clients, decision-makers, and support personnel.

Although my present position is challenging, I am looking to associate myself with a progressive firm that addresses both national and international banking markets. I offer both experience and enthusiasm.

I look forward to hearing from you.

Sincerely,

Chris Smith

Enc. Resume

Vice President of Administration

178 Green Street

Dodge City, KS 67801

(316) 555-5555

July 26, 20--

Pat Cummings

Chief Executive Officer

Any Corporation

1140 Main Street

Wichita, KS 67226

Dear Ms. Cummings:

I have served as Vice President of Administration and Finance at Third Bank of Kansas for the past eighteen years. Although this position has been very challenging, I am interested in a change and feel that my background might be of interest to you.

Please consider the following qualifications:

- Provided handling and record-keeping services for corporate, fiduciary, and personal custody accounts with assets totaling $20 billion.
- Managed administrative sales, which totaled more than $500,000.
- Directed administrative processes for 56 percent of the department's largest and most complex accounts.
- Analyzed new accounting systems to determine customers' needs.
- Developed and maintained strong securities operational knowledge.

In addition to my extensive experience, I am also a member and past president of the Securities Operations Association of the Heartland, speaker/panel member of the Kansas Bankers Association, and past president of the Bank of Heartland Supervisors' Association.

I look forward to hearing from you in the near future.

Sincerely,

Chris Smith

Enc. Resume

Zoologist

178 Green Street
Lexington, KY 21345
(606) 555-5555

June 26, 20--

Pat Cummings
Director
Any Stable
1140 Main Street
New York, NY 10153

Dear Ms. Cummings:

    I am a Zoologist with eight years of experience working primarily with racehorses. I am currently seeking a position in a stable where my expertise in genetics and breeding will contribute to the success of the organization. Perhaps my credentials will interest you.

First, my most recent experience includes work with the following:

- Center for DNA Research, Cambridge, MA; Spring 20--
- Truman Thoroughbred Stables, Hamilton, MA; Spring 20--
- Center for Genetic Research, New York, NY; Summer 20--

    Currently I serve as Genetics/Breeding Specialist for the Uphill Thoroughbred Stables and Stud Farm. In this position, I work directly with doctors of veterinary medicine and racehorse trainers in breeding and grooming top-quality thoroughbreds for racing and dressage. I also investigate genetic factors, forecast crossbreeding, and evaluate artificial insemination considerations of specific mares and studs.

    Although I am quite happy with my present employer and the work is challenging, I am interested in a position where I can conduct more intensive research in a laboratory environment. If my qualifications meet your needs, please call.

    I look forward to hearing from you.

Sincerely,

Chris Smith, D.V.M.

Enc. Resume

178 Green Street
Payne Gap, KY 41537
(606) 555-5555

April 30, 20--

Pat Cummings
Chief Administrator
Any Hospital
1140 Main Street
Sandy Springs, SC 29677

Dear Ms. Cummings:

I recently read about your need for a Cardiologist in the May edition of the bulletin published by the South Carolina Medical Association. Please accept the following summary of accomplishments as my application for this opportunity.

- Two years as Cardiology Fellow with extensive experience covering the full spectrum of clinical cardiology.
- Experience encompasses: cardiac catheterization and angioplasty, cardiac pacing and electrophysiology, echocardiography, exercise testing and nuclear imaging, in- and out-patient hospital care of cardiac patients.
- Two years of experience as a Clinical Instructor in Medicine at St. Martha's Hospital, teaching interns, residents, and medical students.
- Board certified—Internal Medicine, board eligible in Cardiology.

In my current position as Cardiology Fellow at St. Martha's, I have had the opportunity to utilize state-of-the-art systems, procedures, and techniques covering the full spectrum of clinical cardiology. I am also presently involved in research encompassing clinical evaluation of the Bundeen cross-coronary stent, and have just completed a review article dealing with ventricular arrhythmias. Additionally, I received my Doctor of Medicine degree from the Boston College School of Medicine, and a Bachelor of Science degree in Preprofessional Studies from the University of Pennsylvania.

I am planning to move to South Carolina shortly, and I understand that you need a qualified Cardiologist to fill your vacancy. Would you have a few moments to speak with me next week during a scheduled visit to your area? I am sure I could convince you that I have the capabilities and the motivation to join your staff.

I will call your office on Friday to follow up on this inquiry.

Sincerely yours,
Chris Smith, M.D.

Community Center Director

178 Green Street
West Chester, PA 19380
(800) 555-5555

February 29, 20--

Pat Cummings
President and Executive Director
Any Community Center
1140 Main Street
Philadelphia, PA 19114

Dear Mr. Cummings:

I was sorry to hear about your retirement in the article "Community Top Gun to Step Down" featured in the February 28 edition of the *Philadelphia Enquirer*. Your accomplishments as Executive Director at Any Community Center speak for themselves, and I am sure your dedication and vision will be sorely missed.

I understand from a statement you made in the article that you will be personally choosing your successor prior to retirement. As a seasoned Community Center Director myself, I would be honored if you would consider me worthy of continuing your work. Presently, I am working as the Associate Executive Director of the West Chester YMCA.

My responsibilities encompass all aspects of operations:

Supervision: Supervise seven full-time program directors and nonexempt administrative staff. Recruit, hire, train, and evaluate full- and part-time staff. Organize and conduct staff meetings and training events. Responsible for career development for full-time professional staff.

Management: Financial management of a $2 million multidepartment annual budget. Developed and projected new annual budget, balanced and allocated funds, and ensured branch departments met financial goals. Operations management of all program areas, member services, office administration, and facility maintenance. Administered safety and risk-management procedures for the branch.

Fundraising: Chaired 20-- Annual Support Campaign and Community Gifts Chair of the 20-- Annual Support Drive. Organized campaign activities, recruited and trained volunteers, managed telephone solicitations, developed prospects, and implemented related administrative procedures.

Programs/Services: Managed multiprogram areas, scheduling, enrollment, and member evaluations. Established program guidelines and criteria. Managed and supervised membership department and front desk area, program registration, and member services/relations.

Community Relations: Responsible for administration and allocation of scholarship/financial aid funds. Assisted in volunteer development program. Direct responsibility to branch board of directors and program committees. Responsible for public service announcements and public relations via presentations at various community organizations.

I would be very interested in talking with you about your requirements for the position. When would be a convenient time to meet?

Sincerely,

Chris Smith

Director of Information Services

178 Green Street
Clearfield, UT 84016

November 5, 20--

Pat Cummings
Vice President, Operations
Any Corporation
1140 Main Street
Salt Lake City, UT 84104

Dear Mr. Cummings:

I am interested in your advertisement for a Director of Information Services as published in the November edition of the *Salt Lake Tribune*. Several of the qualifications I could bring to this position include:

- Extensive experience in COBOL Programming.
- Proven managerial abilities.
- Self-motivation; able to set effective priorities to achieve immediate and long-term goals and meet operational deadlines.
- Development of interpersonal skills, having dealt with a diversity of professionals, clients, and staff members.
- Ability to function well in fast-paced, high-pressure atmosphere.

For the past eleven years I have had the opportunity to progress in positions of responsibility at my current employer from Programmer to Director of Information Services. In this capacity, I control programming and systems, computer operations, data entry, membership records, and membership promotion and retention departments. I have successfully implemented complete financial reporting systems, inventory, accounts receivable, computerized production of publications, and applications.

In addition to my work experiences, I hold both a Bachelor's and a Master's degree in Business Administration. I am proficient in most computer systems, as well as peripheral equipment and 35 online CRT terminals (COBOL).

I am very interested in learning more about your work at Any Corporation and how I might best apply my skills to your advantage. Please contact me at (801) 555-5555 to schedule a meeting.

Sincerely,

Chris Smith

Hospital Administrator

178 Green Street
Norwalk, CT 06856
(203) 555-555

August 11, 20--

Pat Cummings
Chairperson, Board of Directors
Any Hospital
1140 Main Street
Bridgeport, CT 06605

Dear Mr. Cummings:

Thank you for speaking with me this morning regarding the Hospital Administrator position available at Any Hospital. As per your request, please allow me to present several of my most relevant experiences and accomplishments in health care management/administration.

For the past year, I have been working as Acting Director of the Norwalk Medical Center. In this capacity, I am responsible for the supervision/coordination of all administrative services for the city's public health care program. This includes the health care and hospitalization for indigent, low-income, and welfare patients, consistent with care-afforded insurance and fee-for-service patients. In addition, I troubleshoot staff and general administration conflicts and resolve policy issues, as well as develop reports for budgeting proposals and expenditure control.

Previous to my current position, I spent six years as Central Administrator of Emergency Services for the same institution. I coordinated all administrative details of the department, prepared the department budget, and monitored expenditures. As Administrator, I also supervised ward secretaries, interpreters, and ancillary personnel. This same duty was performed in the position of Unit Manager, which I held from 20-- to 20--. This position gave me exposure to several aspects of administrative support, vendor relations, and inventory control.

My work experience is supported by a Master of Science degree in Health Service Administration, a certificate in Management Development from the Connecticut Hospital Association, and a Bachelor of Arts degree in English.

I am very eager to apply my acquired knowledge of health care administration to the position at Any Hospital. I hope my qualifications match your requirements, and that I will have the opportunity to speak with you again in a personal interview.

Thank you for your consideration.

Sincerely,

Chris Smith

Manufacturing Manager

178 Green Street
Lake City, FL 32056
(904) 555-5555

May 8, 20--

Pat Cummings
Chief Executive Officer
Any Corporation
1140 Main Street
Chicago, IL 60611

Dear Ms. Cummings:

I discovered Any Corporation through your listing in the *Chicago JobBank*. I am an experienced executive with a broad technical as well as management background in the machining and manufacturing fields. Next month, I will be moving permanently to Illinois, and would be very interested in learning of suitable management opportunities at your firm.

With more than sixteen years of training in the manufacturing industry, I possess a proven track record of accomplishment. Some of the experiences I could bring to Any Corporation include:

Manufacturing Manager; Gladstone Motor Company, Lake City, VT
- Oversaw modernization and reorganization of engine plant contracted for remanufacture of Dane Motor Company engines.
- Set up controls for workers in manufacturing departments and the machine shop, which included grinding, boring, and honing operations.
- Initiated an improved quality control system to meet Dane specifications for full-year warranty. System resulted in reduction of rejects to less than 4 percent on 500 to 600 engines completed monthly.
- Classified purchasing details on 80 different production engines; implemented inventory control; greatly improved ordering efficiencies; and set up effective marketing service policies.

Manufacturing Manager; P.I.L. Engineering Company, Tampa, FL
- Supervised the production of a machine shop that subcontracted to manufacture precision machine parts and assemblies for the electronic industry.
- Developed and implemented manufacturing, cost control, and quality control programs; successfully developed business to $8.2 million in annual sales.

General Manager; Ferou Maintenance, Tampa, FL

- Shouldered full responsibility for tractor-trailer maintenance company servicing the Shaw Line Hault Fleet consisting of 500 trailers and 200 tractors traveling between Florida and the mid-Atlantic states.
- Initiated many vehicle design changes that were adopted by the Stanza Motor Company.
- Designed unique field service trucks on which specifications were written for national application.

I will be in the Chicago area during the week of May 22 to 26, and would be very interested in meeting with you at that time regarding possible openings appropriate for my qualifications. Perhaps I could share several of my design and organizational ideas, which I feel might benefit operations at Any Corporation. I will contact you next week to schedule a mutually convenient meeting time.

Sincerely,

Chris Smith

Vice President, Sales and Marketing

178 Green Street
Pigeon Forge, TN 37868
(615) 555-5555

October 14, 20--

Pat Cummings
Chief Executive Officer
Any Corporation
1140 Main Street
Nashville, TN 37211

Dear Ms. Cummings:

In a phone conversation on Friday, my neighbor and your Senior Sales Representative, Milton Farley, informed me of the newly vacant position of Vice President, Sales and Marketing at Any Corporation. Milton felt that my extensive experience as an executive in this area would make me an excellent candidate for this opportunity. In this regard, please allow me to describe my background.

Experience:

Vice President; Littleton and Shelley, Nashville, TN

Company is a $10 million, industry-leading producer of toys and related items manufactured and sold internationally. Started as Purchasing Manager, assuming additional responsibilities for outside sales, and, on the basis of outstanding success in the development and handling of key accounts and general operations, advanced to the current position of Vice President in charge of sales and product development.

Accomplishments:

- Personal sales in excess of $4 million a year, while managing/working with network of more than 46 sales organizations employing 150 sales representatives.
- Managed development, sourcing, manufacturing, and importation of total doll and doll accessory product lines from Far East and Europe. Reduced cost of manufacture by 15 percent.
- Added $350,000 at significant margin to gross sales through establishment of new division marketing line of doll accessories. Developed new fashions projected at $600,000 first-year sales.

- Developed new sales accounts, through establishment of national representative/distributor organization, from annual sales of $250,000 to current volume of $850,000.

Although my time at Littleton and Shelley has provided me with a great deal of challenge and satisfaction, I would like to apply my experience to a new environment. I am familiar with your products and services, and am confident I could provide innovative and cost-effective supervision of your sales and marketing team. Based on my experience, my compensation requirements are between $100,000-$115,000.

Could we meet for further discussion?

Sincerely,

Chris Smith

50-Plus Job Candidate
Product Manager

178 Green Street
Fort Worth, TX 76111
(817) 555-5555

April 11, 20--

Pat Cummings
Vice President
Any Corporation
1140 Main Street
Fort Worth, TX 76101

Dear Mr. Cummings:

Is your corporation in need of a motivated professional with comprehensive product management experience? If so, I would like to present my qualifications for your consideration.

In my vast experience, I have gained valuable insight into all aspects of product/protocol development and management to obtain FDA product approval. As Product Manager for Estrade, Inc., I provided extensive coordination of all product development activities for a large medical supply corporation. This acquired knowledge of clinical research would be especially beneficial to your development team.

I have consistently maintained a strong motivation for developing innovative product design and management, as well as a flexibility toward new approaches and marketing techniques. I am thoroughly proficient in most major computer applications, including Microsoft Word and Excel; I can navigate the Internet with ease. Much of my work has necessitated collaboration with systems consultants on the design and implementation of data management systems, including remote access.

I would be happy to further outline my skills during the course of a personal interview. After you have reviewed my qualifications, please contact me to schedule a time that is convenient for you to meet.

I appreciate your consideration and look forward to speaking with you.

Sincerely,

Chris Smith

Enc. Resume

All Employment at One Company
Inventory Control Manager

178 Green Street

Minot, ND 58702

(701) 555-5555

April 4, 20--

Pat Cummings

President

Any Corporation

1140 Main Street

Grand Forks, ND 58201

Dear Ms. Cummings:

I am currently searching for a position in inventory control and administration, and would like to inquire about suitable opportunities at Any Corporation.

As a member of your staff, I would offer more than twelve years of experience in inventory control management, in positions ranging from Office Manager to Vice President of Inventory Management/Administrative Services. I possess a strong background in customer service, excellent interpersonal skills, and a strong motivation to successfully complete any task put before me. These qualifications are supported by a Master of Business Administration degree, and a Bachelor of Science in Management.

If given the chance, I am confident I could cost-effectively direct your inventory control. Please contact me at your convenience to schedule a meeting. The opportunity to further prove my capabilities is of great interest to me.

I look forward to your reply.

Sincerely,

Chris Smith

Enc. Resume

All Employment at One Company
Materials Manager

178 Green Street
Daytona Beach, FL 32115

August 18, 20--

Pat Cummings
Vice President, Fiscal Affairs
Any Hospital
1140 Main Street
Orlando, FL 32816

Dear Mr. Cummings:

During the past eighteen years, I have progressed rapidly in positions of responsibility from Supervisor of Patient Transportation to Manager of Warehousing/Distribution to my current position as Senior Buyer and Manager of Inventory Control.

Although my prior associations have been growing and challenging experiences, I would like to make a position change and move into materials management within the health care field. I am in search of an opportunity in which I can use my skills to achieve the same meaningful results, but in a broader scope of responsibility.

Through cost-effective negotiations, purchasing, and control, I have been able to reduce the expenditures of all in-house medical and nonmedical supplies substantially each year as Manager of Inventory Control. In addition, I played a key role in automating inventories and providing a functional layout for warehouse locations, which effectively reduced the selection and distribution process for warehoused materials. This also enabled me to provide more stringent controls, thereby reducing shrinkage, damage, and obsolescence—common problems causing great concern in the health care field.

Enclosed is my resume. I would very much like to schedule a mutually convenient interview time. I can be reached at the address cited above or by phone at (904) 555-5555. The opportunity to join your management team is of great interest to me, and I look forward to meeting with you for further discussion.

Sincerely,

Chris Smith

Enc. Resume

At-Home Parent Re-entering the Work Force
Graphic Designer

178 Green Street
Mountain View, CA 92715
(415) 555-5555

July 23, 20--

Pat Cummings
Director
Any Advertising Agency
1140 Main Street
Sausalito, CA 94966

Dear Mr. Cummings:

I am very interested in a freelance or part-time position in graphic design or advertising production. I forward the attached resume for your evaluation.

Please note that in addition to a Bachelor of Arts degree and current enrollment in the Massachusetts College of Art's Graphic Design Certificate Program, I offer more than seven years of valuable experience in the production and traffic areas of print and graphic design, and in related fields including fundraising and direct and mass mailings.

As you can see from my resume, I left the field three years ago with excellent references to raise a family and manage a household. Now, with my family well established, I am highly motivated to return to the work force and contribute the valuable experience gained before and during my hiatus.

I would like the opportunity to make a significant contribution to the success of Any Advertising Agency. I am available at the above address and phone number should you have any further questions.

I look forward to hearing from you.

Sincerely,

Chris Smith

Enc. Resume

At-Home Parent Re-entering the Work Force
Salesperson

178 Green Street
Fort Collins, CO 80525
(303) 555-5555

August 14, 20--

Pat Cummings
Department Manager
Any Store
1140 Main Street
Aurora, CO 80012

Dear Ms. Cummings:

Emmett Puffin recently informed me that you are seeking a full-time addition to your children's department sales staff. I have been observing some very positive changes at Any Store, especially your new campaign to promote back-to-school sportswear. I am anxious to join such a successful sales team.

As my resume indicates, I possess more than three years of experience within the retail and wholesale arenas. I am committed to quality sales and service standards and am eager to continue my record of success with Any Store. As your newest Sales Associate, I would contribute strong interpersonal skills and an enthusiastic selling approach.

I will contact you on Friday to schedule a personal interview. I look forward to discussing how my capabilities could be guided to suit your needs.

Thank you for your time and consideration.

Sincerely,

Chris Smith

Enc. Resume

Bilingual Applicant
Medical Receptionist

178 Green Street
Palm Harbor, FL 34683
(727) 555-5555

April 24, 20--

Pat Cummings, M.D.
Any Pediatric Clinic
1140 Main Street
Tampa, FL 33614

Dear Dr. Cummings:

In response to your ad in Sunday's *Tampa Tribune* for a medical receptionist, I am pleased to enclose my resume for your consideration. A graduate of Plant High School, I have completed courses in medical terminology, billing, and transcription at Hillsborough Community College. For the last two years, I have worked as a receptionist and clerk typist in the Admitting Department at Tampa General Hospital. I am knowledgeable in a variety of software programs, including Microsoft Office, Word, and Excel. My typing speed is 60 wpm.

While I am sure that, like me, most of the applicants for this position can offer a pleasing telephone voice, professional demeanor, and exceptional organizational skills, I bring one competency that few of them probably have—I am fluent in both English and Spanish. A visit to the doctor is stressful enough for children and their parents, but for those who do not speak the language, it is doubly so. I will be able to immediately put them at ease and to help them complete the necessary paperwork as well as assist you and your staff with your translation needs during examinations and treatment.

I believe I could make a positive contribution to your practice and I would welcome the opportunity for an interview. Thank you for your consideration and I look forward to hearing from you.

Sincerely,

Chris Smith

Enc. Resume

Career Changer
Advertising Assistant

178 Green Street
Daytona Beach, FL 32115
(904) 555-5555

August 18, 20--

Pat Cummings
Hiring Manager
Any Advertising Agency
1140 Main Street
Orlando, FL 32816

Dear Mr. Cummings:

I am very interested in pursuing my career in the advertising industry at Any Advertising Agency. While researching area firms, I read an exciting piece in *Ad World* about your recent campaign for Homeloving soups. Congratulations on receiving a Clio Award for your efforts.

I would love to join your winning team in an entry-level, administrative position. I can offer more than eight years of administration, promotion, and communication experience. The following achievements would be especially beneficial to your firm:

Administration: Record keeping and file maintenance. Data processing and computer operations, accounts receivable, accounts payable, and accounting research and reports. Order fulfillment, inventory control, and customer relations. Scheduling, office management, and telephone reception.

Promotion: Composing, editing, and proofreading correspondence and PR materials for my own house-cleaning service.

Communication: Instruction, curriculum and lesson planning, student evaluation, parent-teacher conferences, and development of educational materials. Training and supervising clerks.

Computer Skills: Proficient in Microsoft Word, Lotus 1-2-3, Excel, FileMaker Pro, and ADDS Accounting System.

I would like to request a personal interview to further outline my skills, and how they could be immediately applicable to an administrative position at Any Advertising Agency. I will call your office on August 23 to schedule a convenient meeting time.

Thank you, Mr. Cummings. I look forward to our conversation.

Sincerely,

Chris Smith
Enc. Resume

178 Green Street
Carson City, NV 89706

August 26, 20--

Pat Cummings
Hiring Manager
Any Casino
1140 Main Street
Las Vegas, NV 89109

Dear Mr. Cummings:

Although I have spent the past two years as a medical student and my work experience has been focused in medical research and direct patient care, I am interested in a career change. I am in search of a position where I can use my skills to deal effectively with people, in an exciting and fast-paced environment such as Any Casino.

My work experience and educational discipline have provided me with the ability to rapidly learn new skills and produce solid returns with minimal instruction or supervision. I realize that to become a competent Casino Dealer requires training and experience, and I am willing to devote the time and effort necessary to become a professional in the field.

My professional profile is enclosed. I would like to convince you that I am qualified and strongly dedicated to becoming an effective Dealer for your casino. Can we schedule an interview?

Should you require additional information, please contact me at the above address or by phone at (702) 555-5555. May I hear from you?

Yours sincerely,

Chris Smith

Enc. Professional profile

178 Green Street
Yankton, SD 57078
(605) 555-5555

February 2, 20--

Pat Cummings
Director of Information Systems
Any Corporation
1140 Main Street
Sioux Falls, SD 57117

Dear Ms. Cummings:

After eighteen years in a successful practice of general dentistry, I have decided on a career change. To make the transition into computer programming, I sold my practice and have spent the last four years preparing as both a full-time student of computer programming and a Customer Service Representative and computer operator with the products division of CMZ Incorporated.

Although my present position is interesting and has provided me with the opportunity to apply my technical and computer skills, I am looking for a position with room for merit advancement based on my personal performance and contribution to the cost-effective efficiency of your systems.

The enclosed resume summarizes my background and experience. I am available to discuss my qualifications in a personal meeting. I can be reached at the above address or by phone at (605) 555-5555.

Sincerely,

Chris Smith

Enc. Resume

178 Green Street
Laie, HI 96762
(808) 555-5555

April 6, 20--

Pat Cummings
Credit Supervisor
Any Corporation
1140 Main Street
Honolulu, HI 96816

Dear Mr. Cummings:

Please accept the enclosed resume as an expressed interest in joining Any Corporation to contribute and develop my skills.

My experience lies in customer service and sales, where I have dealt with the public in a sales and assistance capacity in a financial environment. I would now like to expand and advance my career by applying my developed skills to a position as a Credit Analyst. Relevant skills and experience include:

- Bachelor of Science degree in Business Administration.
- Extensive experience in researching, compiling, and analyzing financial reports.
- Exclusive responsibility for customer service for more than 1,000 accounts.
- Opened and serviced 85 new accounts over a one-year period.

I would welcome the opportunity to meet with you to discuss ways in which my capabilities might suit your needs. Please consider my application and direct your response to the address cited above.

Your time and consideration is very much appreciated. I look forward to hearing from you.

Sincerely,

Chris Smith

Enc. Resume

Career Changer
Marketing Executive

178 Green Street
Boise, ID 83725
(208) 555-5555

August 5, 20--

Pat Cummings
Vice President
Any Corporation
1140 Main Street
Chicago, IL 60605

Dear Ms. Cummings:

I am forwarding my resume with regard to the opening in your marketing department as advertised in the August 6 edition of the *Chicago Tribune*.

Although I am currently employed in a management position, I am interested in a career change, especially one that would allow me to combine a thorough knowledge of boating with my sales, marketing, and communication skills. I am an imaginative, well-organized self-starter with a strong interest in boating. As a semiprofessional sailboat racer, I twice won national honors and participated in the races at Cape Cod. In addition, I have made lasting contacts with owners and officials.

After you have had the chance to review my resume, please contact me so that we can further discuss the possibility of my joining your staff. I am confident that my business background and knowledge of boats will enable me to have a favorable impact on both your sales and image.

Thank you for your attention, and I look forward to speaking with you again to learn more about this opportunity.

Sincerely yours,

Chris Smith

Enc. Resume

178 Green Street
Wichita, KS 67202

February 1, 20--

Pat Cummings
Vice President
Any Bank
1140 Main Street
Topeka, KS 66607

Dear Ms. Cummings:

During the past eight years, I have been actively involved as Vice President and Director of Operations of an established, quality, $1.4 million function/recreation complex with total responsibility for creating effective sales programs and assuring the quality of services provided.

Currently, I am seeking a career change and opportunity to associate with a progressive bank where I can effectively apply my creative and innovative talents and capability for developing or increasing new service products.

I am flexible, highly energetic, and adept at initiating promotional advertising and marketing programs that will stimulate growth and profits. I am not afraid of the risk or extra time required to gain valuable banking experience at Any Bank, and I would welcome the challenge.

The enclosed resume summarizes my background and experience. Should you require additional information, please contact me at the above address or phone me at (316) 555-5555. I will contact your office next week to schedule a mutually convenient time to meet.

I appreciate your consideration.

Yours sincerely,

Chris Smith

Enc. Resume

Career Changer
Real Estate Developer

178 Green Street
Norfolk, VA 23529
(804) 555-5555

July 20, 20--

Pat Cummings
Director of Real Estate Development
Any Corporation
1140 Main Street
Alexandria, VA 22312

Dear Mr. Cummings:

After several years of diverse and successful experience as a Municipal Bond Broker, I decided to pursue a career encompassing a broader scope of real estate development. To achieve this objective and establish myself as a professional in the field of real estate development, I have spent the past year completing a comprehensive graduate program and earned a Master's degree in Real Estate Development from the University of Virginia.

Presently, I am investigating career opportunities with a progressive developer emphasizing the financial and field aspects of project management. My experience, prior to entering said graduate program, required extensive involvement in the purchase and sale of bonds for financing public and private developments. These included private and public construction developments and business ventures that required the ability to work with decision makers and financial/investment professionals in the field of real estate development.

I am a dedicated, energetic self-starter who can recognize opportunities and has always been willing to devote the time necessary to complete any task thoroughly. With this attitude, I feel confident that I can readily become a valuable asset as a member of your management team.

I am presently available for an interview, and will be glad to meet with you at a mutually convenient time. My resume is enclosed for your review.

I appreciate your consideration.

Yours sincerely,

Chris Smith

Enc. Resume

178 Green Street
Belle, WV 25015

February 24, 20--

Pat Cummings
Sales Manager
Any Corporation
1140 Main Street
Clarksburg, WV 26302

Dear Ms. Cummings:

If you are in need of a highly motivated achiever skilled in selling products and services and developing client relationships and new business, then we have good reason to meet.

During the past six years, I have owned and operated a photography studio and photo-processing laboratory, both of which require the ability to manage inside production while generating enough outside sales to keep the business profitable. Since accomplishing my objective, I am interested in associating with a firm, such as Any Corporation, that can benefit from my ability to sell, manage, and train others to do a quality job.

I am confident of my ability to handle a sales position requiring innovative thinking for positive results. I would welcome the opportunity to convince you of my enthusiasm and skill in a personal interview. When would be a good time for us to meet?

I can be reached at the address cited or by phone at (304) 555-5555.

Sincerely,

Chris Smith

Enc. Business profile

Displaced Homemaker
Administrator

178 Green Street
Solon, OH 44139

February 25, 20--

Pat Cummings
Human Resources Director
Any Corporation
1140 Main Street
Cleveland, OH 44111

Dear Mr. Cummings:

I would like to offer my skills and experience for your consideration regarding administrative positions available at Any Corporation.

As an addition to your staff, I would bring extensive, varied experience in administration, including staff supervision, meeting planning and direction, and activities scheduling. I have the ability to speak effectively before groups, and communicate well through phone contact or the written word. Additionally, my skills include fundraising, promotion, and bookkeeping.

I am very interested in contributing to the continued success at Any Corporation, and am sure I would meet your expectations. Could we get together for further discussion? Please contact me at the address cited above or by phone at (216) 555-5555.

Thank you for your time.

Sincerely,

Chris Smith

Enc. Resume

178 Green Street

Provo, UT 84603

(801) 555-5555

November 19, 20--

Pat Cummings

Chief Executive Officer

Any Corporation

1140 Main Street

Salt Lake City, UT 84110

Dear Mr. Cummings:

    Todd Duncan, of your operations department, suggested I contact you concerning employment opportunities. Todd mentioned that you were considering expanding your sales staff, and thought you might benefit from a professional with my qualifications.

    I offer more than twenty years of progressively responsible experience in sales, culminating in my most recent position as Director of Sales and Pricing with a $750 million, 120-store chain. As a senior-level manager, I have been responsible for all aspects of store operations, including merchandising management, buying, strategic planning, marketing, and staff development and management.

    Although I have thoroughly enjoyed my present position, corporate downsizing has prompted me to search for a new position. I feel that my years of successful management experience can be more advantageously utilized by a growing and diversifying firm such as Any Corporation.

    If you are looking for a well-organized, innovative individual with the ability to garner results, please contact me. I would be happy to meet with you at your convenience.

Sincerely,

Chris Smith

Enc. Resume

Freelancer
Production Assistant

178 Green Street
Miami, FL 33132

September 21, 20--

Pat Cummings
Executive Producer
Any Production Company
1140 Main Street
Hialeah, FL 33012

Dear Mr. Cummings:

I am writing to express my keen interest in the Production Assistant position, as advertised in the September 20 edition of the *Miami Herald*.

I possess extensive experience in all aspects of video production, including positions as Writer, Researcher, Director, and Editor. For the past three years, I have been a freelance Production Assistant working on several commercial and documentary pieces. As Chief Assistant on *Milk Carton Kids: An American Crisis,* I assisted in preliminary research/writing, scheduling location shooting, and screening potential interview candidates. I also helped in the completion of two public service announcements for Miami Child Services, where my duties also involved camera operation and heavy editing work.

My freelance experience has been diverse and rewarding, and yet, I would like a permanent production position where my skills can be utilized to a greater advantage. I have admired Any Production Company's work for some time, and attended your screening of *Silent Victims* at the Miami Rape Awareness Convention last month. I would like the opportunity to contribute to such remarkable work.

Please contact me at (305) 555-5555 or (305) 555-4444 evenings, if you need any additional information or if you would like to arrange a meeting.

I look forward to hearing from you.

Sincerely,

Chris Smith

Enc. Resume

Frequent Job Changer
Marketing Assistant

178 Green Street
El Segundo, CA 90245
(213) 555-5555

December 14, 20--

Pat Cummings
Director of Marketing
Any Corporation
1140 Main Street
Los Angeles, CA 90089

Dear Mr. Cummings:

I am currently seeking an entry-level opportunity in a successful marketing department, and have learned about Any Corporation through the *L.A. Top Sellers Guide*. Congratulations on such an outstanding year.

As you can see from the enclosed resume, since completion of my Bachelor of Science degree, my professional associations have been extensive and diverse. Throughout my experiences, I have developed several important skills that I believe could benefit your marketing department. I possess solid communication skills, both in person and by phone. I am proficient with Macintosh, PC, and spreadsheet applications, and I can effectively manage all aspects of daily business operations, including inventory management and account maintenance. Above all, I possess a strong work ethic and enthusiasm to learn.

Last month I took an intensive seminar entitled "Marketing for Success!" This investment conclusively confirmed my desire to pursue marketing as a career. I know that, if given the chance, I could quickly prove my worth as a member of your staff. Would you permit me that chance?

I look forward to your response.

Sincerely,

Chris Smith

Enc. Resume

Gaps in Employment History
Assistant Curator

178 Green Street
Tallassee, AL 36078

June 3, 20--

Pat Cummings
Curator
Any Museum
1140 Main Street
Mobile, AL 36633

Dear Ms. Cummings:

If you are in need of a skilled individual to assist you in museum operations, I would like to offer the enclosed resume for your consideration. I am currently seeking a full-time position in which I can apply both my museum and gallery experience and keen interest in fine art.

As you will note from my resume, I have completed two extensive internships for successful art galleries elsewhere in Alabama. In each position, I was exposed to all aspects of operations, from sales to clerical duties. My responsibilities also included assisting customers, setting up displays, and completing mailings for exhibitions. I also possess a Bachelor of Art degree in Art History, and have participated in several related seminars.

In addition, I have spent the last year traveling extensively through Europe, visiting some of the finest museums in the world. This experience has greatly intensified my interest in securing a position in the art world.

I would be available for an interview at your convenience to discuss my qualifications further. Please contact me at the address cited above or by phone at (205) 555-5555.

Sincerely,

Chris Smith

Enc. Resume

178 Green Street
Eagan, MN 55122
(612) 555-5555

September 12, 20--

Pat Cummings
Senior Accountant
Any Corporation
1140 Main Street
Bloomington, MN 55438

Dear Ms. Cummings:

I am currently searching for an accounting position in which I may contribute my financial expertise as well as my ability to interface effectively with the business community on an international scale.

I offer more than twelve years of comprehensive accounting experience, in both public and private firms. My skills include audits, Chapter 11 filings and bank reconciliation, preparation of financial reports, and accounts payable/receivable. In my most recent position as Senior Accountant, I was solely responsible for the setup and modification of a new computer system, and for leading a steering committee to select the general ledger package, which is currently in use.

As you will note from my resume, the majority of my work experience has been focused in Madrid, Spain. Last year, I made the decision to permanently move to the United States with my family, and am very interested in securing a long-term association with a firm such as Any Corporation. Please be assured that although English is my second language, I have been speaking it fluently for more than twenty years. As a Staff Accountant at your firm, I could provide translation services to your international department if needed, and an extensive knowledge of European financial dealings.

I would very much like to meet with you for further discussion. I will call your office next week to confirm a meeting time that fits your schedule. In the interim, please contact me if I can provide you with any additional information.

Sincerely,

Chris Smith

Enc. Resume

Military Background
Transportation Operator

178 Green Street
Provo, UT 84602
(801) 555-5555

January 10, 20--

Pat Cummings
Controller
Any Corporation
1140 Main Street
Provo, UT 84602

Dear Ms. Cummings:

During the past twelve years, my experience has been focused on transportation and sales, and seven of these years were spent with the United States Army. Although my recent experience has been in the sale of intangibles, I am interested in resuming a civilian career in transportation operations or in the sale of products or equipment allied to the transportation field.

I have a Bachelor of Science degree, and I am a graduate officer of the U.S. Army Transportation School—the equivalent of a graduate school. In addition to managing all phases of complete civilian and tactical transportation operations (vehicles from two-and-one-half-ton cargo trucks to ten-ton tractor trailers and petroleum tankers), I have taught courses and have trained troops in the total transportation cycle in the United States and abroad.

The enclosed resume summarizes my educational background and experience in the areas I have cited above. I feel confident that with my qualifications in the transportation field, I can contribute substantially toward the efficient operation of an in-house traffic, transportation, and distribution function, and/or commercial transportation depot.

I would appreciate the opportunity to further discuss my qualifications in the transportation field and the immediate and long-term contribution I could make to Any Corporation.

If my qualifications interest you, please contact me. I will be glad to furnish any additional information you require.

Sincerely,

Chris Smith

Enc. Resume

178 Green Street
Gallup, NM 87301
(505) 555-5555

July 21, 20--

Pat Cummings
Hiring Manager
Any Accounting Firm
1140 Main Street
Albuquerque, NM 87103

Dear Mr. Cummings:

   I am seeking an entry-level position in accounting that will allow me to apply my expertise in both financial management and customer service. While researching area firms, I became very interested in Any Accounting Firm's esteemed training and development program. To such a program, I would bring:

- Bachelor of Science degree, Cum Laude, in Finance.
- Four years of collections experience.
- Successful collection of 90 percent of company's overdue accounts.
- Experience in accounts payable and accounts receivable.
- Computer skills: Lotus 1-2-3, Microsoft Word
- Knowledge of spreadsheets and accounting software.
- Excellent interpersonal skills.
- Strong leadership qualities.

   I am a highly motivated self-starter who has the ability and drive to make a significant contribution to your firm. My resume is enclosed for your review. Would your schedule permit a meeting next week to further discuss my desire to join Any Accounting Firm's staff? I will call you on Friday, July 28, to follow up on this inquiry.

   Thank you for your consideration. I look forward to speaking with you.

Sincerely,

Chris Smith

Enc. Resume

Overseas Employment History
Marketing Assistant

178 Rue Vert
Paris, France
011-331-45-55-55

January 7, 20--

Pat Cummings
Director of Human Resources
Any Corporation
1140 Main Street
New York, NY 10028

Dear Ms. Cummings:

I am looking for a new association with an international service-oriented organization that can benefit from my multilingual and organizational skills in a marketing position.

I have a Bachelor of Arts degree in French (Summa Cum Laude), am fluent in French and Italian, and have strong proficiency in Spanish. In addition, I have experience as an Interpreter and Translator working on international market research with the International Marketing Department at the University of Paris. I concurrently worked as an Administrative Assistant to professors and business executives.

Since 20--, I have been tutoring individuals in foreign languages and English as a Second Language. I am familiar with various cultures and work well with multilingual, multicultural individuals and groups.

The enclosed resume summarizes my experience. I will be in New York from February 14 through February 28 to secure permanent housing arrangements. I would appreciate the opportunity to meet during that time so that we may discuss the mutual benefits of my joining your firm.

I will call your office the week of February 6 to confirm receipt of my application and to schedule an interview. Thank you for your time.

Sincerely,

Chris Smith

Enc. Resume

Part-Time Employment History
Art Instructor

178 Green Street
Marysville, OH 43040
(513) 555-5555

January 28, 20--

Pat Cummings
Principal
Any Elementary School
1140 Main Street
Dayton, OH 45404

Dear Mr. Cummings:

I would like to express my interest in applying for the part-time Art Instructor position advertised in the *Dayton Daily News*.

I am a trained Elementary Art Instructor with expertise in arts and crafts instruction as well as program conception and coordination. For four years, I taught art classes on a part-time basis for the Roosevelt School in Marysville. In addition to my teaching and program management activities, I arranged field excursions and produced an annual district-wide arts competition. Also, I hold a State of Ohio Elementary Education Certificate in Art, and a Bachelor of Fine Arts degree in Art Education.

For the past year, I have been spending weekends as Arts and Crafts Program Director for the Dayton Parks and Recreational Association. I create and facilitate programs for children, control a budget, select and purchase supplies, and supervise aides in various duties. Since this work is restricted to weekends, my weeks would be completely open to fulfill my responsibilities as your Art Instructor. I am confident that I could create and maintain an exciting program at Any Elementary School.

My resume is enclosed for your review. I would welcome the opportunity to discuss my relevant experience further in a personal interview. At such a time, I could provide you with several excellent references attesting to my skills, as well as a portfolio of past programs I have implemented.

I look forward to hearing from you.

Sincerely,

Chris Smith

Enc. Resume

Physically Challenged
Meeting Planner

178 Green Street
Mukilteo, WA 98275
(206) 555-5555

October 3, 20--

Pat Cummings
Director of Human Resources
Any Corporation
1140 Main Street
St. Charles, MO 63302

Dear Mr. Cummings:

I recently learned from your Vice President of Operations, Marsha Ponnif, that you might be in need of a Meeting Planner to join your management structure. I am submitting the enclosed business profile for your review.

During the past sixteen years, I have successfully demonstrated solid troubleshooting and problem resolution skills in management, marketing, and sales. My progressively responsible experience includes:

- Corporate/institutional meeting planning.
- Hospitality service coordination.
- Destination management/program coordination.
- Employee/client incentive programs.
- Sales/customer service.

Although my positions have been fast-paced and broad in scope, I would like to make a change and am very impressed by the products and services offered by Any Corporation. Could we meet for an interview? I will contact you next week to schedule a convenient time for further discussion.

Thank you, Mr. Cummings. I look forward to our next conversation.

Sincerely,

Chris Smith

Enc. Business profile

178 Green Street
Providence, RI 02902
(401) 555-5555

October 4, 20--

Pat Cummings
College Relations Representative
Any Service
1140 Main Street
Hartford, CT 06115

Dear Mr. Cummings:

I am enclosing my resume to apprise you of my interest in working for your airline catering service.

I will receive my Bachelor of Science degree in Food Service from Johnson & Wales University in January. In addition to studying such valuable courses as Chemical Science, Organic Chemistry, Nutrition, and Food Service Administration, I have learned a great deal about the food industry as an active member of the Student Association for Agricultural Science. Further, I offer solid experience in the food industry through working as an Assistant Manager for two summers at a local yogurt shop.

I would be very interested in securing an entry-level position with Any Service. If you feel that my qualifications might meet your needs, please contact me at (401) 555-4444. A message may also be left at the phone number listed above.

Thank you for your attention, and I look forward to your response.

Sincerely,

Chris Smith

Enc. Resume

Recent Graduate
Assistant Museum Director

178 Green Street
Vermillion, SD 57069

June 26, 20--

Pat Cummings
Museum Director
Any Museum
1140 Main Street
Rapid City, SD 57701

Dear Ms. Cummings:

   I am a recent graduate of the University of South Dakota with a well-rounded art history background. I would like to put my skills and knowledge to use in an entry-level position at your prestigious museum, perhaps as an Assistant Director to the Curator.

   As my resume indicates, I participated in an exclusive summer program for art history majors at the Louvre in Paris. There, I studied some of the most significant works of European art and attended a very interesting seminar about the workings of the Louvre itself. I also worked for two summers at the Metropolitan Museum of Art in New York City, where I served as a Museum Assistant at the information booth. My coursework in African-American art, modern art, and museum science has also prepared me well for an entry-level position in a fine arts museum.

   I have long been a lover of art and art museums. I have been visiting your museum since I was a small child and would be thrilled at the opportunity to become a part of your excellent staff.

   Enclosed is my resume for your consideration. I may be reached at (605) 555-5555 after 3 P.M. on weekdays and anytime on weekends. I hope to hear from you soon.

Sincerely,

Chris Smith

Enc. Resume

178 Green Street
New London, CT 06320

July 17, 20--

Pat Cummings
Regional Program Director
Any Environmental Campaign
1140 Main Street
Danbury, CT 06810

Dear Ms. Cummings:

As a recent graduate of Tufts University Environmental Leadership Training Program and a 20-- graduate of Mesa State College with a degree in Biology, I am currently launching my career as an Environmental Campaigner in areas of concern that affect local, national, or world communities.

For the past several years, my elective studies concentrated on biology, chemistry, and the scientific, management, and political issues associated with the environment. In addition, I have organized recycling programs in my hometown and on college campuses. Now I aim to make environmental campaigning my full-time profession. I am anxious to devote my energy to Any Environmental Campaign, and am confident I can make a significant contribution.

I can be reached at the address cited above or by phone at (203) 555-5555.

Looking forward to your response for a better world.

Sincerely,

Chris Smith

Enc. Resume

Recent Graduate
Forester

178 Green Street
Los Angeles, CA 90053
(213) 555-5555

July 30, 20--

Pat Cummings
Director
Any Bureau
1140 Main Street
Oakland, CA 94612

Dear Mr. Cummings:

I am a recent college graduate with a degree in Earth Science and Forestry and am seeking a position in Forestry in the Pacific states.

In June, I graduated from the University of Southern California with a Bachelor's degree in Earth Science and Forestry. I have studied many relevant courses including Forest Economics, Range Management, Ecology, Soil Science, Hydrology, Wildlife, and Agronomy. In 20--, I was recognized for outstanding achievement in the natural sciences when I was awarded the prestigious Lukestrom Badge.

I also offer on-site work experience, having interned last summer for the California State Soil Conservation Service. In this position, I was exposed to all aspects of applied soil science. I provided technical assistance primarily to farmers and ranchers to promote the conservation of soil, water, and related natural resources. Equally important, I helped to develop programs to combat soil erosion and maximize land productivity without damaging the environment.

I gained valuable experience in forestry when I attended Southern California University's Field Camp in Walgreen Falls. I planted and maintained trees and rare natural vegetation and recorded and charted their growth. In addition to testing soil and water samples, I tracked wildlife and worked to preserve natural habitats for endangered species.

If you feel that I am suited for a position with Any Bureau, I would greatly appreciate an interview. I may be reached at the number listing above during the morning hours. Thank you for your consideration.

Sincerely,

Chris Smith

Enc. Resume

178 Green Street
Aston, PA 19014
(215) 555-5555

April 4, 20--

Pat Cummings
Attorney-at-Law
Any Firm
1140 Main Street
Erie, PA 16563

Dear Mr. Cummings:

Justice Ellen Malone of Allentown Courthouse suggested that I contact you regarding an opening you may soon have for a Legal Assistant.

I will be graduating this May from Temple University with a Bachelor of Arts degree in African-American Studies. In addition to my core studies, I have studied in a variety of areas including business administration and computer applications. In 20--, I was awarded the prestigious Lieberman Scholarship.

I also offer a strong background in law, having worked in a variety of legal settings throughout my college years. I was a volunteer for Temple's Student Legal Aid, helping students with a variety of legal problems. I worked part-time over the past three years as a Volunteer Probation Officer for the Allentown juvenile court. And in addition to being an Outside Media Contact for an Aston Outreach Unified Neighborhood Team, I spent one summer as a Research Assistant for the Chief County Clerk of Allentown.

All of these positions have given me a strong sense of the law and extensive knowledge about the American legal system. Moreover, this experience has convinced me that I would like to pursue law as a career. Justice Malone highly recommends your firm as one that might be a good match for my goals and qualifications.

Enclosed is my resume. I will contact you within the week to further discuss the possibility of securing this position. Thank you for your time.

Sincerely,

Chris Smith

Enc. Resume, Writing sample

178 Green Street
White Plains, NY 10604
(914) 555-5555

March 16, 20--

Pat Cummings
Professional Recruiter
Any Photographic Institute
1140 Main Street
Long Island, NY 11747

Dear Ms. Cummings:

Perhaps you are seeking an addition to your excellent team of physicists? A new person can provide innovative approaches and ideas to the challenges of research and development.

As you can see from my resume, I will be graduating in June from New York University (NYU) with a Bachelor's degree in Physics. I also have studied related fields such as chemical engineering, mathematics, and systems applications, all of which I am sure would help me as a physicist with Any Photographic Institute. I offer solid experience, having worked for two summers for the physics department at NYU, both as an intern and a laboratory technician.

Additionally, I have a personal interest in photography, having been an avid amateur photographer for many years. I built my own darkroom and have won several awards for my photographs. Because of this, I feel that Any Photographic Institute is an especially good match for my skills and interests.

Please advise me of any positions that may become available. Your consideration of my credentials is greatly appreciated.

Sincerely,

Chris Smith

Enc. Resume

178 Green Street
Columbia, SC 29202
(803) 555-5555

August 14, 20--

Pat Cummings
Stage Director
Any Production Company
1140 Main Street
Columbia, SC 29202

Dear Mr. Cummings:

Lynne Winchester recently indicated that you may have an opening for a Set Designer and suggested that I contact you. I seek a creative position involving stage design in television.

I graduated last December from Clemson University with a Bachelor of Arts degree in Theatre Arts and a concentration in Studio Art. In addition to modern drama, and music and sound in theatre, I completed courses in set creation and design, intermediate painting, and woodworking. As a member of the drama club, I designed and helped create props for numerous campus productions including *The Tempest* and *Marco Polo Sings a Solo.*

As for my work experience, I co-designed and co-created the props and decorations for a new miniature golf course with a tropical island theme, which turned out to be a big hit. I also gained valuable skills working as an apprentice to a busy carpenter and painting houses for a large company.

Enclosed is my resume as well as some photographs of my work. I have some great ideas for the sets of *Trivia Tunes* and *Videos after Dark* which I would like to discuss with you in a personal interview. I may be reached at the above listed number before 1 P.M. on weekdays. Thank you for your consideration of my application.

Sincerely,

Chris Smith

Enc. Resume, Photographs

Recent Graduate
Translator

178 Green Street
Chicago Heights, IL 60411
(708) 555-5555

July 5, 20--

Pat Cummings
Director
Any Council
1140 Main Street
Denver, CO 80204

Dear Ms. Cummings:

I am writing with the hope that you will consider me for the position of Translator as advertised in today's *Rocky Mountain News*.

I graduated last month with a Bachelor of Arts degree in International Relations and French Language from Northwestern University. Consistently on the dean's list and graduating one year early with honors and advanced standing, I have been recognized throughout my career for excellent scholarship. I was also very active in many extracurricular events and organizations, including a residential honors program studying ethics and politics. By my junior year, I had become a Model United Nations Advisor, an Alumni Ambassador, and President of the International Affairs Society.

In addition, I have work experience in the field of international affairs, having served as an interpreter and translator for a Parisian film corporation. In this position, I interpreted during negotiations regarding film co-productions and translated agreements, film scripts, scenarios, and foreign correspondence. I also worked as the Assistant to the Parisian Correspondent for Desliases Associates, a prestigious import/export company.

I feel confident that an interview would determine that my expertise in international affairs and the French language and culture makes me well qualified for this position. I am not limited by location and would enjoy the opportunity to live and work in Denver for Any Council.

I look forward to meeting you, Ms. Cummings, and will give you a call to follow up on this letter toward the end of next week.

Sincerely,

Chris Smith

Enc. Resume

Retiree Re-entering the Work Force
Math Instructor

178 Green Street
Bartow, FL 33830
(813) 555-5555

August 2, 20--

Pat Cummings
Principal
Any Junior High School
1140 Main Street
St. Petersburg, FL 33716

Dear Mr. Cummings:

Recently I bumped into long-time friend and colleague, Harry Nestor, Superintendent of St. Petersburg Schools. Harry tells me that Any High School is currently searching for a part-time Math Instructor for the upcoming school year. I would like to express my interest in assuming such a position.

As my enclosed professional profile reflects, I possess more than thirty-three years of experience in junior high and high school education. Before assuming my most recent position as Principal of Sacred Heart Junior High School in St. Petersburg, I taught math and science courses to middle school children for thirteen years. My expertise ranges from remedial math to precalculus for advanced students. In addition to my Master's degree in Education, I hold a Florida State Teacher Certification.

Although retired for more than two years, I feel I still have much to offer in the field of education, and would once again like to apply my skills to the personal and intellectual advancement of all students.

I look forward to hearing from you further regarding this position.

Sincerely yours,

Chris Smith

Enc. Professional profile

178 Green Street
Wilmington, DE 19899
(302) 555-5555

February 22, 20--

Pat Cummings
Editor
Any Publishing Company
1140 Main Street
New Castle, DE 19720

Dear Mr. Cummings:

I would like to take this opportunity to express my interest in the Publisher's Assistant position advertised in the February 21 edition of the *News-Journal*.

I am a 20-- graduate of Johns Hopkins University, with a Bachelor of Arts degree in English. Since my graduation, I have accepted several temporary positions with area businesses in order to gain a wide range of skills with the ultimate goal of securing an entry-level position in publishing. While at Curran, Moylan, and Hudson, I developed strong written and interpersonal communication skills. My responsibilities included sorting mail, interfacing with management and clients, and data input. As a temporary Marketing Assistant at Finner and Grant Publishers, I assisted in special project work in the editorial department and with administrative responsibilities.

Each of my experiences has provided me with excellent computer and general office skills, which I could apply to the position of Publisher's Assistant. I would appreciate the chance to discuss my qualifications with you, and to learn more about current projects at Any Publishing Company. I plan to call you within the next several days to arrange a meeting.

Thank you for your consideration.

Sincerely,

Chris Smith

Enc. Resume

Weak Educational Background
Parking Supervisor

178 Green Street
Scottsdale, AZ 85254
(602) 555-5555

May 13, 20--

Pat Cummings
Manager of Operations
Any Airport
1140 Main Street
Phoenix, AZ 85021

Dear Ms. Cummings:

I am currently investigating opportunities to which I can apply my knowledge of, and extensive experience in, the management of large parking facilities.

In my most recent position at Parkinson Hotel, my proven abilities and tireless work ethic resulted in rapid advancement to a management position after only one year of service as a Parking Attendant. As Supervisor of Parking Facilities, I oversaw all financial collections, maintained customer service standards, effectively troubleshot, and managed a large staff. Additionally, I administered work schedules and payroll, assigned duties, and interfaced with hotel management.

I am a self-motivated, people-oriented, responsible individual capable of meeting your expectations for quality supervision. I look forward to a personal interview to further discuss how I can contribute to your parking staff.

Sincerely,

Chris Smith

Enc. Resume

Weak Employment Background
Sales Manager

178 Green Street
Kalamazoo, MI 49006
(616) 555-5555

June 20, 20--

Pat Cummings
On-Site Sales Manager
Any Corporation
1140 Main Street
Roscommon, MI 48653

Dear Ms. Cummings:

    If your company is looking for a self-motivated person who can work well with people, grasp and expand on new ideas, tackle and follow through on difficult projects, and achieve set objectives, then I feel we have good reason to meet.

    Confident in my ability to succeed, I offer you a Bachelor of Science degree in Economics (Cum Laude), a graduate degree in Urban Affairs, experience in sales, and the desire to apply all or part of this background to a structured management training program in your firm.

    The enclosed resume summarizes my background. I am not afraid of hard work, can work under pressure, and honestly feel that within a short time I could be contributing a profitable return on your company's training investment. I am available any time to learn more about Any Corporation and convince you of my desire to join your ranks.

    I look forward to meeting with you. Thank you for your time.

Sincerely,

Chris Smith

Enc. Resume

Response to Print Classified Ad
Assistant Editor

To: *patcummings@anybooks.com*
From: *chrissmith@bluepencil.com*
Subj: Assistant Editor position

Dear Ms. Cummings:

    I am pleased to attach my resume in response to your recent advertisement in the *Boston Globe* for an Assistant Editor. I believe that my strong written and verbal communication skills, as well as my proficiency in both Microsoft Word and WordPerfect and several desktop publishing programs, including PageMaker, make me the ideal candidate for this position. For the last two years, I have worked as a reporter and copyeditor for a weekly newspaper; previously, I was features editor, graphic artist, and reporter for various college publications.

    I would welcome the opportunity to meet with you to further discuss my abilities as they relate to your specific needs. May we schedule an appointment soon? I look forward to hearing from you.

Sincerely,

Chris Smith

178 Green Street
Worcester, MA 01610
(508) 555-5555
chrissmith@bluepencil.com

"Cold" Contact
Civil Engineer

To: *patcummings@anyfirm.com*
From: *chrissmith@digsdirt.com*
Subj: Civil Engineering opportunities

Dear Ms. Cummings:

I have more than ten years of progressively responsible experience acquired during roadway, civil, site, hazardous waste, and waterfront projects, as well as Certification in Surveying Technology and a Bachelor of Science degree in Forest Resource Management. At present, I am investigating new and broader career opportunities that would allow me to put my extensive technical and supervisory skills to work for a progressive firm such as yours.

The attached resume describes my qualifications and accomplishments in greater detail. I am confident of my ability to make a positive and immediate contribution to Any Firm and would welcome the opportunity to personally discuss your current or anticipated staffing requirements face-to-face. I can be reached by e-mail at the address above or by phone at (401) 555-5555. I await your reply.

Sincerely,

Chris Smith

178 Green Street
Providence, RI 02903
(401) 555-5555
chrissmith@digsdirt.com

To: *patcummings@anyzoologyassociation.com*
From: *chrissmith@infosearch.com*
Subj: Membership directory

Dear Mr. Cummings:

    I am currently conducting a search for job availabilities in the field of zoology within the Midwest and would appreciate any assistance you may be able to provide with regard to the members of your association. Do you publish a membership directory that I might use in my job-search efforts, and if so, how may I go about obtaining a copy?

    Thank you for your time. I look forward to your return response.

Sincerely,

Chris Smith

178 Green Street
Tempe, AZ 85285
(602) 555-555
chrissmith@infosearch.com

Address/Phone Number Change
Laboratory Assistant

To: *patcummings@anymedicalassociation.com*
From: *chrissmith@continuedinterest.com*
Subj: New address/phone number

Dear Ms. Cummings:

    I am writing to inform you of a change in my address and phone number. Effective July 1, you may reach me at:

178 Green Street
Shawnee Hills, OH 43965
(216) 555-5555

    For your convenience, I have attached an updated copy of my resume. I continue to look forward to hearing from you with regard to any Laboratory Assistant positions you may have available. Thank you for your consideration.

Sincerely,

Chris Smith
chrissmith@continuedinterest.com

178 Green Street
Yorktown Heights, NY 10598
(914) 555-5555

September 24, 20--

Pat Cummings
Director of Regional Administration
Any Corporation
1140 Main Street
Port Chester, NY 10573

Dear Ms. Cummings:

As per our conversation and your request, I am enclosing my business profile for your review in consideration for the position of Arbitrator with Any Organization.

In addition to a Bachelor of Arts degree and extensive study in arbitration, I have been actively involved as an Arbitrator for the Better Business Bureau for the past four years. My activities during the past thirteen years, as a licensed Auctioneer and Nightclub Manager, have consistently involved skill in new business development, negotiating, listening, weighing facts, and making decisions to resolve disputes in the best interest of all parties concerned.

I have successfully arbitrated cases involving manufacturers, vendors, and customers, chaired arbitration panels, and established a reputation for being able to make fair decisions under stressful conditions.

The enclosed document summarizes my experience. If you feel that my qualifications match your needs, I would like to speak with you further in an interview. I can be reached at the above address and phone, or you may leave a telephone message at (914) 555-4444.

Thank you for your consideration of my application. I look forward to your response.

Yours sincerely,

Chris Smith

Enc. Business profile

Assistant Portfolio Manager

178 Green Street
Parsippany, NJ 07054
(201) 555-5555

March 28, 20--

Pat Cummings
Director of Finance
Any Firm
1140 Main Street
Morristown, NJ 08057

Dear Ms. Cummings:

Our phone conversation yesterday was both informative and valuable for my job search. Thank you for your help. As you know, I am very interested in joining Any Firm, whose progressive approach to financial planning and management has prompted me to forward the enclosed resume.

As I mentioned while speaking with you, I offer considerable work experience ranging from Promotional Sales Representative, Assistant Campaign Manager, and Assistant Budget Analyst to my present position as Assistant Portfolio Manager. I would like to meet and discuss further my qualifications and the opportunities you may have available.

Thank you again for your time. I look forward to your reply.

Sincerely,

Chris Smith

Enc. Resume

178 Green Street
Marylhurst, OR 97036
(503) 555-5555

January 4, 20--

Pat Cummings
Managing Editor
Any Corporation
1140 Main Street
Portland, OR 97201

Dear Mr. Cummings:

Thank you for taking the time to speak with me on the phone yesterday. As requested, I am sending my resume for your review.

As previously mentioned, I am currently an Editorial Intern at the Portland State University Press. My career goal is to become a Managing Editor. I proofread and copyedit on a regular basis at work using *The Chicago Manual of Style,* and recently completed a course in copyediting. I also help our Production Editor prepare manuscripts for turnover to the production department. I am eager to apply my knowledge, develop new skills, and contribute to a growing company.

I plan to contact you again before the summer, when you predicted there might be job openings. In the meantime, I hope that 20-- is a successful year for you and your growing company.

Sincerely,

Chris Smith

Enc. Resume

Concierge

178 Green Street
Warren, MI 48091
(313) 555-5555

July 23, 20--

Pat Cummings
Executive Manager
Any Hotel
1140 Main Street
Port Huron, MI 48060

Dear Mr. Cummings:

I appreciate the time you took yesterday to speak with me concerning the Concierge position at Any Hotel. Your description of the position and its responsibilities was most helpful. I would like to take this opportunity to review my qualifications:

- Promoted to establish concierge department in 350-room luxury hotel.
- Responsible for setting tone and image of hotel as a result of providing guest services, including tourist information, tour arrangements, and hotel and airline reservations.
- Presently supervise and manage 40-person hotel staff, including concierge department assistants, mail and information clerks, bell staff, doormen, valet parking and hotel garage staff, and telephone operators.
- Diplomatically and effectively resolve guests' grievances/problems; compose responses and make follow-up phone contact.

In addition to the outlined experience, I would bring to the position an intimate knowledge of the area and its offerings and the ability to work well under pressure. My formal education includes dual degrees in Restaurant and Hotel Management and in French from Marquette University, as well as a year of study at the Sorbonne University in Paris.

After you have reviewed the enclosed resume, I would appreciate the opportunity to continue our phone conversation in person. Thank you.

Sincerely,

Chris Smith

Enc. Resume

Executive Marketing Director

178 Green Street
Boise, ID 83725
(208) 555-5555

August 3, 20--

Pat Cummings
Vice President
Any Corporation
1140 Main Street
Chicago, IL 60605

Dear Mr. Cummings:

I am forwarding my resume with regard to the opening in your marketing department that we discussed yesterday by phone.

Although I am currently employed in a management position, I am interested in a career change, especially one that would allow me to combine a thorough knowledge of boating with my sales, marketing, and communication skills. I am an imaginative, well-organized self-starter with a strong interest in boating. As a semiprofessional sailboat racer, I twice won national honors and participated in the races at Cape Cod. In addition, I have made lasting contacts with owners and officials.

After you have had the chance to review the enclosed resume, please contact me so that we can further discuss the possibility of my joining your staff. I am confident that my business background and knowledge of boats will enable me to have a favorable impact on both your sales and image.

Thank you for your attention, and I look forward to speaking with you again to learn more about this opportunity.

Sincerely yours,

Chris Smith

Enc. Resume

Export Manager

178 Green Street
New York, NY 10027
(212) 555-5555

July 1, 20--

Pat Cummings
Controller
Any Corporation
1140 Main Street
Chicago, IL 60605

Dear Ms. Cummings:

Thank you for taking time out of your busy schedule to speak with me yesterday regarding the Export Manager position. My interest in this position and in Any Corporation is stronger than ever, particularly because it would afford me the opportunity to become less desk-bound—an occupational hazard in my most recent employment.

Pursuant to our conversation, I have compiled a supplement to my resume, detailing my experience relevant to the position of Export Manager. As I explained to you, my family has been involved in the fashion industry for most of my life. I have actively assisted/advised both my mother and my uncle with their European outlets, acquiring considerable expertise and knowledge of the fashion accessory and perfume industries.

With regard to salary requirements, I did a brief cost survey of the Chicago area and happily discovered a favorable difference between that area and where I reside in New York. I would, therefore, be able to consider a salary somewhat lower than we discussed—perhaps in the low sixties—since my living expenses would be so significantly decreased.

I am very enthusiastic about the prospect of re-entering a field where my interpersonal skills and familiarity with European culture and fashion will be more fully utilized. I look forward to hearing from you again in the near future.

Sincerely,

Chris Smith

Enc. Resume

Flight Attendant

178 Green Street
Mountain View, CA 94039

February 5, 20--

Pat Cummings
Director of Human Resources
Any Airline
1140 Main Street
San Francisco, CA 94104

Dear Mr. Cummings:

   I appreciate the time you took to speak with me today regarding the Flight Attendant opening advertised in the *San Francisco Chronicle*. After considering the requirements you outlined, I am even more confident of my ability to meet your needs:

You require:
- Communication skills
- Customer service aptitude
- Specialized training

I offer:
- A Bachelor of Arts degree in Communications.
- Highly developed interpersonal skills, having dealt with a diversity of professionals, clients, and associates.
- Fluency in Spanish; a knowledge of German.
- More than five years of experience in retail/sales, dealing with a wide variety of clients.
- Skill at handling customer complaints and problem-solving.
- Flight Attendant certification.
- CPR training.
- Participation in three-day intensive seminar, "Reacting in an Emergency."

   I have enclosed a resume for your review. I would welcome the chance to address my skills and enthusiasm for this position in a personal meeting. Please contact me at the above address or (415) 555-5555.

Sincerely,

Chris Smith

Enc. Resume

Laboratory Technician

178 Green Street
Weymouth, MA 02190
(617) 555-5555

September 12, 20--

Pat Cummings
Human Resources Director
Any Corporation
1140 Main Street
Chicago, IL 60605

Dear Mr. Cummings:

It was nice talking with you again today. As requested, I am enclosing my resume for your consideration.

In addition to a Bachelor of Science degree in Biology, I have five years of experience in a laboratory setting. This includes preparation and performance of experiments, as well as analysis, writing, and presentation of results.

Currently, I am investigating new opportunities where I can continue to develop my skills and apply my knowledge toward broader responsibilities and advancement. I look forward to our meeting on Monday, September 18, and learning more about the industry's forecast.

Again, thank you for taking time out of your busy schedule to aid me in my job search. Your confidence in my abilities is greatly appreciated.

Sincerely,

Chris Smith

Enc. Resume

Magazine Publishing Intern

178 Green Street
Phoenix, AZ 85004
(602) 555-5555

March 28, 20--

Pat Cummings
Editor-in-Chief
Any Magazine
1140 Main Street
Little Rock, AR 72203

Dear Ms. Cummings:

Thank you for your time and courtesy during our telephone conversation on Friday, March 24. As I mentioned to you, I am very interested in the summer internship at *Any Magazine*.

I am currently participating in a senior-year internship at a Tucson-based publishing firm, Baker Communications Group. After my graduation in May, I want to expand my experience in the publishing and public relations fields. I feel the *Any Magazine* internship provides that opportunity, and that I can make a valuable contribution as a summer Intern.

I am most interested in discussing the possibility of working for *Any Magazine* this summer. I have enclosed my resume for your review, and I look forward to hearing from you.

Sincerely,

Chris Smith

Enc. Resume

Mailroom Supervisor

178 Green Street
Carey, OH 43316
(419) 555-5555

March 23, 20--

Pat Cummings
Director of Human Resources
Any Corporation
1140 Main Street
Galion, OH 44833

Dear Mr. Cummings:

I enjoyed speaking with you over the phone yesterday and appreciate your consideration of my resume for the Mailroom Supervisor position.

I believe I possess the specific experience you require for this position. As I mentioned during our conversation, I have direct experience in mailroom management. In my current position at O'Keefe and Murphy, my responsibilities include:

- Coordinating all incoming mail, dispersing inter-building correspondence, managing courier services, and shipping/receiving.
- Researching and accounting for certified, registered, and express mail.
- Administering employee evaluations/appraisals, and scheduling hours.
- Obtaining/maintaining lease agreements for electronic machinery and equipment.

I am very interested in applying my skills as your new Mailroom Supervisor. Could we meet for a personal interview? Please contact me when your schedule permits a meeting.

Thank you for your courtesy yesterday. I look forward to speaking with you further.

Sincerely,

Chris Smith

Enc. Resume

178 Green Street
Boise, ID 83730
(208) 555-5555

July 6, 20--

Pat Cummings
1140 Main Street
Boise, ID 83757

Dear Mr. Cummings:

As per your request during our recent phone conversation, I have enclosed several references attesting to my abilities as a Nanny.

Also attached is a professional profile listing relevant activities that might be of interest to you. In addition to my experience as a private day-care provider, I have taught in infant, toddler, and preschool programs, where I was involved in planning curriculums, organizing activities, and communicating regularly with parents and staff.

I have made children's growth and development my career, and would very much like to apply my skills as your Nanny. I would appreciate the opportunity to speak with you further after you have verified my references, and would love to meet your children.

I hope to hear from you soon.

Sincerely,

Chris Smith

Enc. Professional profile, References

Precision Inspector

178 Green Street
Horsham, PA 19044
(215) 555-5555

October 16, 20--

Pat Cummings
Vice President
Any Corporation
1140 Main Street
Reading, PA 19612

Dear Ms. Cummings:

As per our phone conversation this morning, I would like to confirm our interview time of 9 A.M., Wednesday, October 18, for the Precision Inspector position.

In preparation for our meeting, I would like to reiterate my qualifications for this position. I offer more than ten years of experience in:

- First-piece, in-process, and other phases of precision inspection.
- A wide variety of production manufacturing departments shops and associated inspection areas.
- Inspection procedures and methods pertaining to machined and fabricated complex parts from in-plant and vendors.
- Working to industrial and government specifications, and interpreted drawings.
- Making complicated setups and using tools and techniques to inspect finished goods with a maximum amount of efficiency and minimum supervision.

I look forward to our interview and the opportunity to discuss the mutual benefit of our working together.

Sincerely,

Chris Smith

Enc. Resume

178 Green Street
Atlanta, GA 30378
(404) 555-5555

February 6, 20--

Pat Cummings
Superintendent
Any School System
1140 Main Street
Mobile, GA 31776

Dear Mr. Cummings:

Thank you very much for taking the time to speak with me today regarding the Principal position available in your district. As you requested, I have enclosed a resume for your consideration.

I would be very interested in meeting with you and learning more about the position and its requirements. Should you need any additional information, please do not hesitate to contact me.

I look forward to pursuing the next step in the application process.

Sincerely,

Chris Smith

Enc. Resume

Production Assistant

178 Green Street
Tulsa, OK 74103
(918) 555-5555

January 24, 20--

Pat Cummings
Human Resources Director
Any Publishing Company
1140 Main Street
Philadelphia, PA 19130

Dear Ms. Cummings:

    Thank you for taking the time to talk with me on Friday, January 20, about your firm's opening for a Production Assistant. I am very interested in this position and believe it would be an appropriate place to learn more about the publishing field.

    I enjoyed our conversation and look forward to hearing more about this opportunity. Thank you for your time and consideration.

Sincerely,

Chris Smith

Enc. Resume

Psychiatric Nurse

178 Green Street
Racine, WI 53406
(414) 555-5555

May 2, 20--

Pat Cummings
Director of Human Resources
Any Hospital
1140 Main Street
Milwaukee, WI 53203

Dear Ms. Cummings:

Thank you for taking the time yesterday to discuss the Psychiatric Nursing position. I am excited about the opportunity and I am confident that I could make a positive contribution.

As mentioned during our phone conversation, some of my relevant experiences include:

- Work in diverse hospital and human service environments in a range of units from pediatric and medical/surgical, as well as handling mixed adults/adolescents with bipolar or borderline/acute personality disorders.
- Crisis intervention and case management as related to patients suffering from conduct disorders, sexual and physical abuse, acute or chronic psychiatric distress, substance abuse, and physical challenges.
- Supervising three nurses and associated staff, assigning patients for evaluation, working with social service representatives and patients' families and/or guardians, distributing medications, providing emergency medical assistance, and handling associated details of medical administration.

I would like the opportunity to continue our discussion in person. Perhaps we could arrange a mutually convenient time to meet. I will contact your office on Monday, May 8, to set up an appointment.

Sincerely,

Chris Smith

Enc. Resume

Purchasing Agent

178 Green Street
Carlsbad, NM 88220
(505) 555-5555

December 5, 20--

Pat Cummings
Supervisor, Order Entry Department
Any Store
1140 Main Street
Albuquerque, NM 87106

Dear Mr. Cummings:

As you requested during our recent discussion, I am enclosing my resume for you to review and distribute to the administration services department. My interest is in a position in which I can utilize, and the company can benefit from, my strong purchasing and inventory skills.

Although my present position is diverse and secure, there seems to be little room for further growth within the company and I think it is time for a change. I would like the opportunity to rejoin Any Store and I feel that my diverse purchasing, inventory, and traffic skills can be well utilized within the new administration services department.

I want to thank you in advance for your interest and your time, and look forward to a meeting with you to further discuss opportunities with Any Store. Should you require additional information or want to set up an interview, please contact me at the telephone number listed above. I have enjoyed working at Any Store in the past in part-time positions and would welcome the opportunity to join the company on a full-time basis.

Thanks again for your interest and assistance.

Sincerely,

Chris Smith

Enc. Resume

178 Green Street
Akron, OH 44316

August 5, 20--

Pat Cummings, M.D.
Director
Any School for the Deaf
1140 Main Street
Dayton, OH 45404

Dear Dr. Cummings:

Thank you for the opportunity, during our recent phone conversation, to discuss the teaching position available at Any School for the Deaf. As you requested, I am enclosing my resume which reflects my dedication to teaching and counseling hearing-impaired children.

In addition to a Bachelor of Arts degree in Human Development, which includes coursework in child development, psychology of learning, and counseling theories, I have four years of experience working with the severely handicapped. This background, combined with my many years of personal experience as a hard-of-hearing person, can be successfully applied in a teaching capacity to motivate and benefit hearing-impaired children at your institution.

After you have reviewed my qualifications, I would appreciate meeting with you to further explain my interest in, and qualifications for, working within the deaf community. I feel I have the expertise, willingness for further personal development, interest, and patience required to work with your students.

Should you require additional information prior to our meeting, I can be reached at the above address or by phone at (216) 555-5555. I plan to make a follow-up call within a few days.

Once again, thank you for your courtesy.

Sincerely,

Chris Smith

Enc. Resume

Administrative Assistant

178 Green Street
Neptune, NJ 07754
(908) 555-5555

January 22, 20--

Pat Cummings
Hiring Officer
Any Corporation
1140 Main Street
Passaic, NJ 07055

Dear Ms. Cummings:

Thank you for interviewing me for the Administrative Assistant position on Friday. Our meeting was as informative as it was enjoyable.

I was impressed with your product lines and position in the marketplace, as well as your vitality and commitment to growth, and I hope to contribute to the continued growth of Any Corporation.

To this end, I would like to meet Richard Griffin to discuss how I may be of assistance. Organization and administration are two of my strongest skills, and I believe my experience in these areas would be beneficial to your company.

Thank you again for your time and consideration. I look forward to hearing from you.

Sincerely,

Chris Smith

Bank Manager

178 Green Street
Pullman, WA 99164
(509) 555-5555

June 20, 20--

Pat Cummings
Vice President, Northwest Region
Any Bank
1140 Main Street
Sumas, WA 98295

Dear Ms. Cummings:

Thank you for the quality time you extended me during our meeting on June 16 to discuss management opportunities with Any Bank.

I want to express my appreciation to you for providing an overview of the various responsibilities associated with management positions in Any Bank's northwest division. I am confident of my ability to meet your requirements for efficient and quality performance in any position for which I am considered.

Management opportunities with Any Bank are of great interest to me, and I look forward to hearing from your human resources representative for further discussion.

Thanks again for a most pleasant and informative interview.

Sincerely,

Chris Smith

Conference Coordinator

178 Green Street
Fort Smith, AR 72902
(501) 555-5555

August 5, 20--

Pat Cummings
Executive Director
Any Corporation
1140 Main Street
Little Rock, AR 72219

Dear Ms. Cummings:

Thank you for allowing me the opportunity to interview for the Conference Coordinator position. As the result of our informative discussion, my interest in the position has strengthened substantially.

As I mentioned during our interview, I can bring eight years of diverse part-time and full-time experience in positions which required flexibility and the ability to accept and follow through on new assignments and responsibilities. I have had the opportunity to deal with people on all levels in the workplace as an Instructor and Events Coordinator in hospitality and related businesses.

Based on my past work experience, as well as my Master's degree in Administration, I feel confident that I have the qualifications for the position under discussion. Please let me know if there is anything I can do to assist you further in your hiring process.

Thank you again for a most enjoyable interview.

Sincerely,

Chris Smith

Distribution Coordinator

178 Green Street
Flint, MI 48501
(313) 555-5555

December 4, 20--

Pat Cummings
Vice President, Operations
Any Corporation
1140 Main Street
East Lansing, MI 48824

Dear Mr. Cummings:

It is not often that a candidate hears a company and job responsibilities presented as clearly as you did during our conversation last Friday. The Distribution Coordinator position sounds like an ideal opportunity for which I consider myself to be well-qualified. I appreciated the opportunity to discuss my credentials with you in so much detail.

As we discussed, I possess seven years of experience managing a successful and profitable wholesale seafood company which has expanded into retail seafood sales and seafood restaurant operations. In addition, I have since been involved in multistate, retail operations that require cost-effective management of sales and operational activities from development of start-up locations to multistate distribution using all forms of transportation.

My combined experience with fresh seafood, distribution, planning, and scheduling can be successfully applied to areas of interest to you and to the benefit of Any Corporation. I am excited about the challenge this position presents, and I look forward to your response.

Thank you again for the gracious invitation to your offices. I enjoyed my stay and I hope to return soon.

Yours sincerely,

Chris Smith

Doctor

178 Green Street
Luna, NM 87824
(505) 555-5555

December 2, 20--

Pat Cummings, M.D.
Director, Emergency Medicine Fellowship Program
Any Hospital
1140 Main Street
Chicago, IL 60605

Dear Dr. Cummings:

Thank you for allowing me to interview for the fellowship position in your department at Any Hospital. I appreciated the opportunity to meet with the faculty and the staff; everyone was most hospitable.

I was impressed with the program and in particular the thought that has gone into the fellowship curriculum development and research guidance. I came away very enthusiastic about the position.

Please extend my thanks to Dr. Lee, Dr. Murphy, and Dr. Sloat for a thoughtful discussion relative to the Emergency Medicine Fellowship Program. Being part of such a team is, indeed, an enticing prospect.

If you have any further questions please do not hesitate to contact me. I look forward to hearing from you.

Sincerely,

Chris Smith, M.D.
cc: Joan Lee, M.D.
Brian Murphy, M.D.
Susan Sloat, M.D.

178 Green Street
Kingston, MA 02364

July 1, 20--

Pat Cummings
Editor
Any Publishing Company
1140 Main Street
Boston, MA 02106

Dear Mr. Cummings:

I want to thank you for interviewing me yesterday for the Editorial Assistant position you have available. I enjoyed meeting you and learning more about Any Publishing Company and your work on the *Internet Primer*.

This position offers an incredible opportunity to learn the entire editorial and production processes involved in creating a book. I think my education as well as my written and editorial skills are an idea match to the job requirements you outlined. Above all, I am very eager to learn and I know that I could make a significant contribution to your organizaton.

I would like to reiterate my strong interest in this position and in working with you and Daniel Connelly. This is the ideal opportunity I seek. Please feel free to call me at (617) 555-5555 if I can provide you with any additional information.

Again, thank you for the interview and your consideration.

Sincerely,

Chris Smith
cc: Daniel Connelly

Engineering Consultant

178 Green Street
Geismar, LA 70734
(504) 555-5555

January 18, 20--

Ms. Pat Cummings
Vice President
Any Corporation
1140 Main Street
Lafayette, LA 70504

Dear Ms. Cummings:

    It was a sincere pleasure making your acquaintance on Tuesday regarding the position of Engineering Consultant. The personal dynamics that you exude, the predicted corporate growth, and the position's promised personal fulfillment, have left me very enthused.

    Thank you for your consideration. I look forward to meeting with you again in the near future.

Sincerely,

Chris Smith

Export Manager

178 Green Street
Mill Valley, CA 94941
(414) 555-5555

March 22, 20--

Pat Cummings
Vice President, Exports
Any Corporation
1140 Main Street
Minneapolis, MN 55404

Dear Ms. Cummings:

Thank you for taking time out of your schedule to speak with me yesterday regarding the position of Export Manager. My interest in this position, and in Any Corporation, is stronger than ever, particularly because it would afford me the opportunity to become less desk-bound— an occupational hazard in my most recent employment.

I will contact your offices on March 29 to determine the next stage in the application process. In the interim, any questions you have may be addressed to my business phone, (414) 555-4444, or fax, (414) 555-3333.

Sincerely,

Chris Smith

Finance Executive

178 Green Street
Casper, WY 82604

November 15, 20--

Pat Cummings
Hiring Manager
Any Corporation
1140 Main Street
Charleston, WV 25301

Dear Mr. Cummings:

Thank you for a most informative and enjoyable discussion during our meeting on Monday. The knowledge I gained during the interview has certainly enhanced my interest in joining Any Corporation.

With my expertise in strategic planning, international finance, marketing, and general management, I feel confident that I can meet your expectations and significantly contribute to your company's objectives as a member of your management staff.

I want to thank you again for the time and courtesy you extended to me. I look forward to meeting with you again for a continued discussion of marketing opportunities available with your company.

Should you require additional information prior to a second meeting, please contact me at the above address or by phone at (307) 555-5555.

Sincerely,

Chris Smith

178 Green Street
Baltimore, MD 21217

November 9, 20--

Pat Cummings
Vice President
Any Organization
1140 Main Street
Silver Spring, MD 20910

Dear Ms. Cummings:

I wish to thank you and Shannon Rickle for the opportunity to discuss the fundraiser position advertised by your firm. As you requested, I am enclosing a writing sample for your review, and I would like to emphasize that the orientation and purpose of the campaign, as I understand it, is of great interest to me.

I feel that my experience, as outlined below, ideally matches your needs:

Requirements of the position:
- Extensive service and administrative experience.
- Ability to effectively manage personnel.
- Specific fundraising accomplishments.

My qualifications:
- More than eighteen years of strategic planning, administrative, and sales experience in a major service-intensive industry.
- As Director of Agencies, National Sales Trainer, Sales Manager, and Administrator, my responsibilities encompassed the development and management of personnel recruitment, orientation, training, telemarketing, data collection, motivational programs, seminars, and workshops that generated dedicated, highly productive teams.
- During the three years I served as Vice President of Wing Industries, I was responsible for the organization and planning of fundraising campaigns which successfully generated in excess of $800,000 for the reconstruction of a $1.2 million auditorium that had been destroyed by arson.

Based on this background, I feel confident that I have the principal qualifications necessary to manage and administer programs and provide meaningful support to fundraising campaigns that require strong organizational and motivational skills. If I can provide any additional information to assist you in your decision, please do not hesitate to contact me at (301) 555-5555.

Thank you again for a most enjoyable interview. I look forward to hearing from you.

Sincerely,

Chris Smith
cc: Shannon Rickle

Enc. Writing sample

Human Resources Representative

178 Green Street
Gardner, MA 01440
(508) 555-5555

November 15, 20--

Pat Cummings
Director of Human Resources
Any Corporation
1140 Main Street
Winchester, MA 01890

Dear Ms. Cummings:

    I would like to thank you for taking the time to interview me yesterday for the H.R. Representative position. I was very impressed by the size of your staff, and I certainly understand how demanding such a position would prove to be.

    Ms. Cummings, after speaking with you, I am even more eager to join the ranks of your qualified representatives. I believe my education, training, and strong motivation would assist me in successfully completing all aspects of the position.

    Thank you again for meeting with me. I hope your hiring decision will result in our meeting again.

Yours sincerely,

Chris Smith

Inventory Control Analyst

178 Green Street
Little Rock, AR 72203
(501) 555-5555

November 17, 20--

Pat Cummings
President
Any Corporation
1140 Main Street
Chicago, IL 60605

Dear Mr. Cummings:

It was a pleasure meeting you today. I appreciate your taking the time from your hectic schedule to speak with me about your opening for an Inventory Control Analyst.

The position is exciting and seems to encompass a number of diverse responsibilities. I believe that with my experience and skills, I would be able to contribute significantly to your organization.

I look forward to hearing from you in the near future. If you need further information, please feel free to call me.

Sincerely,

Chris Smith

178 Green Street
Boston, MA 02215
(617) 555-5555

April 21, 20--

Pat Cummings, J.D.
Principal
Any Law Firm
1140 Main Street
Woodland Hills, CA 91367

Dear Ms. Cummings:

Thank you for taking the time to interview me on Thursday. I enjoyed meeting with you to discuss the internship at Any Law Firm. I also enjoyed the tour of the office, which I found to be interesting and informative.

Thank you again for your time and consideration. If you have any questions, I would be happy to provide whatever additional information you need. I look forward to hearing from you soon.

Sincerely,

Chris Smith

Personal Secretary

178 Green Street
Nashua, NH 03060
(603) 555-5555

July 14, 20--

Pat Cummings
President
Any Corporation
1140 Main Street
Manchester, NH 03103

Dear Ms. Cummings:

I found our interview this morning to be most refreshing. Your staff was hospitable, your facilities impressive, and our discussion informative. I am very interested in becoming your Personal Secretary.

You mentioned during our meeting that you are looking for an assistant with extensive knowledge of computer systems and applications. My computer literacy includes proficiency in Microsoft Word, WordPerfect, Lotus 1-2-3, dBase Plus, DOS, Windows, and desktop publishing. I also have experience with spreadsheets inventory management.

I believe I have much to offer your company, and I hope I will receive the opportunity to prove my worth to you. Thank you for extending me your time, Ms. Cummings.

Sincerely,

Chris Smith

178 Green Street
Halifax, MA 02338
(617) 555-5555

March 10, 20--

Pat Cummings
President
Any Corporation
1140 Main Street
Lynn, MA 01903

Dear Mr. Cummings:

I am grateful for the time you took this morning to interview me for the Personnel Manager position. Any Corporation sounds like an exciting, fast-growing firm; I would very much like to apply my skills to your continued success.

During our conversation, you mentioned that you were looking for a professional who could adjust human resources policy to the needs of an expanding company. I believe I possess just the qualifications necessary to do this. My prior positions in human resources management have provided me with extensive experience in all aspects of policy conception and implementation. My skills range from training and program development to budget management and employee relations.

If given the chance, I am confident I can restructure your department to meet and exceed your expectations. I hope I will be offered that chance.

Thank you again for a most enjoyable interview.

Sincerely,

Chris Smith

Production Assistant

178 Green Street
Rapid City, SD 57709

September 9, 20--

Pat Cummings
Station Manager
Any Television Station
1140 Main Street
Sioux Falls, ND 57117

Dear Mr. Cummings:

   Thank you for meeting with me yesterday. I appreciate your thorough explanation of the Production Assistant position and, now that I know exactly what it entails, I am confident that I can make a positive contribution to the station.

   I want to re-emphasize my strong interest in joining your team. I believe my degree in Mass Communications, my internship experience, and my winning attitude make me a suitable candidate for this position.

   Please feel free to contact me at (605) 555-5555 with any questions, and I look forward to your reply.

Sincerely,

Chris Smith

Public Records Analyst

178 Green Street
Long Beach, CA 90840
(310) 555-5555

May 28, 20--

Pat Cummings
Senior Analyst
Any Corporation
1140 Main Street
Thousand Oaks, CA 91362

Dear Ms. Cummings:

Thank you for speaking with me on Friday regarding the Public Records Analyst position. I am convinced my experience and training would benefit a progressive firm such as yours.

Please let me reiterate my qualifications:

- Twelve years of professional experience as a Marine Information Specialist and Public Records Analyst.
- Skilled in working with automated and manual record management systems.
- Increased corporation's efficiency by 84 percent with development of broad-based management programs for electronic records.
- Regarded as a specialist in records management systems analysis.
- Conducted workshops and seminars explaining records management and all phases of its practices.

Again, I appreciate your time and consideration. Please contact me at the above address or phone number with any further questions. I look forward to your reply.

Sincerely,

Chris Smith

Publisher's Assistant

178 Green Street
Albuquerque, NM 87109
(505) 555-5555

January 20, 20--

Pat Cummings
Human Resources Director
Any Publication
1140 Main Street
Albuquerque, NM 87109

Dear Mr. Cummings:

I very much enjoyed talking with you today about the position of Publisher's Assistant. I was particularly interested in the position's variety of tasks, which would make the day's work challenging. My experience at Malkmus Press is an excellent foundation for the work required at *Any Publication*.

I was glad to be able to meet Mr. Poska, and have no doubt that I would be an excellent assistant to him. I recognize the importance of making his day more productive; I know I could help to do that.

I am looking forward to hearing from you next week. Thank you for taking the time out of your busy schedule to talk with me. I found it to be a rewarding afternoon.

Sincerely,

Chris Smith
cc: Mr. Poska

Recycling Manager

178 Green Street
Warsaw, IN 46580
(219) 555-5555

December 10, 20--

Pat Cummings
Director
Any Corporation
1140 Main Street
Crane, IN 47522

Dear Mr. Cummings:

    My time spent at Any Corporation yesterday was thoroughly enjoyable. Thank you for taking the time to discuss the position of Recycling Manager with me. After carefully reviewing its requirements, I have composed a brief list of my matching qualifications:

- Sixteen years of broad experience in recycling programs, recyclable materials, and spinoff industries using materials to manufacture products for industrial and consumer markets.
- Solid experience in sales, customer service, and customer relations.
- Ability to promote and/or market products or services provided or produced by related recycling industries.
- Skill as an accomplished communicator who can effectively work with individuals and groups in educational and/or sales environments.

    I am very interested in joining Any Corporation in this capacity. I know I can meet and exceed your expectations.

    I look forward to learning of your decision.

Yours sincerely,

Chris Smith

Retail Sales Associate

178 Green Street
Gary, IN 46402
(219) 555-5555

February 1, 20--

Pat Cummings
Retail Sales Manager
Any Store
1140 Main Street
South Bend, IN 46626

Dear Mr. Cummings:

I want to thank you for meeting with me on January 27 regarding the position of Sales Associate. I enjoyed the opportunity to learn more about the responsibilities and opportunities available at Any Store.

I also want to reiterate my interest in the position. I feel confident that my seven years of acquired sales experience, combined with well-seasoned communication and interpersonal skills, would make me an ideal candidate for this position.

Thank you again. I look forward to hearing your final decision.

Sincerely,

Chris Smith

Sales Representative

178 Green Street
Metairie, LA 70001
(504) 555-5555

January 5, 20--

Pat Cummings
Regional Sales Supervisor
Any Airline
1140 Main Street
Baton Rouge, LA 70803

Dear Ms. Cummings:

I appreciate you taking the time to interview me for the position of Sales Representative with your organization. I found your discussion of the operational procedures at Any Airline, as well as your expectations of the sales staff, to be very informative and interesting. I am confident that, as a Sales Representative, I would make a strong contribution to your staff by increasing profits and expanding your market.

I would like to reiterate the qualifications I possess that would contribute directly to your organization:

- More than twelve years of broad-based experience in travel, hospitality, and retail environment industries.
- Positions in Air Travel ranging from Customer Service Representative to Director of Regional Sales.
- Extensive responsibility handling major corporate accounts on both domestic and international levels.

Again, thank you for taking the time to consider my candidacy. I look forward to learning of your final decision.

Sincerely,

Chris Smith

Staff Accountant

178 Green Street
Eugene, OR 97401
(503) 555-5555

July 24, 20--

Pat Cummings
Human Resource Manager
Any Corporation
1140 Main Street
Portland, OR 97204

Dear Mr. Cummings:

    I would like to thank you for meeting with me on Friday regarding the Staff Accountant position. After considering your needs, as we discussed, I am even more convinced of my ability to make a valuable contribution to your firm.

    For your consideration, I have taken the liberty of matching my qualifications with the requirements of the position offered:

Solid Accounting Background:
Experience in excess of five years with all facets of accounting, including financial statements, budgeting, payroll, and accounts receivable.

Business Office Operation:
Broad experience supervising personnel at all levels. Maintained excellent banking relationships.

Computer Experience:
Broad knowledge of accounting software and PC-based applications including Excel and Lotus SmartSuite. Experience with mainframe systems and payroll services.

    If I can be of additional assistance, please do not hesitate to contact me. I am very eager to apply my skills to the successful ranks of your accounting team, and I look forward to learning of your final decision.

Yours truly,

Chris Smith

178 Green Street
Loganville, GA 30249
(404) 555-5555

April 23, 20--

Pat Cummings
Principal
Any Elementary School
1140 Main Street
Norcross, GA 30071

Dear Mr. Cummings:

I thoroughly enjoyed my afternoon at Any Elementary School and our interview for the sixth grade teaching position. Thank you for taking time out of your day to speak with me.

It was also a pleasure to meet Richard Morrison and to observe his classroom for an hour. His dedication to the children he teaches is evident, and I would be honored to instruct room 160 during his leave of absence.

Thank you again for inviting me to your school. I hope that your hiring decision will result in my returning to Any Elementary in the fall.

Sincerely,

Chris Smith
cc: Richard Morrison

Writer/Researcher

178 Green Street
Middletown, CT 06457
(203) 555-5555

January 16, 20--

Pat Cummings
Staff Writer
Any Publications
1140 Main Street
Waterbury, CT 06723

Dear Ms. Cummings:

Thank you for the opportunity to meet with you again today. It was a pleasure to learn more about the position you have available and your goals for continuing the success of the *Inside Connecticut* publications.

I am very excited about the potential the Writer/Researcher position has to offer. I am confident that my skills, abilities, and interest would contribute to enhance the productivity of this publication.

I hope that you find me a qualified candidate for this position, and I would enjoy the opportunity to contribute to your organization. Thank you for your consideration, and I look forward to hearing your decision.

Sincerely,

Chris Smith

178 Green Street
San Jose, CA 95134
(408) 555-5555

January 27, 20--

Pat Cummings
Director, Public Relations
Any Corporation
1140 Main Street
San Francisco, CA 94120

Dear Ms. Cummings:

I am currently investigating career opportunities in the San Francisco area. In the course of my research, I found Any Corporation to be an industry leader in accounting and financial planning.

Could you send me information concerning your services? I would be especially interested in an annual report and company roster. I have enclosed a self-addressed stamped envelope for your convenience.

I appreciate your attention to my request.

Sincerely,

Chris Smith

Career Planning Services

178 Green Street
Arlington Heights, IL 60004
(708) 555-5555

November 7, 20--

Pat Cummings
Director
Any Woman's Bureau
1140 Main Street
Chicago, IL 60603

Dear Mr. Cummings:

   I am an accomplished loan officer who is finding it very difficult to obtain gainful employment in my field. My resources in the Chicago area have been exhausted and relocation is not an option. In this respect, I would like to ask for your help.

   I would be very eager to participate in any career planning or placement services you might offer. Could you please send any relevant information concerning your programs and services to the above address? I have enclosed a self-addressed stamped envelope for your convenience.

   Many thanks for your assistance. I look forward to hearing from you.

Sincerely,

Chris Smith

178 Green Street
Washington, DC 20071
(202) 555-5555

March 25, 20--

Pat Cummings
Publisher's Assistant
Any Publisher
1140 Main Street
New York, NY 10108

Dear Ms. Cummings:

    I am writing to inquire about Any Publisher. Please send me information regarding your company size and target markets, as well as a catalog of your most recent publications.

    I have enclosed a self-addressed stamped envelope for your convenience. Thank you for your attention.

Sincerely,

Chris Smith

Grants Listing

178 Green Street
Worcester, MA 01610
(508) 555-5555

April 13, 20--

Pat Cummings
Director
Any Research Agency
1140 Main Street
New York, NY 10017

Dear Ms. Cummings:

I would like to request information on research projects currently being conducted at your agency in the area of molecular biology.

I will complete a Doctor of Physiological Chemistry degree from Worcester Polytechnic Institute in May and am searching for a new research association. My doctoral thesis focused on DNA sequence analysis and S1 mapping.

Do you possess a listing of all grants conferred in related areas within the last two years? Any information you could provide would greatly assist me in my search. For your convenience, I have enclosed a self-addressed stamped envelope.

Thank you.

Sincerely,

Chris Smith

178 Green Street
Heston, KS 67062
(316) 555-5555

September 25, 20--

Pat Cummings
President
Chamber of Commerce
1140 Main Street
Topeka, KS 66612

Dear Mr. Cummings:

   I am currently conducting a job search in the greater Kansas area and would appreciate any assistance you could provide me.

   My interest is in the field of computer programming, and I am wondering if you publish a Directory of Members, especially listing the major employers in the technology industry.

   If so, could you possibly send me this information? I have enclosed a self-addressed stamped envelope for your convenience.

Sincerely,

Chris Smith

Membership Listing

178 Green Street
Tempe, AZ 85285
(602) 555-5555

July 18, 20--

Pat Cummings
Director
Any Association of Zoologists
1140 Main Street
Denver, CO 80205

Dear Mr. Cummings:

I am writing to inquire if your association provides a mailing list of members.

I am currently conducting a job search within the Midwest, and would appreciate any assistance you could provide regarding member names, their titles, organizations, addresses, and other relevant information.

Please forward any appropriate materials to the above address in the self-addressed stamped envelope I have provided for your convenience.

I look forward to your return response.

Sincerely,

Chris Smith

178 Green Street
Everett, MA 02149
(617) 555-5555

February 5, 20--

Pat Cummings
Subscription Manager
Careers in Psychology
1140 Main Street
Boston, MA 02118

Dear Ms. Cummings:

    I heard about your publication through the National Association of Psychologists. I understand that *Careers in Psychology* publishes an "Advertised Openings" section at the close of each edition. Could you possibly send me information on subscription prices and an order form?

    I have enclosed a self-addressed stamped envelope for your convenience. Thank you.

Sincerely,

Chris Smith

Laboratory Assistant

178 Green Street
Shawnee Hills, OH 43965
(216) 555-5555

May 31, 20--

Pat Cummings
Research Scientist
Any Medical Association
1140 Main Street
Chicago, IL 60605

Dear Mr. Cummings:

    I am writing to inform you that I have moved to the above address and telephone listing. Enclosed is an updated copy of my resume for your files. I am looking forward to hearing more about any Laboratory Assistant positions you may have available.

    Thank you for your time.

Sincerely,

Chris Smith

Enc. Resume

178 Green Street
Winston-Salem, NC 27113

July 21, 20--

Pat Cummings
Agent
Any Production Studio
1140 Main Street
Durham, NC 27702

Dear Ms. Cummings:

I recently received your kind letter in response to my audition for the lead guitarist position. Since you mentioned that you would be keeping my resume and demo tape on file, I wanted to let you know that, effective August 1, my address will change to the address listed above. My new phone number is (919) 555-5555.

Until August 1, you can reach me at (708) 555-4444 in Aurora, IL.

I am still very interested in the position, and look forward to hearing from you soon.

Sincerely,

Chris Smith

Enc. Resume

Pet Groomer

178 Green Street
Baltimore, MD 21210
(410) 555-5555

September 21, 20--

Pat Cummings
Owner
Any Pet Salon
1140 Main Street
College Park, MD 20742

Dear Mr. Cummings:

    Thank you for meeting with me last week regarding the Pet Groomer position. I remain very interested in this opportunity and, for this reason, wanted to alert you to my address change. Effective October 1, I can be reached at the address and telephone number shown above.

    I look forward to hearing from you.

Sincerely,

Chris Smith

Enc. Resume

Staff Nutritionist

178 Green Street
Tampa, FL 33681
(813) 555-5555

April 6, 20--

Pat Cummings
Human Resources Manager
Any Hospital
1140 Main Street
Ocala, FL 32674

Dear Ms. Cummings:

Last month, I sent my resume in response to your advertisement in the Monday, March 13, edition of the *Tampa Tribune* for Staff Nutritionist. I am still very interested in this or similar openings at Any Hospital.

For this reason, I would like to make you aware of an address change from my previous inquiry. I have since moved from Jacksonville to the address listed above. I have enclosed an updated resume for your convenience.

Thank you. I look forward to hearing from you in the future.

Sincerely,

Chris Smith

Enc. Resume

Wholesale Buyer

178 Green Street
Greenbelt, MD 20770

February 23, 20--

Pat Cummings
Senior Buyer
Any Corporation
1140 Main Street
Landover, MD 20785

Dear Mr. Cummings:

I want to thank you for a pleasant and informative interview last week in reference to the Wholesale Buyer position. I enjoyed meeting with you and Richard Mayes and learning more about your department's successful track record of commercial negotiations.

I would now like to alert you to a change in my phone number. The new listing is (301) 555-5555. My address remains the same.

Please be assured of my continued interest. I have enclosed an updated copy of my resume and look forward to hearing your decision.

Sincerely,

Chris Smith
cc: Richard Mayes

Enc. Resume

178 Green Street
Washington, DC 20016
(202) 555-5555

November 11, 20--

Pat Cummings
Bookkeeper
Any Corporation
1140 Main Street
Washington, DC 20001

Dear Mr. Cummings:

Thank you so much for your great reference regarding my application for the Bookkeeping position at the Baldwin Company.

I am pleased to report that I have been offered, and have accepted, the position. I appreciate your efforts on my behalf.

Sincerely,

Chris Smith

Broker

178 Green Street
Sidney, MT 59270
(406) 555-5555

April 26, 20--

Pat Cummings
Investment Broker
Any Corporation
1140 Main Street
Missoula, MT 59807

Dear Ms. Cummings:

I want to thank you for the excellent reference you provided Denmark Associates. With your generous help, I was offered a position as a Broker.

I am excited about this opportunity and I appreciate your assistance. I look forward to returning the favor.

Sincerely,

Chris Smith

Government Intern

178 Green Street
Albany, GA 31701
(912) 555-5555

November 29, 20--

Pat Cummings
Assistant to the President
Any University
1140 Main Street
Doraville, GA 30340

Dear Ms. Cummings:

I am writing to express my thanks for your kind reference regarding my summer internship application. The selection committee at the State House informs me that you were contacted, and that you spoke highly of my work in the President's office.

I will contact you in early January when my application is processed and I hear of the outcome. Once again, I am very grateful for your help.

Best wishes,

Chris Smith

Nurse

178 Green Street
Mount Vernon, NY 10550
(914) 555-5555

April 14, 20--

Pat Cummings, R. N.
Nursing Administrator
Any Hospital
1140 Main Street
New York, NY 10001

Dear Mr. Cummings:

Kathy Mohagan at West Side Hospital mentioned that she contacted you as a reference and that you spoke highly of my work at Any Hospital.

Thanks so much for your assistance, Pat. Please let me know if I can do anything in return.

With best regards,

Chris Smith

178 Green Street
Santa Clara, CA 95054
(408) 555-5555

June 11, 20--

Pat Cummings, M.D.
General Surgeon
Any Hospital
1140 Main Street
Palo Alto, CA 94304

Dear Dr. Cummings:

Thank you for speaking to Dr. Griffin in support of my credentials. As you know, getting established in the medical community is not easy and I appreciate the confidence you have in my abilities.

I have since been called back to interview with the Board of Directors. I will keep you updated on my progress.

Thank you again for all your help.

Sincerely,

Chris Smith

Teacher

178 Green Street
Triangle Park, NC 27709
(919) 555-5555

May 29, 20--

Pat Cummings
Principal
Any High School
1140 Main Street
Raleigh, NC 27695

Dear Mr. Cummings:

Thank you for agreeing to act as a reference for my teaching application at Martin Luther King Jr. High School. I greatly appreciated your assistance, Pat.

I have been offered the position, and have gladly accepted. I will be teaching two sections of remedial English and one special topics course in journalism. The principal has also asked me to act as faculty moderator for the school newspaper. My year should be very busy, yet also very enjoyable.

Enjoy the remainder of your summer vacation. I hope to see you at association meetings in the fall.

Sincerely,

Chris Smith

178 Green Street
Washington, DC 20007
(202) 555-5555

September 6, 20--

Pat Cummings
Professor of Art History
Any College
1140 Main Street
Worcester, MA 01610

Dear Dr. Cummings:

Knowing how busy you are with different projects, I really appreciate the time you took to write a recommendation for my graduate school applications. I have since received three letters of acceptance and I am confident that your letter contributed to my success.

Again, thank you for your continued support. I will be sure to keep in touch as I pursue my degree.

Sincerely,

Chris Smith

Chemical Engineer

178 Green Street
Medford, WI 54451
(715) 555-5555

October 29, 20--

Pat Cummings
Distinguished Professor of Chemistry
Any University
1140 Main Street
West Bend, MI 53095

Dear Dr. Cummings:

    Thank you for your excellent recommendation for my job-search applications. I feel confident that your acknowledgment of my abilities will contribute to the strength of my candidacy.

    I will keep you informed as the selection process comes to a close next week.

Sincerely,

Chris Smith

Human Resources Representative

178 Green Street
Hesston, KS 67062
(316) 555-5555

April 3, 20--

Pat Cummings
Assistant Director, Career Services
Any University
1140 Main Street
Topeka, KS 66612

Dear Mr. Cummings:

   I received your letter of recommendation in this morning's mail. Thank you for your kind words, and the effort you extended to mail it to me before my interview on April 12.

   I am sure that your letter will greatly assist me in presenting myself as a qualified candidate for the Human Resources Representative position with Any Corporation. I will be sure to inform you of the outcome of my interview.

   Thank you again.

Sincerely,

Chris Smith

Restaurant Manager

178 Green Street
Augusta, ME 04336
(207) 555-5555

July 1, 20--

Pat Cummings
Manager
Any Restaurant
1140 Main Street
Kennebunk, ME 04043

Dear Ms. Cummings:

Thank you so much for taking the time to write me a letter of recommendation for my job search. As you know, I had an interview for the Management Training Program with Fat Dickie's restaurant chain last week.

I have since been asked back for a second interview. I will keep you posted as to the outcome of my application.

Thank you again, Pat. I hope that everything is going well at the restaurant.

Sincerely,

Chris Smith

178 Green Street
Twodot, MT 59085
(406) 555-5555

October 14, 20--

Pat Cummings
Managing Editor
Any Press
1140 Main Street
Chicago, IL 60605

Dear Ms. Cummings:

I am happy to inform you that I have just accepted an offer for employment as an Acquisitions Editor at Dandelion Publishing Group. I should begin work there the first week of November.

I would like to thank you for all of your help during my job search, specifically for putting me in touch with Ninona Punder at Dandelion's billings office.

If there is ever anything that I can do for you, please do not hesitate to contact me. Yours was a favor I shall not soon forget.

Again, many thanks and best wishes.

Sincerely,

Chris Smith

Bank Manager

178 Green Street
Tacoma, WA 98477
(206) 555-5555

June 4, 20--

Pat Cummings
Assistant Vice President
Any Savings Bank
1140 Main Street
Spokane, WA 99201

Dear Mr. Cummings:

I received your letter dated June 2, regarding my initial inquiry for job placement assistance. Thank you so much for providing several names for contact purposes.

I have enclosed another copy of my resume. Please feel free to pass it on to any colleagues searching for a new Branch Manager.

Once again, your assistance is greatly appreciated.

Sincerely,

Chris Smith

Enc. Resume

178 Green Street
Van Nuys, CA 91411
(818) 555-5555

February 16, 20--

Pat Cummings
General Manager
Any Fitness Center
1140 Main Street
Van Nuys, CA 91411

Dear Mr. Cummings:

I am writing to thank you for your wonderful referral to Dani Johnson at Body Beautiful. When I called Ms. Johnson two weeks ago while on a visit to California, she invited me to interview for a Fitness Instructor position. Yesterday, she called to offer me the job!

Thank you so much for your assistance. If there is ever anything I can do in return, please do not hesitate to contact me. I have listed my new address and phone number above, effective March 1.

With best regards,

Chris Smith

Medical Assistant

178 Green Street
Richardson, TX 75083
(214) 555-5555

September 19, 20--

Pat Cummings, M.D.
Ophthalmologist
Any Hospital
1140 Main Street
Irving, TX 75038

Dear Dr. Cummings:

Although I regret that you did not have the need for an Assistant, I would like to thank you for referring me to Dr. Wilson in Richardson. In my meeting with him on Tuesday, I received several other contact names.

Should you become aware of any opportunities for a Medical Assistant, please let me know. I am still very interested in gaining hands-on experience before I begin graduate study in the field.

I hope to speak with you in the future.

Sincerely,

Chris Smith

Photographer

178 Green Street
Monroe, LA 71209
(318) 555-5555

November 1, 20--

Pat Cummings
Director
Any Corporation
1140 Main Street
New Orleans, LA 70130

Dear Ms. Cummings:

    Thank you for referring me to the resources available at the New Orleans Photography Center and especially to its Director, Peter O'Sullivan. The job listings he provided have been invaluable for my career search. I have since made numerous contacts and have scheduled two interviews.

    Thank you again and I would appreciate any assistance you might provide in the future.

Sincerely,

Chris Smith

Publicist

178 Green Street
Anniston, AL 36202
(205) 555-5555

March 4, 20--

Pat Cummings
Director of Public Relations
Any Heart Association
1140 Main Street
Montgomery, AL 36102

Dear Mr. Cummings:

I enjoyed meeting with you on Friday at your Montgomery headquarters. Your work for the Heart Association seems very rewarding.

I would also like to thank you for referring me to Beth Holmes at the Committee on Social Awareness. My discussions with both Ms. Holmes and yourself have definitely confirmed my interest in public relations work for a non-profit organization.

Good luck with your new television campaign.

Sincerely,

Chris Smith

178 Green Street
Wilmington, DE 19803
(302) 555-5555

January 4, 20--

Pat Cummings
Principal
Any School
1140 Main Street
New Castle, DE 19720

Dear Mr. Cummings:

　　Thank you for putting me in touch with Steven Simons and the Wilmington School District. A number of opportunities were available there and I was fortunate enough to be offered a fourth-grade teaching position.

　　Again, I appreciate your assistance.

Sincerely,

Chris Smith

Art Designer

178 Green Street
Radnor, PA 19087
(215) 555-5555

March 25, 20--

Pat Cummings
Art Director
Any Advertising Agency
1140 Main Street
York, PA 17402

Dear Ms. Cummings:

It was a pleasure meeting with you on Tuesday and learning about your work at Any Agency. I especially enjoyed watching you design the promotional sample for Smithe and Resin's new copier.

After spending the day with an art team at an advertising agency, I am sure that I want to pursue a career in art design. I will be sure to contact you upon graduation to follow up on your offer of placement assistance.

Good luck in your future endeavors at Any Agency, and thank you again for your kindness.

Sincerely,

Chris Smith

178 Green Street
Toast, NC 27049
(919) 555-5555

July 26, 20--

Pat Cummings
Associate Professor of Psychology
Any University
1140 Main Street
Chicago, IL 60605

Dear Ms. Cummings:

It was a pleasure seeing you again today. I appreciate the time you found in your busy schedule to meet with me.

It was interesting to learn about the use of interactive toys and models in child psychology. I have already been to the library to borrow the book by Leonard Finn that you recommended so highly. I am looking forward to reading about his ideas on child's play before the latency period.

As per your suggestion, I will be contacting Mr. Hayden within the next few days to set up an appointment. I will let you know how everything is progressing after I have met with him.

Again, thank you for your assistance. You will hear from me soon.

Sincerely,

Chris Smith

Hotel Clerk

178 Green Street
Newark, DE 19713
(302) 555-5555

September 18, 20--

Pat Cummings
General Manager
Any Inn
1140 Main Street
Wilmington, DE 19801

Dear Ms. Cummings:

Thank you for being so gracious with your time on Friday. I found your description of current trends in hospitality very enlightening.

I appreciate the suggestions you made regarding my resume. I think the new version is much improved. I have enclosed a copy in the hope that you will feel free to make any further comments or to share it with anyone in the industry you feel might be interested in someone with my qualifications.

As per your suggestion, I will contact James Moller with Daylight Hotels this week. Again, thank you for all of your assistance.

Sincerely,

Chris Smith

Enc. Revised resume

Marketing Assistant

178 Green Street
Exeter, NH 03833
(603) 555-5555

December 5, 20--

Pat Cummings
Director, Marketing
Any Corporation
1140 Main Street
Keene, NH 03431

Dear Mr. Cummings:

   I appreciate your taking a few moments to meet with me yesterday. I realize that, as Marketing Director of a large support staff, your time is very valuable.

   After visiting Any Corporation and hearing about your experiences, I am even more confident that I would like to pursue a career in marketing upon my graduation next year. In the meantime, I will follow your advice on course selection and summer employment.

   Thank you again for your time, Mr. Cummings. I plan to keep in touch throughout the year, as my job-hunting strategy becomes more focused.

Sincerely,

Chris Smith

Mechanical Engineer

178 Green Street
Norman, OK 73019
(405) 555-5555

November 4, 20--

Pat Cummings
Mechanical Engineer
Any Corporation
1140 Main Street
Tulsa, OK 74102

Dear Ms. Cummings:

Thank you for speaking with me yesterday regarding your work at Any Corporation. Your new design plans for coal-fired boilers sound very exciting. I wish you much success.

As you know, I have been considering a shift in focus within the field of mechanical engineering. Although I have enjoyed my training in costing and standards, my greatest interest has always been transportation. I am sure your insight will help me determine the smoothest transition into this new line of design.

As you requested, I will keep in contact as I pursue new opportunities.

Sincerely,

Chris Smith

Occupational Therapist

178 Green Street
Downers Grove, IL 60515
(708) 555-5555

May 14, 20--

Pat Cummings
Occupational Therapist
Any Rehabilitation Center
1140 Main Street
Evanston, IL 60201

Dear Ms. Cummings:

Thank you for taking the time to meet with me on Friday. I enjoyed meeting you and learning about the programs offered at Any Rehabilitation Center.

Our discussion definitely strengthened my interest in occupational therapy as a career path. I am planning to take your advice and enroll in a graduate program in September. In the interim, I will contact the referrals you provided to inquire about summer internship possibilities.

Thank you again for your assistance.

Sincerely,

Chris Smith

Social Worker

178 Green Street
Jacksonville, FL 32256
(904) 555-5555

February 22, 20--

Pat Cummings
Social Worker
Any Agency
1140 Main Street
Clearwater, FL 34625

Dear Mr. Cummings:

Speaking with you yesterday was very helpful. Thank you for rearranging your busy schedule to offer your advice and experience.

Although I am considering a career in social work, I had not given thought to working exclusively with young adults until I visited your offices. The Early Intervention Program you direct is an amazing venture and I am now very interested in becoming involved with an agency that targets at-risk youth.

Currently, I am applying for an internship with the Jacksonville Teen Clinic. I will keep you updated on the status of my application.

Thank you again for the interest you expressed in my career search. I appreciate your help.

Sincerely,

Chris Smith

Advertising Assistant

178 Green Street
Parsippany, NJ 07054
(201) 555-5555

July 18, 20--

Pat Cummings
Senior Vice President
Any Advertising Agency
1140 Main Street
Ridgefield Park, NJ 07660

Dear Ms. Cummings:

    Congratulations on your recent write-up in the *Advertising Advantage*. Your innovative marketing campaign for Hi-land Products sounds very intriguing. I have no doubt it will be a huge success.

    I am writing to inquire about joining your talented staff. You may recall that I sent a resume in response to the position of Advertising Assistant that appeared in the *New York Times* on May 28, 20--. Although I did not receive a response, I continue to believe that I would make a valuable addition to Any Advertising Agency. If any additional entry-level openings occur, I hope you will again consider my qualifications. I have enclosed a copy of my resume for your convenience.

Sincerely,

Chris Smith

Enc. Resume

Bank Administrator

178 Green Street
Knoxville, TN 37921

May 27, 20--

Pat Cummings
Division Head, Banking
Any Corporation
1140 Main Street
Memphis, TN 38103

Dear Ms. Cummings:

Approximately two weeks ago, I submitted a resume for your review and consideration. As I have yet to receive a response, I am enclosing a second copy of my resume in the event that my previous correspondence did not reach your desk.

As I previously indicated, I am interested in securing a new position with a company where I can apply the knowledge I have acquired during my employment and academic endeavors, along with my exceptional management and administrative skills, to a career in the banking industry.

I have seven years of experience in the marketing and management divisions of two banks, where I have been involved in every aspect of the administration, planning, and direction necessary for success. Accordingly, I feel I could become a valuable asset to your company.

I would appreciate the opportunity for a personal interview at your convenience. Please contact me at (615) 555-5555 during the day or at (615) 555-4444 during evening hours.

Thank you for your time. I look forward to hearing from you soon.

With best regards,

Chris Smith
Enc. Resume

Billings Clerk

178 Green Street
Elko, NV 89801

July 27, 20--

Pat Cummings
Billings Supervisor
Any Corporation
1140 Main Street
St. Louis, MO 63121

Dear Mr. Cummings:

Thank you for considering my resume. Your time is greatly appreciated.

I wanted to inform you that I will be relocating to Missouri in the near future. My plans are to further my career in the accounting and finance industry in the St. Louis area. As an added note, I am taking a computer spreadsheet course, which should enhance my skills in the field.

I am still very interested in furthering my career at Any Corporation and would ask for your consideration regarding any future availabilities. Until my move to St. Louis on August 28, I can be reached by phone at (702) 555-5555. I will call again in six weeks' time.

Thank you again. I look forward to speaking with you.

Sincerely,

Chris Smith
Enc. Resume

Commercial Photographer

178 Green Street
Baltimore, MD 21214
(301) 555-5555

April 20, 20--

Pat Cummings
Hiring Manager
Any Advertising Agency
1140 Main Street
Wheaton, MD 20902

Dear Mr. Cummings:

After speaking with your colleague Michael Hicks yesterday, I understand that your search for a Commercial Photographer is still on. Please allow me to express my continued interest in the position, and to reiterate my qualifications.

In addition to having graduated from the two-year program in all aspects of professional photography offered at the Ziegler School of Photography, I have additional training in graphic and liberal arts, as well as in related areas of advertising and promotion. Examples of my work are currently on exhibit in London, Toronto, New York, Miami, and Los Angeles. My experience also includes diverse aspects of both large and small business operations, which is of great value in selecting subjects and backgrounds appropriate to commercial advertising and promotion, or personnel and public relations.

I have assembled a portfolio of relevant work that I think would be of interest to you. Will you be scheduling interviews soon? I would like to show you my work and express my sincere interest in producing quality products for Any Advertising Agency.

I will follow up this inquiry with a phone call next week. In the interim, I have enclosed another copy of my resume for your review.

Thank you very much for your time.

Sincerely,

Chris Smith
cc: Michael Hicks

Enc. Resume

Computer Programmer

178 Green Street
St. Paul, MN 55164
(612) 555-5555

September 2, 20--

Pat Cummings
Systems Programmer
Any Corporation
1140 Main Street
Minnetonka, MN 55343

Dear Ms. Cummings:

Thank you for taking the time to speak with me in late May regarding entry-level computer programming positions at Any Corporation. Although you indicated that a hiring freeze is in effect at your firm for the immediate future, I would like to update you on several newly acquired skills I think you might find of interest.

During the past summer at the University of Minnesota's Studio, I worked as both a Programmer and Research Assistant, successfully meeting a variety of technical and intellectual challenges. As a Programmer, I learned Windows programming and implemented improvements to ConStats, a Windows-based package of educational software designed to teach introductory statistics. As a Research Assistant, I used the SAS statistical language to produce analyses regarding how ConStats was being used by students. This work resulted in a published journal article, an excerpt of which I have enclosed.

I am very interested in applying my newly acquired skills to your organization and would appreciate the opportunity to talk with you in a personal interview. Thank you for your time and consideration.

Sincerely,

Chris Smith

Enc. Resume
Excerpt from *Computer Programmer,* December 20--

Correctional Officer

178 Green Street
Butte, MT 59404
(406) 555-5555

January 18, 20--

Pat Cummings
Director of Security
Any State Prison
1140 Main Street
Billings, MT 59104

Dear Mr. Cummings:

   This letter regards a resume I faxed to your offices on Thursday, January 4. I have yet to hear if the Correctional Officer position has been filled, and I want you to know that I remain very interested in this opportunity. Please feel free to contact me with any additional questions concerning my qualifications.

   An additional copy of my resume is enclosed for your review.

Sincerely,

Chris Smith

Enc. Resume

Foreign Language Teacher

178 Green Street
Hapeville, GA 30354
(404) 555-5555

May 20, 20--

Pat Cummings
Principal
Any High School
1140 Main Street
Warner Robins, GA 31088

Dear Mr. Cummings:

On May 6, I wrote to you regarding your anticipated opening for a Foreign Language Teacher to be filled in the 20-- school year.

In the event that my original application has gone astray, I have enclosed a packet containing an additional professional profile, proof of certification, and letters of recommendation.

I would appreciate the opportunity to sit down with you face-to-face to further discuss my qualifications and enthusiasm for this or other available positions. I will follow up this letter with a phone call in a few days.

Sincerely,

Chris Smith

Enc. Professional profile, Proof of certification, Letters of recommendation

Freelance Copyeditor

178 Green Street
Shawnee, OK 74801

November 21, 20--

Pat Cummings
Vice President, Editorial
Any Publishing Company
1140 Main Street
Oklahoma City, OK 73125

Dear Ms. Cummings:

Please allow me to update my previous letter to Any Publishing Company with regard to your search for a Freelance Copyeditor. You will notice my resume has been revised to include more relevant experience.

My most recent assignment for Southwestern Publications involved copyediting material intended for educational television and geared for a high school audience. Many of my line corrections, as well as my editorial suggestions for improvements, were used in final versions. My work was found to be thorough, precise, and consistent.

I also edited a Master's thesis in Business Administration for a Langston University student. The text needed many corrections in spelling, grammar, usage, and style. I offered suggestions for improving content as well. The feedback on my work was quite good.

You may also recall that I am proficient in desktop publishing. I print high-quality resumes, essays, and formal letters for clients who contract for my services. I apply strict standards to all of my work and operate in a thoroughly professional manner.

Thank you again, Ms. Cummings, for considering me as a potential freelancer for Any Publishing Company. I will be following up this letter with a phone call in the next few weeks. Should you wish to contact me sooner, my phone number is (405) 555-5555. I look forward to communicating with you in the near future.

Sincerely,

Chris Smith

Enc. Resume

178 Green Street
Norman, OK 73019
(405) 555-5555

August 7, 20--

Pat Cummings
Owner
Any Jewelry Maker
1140 Main Street
Edmond, OK 73034

Dear Ms. Cummings:

On July 12, I sent a resume and small portfolio of samples as my application for a position as a Designer for your jewelry line. Since I have not received a response, I can only assume that you did not have any suitable vacancies at that time. Please allow me to highlight my qualifications again, as I remain very interested in joining your design team:

- Eight years of experience as a model maker and designer for several prominent competitors in the jewelry industry.
- Honors graduate of the National School of Jewelry Design, including an award for outstanding achievement.
- Three years of additional, diverse experience as a Customer Service Representative in the jewelry industry.

Would it be possible to meet with you next week to discuss your needs and present several examples of my past design work? I will call you on Friday to schedule a time that is convenient for you.

Thank you for your continued consideration. I hope that our future discussions will result in our working together.

Sincerely,

Chris Smith

Enc. Resume

Physical Therapist

178 Green Street
Somerville, MA 02145
(617) 555-5555

November 16, 20--

Pat Cummings
Rehabilitation Coordinator
Any Clinic
1140 Main Street
Mansfield, MA 02048

Dear Mr. Cummings:

In a letter dated August 12, I expressed my interest in securing a staff position as a Physical Therapist at Any Clinic. Although I realize that there may not have been any suitable availabilities at that time, I have enclosed a second resume for continued consideration.

Since my initial application, I have been working on an independent research project while continuing my job search. My study evaluated back and shoulder strength of athletes suffering from tendinitis and bursitis. Last week, my results were accepted for publication in the *National Journal of Rehabilitation*.

I have enclosed an excerpt of my article for your review. I hope this strengthens my candidacy for a position at Any Clinic. I would welcome the chance to meet with you should any opportunities for a Physical Therapist become available.

Sincerely,

Chris Smith

Enc. Resume, Excerpt from journal article manuscript

Radio Announcer

178 Green Street
New Rochelle, NY 10801

January 4, 20--

Pat Cummings
Production Manager
Any Radio Station
1140 Main Street
Garden City, NY 11530

Dear Mr. Cummings:

Last week, I spoke with your assistant, Linda McMillian, regarding the initial resume and demo tape I sent as application for the On-Air Announcer position you have available. Although Ms. McMillian could not confirm whether you had had the chance to review my materials, she did inform me that the position is still available.

I would like to take this opportunity to express my continued interest in becoming an Announcer at Any Radio Station. Since I moved to New York three years ago, I have listened to and admired your station's broadcasts. I would love to contribute to the success of what Radio NY considers to be "Westchester's Best News Station."

As your newest Announcer, I would bring almost thirteen years of experience in diverse areas of AM and FM announcing, newscasting, and audio production, including current responsibility for a regular on-air shift with WJBF AM (1170), New Rochelle, New York.

I have enclosed another copy of my resume and tape. After you have reviewed these materials, I would like to arrange a meeting to further discuss the position. I can be reached at (914) 555-5555.

I look forward to speaking with you.

Sincerely,

Chris Smith

Enc. Resume, Demo tape

Sales Representative

178 Green Street
Yuma, AZ 85365
(602) 555-5555

November 7, 20--

Pat Cummings
Vice President of Industrial Relations
Any Corporation
1140 Main Street
Helena, MT 59601

Dear Ms. Cummings:

On October 3, I sent you a letter expressing my interest in a position in professional sales and enclosed my resume for your review. As of today, I have not received a response and I am writing again to reiterate my interest in becoming a member of your sales staff.

My objective is to remain in the health care field with a company that is consistently developing, marketing, and promoting products to help those with chronic diseases. I would like to re-emphasize my education, clinical experience as a medical student, and practical experience in both medical research and direct patient care. Each of these experiences has given me the skills and sincerity to introduce and sell health care products, equipment, instruments, and services to medical professionals and administrators.

I have taken the liberty of enclosing a second copy of my resume. I am free to relocate and/or travel. I hope to hear from you so that I will have the opportunity to convince you that I have the qualifications and motivation to effectively represent your company.

Thank you again for reviewing my application materials. I look forward to your response.

Sincerely,

Chris Smith

Enc. Resume

Sanitation Inspector

178 Green Street
Conshohocken, PA 19428
(215) 555-5555

May 23, 20--

Pat Cummings
Chief Inspector
Any Office
1140 Main Street
Lewisburg, PA 17837

Dear Mr. Cummings:

 I am writing to express my continued interest in the position of Sanitation Inspector advertised in the May 8 edition of the *Express-Times*.

 In the event that you did not receive my original mailing, I have enclosed a second copy of my resume for your consideration. I feel that this position provides the ideal opportunity to apply my thirteen years of experience in the public health and safety industry. I am confident that, given the opportunity, I would be readily able to effectively maintain your strict inspection standards.

 I would be happy to further discuss my qualifications for this position in a personal interview. I am available at your convenience, and look forward to hearing from you.

 In the interim, be assured of my enthusiasm and competence.

Sincerely,

Chris Smith

Enc. Resume

Shipping/Receiving Expediter

178 Green Street
Anchorage, AK 99502
(907) 555-5555

April 17, 20--

Pat Cummings
Supervisor
Any Company
1140 Main Street
Fairbanks, AK 99701

Dear Ms. Cummings:

This letter follows a resume I mailed to your offices last Monday. I am very interested in the Shipping/Receiving Expediter position you advertised in the Sunday, April 9, edition of the *Anchorage Daily News*.

Please note that I offer twelve years of experience with the Alpha Corporation as an Expediter. In this capacity I enter packing slips, invoices, and other material control information into a highly specialized computer system, identify package contents and compare them to packing slips, schedule daily deliveries of incoming traffic, and create and implement an inventory system.

I am confident I can make an immediate contribution to Any Company. If you have any questions, I can be reached at the address and telephone number above.

Thank you for your consideration and I look forward to hearing from you.

Sincerely,

Chris Smith

Enc. Resume

Staff Accountant

178 Green Street
Parsippany, NJ 07054

August 4, 20--

Pat Cummings
Director of Human Resources
Any Corporation
1140 Main Street
New York, NY 10019

Dear Ms. Cummings:

Last year I spoke with Susan Rutter, the Director of Human Resources with your Chicago office, about the possibility of working within that division of Any Corporation as a Staff Accountant.

Since that conversation, I have relocated to the New York area. Consequently, I would like to continue my application process with Any Corporation through your office. I have enclosed a resume for your consideration.

I graduated from the University of Chicago in May with a Bachelor's degree in Accounting and Economics. Both my education and my internship at Gunn and Millstreet have adequately prepared me to begin a career in the corporate arena, and I am very eager to apply this experience to a position at Any Corporation.

I would be happy to further outline my capabilities and learn more about your prestigious training program during the course of a personal interview. I can be reached at the above address or by phone at (201) 555-5555. I look forward to your reply.

Sincerely,

Chris Smith

Enc. Resume

Systems Analyst

178 Green Street
Schenectady, NY 12305

March 2, 20--

Pat Cummings
Supervisor
Any Company
1140 Main Street
Olympia, WA 98505

Dear Mr. Cummings:

Last week I interviewed with Matthew Pratt at Pisces Data Systems, Inc., for a Systems Analyst position. While there were no such positions available with his firm at this time, Mr. Pratt knew of several openings at Any Corporation and he therefore took the liberty of faxing my resume to your attention. I am unsure if you actually received the information so I have enclosed an additional copy. I am very interested in opportunities at Any Company.

Allow me to review my qualifications:
- Set up the interfacing of a minicomputer to a PC in order to archive daily receipts onto optical disks.
- Created a device driver for a new disk system, and developed a new operating system to handle the new driver.
- Qualified all of Devlin software onto a new computer system.
- Built a new method of handling orders within the system.
- Rewrote accounts receivable program system to handle long-term notes.

I will contact your offices this coming Wednesday (March 8) to discuss how my skills can benefit your company. If you have any further questions before this time, please feel free to call me at (508) 555-5555.

Sincerely,

Chris Smith

Enc. Resume

Telemarketer

178 Green Street
Grace City, OH 58445
(216) 555-5555

February 19, 20--

Hiring Manager
P.O. Box 7777
Kent, OH 44242

RE: Advertisement in the February 2 edition of the *Sun Newspaper*

Dear Hiring Manager:

Please consider this letter as a follow-up inquiry regarding my resume sent on February 4, 20--, with regard to the telemarketing position.

Should the advertised position still be available, I would be very interested in discussing my qualifications with you in a personal interview. As the enclosed copy of my resume reflects, I have a proven track record of selling and closing capabilities as a Telemarketer. Last year, I independently generated more than $1.5 million in sales for my employer through cold-calling techniques. I would like to apply the same successful telemarketing abilities to your firm.

When can we meet for an interview?

Sincerely,

Chris Smith

Enc. Resume

Typist

178 Green Street
Gaithersburg, MD 20879
(301) 555-5555

March 3, 20--

Pat Cummings
Executive Hiring Officer
Any Corporation
1140 Main Street
Potomac, MD 20854

Dear Ms. Cummings:

On February 15, I faxed my resume to your office. To date, I have not received a response, but I want you to know that I remain very interested in the typing position. If it has not been filled, I would welcome the opportunity to discuss this job opportunity with you. If, however, the position has been filled, I would appreciate your input as to how I might further my job search with Any Corporation. I have enclosed a SASE for your convenience.

I am also enclosing another copy of my resume with references, in the hopes I might be considered for any other opportunities that may become available in the future.

Thank you for your time.

Sincerely,

Chris Smith

Enc. Resume, References, SASE

Administrative Assistant

178 Green Street
Shawnee, OK 74801
(405) 555-5555

February 27, 20--

Pat Cummings
President
Any Corporation
1140 Main Street
Oklahoma City, OK 73101

Dear Mr. Cummings:

Thanks to you and your enthusiastic staff for all the help offered me while visiting your offices last week. Although I was not selected for the Administrative Assistant position, I would appreciate detailed feedback on how to improve my candidacy for future openings at Any Corporation. Yours is a team I hope to someday join. I hope you will let me know what I can do to achieve this goal.

Again, thank you for your consideration. I look forward to your response.

Sincerely,

Chris Smith

Architect

178 Green Street
Middletown, RI 02840
(401) 555-5555

July 10, 20--

Pat Cummings
President
Any Firm
1140 Main Street
Providence, RI 02912

Dear Ms. Cummings:

Again, thank you for meeting with me last week to discuss the opportunities for Architects at Any Firm. I admire the innovative work you and your staff produce and, although I was not chosen for the position, I would like to be considered for upcoming projects.

I have enclosed an additional copy of my resume for your files. Thank you for your attention and I hope to hear from you in the near future.

Sincerely,

Chris Smith

Enc. Resume

178 Green Street
White Plains, NY 10604
(914) 555-5555

July 1, 20--

Pat Cummings
Editor
Any Publication
1140 West 43rd Street
New York, NY 10036

Dear Mr. Cummings:

    Once again, I would like to thank you for affording me the chance to interview for the Assistant Editor position with *Any Publication*. Although I am disappointed I was not selected for the position, I enjoyed meeting with you and your staff and learning more about your company.

    I am still interested in opportunities with *Any Publication* and would appreciate it if you would keep me in mind for future openings at your publication. Thank you again for your consideration.

Sincerely,

Chris Smith

178 Green Street
Wadesboro, NC 28170
(704) 555-5555

September 5, 20--

Pat Cummings
Head Counselor
Any Center
1140 Main Street
Charlotte, NC 27706

Dear Ms. Cummings:

Thank you for meeting with me last Friday regarding your current vacancy. Although I regret not being chosen for the Counselor position, I found the interview process very informative.

Please note that I have applied for a Master's degree in Social Work program to begin in January of 20--. I would be very interested in pursuing the field work required for my M.S.W. degree in a counseling capacity at Any Center.

I will contact you again in the future to inquire about suitable opportunities.

Thank you again for your consideration.

Sincerely,

Chris Smith

Telemarketer

178 Green Street
Ontario, OR 97914
(503) 555-5555

March 3, 20--

Pat Cummings
Human Resources Director
Any Corporation
1140 Main Street
Albany, OR 97321

Dear Mr. Cummings:

As per receipt of your letter dated March 1, I understand that your search for a Telemarketing Professional has come to an end. Although I am disappointed that I was not chosen for the position, I appreciate your taking the time to interview me. I was impressed by both Any Corporation's products and its friendly staff.

I am still very interested in applying for any current or anticipated availabilities at Any Corporation. I have enclosed another copy of my resume for your convenience. I hope you will consider my qualifications in the future.

I look forward to speaking with you again.

Sincerely,

Chris Smith

Enc. Resume

Firefighter

178 Green Street
Decatur, IL
(217) 555-5555

December 12, 20--

Pat Cummings
Captain
Any Fire Department
1140 Main Street
Palos Heights, IL 60455

Dear Mr. Cummings:

Last week I met with you to discuss your opening for a Firefighter. I was very impressed by the team of people working at Any Fire Department and the facility itself was one of the most technologically advanced I have seen.

Although I am convinced I would have enjoyed the position, I must withdraw my candidacy. My family and I have decided to relocate and the move will take us out of state.

Thank you again and best wishes.

Sincerely,

Chris Smith

178 Green Street
Carthage, MS 39051
(601) 555-5555

June 4, 20--

Pat Cummings
Owner
Any Boutique
1140 Main Street
Jackson, MS 39205

Dear Mr. Cummings:

I would like to express my appreciation for the time you extended to me during our interview on May 30 for the Hairstylist position. I have rarely seen such a friendly and enthusiastic staff, and your customers certainly seem satisfied with your work!

Although the position sounds wonderful, I am writing to withdraw my name from consideration. Since our meeting, my current employer has offered me a promotion that I cannot turn down. I hope my decision does not hinder your hiring process; I know that whomever you choose will prove to be an excellent Hairstylist.

Once again, thank you for your consideration.

Sincerely,

Chris Smith

Nurse's Aide

178 Green Street
Denver, CO 80239
(303) 555-5555

March 11, 20--

Pat Cummings, R.N.
Nursing Director
Any Hospital
1140 Main Street
Stratford, CT 06497

Dear Mr. Cummings:

    I regret to inform you that I am withdrawing my application from the pool of applicants for the Nurse's Aide position. An abrupt change in my personal situation has made relocation to your area impossible at the present time.

    I wish you the best of luck as your search continues.

Sincerely,

Chris Smith

178 Green Street
Newnan, GA 30265
(404) 555-5555

December 12, 20--

Pat Cummings
Owner
Any Preschool
1140 Main Street
Macon, GA 31297

Dear Ms. Cummings:

I would like to thank you for taking the time to interview me last Thursday for the part-time Preschool Instructor position. It was a pleasure meeting you and Jennifer Hedge, as well as the wonderful children you have the opportunity to work with.

As I mentioned during our conversation on Thursday, my prime interest is in obtaining full-time teaching work. Therefore, I have decided to accept a position as a Pre-Kindergarten Teacher in an elementary school near my home. Although I would have enjoyed working with your fine staff, I feel that this position provides an ideal opportunity for me to pursue my goals.

I have no doubt that you will find a qualified instructor to fill your vacancy, as you manage an excellent developmental facility for children. Thank you again for considering my candidacy.

Best of luck in your future endeavors.

Sincerely,

Chris Smith
cc: Jennifer Hedge

Regional Sales Manager

178 Green Street
Kennelworth, NJ 07033
(201) 555-5555

July 1, 20--

Pat Cummings
Human Resources Director
Any Corporation
1140 Main Street
New Brunswick, NJ 08933

Dear Mr. Cummings:

    As you may recall, I spoke with you over the phone several weeks ago regarding the status of my application for the Regional Sales Manager position. Thank you for the time you extended to inform me of the hiring process.

    While I understand that you are still in the process of sorting through resumes, I wanted to notify you that I no longer wish to be considered as an applicant. I have just accepted another offer for a similar position.

    I wish you the best of luck in your search for a qualified candidate.

Sincerely yours,

Chris Smith

178 Green Street
Lexington, MA 02173
(617) 555-5555

December 12, 20--

Pat Cummings
President
Any Travel Agency
1140 Main Street
Allston, MA 02134

Dear Mr. Cummings:

I enjoyed meeting with you yesterday to discuss the Travel Agent position. The prospect of working with you and your staff in such a fast-paced environment was very exciting.

However, after much thought, I have decided to withdraw my candidacy. The extensive travel the position involves is not well suited to my present situation.

Again, thank you for your consideration and best of luck with your search.

Sincerely,

Chris Smith

Archivist

Dental Hygienist

178 Green Street
Terre Haute, IN 47804
(812) 555-5555

May 12, 20--

Pat Cummings, D.M.D.
Any Dental Center
1140 Main Street
Wayne, IN 46802

Dear Dr. Cummings:

I received your letter of May 8, offering me the Dental Hygienist position at Any Dental Center. The compensation and benefits sound very tempting, and I am confident I would enjoy working with your staff.

However, shortly before receiving your letter, I was offered another position, which I have accepted. Thank you for your time and consideration of my candidacy.

Best wishes,

Chris Smith, R.D.H.

178 Green Street
Bartow, FL 33830
(813) 555-5555

September 17, 20--

Pat Cummings
Senior Editor
Any Publishing Company
1140 Main Street
Miami, FL 33173

Dear Mr. Cummings:

   Thank you so much for your generous offer of employment, and for your confidence in my abilities as an Editor.

   As I explained in our phone conversation, a newly arisen personal situation has caused me to rethink my plans to relocate to Miami. After much deliberation, I have decided that I must postpone my plans. I apologize for informing you of this change on such short notice, and I regret not being able to seize the opportunity to work for such a distinguished organization.

   I hope that we will be able to join forces at some point in the future.

Sincerely,

Chris Smith

Law Enforcement Officer

178 Green Street
Chalmette, LA 70043
(504) 555-5555

January 5, 20--

Pat Cummings
Police Chief
Any Police Department
1140 Main Street
Broussard, LA 70518

Dear Ms. Cummings:

    I would like to extend my thanks to you and your squad for meeting with me about the Law Enforcement Officer position. I enjoyed the time I spent at the station. You have a great group of people working with you.

    Although I know I would be proud to serve on your team, I must decline your generous offer. I have accepted a position in a neighboring town.

    Thank you again and best of luck for a safe New Year.

Sincerely,

Chris Smith

Paralegal

178 Green Street
Woodbridge, NJ 07095
(908) 555-5555

March 4, 20--

Pat Cummings
Hiring Manager
Any Law Firm
1140 Main Street
Cherry Hill, NJ 08034

Dear Ms. Cummings:

Thank you very much for offering me the chance to work as a full-time Paralegal at Any Law Firm next fall. I realize what a challenging and gainful experience this opportunity represents.

As I explained in our interview on February 28, I had also submitted law school applications for the upcoming year. Early this week, I received notification of my acceptance at Fordham University.

After weighing my choices, I realized that the best decision would be to begin law school without delay. However, I sincerely wish to thank you for your trust in my skills.

Should you need a summer intern or part-time Law Clerk within the next three years, I would welcome the opportunity to work for your firm.

Sincerely,

Chris Smith

Production Assistant

178 Green Street
Belair, TX 77401
(713) 555-5555

May 27, 20--

Pat Cummings
Producer
Any Production Company
1140 Main Street
Dallas, TX 75227

Dear Mr. Cummings:

It was a pleasure meeting with you last week and learning more about the current film projects underway at Any Production Company. I was pleased to receive your generous offer to assist you on a part-time basis as a Production Assistant.

Since our meeting, however, I have received an opportunity to pursue a documentary film project of my own. As you may recall, I was waiting for a decision on a grant proposal; on Thursday, I received word that I have been granted the necessary funding.

I am afraid this project will consume my energies on a full-time basis, so I must decline the opportunity to work with you on your new film. I admire your work greatly, Mr. Cummings, and know that I would have enjoyed assisting you.

Good luck on your project!

Sincerely,

Chris Smith

Publishing Intern

178 Green Street
Youngstown, OH 44501
(216) 555-5555

July 24, 20--

Pat Cummings
Editor
Any Publishing Company
1140 Main Street
Easton, PA 18044

Dear Mr. Cummings:

    I would like to thank you for taking the time to talk to me about Any Publishing Company and for offering me an internship position. I enjoyed meeting both you and Lee Jones and was very enthusiastic about the type of company Any Publishing appears to be. Being able to participate in the editorial as well as the production side of publishing is quite appealing to me, and I realize how unique this opportunity is. I feel that the internship position and I would have been a perfect fit.

    As you know, an abrupt change in my personal circumstances necessitated my turning down your offer. I want you to know that I sincerely regret this, as I know it would have been both a pleasure and a challenging experience to work for you. I hope I have not inconvenienced you. Thank you again for your time.

Sincerely,

Chris Smith
cc: Lee Jones

178 Green Street
Winterthur, DE 19735
(302) 555-5555

February 14, 20--

Pat Cummings
Vice President, Research and Development
Any Corporation
1140 Main Street
Chicago, IL 60605

Dear Ms. Cummings:

Thank you for taking the time to meet with me on Friday to discuss the opportunities for employment within your research and development department.

While I appreciate your generous offer, I have decided to decline the position. I have accepted a job elsewhere which I feel is better suited to my long-term needs.

Again, many thanks for your time. I wish you the best of luck in your future endeavors at Any Corporation.

Sincerely,

Chris Smith

Sales Representative

178 Green Street
Menomonee Falls, WI 53051
(414) 555-5555

January 30, 20--

Pat Cummings
Vice President, Sales
Any Corporation
1140 Main Street
Milwaukee, WI 53202

Dear Mr. Cummings:

 I truly enjoyed our meeting on Friday to discuss the possibility of my joining Any Corporation in a sales position. Your staff seems very enthusiastic, and I was impressed by your semiannual sales record. That is quite an achievement.

 Although I greatly appreciate your confidence in my abilities, I must decline your employment offer. I realize that in order to generate the quantity of sales necessary to reach mutual goals, I would have to invest a great deal of time in travel. At this point, that is not an allowance I am able to make.

 Once again, thank you for your consideration. Best of luck in the future.

Sincerely,

Chris Smith

178 Green Street

Canton, MA 02024

(617) 555-5555

June 19, 20--

Pat Cummings

Principal

Any Elementary School

1140 Main Street

Billerica, MA 01821

Dear Mr. Cummings:

    Thank you for taking the time to meet with me regarding teaching positions at Any Elementary School, and for offering me the opportunity to fill the vacancy in your fourth-grade classroom.

    As you know, my prime interest is in securing a position where I may apply my newly acquired skills in ESL instruction. I understand that budgetary constraints will not allow you to offer that type of position for the upcoming school year. However, I feel that this is where my interests and abilities best lie.

    I appreciate your offer, and although I cannot join your school at this time, I hope that our paths will cross in the future.

Sincerely,

Chris Smith

Veterinary Assistant

178 Green Street
Kingston, RI 02881
(401) 555-5555

December 5, 20--

Pat Cummings, D.V.M.
Veterinarian
1140 Main Street
Warwick, RI 02888

Dear Dr. Cummings:

Thank you very much for offering me the opportunity to intern at your office for the upcoming semester.

Unfortunately, I have not been able to come to an agreement with the internship coordinator's office at the University of Rhode Island to work the twenty hours per week the position would demand. The University strictly adheres to its maximum commitment of fifteen hours per week.

I truly regret not being able to work with you. I hope that, in the future, circumstances will allow me to be of your assistance.

Again, my thanks for your generous offer.

Sincerely,

Chris Smith

178 Green Street
Greenwich, CT 06830
(203) 555-5555

March 24, 20--

Pat Cummings
Head Architect
Any Corporation
1140 Main Street
Hartford, CT 06106

Dear Ms. Cummings:

Effective April 7, 20--, I will be terminating my employment with Any Corporation. I have allowed two weeks prior to my departure for assisting in the transition process.

I have recently accepted a position as Head Architect with a local office in the public sector. I feel that this new opportunity is well suited to my long-term career goals.

I would be happy to train and assist my replacement, as well as complete any other organizational matters that need my attention.

Sincerely,

Chris Smith

Forester

178 Green Street
Cheyenne, WY 82001
(504) 555-5555

February 15, 20--

Pat Cummings
Executive Director
Any State Park
1140 Main Street
Cheyenne, WY 82001

Dear Mr. Cummings:

As of March 6, I will be terminating my employment at Any State Park.

As you know, my goal has always been to work full-time as an advocate for forestry preservation. Recently, I have been offered, and accepted, a year's appointment with the International Forestry Preservation Corps in Brasilia, Brazil. The chance to work and live among the rain forests of Brazil is a unique and exciting opportunity that I could not turn down.

I have thoroughly enjoyed my time at Any State Park, and regret having to abandon my work here. Please be assured that I will extend every effort to make my departure as smooth as possible.

I appreciate your understanding.

Sincerely,

Chris Smith

178 Green Street
London, NWI 4SA UK
(44) 71 555 55 55

October 20, 20--

Pat Cummings
Vice President, International Division
Any Corporation
1140 Main Street
Los Angeles, CA 90071

Dear Ms. Cummings:

I am writing to inform you that I have decided to return to the United States or Canada to establish a more permanent base for my family as of November 10.

I regret leaving Any Corporation, but as you know, I have asked several times, without success, for relocation to a position in the North American division. I had enjoyed working for Any Corporation and would have liked to continue. However, I have established an excellent reputation and the credentials for quality and profitability in both food and beverage and general hotel operations over the years, and I am confident these will assist me in securing a new position within the industry.

Once again, I regret having to resign from my position. I wish you much success in the future.

Sincerely,

Chris Smith

Medical Technologist

178 Green Street
West Fargo, ND 58078
(701) 555-5555

May 31, 20--

Pat Cummings
Senior Medical Technologist
Any Hospital
1140 Main Street
West Fargo, ND 5878

Dear Ms. Cummings:

Friday, June 16, will be my last day of employment at Any Hospital.

I have accepted a research position in a private laboratory setting. While I have enjoyed working as a member of your staff, my new employment will allow me to pursue hematology, which is, as you know, an area of real interest for me.

Please let me know if there is anything I can do to assist you in locating a replacement.

Sincerely yours,

Chris Smith

Production Assistant

178 Green Street
Pittsburgh, PA 15222
(412) 555-5555

August 4, 20--

Pat Cummings
Internship Coordinator
Any Television Coordinator
1140 Main Street
Allentown, PA 18101

Dear Mr. Cummings:

    With this letter, I would like to offer notice of the termination of my production assistant-ship. As I am preparing to return to school, August 18 will be my last day of employment.

    My experience at Any Television Station has been both educational and enjoyable. I know that the production work I have been involved in will continue to benefit me in the future.

    Thank you for affording me this experience. I am grateful to have contributed to Any Television Station in return for the skills and knowledge I have gained.

Yours truly,

Chris Smith

Speech Pathologist

178 Green Street
Santa Fe, NM 87504
(505) 555-5555

July 3, 20--

Pat Cummings
Principal
Any School
1140 Main Street
Deming, NM 87199

Dear Ms. Cummings:

    I am writing to inform you of my resignation, effective July 15. Although I have enjoyed my position as a Speech Pathologist at Any School, I have accepted another position where I feel my diverse skills will be more fully utilized.

    I want to thank you for the wonderful experience I had here. Both the staff and the students were great to work with. I wish you much luck in the approaching academic year.

Sincerely,

Chris Smith

Vice President, Sales

178 Green Street
Falls Church, VA 22043
(703) 555-5555

August 22, 20--

Pat Cummings
President
Any Company
1140 Main Street
Alexandria, VA 22312

Dear Ms. Cummings:

I have enjoyed serving as Vice-President of Sales, but I have received an offer from another pharmaceutical company that I feel is better suited to my career objectives. Regrettably, I submit this letter as notice of my resignation.

My last day will be September 6. If I can be of any assistance in recommending potential candidates for my position, I would be more than happy to help.

I wish you the best of luck and future success.

Sincerely,

Chris Smith

Accountant

178 Green Street
Cedar City, UT 84720
(801) 555-5555

December 4, 20--

Pat Cummings
Account Manager
Any Corporation
1140 Main Street
Salt Lake City, UT 84110

Dear Mr. Cummings:

Please receive this letter as my formal acceptance of your employment offer. I am very excited about joining the ranks at Any Corporation, and I hope to quickly make a contribution to your qualified accounting staff.

Yesterday, I submitted a formal resignation notice to my current employer, and have arranged a start date of December 9. I will contact you later this week to confirm that date and to provide any additional information you might need.

In the interim, be assured of my enthusiasm about beginning a new phase of my career with Any Corporation. I look forward to working with you.

Sincerely,

Chris Smith

178 Green Street
Mayville, WI 53050
(414) 555-5555

May 1, 20--

Pat Cummings
Principal Architect
Any Corporation
1140 Main Street
Columbia, SC 29208

Dear Mr. Cummings:

I am pleased to accept the offer to assist you on the Glendale Shopping Complex project. The proposal you gave me sounds very exciting, and I am excited about being given the chance to add my expertise to such a challenging endeavor.

As you know, I am in the process of securing housing to facilitate my move to Columbia. I expect to be settled in your area by the end of the month, in plenty of time to start work in mid-June. Should this arrangement present a conflict, please let me know.

I will keep in touch as my start date nears. Thank you again for your kind offer.

Sincerely,

Chris Smith

Customer Service Representative

178 Green Street
South Pasadena, CA 91030
(213) 555-5555

April 1, 20--

Pat Cummings
Customer Service Manager
Any Corporation
1140 Main Street
Los Angeles, CA 90010

Dear Ms. Cummings:

    I would like to thank you and Donald Grasier for offering me the position of Customer Service Representative during our meeting on Friday. As you suggested, I took the weekend to consider your offer, and am pleased to accept its terms.

    This morning I gave notice to my current employer and should be able to begin work at Any Corporation on Monday, April 17. Please let me know if there are any papers we need to go over before my start date.

    Thank you again for providing me with this opportunity. I am very excited to join your sales team!

Sincerely,

Chris Smith
cc: Donald Grasier

178 Green Street
Halifax, MA 02338

July 6, 20--

Pat Cummings
Editor
Any Publishing Company
1140 Main Street
Port Chester, NY 10573

Dear Mr. Cummings:

    As per our telephone conversation, I would like to confirm my acceptance of your employment offer. This position as Editorial Assistant provides exactly the kind of experience I hoped to find. I feel confident that I can make a significant contribution to Any Publishing Company, and I am grateful for the opportunity you have given me.

    As we discussed, I will report to work at 8:00 A.M. on Monday, July 17. I will be moving to New York on July 11. Until then, I can be reached in Massachusetts at (617) 555-5555. Again, I appreciate your confidence in me and look forward to beginning work.

Sincerely,

Chris Smith

Geographer

178 Green Street
St. Paul, MN 55104
(612) 555-5555

May 12, 20--

Pat Cummings
Hiring Coordinator
Any Government Agency
1140 Main Street
Minneapolis, MN 55413

Dear Ms. Cummings:

    I am grateful for the opportunity to be part of such an esteemed department in the agency. I look forward to assuming my post as Geographer, and I am happy to accept the terms of our agreement.

    As discussed, my graduation date is set for May 31, and I will be available to begin the following Monday, June 5. I will contact your offices early next week to schedule my training session.

    Again, thank you. I am very excited to begin.

Sincerely,

Chris Smith

178 Green Street
Kingston, RI 02881
(401) 555-5555

February 25, 20--

Pat Cummings
Chief Statistician
Any Corporation
1140 Main Street
Pawtucket, RI 02862

Dear Ms. Cummings:

    I received your letter, and I am very pleased to accept your offer of employment as a Statistician at Any Corporation. I appreciate your trust in my skills, and will make every effort to contribute to your team.

    I have given notice of my resignation at my current employer and intend to start at Any Corporation on Monday, March 13. As per your request, I have scheduled a physical exam for this week, and will submit the appropriate materials on my first day of work.

    I am very excited to begin working with you and your statistical staff.

Sincerely,

Chris Smith